ROUTLEDGE LIBRARY EDITIONS:
BANKING & FINANCE

# MONEY AND BANKING IN THE UK

# MONEY AND BANKING IN THE UK
## A History

MICHAEL COLLINS

Volume 6

Routledge
Taylor & Francis Group
LONDON AND NEW YORK

First published in 1988

This edition first published in 2012
by Routledge
2 Park Square, Milton Park, Abingdon, Oxfordshire OX14 4RN

Simultaneously published in the USA and Canada
by Routledge
711 Third Avenue, New York, NY 10017

First issued in paperback 2014

*Routledge is an imprint of the Taylor and Francis Group, an informa company*



*British Library Cataloguing in Publication Data*
A catalogue record for this book is available from the British Library

ISBN: 978-0-415-52796-5 (Volume 6)
ISBN: 978-0-415-75182-7 (pbk)

**Publisher's Note**
The publisher has gone to great lengths to ensure the quality of this reprint but points out that some imperfections in the original copies may be apparent.

**Disclaimer**
The publisher has made every effort to trace copyright holders and would welcome correspondence from those they have been unable to trace.

# MONEY AND BANKING IN THE UK: A History

MICHAEL COLLINS

CROOM HELM
London • New York • Sydney

Croom Helm Ltd, Provident House, Burrell Row,
Beckenham, Kent, BR3 1AT

Croom Helm Australia, 44-50 Waterloo Road,
North Ryde, 2113, New South Wales

Published in the USA by
Croom Helm
in association with Methuen, Inc.
29 West 35th Street
New York, NY 10001

British Library Cataloguing in Publication Data

Collins, Michael
Money and banking in the UK: a history.
1. Banks and banking — Great Britain — History — 19th century 2. Banks and banking — Great Britain — History — 20th century 3. Monetary policy — Great Britain — History — 19th Century 4. Monetary policy — Great Britain — History — 20th century
I. Title
332.1'0941 HG2986

ISBN 0-7099-0760-5

Library of Congress Cataloging-in-Publication Data

ISBN 0-7099-0760-5

Printed and bound in Great Britain by Mackays of Chatham Ltd, Kent

# CONTENTS

## PART II: 1914-1939



## PART III: 1939-1986

# LIST OF TABLES

# LIST OF FIGURES

# ABBREVIATIONS

| | |
|---|---|
| billion | = one thousand million |
| the Bank | = Bank of England |
| 'England' | sometimes refers to England and Wales |
| PP | = Parliamentary Papers |
| in tables: | n.a. = not available |
| | - = insignificant amount |

# PREFACE

This study provides a long-term perspective on both the development of banking institutions and the evolution of monetary policy in the UK. Current interest in the history of money and banking remains strong and it is opportune to survey developments in this country. The objective is to provide an historical analysis which incorporates the results of recent research - the aim being to present the material in a form accessible to undergraduates and other students of money and banking, yet to be of use to professional economic historians, economists and bankers.

The years covered by the book - from 1826 to 1986 - correspond to almost the whole period of the UK's experience as an industrial nation, and awareness of the general direction and pace of the country's broad economic development is obviously important to any assessment of long-term monetary change. As will emerge, the course of change in the UK had much in common with other developed nations. This was true, for instance, of the upsurge in the number of banking outlets associated with industrialisation and *per capita* income growth; of the long-term growth in the scale of operations for individual banking units; and - after the early phase of rapid expansion - of the slow-down experienced in the growth of bank deposits relative to other financial assets. Of course, country-specific conditions (national legislation, national economic environment, etc.) render each nation's monetary history unique but, in the UK's case, these unique features are of wide interest. The UK was the leading industrial and commercial power for much of the nineteenth and early twentieth centuries. One consequence was that the City of London's financial institutions gained a prominent position within international money markets and, in particular, the nineteenth century saw the emergence of the pound sterling as the world's key currency. Subsequently, though, Britain's economic performance underwent relative decline as other nations industrialised and achieved faster growth rates and much of the economic history of the present century has been one of (often painful) adjustment to the realities of decline – realities which have had important consequences for Britain's international role, for institutional arrangements within money markets and for the conduct of monetary policy.

The book is concerned with developments in three main areas of monetary history: domestic commercial banking; monetary policy; and the UK's international financial position. For ease of analysis, the 160 years under study are arranged into three clear chronological divisions.

Part I covers the years from 1826 to 1913, a period in which the UK emerged as the world's leading economic power. It was in these years that an extensive and fully-operative domestic banking system was established. The state did attempt to create a legislative framework for the system, but minimum interference was more characteristic of governmental attitudes and the conduct of what passed for a minimal monetary policy was left largely in the hands of the privately-owned Bank of England. Internationally, the UK sought to minimise the potential for discretionary policy decisions by espousing full currency convertibility and stable exchange rates under the gold standard.

In many ways the years from 1914 to 1939 – which are covered in Part II – marked a break in the traditional monetary arrangements of the Victorian and Edwardian eras. The earlier slow-down in the growth of commercial banking was confirmed in the interwar years, but more noticeable changes affected the conduct of policy and the position of the City of London within the world economy. The First World War led to a sharp increase in the state's involvement in financial markets. First, the legacy of large wartime debts and, then, the economic traumas of the 1920s and 1930s forced the Treasury to abandon its traditional stance and become more active in the conduct of monetary policy. Declining exports led to high unemployment and weakened the authorities' ability, and commitment, to maintain the international gold standard. More discretion was called for – and exercised – than ever before.

Part III of the book covers the most recent period, from 1939 to 1986. The dominance of state influence within the domestic money markets was re–established by the Second World War and the immediate requirements of state finance continued to determine the composition of banks' assets for more than a decade after the war. Of even greater long–term significance was the acceptance by the authorities of the obligation to 'manage' the economy, which meant that successive postwar governments took direct responsibility for the conduct of monetary and credit policy. The position that monetary instruments held within different governments' overall economic policy varied but, on trend, monetary policy emerged from relative obscurity in the 1940s to become the central feature of the Thatcher government's economic strategy of the early 1980s. In money markets, the high street banks found themselves losing ground in the provision of domestic retail banking services to non–bank financial intermediaries such as building societies; and, internationally, the opening–up of world money markets from the late 1950s led City institutions into intense competition, particularly with the successful US and Japanese banks. The UK's relative economic decline meant that sterling's role as a key international currency also declined and re–occurring weaknesses on the external account meant that exchange rate considerations had a significant influence on monetary policy decisions throughout the postwar period. This was true of all three main exchange rate regimes experienced since World War II – of the years up to 1958, when the UK was committed to maintaining stable exchange rates but with restricted convertibility; of the period from 1958 to 1972, when there was both exchange rate stability and convertibility; and of the years since 1972 when the authorities maintained convertibility but allowed much greater freedom for movements in exchange rates.

Finally in these introductory remarks it is worth emphasising that the UK commercial banking 'system' has, in fact, comprised three distinct systems: one in England and Wales, another in Scotland and a third in Ireland (or Northern Ireland). Different legal frameworks ensured their co-existence as quite separate entities for a good part of the period, although cross-country links have been more evident in the twentieth century. The main features of all three systems are detailed in the pages that follow but, inevitably, more weight is given to developments in England. This is, in part, recognition of the relative quantitative importance of English banking provision in both domestic and international markets, but it also reflects the fact that it has been in England where the seat of power has been located. In particular, policy was formulated, first, by the Bank of England and, then, by Westminster governments.

ACKNOWLEDGEMENTS

Many thanks to those who read draft chapters and offered comments, with special appreciation to Forrest Capie, Edwin Green, Charles Munn and Gerard Turnbull. Thanks, too, to Teresa Brier and, particularly, Carolyn Weaver without whose patience and skill the manuscript would never have been completed.

# PART I: 1826–1913

Chapter One

# BANKING IN THE EARLY NINETEENTH CENTURY

## INTRODUCTION

The banking sector faced catastrophe at the end of 1825. In the two years, 1825–6, 93 banks in England and Wales found themselves unable to fulfil the most fundamental of all bankers' obligations – they were unable to pay cash to their customers on demand.[1] It is this inauspicious episode that marks the beginning of the present account of the evolution of modern banking in the United Kingdom. The banking crisis had arisen out of more general problems facing the economy and it will be a recurrent theme that economic pressures from the non-banking world often invoked important changes in the environment in which the commercial banks had to operate.

The major 'environmental' change in 1826 came from Parliament, where Lord Liverpool's government successfully introduced two pieces of legislation aimed at bolstering the defective English commercial banking system. The first act[2] forbade, from 1829, the circulation of bank notes of under £5 denomination in England and Wales, and *de facto* stopped immediately the stamping of new notes of this type. The Banking Co-partnership, or Joint-Stock Bank, Act[3] was the second, and more important, of the legislative measures. This act sought to provide greater stability by allowing banks access to larger capital resources.

Since 1708 the Bank of England had been the only English bank able to raise capital from a large body of proprietors, all other banks in England and Wales being restricted by Act of Parliament to a maximum of six partners. The Joint-Stock Bank Act attacked this legislative monopoly and permitted the formation of banks with an unlimited number of partners, or shareholders, outside a radius of sixty-five miles from London.[4] Although there remained many difficulties, and although it was to take the best part of the nineteenth century for the process to be consolidated, with hindsight it can be seen that the Joint-Stock Bank Act of 1826 laid the legal foundation for the emergence of the modern form of bank - a bank whose corporate structure and large capital resources enabled it to build up an extensive national, indeed international, business.

## EARLY BANKING HISTORY

In 1826, of course, legislators had had little inkling of such developments and had merely sought to strengthen an already expanding sector. For England it is useful to distinguish between the expansion that was occurring in London and expansion elsewhere. The earliest English bankers were the London money scriveners and goldsmiths.[5] By the middle of the seventeenth century they were in regular receipt of deposits which, in turn, were lent at interest in the normal manner of financial intermediation; although their clientele was restricted to a select group of wealthy merchants and landowners. In 1694 the importance of the London money markets had been enhanced by the creation of the Bank of England.[6] The immediate reason for the Bank's formation was the need of government to raise finance and, as will be shown in later chapters, the close relationship with the government of the day was to have a critical bearing on the ultimate emergence of the Bank as a truly central bank. The Bank operated the government's main accounts as the government's banker and continued to enjoy a privileged position in consequence. By the early eighteenth century it had already emerged as the largest and most prestigious financial institution in England. From its earliest days one important function was to issue notes. Initially these rivalled those of the London private bankers but through the eighteenth century the Bank established a virtual monopoly of note issuing in London - in the metropolis its notes were generally treated as cash by bankers and public alike, although they were not to become legal tender until as late as 1833.

The London money market was developing in other respects, too. Although many banking partnerships were of a transitory nature and some firms carried on banking and non-banking activities side by side, an increasing proportion of private bankers was specialising. True, their note circulations were falling away but opportunities for financial intermediation were expanding along with the general upward trend in economic activity. Such opportunities were probably greater for those bankers in the City of London who tended to specialise in the handling of mercantile accounts, in contrast to the more genteel West End bankers who relied heavily on the accounts of the aristocracy. One important aspect of the expansion of commercial banking services in the capital was the increased use of cheques. Their use was greatly facilitated by the establishment, by 1773, of the London Clearing House. The Clearing House was to provide an effective means of mutual exchange and cancellation of claims among the London bankers.[7] In this way they were able to minimise the transaction costs involved in operating a cheque system because only the balance of claims need now be paid in cash (most often, in Bank of England notes).

Overall, such developments reflect the continued expansion of London banking through the eighteenth century, a time of consolidation and increased professionalisation. By the opening of the period under study, London had already acquired a well-established commercial banking sector even though the Bank of England's joint stock monopoly had restricted the potential size of individual firms.

Banking changes were bound up with the changing pace of economic development. Britain's Industrial Revolution was marked by a growth in both productive and trading sectors, the greater accumulation of wealth holdings and increased sophistication of economic relations. The pervasive rise in the scale of economic activity made specialisation, including financial specialisation, more feasible and economic development called for more advanced mercantile and financial arrangements. Here, the commercial banker played a central role: in the provision of credit, media of exchange and remittance facilities; as well as providing the more traditional service as a safe repository for valuables.

Economic development was not confined to London and in other parts of the kingdom, too, there was a positive response to the growing demands for financial intermediation. Because of their separate legal and economic identities banking developments in England and Wales, Scotland and Ireland followed three distinct, though not dissimilar, courses. In Ireland, small private banking partnerships had first emerged during the late seventeenth century. The system consisted of about eleven private banks (half of them in Dublin) plus the Bank of Ireland which had been created through legislative charter in 1783.[8] The Bank of Ireland dominated the system, all other banks being puny in comparison. It was the government's bank in Ireland and special privileges, partially modelled on those of the Bank of England, granted it a monopoly of the joint stock form of ownership, guaranteed access to large capital resources and ensured a high volume of business. However, as the Bank of Ireland confined its activities to Dublin, Irish provincial needs were met by the private bankers and by merchants and bill discounters who acted as quasi-bankers.

The severe financial crisis of 1820, in which one-half of the banks in southern Ireland failed, was to be a watershed in Irish banking developments. It 'marked the beginning of the end of the private banks in the south' of the country[9] and provoked legislative changes which were to have important implications for the banks in England. In 1821 the London Parliament responded to the difficulties of the previous year by restricting the Bank of Ireland's privileges and permitting the formation of banks with over six partners outside a radius of fifty (Irish) miles from Dublin.[10] This reform and the Irish Banking Act of 1824, led to the creation in the 1820s and 1830s of joint stock banks with large partnerships and these quickly displaced the smaller, private banks. More widely, these Irish banking reforms were to serve as a model for the English legislation of 1826.

In fact, those favouring reform in both Ireland and England could already draw upon the Scottish example. Banking firms with a large number of partners had appeared much earlier in Scotland. In 1716 the Bank of Scotland had lost its joint stock monopoly, which meant that future developments could proceed unfettered by this particular restriction.

Scottish banks had first emerged in the late seventeenth century and modest growth continued through the first half of the next century. During the third quarter of the eighteenth century, however, Scotland enjoyed a tremendous expansion in banking services. 'By 1772 ... the banking system of Scotland was perhaps the most developed in Europe, ready to respond to the demands of rapid industrialisation.'[11] The most stable elements of the system were the three public (or chartered) banks based in Edinburgh – the Bank of Scotland, the Royal Bank of Scotland and the more recently-formed, British Linen Company.[12] In addition there were private firms operating outside Edinburgh. In the early stages of development some of these private partnerships offered banking services as an adjunct to their normal business (e.g. sugar importers), but by the latter half of the eighteenth century they were operating as specialist bankers. While some of the private firms were akin to the small English country banks, others had quite large proprietorships and, therefore, had access to larger capital resources. All were known as 'provincial banking companies'.

Thus, by 1826 Scotland already had a well-developed system in that its banks had relatively large proprietorships, they often operated more offices than their English counterparts and they were comparatively stable during economic recessions. It was this stability which provided such a persuasive argument for altering English (and Irish) law in such a way as to permit the formation of larger banks.

Specialist banking also came to the English provinces during the second half of the eighteenth century. The lag behind London was due to the capital's early importance in the raising and servicing of government finance and in international financial transactions, and because of the greater scale and significance of much of the metropolis's local economic activity. Outside London some of the banker's functions had long been performed by such professionals as provincial attorneys[13] but it was the second half of the eighteenth century - especially from the 1780s - that witnessed the mushrooming of the provincial specialist, the English country banker.[14]

Even then, the term 'specialist' must be interpreted cautiously, for the turn of the century was a period of very rapid transition. There had been only a handful of provincial bankers in 1750; but this had risen to over a 100 during the 1780s, close to 400 by the beginning of the nineteenth century, and to a staggering 600 or so by the mid-1820s.[15] These banks commonly began as adjuncts to existing, non-bank businesses. Only as the scale of the financial side of their businesses grew did the eighteeth-century industrialist, merchant, or scrivener, move more fully into banking. Some never did so, while others became bankers only temporarily, perhaps abandoning this aspect of their business as partnerships changed or as profits fell. In this transitional period there was a certain degree of flux and, at any one time, there were differences across firms as to the extent of specialisation. Different firms were at different stages of metamorphosis.

The historian of the English country bankers, L.S. Pressnell, has identified three main types of business activity from which they sprang:

> that of industrialists, whose main concern, was to provide a local means of payment; that of financial intermediaries, most notably the money scriveners, who sought or offered outlets for specific sums of money on behalf of their clients; and remitters of funds between London and the country, principally traders and collectors of government revenue.[16]

By 1826 the process of specialisation had advanced enough to identify a large body of firms known as 'country bankers' who conducted a business which would be recognised readily as banking. So, during the Industrial Revolution England's provincial towns and villages acquired an extensive banking system, providing greater opportunities for both savers and borrowers. But the new system contained serious weaknesses. In particular, the country bankers have generally been seen as a contributory cause of the short-term instability experienced in the period. In economic upswings their numbers and businesses expanded, in downswings they contracted. In this they were not unlike most other business concerns, but as suppliers of media of exchange - of money - the role of the banker took on added significance. Expansion of a banker's business directly encouraged expansion of the business community in general, through the greater availability of loans and means of payment; whereas banking contraction added to general deflationary pressures.

## ECONOMIC CRISIS AND THE LEGISLATION OF 1826

For many English contemporaries the case against the country bankers was particularly strong because, unlike their London counterparts, most of them issued bank notes of their own. The banks' customers used these notes to settle debts in their locality and if confidence in the banker was high the notes were an effective substitute for cash. The bankers saw themselves as providing the community with an additional form of payment and, of course, they made a profit by persuading the public to take payment in their 'promise to pay' rather than in the coin of the realm. On the other hand, critics saw this as a dangerous power to print money. It was considered dangerous because there was no close regulation of the amount of each bank's note issue and critics believed that potential fluctuations in these note issues endangered price stability in the economy as a whole.

In 1826 complaints concentrated on the issue of bank notes of 'small' denominations of £1 and £2.[17] Leading critics had already been alerted to the dangers by the price inflation and the falling gold value of the pound during the French Wars when, from the financial crisis of 1797, the legal requirement on issuers to pay gold on demand for their notes had been suspended. In England the previous ban on notes of under £5 (imposed in 1777) had been removed at the same time and there then followed a period in which the total country note issue apparently increased sharply.[18] Small notes had been due to disappear sometime after the war, in 1823, but the political influence of the country bank lobby proved most effective at a time when there was a general fear of deflation. As a result prohibition of small notes was postponed.

The crisis of 1825–6 was to prove decisive in determining the course of banking developments in England. The economy had been expanding from about 1822, with the pace increasing markedly during 1824. In its later stages the recovery turned to boom, with signs of full employment, general inflationary pressures and speculation in both the capital markets (especially in overseas government and mining securities) and commodity markets. For much of the expansionary phase rates of interest remained low and contemporary opinion assumed that bank liabilities expanded. The Bank of England's position was 'permissive to expansionary', doing nothing to inhibit the expansion. The boom ended in 1825, the most dramatic feature of the year being the short internal liquidity crisis which was at its most intense in mid-December. This panic for cash seriously depleted the reserves of the banking system and threatened the legal convertibility of notes to gold. During the crisis the public, not without good reason, lost confidence in the ability of the country banks to meet their obligations. As the pressure for liquidity spread to all parts of the country, bank notes were presented *en masse* and coin or Bank of England notes demanded in return. People preferred to hoard their cash rather than entrust it to a banker. Worst fears were realised, for many bankers had insufficient cash and were forced to close their doors to note-holders and depositors alike. London bankers and other financial institutions were implicated and, at its worst, there was a widespread loss of confidence in all but the most secure forms of money and credit. Only by lending freely at the height of the crisis was the Bank of England able to quell the panic and, by the narrowest of margins, avert the threat to convertibility of its own notes.

Obviously, a means of reducing the vulnerability of the system to 'runs' of this sort would have been generally welcomed. Thus, while there were many factors contributing to the nature of the boom and subsequent slump, the instability of the English country banks exposed them to public scrutiny. Their notes had expanded during the boom; and the crisis had fully revealed the vulnerability of this component of the money supply.[19] Country bankers emerged as the main scapegoats, being held largely responsible for the crisis. This is why Parliament's chief concern with banking reform in 1826 was with the abolition of small notes. In this, the reformers were only partially successful - banning notes of under £5 in England and Wales from 1829. However, forceful lobbying from the Scots prevented the ban being extended to Scotland (or Ireland) where there was a much longer tradition of using small notes and where banking stability during the crisis had contrasted sharply with English experience.[20]

To the Bank of England the right to issue notes of under £5 was unimportant. In fact, since 1821 the Bank had been withdrawing its small notes from circulation and it was only during the liquidity panic itself that this process was reversed. But the directors of the Bank saw any threat to their monopoly of joint-stock formation in a completely different light. This constituted an attack on their privileged position which they naturally opposed. In the aftermath of the crisis, however, the government was determined on reform. The government believed that, in tandem with its new restrictions on small notes, abolition of the Bank of England's joint stock monopoly would strengthen the structure and practice of commercial banking and could well reduce recurrent oscillations within the economy. If nothing else, it would enhance the ability of commercial banks to withstand 'runs'. Larger partnerships should produce larger banks with access to larger capital resources. Moreover, as with the country banks, partners in the new banks would bear unlimited liability for the firms' debts. It was felt that the knowledge that a bank could call on a much larger proprietorship for resources and that, ultimately, creditors could take legal action against the larger number of partners, would instil greater confidence among note-holders and depositors of the new banks.

Public opinion had already become increasingly convinced of the need for reform in the years immediately preceding the financial crisis. Thomas Joplin, a Newcastle timber merchant and of growing importance as a bank promoter, had been to the fore in contrasting the vicissitudes of the English banks with the stability of the Scottish banking system.[21] In Scotland the Bank of England's privilege did not apply and this had resulted in the typical Scottish bank being larger than its English counterpart. Significantly, the Scottish banks were also more stable – in 1825–6 only four Scottish banks stopped, not one a calamitous failure[22] – and it was this contrast which lent immediate poignancy to the arguments of the reformers. The government acted quickly and, though the Bank of England showed some reluctance, it was forced to make concessions. Indeed, the Bank's official historian, J. Clapham, portrays the negotiations as being wholly one-sided, believing that: 'The Bank was never so inert in the hands of ministers, so much ordered about, as in 1826.'[23]

The government introduced its legislation in February and the reform of company structure became law as the Banking Co-partnership Act in May 1826. In detail the act permitted the formation of banks with an unrestricted number of partners outside a 65-mile radius from London; it retained the Common Law obligation of unlimited liability on those partners for the debts of their bank; it allowed the new banks to sue and be sued in the name of Public Officers; it forbade the new banks from issuing small short-dated bills on their London agents, by setting the minimum amount and period of such bills at £50 and six months respectively; it prevented bills and notes issued by the banks from being made payable within the 65-mile exclusion zone; and, more positively, it asserted the right of the new type of bank to participate in the discounting of bills in London and elsewhere, provided such bills were not drawn by, or on, the bank itself.

The act was a clear attack on the Bank of England's privileged position, but the Bank had carefully protected its London business both by preventing other joint-stock banks from operating there and by ensuring that the notes and bills of the new banks could not possibly compete with the Bank's own issues in and around the metropolis.[24] Moreover, by way of compensation the government had included a clause in the act which formally asserted the Bank of England's right to open branches anywhere in England, and the law gave the Bank one advantage over rivals by permitting notes issued at any branch to be made payable in London as well as at the branch of issue. Thus, on the basis of the 1826 legislation alone the Bank had conceded very little - its business had long been confined to London and it had ensured that the new banks were kept well away from the capital. But, as will become clear, the 1826 Act was just the beginning. In the following decades the assault on the Bank's position was to be carried much further.

Finally, before leaving the 1826 legislation, three points should be made about its effectiveness and the implications for future developments. First, on the joint-stock banks themselves the act contained serious deficiences. The most obvious was the ban on their formation in London, but others arose from the lack of detailed regulation. The legislators gave them more or less the same freedom as existing private banks. There were no strictures as to the rights or responsibilities of shareholders. There was no guidance as to share denominations, to the publication and auditing of accounts, or even to the nature of banking business to be conducted. The legal status of the new joint-stock banks was left largely to the courts to interpret under Common Law and this created uncertainty and may well have inhibited early growth. Secondly, it is worth emphasising that the Joint-Stock Bank Act did nothing to alter the law governing the private banks. In England the private partnership continued to be the dominant form of bank for a long time after 1826 and the new joint-stock banks had to establish their businesses in the teeth of opposition from these established firms. Finally, judgement on the 1826 reforms must be that their impact on the amplitude of business fluctuations in the middle decades of the nineteenth century was marginal. Oscillations in monetary conditions and recurrent banking crises continued to occur – the institutional change which was ultimately to moderate the number of bank failures was to be a much more gradual process than the enactment of an Act of Parliament.

## STRUCTURE OF THE BANKING SYSTEM

### *Consolidation*

In the second quarter of the nineteenth century a national system of banking arrangements began to emerge. In many respects it was an imperfect system but it was one which enabled the hundreds of small, individual banks in England to overcome the problems of poor communications inherent in a relatively undeveloped economy, and one which forged greater links between the separate banking systems of England, Scotland and Ireland. It also enabled individual banks to expand their businesses beyond the confines of their own limited resources and, in so doing, greatly enhanced the scale of financial services available to the economy as a whole. In short, the second quarter of the nineteenth century witnessed a quickening in the whole process which was to lead to the creation of a national money market.

This is not to claim that major imperfections did not exist, nor that there were no important gaps in the financial linkages between different towns and regions. Some communities still had no banks and, apart from the very largest customers, local people would have to take whatever terms were offered for deposits, say, in a one-bank rural town or village. But this would be less true in larger towns where rival banks operated and, even before the advent of joint-stock banks in England, very few sizeable communities on the British mainland were more than ten miles or so from a bank. Moreover, as general communications improved, arrangements developed whereby the banks themselves could overcome some of the handicaps of having their office, or offices, confined to a specific locality. Increasingly, in both borrowing and lending they could obtain a more competitive rate of interest, a rate ultimately determined by conditions in the country as a whole.

A critical element in this drawing together of the disparate parts of the money market was the general improvement in communications. For the conduct of day-to-day business, bankers required a speedy and reliable means of remitting cash, securities and other documents, as well as a means of exchanging information. By the end of the eighteenth century mainland Britain already had an effective stage-coach network between major towns. At the start of the period under study the approximate travelling time by coach between London and Liverpool was thirty hours (1821), seventeen hours between London and

Birmingham (1821), and thirty hours between York and Edinburgh (1818).[25] In the 1820s, then, bankers already had access to quick, though not rapid, inter-regional communications. This was to improve dramatically with the establishment of the railway network in the 1830s and 1840s. The steam locomotive was reliable, secure and much faster. Within a short while travelling times along the main lines had been drastically reduced and these continued to improve. By the close of the 1880s, for instance, the fastest trains were taking only four-and-a-half hours from London to Manchester and just eight-and-a-half hours between London and Edinburgh.[26] The bankers quickly recognised the advantages of using the railroads and switched their business away from the highways. Reform of postal services and the introduction in 1840 of a single rate of one pence (ld) for letters, further enhanced internal communications. Finally, the gradual extension of the electric telegraph from the later 1830s ultimately made rapid communication a reality. In other words, from the early nineteenth century the means of communication essential to the creation of a national money market were already present and were to continue to improve, providing an important cohesive influence.

Nevertheless, until well into the second half of the nineteenth century the distinctive feature of the typical English provincial bank – whether a well-established private bank or a new joint-stock bank – was that its business was overwhelmingly local in nature. In this respect the English system lagged behind those of Scotland and Ireland, where the operation of branches in addition to a head office was much more common during the second quarter of the nineteenth century. In England, even those joint-stock banks that began to open branches from the mid-1830s continued to conduct a relatively small, local or regionally-based business. The creation of national banks with extensive branch networks still lay in the future.

Thus, a major problem facing the banks of the early and mid-nineteenth century was how to overcome this inherent isolation. At a practical level they needed a means of remitting funds between different parts of the country and a means of ensuring that they were kept informed as to both the range of investment opportunities available elsewhere and the terms being asked for alternative sources of funds. From the point of view of the national economy both investors and borrowers would benefit if local money markets could be more effectively linked. This would enable more idle funds to be drawn into the banking system and put to active use. It could lead also to important economies for individual bankers as they benefited from the pooling of resources and information. For instance, if a local bank had means of gaining ready access to funds from outside the immediate neighbourhood it could well reduce its own cash holdings. In such circumstances, if an emergency did arise the cash reserve could be readily supplemented from outside. The effective pooling of reserves in this manner would (all things being equal) reduce the aggregate of reserve funds normally held by banks.

*Inter-bank Agencies*

English provincial banks overcame the problem to a certain extent by developing a provincial agency network. By the mid-nineteenth century the banks in major towns were directly linked through the operation of mutual agencies. Although detailed arrangements varied, to a large degree provincial banks were able to arrange among themselves for the purchase and sale of securities and for the payment, or collection, of debts on behalf of customers. In addition, they supplied each other with general information from different parts of the country on investment opportunities, the state of harvests, bankruptcies, frauds, forgeries, and the like. The Scottish banks had similar arrangements with provincial firms in both Scotland and England, but in Scotland the note exchange was a more tangible arrangement linking the various parts of the system.

Here, expense was minimised by bankers sending to Edinburgh the notes of other banks that they had received and arranging for their mutual clearing, or exchange.[27]

However, provincial-based agencies had only a limited impact on bringing together the various components of the money market into a single national system. Much more important was the London money market, if only because of the sheer volume of financial transactions conducted there. The City of London was the natural centre for the lending and raising of funds by the commercial and financial population of the metropolis and, as such, its banks had access to an unrivalled volume of 'retail' banking business (i.e. dealing directly with the public). It was also the centre for the raising and servicing of governmental finance. But of critical importance from the perspective of the national monetary system was the fact that London's financial intermediaries also participated in a growing 'wholesale' money market, where money was lent to, and borrowed from, other financial intermediaries.

Indeed, the City of London's financial institutions have often been portrayed as being at the centre of a national network of financial conduits through which provincial bank funds flowed. This intermediary role within money markets was especially important in those years preceding the establishment of large-scale national banking companies which, ultimately, were able to achieve the extensive transfer of funds through their own branching networks. For most of the nineteenth century banks from districts where the inflow of deposits generally exceeded the outflow of funds, sent their 'surplus' to London for the purchase of securities from, or as deposits and short-term loans to, City financial institutions. Conversely, local banks based in areas where the demands for loans and investments from industry, commerce and other businesses exceeded local deposit resources, regularly raised extra funds in the City of London. Thus, City institutions were able to channel funds from net saving areas to net borrowing areas, making a direct contribution to the greater utilisation of financial resources within the country as a whole. In the market for short-term funds, this business essentially revolved around the London discount houses and the London commercial banks.

*London Discount Houses*

Bills of exchange were a common means of settling mercantile, and other, debt throughout this period and their purchase (or 'discount') was a popular form of investment for bankers. The existence of a national market for such bills - where they could be sold, bought and re-sold - greatly enhanced their attractiveness to the banks; and this national market rested largely with the London discount firms. By the early decades of the nineteenth century a small number of firms, the most important of which was Richardson, Overend & Co, had begun to specialise in bill transactions.[28] Their business was conducted with individuals, industrial and commercial firms, as well as with banks. Initially they operated as true brokers, concentrating on bringing sellers of bills (borrowers) into contact with purchasers (lenders), but gradually some firms began to operate on their own account. They borrowed funds directly from lenders and they bought and sold bills as principals. During the second quarter of the nineteenth century the London discount market consisted of firms at different stages of this development but, in general, the market for bills was growing strongly and becoming more organised. At this time the discount firms had already established contacts with both provincial and London bankers. After 1826 the London banks were a growing source of funds for the discount firms, and the provincial banks were both purchasers and suppliers of bills. It was in this way that the London discount market provided national intermediation for local banks. It received funds on deposit from, and sold bills to, 'net savers'; and bought bills from 'net borrowers'. This was the way in which it contributed to the fuller utilisation of the nation's financial resources and helped break down barriers to local money markets.

*London Banking Agencies*

London commercial banks provided the second force for cohesion within the system. By the early nineteenth century a number of the London banks had already established an important agency network with English provincial bankers. The importance of the London bill and security markets also meant that the Scottish and Irish banks had to have accounts with City banks. These inter-bank links enhanced the business of London banks and broadened the horizons of provincial firms. Moreover, when English joint-stock banks were established in the provinces under the new legislation they, too, quickly opened London agency accounts. In general, therefore, the London-country agency system formed an important part of the unifying process between local money markets and the centre.

The London bank would receive funds from, and make loans to, provincial agents, often through the medium of bills of exchange. In this way they performed some of the same functions as the discount firms. More importantly, however, the London banks conducted a more strictly 'agency' business, providing a number of services for the provincial banker in return for a fee.

Thus, the London bank would meet financial claims on the provincial bank when such claims fell due in London - paying cash for notes, drafts and bills drawn by, or on, the provincial firm. The importance of London in the national economy meant that it was essential for local banks, and many of their customers, to have an efficient means of remitting funds there and drawing bills on a London agent was an effective way of achieving this. London agents would also buy or sell securities on their country agents' behalf (or arrange for, say, a stock broker to do so). In this way, the London bank was in regular correspondence with its provincial contacts and would provide a great deal of information as to conditions in financial markets generally. London agents also provided specific advice on such matters as investment opportunities, the creditworthiness of firms that the provincial banker may have dealings with, implications of government policy, new legislation, and so on. Moreover, if a London bank was at the centre of a large network of provincial agencies (as, for instance, were the two London firms of Glyn & Co., and Loyd, Jones & Co.) then it would be in a position to facilitate the exchange of both information and funds between one locality and another. Finally, in an emergency a provincial bank could augment its local cash resources by either drawing on a special deposit kept with the London agent for that purpose, or by borrowing from the London bank. Provincial banks often treated their London accounts as an important part of their cash, or quasi-cash, reserve.

In general, therefore, the London agency arrangements provided two main means of unifying a fragmented money market. First, they were the channels through which flowed regular information on conditions affecting London and, indeed, national and international money markets. They also provided the provincial bank with ready access to the London money market, either as borrower or investor. Here, the London bank was in a position to act as intermediary between such borrowers and investors, either by directly diverting funds from one of its own provincial agents to another, or by indirectly seeking funds, or borrowers, from other London financial institutions. Inevitably, local money markets became less isolated and conditions there increasingly reflected what was happening in the country as a whole.

*Bank of England*

The other London institution which played an important role in the creation and functioning of the banking system was the Bank of England. The Bank was unique in many respects. As will be shown in later chapters, it was not so much the conduct of its commercial business which distinguished the part it played but rather those features of its business which were to lead to its evolution as a central bank with responsibility for monetary policy. In particular, by the 1820s it had already become the main repository of the nation's specie reserves. Other banks held some cash themselves in order to meet customers' needs for transaction purposes, but there was pressure on them to keep this to a minimum because, as an asset, cash earned no interest for the bank.

The agency network enabled banks to economise here and pool their reserves. In those periods in which the general public wished to hold more cash, the provincial banks could draw on their London accounts by running down their balances with discount houses and London agents, or by selling bills and other securities. Beyond a certain point, however, the London money market could find its own cash holdings falling below desired levels. Higher interest rates could deter borrowers but, ultimately, more cash may have been required and it is here that the Bank of England played a critical supporting role. If the system as a whole required more cash it would borrow from the Bank. The Bank would not only provide gold and silver coin but would also issue its own notes which from an early date were recognised as cash in London and Lancashire and which, from 1833, were legal tender in England and Wales. It was in this sense that the Bank of England held the ultimate cash reserve of the country.

Two institutional aspects should be emphasised. First, after the 1826 crisis few commercial banks borrowed directly from Bank's head office in London. It was rather the culmination of a series of indirect chain reactions. The English provincial, Scottish and Irish banks would borrow from the London banks and London discount houses; the London banks would restore their cash reserves by borrowing from the discount houses; and it was the discount houses who, ultimately, borrowed directly from the Bank.[29] However, a second institutional point modifies this picture somewhat, for two changes enabled the commercial banks, to some extent, to draw directly on Bank of England funds. The first change followed the 1825–6 crisis when the Bank began to open a number of English provincial branches and these provided borrowing facilities for some local banks. The second change was a gradual development that continued throughout the nineteenth century, namely the accumulation of bankers' cash reserves at the Bank of England. As with the provincial bankers' balances at London agents and discount houses, these could be drawn upon directly if necessary.

It was in this manner that, in normal circumstances, the Bank of England acted as a general buttress to the nascent banking system, effecting the pooling of cash reserves and reducing the system's susceptibility to shocks. Moreover, the growing dependence of all banks on the London money market meant that the Bank of England could more easily influence national monetary conditions through its own operations in that market. Again it was not a perfect bond but it was an important additional factor in the formation of a national money market.

## SUMMARY

The following linkages between the most important sections of the banking system of the 1820s and 1830s should be emphasised:

1. The London money market acted as a central intermediary for the whole system – attracting funds from investors throughout the country and providing funds to borrowers.
2. The London bankers' agency business placed them at the centre of a two-way flow of funds and information.
3. The London discount firms dealt directly with the Bank of England, London banks, provincial banks and with private individuals and firms.
4. The provincial banks operated agencies amongst themselves which supplemented their more important London agency arrangements.
5. The Bank of England held the largest

reserve. While it did not borrow money itself by selling bills to the discount market it was prepared to buy bills from, and make loans to, financial institutions (especially the discount houses). Most of its business was confined to London but the opening of branches after 1826 enabled it to supply cash directly to bankers in a small number of major English towns.

6. Three separate banking systems existed in the United Kingdom - in England and Wales, in Scotland and in Ireland - with separate institutional and legal developments. However, commercial ties between the three countries in the form of inter-bank agencies and accounts in London helped provide important institutional links across money markets.

FURTHER READING

W.T.C. King, *History of the London Discount Market* (Routledge & Sons, London, 1936), especially chs. 1–2.

S.G. Checkland, *Scottish Banking. A History, 1695– 1973* (Collins, Glasgow and London, 1975), Parts 1–3.

G.L. Barrow, *The Emergence of the Irish Banking System, 1820–1845* (Gill & Macmillan, Dublin, 1975).

L.S. Pressnell, *Country Banking in the Industrial Revolution* (Oxford University Press, Oxford, 1956).

NOTES

1. *Select Committee on the Bank Acts*, PP 1857 (Sess. 2), vol. 10, Appendix 21, p. 234.

2. 7 Geo. IV, c.6.

3. 7 Geo. IV, c.46.

4. The size of the area within which joint-stock banks were banned was based on a similar exclusion zone of 50 miles from Dublin granted to the

Bank of Ireland in 1821; 65 English miles being roughly equivalent to 50 Irish miles. For further details see T. E. Gregory, assisted by Annette Henderson, *The Westminster Bank through a Century* (2 vols., Oxford University Press, London, 1936), vol. 1, pp. 14–22.

5. W.R. Bisschop, *The Rise of the London Money Market, 1640–1826* (King & Son, London, 1910), chs. 1, 3; Ellis T. Powell, *The Evolution of the Money Market, 1385–1915* (Financial News, London, 1915), ch. 3; R.D. Richards, *The Early History of Banking in England* (King & Son, London, 1929), chs. 2–4.

6. On the Bank's early years see Sir John Clapham, *The Bank of England: A History* (2 vols., Cambridge University Press, Cambridge, 1945), vol. 1, pp. 1–104.

7. Philip W. Matthews, *The Bankers' Clearing House* (Pitman & Sons, London, 1921), ch. 1.

8. This account is drawn from G.L. Barrow, *The Emergence of the Irish Banking System, 1820–1845* (Gill & Macmillan, Dublin, 1975), ch 1.

9. Ibid., p.17.

10. 1 & 2 Geo. IV, c.72.

11. On Scottish banking developments see S.G. Checkland, *Scottish Banking. A History, 1695–1973* (Collins, Glasgow and London, 1975); and Charles W. Munn, *The Scottish Provincial Banking Companies, 1747–1864* (John Donald, Edinburgh, 1981). The quotation is from Checkland, p. 92.

12. The Royal Bank and the British Linen Company were both formed by Royal Charter, and the Bank of Scotland by an Act of the Scottish Parliament in 1695.

13. B.L. Anderson, 'The Attorney and the Early Capital Market in Lancashire' in Francois Crouzet (ed.), *Capital Formation in the Industrial Revolution*, (Methuen & Co., London, 1972), pp. 223–55.

14. Much of the following account draws on L.S. Pressnell, *Country Banking in the Industrial Revolution* (Oxford University Press, Oxford, 1956).

15. Contemporary sources make it impossible to be too precise but the scale of change is clear enough – Pressnell, *Country Banking*, ch. 2.

16. Ibid., p. 13.

17. While contemporaries referred to such note denominations as 'small', it should be borne in mind that £1 or £2 were fairly large sums in the days when skilled male workers may have been earning about £1.00 to £1.40 per week (during the 1830s and 1840s).

18. Arthur D. Gayer, W.W. Rostow and Anna Jacobson Schwartz (assisted by Isaiah Frank) *The Growth and Fluctuations of the British Economy, 1790–1850* (2 vols., Oxford University Press, Oxford, 1953), vol. 1, pp. 79–81, 103–7, 131–5. A brief summary of the main events of the Restriction Period is contained in Edwin Cannan (ed.), *The Paper Pound of 1797–1821. The Bullion Report* (King & Son, London, 1919; reprint Cass & Co., London, 1969).

19. Gayer, Rostow and Schwartz, *British Economy*, pp. 205–6; Frank Whitson Fetter, *Development of British Monetary Orthodoxy, 1797–1875* (Harvard University Press, Cambridge, Mass., 1965) p. 107.

20. For a recent assessment praising the merits of the Scottish note-issuing system see Lawrence H. White, *Free Banking in Britain. Theory, Experience and Debate, 1800–1845* (Cambridge University Press, Cambridge, 1984).

21. For some details of Joplin's early connections with joint-stock banks see Gregory, *Westminster Bank*, vol. 1, pp. 335–53.

22. Checkland, *Scottish Banking*, pp. 315, 406–9.

23. Clapham, *Bank of England*, vol. 2, p. 107. See Gregory, *Westminster Bank*, vol. 1, pp. 17–22, for a brief summary of the formal negotiations.

24. W.F. Crick and J.E. Wadsworth, *A Hundred Years of Joint-Stock Banking* (Hodder & Stoughton, London, 1936), p.17.

25. W.T. Jackman, *The Development of Transportation in Modern England* (Cambridge University Press, Cambridge, 1916; reprinted by Cass &

Co., London, 1962), pp. 696–7.

26. T.C. Barker and C.I. Savage, *An Economic History of Transport in Britain*, 3rd. edn (Hutchinson & Co., London, 1974), p. 99.

27. Munn, *Scottish Provincial Banking*, pp. 21–9, 47–8, 184–92. A Dublin note exchange was established for the Irish Banks in 1845 – See Barrow, *Irish Banking*, pp. 183–4.

28. For the early history of the discount market see W.T.C. King, *History of the London Discount Market* (Routledge & Sons, London, 1936), especially chs. 1–2; Pressnell, *Country Banking*, pp. 84–104; and W.M. Scammell, *The London Discount Market* (St Martin's Press, New York, 1968), ch. 5.

29. This facility was to be greatly reduced in 1858. The system of borrowing outlined here is a generalisation. Obviously some banks did borrow directly from the Bank of England and some, such as the Bank of Ireland, had special arrangements to do so.

Chapter Two

# GROWTH OF THE BANKING SECTOR, 1826–1913

This chapter quantifies the scale of long-term developments in the monetary sector during the ninety years or so to the outbreak of the First World War. The figures to be presented highlight both secular growth and structural change. Naturally they reflect changes in the environment pertaining specifically to banks, but more fundamentally they also capture the impact of long-term trends within the broader economy. Legislation was of some significance, but it was essentially the continuation of economic growth – with the long-term rise in population and *per capita* income – that led to fundamental changes in the kinds of money people wished to hold and use, and in the uses to which they were prepared to put different financial institutions.

The overall growth of commercial banks and the development of new and more appropriate techniques of conducting their business interacted with general economic expansion, being both cause and effect of the spread of the banking habit. Growing demand made the provision of more services economically feasible, whereas the increase in the number of branches encouraged the public to open and use bank accounts. On the one side, savers were increasingly willing to place their funds with the commercial banking sector and, on the other, individuals and firms sought greater financial assistance from outside the small circle of friends and associates to which many had turned in the early nineteenth century.[1] Bargains struck within the money market became less dependent on personal contact and more generally subjected to impersonal, commercial considerations.

Two aspects of these long-term monetary developments are emphasised in this chapter:

1. The size and composition of the money stock.
2. The absolute and relative growth of monetary institutions.

## THE IMPORTANCE AND DEFINITION OF MONEY

The importance within the national economy of the size and composition of the stock of money held by the public is generally appreciated. Indeed, many economists would claim that changes in the size of the domestic money stock have been significant determinants of changes in the overall level of business activity through their effects on output, prices, or both.[2] It could be argued that, on assumptions of full employment, a rise in the stock of money relative to the amount of domestic goods and services available would be inflationary (push up domestic prices) and encourage an increase in imported goods. In such circumstances, information on what is happening to the stock of money becomes important both to an understanding of economic events and, from the point of view of policy, to the control of monetary expansion. For long-term analysis, changes in the money stock during the nineteenth century were one dimension of the growing sophistication of an industrialising and maturing economy, of the switch to more convenient means of making payments and settling debts. They also reveal one aspect of how the public held its assets, by providing a measure of its preference for money balances.

Before changes in the stock of money can be quantified, however, it is first necessary to define 'money'. Of the various functions of money - unit of account, standard of value, and medium of exchange - it is the third which is of most practical use in determining which items should be considered as part of the stock of money. But even if money is defined as 'generally-recognised means of exchange', selection difficulties remain. How 'general' does the use of a particular medium of exchange have to be in order to be classed as money? It would be universally agreed that coins used in everyday transactions were money but what of, say, trade credit facilites used regularly among industrial and commercial firms? What of deposits with bankers? Should both banks' current accounts and deposit accounts be included? For most of the period the former were subject to immediate withdrawal and conversion to coin and notes as well as to chequeing, whereas the latter usually required some notice of withdrawal but, nevertheless, could be converted to cash quickly. And what of deposits or shares held at building societies and other financial institutions?

These examples are given to illustrate that there can be no one, universally-accepted definition of money. Moreover, in an historical study the problems are compounded because the 'monetariness' of particular media of exchange varied over time. For instance, in the nineteenth century the growing use of cheques undoubtedly increased the 'monetariness' of bank deposits on trend. Another major difficulty with an historical study is that of data – in the past data may not have existed, or may not now be available, or may be unreliable. In practice, therefore, decisions as to what items are included as money are guided by commonly-accepted definitions used during the period, and by the availability of relevant data. For present purposes coin, bank notes, and commercial bank deposits are included as components of the domestic money stock; and this chapter is particularly concerned to measure the growth of bank money and to compare what happened to this with the experience of other forms of money.

In this examination of long-term monetary change it will be useful to relate actual experience to a hypothetical development path such as recently expounded by Michael D. Bordo and Lars Jonung.[3]

These writers, following the earlier work by Wicksell and others, have suggested that the normal pattern of long-term monetary change in a developing economy is for there to be, first, an upward trend in the ratio of the money stock to national income (a fall in the income velocity of money) followed by a downward trend in the ratio (rise in velocity). According to this approach the earlier phase of falling velocity results from the process of 'monetisation'. By 'monetisation' is meant a process whereby barter and payments in kind are replaced by money payments. A major driving force is the greater division of labour associated with economic development because this leads to more frequent exchanges and to the use of more sophisticated methods of conducting those exchanges. The increasing use of money results from the growth of commercial banking which provides the public with acceptable forms of money in the shape of notes and deposits. After some time (measured in decades or – depending on the dating of the beginning of the monetisation phase – in centuries) the public's long-term demand for money relative to income begins to wane and the money stock falls in relation to income, due partly to the process of 'financial sophistication' and partly to the greater economic stability and security associated with economic development.

For present purposes, it is the concept of 'financial sophistication' which is particularly interesting. The argument here is that, as an industrial economy continues to mature a growing range of financial institutions and services is developed and these provide increasingly attractive alternatives to the commercial banks. New and more numerous financial assets are evolved – building society shares, insurance annuities, savings bank accounts, bonds and shares – and, as a result, there is a fall in the demand for money as an asset. Economy in the use of money balances also derives from long-term technical improvements in the means of communication and transfer (e.g. the electric telegraph in the nineteenth century).

According to this approach, then, the earlier of

the identified phases is characterised by a rise on trend in the demand for money relative to income (fall in velocity) and the later phase by a fall on trend in the demand for money (rise in velocity). It is accepted by Bordo and Jonung that:

> velocity is influenced by both sets of institutional variables at the same time, but the monetization effect will first dominate, causing velocity to decline. Later, the influence of financial sophistication and economic stability will be stronger than the monetization process causing velocity to rise. The relative strength of these two sets of forces will determine the dating of the turning point of velocity.[4]

The thesis, thus, provides a meaningful framework in which to examine long-term trends within the main components of the money stock in the UK.

## COMPONENTS OF THE STOCK OF MONEY

### *Coin*

During the nineteenth century coins (composed mainly of gold or silver) remained an extremely important part of the total money supply. The gold standard under which the banks operated applied to the domestic economy as well as to international transactions. Thus, the Bank of England was obliged by law to keep a reserve of gold (and silver) coin to pay note holders and depositors when they required it. The commercial banks, too, held a stock of coin in order to meet customers' needs and, of course, at any one time the general public would have coin in its own possession. Indeed, as the smallest bank note denomination in England and Wales was £5 and the use of cheques was still in its infancy at the beginning of the period, it is assumed that most retail transactions were settled in coin in these years. Even in Scotland and Ireland the smallest bank notes were for £1, which was quite a large sum at a time (e.g. the 1830s and 1840s) when skilled workers earned something in the region of £1 to £1.8s. per week. Obviously legal restrictions here helped maintain the importance of coin and limited the role of bank money within the monetisation process as it affected retail transactions.

No fully accurate estimates exist as to the size of the stock of coin in the hands of the public during the nineteenth century. One major problem with making any calculation lies in the fact that holders of coin were free to import and export it, and to melt it down, say, for jewellery. Thus, the figures in Table 2.1 are for guidance only. Nevertheless, these emphasise the importance of coin throughout the nineteenth and early twentieth centuries, while illustrating its failure to grow as fast as bank liabilities. As both the population and the standard of living rose, the need for cash obviously increased and the supply of coin continued to provide a basic medium for retail transactions, wage payments and the like; and despite the growth in bank money, coin was still contributing about 12 per cent of the total money supply by the early years of this century.

*Bank Notes*

*Bank of England Notes.* The Bank of England issued notes payable to bearer on demand in denominations of £5 and over, redeemable in specie at the Bank. From 1833 they were legal tender in England (though not in Scotland) and, as such, formed a critical part of the commercial banks' cash reserves and circulated widely among the public.[5] However, as column 3 in Table 2.1 shows, in absolute terms Bank of England notes were a fairly stable element in the long-term growth of the money supply (especially from the 1870s), and a small and declining proportion of the total. They had enjoyed some expansion in the 1860s and 1870s in response to the increased demand for money of all kinds, and at that time legal restrictions in England meant that only the Bank of England could expand its note circulation to any degree. An increase in the Bank's specie and bullion reserve provided the means to push up this circulation by about 22 per cent

Table 2.1 : U.K. Money Stock and its Main Components, 1825-1913

£ million. Ratio (%) of each component to the total money stock is given in parentheses.

| Date[a] | Coin in Circulation | Bank of England Liabilities | | | | Comm. Bank Note Liabilities | | | | Comm. Bank Deposit Liabilities | | | | Total Commercial Bank Notes & Deposits [10+14] | Total Money Stock [2+3+4+15] |
|---|---|---|---|---|---|---|---|---|---|---|---|---|---|---|---|
| | | Notes in Circul- | Deposits held by General Public[b] | Government Deposits | Bankers' Balances | England and Wales | Scotland | Ireland | Total | England and Wales | Scotland | Ireland | Total | | |
| 1 | 2 | 3 | 4 | 5 | 6 | 7 | 8 | 9 | 10 | 11 | 12 | 13 | 14 | 15 | 16 |
| 1825 | - | 19.7 | 11.3[c] | - | 0.8 | - | 3.3 | - | - | - | 14.5 | - | - | - | - |
| 1850 | 61.0 (23.9) | 18.9 (7.4) | 9.4 (3.7) | 9.8 | 1.5 | 6.3 (2.5) | 3.2 (1.2) | 4.6 (1.8) | 14.1 (5.5) | 106.6 (41.7) | 35.0 (13.7) | 10.4 (4.1) | 152.0 (59.5) | 166.1 (65.0) | 255.4 |
| 1875 | 105.1 (16.5) | 25.6 (4.0) | 11.7 (1.8) | 7.6 | 9.3 | 4.8 (0.8) | 5.9 (0.9) | 7.1 (1.1) | 17.8 (2.8) | 366.4 (57.4) | 79.8 (12.5) | 32.3 (5.1) | 478.5 (74.9) | 496.3 (77.7) | 638.7 |
| 1900 | 119.9 (12.0) | 27.6 (2.8) | 21.7 (2.2) | 10.1 | 24.1 | 1.2 (0.1) | 7.8 (0.8) | 6.6 (0.7) | 15.6 (1.6) | 664.4 (66.3) | 104.7 (10.4) | 48.6 (4.8) | 817.7 (81.6) | 838.6 (83.7) | 1002.5 |
| 1913 | 144.3 (12.0) | 27.7 (2.3) | 13.3 (1.1) | 29.9 | 39.3 | 0.2 (0.02) | 8.2 (0.7) | 9.2 (0.8) | 17.6 (1.5) | 803.7 (66.8) | 125.9 (10.5) | 71.1 (5.9) | 1018.7 (83.1) | 1018.3 (84.6) | 1203.6 |

*Sources and Notes:* **over page**

Table 2.1 (Cont'd)

*Notes*

a. All figures are five-year averages centred on the dates shown *except* for Scottish bank liabilities, 1825 and 1850; Irish bank deposits, 1850–1913; and for 1913 when an average for 1910/13 is used.
b. Includes seven-day and other short-dated bills.
c. Includes government deposits (1825 figure only).

*Sources*

1. Bank of England liabilities – 'Bank of England Liabilities and Assets: 1696 to 1966', Appendix to *Bank of England Quarterly Bulletin*, vol. 7, June 1967; contemporary issues of *The Economist*.
2. Commercial bank notes – B.R. Mitchell and P. Deane, *Abstract of British Historical Statistics* (Cambridge University Press, Cambridge, 1962), pp. 450–1 *except* for Scotland, 1825.
3. Scottish deposit liabilities and notes (1825) – S.G. Checkland, *Scottish Banking. A History, 1695–1973* (Collins, London, 1975), pp. 424, 426, 743–7.
4. English deposit liabilities – Michael Collins, 'Long-term Growth of the English Banking Sector and Money Stock, 1844–80', *Economic History Review*, 2nd ser., vol. 36, 1983, Appendix 4, p. 394, for 1850 and 1875; Forrest Capie and Alan Webber, *A Monetary History of the United Kingdom, 1870–1982* (Geo. Allen & Unwin, London, 1985), vol. 1, p. 130, for 1900 and 1913.
5. Coin – Forrest Capie and Alan Webber, 'Total Coin and Coin in Circulation in the United Kingdom, 1868–1914', *Journal of Money, Credit and Banking*, vol. 15, 1983, pp 30–31. The 1850 estimate has been made by the author on the basis of backwards extrapolation using the figures for bullion movements in Albert H. Imlah,

*Economic Elements in the Pax Britannica* (Russell & Russell, New York, 1958) p. 71.

6. Irish deposit liabilities – 1850 figure from W. Newmarch, 'An Attempt to Ascertain the Magnitude and Fluctuations of the Amount of Bills of Exchange ... 1828–1847', *Journal of the Statistical Society*, vol. 14, 1851, p. 169, where he estimates deposits and 'private capital' to be £12.4 m. – £2 m. has been deducted here for 'private capital'. 1875 figures from S. Nishimura, 'The Estimates of Bank Deposits in the UK, 1870–1913' (unpublished typescript, University of Hosei, 1976) p. 20. 1900 and 1913 figures from David K. Sheppard, *The Growth and Role of UK Financial Institutions, 1880–1962* (Methuen & Co., London, 1971), pp. 180–1.

between 1865 and 1875. However, the Bank's note issue then stabilised at some £26 million–£28 million and its relative importance plummeted (dropping from 4 per cent of the money supply to about 2 per cent, 1875–1913) as other components of the money stock expanded. Nevertheless, the fact that Bank notes were legal tender and were part of the commercial banks' cash reserves, continued to afford them a special status.

*Commercial Bank Notes.* Many English commercial banks outside London also issued bearer notes during the nineteenth century, although by the early twentieth century the practice had declined so much that the handful of surviving issuers kept up their circulations largely as a matter of prestige and public relations. These notes were used for retail and other cash transactions within the locality of the issuing bank. They were not legal tender but depended upon public confidence for their circulation. Over the long run notes were replaced by deposits and the use of cheques, or by Bank of England notes which were more secure and more widely accepted. The prestige of the Bank of England and the fact that its notes were legal tender ensured that they eventually circulated throughout the country. Legal restrictions were also important in the early demise of the private note issue in England. As with Bank of England notes, the abolition of notes under £5 denomination in 1826 meant that bankers lost any chance of supplying notes for the great bulk of retail transactions. Moreover, the 1844 Bank Charter Act fixed the maximum value of notes that individual banks could circulate and encouraged the eventual disappearance of the English commercial bank note. In consequence, English notes which in 1850 were already only about 2.5 per cent of the money supply as defined in Table 2.1, were down to a minute 0.02 per cent by 1913.

Scottish and Irish experience was somewhat different. Notes of 'small' denomination (between £1 and £5) were not banned in 1826, nor were Bank of England notes made legal tender. This partly accounts for the wider circulation enjoyed by commercial bank notes in both Scotland and Ireland. Notes in these countries enjoyed expansion in the period as a whole, despite the severe blow to confidence suffered in the wake of the City of Glasgow Bank's failure in 1878 and despite the restrictive legislation of 1845. Two separate acts of 1845 (one for Scotland, and one for Ireland) had imposed limits to the 'authorised' circulation of individual banks, any excess to be matched – £ for £ – by an increase in the size of the bank's specie (largely gold) reserve. But, as Table 2.1 shows, although both Scottish and Irish bank notes in total continued to grow (and have done so through the twentieth century) they were declining in relative importance. By the mid-nineteenth century notes were already only about one-tenth of the value of Scottish deposit liabilities, and the faster growth of deposits confirmed the dwindling significance of notes among commercial bank liabilities and in the total money stock. This experience was shared by Irish notes – they continued to grow through the period as a whole, but declined relative to deposits. Thus, in all three countries – England, Scotland and Ireland – commercial bank notes were of declining importance and, by the 1870s, were already only a very small part of the money stock held by the public.

*Bank Deposits*

*Bank of England Deposits.* It is useful to distinguish three types of Bank of England deposits: deposits held by the general public; government deposits (known as 'public deposits'); and bankers' balances. Although it came to act as a central bank, the Bank of England was formally a non-government institution with private customers of its own and it was the balances of these customers which formed part of the general money supply. However, during the nineteenth century the Bank's commercial banking business was rarely competitive enough to share in the general expansion of banking services – for instance, unlike most other banks it did not normally pay interest on deposits. In consequence, compared to the commercial banks its private deposits experienced only modest growth or even decline (after 1900 in Table 2.1), and they were not a significant factor in the growth of the general money supply.

Government balances at the Bank arose from its function as the government's banker and these continued to be an important, long-term source of revenue for the Bank. In calculating the size of the money stock in the hands of the general public these deposits are excluded, however, as the government must be included among the 'monetary authorities' and, as a result, its deposits were inter-authority liabilities.

Bankers' balances at the Bank are also excluded when calculating the money supply as they did not form part of the balances in the hands of the general public. Together with coins and Bank of England notes, these balances were part of the commercial banks' reserves because they could be converted quickly to cash or used to settle inter-bank debts. Thus, they were part of the supply of 'high-powered money' – that is, part of the supply of cash held by the banks as reserves against note and deposit liabilities. As can be seen from Table 2.1, it was this item which experienced the greatest growth among the Bank's liabilities as the commercial banks, discount houses and other financial institutions found it increasingly convenient to build up their balances at the Bank.

*Commercial Bank Deposit Liabilities.* As with the coin circulation, when it comes to measuring commercial bank liabilities, data deficiences, particularly in the earlier period, mean that only estimates can be made. Data constraints also necessitate the lumping together of all types of deposits – including both current and deposit accounts – and, therefore, obscure the fact that over this period the 'monetariness' of deposits changed significantly. As already noted, the growing popularity of cheques meant that current account deposits would have been a more readily-recognised medium of exchange than, say, deposit accounts whose encashment and withdrawal was subject to a variety of restrictions. Be that as it may, when it comes to the statistics it is necessary to consider deposits as a single group.

Of all the major items of the money stock it was these commercial bank deposit liabilities that contributed the greatest growth by far. It was the change in deposits that captured the extent of the monetisation process in the UK. Tables 2.1, 2.2 and 2.3 show that in total they rose almost seven-fold from 1850 to 1913. Deposits per head of the population rose from £5.50 to £22.30 and whereas just £27.10 of bank deposits had been held in 1850 for every £100 of Gross National Product, this was up to £43.60 by the First World War. Similarly, deposits became more important within the total money supply: rising from some 60 per cent in 1850, to 75 per cent by 1875 and still further to over 83 per cent by 1913. In other words, during this period it was the commercial banks who were contributing the bulk of the new money needed by the developing British economy. Of the three countries, English bank deposits grew the fastest in absolute terms and within the English sector it was the joint-stock banks, with large capital resources and expansionary branching

Table 2.2 : U.K. Monetary Change, 1850–1913

| Date[a] | a) Commercial Bank Deposits per head of population (£) | | | | | b) U.K. Commercial Bank Deposits per £100 of GNP at factor cost (£) | c) Money Stock as Ratio to GNP (%) (the reciprocal, Velocity, is given in parentheses). |
|---|---|---|---|---|---|---|---|
| | England & Wales | Scotland | Ireland | U.K. Current Prices | U.K. Constant Prices[b] | | |
| 1 | 2 | 3 | 4 | 5 | 6 | 7 | 8 |
| 1850 | 6.00 | 12.20 | 1.40 | 5.50 | 6.00 | 27.10 | 45.5 (2.2) |
| 1875 | 15.20 | 22.70 | 6.10 | 14.60 | 13.30 | 38.20 | 50.9 (2.0) |
| 1900 | 20.70 | 23.60 | 10.90 | 20.00 | 20.50 | 45.20 | 55.4 (1.8) |
| 1913 | 22.40 | 26.60 | 16.20 | 22.30 | 21.50 | 43.60 | 52.4 (1.9) |

*Notes:*

a Where possible all figures are five-year averages centred on the dates shown, *except* for 1913 when an average for 1910/13 is used.

b The price index used is Phyllis Deane's implicit price deflator (GNP at factor cost), 1900 = 100.

[over]

Table 2.2 (Cont'd)

*Sources*:

1. Monetary data from Table 2.1.
2. Population figures from B.R. Mitchell and P. Deane, *Abstract of British Historical Statistics* (Cambridge University Press, Cambridge, 1962), pp. 8–10.
3. GNP figures are from Phyllis Deane, 'New Estimates of Gross National Products for the United Kingdom, 1830–1914', *Review of Income and Wealth*, ser. 14, 2, June 1968, pp. 104–7. These have been preferred to those in C.H. Feinstein, *National Income, Expenditure and Output of the United Kingdom, 1855–1965* (Cambridge University Press, Cambridge, 1972) solely on the grounds that they cover more of the period. Use of Feinstein's figures for the later dates produced the following results:

| | Commercial Bank Deposits per £100 of GNP (£) | Money Stock as Ratio to GNP (%) |
|---|---|---|
| 1875 | 42.00 | 49.7 |
| 1900 | 47.40 | 53.1 |
| 1913 | 46.20 | 50.7 |

policies, which experienced the most rapid growth.[6] In general, although the coin circulation remained fairly buoyant, the rapid expansion of bank deposits is clear evidence of a growing sophistication and maturation of the economy and its means of settling debts. The figures emphasise the importance of the commercial banks within the history of British economic development.

*Total Money Stock*

Combining the various monetary items enables the production of estimates for the total stock of money

Table 2.3: U.K. Monetary Growth, 1850-1913 (per cent per annum, continuously compounded)

| Period | UK Commercial Bank Deposits | | Total Money Stock | |
|---|---|---|---|---|
| | Current Prices | Constant Prices | Current Prices | Constant Prices |
| 1848/52-1873/77 | 4.7 | 4.0 | 3.7 | 3.0 |
| 1873/77-1898/1902 | 2.2 | 2.7 | 1.8 | 2.3 |
| 1898/1902-1910/13 | 1.6 | 1.1 | 1.4 | 0.1 |
| 1848/52-1910/13 | 3.0 | 2.8 | 2.5 | 2.3 |

*Source:* As Table 2.1

---

held by the public for the period since 1850. The figures are given in Table 2.1, column 16. Overall the money stock grew somewhat less than five-fold between 1850 and 1913, at an annual compound rate of growth of 2.5 per cent (Table 2.3).

Significantly, the figures in Table 2.2, column 8, conform to the pattern predicted by the Bordo/Jonung hypothesis – at first, the ratio of money to Gross National Product shows a long-term tendency to rise (from 45.5 per cent in 1850, through 50.9 per cent in 1875, to 55.4 per cent in 1900) and, then, falls (to 52.4 per cent in 1913). In fact, the study by Bordo and Jonung, as well as a similar one by Forrest Capie and Geoffrey Wood[7], failed to find the expected 'U-shaped' movement in income velocity for the UK. Their data series did not begin until the 1870s, however, and the inclusion here of earlier figures makes the pattern clearer.

The growth in money balances was strongest in

the middle decades of the nineteenth century when the commercial banks were expanding rapidly, reaching out to new customers and extending their branch networks. But this growth was already levelling off by the late nineteenth century. Table 2.3 shows that real monetary growth was very high, in historical terms, during the third quarter of the century when an annual growth rate of 3 per cent (3.7 per cent in nominal terms) was achieved. It is also clear that the main contribution to this aggregate figure came from the sharp expansion of bank deposits, which grew at 4 per cent per annum (4.7 per cent at current prices). However, both bank deposit and money stock growth rates eased noticeably in the last quarter of the century and this decline went even further in the Edwardian years, when real monetary growth was very close to zero and the trend in income velocity was reversed. The *per capita* and other figures in Table 2.2 provide strong corroborative evidence of a sharp slow–down in banking expansion around the turn of the century.

There are two ways of looking at this relative stagnation. From the public's point of view it could well have been that alternative forms of holding liquid assets were becoming more plentiful and more attractive (in terms of security, accessibility and profitability). In other words – as Bordo and Jonung suggest – the process of financial sophistication was becoming more powerful. In particular, the expansion of the savings bank and building society movements (and, more selectively, of the overseas banking sector in London) may have attracted proportionately more of the funds which had previously gone to the commercial banks. Such deposits in other financial institutions are not included in the definition of the money supply used here and, thus, do not add to its growth. From the point of view of the banks, the levelling–off of growth may have been a sign of market 'maturation'. Perhaps by 1900 the more readily exploitable parts of the retail deposit market had already been tapped and new branches were opening up in less densely–populated and less wealthy areas, or were duplicating existing facilities operated by rival banks in the same town. For the future, growth of bank deposits would proceed more steadily, depending largely on the rates of population and income growth, as well as on the rate of inflation. The fruits of expansion derived from the initial exploitation of new markets as the banking habit had spread in the nineteenth century were no longer available, at least not until there had been a revolution in social attitudes towards who should hold a bank account.

Other long–term institutional and market factors may have had an important part in the banks' relative stagnation. As will be shown in Chapter 3, the turn of the century was marked by a greater concentration of market power into fewer and fewer banking companies. In addition, there is evidence of an inclination on the part of the larger banks to suppress price competition, a tendency to oligopoly. Moreover, a fairly inflexible consensus emerged as to what constituted 'proper' banking business, thus restricting the exploitation of new forms of business and encouraging the segmentation of the UK monetary sector into groups of institutions specialising in the provision of a limited range of services. The restrictive and defensive attitudes of the London and Scottish clearing banks in particular may have stunted their ability to capture a larger share of the provision of the broader range of financial assets and services sought by the public.

*Other Media of Exchange*

The financial assets considered in this chapter as part of the money supply have been closely confined, but it could well be argued that during the period other assets were also used as money. For instance, commercial or trade credit, whereby suppliers granted firms credit for materials purchased, was (and is) a common form of conducting business. In other words, trade credit could be seen as providing an important medium of exchange. In particular, the bill of exchange was a widely–accepted means of settling debt within the domestic economy, at least in the early and middle decades of the nineteenth century.[8] Indeed, until the cost of using them became prohibitive with the imposition of stamp duties (in 1826 and 1833) in some areas, such as Lancashire, small bills of exchange were even used in retail transactions. The bill of exchange was also attractive to commercial banks and other financial institutions as a portfolio asset because it could be quickly converted to cash. It could be argued, then, that the bill had many of the attributes of what is generally considered to be 'money'.

Similar difficulties arise over the exclusion from the money stock of deposits at financial institutions other than commercial banks – institutions such as discount houses, merchant banks, building societies and savings banks. The omission of such financial liabilities (assets for deposit holders) from Table 2.1 serves to emphasise the arbitrariness of any exclusive list of money stock components. The figures are to be interpreted liberally, as an indication of the changing dimensions of the monetary sector during this period but in the knowledge that there also existed a whole edifice of quasi-money and credit which has not been quantified.

## FINANCIAL INSTITUTIONS

A survey of the changing quantitative significance of the country's major financial institutions provides another important means of assessing long-term developments in the UK banking sector.

### *The Commercial Banks*

A commercial bank is defined here as a financial intermediary which accepted money on deposit subject to cheque. It has already been seen that, outside London, many of them also issued demand notes to the public although in England this practice was on the decline from as early as the end of the 1830s. For the period as a whole, the main distinction drawn between different types of English commercial banks is that between those that were private partnerships and those that were joint-stock banks (or banking

Table 2.4 : Number of Banks and Banking Offices, 1825-1913

| Date | England & Wales | | | | Scotland | | Ireland | | U.K. | |
|---|---|---|---|---|---|---|---|---|---|---|
| | Private Banks | | Joint-Stock Banks | | | | | | | |
| | Banks | Offices | Banks | Offices | Banks | Offices | Banks | Offices | Banks | Offices |
| 1825 | 650 | 650[a] | 0 | 0 | 36 | 173 | 15 | 25[a] | 715 | 848 |
| 1850 | 327 | 518 | 99 | 576 | 17 | 407 | 16 | 184 | 459 | 1685 |
| 1875 | 236 | 595 | 122 | 1364 | 11 | 921 | 12 | 440 | 381 | 3320 |
| 1900 | 81 | 358 | 83 | 4212 | 10 | 1085 | 10 | 614 | 184 | 6269 |
| 1913 | 29 | 147 | 41 | 6426 | 8 | 1248 | 10 | 789 | 88 | 8610 |

a Assuming one office per private bank.

*Sources:*

*England and Wales*

1825 Rondo Cameron, *Banking in the Early Stages of Industrialisation* (Oxford University Press, London, 1967), P. 33.

1850-1913 *Banking Almanac* - See Michael Collins, 'The English Banking Sector and Monetary Growth, 1844-80', University of Leeds Economics Discussion Paper, No. 102, 1981, pp. 5-6; and Shizuya Nishimura, *The Decline of Inland Bills of Exchange in the London Money Market, 1855-1913* (Cambridge University Press, Cambridge, 1971) pp. 80-1.

*Scotland:* S.G. Checkland, *Scottish Banking. A History, 1695-1973* (Collins, London, 1975), pp. 424, 497, 530, 743-6.

*Ireland:*

1825 G.L. Barrow, *The Emergence of the Irish Banking System, 1820-1845* (Gill and Macmillan, Dublin, 1975), Appendices 2 and 4.

1850-1913 Banking Almanac.

Table 2.5 : Growth of the Banking Sector, 1825-1913

| Date | Number of Offices per Bank | | | | | No. of Banking Offices per 10,000 of Population | | | |
|---|---|---|---|---|---|---|---|---|---|
| | England & Wales | | Scotland | Ireland | U.K. | England | Scotland | Ireland | U.K. |
| | Private Banks | Joint-Stock Banks | | | | | | | |
| 1825 | 1.0(?) | - | 4.8 | 1.7(?) | 1.2 | 0.50 | 0.78 | 0.04 | 0.38 |
| 1850 | 1.6 | 5.8 | 23.9 | 11.5 | 3.7 | 0.62 | 1.42 | 0.27 | 0.61 |
| 1875 | 2.5 | 11.2 | 83.7 | 34.2 | 8.6 | 0.81 | 2.62 | 0.78 | 1.00 |
| 1900 | 4.4 | 50.7 | 108.5 | 61.4 | 34.1 | 1.42 | 2.45 | 1.37 | 1.52 |
| 1913 | 5.1 | 156.7 | 156.0 | 78.9 | 97.8 | 1.80 | 2.64 | 1.82 | 1.83 |

*Sources:* Banking Data as Table 2.4. Population Data from B.R. Mitchell and P. Deane, *Abstract of British Historical Statistics* (Cambridge University Press, Cambridge, 1962), pp. 8-10.

companies) which had a large body of shareholders.

Tables 2.4 and 2.5 provide an empirical survey of banking institutions over the period from 1825 to 1913. For England, two features of the total number should be stressed. The first is the very large number of banks which existed at the start of the period – with over 600 in 1825, and still more than 400 in 1850. The existence of so many banks emphasises the importance of the agency networks in drawing together the various parts into, at least, the semblance of a 'system'. It also meant that during that period any attempt by the monetary authorities to impose a change in policy was likely to be indirect – face-to-face contact was a practical impossibility. Certainly the degree and nature of contact between the Bank of England and the commercial banks was, of necessity, wholly different from that of the twentieth century when only a small number of very large banks came to dominate the money market.

The second point arising from the figures is that, on trend, the number of English banks decreased. This was a fairly gradual process, arising partly out of a steady trickle of liquidations but, more significantly, it was the result of bank amalgamations. Table 2.4 also shows that the number of private banks fell in relation to the joint-stock banks. Before 1826 all banks were private partnerships, but by 1850 private firms were down to 77 per cent of the total; and with the pace of the decline quickening from the 1890s, by 1913 they were only 41 per cent.

The relative decline of the English private bank is even more apparent from the figures on the number of banking offices. From the beginning, joint-stock banks were more inclined to operate branches and, therefore, were more likely to have larger businesses than the private bankers. This distinction became more pronounced over time. Thus, in 1850 private banks operated just under one-half of all English bank offices, but this had fallen to less than one-third by 1875, and to only some 2 per cent by 1913. This change in the share of banking outlets was due less to private banks closing down than to a greater willingness on the part of joint–stock banks to operate branch networks and a greater concentration of ownership through inter–bank mergers. By the turn of the century, in particular, the larger banking companies were operating an aggressive branching policy which more than trebled the number of banking offices in just two–and–a–half decades. As a result, although the figures show the total number of banks on the decline, 1826–1913, the number of outlets through which commercial banking services were offered to the public increased markedly (see Table 2.5). The number of banks may have been declining, but they were larger and financially stronger.

Table 2.5 also provides one measure of the size of the business of different types of banks (i.e. the number of offices per bank) and emphasises the distinction between English private and joint–stock banks. While both types of bank were, on average, operating more branches in addition to their head office, the number of offices per private bank increased only from 1.6 to 5.1 between 1850 and 1913. In other words, the great bulk of private banks operated a very limited number of retail outlets. Even successful partnerships such a Leatham, Tew & Co. of the West Riding had only three offices in 1880; and the more important Yorkshire partnership of Beckett & Co. were operating just eight offices in the same year. Exceptionally, more than ten offices may have been managed by a private bank, but less than half–a–dozen was typical. This is what we might expect from enterprises with access to only a restricted amount of proprietor capital. In contrast, the large body of shareholders in the joint–stock banks enabled them to draw on a greater range of capital resources. True, by the mid–nineteenth century even these joint–stock banks were still typically small, with just a handful of local branches. By the last quarter of the century, however, there were already examples of the national–based, commercial bank with a provincial branch network and a City of London head office. Representative of these was the London and Provincial Bank Ltd, which had a large network of 80 offices in

1880; and the National Provincial Bank of England Ltd with 150 offices. These were to provide the pattern for the future, so that by 1913 the average joint-stock bank was operating 156 offices, or over 30 times as many as its private counterpart. They were wholly different types of business enterprises.

In addition to the English banks, of course, there existed an important Scottish commercial banking sector. Scottish bank liabilities accounted for a significant, if declining, proportion of the national total. They were equivalent to about 23 per cent of total UK bank liabilities in 1850, some 17 per cent in 1875 and around 12-13 per cent at the beginning of the twentieth century.

As was noted in the previous chapter, by the second quarter of the nineteenth century the Scottish and English money markets were becoming more closely integrated in the sense that inter-bank accounts meant that short-term funds could be viewed as part of a national pool, with effective arbitrage standardising interest rates across regions. But in other respects the Scottish system remained separate - its institutions, banking practice and governing legislation differed from that of England. By the 1820s banks with larger numbers of shareholders than their English counterparts already dominated the Scottish system. As a result the distinction between private and joint-stock banks is not very helpful and the Scottish figures in Tables 2.4 and 2.5 refer to the totality of banks.[9] As for England, the total number of banks declined over the period as a whole and the number of offices increased in absolute and *per capita* terms. However, the significant contrast lies in how 'advanced', even at the beginning of the nineteenth century, the Scottish system was in the proliferation of offices. Until the very end of the period under study the average Scottish bank operated many more branches than its English counterpart. The figures in Table 2.5 also show that the Scottish system operated more branches per head of the population. By the twentieth century this may have merely reflected the fact that the Scottish population was geographically more dispersed, the English population more urbanised. Thus, in order to reach the public the Scottish banks may have needed to operate more branches, spreading them around many more small towns. Certainly, by 1913 English bank deposits per head of the population had more or less caught up with the Scottish (Table 2.2). However, such an explanation fails to explain why 'rural' Ireland had no more bank offices *per capita* than 'urban' England.

In Ireland a small number of joint–stock banks was already established by 1825. In 1850 they were outnumbering private firms by eleven to five and they have dominated ever since.[10] Thus, the figures in Tables 2.4 and 2.5 refer largely to the Irish joint–stock banks. It was these banking companies that operated fairly large branch networks compared to their English counterparts (though fewer than the Scottish banks). In *per capita* terms, Table 2.5 shows that Ireland was the 'least developed' banking system in 1825, with only 25 offices available for over seven million people – the lack of banking facilities presumably reflecting the low level of incomes and economic development in that country. However, rapid expansion occurred in the next half–century and (coupled with the fall in the Irish population) by 1875 the number of banking offices *per capita* had reached a level very similar to that in England.

All in all, then, the experience of the British commercial banking system over the years from 1825 to 1913, was of a very sharp contraction in the number of firms, yet an equally sharp rise in the number of retail outlets or branches. In all three countries banks grew in size and market power became concentrated into fewer and fewer firms. In terms of numbers, the 715 banks of 1825 had dwindled to 88 by 1913, while the number of offices had risen from 848 to over ten times that number.

### *Bank of England*

At the beginning of the period the Bank of England was the most prestigious of all British banks and when it chose to do so it could dominate the short–term money market in London. This dominance reflected not only the Bank's special status (e.g. as the government's bank) but also its sheer size. As Table 2.1 illustrates, in 1850 the Bank's note and deposit liabilities to the general public were some 17 per cent of total commercial bank liabilities. But compared to the commercial banks, the Bank of England's liabilities stagnated and by the early twentieth century the Bank's influence was no longer based on the volume of its business. In fact, at the outbreak of World War I it accounted for only 4 per cent of bank liabilities.

The decline relative to commercial banks is not difficult to explain. Indeed, in many respects it was the Bank's dominance in the early and mid-nineteenth century which was extraordinary. This had resulted from its legal monopoly of joint-stock formation in England and Wales and from the broad acceptance of its notes. The removal of these legal privileges, the greater use of cheques and bank deposits compared to notes and the Bank's lack of commercial orientation when it came to developing new banking services, all served to constrict its growth relative to the commercial banks. Potentially, the Bank's ability to intervene in security markets and to influence interest rates was reduced, with important consequences for the conduct of monetary policy.[11] Here we need only note that this was happening and postpone further consideration until Chapter 6.

### *Non-bank Financial Intermediaries*

Accompanying the growth of the British commercial banking sector was an expansion in other savings and deposit institutions, known collectively as 'non-bank financial intermediaries'. Although there was some overlap, delineation of function was a more obvious characteristic of these institutions during the nineteenth century. In most cases legislation encouraged early demarcation, and eventual cartelisation within particular groups (such as building societies) consolidated it. Much of the early legislation – especially the Friendly Society Acts, 1793–1855, and the Trustee Savings Bank

Acts, 1817–80 – was aimed at encouraging and protecting small savings within charitable, or non-profit making, institutions. Thus, friendly societies and trustee saving banks were granted tax exemptions although the maximum amounts deposited and the use to which funds could be put were closely regulated by government.[12] The government also set up its own Post Office Savings Bank in 1861, again with prescribed functions. Individual deposits were limited to a £150 maximum, the interest rate on deposits was fixed at two-and-one-half per cent per annum and all investment funds had to be placed with the National Debt Commissioners. To some extent these savings banks competed with the commercial banks for the funds of small savers – by 1904 there were over 15,000 branches of the Post Office Savings Bank and some 400 trustee savings banks' offices[13] – but it was never the intention to compete actively in the commercial money markets; nor did the commercial banks actively court small savers.

The middle decades of the nineteenth century also witnessed a sharp expansion in the number of building societies and a growing number of these were established as 'permanent' institutions rather than the temporary, or 'terminating', societies of the early part of the century.[14] By 1873 there were about 1,500 societies but direct competition between the building societies and the commercial banks was prescribed in a similar manner to that with savings banks. For example, the Building Society Acts of 1874 and 1894 granted certain legal privileges and tax exemptions to the societies but, in return, the societies' range of activities was restricted. The 1894 Act, in particular, 'had the effect of firmly channelling the building society business towards the promotion of low-income group home ownership ... they were incorporated within the charitable institutional framework.'[15] Of some importance from the commercial banks' point of view, was the eventual legal requirement that the savings banks and building societies should confine their deposits to term accounts requiring notice of withdrawal. In other words, the development of a 'building society cheque', or some such equivalent, became impossible. This illustrates the general tenor of the legislation of the period. Little wonder, therefore, that it was the commercial banks whose deposits supplied the lion's share of new liquid balances in the hands of the public.

Throughout the nineteenth century other specialist institutions emerged, or continued to develop, in response to particular needs in the money market. Obviously the great expansion in insurance business played an important role in the general savings movement.[16] Within the City of London, specialisation became the 'order of the day' in both long- and short-term money markets. Among the most important of these City institutions were the discount houses which specialised in the purchase and sale of bills of exchange. They were to constitute an important link in the money market arrangements of the UK – providing a safe means of depositing funds at short notice for the commercial banks and supplying a specialist service in bill investments. Also from the mid-nineteenth century a number of merchant bankers began to perform specialist functions which were to prove permanent features of the London money market. Thus, the acceptance houses specialised in the creation of short-term credit in foreign trade and finance in the form of the 'bill on London'; and the issuing houses offered specialist services in the issuing of securities (often for overseas customers) on the London Stock Market.

Finally in this survey of monetary institutions, mention must be made of foreign banks with offices in London. An increasing number were established from the mid-nineteenth century. They participated in the expansion of the City's role as an international financial centre, sharing in the provision of both long- and short-term credit, although they competed directly with the domestic banks to only a limited extent.

## CONCLUSION

The period from 1826 to 1913 witnessed strong,

long-term monetary growth. This is to be expected for a country experiencing general economic expansion. Similarly, as the economy matured so, too, did the means of payment used. In particular, the period saw the continued development of the commercial banking sector and the extension of the banking habit. The banks themselves became larger and more secure institutions, their branch offices reaching a much broader section of the population. Quantitatively, commercial bank deposits became the dominant component of the domestic money stock. However, concentration on the commercial banks must not obscure the fact that British economic development was also accompanied by increased institutional specialisation in the money markets, and by the existence of financial assets other than those defined here as 'money'. These developments, too, were important features of Britain's continuing financial maturity and sophistication.

## FURTHER READING

Michael Collins, 'Long-Term Growth of the English Banking Sector and Money Stock, 1844–80', *Economic History Review*, 2nd ser., vol. 36, 1983, pp. 374–94.

Forrest Capie and Alan Webber, *A Monetary History of the United Kingdom, 1870–1982* (Geo. Allen & Unwin, London, 1985), vol. 1.

David K. Sheppard, *The Growth and Role of UK Financial Institutions, 1880–1962* (Methuen & Co., London, 1971).

## NOTES

1. On the 'personal' nature of the late eighteenth/early nineteenth-century capital market see Francois Crouzet (ed.), *Capital Formation in the Industrial Revolution* (Methuen & Co., London, 1972), especially the editor's introduction.

2. There is a voluminous literature on the importance of money. Professor Milton Friedman is

the leading exponent of modern monetarist theory and a recent statement of his views can be found in Milton Friedman and Anna J. Schwartz, *Monetary Trends in the United States and the United Kingdom* (University of Chicago Press, Chicago and London, 1982), ch. 2. A textbook survey of the issues is contained in Howard R. Vane and John L. Thompson, *Monetarism: Theory, Evidence and Policy* (Martin Robertson, Oxford, 1979), chs. 1 and 8.

3. Michael David Bordo and Lars Jonung, 'The Long Run Behavior of the Income Velocity of Money in Five Advanced Countries, 1870–1975: An Institutional Approach', *Economic Inquiry*, vol. 19, no. 1, 1981, pp. 96–116.

4. Ibid., p. 99.

5. On the ambiguous legal position of Bank of England notes in Ireland see G.L. Barrow, *The Emergence of the Irish Banking System, 1820–1845* (Gill and Macmillan, Dublin, 1975), pp. 142–5.

6. As the Irish population was declining, it could be argued that in *per capita* terms Irish deposit growth was stronger (Table 2.2) although, of course, the absolute amount was much smaller.

7. Forrest H. Capie and Geoffrey E. Wood, 'The Long Run Behaviour of Velocity in the UK', City University Study of Monetary History Discussion Paper, no. 23, 1986.

8. W. Newmarch, 'An Attempt to Ascertain the Magnitude and Fluctuations of the Amount of Bills of Exchange ... 1828–1847', *Journal of the Statistical Society*, vol. 14, 1851, pp. 143–83; and T.S. Ashton, 'The Bill of Exchange and Private Banks in Lancashire, 1790–1830' in T.S. Ashton and R.S. Sayers (eds.), *Papers in English Monetary History* (Oxford University Press, Oxford, 1953), pp. 37–49.

9. On the position of the provincial banking companies and public banks in Scotland in the early nineteenth century see Charles W. Munn, *The Scottish Provincial Banking Companies, 1747–1864* (John Donald, Edinburgh, 1981), chs. 3–4; and S.G. Checkland, *Scottish Banking. A History, 1695–1973*, (Collins, Glasgow and London, 1975), chs. 10–12.

10. Barrow, *Irish Banking*.

11. For contemporary anxieties about this situation see Walter Bagehot, *Lombard Street*, (King, London, 1873), and R.H. Inglis Palgrave, *Bank Rate and the Money Market* (John Murray, London, 1903), especially pp. 217–26.

12. H. Oliver Horne, *A History of Savings Banks* (Oxford University Press, London, 1947).

13. David K. Sheppard, *The Growth and Role of UK Financial Institutions, 1880–1962* (Methuen & Co., London, 1971), p.8.

14. For a general history of building societies see E.J. Cleary, *The Building Society Movement* (Elek Books, London, 1965); and Sir Harold Bellman, *Bricks and Mortals* (Hutchinson & Co., London, 1950).

15. Sheppard, *Financial Institutions*, pp. 6–7.

16. Barry Supple, *The Royal Exchange Assurance* (Cambridge University Press, Cambridge, 1970); H.A.L. Cokerell and Edwin Green, *The British Insurance Business, 1547–1970* (Heinemann, London, 1976), especially ch. 5; and G. Clayton, *British Insurance* (Elek Books, London, 1971), chs. 6–8.

Chapter Three

# COMMERCIAL BANKS: INSTITUTIONAL CHANGE, 1826–1913

This and the following chapter concentrate on the commercial banks. Chapter 4 details the type of business undertaken by the banks, but the present purpose is to examine institutional developments. These are viewed as the joint-product of the legal and economic environment in which the banks found themselves operating, the interactions involved forming the substance of the chapter.

## MAIN TRENDS

Two main, closely-related themes permeate commercial bank developments in the nineteenth century: the growth in scale, and the increase in stability. Through the century to 1914, not only was individual bank size growing – in terms of the number of offices operated and value of assets and liabilities – but also there was a considerable concentration of market power as fewer banks gained a larger share of the commercial banking business. The two main vehicles through which this was achieved were the wider adoption of the corporate structure by banks and the amalgamation movement. The increase in scale in itself partly explains the growing stability of the banking system – the bigger the bank, the greater the potential for spreading risks. Stability was also concomitant with greater experience, for the lessons learnt from survival through one economic recession could alter business practice in such a way as to enhance the chances of survival in the next. Also as banks and bankers as a group gained greater experience, an element of professionalism was added to their business practices and this, too, increased stability. Legislation also played some part, yet it rarely took a leading role. Obviously the legal framework was one of the broad parameters governing bank operations but, on the whole, the law was permissive and, with the exception of note–issuing, it placed few restrictions on the type of business that bankers could undertake.

## THE CORPORATE STRUCTURE

The separation of private banks from the joint–stock companies is a major division which needs to be drawn for this period. The distinction relates to differences in the form of ownership. Private banks were one–man firms or small partnerships, and joint–stock banks were companies whose shares were more widely–owned and more widely–marketed. The distinction accounted for major differences in internal organisation, sometimes in the nature of business conducted and, ultimately, in the long–term growth of the firm.

As was emphasised in Chapter 1, until 1826 the Bank of England held a monopoly on joint–stock formation among English and Welsh banks but the privilege was removed in that year as part of a parliamentary reform package aimed at stabilising the commercial banking system. The economy had been subjected to major oscillations during the previous three decades – with recurring large–scale bankruptcies among private banks – and the hope was that reform would lead to the creation of larger commercial banks with greater capital resources, thus enabling them more readily to withstand fluctuations in business.[1]

The hopes of the legislators were partly pinned on the relatively better performance of the Scottish banks. The Bank of England's privilege did not extend to Scotland, so banks with large partnerships already existed there. These were the three

Edinburgh-based 'public banks' – the Bank of Scotland, the Royal Bank of Scotland and the British Linen Company – and the so-called provincial banking companies, some of which were similar to the English private banks in that they had a small number of proprietors, but some of the more successful of which were, in fact, large co-partnerships with up to about 200 proprietors.[2] These larger Scottish banks seemed to weather the economic storms of the early nineteenth century much better than their smaller English or Irish brethren, and this was a powerful factor in the reforms of the 1820s. Initially, acts of 1821, 1824 and 1825 extended the 'Scotch system' to Ireland by restricting the privileges of the Bank of Ireland and allowing the formation of joint-stock banks in that country.[3] In 1826 the same principle was applied to England and Wales and, henceforth, banks with over six partners were permitted.

As in many other sectors of the economy, in the long-term the joint-stock enterprise was successfully adapted to banking and marked the demise of the private firm. In fact, the commercial banking sector was one of the leaders in the adoption of the corporate enterprise in Britain. Essentially, success was a direct result of the ability to raise larger share capital. By issuing shares the banking company could broaden its catchment of proprietors, even if in the early days the shares were neither freely marketable nor directly on sale to the general public.[4] In contrast, the private bank was of necessity restricted to the resources invested by a small number of partners. This contributed directly to the stability of joint-stock banks, a major element in any attempt by a bank to win public confidence and to expand its note and deposit liabilities. Greater capital resources allowed a higher turnover of business, enabling economies of scale – another major element in the successful conduct of a commercial banking enterprise. One particular feature was to be the development of branching networks by some of the larger banking companies while, in contrast, exceptionally few private banks operated more than a couple of offices.

More general features associated with corporate enterprise can also be assumed to have benefited the banking company. Compared to many private firms there was at least the potential for less nepotism in making senior managerial appointments. Moreover, the management and direction of companies was less dependent on the interests and lives of senior partners. For the private firm the interests and business of the bank were very much intertwined with those of the partners and adverse conditions affecting the latter would also damage the firm. In many of the banking companies there was a much greater separation of identities between the company itself and its managers, the more so as the century progressed. Thus, the death of a joint–stock bank manager might have little impact on the business of his branch, but the death of a partner could drastically affect a private bank, and even lead to its closure.

Despite these differences joint–stock and private banks continued to share many common traits throughout much of the nineteenth century. Up until at least the 1870s, both types of bank in the English provinces were essentially local concerns and both augmented local contacts through the use of London and country agencies. Moreover, not all of the successful banking companies were new enterprises. Many were, but others were formed from already–established private banks 'going public' or from amalgamations involving private firms. In such cases, many aspects of the business of the two types of enterprise could be indistinguishable. Thus, the issue is far from clear–cut and even though it is correct to portray the nineteenth century on the whole as one in which joint–stock banks expanded at the expense of private firms, in England, at least, the latter neither disappeared quickly nor were they always unwilling participants in the process.

The course of joint–stock development, in fact, was far from being a smooth progression. Legal sanction in 1826 did not produce an immediate outburst of activity in England – the first banking company was established there in 1826, but even as late as 1830 there were still only fourteen.[5] The slow start is partly explained by the antagonism of the established rivals, the private bankers and the Bank of England. A further factor was the uncertain condition of company law. While the Act of 1826 sanctioned the formation of English joint–stock banks it said little of the duties, rights and privileges of the new corporations.

> No provision was made as to share denominations or amounts to be paid up on shares; no regulation was placed upon note issues; and no attempt was made to lay down directives regarding the deeds under which the co–partnerships were to operate.[6]

The rights and responsibilities of shareholders, directors, officers of the banks and of the companies as legal entities, were all largely undetermined. The legislature left such details to the new banking practitioners themselves, with the precise legal position to be determined in the courts under Common Law. Naturally, uncertainties took some time to dissipate and may have hindered expansion in the very early years; and it was not until 1838 that legislation attempted some general clarification.

Another important explanation of the slow start made by joint–stock banks was the unfavourable nature of economic conditions in the late twenties and early thirties. In fact, it was not until the economy was experiencing a sharp expansion in the mid–1830s that the new companies were able to assail successfully the entrenched positions of existing banks. One important advance had been the provision under the 1833 Bank Act which further weakened the Bank of England's privileged position by confirming the view that the formation of other joint–stock banks in London was lawful provided they did not issue notes. In other words, the act emphasised that the Bank of England's London monopoly referred to its note–issuing powers, not to its joint–stock structure.[7] The London and Westminster Bank, which was formed in 1833, was the first company to take advantage of this interpretation of the law[8] and others, such as the London Joint-Stock Bank and the National Provincial Bank of England, quickly followed. Despite early legal problems the business of these banks expanded sharply. In general, their capital resources were large, their directors wealthy and their management enterprising. One important innovation was the regular payment of interest to depositors in London, a practice the private banks had not followed. Not surprisingly, they quickly won new customers.

In fact, the mid-1830s witnessed a major expansion of joint-stock banks throughout Britain. Indeed in its later stages the expansion took on the proportions of a banking mania, with 59 English banking companies being formed in the one year, 1836.[9] Many of the new English firms were based in the industrial and commercial towns of the North and the Midlands, areas directly involved in the general economic boom. Ireland and Scotland also shared in this 'mania' for joint-stock banking. But the expansion in all parts of the kingdom came to an abrupt end in the second half of 1836. A number of banks failed as the wider commercial boom collapsed and the economy entered a recession; and further economic troubles in 1839 produced another crop of failures among both joint-stock and private banks. In particular, such failures as those of the Northern and Central Bank of England, the Commercial Bank of England and the Agricultural and Commercial Banking Company of Ireland revealed poor business practice and even outright fraud. Naturally, such revelations deterred new investors and promoters, and discouraged existing management from undertaking ambitious expansion plans. Moreover, the fortunes of the banks were once more directly affected by the general business cycle as the economy experienced a very severe recession in the early years of the 1840s. In fact, between 1844 and 1861 only seven new banking companies were established in England and the rate of new company creation was not to approach that of the mid-1830s again until the 1860s.

Nevertheless, the first period of expansion had produced a significant number of new joint-stock banks - Table 2.4 (page 52) shows that by the end of 1850 there were 99 companies with 576 offices in London and the English provinces. These were still far outnumbered by the 327 private banking concerns (although this non-corporate sector operated just 518 offices) and the private firms still accounted for about one-half of total English commercial bank liabilities. So, to reiterate an earlier point, while the English companies made rapid inroads into the country's banking business, the private firms continued to be responsible for a significant proportion of that business for some considerable time to come. In Ireland and Scotland, in contrast, the company structure now predominated. The new joint-stock structure had taken a tight grip in Ireland where eleven banking companies (including the Bank of Ireland) dominated commercial banking business, with just five private banks remaining by 1850. In Scotland, too, there had been a wave of new joint-stock bank formations which by the middle of the century had resulted in the absorption of many of the smaller provincial banking companies and the creation of banks with larger numbers of shareholders.

The robustness of private banks in England needs further explanation. In some ways it is not all that surprising in that, unlike Scotland, the legal restrictions first imposed in 1708 on the number of partners meant that private banks had long had the market to themselves and were already well-entrenched by 1826. It is true that Ireland had similarly been denied joint-stock banks, but the private banks in that country were much less firmly established and the extensive failures suffered by them in 1820 and 1825/26 meant that their survival was much more precariously balanced than in England. It was in England that the joint-stock newcomers faced more of an uphill struggle, having either to win over the established private banks' customers or to widen the pool of bank clientele so as to include people who had not previously held banking accounts. They had more success in the towns than in the countryside. The continuation of private banking proved quite resilient among rural communities and it was here that three–quarters of them were to be found by the mid–nineteenth century. The adoption of a corporate structure, then, provided no guarantee of success. In fact, for most purposes, restricted access to capital resources was no obvious drawback to the private banks because in the early and middle years of the nineteenth century most of their business was conducted locally and most of their industrial, agricultural and commercial customers' firms were also small, with financial requirements well within the capabilities of private banks. Moreover, if the private bank needed to supplement resources it could, of course, always draw on its agency connections in London and elsewhere.

The private bank also had some positive advantages over the banking company and these retained some, though waning, validity into the second half of the century. Apart from the goodwill generated by a bank having been established for some time, the private bank could also offer a 'personal' service, a factor perhaps more significant in a rural community. Usually the scale of the business was small enough for the banker to have close relationships with at least the more important customers, whereas customers themselves were in a position to assess the safety of their deposits through their direct knowledge of the banker's personality and public displays of wealth (size of house and estate, carriages, number of servants, philanthropic works, etc.). It was often claimed by private bankers that such personal contact was impossible for a large corporation employing salaried managers. While industrial and commercial concerns were themselves operating on a small–scale such considerations may well offer an important explanation for the continued success of the private bank and, indeed, probably account for the relative smallness and parochialism of most English banking companies up until the last quarter of the nineteenth century.

However, the failure of the corporate structure to maintain its earlier rate of expansion was not due solely to the continued validity of the private firm. Legislative restriction was also significant. A series of acts of Parliament in 1844 and 1845 directly affected joint–stock bank formation. Thus among the provisions regulating the issuing of notes, the Bank Charter Act of 1844 declared that there were to be no new note–issuers anywhere in Britain; and that lapsed issues could not be revived. This act also limited the size of individual English bank note issues to those existing in 1844 and allowed for the loss of issuing rights in future bank mergers where the number of partners exceeded six. Separate acts of 1845 placed similar restrictions on Irish and Scottish banks although they were allowed to exceed the new limits if (and only if) they covered each extra issue of notes by an equivalent increase in their bullion reserves. In this way a potential source of growth for banking firms in all three countries was lost. In England the 1826 ban on notes of under £5 denomination had already reduced the importance of note–issuing, but in Scotland and Ireland it was still an integral part of every commercial bank's business. Therefore, the 1844 ban on new note issuers had a greater impact in these two countries. Moreover, in Scotland and Ireland any proposed new bank would not only be unable to issue its own notes but would also find it impossible to substitute Bank of England notes – an option available to new English banks – because these notes did not freely circulate outside England and Wales. In effect, the restrictions on note issues removed the threat of new competition for the Irish and Scottish banks and the structure of these banking systems was to remain more or less fixed until the twentieth century.

In England it was still possible for newcomers to carry on a banking business with the use of Bank of England notes and coin. However, new bank creations were stifled there also, due to another piece of legislation – the Joint–Stock Bank Act of 1844.[10] This imposed severe restrictions on the formation and operation of new joint–stock banks, although regulations governing existing banks remained intact. In future new banking companies would have to meet much tighter criteria:

> The minimum nominal capital was to be £100,000, no share was to be of lower denomination than £100, and no company thus formed could begin business until all the shares had been subscribed and at least one-half of their nominal amount paid-up. It was required that the deed of partnership should be in a form approved by the Privy Council and that it should contain, among other clauses, provisions forbidding the company to purchase or lend upon the security of its own shares, requiring a statement of assets and liabilities to be published once a month, and arranging for the annual accounts to be examined by auditors elected by shareholders.[11]

Many of the provisions may have been laudible in themselves but in total they were largely responsible for creating a hiatus in bank company formation: in England only one new company was formed in the five years to the end of 1849, and only five during the whole of the next decade.[12] Indeed it was not until the legislation was repealed in 1857 that the path was cleared for further English expansion of joint-stock banking, in the 1860s.

The 1860s joint-stock bank 'boom' was, indeed, largely an English experience. As has been shown, the earlier expansionary phase had already established the overwhelming predominance of the joint-stock firm within the Irish and Scottish banking systems, and the 1845 ban on new note-issuers imposed an effective deterrent to newcomers. The acceptability of Bank of England notes meant that the impact of the ban was much less serious in England and Wales, however, and the repeal of the 1844 Joint-Stock Bank Act in 1857 cleared the way for further assaults on the position of the private banks. In this subsequent expansion other factors also played a part. One favourable event had been the admission in 1854 of the first joint–stock banks to the London Clearing House which, until then, had been an exclusive private bankers' preserve. The event has been lauded as: '...a landmark...since it simplified and cheapened and therefore assisted the process of cheque clearing.'[13] Also legislation of 1858 removed the discriminatory stamp duty on cheques drawn more than fifteen miles from the bank of issue. Another – more important – influence was the enabling legislation of 1858 and 1862 which permitted banking companies to extend limited liability to their shareholders. While few existing companies took immediate advantage of its provision, the consolidation and clarification of company law created a major stimulus for new joint–stock bank creations. As in the 1830s, cyclical movements within the economy were also important: the boom in bank formation taking place within a period of general economic growth. The scale of English joint–stock expansion was such that during the years, 1862–66, the number of joint–stock bank offices increased by over one–half; the number of banks rose by almost one–fifth; and there was a massive jump – of something like 80 per cent – in note and deposit liabilities. By comparison the number of private bank offices stagnated and their liabilities rose by less than one–fifth over the same five–year period – by the late 1870s the private banks' share in the number of English banking offices and in the total of deposit and note liabilities was down to less than one–third.[14] The private bank was still important, but the dominance that joint–stock banks had long enjoyed in Scotland and Ireland had, at last, reached England.

For the rest of the period up until the First World War the number of private banks steadily, if undramatically, contracted and joint–stock banks continued to consolidate their position by actively expanding their branch networks, especially around the turn of the century. By 1913 there were 41 English joint–stock banks operating 6,426 offices, and only 29 private banks with 147 offices.[15] By this time eleven of the English joint–stock banks operated over 100 offices each, accounting for some 31 per cent of the total. The system in England was no longer a loose amalgam of small, locally-based banks, but was dominated by a few national giants such as Barclay & Co. Ltd and the National Provincial Bank Ltd, which operated head offices in London and extensive branch networks throughout the country. So, for the United Kingdom as a whole there were now three, highly-concentrated banking systems dominated by large, corporate enterprises.

## BANK BRANCHING

Bank expansion came from both internal and external growth. Obviously, one important source for internal growth was the opening up of new branches or offices; whereas external growth occurred when two or more banks merged their separate identities to form a new, larger business. Amalgamations proved to be the most rapid means of expanding. Both the formation of branch systems and amalgamations were present throughout most of the nineteenth century and both were associated largely with joint-stock banks rather than private firms.

Eighteenth-century Scottish banks were the innovators when it came to the use of branches to supplement the business of head office. By the end of the 1780s a typical Scottish bank was already operating a small branch system which was generally confined to a particular region of the country and which rarely involved more than four or five offices per bank.[16] The middle decades of the nineteenth century saw a tremendous extension of this branching system by both the dominant joint-stock banks and public banks – by 1875 the number of offices per bank was over eight times the number being operated by joint-stock banks in England.[17] Moreover, by this time the main banks had established 'national' systems of branches covering most of Scotland and they were in the process of opening offices in London in order to participate more directly in the business of the world's largest financial centre.[18] According to the historian of the Scottish banking system, S.G. Checkland, the Scottish banks' leadership in branch formation was partly the result of a long tradition of using agents. Initially these agents were local businessmen or professionals who acted on behalf of the bank in a part-time capacity within their own community. In this way costs were kept to a minimum, making it economically feasible to maintain a presence in a number of localities even at an early stage of economic development. For the nineteenth century, the fact that the Scottish system was dominated by a small number of large banks which exercised oligopoly powers and closely controlled interest rates was another important factor.[19] In effect Scottish banks chose not to compete on price, concentrating instead on the services offered, and the extension of retail outlets through branching was an important part of this type of competition.

Irish and English branch development remained retarded relative to Scotland for much of the century. In Ireland, the Bank of Ireland and the Provincial Bank of Ireland both operated a number of branches from the mid–1820s, and there was a sharp boost in the mid–1830s with the establishment of new banks such as the National Bank and the Northern Bank which set up permanent branching networks. So, although by the middle of the nineteenth century Ireland had many fewer bank offices per head of the population than either England or Scotland, there was no comparable system to that in England with its large number of private banks most of which operated only a few offices. The typical Irish bank for most of the nineteenth century was a bank with a branch system; and this typical Irish bank was running some 60–80 offices by the beginning of the twentieth century.

Even in England there had been some examples of early joint–stock banks such as the Northern and Central Bank of England which had operated large branch networks during the 1830s, but they had been very much the exception. As has already been stressed, the typical English bank in the early and mid–nineteenth century was locally–based with a limited number of offices. Moreover, most of the branch networks that began eventually to emerge tended to be concentrated in the same geographical regions, with offices in towns close to the head office. This was the case, for instance, for the Manchester and Liverpool District Bank and the Wiltshire and Dorset Bank. Geographical proximity would have made communication between the branches and head office easier, facilitating central control. Also it was often the case that the local economies of satellite towns were similar, or supplementary, to that of the main town(s) in the district. Thus, the business of satellite branches could have been largely an extension of the business of head office – that is, of the type with which the bank was familiar. But even in the 1840s there were wholly exceptional London-based banks such as the National Provincial Bank of England which had ninety offices throughout the country.

Through the half-century to 1914 this indeed was to become the normal pattern, as London banks extended their provincial offices and as provincial banks were obliged to open up City offices if they were to lay serious claim to being 'national' banks. General improvements in communications were an important underlying factor. Another was the general pressure for economies of scale. In the case of banks, as for other financial institutions, the sheer attractiveness of 'bigness' as an advertisement of security and prestige may in itself have been a factor. Fundamentally, though, domestic banking was a 'retail' business, with the banks at this time concentrating on deposit-gathering and on the provision of money transmission facilities. Therefore, it was essential for them to establish extensive branch networks both for the convenience of customers and in order to attain economies of scale. For these long-term and undramatic reasons the extension of branch networks in England and Wales continued throughout the century, with the number of bank offices rising faster than the population. It was a process closely related, of course, to the rise of the joint-stock bank and decline of the private bank. It meant that on the eve of the First

World War, the average English joint-stock bank was at last operating the same number of offices (some 157) as the average Scottish bank, although Scotland still had significantly more offices per head of the population than either England or Ireland.[20]

## BANK AMALGAMATIONS

Mergers and take-overs were the main means by which a bank could directly increase the number of its branches, and for the commercial banking sector as a whole they proved to be major techniques for achieving growth in scale and of concentrating market power into the hands of fewer and fewer firms. Scotland again led the way. The Scottish banks were involved in a major phase of amalgamations in the 1830s and 1840s and these, together with bank failures, reduced the number of banks from 36 in 1830, to just 17 in 1850.[21] By 1879 more failures and a number of minor amalgamations had reduced the number still further, to a mere ten – seven 'national' and three 'regional' banks – and this effectively remained the pattern until 1950.[22]

In England, amalgamation was also the main method by which a system consisting of over 600 banks in 1825 had contracted to just 70 by 1913, and by which the 'Big Five' London clearing banks came to dominate the market by 1918.[23] Joint-stock banks were usually the more active and dominant partners in any merger or takeover, but not always. Thus, over half of the amalgamations between 1870 and 1920 involved private banks joining with joint-stock banks; but the merging of two private firms (as defence against joint-stock takeover?) and the combining of two joint-stock banks (seeking economies of scale?) were also common.[24]

English bank amalgamations had occurred early in the nineteenth century and they continued to account for a steady, gradual disappearance of individual firms throughout the period.[25] But a 'merger movement' proper did not develop until the early 1860s, with the peak of activity (as measured in terms of the number of amalgamations per annum) occurring in the late 1880s and early 1890s. In the seven years from 1888 to 1894 there were 69 mergers in all, more than had taken place in the whole of the previous 18 years (since 1870). Thus, the Birmingham and Midland Bank (eventually emerging as the Midland Bank in 1924) was involved in a total of ten mergers during these years, mergers which led to its creation as one of the country's leading banks with offices in the City and with an extensive network of branches in the Midlands and North. The other major banks also participated in the merger boom. The rate of mergers then settled back somewhat, to a steady half-dozen or so each year, although the size of the banks involved grew steadily so that by 1918 the emergence of the 'Big Five' – Barclays, Lloyds, the National Provincial, the Midland and the Westminster – had already fixed the competitive structure of twentieth-century domestic banking in England.

Concentration of banking business into fewer and fewer hands was the most obvious effect of amalgamations. It has already been noted that a high degree of market concentration was achieved by the middle of the nineteenth century in Scotland and one important corollary was the establishment, in 1840, of the General Managers' Committee which sought to consolidate earlier bank co-operation and reduce price competition. The smaller number of large banks made possible the maintenance of cartel arrangements to stifle competition on rates paid to depositors and charged to borrowers. 'By 1850, it would seem, the Scottish banks had arrived at a fairly firm agreement about rates...' and they were to operate an effective cartel into the twentieth century.[26]

A recent study by Forrest Capie and Ghila Rodrik-Bali has shown a sharp shift towards market concentration in England, too, mainly as a result of bank amalgamations over the period from 1870 to 1920.[27] Thus, while the largest five banks accounted for one-quarter of English and Welsh deposits in 1870, the 'Big Five' were holding four-fifths of deposits by 1920. In other words, by the end of the First World

War Barclays, Lloyds, the Midland, the National Provincial and the Westminster were in a position to dominate English commercial banking business.

They were also operating an effective cartel which limited competition on interest rates. Indeed, the rise in the degree of concentration had been associated with greater co-operation among English banks from the 1860s, with a number of formal and informal agreements to restrict competition.[28] Thus, the London joint-stock banks first agreed to pay one per cent below Bank rate on deposits on current accounts and, then, in response to a general fall in interest rates, they abolished such payments altogether in 1877.[29] On deposit accounts (which were subject to notice of withdrawal) they paid a common rate, set at a fixed margin of 1.5 per cent below Bank rate by 1886. It has been suggested that these agreements arose not merely from the desire of the largest banks to avoid price competition, but also out of the acquiescent policy of the authorities. As in other markets, concentration in banking benefited from the *laissez-faire* attitude adopted by successive British governments to the rise of oligopolies and cartels; and there was no serious attempt at anti-trust legislation in Britain until after the Second World War. But more active collusion from the authorities has been alleged by Brian Griffiths on the grounds that the Treasury and the Bank of England found it easier to implement interest rate policy when dealing with a small number of cartelised banks.[30] The restriction of competition may have been the price paid for commercial bank compliance in the sale of government securities and in effecting interest rate controls. In fact this was more obviously true after the First World War when the needs of government finance became so pressing, but Griffiths suggests it may have also been a general factor from the late nineteenth century. Irrespective of the extent of overt official involvement, the nature of the long-term transformation of the English banking sector is clear: the competitive system of the early nineteenth century which had consisted of numerous small units had been replaced by the 1920s by a highly concentrated and cartelised system.

## THE STABILITY OF BANKS AND ECONOMIC FLUCTUATIONS

There has always been the closest of links between the business of bankers and fluctuations in the general economy. If the economy is expanding, bankers find demand for loans rising and are more inclined to lend; whereas in a period of recession the public may seek fewer loans and the banks become more cautious. During the formative years of the nineteenth century this interaction between the intensity of economic fluctuations and the experience of bankers in coping with it, was to be one of the most important elements both in long-term legislative and institutional change and in influencing the type of banking business conducted.

In the first half of the nineteenth century a very close connection existed. Thus, the sharp economic upswings of the mid-1830s and early 1860s were also periods of joint-stock bank boom. During recessions, too, bank performance seemed to correspond with, if not actually intensify, the downswing. In particular, some recessions were marked by dramatic, if short-lived, 'runs' on the banks as customers *en masse* lost confidence and sought to convert their holdings of commercial bank notes and deposits to coin and Bank of England notes. The consequence was a series of bank pressures involving some notable failures – in 1825/26, 1837, 1839, 1847, 1857, 1866 and 1878.[31] Whether bank instability was chiefly a cause or result of the sharpness of general economic fluctuations is debatable, but the close correlation was important in provoking a spate of banking legislation up to the middle of the 1840s. As has already been shown, one major objective of the reforms of the 1820s and 1830s was to remove restictions imposed by the privileges granted to the Bank of England and the Bank of Ireland and to encourage the spread of the 'Scotch system' by permitting the formation of larger – and it was hoped – more stable banks in England, Wales and

Ireland; and although the 1844 Joint–Stock Bank Act was to prove too restrictive it, too, had attempted to instil greater stability through tighter regulations on share capital and on the publication and auditing of accounts.

The restrictions placed on the banks' powers to issue notes had similarly aimed at greater stability. For many in the early nineteenth century, money was synonymous with coin and notes and it was believed that the variations in the note circulation of the commercial banks added to general fluctuations. Thus, critics claimed that in prosperous times bankers tended to encourage inflation and speculation by over–issuing their notes; while in recessions, contractions of the note–issue added to the gloom. As has already been outlined, Parliament attempted a number of controls, although at first there was more success against the English rather than the Scottish or Irish issuers. Small notes of under £5 denomination had been allowed to circulate since 1797, but they were completely banned in England and Wales in 1826.[32] Moreover, in 1833 the prestige of Bank of England notes, which rivalled those of the commercial banks, was further enhanced by the terms of the Bank Charter Act which declared them legal tender in England and Wales (though not in Scotland or Ireland). Finally, as was shown previously, acts of 1844 and 1845 banned all new banks from issuing notes, limited existing circulations and paved the way for the gradual dwindling of the English commercial bank note issue altogether.

So, by the mid–1840s experience of economic oscillation and corresponding banking fortunes, especially in England, had produced a number of legislative reforms aimed at establising a more stable system. However, the overwhelming importance of deposits among the banks' liabilities, and the fact that this part of their business was left unregulated, rendered the controls on notes largely irrelevant except for the deterrent effect on new bank formations in Scotland and Ireland. The impact of the reforms in company legislation, particularly the sanctioning of joint–stock banks in England and Ireland, were more obviously beneficial and we have identified these as major factors in the long-term stabilisation of the system.

After the 1840s, banking legislation largely followed in the wake of general company law reform. Thus, in 1857 the tight restrictions imposed on joint-stock banks in 1844 were repealed and a series of Acts, 1858–62, extended the right of limited liability to bank shareholders, and the Companies Act of 1879 introduced a general reform of banking shares by permitting the adoption of 'reserved liability' and further strengthened the rights of shareholders (see pages 100–1).

Although it was to induce fewer pieces of legislation, the connection between banks and economic fluctuations did not disappear, of course, and, indeed, remains today. In fact, some commentators such as H.P. Minsky continue to argue 'that the larger a financial system grows in relation to the economy and the more complex and layered it becomes, the greater its fragility and its proneness to financial crisis, and the more serious its effects on economic development.'[33] But this was not true of the institutions conducting domestic banking in the UK during the late nineteenth and early twentieth centuries. Over time, institutional survival and resilience was enhanced. For the banks, banking became a safer business. Even so, there were still occasions when the word 'crisis' was to be used to describe conditions in the money markets – as when the discount house of Overends failed in 1866; at the time of the City of Glasgow Bank failure in 1878; and during the 'Baring Crisis' of 1890 when one of Britain's leading merchant banks was unable to meet its immediate cash liabilities without help from the Bank of England and a broadly-based consortium of bankers. The frequency and severity of banking crises were diminishing, however. On trend, the institutions at the core of the banking business in the UK became more stable, more secure, and these banks were a less obvious source of economic fluctuations.

Apart from their effect in initiating early bank

legislation, economic crises may have added to the long–term stability of the banking sector in a much less obvious, but perhaps more important, manner by inducing new business practices amongst the banks. Thus, after the first flush of success for the new joint–stock banks in the 1830s, there were signs of greater caution.[34] After the banking crises of 1837 and 1839 the more adventurous, fraudulent, or simply foolhardy, banks went out of business. In England the most notorious had been the Northern and Central Bank and in Ireland, the Agricultural and Commercial Bank. Both had enjoyed a mushrooming of business in the mid–1830s but incompetent management and an extension of business far beyond the confines of their capital and personnel resources had led to their equally dramatic collapse. While these were two of the most prominent examples, successive economic recession and banking crises undoubtedly took their toll of others. In this way, some of the more adventurous, but also more unstable, elements in the banking sector were gradually eliminated.

Even if banks did not go into liquidation, the experience during crises of sudden demands for cash, of accumulating bad debts and of damaging losses, induced greater caution for the future. This seems to have been the case for the Manchester and Liverpool District Bank in 1839, and the North and South Wales Bank which was forced temporarily to refuse cash payments in 1847 – both banks were to become more conservative in their lending and investment, and both were to survive as successful businesses. The assumption is that this was a general, long–term process: incautious banks went out of business and survivors improved their business practices. It is apparent, for instance, that over the whole century the size of balances kept by bankers at the Bank of England increased, thus building up the system's cash reserves; and that it was immediately following 'crises' that these balances were added to.[35] Similarly, after the major failure of the City of Glasgow Bank in 1878 Scottish banks seem to have become much more cautious and British banks in general held larger cash reserves.[36] In addition, we have seen, that on trend amalgamations were contributing to the absorption of the smaller and, perhaps, weaker banks.

Since 1878 there have been no significant failures among important domestic banks in Britain. Here is a sure sign of success for the spread of the corporate structure, the growth in scale and the adoption of changed business practices. It is also a reflection of the process of professionalisation which was to permeate British banking in the course of the nineteenth century. During the latter half of the eighteenth century many firms had still been quasi–bankers, conducting another form of business in addition to that of banking. By 1826, the specialist banker dominated. Many bankers were still relatively inexperienced, however, with no easily–accessible and well–established body of knowledge as to what constituted 'good banking practice'. Survival depended on partners' business acumen, lessons drawn from the experience of the banker's own firm, and luck. Not surprisingly, the new joint–stock banks of the 1830s seem to have had difficulty in recruiting suitable staff – for some, the rapid expansion of business severely tested the ability of management and, as has been noted, this was one source of weakness. In contrast, by the end of the nineteenth century, banking had become an established profession, with a recognised career structure and minimum technical training for staff employed by many of the major banks.

The century had seen a growing awareness among bankers of a common interest in the propagation and spread of sound business practices. Early on, this had resulted in the appearance of specialist banking journals (such as the monthly *Bankers Magazine* which was first published in 1844) and even in the publication of a number of early 'textbooks' on how practical banking should be conducted (especially, J. Dalton's *The Banker's Clerk* in 1843, and J.W. Gilbart's *Practical Treatise on Banking* from 1827). Many more were to follow as the century progressed. There had even been early, though abortive, attempts at creating a professional association. There was to be no success at establishing permanent representative bodies, however, until the 1870s – with the foundation of the Institute of Bankers in Scotland in 1875 and of the English Institute of Bankers in 1879; although the Institute of Bankers in Ireland was not formed until 1898.[37] The various institutes have continued to provide advice and supervision on the education and training of staff, establishing minimum qualifications and organising professional examinations. In this manner, experience and knowledge were pooled and minimum standards raised. Conformity in business practice may have led to British banks being less daring than some critics wished, but it also instilled greater security into the system as a whole.

Two other factors need to be singled out as important elements leading to greater stability. The first was the spread of the cheque clearing system which reduced costs and pooled resources in a specialised manner. As already noted, joint–stock banks were admitted to the London Clearing House in 1854.[38] The admission of the Bank of England ten years later helped pave the way for the creation of an effective, national cheque clearing system, with bankers drawing on their balances at the Bank of England to settle debts among themselves.[39] North of the border, the Edinburgh Clearing House was set up in 1865 to facilitiate the clearing of cheques in much the same manner as was already being done for notes (begun in 1771); and, in Ireland, the Dublin Clearing House was established in 1845 and was soon being used by the main banks to clear notes and cheques.[40]

The final factor to be stressed here as affecting stability, operated on the general environment in which commercial banking was conducted – namely, the evolution of banking policy and the gradual emergence of the Bank of England as a central bank with responsibilities for the 'soundness' of money markets in Britain. Bank of England action was to impose certain constraints on the business of the banks but, ultimately, the Bank of England's willingness to 'manage' the gold standard in such a way as to reduce the degree of pressure on domestic money markets and its general willingness to provide funds to the banks during liquidity pressures, created an important element of stability which had been missing in the early nineteenth century.[41]

## CONCLUSION

The years from 1826 to 1914 saw tremendous change in British domestic banking, with the emergence of a mature and sophisticated commercial banking sector. The timing of developments differed in different parts of the kingdom and, indeed, there were important regional variations with, in particular, the greater resilience of private banks in the rural communities of England. Although stronger links were being forged between the separate systems in England, Scotland and Ireland, the banks in the three countries remained largely independent of one another. Nevertheless, many of the general institutional and structural changes were commonly shared. In all three, the joint-stock bank came to dominate, branch banking became the normal form of conducting business, there was a sharp growth in the scale of business, and there was a greater concentration of market power which lent itself to co-operation among existing banks and a stifling of new competition. By the late nineteenth century some English customers were facing cartel arrangements on rates of interest, an experience endured by the Scots since the middle years of the century. In the absence of price competition the banks were giving greater weight to the provision of better and more extensive customer services. The opening of new branches thus enhanced the convenience of having a bank account and at an increasing number of these offices the banks were undertaking a wider range of work such as acting as trustees and executors, and in broadening their overseas business. The main benefit deriving from these institutional changes, however, was an increase in stability. The threat of British bank failures of the sort common in the early and middle nineteenth-century had disappeared and the dominant, nationally based banks which emerged by the time of the First World War were sound enough to withstand even the financial traumas of war and the economic upheavals which were to be a feature of the following two decades.

FURTHER READING

W.F. Crick and W.E. Wadsworth, *A Hundred Years of Joint–Stock Banking* (Hodder and Stoughton, London, 1936).

S.G. Checkland, *Scottish Banking. A History, 1695–1913* (Collins, Glasgow & London, 1975).

Forrest Capie and Ghila Rodrik–Bali, 'Concentration in British Banking, 1870–1920', *Business History*, vol. 24, 1982, pp. 280–92.

NOTES

1. W.T.C. King, *History of the London Discount Market* (Routledge & Sons, London, 1936), ch. 2; W.F. Crick and W.E. Wadsworth, *A Hundred Years of Joint–Stock Banking* (Hodder and Stoughton, London, 1936), pp. 9–17; Frank Whitson Fetter, *Development of British Monetary Orthodoxy, 1797–1875* (Harvard University Press, Cambridge, Mass., 1965) pp. 120–2; and T.E. Gregory (assisted by Annette Henderson) *The Westminster Bank Through a Century* (2 vols., Oxford University Press, London, 1936), vol. 1, pp. 1–22.

2. Charles W. Munn, *The Scottish Provincial Banking Companies, 1747–1864* (John Donald, Edinburgh, 1981), especially ch. 7. For a recent championing of the 'free' Scottish system see Lawrence H. White, *Free Banking in Britain. Theory, Experience, and Debate, 1800–1845* (Cambridge University Press, Cambridge, 1984).

3. G.L. Barrow, *The Emergence of the Irish Banking System, 1820–1845* (Gill and Macmillan, Dublin, 1975), ch.3.

4. B.L. Anderson and P.L. Cottrell, 'Another Victorian Capital Market: A Study of Banking and Bank Investors on Merseyside', *Economic History*

*Review*, 2nd ser., vol. 28, 1975, pp. 598-615.

5. S.E. Thomas, *The Rise and Growth of Joint-Stock Banking* (Pitman, London, 1934), vol. 1, Appendix M, p. 656.

6. Crick and Wadsworth, *Joint Stock Banking*, p. 16.

7. This was directly parallel to the Bank of Ireland's privileged position in Dublin. There, the 1824 Irish Banking Act had already confirmed that the Bank's monopoly within 50 miles of Dublin applied only to its note issue.

8. See Gregory, *Westminster Bank*, especially vol. 1.

9. Thomas, *Joint-Stock Banking*, pp. 658-62.

10. 7 and 8 Vict. c. 113.

11. Crick and Wadsworth, *Joint-Stock Banking*, p. 26.

12. Thomas, *Joint-Stock Banking*, pp. 662.

13. Joseph Sykes, *The Amalgamation Movement in English Banking, 1825-1924* (King & Son, London, 1926) p. 22.

14. All data are from Tables 2.1 and 2.4.

15. Shizuya Nishimura, *The Decline of Inland Bills of Exchange in the London Money Market, 1855-1913* (Cambridge University Press, Cambridge, 1971), pp. 60-5 for figures on the years 1855-1913.

16. Munn, *Scottish Provincial Banking*, ch. 9; and S.G. Checkland, *Scottish Banking. A History, 1695-1973* (Collins, Glasgow & London, 1975), pp. 196-9.

17. Table 2.5.

18. See Checkland, *Scottish Banking*, ch. 15.

19. Ibid., pp. 526-7.

20. Table 2.5.

21. Checkland, *Scottish Banking*, ch. 11.

22. Ibid., p. 465.

23. The 'Big Five' were Barclays, Lloyds, the National Provincial, the Midland, and the Westminster.

24. Forrest Capie and Ghila Rodrik-Bali, 'Concentration in British Banking, 1870-1920', *Business History*, vol. 24, 1982, p. 282.

25. See Sykes, *Amalgamation Movement*, pp.

1–93, for an historical survey.

26. Checkland, *Scottish Banking*, pp. 391–2.

27. Capie and Rodrik–Bali, 'Concentration in British Banking'.

28. Brian Griffiths, 'The Development of Restrictive Practices in the U.K. Monetary System', *Manchester School*, vol. 41, 1973, pp. 3–18.

29. *The Economist*, vol. 35, 1877, pp. 91–2.

30. Griffiths, 'Restrictive Practices', pp. 3–18.

31. Michael Collins, 'English Banks and the Mid–Nineteenth Century Business Cycle', in P.L. Cottrell and D.E. Moggridge (eds.), *Money and Power* (Macmillan, London, 1987).

32. 7 Geo. IV, c.6.

33. Raymond W. Goldsmith paraphrasing Minsky in Charles P. Kindleberger and Jean–Pierre Laffargue (eds.), *Financial Crises. Theory, History and Policy* (Cambridge University Press, Cambridge, 1982), p. 42. For formal discussion of the model see Hyman P. Minsky, 'The Financial Instability Hypothesis: Capitalist Processes and the Behaviour of the Economy', ibid., pp. 13–39; and Hyman P. Minsky, *Can 'It' Happen Again? Essays on Instability and Finance* (M.E. Sharpe Inc., New York, 1982), chs. 5–6. Also see Charles P. Kindleberger, *Manias, Panics and Crashes* (Macmillan, London, 1978).

34. One of the best detailed accounts of the early years of joint–stock banking in England is that in Thomas, *Joint–Stock Banking*.

35. 'Bank of England Liabilities and Assets: 1669 to 1966', appendix to *Bank of England Quarterly Bulletin*, vol. 7, June 1967. Also see Michael Collins. 'The English Banking Sector and Monetary Growth, 1844–80', University of Leeds, Economics Discussion Paper, no. 102, 1981, pp. 26–9.

36. On Scotland see Checkland, *Scottish Banks*, pp. 478–81. On England see Michael Collins, 'The Business of Banking: English Balance Sheets, 1840–80', *Business History*, vol. 26, 1984, pp. 43–58. It has been suggested by William P. Kennedy in 'Institutional Response to Economic Growth: Capital Markets in Britain to 1914' in Leslie Hannah (ed.), *Management*

*Strategy and Business Development. An Historical and Comparative Study* (Macmillan, London, 1976), p. 160, that: 'After 1878, no longer would banks become willingly involved in the long-term financing of industry.'

37. R.N. Forbes, *The History of the Institute of Bankers in Scotland, 1875–1975* (Institute of Bankers in Scotland, Edinburgh, 1975); Edwin Green, *Debtors to their Profession: A History of the Institute of Bankers, 1879–1979* (Methuen & Co., London, 1979); Noel Simpson, *The Belfast Bank, 1827–1970* (Blackstaff Press, Belfast, 1975), p. 189.

38. Philip W. Matthews, *The Bankers' Clearing House* (Pitman & Sons, London, 1921) pp. 22–6, 49–50.

39. Provincial clearings were also to be established in major towns such as Manchester, Liverpool, and Birmingham around the turn of the century, and these supplemented the London-based arrangements.

40. Checkland, *Scottish Banking*, pp. 486–7; and Barrow, *Irish Banking*, pp. 183–5.

41. See Chapter 6 on Bank of England policy. On the general issue of lender of last resort action to moderate crises see Forrest Capie and Geoffrey E. Wood (eds.), *Financial Crises and the World Banking System* (Macmillan, Basingstoke, 1986) – in particular see Roy A. Batchelor, 'The Avoidance of Catastrophe: Two Nineteenth Century Banking Crises', ibid., pp. 41–76 [including Comment by L.S. Pressnell] for developments in this period.

Chapter Four

# THE BUSINESS OF COMMERCIAL BANKING, 1826–1913

The basic function of a commercial bank is that it acts as a financial intermediary between borrower and lender. To the lender it offers a place of safe deposit where interest can be earned, while providing loans and credits to the borrower. By using a bank the borrower and lender do not have to know each other personally, and the bank itself incurs much of the risk involved in making a loan. A bank is able to employ specialist staff, building up a great deal of expertise over time. The resultant economies of scale enable it to make a contribution to economic welfare by ensuring the wider dispersal and utilisation of savings. A bank will have its own proprietors' capital, of course, and this, too, can be lent to borrowers. But for the great majority of banks, even in the nineteenth century, proprietors' capital provided but a small proportion of the funds available for bank loans. Fundamentally, nineteenth-century banks (as now) lent other people's money, not their own. Thus, the modern British banking system is a 'fractional reserve system' in the sense that, of the funds attracted from depositors only a very small percentage is retained in the form of cash, the rest is passed on to borrowers. In essence, this was the case throughout the nineteenth century, too: the UK had already developed the 'fractional reserve system' by 1826.

One general way of looking at the business of

these banks is to consider, in turn, the main liabilities they incurred and the main assets in which they invested during the course of their business. Table 4.1 lists the major items involved, and it should be useful for the reader to refer to it during the discussion below. Regarding terminology, when a bank 'borrows', it incurs liabilities (such as deposits) and when it makes loans or investments, these form the bank's assets.

## BANK LIABILITIES

### *Notes*

The function which is often seen as most peculiar to banks is the provision of media of exchange, as their note and deposit liabilities form a large part of the money supply in the hands of the public. Note liabilities were perhaps the most obvious contribution the commercial banks made to the types of money available, for in the last century many Scottish, Irish and English provincial banks issued their own notes which were used as cash by their customers.

Notes were also the most immediate of a bank's liabilities in that note-holders could, without notice, insist on the issuer converting them to legal-tender coin or (in England and Wales from 1833) to Bank of England notes. From the bank's point of view, profit could be made from persuading customers to hold its 'promises to pay'. Effectively, note-holders were lending to the bank an amount equivalent to the face value of the notes; the main cost to the bank being that of printing the notes. In practice the circulation of any one bank's notes was closely circumscribed, being largely confined to the locality where its name was well-known and its 'promise' trusted. In Scotland, in particular, the operation of the note exchange (since 1771) helped ensure a rapid clearing of notes amongst the banks and deterred 'excessive' issues. Moreover, as the figures in Chapter 2 showed, legal restrictions and the availability of alternatives, meant that notes were of dwindling importance compared to other means of payment. They were already less than four per

Table 4.1 : Main Classes of Balance Sheet Items held by a Commercial Bank

| *LIABILITIES* (i.e. claims on the bank) | *ASSETS* (i.e. claims by the bank on others) |
|---|---|
| 1. Notes | 1. Cash |
| 2. Deposits | 2. Money at call and short notice |
| 3. Acceptances and endorsements | 3. Bills discounted |
| 4. Proprietors' capital | 4. Overdrafts and loans (advances) |
| | 5. Investments |

cent of commercial bank deposits by 1875, and under two per cent during the early years of the twentieth century. The important London-based banks and many English provincial banks never issued notes, and the number of those that did continually declined; and although in absolute terms the note circulations of Scotland and Ireland rose they were dwarfed by the expansion in bank deposits.

*Deposits*

Through their willingness to accept money on deposit, commercial banks offer places of safekeeping (customers no longer need to keep savings under their beds!) and a form of investment (as customers can earn interest on those deposits). Deposits formed the great bulk of commercial bank liabilities, even in the nineteenth century. A large proportion of these deposits was on 'current account' and, therefore, could be withdrawn immediately by customers. The rest of deposits were on a variety of 'term accounts', or 'deposit accounts', and here, notice of withdrawal had to be given. The distribution between current accounts and other deposits during the nineteenth century is not certain. But as can be seen from Table 4.2 the figures that are available for England – for just a few banks – suggest that during the 1850s, 1860s and 1870s some two-thirds of deposits were held, on average, in the form of current accounts. On the basis of similarly scant evidence for four large London-based banks, Charles Goodhart has shown that for the 1890s current accounts ranged from some 50 per cent to 75 per cent of total deposits.[1] While it is not certain just how representative these data may be for nineteenth-century banks in general, they do highlight the nature of deposit liabilities for the banks concerned – deposits subject to immediate withdrawal formed the bulk of bank liabilities.

Table 4.2 : Composition of English Bank Deposits, 1850-1880 (decadal averages)

| | Proportion of deposits held as current accounts | Number of banks in sample |
|---|---|---|
| | % | |
| 1850/9 | 63 | 6 |
| 1860/9 | 64 | 10 |
| 1870/9 | 64 | 10 |

*Source:* London clearing bank archives - see Michael Collins, 'The Business of Banking: English Bank Balance Sheets, 1840-80', *Business History*, vol.26, 1984, pp. 43-58.

The nature of the historical evidence means there is some uncertainty as to the interest rates paid to depositors in the nineteenth century. In the English provincial towns it had been common for banks to pay interest on deposits even before the new joint-stock banks were created and in some places, such as Lancashire, interest was paid on both current and deposit accounts.[2] In London, on the other hand, the private banks normally paid no interest on their deposits. However, the arrival of the joint-stock banks in the 1830s changed this, as they sought to compete with established firms and to attract new customers by offering interest payments on deposit accounts. In Scotland all banks had long sought to maintain resources by offering interest payments on a variety of deposits. Here, too, a distinction could be drawn between current account balances and deposits subject to various terms governing withdrawal.[3] Evidence for Ireland is very scanty but by the middle years of the nineteenth century practice seems to have been similar to that in the English provincial towns.[4]

The terms governing deposit accounts varied across banks and over time, but it was common practice for a bank to insist on a period of deposit (say, three to six months) and, then, on a fairly short notice of withdrawal (say, one or two weeks) after that period. In the case of the London and Westminster Bank, for instance, during the mid-nineteenth century interest was paid on deposits made for three months, sums under £1,000 were payable on demand, while greater amounts required a week's notice of withdrawal.[5] In practice, however, this bank worked on the assumption that all deposits were 'on call' – if customers wished to withdraw immediately, they could do so.[6]

Current account deposits could not only be withdrawn in the form of cash but – of long-term significance – could also be transferred easily through the use of cheques and bankers' drafts. Here the banks were making a fundamental contribution to the economy's development, by providing a new form of money. We already know that deposits were the most rapidly expanding component of Britain's total money stock; and by the end of the nineteenth century payment by cheque was very common.[7]

The manner in which note and deposit liabilities could be readily encashed provided another essential feature of the business of commercial banking. It necessitated that a large proportion of a bank's assets be held in fairly liquid form. Banks had to hold both an adequate cash reserve and a portfolio of assets which, if necessary, could be sold quickly and at little loss. As the banks grew in size, developed better business practices and built up greater resources – and as the banking habit spread among the general public – note and deposit holdings became less volatile. Nevertheless, a fundamental characteristic of British banking remained: a substantial proportion of resources continued to be invested in liquid assets.

*Acceptances and Endorsements*

These liabilities arose out of banks financing bills of exchange. They were only contingent liabilities in the sense that a bank could be called upon to meet its commitments to pay only if the principal parties to the bill transaction should fail to do so. All banks bought (or 'discounted') customers' short-term bills of exchange as part of their normal business and, as will be shown shortly, these formed a prominent part of the assets held. However, banks did not have to add bills bought from customers to their portfolios; bills could usually be readily re-sold (or rediscounted). Indeed, some English provincial private banks had been regular rediscounters even very early in the nineteenth century, but it was to be the provincial joint-stock banks which, from the 1830s, popularised the practice and made it an important part of the growing business of the money market in the mid-nineteenth century.[8] In contrast, the London banks did not rediscount their bills and the Scottish banks rarely did so.[9]

The emergence of a formal discount market in London during the second quarter of the nineteenth century both encouraged and benefited from this expanding rediscount business. From the point of view of the national economy the growth of rediscounting provided an important method by which commercial banks could finance the short-term capital needs of their customers. Indeed, during the middle decades of the nineteenth century it became a means by which commercial banks confined to particular localities could draw on funds from all over the nation. For instance, a bank located in a trading area such as Bristol or Liverpool might find that the volume of commercial bills discounted with it was so great that it would quickly exhaust its supply of funds from local depositors. However, ability to resell the bills to financial institutions outside the area (most notably in London) meant customers' needs could be met, the bank fulfilling its important function as provider of short-term finance. The bank's profit was made on the difference between the discount rate it charged to customers and the rate charged to it by other financial institutions. The latter was generally lower as the bank endorsed the bill in its own name before re-sale; thus, making the bill a more secure asset for the new purchaser. But it was here that the bank incurred its own liability, no matter how slight. On maturity the bill would be payable by the original acceptors, but if they should fail to meet the debt successive endorsers of the bill, including the bank, could be held responsible. In other words, the bank was liable to pay the bill only if all previous parties to it failed to do so – hence, the contingent nature of the liability – and careful scrutiny by the bank of bills and discounters kept the risk to a minimum.

The precise volume of bank rediscounting is unknown. Some banks never undertook it to any large extent, either because their funds from local deposits and note circulations were adequate, or because they viewed it as a sign of 'weakness' that a bank should not be able to cope from its own resources. Also the practice fell away sharply among even the provincial joint-stock banks during the 1860s and 1870s. This was partly a reaction to the difficulties incurred by some large rediscounters during the 1857 financial crisis and to the restrictions imposed by the Bank of England on discount house activity in the aftermath of that crisis. It also reflected long-term changes in the nature of banking business – as local banks built up their own deposit resources and, therefore, became less dependent on 'outside' funds and as overdrafts rather than bill discounting became a more common form of borrowing from banks.[10]

Acceptances arose out of similar short-term credit transactions to rediscounts and created similar contingency liabilities for the bank. Here, the bank permitted customers to draw bills directly on it, with the bank formally accepting responsibility to pay when the bill fell due. Customers could then use the bank acceptance to meet commercial debts or conduct financial transactions. The advantage to the customer was that a bank's acceptance would be more readily acceptable in payment because of its greater marketability compared to a normal trade bill. The bank, of course, would charge for the service and would ensure that the customer placed it 'in funds' before payment on the bill was due. Again, as the bank's liability was contingent, it would have to pay only if the customer should fail to honour the agreement. In this way bank acceptances provided a flexible, alternative means of financing short-term credit. It was for the London banks in particular that the acceptance business became important: they accepted bills on behalf of the customers of their provincial agents and, during the early years of the twentieth century, the London joint-stock banks became much more active in the international acceptance business.[11]

*Proprietors' Capital*

Proprietors' capital represents the liabilities of a bank to its owners in the form of partners' or shareholders' investments in the business. It includes original shareholdings, undistributed profits and any reserve or contingency funds accumulated from past profits and held against uncertainties, specific projects (e.g. constructing a new building) or bad debts. Generally these were only a small proportion of the resources available to a bank from deposits and notes, but capital funds were of critical importance in a more fundamental sense. In the last resort it was they that ultimately ensured a bank's solvency by providing an excess of assets over liabilities. They also represented a contingency reserve of resources on which the bank could draw to protect depositors and note-holders against commercial risks and losses. The adequacy of capital funds was important, too, in maintaining general confidence in the enterprise. The success of the early banks largely depended on the trust of note and deposit holders, and this trust rested to no small degree on the standing and wealth of the banks' partners and shareholders. Obviously for a private banking partnership, the greater the perceived wealth of the partners the more likely the public would entrust money to the bank's safe-keeping. In the case of banking corporations or large co-partnerships, greater publicity was given to the banks' accounts and frequent reports were made to shareholders. Thus, the number and (perhaps) names of shareholders would be known to the banking public, as well as the extent of proprietors' aggregate investment in the business. It is perhaps here that part of the explanation lies for the continuing large local interest in bank shareholdings, because local dignatories would obviously be well-known in the neighbourhood.[12] The continuing local nature of the English banking system until the closing decades of the nineteenth century also meant that it was some time before an extensive national market in bank shares emerged. Nevertheless, for the discerning investor they generally provided a secure alternative to railway and insurance company shares.[13]

Initially all bank shares were subject to 'unlimited liability' (except, it seemed, for those of the three chartered Public Banks of Scotland) and, thus, in the event of a bank's liquidation shareholders were liable for *all* the firm's debts even if this meant paying a sum in excess of their original shareholding. However, a series of company law reforms, 1857–62, was to change this and permit banks to register as limited liability companies. But it was the 1879 Companies Act which especially eased the transition to limited liability status by permitting bank proprietors to acquire a special form of 'reserved' liability. Under this act unlimited liability was retained for note issues, but for other liabilities and debts the amount that shareholders could be called upon to contribute in normal circumstances was restricted to a fixed sum – the liability was no longer unlimited. However, in the event of liquidation shareholders would be responsible for paying up to an extra, specified amount in order to cover the company's debts. This extra amount represented the new 'reserved' liability, a reservoir of capital resources not available under normal commercial conditions, but resources which could be drawn upon only in the last resort. Thus, a compromise had been devised between those who argued that full limited liability (where shareholders were liable only to the book value of their shares) might deter the public from placing deposits with a bank; and those who stressed that the unlimited nature of a proprietor's liability under old legislation was restricting the pool of potential investors. The failure of the 'unlimited' City of Glasgow Bank in 1878 – a failure which entailed shareholders having to pay sums far in excess of their normal share commitment – provided the impetus for the 1879 reform and encouraged a general switch to the new, 'limited' form of joint-stock shareholding.

The changing nature of proprietors' liability would obviously have to temper the use of figures in assessing the 'capital adequacy' of banks during the period. However, what figures there are reveal reasonable long-term stability in capital ratios from the 1850s although there was a decline in the 'capital to public liabilities' ratio by the end of the nineteenth century. Part A of Table 4.3 gives figures for samples of English banks (mainly joint-stock banks) over the middle decades of the century. These show an historically high ratio of 35 per cent for the 1840s, which dropped to 20 per cent in the 1850s and there it remained through the 1860s and 1870s. David Sheppard's figures in Part B indicate a decline on trend for the UK as a whole, down from 20 per cent in the 1880s to some 13 per cent in the decade prior to the First World War; and Sidney Checkland's figures show that for Scottish banks (in part C) there was a fall in capital ratios from the late 1860s to the 1870s from whence there was long-term stability at the 15–16 per cent level.

There were to be sharp falls in capital ratios across both world wars – down to about 6 per cent by the 1920s, and to some 3 per cent by the 1950s. So, the size of nineteenth-century bank capital ratios was high when compared to those of more recent times, and on trend the ratio was falling. This is what

Table 4.3: Bank Capital Ratios, 1840-1909 (decadal averages)

| | | | Ratio of Capital Funds (Paid-up Capital and Reserve Funds) to Public Liabilities (%) |
|---|---|---|---|
| A | England and Wales* | | |
| | 1840/9 | (8) | 35 |
| | 1850/9 | (13) | 20 |
| | 1860/9 | (20) | 19 |
| | 1870/9 | (24) | 20 |
| B | United Kingdom | | |
| | 1840/9 | | 20 |
| | 1890/9 | | 15 |
| | 1900/9 | | 13 |
| C | Scotland | | |
| | 1865/9 | | 18 |
| | 1870/9 | | 16 |
| | 1880/9 | | 16 |
| | 1890/9 | | 15 |
| | 1900/9 | | 15 |

* Samples only. The number of banks in each sample is given in parentheses.

*Sources:*

A London clearing bank archives - see Michael Collins, 'The Business of Banking: English Bank Balance Sheets, 1840-80', *Business History*, vol. 26, 1984, pp. 43-58.

B Calculated from David K. Sheppard, *The Growth and Role of UK Financial Institutions, 1880-1962* (Methuen & Co, London, 1971), pp. 743-6.

C Calculated from S.G. Checkland, *Scottish Banking. A History, 1695-1973* (Collins, Glasgow and London, 1975), pp. 743-5.

would be expected. As individual banks grew in size (through mergers, branching, etc.) and as the business of banking became more secure, a smaller capital base would have sufficed for the maintenance of public confidence and for the provision of buffer reserves held against the vicissitudes of business.

## BANK ASSETS

### *Cash*

One strict definition of a banker's cash in the nineteenth century would include only coin, Bank of England notes, and balances at the Bank of England. In practice, a banker may have looked also upon a number of other assets as being 'as good as cash'. Thus, notes and cheques of other bankers or even deposits at other banks could be part of a banker's cash holding, perhaps more especially in Scotland and Ireland where Bank of England notes were not legal tender and the notes and deposits of the 'public banks' of Edinburgh, or the Bank of Ireland, were *de facto* cash. Ultimately, of course, it was customers who determined what constituted 'cash' – if they were willing to accept it in payment from the bank, then all was well.

A banker would have to maintain a certain amount of 'till money' to meet the everyday cash needs of customers (for paying wages, retail transactions, etc.). Yet, as no interest was paid to the bank on its holdings of notes and coin, the need to make a profit would dictate that these be kept to a minimum. But what constituted a minimum during the nineteenth century? There were no legal reserve requirements imposed on British banks and, therefore, practice could vary a great deal from bank to bank. Obviously a major consideration would be the immediate nature of note and deposit liabilities – the greater the proportion of its liabilities that were subject to immediate encashment, the larger the cash reserves a prudent bank might wish to hold. There was, thus, a potential conflict between the dictates of profitability and security. All things being equal, the higher the rate of interest to be earned in the money market, the greater the incentive to keep holdings of non-interest-bearing cash to a minimum; but the greater the risk from sudden demands for cash from customers, the more cash that would have to be held. The paucity of nineteenth century records does not enable us to say confidently what proportion of resources banks kept as cash. It might be thought that over the whole period, as the banking system became more secure and the frequency of banking panics decreased, the amount of cash considered necessary to hold against 'extraordinary' demands would have fallen. However, what few figures there are suggest the reverse – on trend cash reserves seem to have risen.[14] If a true reflection of the banking sector as a whole, these figures are perhaps a further indication of the growing conservatism of British banks and of the increasing emphasis they placed on liquidity. By the last decades of the nineteenth century there was much public debate as to the adequacy of the banking system's cash holdings, and the wider publicity given to banks' accounts probably influenced banking practice towards a greater degree of caution in this respect.[15]

Even more difficult to gauge is whether bankers did indeed operate with a minimum cash reserve or if, in fact, there was a significant degree of variability. The absence of legal regulations and the fact that, for most of the century, cash reserve figures did not have to be published certainly meant that variability was possible. This is a very important issue in assessing whether commercial banks had any significant, autonomous impact on fluctuations in the money supply (and, therefore, on the economy at large) or whether they were merely passive agents, victims of changes in their cash reserves induced from the 'outside' (through changes in Bank of England policy, through the external operation of the gold standard, etc.). For instance, if commercial banks always sought to operate very close to a minimum cash reserve, then a balance of payments deficit causing a loss of gold overseas – or a reduction in Bank of England lending in the money markets – would cause their cash holdings to fall below this desired minimum and the banks would be compelled to correct the situation by, say, making it more difficult for customers to borrow. Thus, the balance of payments' drain, or Bank of England action, would directly affect the volume of commercial bank loans, reinforcing any effects on the real economy. However, if commercial bankers were relatively indifferent to changes in their cash holdings they could, perhaps, absorb the fall in reserves and leave their loans to customers unchanged. In this case, the ultimate impact on the real economy could be much less or, at the least, delayed. In practice, of course, it is likely that there were limits (upper and lower) within which banks were prepared to permit some variation and these limits could well have varied according to circumstances (seasonal factors, money market conditions, etc.) but the less rigid the banks' cash ratios the less immediate would have been the impact on bank lending of changes in the supply of cash.

Again, comprehensive figures are not available to resolve these issues. However, what data there are suggest that for the middle decades of the nineteenth century, for some banks at least, the ratio of cash to public liabilities was, indeed, quite variable. Thus, during the 1860s the ratio ranged from 8 per cent to 13 per cent for a group of twelve English banks; and, during the 1870s from 11 per cent to 17 per cent for a group of fourteen banks.[16] But by the end of the century available figures suggest much greater stability.[17] Therefore, the evidence is somewhat mixed, if indicating a growing rigidity over time.

*Money at Call and Short Notice*

This refers to loans made by banks for very short periods ('at call', overnight or for a week or so). They were loans made to other financial institutions; and, for London–based banks, loans to the discount houses and to brokers on the Stock Market were particularly important.[18] Such loans came to form a significant part of commercial banks' near–cash assets.

If need be they could be recalled very quickly and converted to cash yet, unlike cash, they earned interest for the bank. The practice of making such loans to the discount houses began in a small way after the 1825 financial crisis, when the London private banks decided to take action to avoid a repetition of the situation where, in a general pressure for cash, they had been forced to rediscount their bills of exchange on a large scale.[19] Such a situation had been fraught with the dangers of a general collapse of the market. As each bank unloaded its bills, interest rates were forced up and a severe shortage of cash emerged, raising the real possibility of good bills being unsaleable altogether and threatening the very solvency of the banks. Once the crisis had passed, the London bankers decided that in future they should build up their own reserves of cash and near-cash assets. Thus, the development of large bill brokers in London and their willingness to borrow funds at short notice provided an ideal opportunity. The banks found they could earn a modest rate of interest on loans returnable either on demand or very close to it. Here was a new reserve asset. It was not quite cash, but it was almost as good; and it earned some interest. The practice expanded greatly over the century as a whole and spread to all other banks in Britain. By the First World War the banks in the UK in total held about 14 per cent of their assets in the form of 'money at call and short notice', an amount equivalent to twice their cash holdings and one-and-a-half times their holdings of bills.[20] It seems obvious, therefore, that an increasing proportion of the country's total bill discounts was being financed by the commercial banks 'at one removed' – they were lending to the London discount houses who by this time were the direct buyers of the bills.

*Bills*

At the beginning of the nineteenth century bills of exchange were already a very common form of granting commercial credit in domestic trade. They were a sort of IOU by which a supplier granted credit to a purchaser. For instance, in the Lancashire cotton trade in the 1830s a cotton spinner – say, from the Manchester area – would customarily pay a Liverpool broker for his supply of raw materials within ten days of the purchase with a bill of exchange drawn at up to three months' date. Here, the Liverpool supplier would normally draw up the bill, naming the creditor and debtor; and stating the amount, place (often London) and date of payment. Once the Manchester spinner 'accepted' the bill by signing it, he returned it to the Liverpool broker in payment for the goods. Thus, the Manchester manufacturer received the raw materials straight away but would not have to pay cash until the bill was due, in three months; whereas the Liverpool broker who was granting the credit held the bill as legal proof of the debt. In other words, the bill of exchange was a ready means of one firm giving credit to another.

The brokering firm could keep the bill if it so wished, arranging to collect the cash when the bill became due; or it could sell (i.e. 'discount') it. In law the ownership of the bill could be easily transferred, through the holder endorsing it (i.e. signing his/her name on it) which would then entitle the new holder to the cash when it became due. In the example, the brokering firm may have been able to persuade another merchant to accept the endorsed bill in payment of its own debts; or the bill could be discounted with the firm's bank in order to obtain cash immediately. If a banker became involved in this way, then it became the bank which was effectively providing credit for the original commercial transaction between Liverpool and Manchester – the broker gave credit to the spinner, but the broker financed the credit by borrowing from the bank.

Bill discounting of this sort was a very common means by which the mid-nineteenth-century banker granted short-term loans, and by which businessmen financed their short-term capital needs covering such costs as the purchase of raw materials and the financing of goods in store or in transit. The bank, of course, charged for the service (at an annual rate of interest, or 'rate of discount'). In the process the bank acquired what was technically a self-liquidating asset, in the sense that at the end of the credit period the commercial transaction underlying the bill's creation should have been completed, releasing the money necessary to clear the debt. Bills could be highly liquid assets for the banker. This is not to claim that before the First World War bills were viewed by bankers in any formal sense as part of a 'liquidity reserve'. Such a concept belongs to the twentieth century, even to the post-1945 period. However, even in the nineteenth century the general issue of liquidity – of the negotiability of assets – was of obvious importance to the everyday business of banking and bills played an important role here. Some bills held by banks would be as illiquid as overdrafts in that they could not normally be turned into cash until the customer repaid the loan, especially if the bank concerned did not practise rediscounting in the London money market. But at any one time a bank would hold many of its customers' bills, all falling due for payment at different dates – from within one or two days to within a few months (commonly bills ran for only some three months from the day they were drawn up). Thus, in a judiciously-managed bill portfolio there was a regular turnover of bills, with a certain proportion due to be encashed in any one day. Another important point for the bank was that, even if bills were not rediscounted, they could readily be used as collateral to secure loans from other banks (especially from London agents). Moreover, as has already been noted, where a bank was prepared to rediscount bills, then their liquidity as assets was greatly increased by the willingness of the London discount houses and other financial institutions to buy them.

In this way, many of the bills held by a banker provided a third line of liquidity, certainly some way behind cash and money at call, and perhaps behind holdings of UK government securities (essentially Consols) which also had a ready market in Britain.[21] The existence of a national discount market meant, too, that any one bank was not solely dependent on the local supply of bills, for it could always buy from the discount houses bills originally drawn up outside its own locality.

The bill of exchange was a very common means of meeting the short-term capital needs of many mid-nineteenth-century businesses, with the banks at that time committing a high proportion of their resources to this type of investment. It can be seen from Table 4.4 that for the groups of English banks for which figures are available, net bill holdings were very close to the value of all loans and overdrafts. For these banks bill discounting was a major means by which credit was granted to customers. For a number of Scottish banks, too, despite the early development of the 'cash credit' or 'overdraft', bill discounting during the first half of the nineteenth century appears to have been at least as important a means of extending credit to customers.[22]

Research suggests that for businessmen, short-term capital needs during the early years of industrialisation were often paramount, even for manufacturing concerns.[23] Many firms financed part of these needs out of internal funds but the willingness of commercial banks and discount houses to purchase bills and provide credit created a generally supportive environment and, thus, played an important role in the financing of British economic development. Obviously, as the scale of business grew during the nineteenth century, and as more of a firm's capital was committed to fixed assets such as buildings and machinery, the granting of short-term credits became relatively less important. Nevertheless, this was only a relative decline: short-term capital needs continued to be of importance, and bank credit continued to meet these needs.

The type of bills held by bankers changed markedly over the nineteenth century. Initially inland bills based on internal trade dominated, but from the 1870s foreign bills arising out of overseas finance and trade became more important (see Chapter 5). By 1913 inland bills were only about one-third of all bills

Table 4.4 : Ratio of Bill Holdings to 'Loans and Overdrafts' in English Bank Balance Sheets, 1840-80 (per cent), decadal averages

| | % | Number of banks in sample |
|---|---|---|
| 1840/9 | 100 | 5 |
| 1850/9 | 86 | 10 |
| 1860/9 | 104 | 11 |
| 1870/9 | 64 | 12 |

*Source:* London clearing bank archives - see Michael Collins, 'The Business of Banking: English Bank Balance Sheets, 1840-80', *Business History*, vol. 26, 1984, pp. 43-58.

created in the UK.[24] There was also a sharp decline in the volume of inland bills as overdrafts became a more popular means of obtaining bank finance and as general improvements in communications reduced the need for businessmen to keep large stocks of materials (thus obviating the need for short-term credit to pay for them).[25] One consequence was that bills in total became a much less important means of granting bank credit. Table 4.4 has already shown that there was a sharp decline during the 1870s in the importance of bills to the English banks for which data are available, and by the early years of the next decade it has been estimated by Sheppard that bills had shrunk to just 13 per cent of total UK bank assets.[26]

Finally, the late nineteenth century saw the creation of the Treasury bill which was to become such a popular form of investment for the commercial banks from the First World War. They were first issued by the Treasury in 1877 as a means of raising short-term loans for the government, and they were drawn up in such a way as to resemble bills of exchange as much as possible.[27] The banks bought them as other bills, although there were never enough of them to represent but a small proportion of total bill holdings before the First World War. For instance, it has been estimated that Treasury bills were only some six per cent of the total bill holdings of UK bankers, 1910/12; and by this time bills in total were down to nine per cent of total bank assets.[28]

*Overdrafts and Loans*

This group of assets covers all advances made to non-bank customers other than through the purchase of bills. As such, it is a catch-all category covering a very broad spectrum: from advances secured by the deposit of collateral to unsecured loans where the bank trusted to its judgement as to the customer's ability to repay; from very short advances to medium- or long-term loans; from overdrafts where the customer was free to draw up to an agreed maximum and was charged only on the sum outstanding, to fixed-amount, fixed-period loans with little flexibility, and from loans made to an individual for the purchase of an everyday household gadget to loans to a manufacturer for investment in new machinery. Here was the bread-and-butter business of every banker – the main means by which the banker accommodated the community, especially after the use of inland bills went into decline from the 1870s.

It has been estimated that by the end of the nineteenth century and beginning of the twentieth, the size of advances made by UK banks in aggregate was equivalent to somewhere over one-half of their deposit and note liabilities.[29] For earlier decades, too – in the middle of the nineteenth century – what evidence there is suggests that the English banks employed about one-half of their resources in the form of overdrafts and loans.[30]

Yet despite the importance of bank lending, extremely little is known about it in detail. Within any study of the determinants of Britain's long-term economic development, the extent to which banks lent to businessmen, the type and duration of the loans, and the sort of investment projects they financed, could all be critically important. Did British banks actively participate in the accumulation of capital resources in the productive sectors of the economy? Or was it that they 'failed' the country, by neglecting to finance new technological development, by giving inadequate support to the innovators who were so vital to the maintenance of a high growth rate? Unfortunately, the answers to such questions are unknown.

Nevertheless, it has been common to claim that British banks did indeed neglect the needs of the businessman, especially those of the industrialist, by being overly concerned with liquidity.[31] In one sense this was the price the country paid for having developed deposit banking and the cheque system to such a high degree. Large deposit liabilities readily convertible to cash instilled caution, encouraging the banker to seek 'safe' loans. Thus, in contrast to a number of continental banks, British banks failed to become involved in financing investment projects to any large extent. Indeed, there is some indication that as time went on the banks became *less* involved with industry. There are signs that the smaller banks of the late eighteenth and early nineteenth centuries may have had a greater affinity with their local business communities. They were created by those communities (local businessmen) and their commercial viability was inextricably bound up with the fortunes of local firms. In contrast, by the beginning of the twentieth century large national, or regional, banks were the norm, and through the London money markets they had many more opportunities to invest in short-period, highly-liquid assets. Institutional change confirmed the British banker's prejudice for liquidity.

But this is not the full story. Throughout the period there are many examples of banks making long-term loans to businessmen; and it is also obviously true that even where the banks were providing only short-term credits, the fact that firms did not have to find the funds out of their own resources must have meant more was available for longer-term projects. Moreover, short-term credits could be continually renewed and, thus, effectively become long-term loans. The picture is far from clear, therefore. As has already been emphasised, more research is required. A much more detailed analysis of bank lending is needed before any firm conclusions can be drawn about the extent of bank involvement in business finance during the nineteenth century.

*Investments*

Again due to lack of basic information, many of the comments made about advances and bank involvement in financing British industry can be extended to cover bank investments. Although particular examples exist, it seems that the commercial banks of the nineteenth and early twentieth centuries made very little direct investment in British industry and commerce through the purchase of stocks and shares. This partly reflects the relatively undeveloped state of industrial financing on the organised capital markets – as most firms were private partnerships, and/or family concerns, which financed growth from internal funds, few industrial shares were actually available for purchase. But it also reflects the prejudice of bankers for liquid assets. Certainly, by 1890 investments by the London banks were 'largely held in British government securities, especially Consols...'[32] This conservatism stemmed from the view of most London bankers that investments be treated as part of their liquidity reserve. As there was no danger of default by the British government and as a ready market for Consols had long existed, they seemed ideal securities for a bank to hold. However, the fall in the market value of Consols from the late 1890s raised the possibility of capital loss on resale of such securities, encouraging some banks to become more active participants in the securities market and to diversify their investment portfolio somewhat, embracing the stocks of colonial governments, British local authorities, railways, some public utilities and even the occasional brewer. It was partly for this reason that there was a shift in bank opinion away from treating investments as part of the reserve assets, towards viewing bills more firmly as the most liquid assets after cash and money at call. But the changes were still fairly modest and as one analyst, C.A.E. Goodhart, concludes: 'The major gap in bank portfolios was...[still]...the absence of industrial, especially domestic industrial stocks...'[33]

## BANKING ADVICE AND FINANCIAL SERVICES

The asset/liability approach outlined above does omit one important aspect of a bank's business, namely its role as provider of general financial services. In the nineteenth century specialist institutions existed (such as the stockbroker, discount house, or issuing house) but for many customers, the local bank manager was much more accessbile and he came to offer a range of miscellaneous services. As part of a national (and, indeed, international) financial community the local banker provided a ready means by which customers could remit funds and documents at a minimal cost. Such provision now seems matter-of-fact, but before the nineteenth century it was a major concern for businessmen, especially merchants who regularly had to arrange for bills to be paid, documents to be delivered, and so on. The commercial banking system provided the solution. Banks also offered customers general advice on investment opportunities, insurance and other financial dealings. Initially such services were provided on an informal basis, but as banks grew larger and their businesses became more 'professional', by the turn of the century they were offering a broad range of services. Through them their customers could gain access to foreign currencies, extraordinary supplies of coin and, indeed, a whole range of minor services integral to retail banking.

## THE COMMERCIAL BANKS AND ECONOMIC DEVELOPMENT

As the survey of bank asset holdings indicates, much of British bank involvement with business was in the form of short-term credits via bill discounts or short-period loans. This is corroborated by a variety of indirect sources such as individual histories of industrial concerns, histories of the capital market and the expressed opinion of contemporary bankers, financial journalists, and the like. True, lack of quantitative data prevents detailed assessment of the role commercial banks played in promoting industrial growth and economic development, but it is generally accepted that there was no great involvement in the provision of capital for long-term investment projects. This was in sharp contrast to a number of continental banks, especially those in Germany – a contrast particularly emphasised by Gerschenkron in his study of European economic development.[34]

Gerschenkron saw the contrast as reflecting significant differences in the timing of industrialisation in the UK and Germany. Germany's Industrial Revolution occurred in the middle decades of the nineteenth century and, thus, it came after a prolonged period of technological development in Britain which had given her manufacturers competitive dominance in world markets. Therefore, when German firms were being established in the iron and steel, coal, engineering and chemical industries, they had to invest large amounts in technically-advanced machinery and other fixed capital, and had to begin production on a large enough scale as to be competitive with existing world suppliers. Consequently, their fixed capital needs were large, much larger than had been the case for the early British industrial concerns at a similar stage of development in the late eighteenth and early nineteenth centuries. Thus, in mid-nineteenth-century Germany the need for 'outside' capital supplies to augment the industrial concerns' own resources became critical, and some banks developed their business to meet these needs. They became directly involved in financing capital investment projects and even installed their own personnel among the top management of industrial firms. A very close financial-manufacturing axis developed – an axis of the sort not seen in the UK.

The Industrial Revolution in England and Scotland had not only come much earlier (beginning in the second half of the eighteenth century) but had also been the first. Therefore, the technological and market conditions facing British firms in the early stages of industrialisation had been starkly different than those for the Germans. Many of the new machines at the time were not very sophisticated, nor very expensive, and the progressive nature of technological change meant that most firms had no great difficulty in financing their adoption. Thus, while bank finance seems to have been occasionally used, a firm's internal funds, or borrowings from friends and relatives, were normally adequate to meet its fixed capital needs.[35] Anyway, at the close of the eighteenth century the state of technology was such that the bulk of most manufacturing firms' capital was 'floating capital' such as inventories; and it was here that they sought and gained 'outside' credit from the banks. Thus, in Gerschenkron's view, *at the time of the Industrial Revolution* British commercial bank concentration on short-term financing was as appropriate to the needs of the economy as the German banks' long-term loans were to be in a later period. But once established, the British bankers' concern with short-term credits persisted long after the needs of British industry had altered.

There are two points of interest in this comparison between the British 'credit bank' and the Continental 'investment bank'. First, was it indeed true that British banks concentrated so heavily on short-term loans during the economy's period of rapid industialisation? As a generalisation it probably was true, but there is also growing evidence of direct involvement in other than very short-term financing in this early period – Gerschenkron's assumptions need some qualification.[36]

The second point is of more interest for the period under study. Even if it is accepted that during the nineteenth century British bank lending became inflexible – even 'ossified' in the eyes of some critics – it is still no easy matter to assess whether or not this was damaging to British economic growth. For instance, the emphasis on liquid assets in bank portfolios incorporated a strong element of stability, and it seems a safe assumption that a stable banking system would be conducive to general economic growth. In addition, the short-term credit and remittance facilities offered by the banks were obviously of continuing importance to British industry and commerce; and, from a national viewpoint, by the late nineteenth century the extension of this form of banking business to overseas trade and finance was making a significant contribution to invisible earnings on the balance of payments. Also, on present evidence it would be difficult to sustain the argument that British industry was actively seeking long-term funds from the banks, but being turned away. Rather the indications are that the typical British manufacturing firm was a family concern dependent on internal funding and only rarely seeking infusions of outside capital.[37] Moreover, some financial institutions independent of the commercial banks, such as the finance and trust companies and the London Stock Market, did develop businesses more directly geared to the supply of long-term capital. Even here there was little industrial involvement and, in general, the City more closely embraced overseas investment (mainly in state and public utility securities).[38] Thus, if by the late nineteenth century British industry was not sustaining a high enough investment rate and if this was detrimental to economic growth, the fault did not obviously lie with the domestic banks. In this passive sense – with the constant proviso about the need for more research into the nature of bank lending – there does not seem to be a strong case for condemning the banks. Even so critics could argue that what was required was *positive* involvement, with the active mobilisation of bank deposits for the cause of industrial development. If necessary this would have required much greater involvement with industry, with the banks becoming actively involved in the promotion of new firms and in the financing of mergers and take-overs. This did not happen.

## FURTHER READING

Michael Collins, 'The Business of Banking: English Bank sheets, 1840–80', *Business History*, vol. 26, 1984, pp. 43–58.

C.A.E. Goodhart, *The Business of Banking, 1891–1914* (Weidenfeld and Nicolson, London, 1972).

P.L. Cottrell, *Industrial Finance, 1830–1914* (Methuen, London, 1980).

## NOTES

1. Here 'total deposits' means the sum of current accounts and deposit accounts. Data for the 1860s and 1870s are from the archives of the London clearing banks; and for the 1890s from C.A.E. Goodhart, *The Business of Banking, 1891–1914* (Weidenfeld and Nicolson, London, 1972) pp. 174, 417–23, 436–43, 459, 534.

2. T.E. Gregory, (assisted by Annette Henderson), *The Westminster Bank Through a Century* (2 vols., Humphrey Milford for Oxford University Press, London, 1936), vol. 1, pp. 28–31; R.S. Sayers, *Lloyds Bank in the History of English Banking* (Oxford University Press, Oxford, 1957), p. 162; and Michael Collins, 'The Bank of England and the Liverpool Money Market, 1825–50', unpublished Ph.D thesis, University of London, 1972, pp. 246–8.

3. Charles W. Munn, *The Scottish Provincial Banking Companies, 1747–1864* (John Donald, Edinburgh, 1981), pp. 145–6, 148; and S.G. Checkland, *Scottish Banking: A History, 1695–1973* (Collins, London and Glasgow, 1975) pp. 188–9.

4. G.L. Barrow, *The Emergence of the Irish Banking System, 1820–1845*, (Gill and Macmillan, Dublin 1975), pp. 34–6.

5. Gregory, *Westminster*, vol. 1, pp. 108–9, 114.

6. Gregory, ibid., vol. 2, p. 197. The influential manager of the North and South Wales Bank made the same point – see George Rae, *The Country Banker*, 7th edn (John Murray, London,

1888), pp. 129–32.

7. J.W. Gilbart (ed. Ernest Sykes), *The History, Principles and Practice of Banking*, new edn (2 vols., G. Bell and Sons, London, 1911), vol. 1, p. 137; and W.F. Crick and J.E. Wadsworth, *A Hundred Years of Joint Stock Banking* (Hodder & Stoughton, London, 1936), p. 35.

8. W.T.C. King, *History of the London Discount Market* (Routledge & Sons, London, 1936), pp 42–7; Goodhart, *Business of Banking*, p. 144.

9. King, *Discount Market*, pp. 62–70; Checkland, *Scottish Banking*, pp. 446, 469; and Munn, *Scottish Provincial Banking*, pp. 125–6.

10. Shizuya Nishimura, *The Decline of Inland Bills of Exchange in the London Money Market, 1855–1913* (Cambridge University Press, Cambridge, 1971), p. 53.

11. See pages 151–3.

12. B.L. Anderson and P.L. Cottrell, 'Another Victorian Capital Market: A Study of Banking and Bank Investors on Merseyside', *Economic History Review*, 2nd. series, vol. 28, 1975, pp. 598–615; and M. Collins and P. Hudson, 'Provincial Bank Lending; Yorkshire and Merseyside, 1826–60', *Bulletin of Economic Research*, vol. 31, 1979, pp. 69–72.

13. For the middle years of the nineteenth century see Anderson and Cottrell, 'Banking on Merseyside', pp. 598, 600–4; and for Scotland, Checkland, *Scottish Banking*, pp. 377–8.

14. For the mid-nineteenth century see Michael Collins, 'The Business of Banking: English Balance Sheets, 1840–80', *Business History*, vol. 26, 1984, pp. 49–51.

15. Goodhart, *Business of Banking*, pp. 100–8.

16. Unpublished data from the London clearing banks. See Michael Collins, 'English Banks and the Mid-Nineteenth Century Business Cycle' in P.L. Cottrell and D.E. Moggridge (eds.), *Money and Power* (Macmillan, London, 1987).

17. Goodhart, *Business of Banking*, pp. 116–7, 212–3.

18. For details on the 1891–1914 period see

Goodhart, ibid., ch.7.

19. King, *Discount Market*, pp. 62–70.

20. David K. Sheppard, *The Growth and Role of UK Financial Institutions, 1880–1962* (Methuen & Co., London, 1971), p. 116.

21. In practice, ability to sell individual bills quickly and at little loss would depend upon the quality of the bill. The more prestigious and creditworthy the drawer, acceptor and endorser(s) of a bill, the easier it was to dispose of. Also the particular group of assets a banker might include among his reserves would vary from bank to bank – thus some may have seen their holdings of government securities as more liquid than bills.

22. English data are from the archives of the London clearing banks, and some Scottish figures can be seen in Munn, *Scottish Provincial Banking*, Appendix A, *passim*, and in Checkland, *Scottish Banking*, Appendix 3, *passim*.

23. Sidney Pollard, 'Fixed Capital in the Industrial Revolution in Britain', *Journal of Economic History*, vol. 24, 1964, pp. 299–314; and Francois Crouzet (ed.), *Capital Formation in the Industrial Revolution* (Methuen & Co., London, 1972), especially pp. 39–52.

24. Nishimura, *Inland Bills*, p. 25.

25. Ibid., especially Nishimura's concluding remarks on pp. 77–9.

26. Sheppard, *Financial Institutions*, p. 116.

27. Gregory, *Westminster Bank*, vol. 2, pp. 257–8; and 'The Treasury Bill: The Story of an Economist's Invention', *Midland Bank Review*, February, 1961, pp. 3–4.

28. Sheppard, *Financial Institutions*, p. 116 – although it is also assumed that most of the 14 per cent of assets held as 'money at call' was on loan to the London discount market and, therefore, indirectly invested in bills.

29. Goodhart, *Business of Banking*, pp. 158–9; and Sheppard, *Financial Institutions*, pp. 116–7.

30. Unpublished data from the London clearing banks.

31. For instance, see H.S. Foxwell, 'The Financing of Industry and Trade', *Economic Journal*, vol. 27, 1917, pp. 502–22; Alexander Gerschenkron, *Economic Backwardness in Historical Perspective. A Book of Essays*, 2nd impression (Harvard University Press, Cambridge, Mass., 1966), pp. 13–16; and William P. Kennedy, 'Institutional Response to Economic Growth: Capital Markets in Britain to 1914', in Leslie Hannah (ed.), *Management Strategy and Business Development* (Macmillan, London, 1976), pp. 151–83.

32. Goodhart, *Business of Banking*, p. 168 – the following comments draw heavily on Chapter 8 in Goodhart. On the role of Consols in the reserve also see Rae, *Country Banker*, pp. 207–24.

33. Goodhart, *Business of Banking*, p. 135.

34. Gerschenkron, *Economic Backwardness*. For a critical appraisal of Gerschenkron's views on the role of banks see David F. Good, 'Backwardness and the Role of Banking in Nineteenth Century European Industrialisation', *Journal of Economic History*, vol. 33, 1973, pp. 845–50; and Rondo Cameron (ed.), *Banking and Economic Development. Some Lessons of History* (Oxford University Press, London, 1972), pp. 9–15. For a more general discussion on the Anglo–German comparison see P.L. Cottrell, *Industrial Finance, 1830–1914* (Methuen, London, 1980), pp. 236–44.

35. Pollard, 'Fixed Capital', especially see pp. 307–12 which deal specifically with the role of banks.

36. Rondo Cameron (ed.), *Banking in the Early Stages of Industrialisation* (Oxford University Press, London, 1967), especially chs. 2 and 3; Francois Crouzet (ed.), *Capital Formation*, pp. 46–54; Collins and Hudson, 'Provincial Bank Lending', and Cottrell, *Industrial Finance*, ch.7. But also see S.D. Chapman, 'Financial Restraints on the Growth of Firms in the Cotton Industry, 1790–1850', *Economic History Review*, 2nd. series, vol. 32, 1979, pp. 50–69.

37. A.K. Cairncross, *Home and Foreign Investment, 1870–1913* (Cambridge University Press, Cambridge, 1953), pp. 95–102. In the case of the

Stock Market, too, A.R. Hall in 'A Note on the English Capital Market as a Source of Funds for Home Investment before 1914', *Economica*, new series, vol. 24, 1957, pp. 59–66, suggests it was less a case of market imperfections denying funds to British industry than British industry not seeking the funds. Also see Cottrell, *Industrial Finance*, pp. 179–90. However, Kennedy, 'Institutional Response', lays most stress on the detrimental effect of the institutional structure and practice of capital markets.

38. For example, see Stanley Chapman, *The Rise of Merchant Banking* (Allen & Unwin, London, 1984), pp. 98–103.

Chapter Five

# THE MONETARY SECTOR AND THE INTERNATIONAL ECONOMY

## THE IMPORTANCE OF INTERNATIONAL FACTORS

Britain's industrialisation, and her extensive overseas commercial and financial connections, meant that during the nineteenth century she played a significant role in the world economy. From a national perspective, too, international factors were of continuing importance in the development of the domestic economy. As a proportion of Gross National Product, exports of goods and services rose from over 15 per cent in the 1840s, to a peak of about 35 per cent in the 1870s, falling back only slightly to under 30 per cent just before the First World War.[1] An early technological lead helped the UK to achieve international economic hegemony as the world's leading commercial nation and, despite relatively faster growth among industrial competitors as they 'caught up' from the latter half of the nineteenth century, the UK remained the largest international trader at the outset of the First World War.[2] Many of the world's most important commodity markets for raw materials and foodstuffs were based in Britain and a high proportion of the world's trade was carried by Britain's growing merchant fleet. A heavy dependence on overseas raw materials and food, a free trade policy from the 1840s, and worldwide imperial connections, all ensured that the UK remained the most important single consumer of internationally-traded primary produce. Obviously, in such circumstances external trade factors were highly influential within the domestic economy and, indeed, were critical for individual manufacturing sectors such as textiles, iron and steel, and coal.

This close connection between the domestic and international economies also applied to financial markets. Accompanying the expansion of trade, Britain's financial institutions increased the range and extent of services geared to the needs of the international community. Foreigners and residents who were engaged in international transactions could readily obtain insurance, short-term and long-term borrowing facilities, places of safe deposit which paid competitive rates, remittance facilities, collection services, and a whole spectrum of specialist financial advice and guidance from within the London money and capital markets. The lack of state restrictions permitted the free flow of credit and investment funds in and out of the country; and with Britain's importance as an industrial trading nation, the pound sterling was extensively used in international transactions, financing some two-thirds of world trade by the turn of the century. By then the City of London was well established as the most important financial centre in the world.

However, a parallel can be drawn with the country's experience in international trade: early industrialisation and concomitant financial development, especially in London, enabled British bankers and financiers to capture a large share of the world's financial markets, but similar developments in other advanced nations from the last quarter of the nineteenth century signalled a relative decline for the City. Paris, Berlin and even New York were all taking a more active role in international finance. Even so, by 1913, London was still the most important of this select band of financial centres.

A specific feature of the pre-1914 period which should be emphasised is that, as with her trade in goods, Britain maintained an open market in finance. Bullion, cash, short-term credits and long-term investment funds could be freely raised in London, and could be freely imported into and exported out of the country. During the period, worldwide improvements in communications and continuing overseas economic development drew the world's major money markets closer together, permitting the easier transfer of both funds and information across international boundaries. In this sense, British financial institutions and markets were but a part of world money markets – financial conditions in Britain could influence conditions overseas but, in turn, external factors could impose important constraints on domestic markets.

One aspect of Britain's international role that must be examined, therefore, is the interplay between her contribution to world finance and the impact of international development on domestic monetary institutions. This chapter explores the institutional changes and specialist practices which emerged to cater for the City's international business; dealing with the international bill market, the role of sterling, and overseas investment. There is also a need to consider the more general issue of whether or not such developments were beneficial to the national economy.

## BRITAIN'S ADOPTION OF THE GOLD STANDARD IN THE EARLY NINETEENTH CENTURY

During the French Wars the government had suspended the gold standard. However, once hostilities ceased, two acts of Parliament, passed in 1816 and 1819, prepared the way for Britain's return to a stable exchange rate in terms of gold.[3] They allowed for the gradual resumption of convertibility for sterling banknotes, with the adoption (by May 1823 at the latest) of a Mint price of £3 17s 10d per standard ounce of gold. The melting down of coin and the free export and import of precious metals and specie were also permitted. For the Bank of England convertibility became effective from February 1821 and, henceforth, the Bank had to hold sufficient gold reserves to ensure that convertibility. At first, all note-issuers had to maintain convertibility of their notes into gold on demand but (as previous chapters have shown) from 1833 Bank of England notes became legal tender in England and Wales. This meant that note issuers in those countries could now pay in Bank of England notes, although the requirement to pay gold still applied to the Bank, of course. This confirmed the existing practice whereby the Bank had effectively become the repository for the nation's gold reserve, for there was little need for English banks to hold much gold (they could use Bank of England notes instead) and Scottish and Irish banks could always draw on London if the need arose. The Bank Charter Act of 1844 completed the legislative framework of Britain's pre-1914 gold standard. In an attempt to regulate the domestic note issue this Act imposed further restrictions on the Bank by obliging it to maintain a 100 per cent specie reserve against all notes issued above a permitted fiduciary issue which was initially fixed at £14 million.[4] The Bank not only had to maintain full convertibility but also had to alter its note issue - £ for £ - only in line with changes in its gold reserve.

Thus, under the British gold standard the public's holdings of cash consisted of coins and notes, the latter being freely convertible to gold coin (either directly or, indirectly, through Bank of England notes). Finally, the value of this currency was guaranteed by the government's obligation to maintain a fixed weight of gold in its minted coins.

## INTERNATIONAL EXCHANGE RATES

During the middle years of the nineteenth century the UK's adherence to a gold standard placed her very much in a minority amongst trading nations. At first, the USA was nominally on a bimetallic standard based on both gold and silver and, then, had an inconvertible paper currency (the Federal 'greenback') from 1862 to 1879, although in international trade the gold dollar remained the standard measure of value.[5] On the Continent experience was mixed. France operated a nominal bimetallic standard, although a growing divergence in gold and silver prices was to put the franc on a *de facto* gold standard from the 1850s. The currencies of Holland, Spain, Switzerland, Belgium, and the main German states were tied to silver in one form or another. Indeed, almost all the major European states and a number of important non-European countries, such as India and China, operated monetary standards linked to silver.

An international system of currency exchange rates based on gold emerged only during the last quarter of the nineteenth century. The change to gold was initiated by altered demand and supply conditions on world markets for gold and silver – conditions which by the 1870s were significantly reducing the price of silver in terms of gold. On the supply side, the rate of output at existing gold mines began to decrease, and there were no new major discoveries until those in South Africa in the 1890s. Meanwhile silver output increased with new finds, most notably in Nevada. The estimates of world output given in Table 5.1 give a clear indication of how significant supply side changes were. Through the 1870s the share of gold in the combined production of precious metals (gold and silver) fell from over 70 per cent to under 60 per cent.

There were important changes in demand as well. These led to the sterilisation of a large proportion of the world's monetary gold and a fall-off in the demand for silver. In particular, the 1870s saw a switch by a number of leading countries from silver or silver-related currencies to gold-based currencies. Most significantly, the newly-united Germany led the way by providing for the issue of gold coins in 1871 and by establishing a gold standard for the mark in 1873. This necessitated the purchase and accumulation of gold reserves by the German central bank, the *Reichs-bank*, while allowing the release of silver.

The growing 'glut' and falling price of silver (rising price of gold) added to the existing pressure on those countries operating silver and bimetallic currencies. The pressure arose because official and market prices of silver were no longer close together,

Table 5.1: World Production of Precious Metals, 1841-80

| Period | Weight (tonnes) | | Value | | | |
|---|---|---|---|---|---|---|
| | Gold | Silver | Million Marks | | Percentage share | |
| | | | Gold | Silver | Gold | Silver |
| 1841-50 | 54.8 | 780.4 | 152.8 | 137.4 | 53 | 47 |
| 1851-60 | 401.2 | 1791.1 | 1119.2 | 325.1 | 77 | 23 |
| 1861-70 | 380.1 | 2440.3 | 1060.4 | 439.0 | 71 | 29 |
| 1871-80 | 346.3 | 4419.7 | 966.2 | 726.7 | 57 | 43 |

*Source* *Report of the Royal Commission ... [on] Recent Changes in the Relative Values of the Precious Metals ...*, PP 1887, XXII, Appendix III, p. 318, original data from A.D. Soetbeer "Materialien...'

Table 5.2: The Value of Silver,1851-80

| | a) Silver/Gold Ratio | b) London Price of 1 oz. of Standard Silver (pence) |
|---|---|---|
| 1851-55 | 15.3 | 61.2 |
| 1856-60 | 15.3 | 61.7 |
| 1861-65 | 15.3 | 61.3 |
| 1866-70 | 15.4 | 60.6 |
| 1871-75 | 15.9 | 59.1 |
| 1876-80 | 17.9 | 52.7 |

*Sources:* a) Calculated from Table 2 of A.D. Soetbeer's paper contained as Appendix XVI of the *Report of the Royal Commission ... [on] Recent Changes in the Relative Values of the Precious Metals...*, PP 1888, XLV, p. 620

b) Calculated from Appendix 1 (presented by Pixley) of the *Report of the Royal Commission ...[on] Recent Changes in the Relative Values of the Precious Metals...*, PP 1887, XXII, pp. 314-5.

yet these countries had fixed the official price of silver in terms of their own currencies (and, or, in terms of gold) in the light of the old, high market value of silver. The market value of silver now fell sharply. The figures in Table 5.2 suggest that the price of silver fell by about 11 per cent on the London market in the second half of the 1870s with the market ratio of silver to gold rising from 15.4 to 17.9 between the late 1860s and late 1870s. In such circumstances it became profitable for merchants, financiers, and other traders, to buy silver cheaply on world markets and sell it in the countries concerned at the higher, official price. Silver flowed into these countries, disrupting domestic monetary arrangements and threatening inflation. In bimetallic countries, official rates of exchange between gold and silver reflected out-of-date market conditions and arbitrageurs could make a profit by importing silver and exporting gold. In general, as the metal in silver currencies was now worth less in terms of gold on world markets, and the metal in gold currencies worth more in terms of silver, silver currencies depreciated relative to gold currencies. For instance, British goods valued in gold pounds were more expensive for Indians who were buying with silver rupees.

In this way international trading and financial relations were disrupted and it became increasingly attractive for the nations of the world to follow the example of Europe's two leading powers, Britain and Germany, by joining the gold standard. Adoption of gold offered the prospect of more stable exchange rates and more certainty in international transactions. Holland (between 1872 and 1877) and a number of other European states soon realised this. France (1873–8) and her Latin Union partners, Italy, Belgium and Switzerland, while still formally wedded to a bimetallic system, formulated the so-called 'limping' gold standard (with convertibility to gold at the authorities' option). In 1879 the USA, too, adopted gold convertibility. So, by 1880, the basis of an international 'club' of gold standard currencies was already established and in the following decades many more countries joined. The club had been created not as a result of decisions taken at multinational conferences, but rather in the culmination of largely individual decisions by states to protect amd promote their own national interests.

## STABLE EXCHANGE RATES AND THE FOREIGN EXCHANGE MARKET

The more countries that adopted the gold standard, the more rigid became the international value of currencies in terms of each other. In other words, the international gold standard became a system of fixed exchange rates. This stability reduced risk to those involved in international transactions, for in negotiating contracts and striking bargains they did not have to contend with the uncertainty of fluctuating values in the currencies in which they were dealing. Indeed, this was often claimed as one of the main advantages of the gold standard.

In normal circumstances, official obligations to exchange national currencies at (or for) a fixed weight of gold, and relative freedom to import and export bullion, specie and currency, were sufficient in themselves to ensure stable exchange rates over the short-term between currencies of participating countries. This was true even in the absence of direct official intervention in foreign exchange markets.

In a completely free market the rate of exchange between two currencies would be determined by demand and supply. Thus, the demand for pounds relative to dollars might increase if, in net terms, Americans were buying more British goods and services than Britons were importing from America. In this case traders would be seeking to convert more dollars to pounds than *vice versa*, and a relative scarcity of sterling would develop. As a result the pound's value would appreciate in terms of dollars. A similar effect would be produced by an increase in American investment in Britain compared to British investment in the USA – say, because of a rise in London interest rates or London dividend rates. Or a currency might appreciate for political, or other non-economic, reasons – such as an election, *coup d'état* or threat of war – as exchange dealings reflected the anxieties and preferences of the various individuals engaged in the market.

Thus, a freely floating exchange rate would oscillate in response to changing market conditions. Under the international gold standard, however, the degree of oscillation was strictly limited. A foreign exchange market free of direct intervention from the authorities still existed, but official guarantees to pay a fixed amount of gold for national currencies ensured that the market rate did not deviate greatly from the official, 'par', rate of exchange.

In the nineteenth century the British pound was officially valued at 113.0016 grains of fine gold, and the American dollar at 23.22 grains of fine gold. Thus, the official, mint, or par, rate of exchange between the two currencies was £1 : $4.866, or $1 : £0.205.[6] In other words, holders of currency were guaranteed the equivalent of this rate of exchange at the US Treasury or the Bank of England and, in the absence of other considerations, they would not be prepared to accept anything less in the foreign exchange markets. It was for this reason that market rates deviated so little from official rates. Indeed, any deviation at all was only possible because the act of remitting gold was not costless. In practice, those engaged in international transactions were prepared to condone a slightly 'inferior' rate (or not take advantage of a slighty 'superior' rate) provided the 'loss' was not greater than the cost of shipping gold.

A simple illustration will make the point clear. Assume an increase in the demand for British pounds relative to US dollars, with a subsequent rise in the market rate of exchange to £1 : $4.885 (or $1 : £0.204). Obviously, at such a rate, it should have paid dollar holders to convert their dollars to gold at the American Treasury, ship the gold to London and convert it to sterling at the Bank of England (at the official rate of $1 : £0.205). In this way they would have obtained £0.001 more for each of their dollars and provided the freight charges, handling costs, insurance, and other expenses incurred in shipping the gold did not exceed the difference between the official and market rates (at £0.001 per dollar) then gold would have flowed from America to Britain. The subsequent fall-off in demand for sterling (as gold was now being used instead) would prevent its market price rising any further. The argument can be reversed, of course, in the case of a market depreciation of sterling. Here, gold would have flowed from Britain to America. In normal circumstances, therefore, the extent of market oscillations around official currency values was limited to a very narrow range within the points where it became profitable to either import or export gold. In the case of the pound and the dollar, for instance, it has been estimated that by the late nineteenth century the actual gold export point for Britain was about £1 : $4.857, and the gold import point at where the pound rose to £1 : $4.872.[7]

Obviously, adoption of such a system of external currency regulation by a growing number of nations during the last quarter of the nineteenth century instilled a greater fixity in world exchange rates. However, even in the half-century up to the 1870s, adherence by most of the world's leading nations to one form or other of metallic base, with more or less convertibility, had ensured a reasonable degree of stability. For instance, in the case of sterling its value against the currencies of the UK's major trading partners as a whole, varied by only some three per cent during the 1850s and 1860s.[8] Compared to other periods of modern British history this is evidence of a high degree of exchange rate stability. Thus, for the whole century up to the First World War, Britain's expanding role in international commerce and finance occurred against the background of reasonably orderly exchange rate conditions. On occasions there were crises (such as during the Franco-German War of 1870) which disrupted exchange transactions, but in normal circumstances exchange markets were characterised by stable exchange rates.

## ADJUSTMENT MECHANISMS

It is important to appreciate that, so far, the discussion has been confined to just one aspect of the mechanics of a fixed exchange rate system – namely, the role of bullion arbitrage in tying market currency rates to official rates. But the successful maintenance over time of such an international monetary system geared to stable exchange rates depended upon much broader and more fundamental factors. Thus, the coexistence of silver, gold and bimetallic currencies in the mid–nineteenth century was able to produce relatively stable exchange rates only while there was a reasonable balance between the world supply of gold and silver. Once this balance altered in the 1870s in such a way that the market price of gold relative to silver shifted markedly from conventional or official price ratios, then strains appeared which eventually caused a major realignment of currency values. Similarly, the success of the international gold standard of the late nineteenth and early twentieth centuries in sustaining fixed exchange rates among the currencies of the world's leading traders, was underpinned by the general expansion in international trade and the continuation of world economic development. Expansion in the real economy eased monetary adjustments. It was not until the aftermath of the First World War that the pace of the world's long–term economic progress suffered a serious check and, then, the whole monetary system came under threat.

Before 1914 the maintenance of the gold standard was helped, too, by the provision of arrangements which created new means of international payment and, thus, freed the world's money supply from a slavish dependence on the output of gold mines. Most notably, the widespread use of sterling as a world currency greatly increased the supply of international liquidity. Important market arrangements also developed which enabled funds to be circulated from international creditors to those who required them – thus, increasing the utilisation of world liquidity supplies.

Obviously, though, the formal exchange arrangements adopted by individual nations would have been insufficient on their own to ensure currency convertibility and a stable exchange rate, say, for a country with persistent deficits on the current account of its balance of payments. The continuing net outflows of bullion needed to pay for such an excess of imports would eventually have depleted such a country's bullion reserves and forced devaluation or the abandonment of convertibility. If exchange rate stability were to be maintained, then, effective international arrangements were needed to permit the financing of the deficit and, or, adjustments were needed within the domestic economy to correct that deficit. Such arrangements were, indeed, an integral part of the international gold standard and it is to the means of implementing both internal and external adjustments that attention is now directed. Throughout the nineteenth century the emphasis from most commentators was on adjustment through changes in the stock of money and the level of prices. These adjustments came to be seen in the context of two formulations: the price/specie-flow mechanism; and the rules of the game.

*Price/Specie-Flow Mechanism*

Within the simplest form of price/specie-flow analysis, a country's adherence to the gold standard served to provide both an automatic adjustment to balance of payments disequilibria, and a means of instilling domestic monetary discipline and price stability.[9]

For instance, if a gold standard country were to develop a deficit on its current account balance and suffer a fall in its exchange rate to the point where gold was persistently lost overseas, the necessary longer-term adjustment would occur through changes in the domestic money stock, within a sequence along the following lines:

| | | | | | |
|---|---|---|---|---|---|
| current account deficit | → | fall in exchange rate | → | gold lost overseas | → |

| | | | | |
|---|---|---|---|---|
| fall in domestic money stock | → | fall in domestic prices | → | rise in exports/ fall in imports and correction of deficit |

Within such a model, the outflow of gold would contract the domestic money supply directly as coins were withdrawn from circulation and exported and, indirectly, by reducing the cash reserves of the domestic banks which would then be obliged to cut back on loans to the general public (e.g. by raising interest rates). The monetary contraction at home would, in turn, reduce the demand for goods and services, forcing domestic prices to fall. Thus, the country would become more price competitive on international markets, exports would rise and imports fall. The process would continue until the original current account deficit was eliminated and the specie loss checked – at which point the country's share of world gold would have returned to its 'natural' level, determined by real income and money–holding conventions. Moreover, it was thought that the adjustment process worked just as well in the reverse case where a country had a trading surplus. Here, the domestic money stock and price level would rise, competitiveness fall, and the surplus be eliminated. In other words, the price/specie–flow analysis envisaged a see–saw pattern for international price adjustment – surplus countries were subjected to inflationary pressure, deficit countries to deflation.

The same adjustment process was also credited by supporters with providing a greater degree of domestic price stability because, under the assumptions made, the price level within an individual gold standard country could not digress to any great extent from that of other gold standard countries. Thus, it was argued that the potential for domestic price instability would be greatly reduced by adoption of a fixed exchange rate. The same price/specie–flow mechanism was seen to provide stability. For instance, assume equilibrium on the balance of payments of a gold standard country when the domestic money supply is expanded (say, through the expansionary policies of the monetary authorities, or through commercial banks making loans cheaper and easier to obtain). The following sequence was envisaged:

| | | | | | |
|---|---|---|---|---|---|
| rise in domestic money stock | → | rise in domestic prices | → | fall in exports/ rise in imports | → |

| | | | | | | |
|---|---|---|---|---|---|---|
| current account deficit | → | fall in exchange rate | → | gold lost overseas | → | fall in domestic money stock |

According to the classical analysis, monetary expansion would increase domestic prices, making exports relatively dearer, imports relatively cheaper. A trading deficit with the rest of the world would emerge, causing a loss of specie overseas and enforcing monetary contraction at home. The process would continue until equilibrium was restored and the effects of the initial monetary expansion eliminated. The discipline imposed in this manner by the gold standard was seen as an important corrective to the dangers of 'monetary abuse' (essentially inflationary expansion of the money supply by the monetary authorities). Indeed, the need to constrain the powers of the Bank of England (and the commercial banks) to create money was a major consideration in the arguments for Britain's adoption of the gold standard after the Napoleonic Wars. During hostilities, when the gold standard had been suspended, the currency had depreciated against gold and the economy had been subjected to domestic price inflation. At the time the so–called 'Bullionists' saw this as proof of the dangers inherent in inconvertibility and successfully sought the return to gold in order to reverse the process.[10]

However, even the most fervent supporters of the price/specie-flow mechanism would have seen it only as an approximation to adjustments occurring in the real world. Subsequently, many of the assumptions underlying the analysis have been the subject of much criticism. Here we need only note the most important weaknesses. First, was the belief in a high degree of flexibility (in an upward and downward direction) in the prices of goods and services (including the price of labour). In practice, the degree of flexibility would vary greatly: some prices such as those of internationally-traded commodities, like cotton or wheat, would change quite freely, but others such as wages and rents were relatively inflexible. Secondly, the adjustment process assumed that demand for imports and exports was sensitive to price changes while, in reality, there could be a great deal of variation depending on the commodity demanded. Thus, the demand for imported foodstuffs such as grain and flour might be little affected by price changes - people would have to eat regardless of price - whereas imports of consumer goods (e.g. bicycles) could have been much more price-sensitive. Finally, the price/specie-flow mechanism depends on the efficacy of monetary changes in bringing about domestic price changes in a relatively short period. Again, this assumption was (and is) debatable. Indeed many economists would deny that monetary changes were the main means by which adjustments were transmitted, and would place the emphasis elsewhere, in particular with income flows.

Even so, something akin to the price/specie flow adjustment process still has important present-day champions. A recent study on the UK and the USA by Milton Friedman and Anna J. Schwartz has emphasised that while in the short-term (within a few years) it was possible under the pre-1914 gold standard for each of the countries to exercise some degree of independence in the pursuit of domestic monetary policy, this was not true in the longer term.[11] Over this longer period, price unity between the two countries was the norm and the growth of the money stock relative to nominal income in one country could not diverge greatly (barely at all according to their estimates) from that in the other. In effect, as both countries were on fixed exchange rates (from 1879 for the USA) and as both permitted a fair degree of freedom for financial and trade flows, the USA and the UK shared a common financial system; and the presumption is that this may have been true of others on the gold standard. According to Friedman and Schwartz:

> Before World War I, the United States and the United Kingdom almost literally had a single monetary system; the quantity of money in each was determined by requirements of external equilibrium which necessitated that their price levels moved roughly in step. Their capital markets were linked, with little scope for interest arbitrage since exchange rates could not differ between the two countries. So rates of change in both prices and interest rates were linked.[12]

> ...the influence of each country on the other country's nominal income was manifested entirely through this influence on the other country's money – the classical specie-flow process.[13]

*Rules of the Game*

One factor which the classical analysis did allow for was the intervention of the monetary authorities in the adjustment mechanism. But, traditionally, little scope was given for discretionary action by the authorities – rather, domestic monetary policy was viewed as being subject to the 'rules of the game' of the international gold standard. The actual phrase, 'rules of the game', seems to have been used first in the 1920s and the notion that the actions of the world's central banks were governed by a set of rules had wide currency in the early decades of the twentieth century. It was recognised that the rules had never been the subject of international agreement and, therefore, it must be assumed that (if they had any validity at all) they would have been open to wide differences of interpretation. Even so, the traditional view has been that the common feature for all gold standard countries and their respective monetary authorities was the obligation to maintain convertibility and this, together with the logic of the price/specie–flow mechanism, would have ensured that, in essence, the response to exchange rate and balance of payments disequilibria would have been stereotyped. For instance, in the case of exchange depreciation and a gold outflow it was assumed that the monetary authorities would take such corrective measures as increasing interest rates and, or, reducing the size of their security holdings (i.e. helping to bring about the contraction to the money supply necessary within the price/specie–flow adjustment). Generally, intervention within the 'rules' was seen as quasi–automatic and as serving to reinforce the price/specie–flow adjustment process.

In recent decades a great deal of research has been conducted into the operation of the so–called 'rules'.[14] Much of this work has been the responsibility of A.I. Bloomfield and his general remarks provide a convenient starting point for any assessment. He found that in practice '... monetary authorities showed little or no overt awareness of a mutual responsibility for the smooth functioning of the international gold standard, or the need for collaboration in any form.[15] In other words, in the nineteenth century the monetary authorities of individual nations acted in their own national, or private, interests, and any sustenance these actions may have given to the international monetary system was incidental to their motives. Bloomfield also emphasises that conclusions on whether or not the authorities systematically abided by a set of (even implicit) rules depends upon how the rules are defined.[16] If a fairly strict definition is applied, whereby the authorities have to be seen to be actively *reinforcing* the impact of changes in gold reserves by taking action to alter the domestic money supply within the specie–flow mechanism in the desired direction (with, for example, gold losses leading to a reduction in the money supply) then, most central banks did *not* follow the rules of the game in the period from 1880 to 1914.

However, if the rules are interpreted in the most passive sense, to mean that the authorities did not consciously off–set the impact of gold flows, then, it can be accepted that the authorities in many gold standard countries, including the UK, did indeed abide by a set of 'rules'. The legal commitment to convertibility and the relative openness of these economies meant that international gold flows directly affected internal monetary conditions in participant countries. However, even here, central banks still exercised a fair amount of discretion as to the magnitude and timing of any change in their policy, as well as to the most appropriate means by which to implement the change. One source of national differences was that legal and institutional requirements varied a great deal from country to country.[17] For instance, in the face of a gold outflow the Bank of France was much more inclined to leave its interest rate unchanged, relying on the use of restrictions on the export of gold and on the comparative safety of its very large gold reserve which could cushion the impact of external losses. In contrast, the Bank of England's reserve was small – its safety margin that much less – and by the early years of the twentieth century the Bank's normal reaction to a gold loss was to increase its discount rate, thereby pushing up money market rates – in effect abiding by the rules.[18] However, even for the Bank of England some doubts have recently been raised. If adherence to the rules of the game is interpreted more strictly – to mean that the monetary authorities should not react counter–cyclically to domestic activity or price changes – then, John Dutton claims that there is some evidence of partial violation of the rules by the Bank.[19] Nevertheless, Dutton's results confirm the sensitivity of Bank rate to alterations in the reserves.[20]

The historical evidence also shows that central banks were more sensitive to gold outflows than inflows because outflows threatened their reserves and, ultimately, their ability to maintain convertibility. Such direct pressure was absent with gold inflows because the authorities could always choose to allow reserves to accumulate. Thus, there was a general tendency for the rules to work more effectively in one direction than in the other. They were asymmetric.

In summary, it seems that during the heyday of the nineteenth-century gold standard, from 1880 to 1914, there was no slavish adherence by national monetary authorities to any set of international rules. Less is known about the earlier years of the nineteenth century, but it is barely conceivable that individual authorities would have exercised any less discretion than in later years. Nevertheless, the commitment during the late nineteenth century by most nations to currency convertibility and exchange rate stability meant they were prepared to permit external pressures to operate on their domestic economies in a manner not inconsistent with the classical price/specie-flow adjustment process. This still leaves open the question of whether or not such a process ever operated, and it is to this issue that we now turn.

## ASSESSMENT OF TRADITIONAL ADJUSTMENT MECHANISM UNDER THE INTERNATIONAL GOLD STANDARD, 1870–1913

Strangely enough, under the international gold standard relatively little gold ever flowed between countries. Indeed, it is generally accepted that the amounts of gold involved were such as to be wholly inadequate to account for the necessary balance of payments adjustments envisaged by the simple price/specie-flow mechanism outlined above. Yet exchange rates remained remarkably stable. In other words, although little gold flowed between nations exceedingly few countries found themselves with insufficient gold reserves to maintain convertibility. It might be argued that this was a tribute to the efficiency of central banks in anticipating disequilibria and in taking evasive action in such a way as to minimise gold flows, but it has already been shown that central banks only played to the rules of the game in a minimal fashion. The truth is, in its most naive form the classical explanation is deficient as an accurate description of the historical record, and adjustment to changes on the external account involved more than the money and price changes of the specie-flow hypothesis.

Traditional analysis of adjustment under the international gold standard envisaged a 'see-saw' pattern between deficit and surplus countries. As the former lost gold, interest rates would rise and domestic prices would fall; while countries gaining gold would experience cheaper money and price inflation. In reality, though, there was no see-saw. Indeed, there was a high degree of parallelism in both price and central bank interest rate movements.[21] That is, periods of inflation and deflation seem to have been commonly-shared among the main gold standard countries. This fact alone weakens the use of the crudest form of the classical adjustment mechanism. Of course, there remains the possibility that adjustment occurred in a manner akin to the traditional picture, whereby the see-saw pattern was not between relative price levels but relative rates of price change. In other words, it is possible that in periods of international price inflation a deficit country may have experienced a *rate* of inflation which was lower than that for a surplus country. In such a case, both countries could be experiencing price rises but adjustment could still take place in a manner similar to that of the classical price/specie-flow analysis.

Indeed, from the monetarist perspective presented by Milton Friedman and Anna Schwartz the close correlation in aggregate price changes is fully compatible with the price/specie-flow mechanism. Their recent study of the USA and UK confirms that there was a very close correlation in price movements and in monetary growth in the two countries over the long term, but they also find that in the short term there was scope for autonomous, national monetary policy. According to Friedman and Schwartz, over periods of up to a few years, action by monetary authorities could have had significant effects on domestic activity.[22] Therefore, the type of policies pursued, and whether or not there was adherence to the rules of the game, continue to be important issues for monetarists. What is envisaged by these writers is a specie-flow mechanism which was not instantaneous, but which, on the contrary, operated under important time-lags. Thus, it is quite acceptable - indeed essential to the efficacy of the price/specie-flow model - that prices and interest rates in individual countries were able to diverge for some time from the levels prevailing in the rest of the world. It was in this way that, first, gold flows and, then, money stock changes, were induced to bring about corrective price changes. There was conformity in the long term, but divergence in the short term. As Professor Friedman has emphasised:

> It should be noted ... that while the quantity of money is ultimately an endogenous variable, there can be and is much leeway in the short run, before the external forces overwhelm the independent internal effects. And we have repeatedly been surprised in our studies by how much leeway there is and for how long - frequently a number of years.[23]

Non-monetarists stress different aspects of the adjustment process. In particular, it is often claimed that one of the major deficiencies of the classical theory was its failure to take account of income flows which could have been operating in the same direction as money flows and which could well have been more important in effecting adjustment to balance of payments disequilibria. If true, this may go some way to explain the relatively small size of observed gold flows. Thus, while a deficit may have given rise to a monetary outflow in the manner suggested by the specie-flow mechanism, the same deficit would also cause a direct, and perhaps speedier, contraction of domestic income as export sales fell and, or, expenditure on imports rose. It could well have been this loss of income which deflated the economy rather than - or in addition to - any monetary deflation, and so have brought about a quicker adjustment. As one advocate of this sort of Keynesian analysis, W.M. Scammell, has emphasised:

> What is important ... is that the adjustment attributed to price changes and gold flows in the nineteenth century was swift and smooth, not because of the power of price changes to effect adjustment, but because income changes were always acting in the same direction to reinforce the price changes.[24]

One other important aspect of balance of payments adjustment which the traditional view barely mentioned concerns international flows of long-term capital. For many countries these could have had important monetary and income effects on domestic economies. For large capital exporters like France and Britain, relatively small fluctuations in the extensive amount of overseas loans undertaken annually could well have offset (or reinforced) any short-term disequilibria arising on the trading account. In Britain's case, A.G. Ford has argued that changes in overseas investment flows played a critical role.[25] He found that high levels of British overseas investment (say, in Argentina) generated higher income levels in the recipient country and this, in turn, pushed up the demand for British goods. The increase in demand consequently increased the price paid for British goods by foreigners relative to British import prices, leading to an improvement in British earnings on the current account. Thus in such periods the burden of heavy outflows of capital was greatly eased by improvements on the current account which had arisen directly out of the impact of the capital flows themselves. Over the long-term, too, failure to take account of overseas investment would leave unexplained much of a country's adjustment to world conditions. In Britain's case persistent surpluses on the current account of the balance of payments were offset by the large amount of overseas investment undertaken each year.[26] In this way, adjustment to the trading surplus came via the recycling of capital funds into the international economy rather than through the price changes of the specie-flow mechanism. Similarly, many developing countries of the nineteenth century (e.g. USA, Argentina and Australia) were able to sustain persistent trading account deficits over long periods by offsetting them with imports of capital from Europe.[27] Again, long-term capital movements eased adjustment to trading account disequilibria. It is obvious, therefore, that any analysis which fails to take account of this aspect must be deficient.

The classical view did, of course, recognise the important role played by short-term capital flows. By the late nineteenth century it was readily admitted that the extent to which the domestic economy needed to adjust to disequilibria on overseas trade could be greatly offset by changes in flows of short-term capital. For instance, if a trading deficit arose it could well initiate a series of changes in the money and foreign exchange markets which could attract enough short-term funds into the country to counter-balance any losses on the trading account. This would be partially automatic. Thus, if the emerging trade deficit led to a decline in the market rate of exchange of the gold standard currency involved, 'speculators' could be enticed to purchase the cheaper currency in anticipation of a fairly quick recovery in value (because of the official commitment to maintaining par-value).[28] Increased speculative demand would, in itself, serve to check the depreciation of the currency to some extent. If gold was lost overseas, however, this would curtail the domestic money stock which would, in turn, raise domestic interest rates. All things being equal, higher rates would make it more attractive for both residents and foreigners to increase deposits and loans to the monetary institutions of the country concerned. There would, thus, be an inflow of short-term funds offsetting the loss of funds on the trade account and obviating the need for further adjustment. Moreover, the authorities could well have an important role to play by initiating, or reinforcing, such interest rate changes. Thus, the traditional view supplemented the adjustment mechanism of specie flows and money stock changes with short-term capital flows (whether reinforced or not by the authorities operating interest rate policy in conformity with the rules of the game).

It should be emphasised, though, that for the most part changes in international short-term capital assets were seen as a short-term adjustment mechanism. It was recognised that these type of adjustments were dependent on the ability of the country concerned to persuade foreigners to increase their loans; and that if the trading loss proved to be symptomatic of an underlying disequilibrium (say, through a decline in competitiveness) then, eventually, other adjustments would be needed.

Nevertheless, with the great increase in world capital mobility during the nineteenth century, keen advocates of the gold standard were to portray the role of short-term capital flows - and, in the UK, the part played by the monetary authorities - as smooth, efficient and equilibratory. The Cunliffe Report of 1918, for instance, described it as operating quickly and unambiguously in the British case:

> When the balance of trade was unfavourable and the exchanges were adverse it became profitable to export gold. The would-be exporter bought his gold from the Bank of England...and the...reserve...fell. If the process were repeated sufficiently often...the Bank raised its rate of discount. The raising of the discount rate has the immediate effect of retaining money here which would otherwise have been remitted abroad and of attracting remittance from abroad to take advantage of the higher rate, thus checking the outflow of gold and even reversing the stream.[29]

Subsequently, this traditional view has been modified in a number of important respects. For a start, there was no guarantee that changes in short-term capital flows would be equilibratory in either direction or amplitude.[30] Thus, if a central bank raised interest rates to offset a trading loss, the resultant capital flow could well be larger, or smaller, than the original deficit. So the neatly-balanced equation implicit in the Cunliffe Report would not normally apply. Similarly, in the case where a trading account was already in balance, then an autonomous short-term capital flow (for instance, in response to war or war scares, such as occurred with the run against the rouble during the Russo-Japanese War of 1905–6, or the withdrawal of French funds from Germany during the 1911 Morocco Crisis) could have been disequilibratory. Or, again, a change in interest rates due to purely domestic circumstances could well *initiate* international short-term capital flows with important consequences for the external account. Moreover, as central banks did not always play to the rules of the game, interest rates were not uniformly altered in the manner required by the rules. Indeed, there was a great deal of variation – the central banks of France and Belgium, for instance, altered their rates so little that the traditional picture could have barely applied to those countries.

The truth is that there has been too much generalisation from the British case. In the UK the Bank of England chose to keep its gold reserves low and to rely upon interest rate changes to bring about short-term capital flows to offset any adverse movements in the value of sterling or to prevent losses of gold on the trading account. For many decades Britain – and, indeed, Germany – was very successful in persuading foreigners to hold short-term liabilities of the country's monetary institutions whenever the exchange rate required it. But Britain's position in the international economy was very special, if not unique. Other countries were much less successful.

Generally, the smaller a country was as an international trader and financier, the smaller its influence on the decisions of holders of short-term assets. The strictures of the gold standard seem to have been more malleable for the 'core' of large, developed European countries than for the smaller countries of either Europe or the developing areas on the periphery of the world economy (for instance, in Latin America). In terms of the effectiveness of interest rate policy in attracting short–term capital, for example, there seems to have been a sort of league table of investors' or lenders' preferences. At the top of the table was the UK where any change in the rate of interest was the most potent in causing a change in the supply of 'overseas' funds[31]; then France, followed closely by Germany; the lesser countries of Europe and the periphery made up the base of the hierarchy where interest rate changes had much less effect.[32]

Here the distinction between the 'core' and 'periphery' had real meaning. While it was possible for the Bank of England and other major central banks to ease their trading account adjustments by attracting short–term capital, interest rate changes in countries such as Austria or Chile were much less effective. In fact, these developing countries could find themselves at the mercy of rate changes in the core countries. Thus, if rates rose in Western Europe, 'footloose' international funds would be drawn to the developed countries from the less developed. Equilibratory changes at the centre of the system could be destabilising for countries at the periphery.

So, in the case of short–term capital, too, the traditional picture of gold standard adjustment requires modification. Movements of short–term funds were not necessarily stabilising, nor such a finely–balanced counterpoise to disequilibria elsewhere on the balance of payments. More particularly, it has been a mistake to generalise from the experience of the developed European nations, especially Britain; their position at the core of the world economy bestowed special characteristics.

## THE ROLE OF STERLING

British money markets were intimately linked to the international economy. By the late nineteenth century a number of important foreign and colonial banks had established London offices, a group of London-based merchant banks were actively engaged in overseas financial transactions and international bills had become the mainstay of the London discount market.

It has been estimated that in 1900 there were 18 foreign banks operating London offices and that by 1910 the number had risen to 28.[33] They were mainly continental banks such as the Deutsche Bank, Dresden Bank, Credit Lyonnais and Swiss Bankverein. All were actively engaged in foreign exchange dealings and overseas remittance business. At the time US legislation forbade American banks from opening foreign offices, so they had no presence in London. In addition to these foreign banks there were a number of colonial banks, most of which had been formed from British capital and which specialised in particular regions or countries of the world. The most successful was probably the Hong Kong and Shanghai Banking Corporation which had been founded in 1865 and which by the early twentieth century had a well-established position in China and Japan.

It is assumed that the London business of these foreign and colonial banks was concerned largely with servicing financial and commercial transactions centred on their geographical area of interest (be it the Continent, the Far East, or wherever). They did operate deposit accounts at their London offices and it was said at the time that they offered competitive rates for funds, but the proportion that may have been held in the form of sterling, or by British residents, is unknown and, therefore, it is impossible to know the significance of their liabilities within the domestic money stock. There is, nevertheless, no doubt as to their overall importance. At the time *The Economist* published deposit figures for the foreign and colonial joint-stock banks in London and these show that they held some £112 million of deposits in 1880; £507 million in 1905; and £1,855 million in 1914. In turn, Forrest Capie and Alan Webber, have recently estimated that these were equivalent to 23 per cent, 63 per cent and 157 per cent of total deposits held by (domestic) UK banks at the respective dates.[34] In other words, by the turn of the century the overseas banking sector in London had become significant in quantitative terms and was growing strongly relative to the domestic banking sector. Thus, the decisions taken by overseas banks on the transfer of funds overseas and the purchase and sale of securities within London could be of significance for internal monetary conditions. On occasions they could well provide some element of flexibility for the Bank of England if it could influence them in such a way as to bring about short-term capital flows in the manner outlined by the Cunliffe Report. On the other hand, a large part of their business must have been independent of British internal conditions and, therefore, potentially more volatile - perhaps less responsive than the domestic banks to attempts by the Bank of England to influence interest rates or the foreign exchange markets.

With few exceptions, the domestic banks were tardy in their response to growth of the overseas banking sector. They were slow and cautious in developing similar financial services. As worldwide communications improved over the course of the nineteenth century the larger deposit banks had joined widespread overseas agency networks, whereby banks in different countries acted on each other's behalf in the local centre, thus giving their customers access to overseas remittance and other foreign business. In fact, for the most part British banks were content to rely upon such agency networks and more direct involvement through the operation of branches overseas was non-existent until the twentieth century.[35] In 1911, however, Lloyds Bank broke new ground with the purchase of Armstrong & Co. of Paris, renaming the subsidiary, Lloyds Bank (France) Ltd. In 1913 the London County and Westminster Bank followed this lead and bought a Paris-based subsidiary. A few years earlier - in 1905 - the Midland Bank had initiated another new area of business for UK clearing banks by opening up its own foreign exchange department, rather than relying (as it had previously done) upon the services of foreign banks.[36] Also by the early years of the new century, the large London clearers were becoming more directly involved in the international acceptance business.

The international intermediation of short-term credits was one area of business that many of London's money market institutions as a group found profitable. In some ways international bill discounting bore important similarities to the traditional form of banking business conducted for the domestic economy, but the international business was to provide the world economy with extensive supplies of short-term liquid assets in the form of 'bills on London' (or 'sterling bills'). Two specialist institutions were particularly significant here: the acceptance house and the discount house.

The bill of exchange was a common form of granting mercantile credit. It was a sort of IOU from an importer to an exporter which, once 'accepted' (or signed) by the importer, legally obliged him/her to pay cash on the date of the bill's maturity (say, 60–90 days after it was first drawn up).[37] In this manner the importer gained 60–90 days' credit as payment was made by bill, not by cash; whereas the exporter who was extending the credit, obtained legal proof of the debt (i.e. the bill itself) which could be sold at once, say, to a bank. The bank would pay less than the maturity value of the bill so as to allow for interest during the period pending payment, and to allow for any risk of default by the debtor. The degree of risk and, therefore, the rate of discount charged by the bank was directly related to the prestige and creditworthiness of the acceptor (the importer in the example). The more prestigious the acceptor, the more readily a bill could be sold (or discounted) and the lower the charge. From early in the nineteenth century, therefore, some large merchant banks in London (and Liverpool initially) began to accept bills on behalf of customers, charging a commission for the service.[38] In this way, the debtor found it both cheaper and easier to obtain credit, while the creditor obtained a safer and more saleable security. From the 1830s credit in the American trade seems to have been most important, but the acceptance business became more diversified through the century. The London acceptance became a very common form of effecting commercial and financial transactions in the world economy. Indeed, sterling bills drawn on London were used as a form of credit even for international transactions not involving Britain.

By the end of the nineteenth century the great bulk of London acceptances were being drawn on specialist acceptance houses which had evolved from a small number of merchant banks (such as Rothschilds, Barings and Hambros) and on the London offices of overseas banks. Even so, from the 1860s the use of the international telegraph to transfer funds, including sterling balances held by foreign and colonial banks in London, increasingly rivalled the use of sterling bills.[39] There is some uncertainty as to the relative importance of the two methods of transfer, but we do know that the volume of foreign bills on London received a strong fillip in the decade or so before the First World War when the major London clearing banks, for the first time, entered the international acceptance business on a large scale.[40] The guarantees of such prestigious institutions obviously enhanced the general attractiveness of using sterling bills, and it has been estimated that at this time the proportion of foreign bills on London rose to twice the value of bills created for domestic use.[41]

In addition to the provision of this common form of international short-term credit, the City of London also provided a ready market for the buying and selling of such credit – a secondary money market specialising in bills. From early in the nineteenth century some London institutions had specialised as brokers for the purchase and sale of bills of exchange on behalf of clients. By the middle of the century these 'discount houses' were operating as dealers, buying and selling bills in their own right. Initially the bulk of bills had arisen out of internal trade but as the international use of sterling bills became widespread the discount houses participated fully in the new business. The existence of an open London discount market organised on such a large scale that bills could be readily purchased and sold at a competitive rate, offered support to the whole system of sterling bills. Sterling bills became a generally accepted means of international payment not only because they bore the guarantee of prestigious acceptors but also because the bills could be readily sold in the London money market. True, other financial institutions, or even individuals, might buy such bills but it was the London discount houses which formed the main bulwark to the markets; they *always* stood ready to buy 'good' bills. The system was so international in character by the late nineteenth century that, as with the creation of the bills themselves, the sale of bills on the London discount market might not necessarily involve British firms in the net transfer of funds. Thus, it could be that, say, a German firm would sell the bill to a discount house which would, then, re-sell to a French firm - the net transfer of funds being from France to Germany, even though the transaction was conducted via a sterling bill.

It is clear from the above account that by the end of the nineteenth century there existed a sophisticated international system of short-term credits based on London.[42] The robustness of the system depended not only on the institutional arrangements outlined but also - and in a more fundamental sense - on the greater involvement of Britain in international trade and finance, for this meant that there was a regular demand for sterling from abroad. Of fundamental importance, too, was the stability of the value of the pound. Bills were denominated in sterling; therefore, the fixed value of the pound in terms of gold and the absence of any risk of devaluation provided the general underpinning to the system. Sterling, in effect, became as good as gold because its value was guaranteed and it was readily acceptable as a means of settling international debt. In one important respect it was even better than gold: an international creditor leaving balances on deposit in London, or purchasing sterling bills, earned interest on the assets; holding gold earned none.

Apart from the financing of international

commerce, the City of London also performed an important task as the major supplier of long-term capital to the world economy - providing investment funds for overseas governments, railroads and other public utilities, and commercial and industrial enterprises. The great bulk of the loans were made in the form of portfolio investments through the purchase of stocks and shares.[43] By 1914 it has been estimated that the UK held about 40% of the world's foreign-owned debt (France and Germany were the other two main suppliers) and most of it had been lent to the developing countries of North America, Latin America, Australia, New Zealand, India and South Africa. Foreigners had free access to the London capital market and British investors were eager participants in overseas issues. It was often those same institutions that were providing international short-term credit facilities, that also specialised in the management and supervision of foreign loan issues. From the middle of the nineteenth century the large merchant banks were of most importance, but with the establishment of a growing number of foreign and colonial banks in London, and with the widening interests of the London joint-stock banks, more of the business passed into the hands of these other institutions.[44]

From a global point of view, therefore, there was at any one time a very high volume of short-term and long-term capital being borrowed and lent in the City of London. International funds both flowed into the country (in the form of trading account surpluses and short-term loans from overseas) and out of the country (as both short- and long-term investments). The City formed the pivotal point of a great cycle of international capital; the City's specialist institutions provided the means of intermediation between international borrower and lender.

For this reason it has often been claimed that by the end of the nineteenth century the role of sterling in the international economy was unique, and that the Bank of England was uniquely placed to influence, or even 'manage', the international gold standard. If the

Bank needed to react to changes in the exchange markets or the gold reserve by altering its interest rate, this in turn would alter conditions in the London money market in such a way as to affect the continuous cycle of international funds flowing through the City. The scale of the flow was such that only a marginal adjustment would be necessary to effect the change required by the Bank. Here lies the secret of the Bank's ability to maintain convertibility with a relatively small gold reserve.[45]

From the vantage point of the 1920s, J.M. Keynes claimed that the Bank of England had acted as 'the conductor of the international orchestra', and his view has been echoed many times since.[46] In essence, this view argues that the stability of the international gold standard derived from its growing independence from gold and its heavier reliance on the other main form of international liquidity, sterling. In the first instance, the greater use of sterling to settle international debts freed the world economy from its reliance on a relatively fixed supply of precious metal. Thus, an unprecedented growth in world income could occur without being unduly constrained by a restricted supply of acceptable international money. Indeed, the use of sterling became self-generating: the more common it was to accept the settlement of debts in sterling, the more attractive it became to hold sterling; and the less the need to use gold.

Nor was the role of London confined to supplying a more flexible means of payment. It is claimed that London performed the critical task of re-cycling funds from 'surplus' countries to 'deficit' countries and, thus, was instrumental in avoiding international payment and credit crises on the scale of those that were to shatter the international economy in the 1920s and 1930s. Thus, by the last quarter of the nineteenth century countries experiencing trading deficits on their balance of payments could seek to offset them by raising loans in the London money markets. Such capital borrowing would obviate the need to deflate the domestic economy of the deficit country. Part of the extra demand for loans would be met by British funds, but if it were to persist, so that it endangered the sterling exchange rate or the gold reserve, London interest rates could well rise as the Bank of England took action and this, in turn, would attract an inflow of funds from countries, especially in Europe, with a 'surplus' on trading account. In this way, the City of London, under the direction of the Bank of England, was able to draw on Continental reserves of international liquidity, including gold (especially from France), and redistribute them to those parts of the world where they were in demand. In other words, London helped modify the extent of recessions, particularly in developing countries. As David Williams has represented the position:

> London not only helped to finance the various upswings in economic activity but made a vital - perhaps more significant - contribution to the international economy by helping to cushion downswings in economic activity. London was always a source of finance for developing countries. When her own funds were really stretched she was able to draw on - through the mechanism of interest rates - the liquid resources of other countries - outstandingly European - not normally engaged in extensive international short-term lending.[47]

Within this schema, therefore, by the closing decades of the nineteenth century British monetary conditions had important implications for world money markets and Bank of England policy directly influenced the flow of international funds. This stress on the omnipotence of the City of London needs some modification, however. For a start, Britain's deep involvement in the international economy also meant that domestic monetary conditions were open to buffeting from overseas influences. At that time economic policy ruled out the use of trade restrictions or variations in exchange rates in response to balance of payments problems - free trade and exchange rate stability were at the very heart of British gold standard philosophy. Thus, the absence of controls on international capital flows and the small size of the Bank of England's gold reserve meant inevitably that shocks from international money markets were transmitted quickly to the domestic economy. The City's international involvement created a two-way channel for monetary impulses: into, as well as out of, the country.

Recent findings have also emphasised the dangers of an Anglophile approach to the study of the pre-1914 gold standard. Sterling was of great importance, but other currencies, particularly the franc and mark, played a similar international role, if on a much reduced scale. For instance, Lindert's estimates suggest that whereas a wide range of countries held foreign currency assets (as well as bullion) in central bank reserves by 1913, and that for the world as a whole sterling was the most important of these - forming somewhat less than one-half of such reserves - the mark and the franc were also commonly held.[48] In fact, for *European* central bank reserves these two currencies were more important than sterling.

It is also possible to argue that the focus of attention should not be concentrated solely on London when examining the process by which funds were re-cycled from Europe to deficit countries. It could be argued, for instance, that it was the Bank of France which acted as the lender of last resort and general buttress to the whole system. It was only because the Bank of France maintained a large gold reserve and was prepared to allow it to run down at times of heavy international demand for liquidity, that the necessary cash flowed into London and the international economy in general. In contrast, the Bank of England's cash reserve was so small that it could not possibly meet such demands from its own resources.

## THE BANK OF ENGLAND AND THE MONETARY INTERPRETATION OF BALANCE OF PAYMENTS

The denigration of sterling's role and of the ability of

the Bank of England to influence the international economy has reached its extreme with those who base their analysis on a monetary interpretation of balance of payments adjustment.[49] This approach is based on an equilibrium model - it assumes a tendency to full employment and to perfect international commodity arbitrage, with equality of prices for similar traded goods and securities (after allowance for transport costs and trade restrictions). D.N. McCloskey and J.R. Zecher have been the chief advocates for the use of such a model when explaining the operation of the pre-1914 gold standard.[50] Both the traditional price/specie-flow adjustment and the Keynesian income-flow mechanism are rejected by these commentators and the influence of domestic monetary policy is belittled. Instead the assumption is that the general level of world prices is determined by the world supply of money and, therefore, any one central bank can influence world prices only to the extent that it can alter the world money supply. As the Bank of England's total reserves were but a tiny proportion of the world gold stock it is obvious, according to McCloskey and Zecher, that the Bank's influence on world prices between 1880 and 1913, must have been tiny. Moreover, under the normal assumptions of the monetary interpretation a particular central bank could neither operate a domestic policy independent of the balance of payments nor neutralise the monetary impact of changes in the balance for any significant time period. Even the few years' autonomy claimed for national monetary policy by Friedman and Schwartz is denied. Instead, it is claimed that while the authorities could influence the composition of the money supply between foreign exchange reserves (specie for Britain) and domestic credit, they could not control the overall size of the money stock within their domestic economy. In other words, the Bank of England was just a pawn within the international gold standard; or, referring to Keynes's musical metaphor, McCloskey and Zecher reduce the 'conductor' of the international orchestra to the 'triangle player'.

The conclusions reached by McCloskey and Zecher

are controversial and their validity depends upon the truth of their assumptions: that tendencies to full employment and perfect international arbitrage existed; that there were no significant time-lags in the adjustment process; and that the effect of changes in Bank of England credit and interest rate policies on the level of outstanding sterling assets and liabilities – and on overseas investment – was unimportant to the supply of world money. All these points are keenly disputed.

Nevertheless, this viewpoint, taken in conjunction with the empirical work of Bloomfield and Lindert, does warn against over-emphasising the role of sterling. The picture of just one financial centre and one reserve currency is a distortion of the truth. Britain and sterling were of critical importance in the pre-World War I international financial system but other countries and currencies were not insignificant. From a British point of view, however, there is universal agreement on the importance of the external account. London's international role created one of the critical parameters governing the development of domestic monetary practice and policy.

## FURTHER READING

Anna Jacobson Schwartz, 'Monetary Trends in the United States and the United Kingdom; 1873–1970: Selected Findings', *Journal of Economic History*, vol. 35, 1975, pp. 138–59.

Michael D. Bordo and Anna J. Schwartz (eds.), *A Retrospective on the Classical Gold Standard, 1821–1931* (University of Chicago Press, Chicago and London, 1984).

Arthur I. Bloomfield, 'Rules of the Game of International Adjustment?' in C.R. Whittlesey and J.S.G. Wilson (eds.), *Essays in Money and Banking* (Oxford University Press, Oxford, 1968), pp. 26–46.

W.M. Scammell, 'The Working of the Gold Standard', *Yorkshire Bulletin of Economic and Social Research*, vol. 17, no. 1, 1965, pp. 32–45.

Barry Eichengreen (ed.), *The Gold Standard in*

*Theory and History* (Methuen, New York and London, 1985).

NOTES

1. C.K. Harley and D.N. McCloskey, 'Foreign Trade: Competition and the Expanding International Economy' in Roderick Floud and Donald McCloskey (eds.), *The Economic History of Britain since 1700*, (2 vols., Cambridge University Press, Cambridge, 1981), vol. 2, p. 51. Estimates in C.H. Feinstein, *National Income, Expenditure and Output of the United Kingdom, 1855–1965* (Cambridge University Press, Cambridge, 1972) – p. T8, show exports and property income from abroad rising in the latter half of the period – from 35 per cent of Gross National Product, 1870/4, to 39 per cent, 1908/12.

2. An illuminating survey of Britain's international position up to the First World War is contained in S.B. Saul, *Studies in British Overseas Trade 1870–1914* (Liverpool University Press, Liverpool, 1960), chs. 1 and 2. His analysis of international economic developments places the UK very much at the centre of the world economy (see chapter 3 especially). Also see his 'The Export Economy 1870–1914', *Yorkshire Bulletin of Economic and Social Research*, vol. 17, 1965, no. 1, pp. 5–18.

3. 56 Geo. III, c. 68 and 59 Geo. III, c. 49. See R.S. Sayers, 'The Question of the Standard, 1815–44', *Economic History*, vol. 3, Feb. 1935, pp. 79–102; and J.K. Horsefield, 'The Bankers and the Bullionists in 1819', *Journal of Political Economy*, vol. 57, 1949, pp. 442–8.

4. The Bank Charter Act of 1844 is discussed in more detail on pages 172–8.

5. Michael Collins, 'Sterling Exchange Rates, 1847–80', *Journal of European History*, vol. 15, 1986, pp. 516–7.

6. That is, $£1 = \frac{\$113.0016}{23.22} = \$4.8665$; and $\$1 = \frac{£23.22}{113.0016} = £0.2055$.

The detailed figures are from A.G. Ford, 'International Financial Policy and the Gold Standard, 1870–1914', University of Warwick Discussion Paper in Economics, no. 104, Jan. 1977, p. 4.

7. Oskar Morgenstern, *International Financial Transactions and Business Cycles* (Princeton University Press, Princeton, 1959), p. 177, quotes a variety of sources giving a range of $4.827 - $4.857 for the export point and $4.8762 - $4.90 for the import point, 1877–1913.

8. Collins, 'Sterling', pp. 517–21.

9. For an early classical formulation of the thinking behind the price/specie–flow mechanism see David Hume, 'On the Balance of Trade' (1752), reprinted in Barry Eichengreen (ed.), *The Gold Standard in Theory and History* (Methuen, New York and London, 1985), pp. 39–48. Recent surveys of the literature can be found in Marcello De Cecco, *Money and Empire: The International Gold Standard, 1890–1914* (Blackwell, Oxford, 1974), pp. 1–21; and Michael D. Bordo, 'The Gold Standard: The Traditional Approach' (and subsequent discussion) in Michael D. Bordo and Anna J. Schwartz (eds.), *A Retrospective on the Classical Gold Standard, 1821–1931* (University of Chicago Press, Chicago and London, 1984), pp. 23–119.

10. Frank Whitson Fetter, *Development of British Monetary Orthodoxy, 1797–1875* (Harvard University Press, Cambridge, Mass., 1965), ch. 2, especially pp. 39–54.

11. Milton Friedman and Anna J. Schwartz, *Monetary Trends in the United States and the United Kingdom* (University of Chicago Press, Chicago and London, 1982).

12. Anna Jacobson Schwartz, 'Monetary Trends in the United States and the United Kingdom; 1878–1970: Selected Findings', *Journal of Economic History*, vol. 35, 1975, pp. 148–9.

13. Friedman and Schwartz, *Monetary Trends*, p.337.

14. Arthur I. Bloomfield, *Monetary Policy under the International Gold Standard, 1880–1914*, (Federal

Reserve Bank of New York, New York, 1959); Arthur I. Bloomfield, 'Rules of the Game of International Adjustment' in C.R. Whittlesey and J.S.G. Wilson (eds.), *Essays in Money and Banking* (Oxford University Press, Oxford, 1968), pp. 26–46; Peter H. Lindert, *Key Currencies and Gold, 1900–1913*, Princeton Studies in International Finance, no. 24 (Princeton University Press, Princeton, 1969); Robert Adolphe Triffen, *The Evolution of the International Monetary System: Historical Reappraisal and Future Perspectives*, Princeton Studies in International Finance, no. 12 (Princeton University Press, Princeton, 1964)

15. Bloomfield, 'Rules', p. 27.

16. In a reformulation of the 'rules of the game' as applied to the post–1945 period, Michael Michaely, *The Responsiveness of Demand Policies to Balance of Payments: Postwar Patterns*, Studies in International Relations, no. 5 (National Bureau of Economic Research, New York, 1971), broadens the concept of the 'rules' to encompass aggregate demand policy as applied in nine different developed economies. Also see Kenneth Dam, *The Rules of the Game* (University of Chicago Press, Chicago and London, 1982), ch. 1.

17. A collection of studies (with discussion) on 'national' experience under the pre–1914 gold standard appears in Bordo and Schwartz, *Classical Gold Standard*, namely: Paul McGouldrick, 'Operations of the German Central Bank and the Rules of the Game, 1879–1913', pp. 311–59; Lars Jonung, 'Swedish Experience under the Classical Gold Standard, 1873–1914', pp. 361–404; and Michele Fratianni and Franco Spinelli, 'Italy in the Gold Standard Period, 1861–1914', pp. 405–51. Also see Georg Rich, 'Canada without a Central Bank: Operation of the Price–Specie–Flow Mechanism, 1872–1913', pp. 277–309.

18. For evidence from the bankers themselves see *Interviews on the Banking and Currency Systems of England, Scotland, France, Germany, Switzerland and Italy*, National Monetary Commission, US Senate, 61st Congress, 2nd Session, Document no. 405

(Government Printing Office, Washington, 1910).

19. John Dutton, 'The Bank of England and the Rules of the Game under the International Gold Standard: New Evidence' in Bordo and Schwartz, *Classical Gold Standard*, pp. 173–95; and 'Comment' by Donald E. Moggridge, ibid., pp. 195–9.

20. John Pippenger, 'Bank of England Operations, 1893–1913' in Bordo and Schwartz, *Classical Gold Standard*, pp. 203–22; and 'Comment' by Charles A.E. Goodhart, ibid., pp. 222–7.

21. Bloomfield, *Monetary Policy*, pp. 35–6; Triffin, *International Monetary System*, pp. 3–4.

22. Anna J. Schwartz, 'Introduction' in Bordo and Schwartz (eds.), *Classical Gold Standard*, p. 4; Milton Friedman, 'Comment', ibid., pp. 157–62; and Milton Friedman and Anna Jacobson Schwartz, *A Monetary History of the United States, 1867–1960* (Princeton University Press for NBER, Princeton, 1968), *passim*.

23. 'Comment', in Bordo and Schwartz, *Classical Gold Standard*, p. 157.

24. W.M. Scammell, 'The Working of the Gold Standard', *Yorkshire Bulletin of Economic and Social Research*, vol. 17, no. 1, 1965, p. 43. For similar views see Ford, 'International Financial Policy', pp. 14–18.

25. A.G. Ford, 'The Transfer of British Foreign Lending, 1870–1913', *Economic History Review*, 2nd ser., vol. 11, 1958, pp. 302–8; Ford, International Financial Policy', pp. 49–53, for a more general discussion. Also see his *The Gold Standard, 1880–1914: Britain and Argentina* (Oxford University Press, Oxford, 1962).

26. On the scale of overseas investments see Matthew Simon, 'The Pattern of New British Portfolio Foreign Investment, 1865–1914' in A.R. Hall (ed.), *The Export of Capital from Britain, 1870–1914* (Methuen, London, 1968), especially pp. 15–44; P.L. Cottrell, *British Overseas Investment in the Nineteenth Century* (Macmillan, London, 1975), pp. 11–15, 27–30; and D.C.M. Platt, 'British Portfolio Investment Overseas before 1870: Some Doubts', *Economic*

*History Review*, vol. 33, 1980, pp. 1–16.

27. Triffen, *International Monetary System*, pp. 6–8; and Arthur I. Bloomfield, *Patterns of Fluctuation in International Investment before 1914*, Princeton Studies in International Finance, no. 21 (Princeton University Press, Princeton, 1968), pp. 5–13, 42–6.

28. If it were a well-established gold currency the risks involved were not great because the market value could not fall very much and experience would show a tendency for depreciating values to recover.

29. *First Interim Report of the Committee on Currency and Foreign Exchanges*, Cd. 9182 [Cunliffe Committee], PP 1918, vol. 7, p. 855.

30. Arthur I. Bloomfield, *Short-Term Capital Movements under the Pre-1914 Gold Standard*, Princeton Studies in International Finance, no. 11 (Princeton University Press, Princeton, 1963), pp. 44–5.

31. In practice, a change in domestic interest rates would affect supplies of both foreign funds to the UK and British funds to the rest of the world. So a rise in London rates would encourage foreigners to lend more to British institutions and discourage Britons from lending to foreigners.

32. See the intriguing results in Lindert, *Key Currencies*, pp. 48–57; and in Hugh M. Neuburger and Houston H. Stokes, 'The Relationship between Interest Rates and Gold Flows under the Gold Standard: A New Empirical Approach', *Economica*, vol. 46, 1979, especially pp. 269–76, where they present the results of an investigation into the relationship between rates of interest and gold flows between London, Paris and Berlin.

33. W.F. Spalding, 'The Establishment and Growth of Foreign Branch Banks in London...', *Journal of the Institute of Bankers*, Nov. 1911, p. 438, reproducing figures from *The Economist*.

34. Forrest Capie and Alan Webber, *A Monetary History of the United Kingdom, 1870–1982*, (Allen & Unwin, London, 1985), vol. 1, p. 254.

35. Geoffrey Jones, 'Lombard Street on the Riviera: The British Clearing Banks and Europe, 1900–1960', *Business History*, vol. 24, 1982, pp.

186–210.

36. Edwin Green, *The Making of a Modern Banking Group*, (St. George's Press for Midland Bank Ltd., restricted circulation, London, 1979), pp. 66–71.

37. For more details see Gillett Brothers Discount Co. Ltd, *The Bill on London* (Chapman & Hall, London, 1952).

38. Stanley Chapman, *The Rise of Merchant Banking* (Allen & Unwin, London, 1984), ch. 7.

39. W.T.C. King, *History of the London Discount Market*, (Routledge & Sons, London, 1936), p. 269.

40. King, ibid., pp. 280–2; see Shizuya Nishimura, *The Decline of Inland Bills of Exchange in the London Money Market, 1855–1913* (Cambridge University Press, Cambridge, 1971), p. 93 for detailed estimates of the amount of foreign bills.

41. Nishimura, ibid., p. 25. The ratio of foreign to total bills rose from 47% in 1870;, 56% in 1893; to 65% in 1913.

42. Bloomfield, *Short–term Capital*, pp. 35f. emphasises that sterling bills were by no means the only form of international liquidity, nor the London acceptance the only means of creating short–term credits, and discusses the alternatives.

43. Bloomfield, *International Investment*, pp. 4–5; and Simon, 'British Portfolio Foreign Investment' in Hall (ed.), *Export of Capital*, pp. 23–7.

44. A.K. Cairncross, *Home and Foreign Investment 1870–1913* (Cambridge University Press, Cambridge, 1953), pp. 90–5; and Cottrell, *British Overseas Investment*, pp. 30–4.

45. In practice the Bank was prepared to use techniques other than changes in Bank rate. See Chapter 6.

46. John Maynard Keynes, *A Treatise on Money* (2 vols., Macmillan, London, 1930), vol. 2, p. 307.

47. David Williams, 'London and the 1931 Financial Crisis', *Economic History Review*, 2nd ser., vol. 15, 1963, p. 517.

48. Lindert, *Key Currencies*, pp. 16–21.

49. On the theory see Harry G. Johnson, 'The

Monetary Approach to Balance-of-Payments Theory', in his *Further Essays in Monetary Economics* (Allen & Unwin, London, 1972), pp. 229–49.

50. Donald N. McCloskey and J. Richard Zecher, 'How the Gold Standard Worked, 1880–1913' in Donald N. McCloskey, *Enterprise and Trade in Victorian Britain* (Allen & Unwin, London, 1981), pp. 184–208; and their 'The Success of Purchasing-Power Parity: Historical Evidence and its Implications for Macroeconomics' in Bordo and Schwartz, *Classical Gold Standard*, pp. 121–70 (including 'Comments' by Robert E. Lipsey and Milton Friedman).

Chapter Six

# THE BANK OF ENGLAND AND MONETARY POLICY, 1826–1913

Gaining special privileges from the Crown in a time of war, the Bank of England was established in London in 1694.[1] After weathering the first few turbulent years, the Bank has since been the country's major financial institution, having close links with both government and the City. Until the middle of the nineteenth century a not insubstantial part of this influence stemmed from the Bank's sheer size relative to that of other banks, but it was its evolution as a central bank – discernible from the eighteenth century – that ultimately ensured the Bank of England's unique status. This chapter examines how and why this happened.

## WHY DID THE BANK OF ENGLAND BECOME A CENTRAL BANK?

From its inception in 1694 until nationalisation in 1946 the Bank of England remained a privately-owned joint-stock bank whose bondholders expected a reasonable return on their capital. In any formal sense it was neither a government agency nor a department of state yet by the end of the nineteenth century it had emerged as a central bank. This is not to say that the Bank at that time operated in the same manner as the central banks of today, with their close control and regulation of monetary affairs on behalf of governments. Rather, the Bank's portrayal as a central bank around 1900 rests on the fact that it had accepted broad, public responsibilities for the maintenance of 'sound finance' by acting to avoid threats to the value of the pound sterling, by discouraging speculative and other 'disreputable' practices and by its general willingness to act as lender of last resort to the country's commercial banks. Indeed, the non-interventionist approach of British governments at that time had given the Bank almost sole responsibility for whatever monetary policy there was in the country.

In order to understand how this occurred a number of important features should be emphasised. First and foremost, it was not a consequence of considered planning. Rather it was an evolutionary process as the Bank management of the day responded to legal constraints and obligations, and to immediate economic pressures. Occasionally those in charge may have had more firmly-held views on the Bank's broader responsibilities, or even on how they would like to see its business develop in the long-term, but on the whole the emergence of policy objectives and techniques came about in a piecemeal manner after much trial and error. The metamorphosis of the profit-seeking institution of the eighteenth century into the central bank of the late nineteenth century was far from being a smooth progression: blind alleys were explored, inappropriate measures adopted and later abandoned, and at times sharply retrograde steps were taken before the Bank was to become generally recognised as having wide responsibilities for the conduct of monetary affairs.

One influence of a negative character was the absence of rivals. While the Crown retained responsibility for the coinage, during the nineteenth century it never seriously considered establishing a State Bank for the issue of notes or the conduct of other commercial banking business. Thus, the emergence of a dominant bank in the private sector was always likely to attract some public duties. In terms of sheer size, the Bank did indeed dominate the

English banking system by 1826. It was by far the largest British bank, with liabilities of over £50 million, and the scale of its business was such that it could greatly influence transactions on the London money markets.

The Bank's relative size and prestige owed a great deal to its general relationship with the state, and this was to be a continuous factor in its evolution. It had been created out of the need for state finance, providing loans in return for the special privileges incorporated in its charter; and it continued to supply funds and handle the government's accounts. It was, and is, the government's banker and at a practical level the services it performed for the government provided one source of income – income independent of its commercial banking activities. Among the more important of the privileges conferred on the Bank by the state was its monopoly of joint–stock banking in England and Wales. A parliamentary resolution of 1697 had denied charters to any other banks, and an act of 1709 had limited the number of partners in all other banks to a maximum of six. This privilege remained until 1826. Another privilege enjoyed by the Bank was the special status granted to its notes – here the government gave general support (e.g. in 1696 the death penalty had been introduced for forgers of Bank notes) and this culminated in Bank notes being declared English legal tender in 1833. The Bank's position as the main note–issuer was also important in establishing its high prestige. At the beginning of the nineteenth century notes were far more important than cheques as a means of payment. Thus, the fact that the Bank was the largest issuer in the country – with a monopoly in London – in itself lent weight to its unique position. And while notes were to become less important relative to cheques, the use of Bank of England notes was to spread from London to the rest of the country.

The Bank also became the effective repository of the nation's gold reserve. This resulted partly from its status as a dominant bank with close governmental ties but it also reflected the need of the Bank to hold a reserve of coin and bullion against its note and deposit liabilities. The accumulation of reserves at the Bank meant that for the commercial banks, especially in London – and, as communications improved, throughout the country – there was less need to hold gold themselves. Eventually, more of their cash holdings were to consist of Bank notes and deposit balances at the Bank of England. These they found convenient to use in meeting inter-bank debts and, if need be, they could always be converted quickly to coin. In this way the Bank of England became the bankers' bank. In times of liquidity pressure on the financial system as a whole, the Bank found itself acting as the ultimate supplier of cash, as the banks (and discount houses) drew on their accounts or borrowed from the Bank in order to meet their own customers' needs. It was here that the Bank was called upon to act for the public good by becoming a lender of last resort.

In essence, it is the interplay of pressures arising from these various functions that forms the history of nineteenth-century monetary policy. Here are the reasons why the Bank was to develop central bank functions. As the largest note-issuer and repository of the country's gold reserve it was obliged by law to maintain convertibility of sterling by ensuring that the reserve was adequate to meet the demands on it. Yet, at times, it was also called upon to step forward as lender of last resort by running down that reserve and making advances to the rest of the banking system so as to avoid any general collapse. The execution of these public duties was left to a private institution with a responsibility to pay dividends to its shareholders. Moreover, it was an institution which was waning in quantitative importance throughout the nineteenth century as the commercial banking sector expanded rapidly and the Bank's conservative habits excluded it from a share in much of this new business. Methods of influencing money markets were to become less obvious than when the sheer volume of its business dwarfed that of other banks. Legislation was to provide some guidelines but, in the main, it was left to the Bank's own judgement – and chance – to produce new techniques of implementing policy.

## LEGISLATION

The Bank's importance meant that its actions attracted public interest, and this occasionally invoked official inquiries or even legislation. In many ways the most important legal constraint was the obligation to maintain convertibility of its notes into coin. Acts of 1816 and 1819[2] had placed Britain on a stable exchange rate in terms of gold, and for the Bank full convertibility of its notes on demand became effective from February 1821 and remained so until the outbreak of World War I. It was the need to keep and protect a sufficiently large gold reserve as security against the threat of inconvertibility that was to be at the core of the Bank's development of monetary controls. However, on detailed guidance as to how the objective was to be attained, the gold standard legislation was silent.

The next important legislation came in 1826.[3] As was shown in earlier chapters, under the reforms of that year other English joint-stock banks were permitted outside London and (as part consolation) the Bank was encouraged to open branches in the provinces. The 1826 legislation brought little change in the Bank's formal position regarding the money supply but subsequent reviews of the Bank's charter were to provide periodic opportunities to discuss and implement reforms. In the 1830s and 1840s, in particular, action was taken to strengthen the general structure of money markets. To many contemporaries the economic fluctuations then being experienced seemed particularly noticeable in, and were perhaps aggravated by, the acute oscillations in monetary variables. These had been most apparent in the sharp changes in the cost and availability of bank credit, in gold flows and in the number of bankruptcies or closures amongst banks – especially in 1825/6, 1837, 1839, 1847 and (later in the century) in 1857 and 1866. To many, the Bank's role in this instability was not neutral; and legislators sought greater regulation. They were to meet with only limited success, however.

Most concern was directed towards the Bank's note issue because, together with coin, it was this that constituted cash to the general public and the commercial banks alike. But significantly, another component of cash holdings, the Bank's deposit liabilities, were not controlled in the same way. Thus, the Bank Charter Act of 1833 added to the Bank's standing by making its notes legal tender in England and Wales for amounts in excess of £5, except at the Bank itself which still had to pay in specie.[4] The effects of this were not startling, however, as Bank notes were already widely accepted as cash, although it did confer official recognition to their special status. In the long-term, a more important provision of the 1833 Act was to abolish the legal maximum (of 5 per cent per annum) imposed by the Usury Laws on the rate of interest charged on promissory notes and bills of exchange drawn at or under three months' duration. It was this measure which was to give the Bank freedom to operate a more effective interest rate policy, especially when it wished to raise rates and restrict borrowing. Previously when the rate was already at 5 per cent the Bank had had little choice but to resort to the rationing of loans. From 1833 onwards more flexibility was possible in that the Bank could now charge higher, punitive rates in order to choke off the demand for funds. While there was an inevitable learning phase marked by uncertainty and some anxiety to avoid the unpopularity of charging high rates, Bank rate movements of this sort were to become an essential element in the Bank's armoury of policy instruments. Thus, the 1833 reform of the Usury Laws made an important contribution to this aspect of the Bank's development.

The Bank Charter Act of 1844 attempted a more comprehensive reform.[5] This act incorporated many of the ideas on monetary affairs that were being promoted forcibly by the so-called 'Currency School' of economic commentators. Administratively, the main provision was to divide the Bank of England, creating a Banking Department and an Issue Department. The former was to handle the bulk of the Bank's general business such as the management of government accounts, arranging remittances, receiving deposits, paying cheques, investments, making loans and discounting bills. This part of the business was left almost completely unregulated – the main strictures of the act concerned only the Issue Department. This department was given sole responsibility for the Bank's note issue, but its powers were closely circumscribed. The new regulations were based upon two main assumptions derived largely from the writings of David Hume and David Ricardo:[6]

a. that the correct operation of an international gold standard minimised the extent of general fluctuations in the economy; and
b. that only coin and banknotes could be classed as 'money'.

Supporters of the act stressed that if only precious coins were used as money, then alterations in foreign exchanges and subsequent international flows of specie or bullion would directly affect the size of the domestic money stock. If the foreign exchanges were moving favourably and increasing the value of the pound – say, in response to increased export sales – there would be an influx of coin (or bullion which could be converted to coin) and this would directly increase the stock of money in the country. Conversely, pressure against sterling would result in coins being withdrawn from domestic circulation and exported. Such responses to the foreign exchange market were considered beneficial to the economy as a whole. Thus, in the case of specie being lost to foreigners the benefit derived from the downward pressure on domestic prices due to the effects of domestic monetary deflation, and this, in turn, would improve Britain's competitiveness, increasing demand for British goods and reducing that for imports – thus reversing the pressure on sterling.

The attraction to many contemporaries of this

price/specie–flow model of international adjustment was that it was thought to be fairly rapid in its operation, largely self–regulatory (as it required no discretionary action on the part of governments or their agents) and it minimised fluctuations in exchange rates.[7] Theoretically, if all nations operated a gold standard based on domestic money stocks consisting solely of precious coin, and permitted free trade in bullion and coin, then disruption to exchange rates and international commerce would be minimal. However, if those nations on a gold standard permitted the use of media of exchange other than specie, such as notes, there then existed a potential break in the sequence of reactions connecting the foreign exchange markets and the domestic economy. Thus, if the size of the note circulation were left to the discretion of the commercial banks and their customers an unknown element would be introduced into the regulatory mechanism which could hinder speedy adjustment. In the case of adverse exchanges and an outflow of gold, for example, any contraction of the domestic stock of coin could well be offset by an expansion by the banks of their note circulations. Even if it were accepted that the domestic banks could continue to expand (or fail to reduce) their notes in the face of a growing coin shortage for a limited period only, such delays were seen as aggravating the eventual disruption.

Currency School supporters placed such an interpretation on monetary events in the years from 1825 to 1844, and through the 1844 legislation they sought to remove the abuse. In particular, they tried to ensure that note issuers (including the Bank) could no longer circulate the same, or a greater volume of notes, in the face of an external bullion drain. Yet the reformers recognised that paper money served a useful function in economising on the use of specie. Political expediency also required some recognition of the rights of existing note issuers. Therefore, the Bank Charter Act did not abolish the note circulation, rather it tried to ensure that the note circulation behaved as if it were coin.

For the Bank of England the Issue Department

was allowed an issue of £14 million based on a reserve of government securities – known as the 'fiduciary issue' – but all notes beyond this amount could only be issued in exchange for gold coin and gold or silver bullion, with the specie and precious metal being retained as a full (100 per cent) reserve. Beyond the £14 million, Bank notes issued by the Issue Department varied directly – £ for £ – with that department's reserves of precious metal. It was a principal aim of the act, therefore, that the note issue could be increased only if the Issue Department's cash reserve rose. As shown in Chapter 3, the act also fixed the maximum size of the commercial bank note circulation and introduced changes which prepared for the eventual disappearance of 'private' notes in England and Wales.[8]

However, as an attempt to regulate the money supply the 1844 Bank Charter Act suffered from a number of serious deficiencies. It had ensured that the note issue of the Issue Department varied directly with that department's gold reserve, but not that the value of notes in the hands of the public did so. The Issue Department issued notes directly only to the Bank's own Banking Department, with these notes, in turn, entering into general circulation as customers drew on their accounts and borrowed from, or sold securities to, the Bank. At any one time the Banking Department retained a reserve of notes and the extent to which they were passed to customers would depend on many factors such as rates of interest and the public demand for legal tender. The 1844 Act did not fix the ratio of the Banking Department's reserve to its note liabilities. Thus, it was possible for the Banking Department to pay out notes to the public – or take them in – with some degree of independence from the size of the 'regulated' reserve in the Issue Department. In other words, the purity of the direct link that the Currency School had sought to establish between the gold reserve and the note circulation was never attained.

This is illustrated in Table 6.1 which shows relevant Bank assets and liabilities for the first few

Table 6.1 : Changes in Bank of England Liabilities and the Bullion Reserve, 1845-50 (annual)
£ millions

Changes in:-

| Date (end Feb. to end Feb.) | Coin and Bullion | Total Notes (in circulation and held in the Bank) | Notes in Circulation (outside the Bank) | Notes in Circulation and Deposits* | Notes in Circulation and Deposits* *minus* Bankers' Balances |
|---|---|---|---|---|---|
| | (1) | (2) | (3) | (4) | (5) |
| 1845/46 | -1.7 | -1.7 | 0.2 | 14.0 | 13.1 |
| 1846/47 | -1.8 | -1.8 | -0.7 | -14.4 | -13.7 |
| 1847/48 | 2.8 | 2.8 | -1.2 | - 0.5 | - 1.5 |
| 1848/49 | 0.5 | 0.4 | 0.0 | 0.0 | - 1.9 |
| 1849/50 | 1.8 | 1.9 | 0.7 | 2.1 | 0.6 |

* Includes public sector and private sector deposits.

*Source:*

'Bank of England Liabilities and Assets: 1896 to 1966', *Bank of England Quarterly Bulletin*, vol. 7, June 1967, Appendix.

years of the act's operation. As a comparison of columns 1 and 2 shows, the effect of the 1844 legislation was to ensure an exact correspondence between changes in the coin and bullion reserve and in the total of notes held both inside and outside the Bank. However, of this latter total only those 'in circulation' – held outside the Bank – can be considered to have been part of the money supply and as column 3 clearly shows, there was no close, simultaneous correspondence between changes in 'notes in circulation' and in the bullion and coin reserve. Moreover, as deposits at the Bank were treated as cash by both bank and non-bank sectors, it could be argued that the aggregate of Bank liabilities (notes and deposits) – rather than notes alone – would have been more relevant to any consideration of money supply changes. The figures in columns 4 and 5 of Table 6.1 again illustrate the lack of direct and immediate correlation between changes in the reserve and in liabilities (including and excluding bankers' balances).[9] However, this is not to claim that the size of the reserve did not significantly affect Bank liabilities in a more general sense (and after a time-lag) but the figures do show the failure of the 1844 Act to establish a close 'arithmetic' link – there was still room for discretionary action by the Bank.

The concentration on notes constituted a more general weakness of attempts at tight regulation of the money supply. The act operated on a very narrow definition of money, and its omission of controls over other media of exchange – especially bank deposits which were being used increasingly as money in the form of cheques and bankers' drafts – meant that the degree of control was much less than might first appear.

Nevertheless, the act did serve to re-emphasise the Bank's obligations under the gold standard – in future it not only had to ensure a reserve adequate to maintain convertibility but also had to meet the rigours of the act. After the first few years when it was hoped, forlornly, that the operation of the price/specie-flow mechanism would ensure this automatically, the Bank's new legal obligations meant that it had to monitor closely the size of its gold reserve, the extent of gold flows and the state of foreign exchange markets. It also had to act on such information when necessary.

One main aim of the new regulations, of course, had been to reduce the amplitude of economic fluctuations, but the Act's contribution here was slight. In fact, the note regulations proved so tight that on three occasions (1847, 1857 and 1866) they had to be suspended temporarily; and it may well have been the case that the extra burdens placed on the Bank added to public anxieties about bank liquidity during these monetary pressures of the mid–nineteenth century.

As regards the Bank's evolution as a central bank, the whole thrust of the act was initially against the exercise of discretionary judgement in monetary affairs. Indeed, it had tried to impose strict, non–discretionary controls. However, in practice the extra burden of the 1844 Act obliged the Bank to become more keenly aware of the consequences of its action, or inaction. Also the regular publication of accounts which had been initiated by the 1833 Act, provided public opinion with a yardstick by which to assess Bank performance. Informed public opinion was to serve as an additional means of inducing the Bank's management to give some thought to the broader effects of policy. Finally, in the event it was the failure of the 1844 Bank Charter Act to regulate the Bank's non–note issuing business that permitted it to experiment with and develop its own means of monetary controls. There was still enough freedom in the use of deposits, and in the conduct of the borrowing and lending side of its business, for the Bank to evolve what were to become the more important techniques of monetary policy, techniques which were not incorporated in any act of Parliament.

## THE BANK AND THE GOLD STANDARD

As the previous chapter emphasised, the importance of imports and exports to Britain and the extensive involvement of City institutions in financing world trade and development, meant that the British economy was subjected to much buffeting from external forces. The money markets were no exception in this respect, and the Bank of England's prominent position in the City of London meant that it, too, was frequently called upon to react to overseas influences.

The Bank's obligations under the gold standard played a crucial role in how the Bank was to cope during the nineteenth century. As the main repository of the country's gold reserve any major change in the direction and scale of international payments could alter the size of the Bank's holdings of gold. Thus, all things being equal, an excess of imports over exports on the current account would mean that unless Britain's importers, in aggregate, could persuade foreign suppliers to grant them more credit, then there would be a net flow of funds overseas in the form of payments to foreigners. At an individual level, an importer would go to his/her bank for foreign currency assets (including gold) with which to pay the foreign supplier and the bank, in turn, could draw on its London accounts for the specie. If the demand for cash were general, then it could lead eventually to the London banks and discount houses as a group replenishing their reserves by going to the Bank of England for gold. Before this happened, however, the general pressure for cash could push up interest rates, as bankers responded to the higher demand for loans. This in itself could provide some of the gold required to pay for the excess of imports by inducing private hoarders of gold to place it on deposit with the banks, and by inducing an inflow of funds from abroad as holders of international assets sought to earn the higher interest rates now available in London. It was also feasible that part of the import bill might be met by the direct export of British coin.

In these three ways (release of private hoards, inflow of gold from overseas, and the export of coin) the demand on the Bank of England's gold reserve would not reflect fully the excess of imports over exports. Nevertheless, as it was the main repository of gold, the Bank's reserve would be drawn upon to some extent and its cash position would deteriorate. As for any other bank, if the deterioration should continue, then at some point the Bank's ability to retain the confidence of its customers and to pay cash on demand would be threatened. Obviously preventive measures would be required long before such a situation developed. Indeed, the Bank's legal obligations would necessitate some action, for it had no choice but to pay gold at a fixed rate to note holders on demand. Thus, neither abandoning cash payments nor reducing the amount of gold per note (i.e. devaluation) was an option available to the Bank.[10] Instead the realities of its legal obligations and the nature of external pressures forced it to find means of modifying the impact of these pressures on its cash reserve.

The necessity to take preventive action was greater in the case of a gold loss. If the reserves were rising (say, as a result of an increase in export sales) there would be no threat to the Bank's legal position and, therefore, less urgency. Gold flows were asymmetrical in their impact on Bank policy. Even so, commercial self-interest would have deterred the Bank from accumulating too big a gold reserve because more profit could be made by investing the new gold in government securities or bills of exchange rather than by keeping it in the vaults. In practice, the reserve was kept relatively low (relative, that is, to other central banks such as the Bank of France, and to the liabilities of the banking system) which in itself added to the asymmetry of responses, for low reserves heightened the Bank's sensitivity to gold losses.

In responding to changes in its reserve, the Bank was acting essentially in a self-interested manner, seeking to maintain the convertibility of its own notes and the viability of its own business. However, its position in the money market meant its reserve policy came to be seen as that of the nation. Bank notes were legal tender and as other bankers held Bank notes (and balances at the Bank) as part of their reserves, the Bank held the ultimate source of cash for the whole banking system. Thus, if the Bank should have found itself unable to convert its liabilities to gold on demand, the other banks would have had to abandon convertibility too, and it would have meant the *de facto* abandonment of the gold standard.

Not unnaturally, such considerations drew parliamentary and press comment; and this broader context of 'public opinion' and the 'public interest' also became important in moulding the long-term development of central banking in Britain. Throughout the period there were always strong views as to what constituted the 'correct' policy to be adopted in the light of changes in the exchange rates and the balance of payments. In particular, the orthodox price/specie-flow mechanism called for the Bank to contract its lending in the face of adverse exchanges and balance of payments deficits; and *vice versa* for surpluses.[11] What records there are suggest that over the period as a whole the Bank did not accept or adhere explicitly to such a quantity theory of money. In its central banking function the Bank was more narrowly concerned about the impact of gold flows on its own reserves rather than about the state of the balance of payments, the general level of prices, movements in the money supply, or other national economic indicators.[12] Even so, the need to protect its reserves meant that Bank action generally conformed to what was to become the orthodox view. That is, although it operated some discretionary policy the Bank took no deliberate action to offset the impact of gold flows on the commercial bank's reserves. Thus, when there was a significant fall in the value of sterling and gold was being lost from the reserves, the Bank would normally 'tighten' monetary conditions at home; and 'relax' conditions when the exchange rate was rising and the reserves growing.[13]

## TECHNIQUES OF MONETARY CONTROL

It is with the development of techniques by which to influence demand on the Bank's reserves and the international value of sterling - techniques for 'tightening' and 'relaxing' monetary conditions – that the evolution of central banking is largely concerned.

Gold was drawn from the Bank by customers (including other financial institutions) withdrawing their deposits and converting notes to gold, or by borrowing from the Bank and asking to be paid in gold.[14] Thus, one of the most direct means of affecting the demands on it was for the Bank to alter its willingness to make discounts and advances, either by changing the terms of such loans or by varying the cost of them.

In certain circumstances the Bank exercised outright rationing by setting a limit on the loans to individual borrowers or by imposing a general ceiling for all borrowers. Such rationing was more frequent in the first half of the nineteenth century – as during the liquidity pressures of the 1830s and 1840s – and it could be coupled with changes in the duration of loans granted and in the type of securities deemed acceptable.[15] Active discrimination against what the Bank considered 'unstable elements' in the money market was also a part of its lending strategy. For instance, during the 1830s the Bank refused to discount the bills of joint-stock banks that were issuing their own notes because it saw them as both commercial rivals and as inflationary elements within the economy. Similarly, during the financial crisis of 1836/7 much of the blame for the crisis was placed on speculation in the American trade and on the role played by a group of large Anglo-American merchants whose finance business had expanded rapidly during the mid-1830s boom.[16] The Bank reacted to the growing crisis by adopting an extremely wary attitude to the discounting of any bills drawn on these firms – a form of discriminatory rationing. Again, after the financial crisis of 1857 the Bank decided that a major disruptive element had been the large amount of rediscounting of bills of exchange by provincial banks and the London discount houses, so it determined to discourage such business by refusing to buy bills from the discount houses.[17]

The problem with discrimination and rationing of

this sort was that it often led to public recrimination once a crisis had passed; and the Bank was not an institution to court controversy. More critically, rationing of its loans during a crisis could be self-defeating. During periods of uncertainty and growing liquidity pressure the knowledge that a lender of last resort always stood ready to provide cash against sound securities was an important factor in maintaining public confidence in the ability of the banks to pay on demand. The Bank of England was the most obvious lender of last resort and when the Bank imposed rationing it was possible for solvent firms with excellent securities, but suffering from a temporary shortage of cash, to find themselves being turned away. In such circumstances the large-scale suspension of cash payments and a panic run on the banks might be but a short step away. Obviously any internal panic of this sort would *increase* the demands for gold upon the Bank. With such disadvantages, rationing was to become a less common form of restricting Bank loans as the nineteenth century progressed.

The other main means of influencing the demand for loans was through changing the rate of interest charged. As has been noted, before the passing of the 1833 Bank Charter Act the Bank's powers to change the rate for discounting bills (known as 'Bank rate') was limited as the law set a maximum of 5 per cent per annum. Bank rate was first raised above 5 per cent during 1839, but it was during the 1847 liquidity crisis – when Bank rate reached 8 per cent – that the Bank began to impose punitive rates during periods of heavy demand for loans. The advantage over rationing was that by increasing its discount rate the Bank could deter people from borrowing yet avoid the dangers inherent in rationing. The imposition of higher rates reduced the danger of adding to money market anxieties by refusing to lend to solvent firms on sound securities. Financial institutions and other customers were still able to use the Bank as a source of cash, even if at the cost of higher interest rates.

From the late 1840s the Bank began to vary its

discount rate more frequently and these changes in Bank rate directly affected demand for its loans. Therefore within a narrow interpretation of the Bank's responsibilities, Bank rate changes could have been adequate to protect its cash reserves in the first instance. Even here, however, the level of Bank rate would be intimately affected by the rate of interest prevailing in commercial money markets. For instance, it may seem apparent that a rise in Bank rate from, say, 2 to 3 per cent would deter people from borrowing from the Bank, but this would be less obvious an outcome if commercial rates also rose, say to 6 per cent. Why borrow at 6 per cent when there was cheaper money to be had at the Bank? In fact, it was this relationship between Bank rate and market rate which was critically important in determining the extent of pressure on the Bank's reserve. Moreover, within the broader context of general monetary conditions it was the market rate, rather than Bank rate, that was of most direct relevance because very few businessmen or financiers borrowed directly from the Bank. Instead it was the rate charged by the commercial banks, discount houses and other financial institutions which determined the cost of their loans. Thus, when a provincial firm was contemplating taking out a loan – or placing funds on deposit – it was the rate of interest prevailing at the local bank which was most likely to be important. Similarly, on deciding in which country to invest short-term funds, a comparison of market rates in London and other international centres would be a major consideration to those engaged in international finance. Consequently, if the Bank wished to use Bank rate to alter the general demand for money, or to influence the scale of international capital flows, then it had to develop means of inducing other financial institutions to alter their rates in line with Bank rate. Bank rate had to be made more relevant to business in the commercial money markets.

Even if there were a clearly-perceived objective of altering market rates through Bank rate changes, this would have still been an extremely difficult task for a central bank operating in an open, international economy because interest rates would reflect changes in the general demand and supply of money at home and abroad. For much of the nineteenth century, of course, the Bank had no such well-perceived objective: it was not an authorised, public body with a commitment to manage the currency. Indeed, for a time during the middle years of the nineteenth century the Bank sought to reduce its involvement with the rest of the money market, an actual negation of the view that it had broader responsibilities for influencing the market rate. As has already been discussed, the 1844 Bank Charter Act tried to reduce gold standard management to a set of rules and the Bank was encouraged to operate as other banks in conducting its non-note-issuing business. There was even the suggestion that its responsibility as the ultimate source of cash during liquidity pressures could be relinquished, and in the crisis of the spring of 1847 Bank action came very close to denying its historical role as lender of last resort.[18]

In 1858 the policy of aloofness from other financial institutions was carried much further by the ban on buying bills from the London discount houses. At this time few commercial banks discounted directly with the Bank; instead the banks borrowed from the discount houses which, in turn, sought funds from the Bank. Thus, the 1858 ban affected the supply of Bank funds to the whole money market. However, the disadvantages of such a move were to become apparent over the next three decades. It was increasingly recognised that a great proportion of short-term funds entering into international finance passed through the London bill market and that the key to short-term capital flows was the rate of interest prevailing in that market. Yet for the Bank of England, less contact with the market meant less influence over market rates and, therefore, less influence over gold and capital flows. This waning influence became more obvious during the 1870s and 1880s as the scale of the Bank's own transactions dwindled relative to that of the growing joint-stock banks. The Bank found itself 'chasing rather than governing those market rates of interest which had become critical in the working of the gold standard'[19], and its (admittedly) half-hearted attempt to disassociate itself from the money markets left it 'groping' for other forms of influence.[20]

Ultimately, it had to re-establish links with the market and seek ways of making Bank rate relevant to the other financial institutions during ordinary times as well as in crises. Thus, in 1890 the discount houses were once again permitted to discount regularly at the Bank. Henceforth the Bank sought more frequent, personal contact with the discount houses and commercial banks, consolidating the linkages through which it operated its Bank rate policy. In the first instance Bank rate was made more 'effective' by keeping it close to – though slightly above – the level of market rate. Secondly, the Bank used 'open market operations' when it wished to make money market institutions borrow from it and, therefore, force them to take account of the rate of interest it was charging.[21] Typically, with an increase in Bank rate the Bank would act to reduce the supply of funds available to the discount houses by selling securities (not bills) or by borrowing itself.[22] The discount houses finding themselves short of funds would borrow from the Bank (as the ultimate source of cash in a 'pressure') at the new, higher rate of interest. In order to protect profits the discount houses would, in turn, raise rates charged to commercial banks and other borrowers, while offering more to their depositors. With a general 'tightness' developing in short-term money markets the commercial banks would follow suit by raising their rates. This general increase in rates would obviously affect many more borrowers than the change in Bank rate alone and, therefore, the impact on the demand for money in the domestic economy and on the foreign exchanges would be much greater. Here was the sequence of money market interactions that the 1918 Cunliffe Report saw as such a potent means of managing the gold standard: if the exchange rate fell and the gold reserve was threatened, then an increase in Bank rate would push up market rates and these would attract short-term capital from abroad, easing the pressure on sterling.[23]

The potency of Bank rate was enhanced by the quasi-automatic element that changes in business practice added to market response. Thus, an increasing number of banks began to fix their own deposit or loan rates with reference to Bank rate ('1 per cent above Bank rate', etc.). By the turn of the the century Bank rate was generally recognised as an index of conditions in the short-term money market. Thus, any change in the rate could elicit immediate response from financiers as their expectations altered. Moreover, the greater concentration of market power in the commercial banking sector made it easier for the Bank to seek the co-operation of the largest banks, and the small number of London discount houses ensured regular contact with Bank officials. Such contacts enabled the Bank to exercise direct influence – 'moral suasion' – on the men who made many of the decisions in the commercial money markets and, thus, helped oil the wheels of the Bank rate mechanism.

In the two decades before the First World War the Bank occasionally employed the 'gold devices' as a supplement to its main management technique of Bank rate.[24] It did this by operating directly on the gold market in order to influence international gold flows. The aim was to broaden the gold import and export points by facilitating and cheapening the import of gold and by deterring its export. Under the law the Bank was obliged 'to purchase with its own notes any gold, melted and assayed, at the rate of £3.17.9 per standard ounce.'[25] This still left it the freedom to alter the price at which it bought and sold foreign gold coins and bar gold; and freedom to encourage importers of bullion by offering them interest-free loans and by transferring the cost of melting down the bars from its customers to itself. Each of these devices was used at times for the good of the reserve. They may not have been in the spirit of the price/specie-flow mechanism, nor in line with the international rules of the game, but for a short period they provided a little flexibility in the practical application of reserve policy. Yet they were never more than a marginal auxiliary to Bank rate policy, which by the turn of the century had become the Bank's main technique of monetary management.

## LENDER OF LAST RESORT

There was a long tradition of the Bank coming to the rescue of the banking sector in periods of heavy demand for cash. During the nineteenth century the most extreme of such pressures were often the culmination of a phase of growing economic difficulties – with increasing bankruptcies, deterioration of the balance of payments, and a dwindling of cash reserves at the Bank of England – and they were marked by an intense period of a few days' duration during which there was great public anxiety about the ability of the banks to meet the demands of note and deposit holders. Uncertainty would be so great during these so-called 'crises' or 'panics' as to increase dramatically the demand for cash, creating a serious drain on the resources of the commercial banks. At such times the very viability of the banking system depended upon its ability to draw upon additional reserves of cash, and it was here that the Bank of England acted as a lender of last resort.[26]

As with other aspects of its broader responsibilities the Bank's acceptance of this duty was partly thrust upon it, was not explicitly acknowleged by the Bank itself and, yet, was accepted in practice. The fact that the banks and discount houses held little gold themselves – but instead built up cash balances at the Bank – made it natural that they should turn there during periods of liquidity pressure. The special status of Bank notes also meant that during a crisis it was these as well as coin that the public demanded. Anyway, in such circumstances it could barely have been in the Bank's own interests to refuse loans to reputable and solvent banks. Thus, in periods of pressure the Bank could find itself increasing its loans and discounts as the demand for cash rose. Even so, true to its tradition as a private institution, the Bank never made a public pronouncement to the effect that it was a lender of last resort. Yet there was a wide acknowledgement of the fact and after the publication of Walter Bagehot's *Lombard Street* in 1873 had made plain the advantages to the stability of the banking system as a whole, few seriously disputed the Bank's *de facto* acceptance of the responsibility.[27]

The Bank's willingness to act as lender of last resort was not unqualified, however. It did not mean a willingness to lend to all those who sought loans, but rather a preparedness to lend to 'sound' firms on the best securities. Requests from disreputable or dishonest firms could be rejected without breaching the principle. Thus, in the crisis of 1837 the Bank insisted on the winding-up of the Northern and Central Bank of England whose incompetent and dishonest management had over-extended their business; and in 1866 it refused to save Overend's discount house when it became clear that that firm had become little more than a financial shell. Moreover, when it did rescue a firm in difficulties it had to be sure that its own proprietors would not suffer any financial loss. Thus, even as late as 1890 its rescue of the large merchant banker, Barings, was contingent upon a consortium of commercial bankers offering guarantees against loss. It may have recognised a general responsibility to the money markets but it was not as uninhibited a responsibility as might be exercised by a modern central bank.[28]

## THE BANK AND THE MONEY MARKETS

As has been emphasised, the Bank of England operated through commercial money markets and its relationship with market institutions had a direct bearing on its development as a central bank and on the effectiveness of its policies. The commercial banks were the most important of these institutions. While the Bank was normally able to co-operate with the larger of the commercial banks, especially those based in the City of London, at the beginning of the nineteenth century an important element in the relationship was a degree of competition. The Bank's 'private' functions made the other banks commercial rivals in the business of deposit-raising and the granting of loans. This rivalry was most apparent in the case of note-issuing banks (as the Bank sought an ultimate monopoly of the note circulation) and it was most acute when large joint-stock banks, such as the London and Westminster Bank, were first permitted to operate in the City during the 1830s.

Over time the tremendous growth of the joint-stock banks and the failure of the Bank to share in this expansion of retail deposit banking, reduced the degree of commercial rivalry. But this, too, was to create its own difficulties for the Bank. Its command over market assets - and, therefore, its ability to influence interest rates directly - waned and a number of the larger financial institutions came to see themselves as equals to the Bank and resented attempts at 'monetary control'.[29] Ultimately, however, the decline in rivalry eased the Bank's transition as a central bank because it allowed for the greater co-operation essential to the effective implementation of Bank rate policy. The Bank's membership of the Clearing House from 1864 was part of this closer relationship. After the shock of the 1890 Baring Crisis the advantages of co-operation were even more obvious to a growing number of bankers as well as to the Bank itself;[30] and in 1911 the relationship between the Bank at Threadneedle Street and the commercial bankers in Lombard Street was placed on a more formal footing with the first of what became quarterly meetings of the Committee of the Bankers' Clearing House at the Bank.

The key intermediary position of the London discount houses - placed as they were between the commercial banks on the one hand and the Bank of England on the other - made them important to the implementation of Bank policy. Yet, as with the commercial banks, the degree of co-operation between the Bank and the discount houses varied over time.

In the first half of the nineteenth century there was an element of rivalry as both competed for discount business, but this was to fall away as the Bank concentrated on accepting only the best securities and as Bank rate was normally set at a level above that charged by the discount houses. At times the discount houses themselves were important customers - as they rediscounted at Threadneedle Street in periods of pressure for funds - and were, therefore, a source of income for the Bank. As has been shown, it was this relationship which was to give the Bank a significant leverage in the bill market through changes in Bank rate, but in the early years the Bank viewed the discount houses' business as an ordinary commercial venture. This stopped in 1858 with the Bank's ban on bill discounting for the discount houses, and a decided frostiness permeated the relationship.[31] Many years passed before the thaw set in, by which time the discount market had been transformed from a structure comprising a small number of private firms dominated by the one giant, Overend's, to a situation where, in 1890, there were just two ascendant public companies (the National and the Union) plus twenty or so small private firms.[32] The business of the market had also become much more internationally-orientated, providing the Bank with both a greater need, and incentive, to sharpen its influence. The re-admittance of the discount houses to Bank discounting facilities in 1890 confirmed the growing *rapprochement* and marked the beginning of a settled phase in which the Bank operated a system of close, personal contacts with the discount houses in order to effect Bank rate policy.

## PRIVATE v PUBLIC INTERESTS

It is appropriate in this last section to re-emphasise the fact that throughout the period from 1826 to 1914, the Bank was a privately-owned institution. It had private bondholders who expected a reasonable return on their investment. Its Court of Directors were not government nominees but businessmen (essentially merchants and merchant bankers though not commercial bankers) chosen by the stockholders, and in everyday management the need to raise revenue and make a profit was a constant factor. In certain circumstances the private interest could run counter to, or even conflict with, the Bank's public responsibilities. Indeed, on occasions during the nineteenth century Bank action was criticised on precisely these grounds. Thus, during the economic troubles of 1836/7 some critics believed the Bank should have been more willing to sell off its holdings of government securities in order to reduce the supply of cash to the money markets, but that the low market price of stocks at that time was deterring it from doing so.[33] Similarly in the run-up to the 1847 crisis, the Bank was criticised for being too concerned to increase its own discount business by keeping Bank rate at a competitively low level for too long.[34]

In more normal circumstances the main problem interest rate policy posed for Bank profits was that if Bank rate was to remain above market rate then the Bank would win few customers. This difficulty was not resolved until 1878, when the Bank began to operate a dual interest rate system: Bank rate, which set the minimum price at which the Bank would discount for the money market in general; and its private rate, which was set at a more commercially competitive level for regular customers.[35]

Within the broader, international context the Bank faced growing criticism from the 1870s for not holding large enough gold reserves to meet safely Britain's international liabilities in a crisis.[36] On the other hand, the Bank could argue legitimately that these liabilities were not its alone to bear but those of the whole banking sector, and why should it forego revenue by amassing gold? The 'reserve debate' was never fully resolved, and in the event the solution stemmed from the increased world output of gold from the 1890s and from the Bank developing other techniques, such as Bank rate policy, to protect its reserves. Gold reserves remained relatively low and although convertibility was successfully maintained, low reserves meant a greater sensitivity to gold flows.

The debate over the appropriate level of reserves, in fact, illustrates the general nature of the problem facing the Bank in this period. Those in charge of its everyday business would be barely aware of the trend in its policies towards central banking functions, but public opinion often expected more than would be demanded of a commercial bank. In practice, Bank Governors accepted this and from the late 1870s questions of profit were never allowed to stand in the way of duty: 'When one interest seemed to grate against the other, the public interest had to prevail...'[37] However, the 'public interest' remained narrowly-defined. By the end of the nineteenth century the Bank accepted that it had responsibility as the government's bank to service the National Debt, that it had a duty to maintain sterling convertibility and that it had a general obligation to avoid instability in the money markets. In turn, convertibility was to be achieved mainly through Bank rate policy. Thus, the Bank did not operate a full-blown monetary policy aimed explicitly at controlling the money supply, or bank reserves; and it certainly did not attempt wider economic management. Both its responsibilities and its policy techniques were strictly confined.

## FURTHER READING

R.S. Sayers, *The Bank of England, 1891–1944* (3 vols., Cambridge University Press, Cambridge, 1976), vols. 1 and 2.

Frank Whitson Fetter, *The Development of British Monetary Orthodoxy, 1797–1875* (Harvard University Press, Cambridge, Mass., 1965).

## NOTES

1. Many histories of the Bank of England have been written, the two most notable having been commissioned by the Bank itself: Sir John Clapham, *The Bank of England: A History* (2 vols., Cambridge University Press, Cambridge, 1944); and R.S. Sayers, *The Bank of England, 1891–1944* (3 vols., Cambridge

University Press, Cambridge, 1976). Throughout, the terms 'the Bank' and 'the Bank of England' are interchangeable.

2. 56 Geo. III, c. 68; and 59 Geo. III, c. 49.

3. 7 Geo. IV, c. 6; and 7 Geo. IV, c. 46.

4. 3 and 4 Will. IV, c. 98.

5. 7 and 8 Vict., c. 32.

6. For more detail on the nature of the debate see Frank Whitson Fetter, *The Development of British Monetary Orthodoxy, 1797–1875* (Harvard University Press, Cambridge, Mass., 1965), ch. 6; J.K. Horsefield, 'The Origins of the Bank Charter Act, 1844', and P. Barrett Whale, 'A Retrospective View of the Bank Charter Act, 1844', both in T.S. Ashton and R.S. Sayers (eds.) *Papers in English Monetary History* (Oxford University Press, Oxford, 1953), chs. 8 and 9 respectively.

7. See pages 134–8 for further discussion of the price/specie–flow mechanism.

8. Page 72.

9. For a recent analysis of the Bank's behaviour in the 1840s see Rudiger Dornbusch and Jacob A. Frenkel, 'The Gold Standard and the Bank of England in the Crisis of 1847' in Michael D. Bordo and Anna J. Schwartz (eds.), *A Retrospective on the Classical Gold Standard, 1821–1931* (University of Chicago Press, Chicago and London, 1984), pp. 233–73 (including Comment).

10. The government's 'suspensions' of the Bank Act in 1847, 1857 and 1866 were not measures to suspend gold payments but rather the temporary lifting of the rules governing the note issue and the size of the reserve.

11. See pages 138–41.

12. Sayers, *Bank of England*, vol. 1, p. 29.

13. *Interviews on the Banking and Currency Systems of England, Scotland, France, Germany, Switzerland and Italy*, National Monetary Commission, US Senate, 61st congress, 2nd Session, Document no. 405 (Government Printing Office, Washington, 1910), pp. 26–30; and *Committee on Currency and Foreign Exchanges, First Interim Report*, Cd. 9182, PP 1918,

vol. 7, pp. 855–6. Arthur I. Bloomfield, *Monetary Policy under the International Gold Standard, 1880–1914* (Federal Reserve Bank of New York, New York, 1959) has shown that while this tendency was true a fair amount of discretion was employed. For recent assessments see John Dutton, 'The Bank of England and the Rules of the Game under the International Gold Standard: New Evidence' in Bordo and Schwartz, *Classical Gold Standard*, pp. 173–95, and 'Comment' (pp. 195–9) by Donald E. Moggridge; and John Pippenger, 'Bank of England Operations, 1893–1913', ibid., pp. 203–22, and 'Comment' by Charles A.E. Goodhart (pp. 222–7). Although there is evidence that the Bank was no mere automaton when responding to changes in its reserves Goodhart expresses the consensus view: '...the Bank played the gold standard game faithfully in respect of varying short–term interest rates in response to changes in its liquidity position.' (ibid., p. 223).

14. The following is written in terms of the Bank reacting to gold losses, but in most cases the argument can be reversed for gold inflows.

15. For example, in April 1847 the duration of acceptable bills was reduced from three months to one or two months (Clapham, *Bank of England*, vol. 2, p. 201).

16. Peter Temin, *The Jacksonian Economy* (W.W. Norton and Co., New York, 1969), pp. 136–49 for the general background and for an assessment of the impact of Bank policy on America. Also see R.C.O. Matthews, *A Study in Trade–Cycle History. Economic Fluctuations in Great Britain, 1833–1842* (Cambridge University Press, Cambridge, 1954), pp. 57–9.

17. W.T.C. King, *History of the London Discount Market* (Routledge & Sons, London, 1936), pp. 199–205.

18. Clapham, *Bank of England*, vol. 2, pp. 201–2; and Fetter, *Monetary Orthodoxy*, pp. 204–5.

19. Sayers, *Bank of England*, vol. 1, p.11.

20. E. Victor Morgan, *The Theory and Practice of Central Banking, 1797–1913* (Cambridge University

Press, Cambridge, 1943), pp. 191–9; and R.S. Sayers, *Bank of England Operations, 1890–1914* (King & Sons, London, 1936), ch. 1.

21. Sayers, *Operations*, ch. 2.

22. From the 1890s borrowing became the more common method. (Sayers, *Bank of England*, vol. 1, p. 38).

23. *Report on Currency*, pp. 855–6.

24. Sayers, *Bank of England*, vol. 1, pp. 47–53, Sayers, *Operations*, ch. 4; and R.S. Sayers, *Central Banking after Bagehot* (Oxford University Press, Oxford, 1957), pp. 17–18.

25. Sayers, *Bank of England*, vol. 1, p. 47.

26. Forrest Capie and Geoffrey E. Wood (eds.), *Financial Crises and the World Banking System* (Macmillan, Basingstoke, 1986) provides a useful collection of essays which discusses both the conceptual and historical nature of crises, and which highlights the role of a lender of last resort. For a different perspective see Charles P. Kindleberger and Jean-Pierre Laffargue (eds.), *Financial Crises. Theory, History and Policy* (Cambridge University Press, Cambridge, 1982).

27. On the views of the main dissenter and former Governor of the Bank, Thomas Hankey, see Clapham, *Bank of England*, vol. 2, pp. 283–90.

28. R.G. Hawtry, *A Century of Bank Rate*, 2nd edn (Cass & Co., London, 1962), pp. 107–8; Morgan, *Central Banking*, p. 163; and Sayers, *Bank of England*, vol. 1, p.3.

29. Morgan, *Central Banking*, pp. 167–8, 192–3.

30. Although the relationship was not always the most cordial – see L.S. Pressnell, 'Gold Reserves, Banking Reserves, and the Baring Crisis of 1890' in C.R. Whittlesey and J.S.G. Wilson (eds.), *Essays in Money and Banking* (Oxford University Press, Oxford, 1968), pp. 217–24.

31. Clapham, *Bank of England*, vol. 2, pp. 239–46; King, *Discount Market*, ch. 6.

32. 'The discount market after 1911 consisted of three strong public joint-stock companies, Alexander's,

the Union and the National, and about twenty private firms who, on the strength of money borrowed short from the bankers, bought bills for bill brokers, the so-called running brokers, who brought together buyers and sellers of bills for a commission.' – W.M. Scammell, *The London Discount Market* (St. Martin's Press, New York, 1968), p. 170.

33. For instance, see the criticism of one of the leading London bankers, George Carr Glyn, in Michael Collins, 'The Langton Papers: Banking and Bank of England Policy in the 1830s', *Economica*, vol. 39, 1972, pp. 55–7.

34. Fetter, *Monetary Orthodoxy*, pp. 201–4.

35. The private rate applied to those who kept 'their sole current account with the Bank' (Clapham, *Bank of England*, vol. 2, p. 322. Also see pp. 310–11).

36. Two of the keenest advocates for large reserves were Walter Bagehot, *Lombard Street* (King, London, 1973); and R.H. Inglis Palgrave, *Bank Rate and the Money Market* (John Murray, London, 1903). For the general background see Pressnell, 'Gold Reserves', pp. 179–86.

37. Sayers, *Bank of England*, vol. 1, p. 11.

# PART II: 1914–1939

Chapter Seven

# DEPOSIT BANKING AND OTHER FINANCIAL INSTITUTIONS, 1914-1939

This and the following chapter highlight trends in deposit banking during the years from 1914 to 1939. Overall in this period there was a marked increase in private sector liquidity, including bank deposits. However, although the clearing banks (namely the London and Scottish clearers and Northern Ireland banks) shared in this expansion to some extent, they were no longer the most forthright innovators in the provision of financial services; growth was faster elsewhere. By the beginning of the period the clearing banks were the undisputed suppliers of services associated with retail banking (essentially money provision and transmission on behalf of the general public) but the following decades were to see a strong and growing demand for financial services and assets of a type not traditionally supplied by the clearers. In general the clearers did not seek to satisfy, or were ineffective in meeting, the new demands. It was to be other institutions such as building societies and insurance funds that attracted the business. As a result there was a decline in bank deposits relative to the total of money and near-money assets.

Over the long-term this was a consequence of the greater financial sophistication associated with Britain's advanced state of economic development, as a broader range of financial instruments was devised by the private sector.[1] But the banks' relative decline in the provision of 'encashable assets' (see below) also coincided with the emergence of strong oligopoly influences in retail banking, influences which suppressed price competition. A question arises, therefore, as to the extent to which the relative decline of the banks was self-induced. The argument presented in the following pages is that whereas the root-cause lay in the long-term process of financial sophistication, the banks' competitive stance was an important contributory factor. With only minor exceptions, the clearers recognised and maintained a compartmentalised view of money markets in which the provision of such things as mortgages or annuities was seen as being in the province of the building societies and insurance funds respectively – the banks kept to the business they knew best. Moreover, the rates fixed by the clearing banks for both deposits and advances became uncompetitive in a number of critical instances and, more generally, the suppression of price competition and the greater cartelisation of retail banking did not create a business atmosphere conducive to innovation. Such an approach by the clearing banks was strongly reinforced by a similar attitude among other major financial institutions and by the collusion of the monetary authorities who looked favourably on both institutional specialisation and the suppression of price competition.

For bank assets the main change in the period was a significant shift in composition, from private sector to public sector securities. Two aspects need emphasising. First, was the growth in scale of the public sector. For money markets, the First World War was critical because it massively increased the size of the National Debt, and the clearing banks (as major participants in the market) inevitably took up a large proportion of the Debt. Indeed they often had little choice – during wartime official entreaties to help the 'national interest' were all-persuasive, but even after 1919 the monetary authorities were anxious to nurture close co-operation with the clearers in order to safeguard the market in public securities. Thus, pressure from the authorities (in terms of the supply of financial instruments and in the form of direct 'suasion') was the first inducement for banks to hold more public sector debt. The second factor was a fall–off in private sector demand for bank accommodation. At times, this obviously reflected problems facing the real economy but another general determinant was that bank advances became expensive relative to other forms of borrowing, especially in the 1930s. For both assets and liabilities, then, it is argued that the banks' pricing policy was important.

## DEPOSIT BANK EXPANSION

In terms of assets and liabilities the deposit banks continued to grow between the wars. Table 7.1 shows a rise in the value of total deposits (net of inter–bank balances) from just under £1 billion immediately prior to the First World War to £2.7 billion by the end of the 1930s. This was ahead of population growth, with the average amount of deposits per head rising from £21.2 to £57.7 in the same period (or from £46.6 to £57.7, 1923/25–1936/38, if the impact on the figures of Irish independence is to be avoided). However, the scale of the increase was not as favourable to the banks as at first seems. A great deal of the increase merely reflected price changes, especially the sharp inflation during and immediately after World War I, when prices almost trebled between 1913 and 1920.

In 'real' terms (allowing for price changes) the growth in bank deposits was more modest, rising by some two–thirds from 1911/13 to 1936/38 (column 4, Table 7.1). If measurement is confined to the inter–war years, however, the *rates* of growth achieved were moderately high compared to some previous periods (Table 7.2). An annual growth rate of 2.8 per cent was achieved for price–adjusted deposits during the period as a whole (measuring between the business cycle peaks of 1924 and 1937). This was much higher than the stagnant rates of the early twentieth century although some way behind the very high rates of the middle and late nineteenth century. The figures in Table 7.2 also highlight differences

Table 7.1: U.K. Bank Deposits, 1911/13 - 1936/38*

| | Net Deposits, Current Values (£m) | Deposits per head of population (£) | Net Deposits as a Ratio to Net National Product (%) | 'Real' Deposits, values adjusted for price changes (1929 price=100) (£m) | 'Real' Deposits per head of population (£) |
|---|---|---|---|---|---|
| | (1) | (2) | (3) | (4) | (5) |
| 1911/13 | 961 | 21.2 | 45.3 | 1712 | 37.7 |
| 1923/25 | 2092 | 46.6 | 56.1 | 1979 | 44.1 |
| 1928/30 | 2190 | 48.0 | 53.9 | 2190 | 47.9 |
| 1936/38 | 2731 | 57.7 | 60.2 | 2835 | 59.9 |

*Notes:*

* Data are affected by Irish independence in 1922

a. All figures are three-year averages.
b. Feinstein's implicit price deflator for GNP (converted to 1929 base) has been used to calculate 'real' deposits.
c. Deposits are net of inter-bank balances.

*Sources:*

1. Deposits - Forrest Capie and Alan Webber, *A Monetary History of the United Kingdom, 1870-1982* (George Allen & Unwin, London, 1985), vol. 1, pp. 130-1.
2. Net National Product - C.H. Feinstein, *National Income, Expenditure and Output of the United Kingdom, 1855-1965* (Cambridge University Press, Cambridge, 1972), pp. T5-T6.
3. Population - C.H. Feinstein, ibid., p. T121.

Table 7.2: Rates of Growth of U.K. Bank Deposits, 1923/5 - 1936/8 (continuously compounded, per cent per annum)

| | Net Deposits, current values | 'Real' Deposits, values adjusted for price changes | 'Real' Deposits per head of population |
|---|---|---|---|
| | (1) | (2) | (3) |
| 1923/25-1928/30 | 0.9 | 2.0 | 1.7 |
| 1928/30-1936/38 | 2.8 | 3.3 | 2.8 |
| 1923/25-1936/38 | 2.1 | 2.8 | 2.4 |

*Sources:*

As Table 7.1

between the 1920s and 1930s with annual growth of 0.9 per cent (2.0 per cent if adjusted for price changes) over the 1923/25 to 1928/30 years, compared to 2.8 per cent (3.3 per cent price-adjusted) in the 1930s. Two factors were of general importance here. The later decade witnessed a recovery (from 1932/33) in those industries and services supplying the domestic economy and overall economic growth was somewhat higher in the 1930s than the 1920s. The second general change was the turnround in the authorities' policy stance. In the 1920s monetary policy was dominated by the decision to re-establish the gold standard (achieved in 1925) and this meant that policy was generally deflationary. In contrast, abandonment of sterling convertibility in 1931 and the espousement of a low interest rate policy in the 1930s created a more expansionary environment for the banks.

The figures given in Table 7.3 on the number of banks and banking offices show clearly the continuation and consolidation of pre-war trends.[2] In effect, the commercial banks continued to expand their branch networks, and market power became even more highly concentrated. The Irish figures are complicated by the creation of the Irish Free State (Eire) in 1922 which left only three banks - the Belfast Banking Company, the Ulster Bank and the Northern Bank - whose businesses were largely conducted within Northern Ireland and, therefore, within the United Kingdom, although the province was also serviced by the branches of Dublin-based banks. The three Northern Ireland banks barely increased the number of offices they were operating during the period. The banks in England and Wales, on the other hand, opened up many new branches in the 1920s. There was a pause during the next decade, though, when the number of offices stabilised at about 10,000. This meant that the banks were operating one office per 4,000 or so of the population (Table 7.3). It is obvious from these figures, then, that the large-scale amalgamations that had continued up to 1918 did not lead to the close-down of duplicate offices (one of the more apparent means of reducing costs) on a scale large

Table 7.3 : Number of Banks and Banking Offices, 1912-37

| | England and Wales | | | Northern Ireland | | | Scotland | | | United Kingdom | | |
|---|---|---|---|---|---|---|---|---|---|---|---|---|
| Date | Banks | Offices | Offices per 10,000 population | Banks | Offices | Offices per 10,000 population | Banks | Offices | Offices per 10,000 population | Banks | Offices | Offices per 10,000 population |
| 1912 | 57 | 5634 | 1.55 | 9* | 692* | 1.58* | 9 | 1234 | 2.60 | 75* | 7560* | 1.66* |
| 1924 | 24 | 8700 | 2.24 | 3 | 252 | 2.00 | 8 | 1476 | 3.04 | 35 | 10428 | 2.32 |
| 1929 | 23 | 9838 | 2.48 | 3 | 259 | 2.09 | 8 | 1641 | 3.40 | 34 | 11738 | 2.57 |
| 1937 | 21 | 10118 | 2.47 | 3 | 262 | 2.05 | 8 | 1897 | 3.81 | 32 | 12277 | 2.60 |

*Source:*

David K. Sheppard, *The Growth and Role of U.K. Financial Institutions, 1880-1962* (Methuen & Co., London, 1971). Details differ from those in Table 3.4, pp. 116-25. For 1937, Sheppard's list of English joint-stock banks consists of Barclays, Barings, British Mutual, Coutts, District, Glyn Mills, Isle of Man, Lloyds, London Merchant, Martins, Midland, National Provincial, Union of Manchester, Westminster and Williams Deacons.

* It is important to note the break in the Irish and U.K. series due to the creation of Eire in 1922. In the table, the 1912 figures refer to the whole of Ireland.

enough to reverse the long-term net expansion.[3] Instead, in the absence of effective price competition, the expansion of retail networks became one of the more overt forms of competition practised by the new banking conglomerates. This was even more obvious in Scotland where, despite the already-widespread fears of 'overbanking', the number of offices rose by one-half between 1912 and 1937, so that by the end of the period the banks were operating at a very high density of one branch per 2,600 of the population.[4]

The size of branch networks emphasises the massive scale of individual banking enterprises by the 1920s. In 1921 the largest eleven banks were operating over 7,500 branches and had deposits in excess of £1.9 billion and, in total, the English banks employed a workforce of some 50,000.[5] The process of amalgamation which was largely responsible for this had been almost completed by 1918. The creation of the new Midland Bank is a case in point. Through amalgamations with the Sheffield and Hallamshire (1913), the Lincoln and Lindsey (1913), the Metropolitan Bank (1914) and the London Joint Stock Bank (1918), the Midland emerged as the largest of the British banks. It was indeed the biggest in the world by the early twenties, with almost £22 million of proprietors' capital, £372 million worth of deposits and some 750,000 current account holders.[6] The remaining four of the 'Big Five' were operating on a similar scale and by the end of the inter-war period even the 'second division' of English banks included such large concerns as Martins and the District Bank.

## AFFILIATIONS AND AMALGAMATIONS

Although the English, Scottish and Northern Irish systems continued to operate under separate banking legislation and business practices in the three countries retained some important differences, the period saw the forging of more formal links. In particular, the massive resources of the London clearing banks (LCBs) enabled a number of them to extend their businesses into Scotland and Ireland through the purchase of existing banks in those countries. The Midland led the way with the purchase of the Belfast Banking Company in 1917, and it also affiliated with the Clydesdale Bank (1920) and the North of Scotland Bank (1923).[8] In 1917 the Ulster Bank was taken over by the Westminster, and in the following year the British Linen Bank was affiliated with Barclays, and the National Bank of Scotland with Lloyds. Finally, Scotland's largest bank, the Royal Bank of Scotland, reversed the normal English dominance by taking over the small London private bank of Drummonds' in 1924 and, more importantly, by acquiring the London clearing banks of Williams Deacon's (in 1930) and Glyn, Mills and Co. (in 1939). In all these 'cross-border' unions great sensitivity was shown for the possible adverse effects on business of antagonising local patriotism, and outright mergers were avoided. Instead, the forms of affiliation adopted allowed constituent banks to operate with a fair amount of independence. Patriotism apart, this form of affiliation also meant that the Scottish banks could continue their note issue and it may well have made general organisational sense given the detailed differences in conducting business in the separate parts of the kingdom.

Takeovers and affiliations were also used by a number of the LCBs to extend their overseas interests.[9] The London banks had expanded their foreign exchange and acceptance operations in the decade prior to the First World War and their acceptance business was to expand still further in the 1920s and 1930s, so much so that they were to become formidable competitors to those merchant banks specialising in the acceptance business. As Chapter 5 noted, for other forms of foreign business British banks had traditionally used overseas correspondents – foreign banks acting on their behalf – but shortly before the First World War Lloyds Bank had marked an innovation in the growing internationalisation of banking business by acquiring a direct interest in overseas banking operations through the purchase of the bank of Armstrong and Co. of Paris and Le

Havre. The Midland Bank continued to rely upon foreign correspondents but the other three of the 'Big Five' followed Lloyds and began acquiring direct foreign interests over the following decades, either by the outright purchase of, or affiliation with, foreign firms or through the creation of new companies. In this way banking interests were acquired in South and West Africa, the Middle East, Australasia, Canada, India, Argentina and Continental Europe. In the troubled decades between the wars not all of the ventures were successful,[10] but this outward expansion of commercial bank interests marked a major and permanent departure from traditional operations.

Overseas expansion was a direct consequence of the massive scale and strength of resources available to the LCBs. But it was this strength, and the fact that it was concentrated into the hands of so few firms, which was to bring widespread criticism. Contemporaries feared the emergence of a bankers' trust which could operate monopoly powers over domestic money markets and it was such anxieties that were to check the momentum of the bank merger movement immediately after World War I. Public concern led to the setting up of a Treasury Committee on Bank Amalgamations in 1918.[11] Since most members of the Committee were bankers it is not too surprising that they took a favourable view of past mergers. Their Report pointed to the advantages of establishing large commercial banks: they gained economies and stability by spreading their business throughout the country; they were better placed to make large advances safely to individual customers; and, more generally, the increase in the scale of operations of British industry required a corresponding growth in size from the banks. These had long been the arguments used by the bankers themselves and the war had given them added weight. The cause of 'national interest' had been invoked, with larger banks required to help industry during the difficult period of reconstruction – to help meet the challenge of foreign banking-industrial conglomerates, particularly those of Germany.

However, while acknowledging the advantages from past mergers the Committee was more anxious about the impact of the more recent ones:

> amalgamations have changed their type and consist no longer in the absorption of a local bank by a larger and more widely spread joint–stock bank, but in the union of two joint–stock banks, both already possessing large funds and branches spread over a wide area.[12]

In other words, public anxiety was aroused by the dangers from over–concentration of market power. The fear was that reduced competition would give undue influence to particular banks which, in turn, could distort the allocation of financial resources and undermine the power of the Bank of England to conduct monetary policy. The Committee felt that such a position had not yet been reached but that genuine fears existed. In addition, concern was expressed over the writing–down of capital resources by amalgamated banks and over the problems that might arise if London's international acceptance business should become monopolised. As a result the Committee concluded:

> that the possible dangers resulting from further large amalgamations are material enough to outweigh arguments against Government interference, and that, in view of the exceptional extent to which the interests of the whole community depend on banking arrangements, some measure of Government control is essential.[13]

Legislation to confine future bank mergers within strict guidelines was recommended. In the event, though, no law was ever enacted. However, the clearing banks were obliged to seek an understanding with the Treasury which, in effect, meant that mergers were to be restricted to those which significantly extended customer services and, or, extended the geographical coverage of the merging banks' business. Unions of overlapping institutions – with similar types of business and with operations in the same localities – were to be avoided. Thus, while most of the few remaining private banks were absorbed and such amalgamations as that of Martins with the Lancashire and Yorkshire (1928) and that of the District with the Manchester and County (1935) went ahead, sensitivity to charges of a 'Bankers' Trust' prevented serious contemplation of a merger between any of the 'Big Five' until after the Second World War.

## COMPETITION IN BANKING

Despite contemporary concerns about a bankers' trust, the London clearing banks continued to operate an effective price cartel. Regular meetings of the London Clearing Bankers' Committee fixed the rate on deposits and advances in relation to Bank rate. From 1920 the 'normal' deposit rate was set at two per cent below Bank rate, whereas previously it had been one-and-a-half per cent below.[14] Strictly these rates applied only to the London area, and some variation still occurred in the provinces (e.g. branches in some areas continued to pay interest on current accounts, whereas none was paid in London). Also some discretion was exercised in attracting large deposits.[15] However, the amalgamation movement had been a powerful force for standardisation and the clearing banks' oligopolistic influence spread in the period. In 1936 the District was admitted to the London Clearing House. Since Martins was already a member, all the large English banks were now represented on the Committee. The price cartel in Scotland was also re-affirmed after the war and held throughout the interwar years.[16] The government did nothing to intervene with these traditional arrangements and effective representation and lobbying through such organisation as the Bankers' Information Service, the Institute of Bankers (the professional association), the British Bankers' Association (which brought together the English, Irish, Scottish and London-based overseas banks) and the London Clearing House itself, ensured that the bankers' viewpoint was professionally presented and their interests protected. Wartime experience and the need for the Bank of England to ensure that its public debt operations worked smoothly, helped develop the lines of communication between the Bank, the government and the commercial banks. A 'Treasury Committee' of bankers kept in touch with the Chancellor of the Exchequer and the Governor of the Bank met regularly with representatives of the clearing banks.[17]

Nevertheless, there was some disquiet. One source of criticism was from the Labour Party which adopted a resolution at its 1932 Conference advocating nationalisation of the banks.[18] A widespread concern was over the willingness and ability of the clearing banks to alter their traditional lending policies in order to rejuvenate the ailing British economy. Many perceived the problem of mass unemployment to be that of uncompetitiveness and the solution to lie in re–equipping British industry, with the banks providing the necessary finance. Such anxieties were to lead to a close scrutiny of the nature of deposit bank lending – a topic to be taken up in the next chapter.

Although the banks controlled price competition they continued to compete amongst themselves in the provision of services. The extension of branch networks and the amalgamation movement were important here. So, too, was the broadening of the range of customer services offered. There was also significant competition from outside the deposit bank sector, from non–bank financial intermediaries. The banks' heavy commitment to government securities and their persistence in holding to traditional lines of short–term finance for industry and commerce, combined with their minimum charge of 5 per cent per annum on overdrafts (especially in the 1930s when other rates were low) meant that they did not participate fully in many of the more important growth areas within institutionalised financial markets. Institutional demarcation remained the rule in Britain, and between the wars deposit banking did not grow as fast as some other financial sectors.

## PRIVATE SECTOR LIQUIDITY AND NON-BANK FINANCIAL INTERMEDIARIES

During the inter–war period there was a sharp increase in the liquid asset holdings of private firms and individuals.[19] This may have resulted, in part, from the economic and political uncertainties of the period which may have raised the precautionary demand for liquid balances, especially during the 1930s. Part of the explanation, too, could have been the historically low interest rates prevailing from 1932, for these raised the market price of fixed–interest securities, increased the danger of capital losses to existing bondholders and, thus, provided a greater incentive to hold liquid (non–bond) assets for speculative reasons, at least while fears of further price falls (interest rate rises) persisted.[20] Growth in bank deposits was part of this greater accumulation of cash and near–cash assets. In fact, the ratio of bank deposits to Net National Product rose from about 45 per cent immediately before World War I, to some 56 per cent after the sharp deflationary pressures of the early 1920s,[21] and reached 60 per cent during the cheap money period of the late 1930s (see Table 7.1). However, rising bank deposits were but one element in the general growth in liquidity. Alternatives to bank deposits included National Savings Bonds, building societies' shares and deposits, savings banks' deposits and insurance annuities. Not all of these were as good a money substitute as a bank deposit but they were close alternatives in certain circumstances, and in the climate of the interwar years it proved to be the building societies and the insurance companies which were the most important sources of new personal savings. Table 7.4 reproduces estimates made by David K. Sheppard of the share of net bank deposits in the total stock of household encashable assets. This underwent a long–term decline in the period, from over 50 per cent down to 44 per cent. The banks were losing ground to other financial intermediaries.

Table 7.4 : Share of Net Deposits in Total Household Encashable Assets (%), 1923/5-1936/8

| | |
|---|---|
| 1923/25 | 50.8 |
| 1928/30 | 48.4 |
| 1936/38 | 44.3 |

*Notes:*

a. Figures are three-year averages of December data centred on the cyclical peaks of 1924, 1929 and 1937.
b. Encashable assets include 'currency, bank deposits and shares, life and annuity funds, national savings certificates, defence bonds...and other bonds recorded on the Post Register.'

*Source:* David K. Sheppard, *The Growth and Role of UK Financial Institutions, 1880-1962* (Methuen & Co., London, 1971), pp. 18-19.

-------------------

*Building Societies, Savings Banks and Finance Companies*

There was a great boom in housebuilding between the wars when some four and a half million properties were built which, after allowing for demolitions, increased the housing stock by one–third.[22] Many were built for private owners, especially during the 1930s, and it was the building societies which provided the bulk of funds through their mortgage facilities. In E.J. Cleary's view:

> Altogether the inter–war years offered a very favourable environment for the growth of the building society movement. The demand for mortgages was based on rising incomes and a continuing shortage of houses to let. At the

> same time changes in taxation, together with low interest rates and general uncertainty elsewhere in the capital market, ensured there was a strong flow of funds into building societies.[23]

In all, building societies' assets rose by about ten-fold between the wars.

The societies' privileged tax position was important to their expansion. The government's main concession permitted societies to pay tax 'on behalf of' depositors and shareholders, and the aggregation in compounding tax in this manner meant that customers were being subsidised by the Treasury. The rising rate of personal taxation during these years increased the real value of such concessions and, naturally, made the accumulation of building society funds more attractive. The societies' interest rate structure played an important part, too, especially during the 1930s. In this decade the rates charged on mortgages fell relative to borrowers' incomes, thus reducing the relative burden of borrowing. Moreover, the rates paid to depositors and shareholders failed to fall to the same extent as other market rates, thus making building society balances a relatively more remunerative investment. It is not surprising, therefore, that in the inter-war period as a whole the societies experienced such a sharp increase in their assets (90 per cent of which were held as mortgages) with a corresponding rise in shares and deposits, from about £80 million to some £700 million between 1920 and 1939.[24] With the number of societies falling from 1,271 to 960 the typical institution was becoming larger although still dwarfed by the scale of the LCBs' operations. As a sector, the building societies were supplying a significant, and growing, proportion of the money and near-money assets held by the public. The statistics highlight the deposit banks' relative decline: society shares and deposits were equal to just 6 per cent of bank deposits in 1923/5, but by 1936/8 the ratio had risen to 23 per cent. Here was a rapidly growing area of deposit accumulation in which the banks were not directly sharing.

The building societies were not the only successful rivals for deposits. The Post Office Savings Bank and the trustee savings banks' deposits rose from £112 million in 1919, to £162 million in 1929 and then to £293 million in 1939. By the time of the Second World War there were almost 2,500,000 depositors.[25] If the size of individual enterprises is a reasonable measure of the activity and range of services offered to customers, these too increased as amalgamations reduced the number of savings banks from 163 (in 1919) to 99 (in 1939). Moreover, after stagnating during the 1920s the Post Office Savings Bank's deposits also expanded from the early 1930s.

Among the clearing banks there had been relative neglect of small deposits but from the First World War there was greater awareness of their potential. For instance, a campaign by Lloyds Bank to encourage savings clubs, 'school banks' and individuals to open savings accounts was successful in increasing the number of such accounts from under 50,000 in the early 1920s to some 246,000 by the end of 1929.[26] The most dramatic rise coincided with a vigorous recruiting campaign in 1928 and 1929 but, even then, total balances increased by just £796,000 (at a time when total deposits were some £350 million). Evidently the attraction to the bank of small deposits was less as a new source of funds than as a means of introducing a growing number of customers to the clearer's services.

In fact, more generally it was the operation of interest rate differentials that proved critical in determining which institutions captured the lion's share of the small deposit market. As a general rule the savings banks maintained relatively stable interest rates on deposits in order to encourage small savers and this policy had a see-saw effect on deposit accumulation during the period. In the 1920s only those of the larger trustee savings banks which operated special 'investment accounts' and offered up to 4 per cent per annum to depositors, were able to attract more funds.[27] However, with the general fall to low market rates of interest in the 1930s and 1940s, the two and a half per cent paid by the savings banks on ordinary accounts meant that they became an attractive haven for liquid funds. Indeed, they proved so attractive that it seems they not only encouraged the conventional 'small saver' but also enticed bondholders to sell securities and place the proceeds on deposit within the savings bank movement. According to Edward Nevin:

> The margin between the yield on such deposits, which carried no capital risk, and on Consols, which carried a great deal, was such that it would have been surprising if many investors had not thought it less than worth while to hold securities.[28]

As in the case of the building societies, therefore, institutional rigidities in maintaining interest rates at relatively high levels during the era of cheap money ensured that the savings banks won a disproportionate share of the general increase in the public's holdings of liquid assets. Their success was another reason for the commercial banks' relative decline as providers of safe deposit for highly liquid funds.

The provision of finance for hire-purchase was another growth area. True, this form of credit remained just a small part of the total financial provision[29] but a number of finance companies were to nurture this underdeveloped section of the financial markets and to enjoy rapid expansion as a result.[30] These firms provided finance for both producers and consumers to buy goods on instalments. The aid to industry won official support which, in turn, helped secure the position of the finance companies in Britain's financial hierarchy. By the second half of the 1920s the Treasury and Bank of England believed that the solution to contracting export markets and large-scale redundancies lay in a 'rationalisation programme' to re-equip industry and reduce production costs – the enlargement of a new area of credit for businessmen could help here, and was to be encouraged. Thus, in 1930 the Bank of England publicly supported the United Dominion Trust, through the direct purchase of £250,000 of its shares. Official blessings of this nature naturally boosted the status of the new finance companies and added to their success. Success was also a consequence of the buoyancy of the domestic market for consumer goods, with a number of the new consumer durables such as cars being bought increasingly on hire-purchase. Despite this rapid growth, hire-purchase provision remained in its infancy during the inter-war years and was to suffer a severe contraction during World War II. It was not to become a significant part of Britain's financial provision until the post-war expansion of the 1950s.

*Discount Houses*

The fortunes of other money market specialists were somewhat mixed. The discount houses did well in the 1920s but came under increasing pressure during the 1930s. In the earlier decade the sluggishness of world trade and structural changes in the methods used to finance international transactions restricted the supply of commercial bills coming on to the London market. However, this was largely offset by the large volume of short-term government debt which had been incurred during the war.[31] In particular, Treasury bills replaced commercial bills as the normal asset traded in by the discount market, and as 'a proportion of all bills in the market Treasury bills never accounted for less than two-thirds and often for three-quarters or more.'[32] Government bond transactions also provided a growing area of business. In any case, the commercial position of the discount houses was cushioned against the most severe buffeting of market forces because of their peculiar, intermediate position between the Bank of England and the clearing banks. As was emphasised in an earlier chapter, by offering to take loans from clearing banks (and others) for very short periods, the discount houses provided the banks with the opportunity to build up a second line of reserves – 'money at call and short notice' – which, while not as liquid as cash itself, could be converted to legal tender very quickly and, yet, still earn interest for the banks. The Bank of England was also keen to safeguard this traditional position because the discount houses' operations enabled it to implement changes in short–term monetary policy quickly via a very small number of market operators. In effect, all three parties – the discount houses, the clearing banks and the Bank of England – found it in their longer–term interests to co–operate and, if need be, to forego immediate commercial gains earned at the expense of one of the others.

The importance of such sentiments to the discount houses was most obvious during the 1930s when low interest rates threatened their commercial viability. The very sharp contraction of world trade after 1929 greatly reduced the supply of commercial bills and, therefore, reduced the volume of business conducted by the discount market. The discount houses also found that other financial institutions, and especially the clearing banks, were very keen to purchase what acceptable short–term assets there were. Competition for Treasury bills became intense. Moreover – as has been mentioned already – after Britain abandoned the gold standard in 1931 and the government decided to reinforce market tendencies by instigating a cheap money policy, short–term interest rates fell to historically low levels. Bank rate was held at 2 per cent per annum for almost all the time from 1932 to 1951, and the rate on Treasury bills was down as low as 0.35 per cent per annum in 1935.[33]

The discount houses' profits depended essentially on the margin between the rate of interest they paid for funds (or at which they could re–sell bills) and the rate they had to pay on bills. Because interest rates were so low the scope for operating a profitable rate differential was reduced. In particular, by 1933 the cartel agreement made by the LCBs in 1929 (when market rates had been higher) to keep the rate they required on money at call with the discount houses at 1 per cent below Bank rate, had eliminated the discounters' profit margin on loans from these clearing banks. The discount houses were forced to stop taking funds from their traditional suppliers and the lack of profits threatened their commercial viability.

However, their position was bolstered by support from the Bank of England. The Bank Governor, Montagu Norman, believed that survival of the discount houses was beneficial to the operation of Bank policy.[34] By operating through a small number of discount houses (there were twenty or so in the 1930s) the Bank was not only able to effect regular sales of government short–term debt but could also influence short–term money markets in the most direct fashion. The Bank, therefore, encouraged the clearing banks to co–operate and fostered collusion on price–fixing. A series of agreements, whereby the London clearing banks accepted lower interest rates on money at call and restricted direct competition with the discount houses for newly–issued Treasury bills, was concluded by the end of 1935.[35]

Within the discount market itself, 1935 saw the creation of the so–called 'syndicate', which formalised earlier attempts to restrict competition.[35] By this arrangement the discount houses submitted a joint bid for the weekly issue of Treasury bills at a fixed maximum rate of interest (minimum price) and allocated bills on a strict quota basis according to the capitalisation of each firm. The Bank of England's support was an essential feature of the arrangement and in these years the authorities met regularly with discount house representatives in order to communicate the official view on market conditions and likely trends. In 1940 the syndicated tender system was extended so as to ensure the sale of all Treasury bills issued. By this agreement the discount houses guaranteed to take up all the bills on offer (after 'outside' purchases) at the arranged price and, as a counterpart, the Bank undertook to ensure the discount houses would always have access to adequate funds. Thus, the inter–war years saw a marked shift to regulation and cartelisation in the discount market, a process determined by trying economic circumstances and by the dictates of the monetary authorities. In the event, these new arrangements long outlived the immediate circumstances of their creation and were not abandoned until 1971.

*Merchant Banks*

Economic pressures also brought changes amongst the merchant banks.[37] The long-term decline in the use of sterling bills for international transactions and the contraction of world trade, especially after 1929, drastically curtailed their international acceptance business and forced them to seek other commercial outlets. The banking crisis in central Europe in 1931, in particular, led to the freezing of substantial amounts of bills that had been accepted by British merchant and clearing banks on behalf of German, Austrian and Hungarian institutions. Initially London firms were liable for some £54 million of outstanding acceptances, with an unpaid 'central European' debt of some £66 million (down to £36 million by the outbreak of war). As a result, it was to take a complicated series of tortuously-negotiated Standstill Agreements to prevent possibly extensive failures in the London market. To this limited extent the market coped, but, not surprisingly, throughout the 1930s the international acceptance business languished.[38] London's merchant banks were to rely more on business elsewhere. Thus, they participated more freely in foreign exchange and bullion dealing, deposit raising and investment advice. The collapse of overseas projects and the continuation of official constraints on the outflow of funds overseas also encouraged a number of merchant banks to become more active in the raising of capital for domestic industry, acting as issuing houses and underwriters. Moreover, as issuers they took on increasing responsibilities, buying the issues direct and re-selling to the public rather than the earlier practice of operating merely as agents for the firms raising the capital. Thus, economic circumstances obliged this section of the financial community to move in the direction many critics were seeking – that is, reducing their involvement with overseas borrowers and providing more finance for the domestic economy. But it was only a beginning and criticism continued.

## CONCLUSION

It is clear that not all of the expansion of non–bank financial intermediaries was directly at the expense of the commercial banks. In many respects the money market was segmented into a series of adjacent sub–markets, and specialisation meant that the various financial institutions did not often compete directly except where their particular spheres of market interest overlapped. The conventional clearing banker did not deal in the house mortgage, insurance annuity, or (to a lesser degree) the small deposit markets – and those institutions that did were clearly not seen as rivals. Even where rivalry was more obvious – as with the discount houses over the purchase of Treasury bills or, more generally, amongst the clearing banks themselves – agreement was preferred to competition.

The commercial banking sector as a whole lost the impetus enjoyed in the nineteenth century as financial innovator, although as an earlier chapter argued this may have already been on the wane by the beginning of the new century. The rapid growth areas within the financial market were elsewhere and the clearing banks' relative position continued to decline. Indeed, relative deterioration would be even more apparent if account were taken of such institutions as the foreign banks based in London or the insurance companies whose expansion has not been detailed here. The clearing banks settled for a regime of compartmentalisation and chose to restrict price competition within their own sphere of the market. This response is partly understandable in the uncertain conditions prevailing between the wars. Restriction of competition and protection of market share was widely practised throughout industry and commerce and it was a response that received official approval.

It would be a mistake, however, to leave the impression that the banks were merely marking time in the 1920s and 1930s. In fact, they enjoyed reasonable deposit growth, especially in the 1930s, and they introduced several important changes in business practice (Chapter 8). It should be stressed also that in the retail banking business and in the short-term money market they remained dominant. Nevertheless, rapid expansion had gone, to be replaced by greater emphasis on consolidation and closer co-operation.

## FURTHER READING

T. Balogh, *Studies in Financial Organization* (Cambridge University Press, Cambridge, 1947).

## NOTES

1. For a formal consideration of the impact of financial sophistication in a number of countries see Michael David Bordo and Lars Jonung, 'The Long-Run Behaviour of the Income Velocity of Circulation of Money in Five Advanced Countries, 1870–1975: An Institutional Approach', *Economic Inquiry*, vol. 19, 1981, pp. 96–116.
2. See Chapter 2.
3. Walter Leaf, *Banking* (Williams & Norgate, London, 1926), p. 239; T. Balogh, *Studies in Financial Organization* (Cambridge University Press, Cambridge, 1947), pp. 12–14; and W.F. Crick and J.E. Wadsworth, *A Hundred Years of Joint-Stock Banking* (Hodder & Stoughton, London, 1936), pp. 333–4.
4. G.G. Checkland, *Scottish Banking. A History, 1695–1973* (Collins, Glasgow and London, 1975), pp. 569–71. See Joseph Sykes, *The Amalgamation Movement in English Banking, 1825–1924* (King & Son, London, 1926), pp. 143–6, on England.
5. Sykes, ibid., pp. 145, 159.
6. Crick and Wadsworth, *Joint-Stock Banking*, pp. 335, 345–7.
7. On amalgamations generally, see Sykes, *Amalgamation Movement*, pp. 63–93, 187–91.
8. A.R. Holmes and Edwin Green, *Midland. 150 Years of Banking Business* (Batsford, London, 1986), pp. 157–63.
9. Balogh, *Financial Organization*, pp. 112–5;

and R.J. Truptel, *British Banks and the London Money Market* (Jonathan Cape, London, 1936), pp. 78–81.

10. For instance, see Geoffrey Jones, 'Lombard Street on the Riviera: The British Clearing Banks and Europe, 1900–1960', *Business History*, vol. 24, 1982, pp. 186–210. Also see J.R. Winton, *Lloyds Bank, 1918–1969* (Oxford University Press, Oxford, 1982), pp. 57–9, 119f.

11. *Report of the Treasury Committee on Bank Amalgamations*, Cd. 9052, PP 1918, vol. VI, pp. 333–339. The Report is reproduced in T.E.Gregory, *Select Statutes, Documents and Reports Relating to British Banking, 1832–1928*, (2 vols., Cass & Co., London, reprint 1981), vol. 2, pp. 323–33.

12. *Report on Bank Amalgamations*, p. 335.

13. Ibid., p. 339.

14. Balogh, *Financial Organisation*, pp. 90–1; Edward Nevin and E.W. Davis, *The London Clearing Banks* (Elek Books, London, 1970), pp. 125–6.

15. Winton, *Lloyds*, p. 46.

16. Checkland, *Scottish Banking*, pp. 569–70.

17. Leaf, *Banking*, pp. 87–9.

18. Barnard Ellinger, *The City. The London Financial Markets* (King & Son, London, 1940), pp. 205–17; J.F. Ashby, *The Story of the Banks* (Hutchinson & Co., London, 1934), pp. 263–70.

19. E. Victor Morgan, 'The National Debt and Monetary Policy', *Lloyds Bank Review*, vol. 37, 1955, pp. 18–33.

20. Nevin and Davis, *Clearing Banks*, p. 130.

21. In the early 1920s both nominal NNP and net deposits fell, the rise in the ratio being a consequence of a greater fall in the former.

22. Harry W. Richardson and Derek H. Aldcroft, *Building in the British Economy Between the Wars* (Allen & Unwin, London, 1968), pp. 55–61, 206.

23. E.J. Cleary, *The Building Society Movement*, (Elek Books, London, 1965), p. 191.

24. David K. Sheppard, *The Growth and Role of U.K. Financial Institutions, 1880–1962* (Methuen &

Co., London, 1971), pp. 150–1.

25. H. Oliver Horne, *A History of Savings Banks* (Oxford University Press, London, 1947), pp. 390–1.

26. Winton, *Lloyds*, p. 46. Also see Holmes and Green, *Midland*, p. 168. and Checkland, *Scottish Banks*, p. 570.

27. Horne, *Savings Banks*, pp. 238–31.

28. Edwin Nevin, *The Mechanism of Cheap Money* (University of Wales Press, Cardiff, 1955), p. 260.

29. Even as late as 1939 hire-purchase firms held only some 0.2 per cent of the total assets of British financial institutions (Sheppard, *Financial Institutions*, pp. 3, 184–5).

30. The largest finance companies of the period were the United Dominion Trust, the Mercantile Credit Co., and Bowater.

31. Detailed figures are given in F.W. Paish, 'The Floating Debt, 1914–39, and its Effects on the British Banking System', Appendix to Part II of Balogh, *Financial Organization*, pp. 191, 202. See Shizuya Nishimura, *The Decline of Inland Bills of Exchange in the London Money Market, 1855–1913* (Cambridge University Press, Cambridge, 1971), p. 93, for pre-1914 figures.

32. G.A. Fletcher, *The Discount Houses in London* (Macmillan, London, 1976), p. 41. Also see W.M. Scammell, *The London Discount Market* (St. Martin's Press, New York, 1968), ch. 7.

33. Sheppard, *Financial Institutions*, p. 190; Susan Howson, *Domestic Monetary Management in Britain 1919–38* (Cambridge University Press, Cambridge, 1975), p. 151.

34. Sir Henry Clay, *Lord Norman* (Macmillan, London, 1957), pp. 465–62. For the Bank's general attitude to the discount market see R.S. Sayers, *The Bank of England, 1891–1944* (3 vols., Cambridge University Press, Cambridge, 1976), vol. 2, pp. 536–44.

35. Balogh, *Financial Organization*, pp. 132–8.

36. B. Griffiths, 'The Determination of the

Treasury Bill Tender Rate', *Economica*, n.s., vol. 38, 1971, pp. 180–4.

37. Stanley Chapman, *The Rise of Merchant Banking* (George Allen & Unwin, London, 1984); Ellinger, *The City*, chs. 31, 32, 39; and Balogh, *Financial Organization*, pp. 241–60.

38. Sayers, *Bank of England*, vol. 2, pp. 503–12; and C.S.R. Harris, *Germany's Foreign Indebtedness* (Oxford University Press, London, 1935), ch. 3.

Chapter Eight

# THE BUSINESS OF COMMERCIAL BANKING, 1914–1939

The type of business conducted by the banks changed significantly between 1914 and 1939 as a consequence of fundamental changes within the economy itself. These years saw a fall-off in the banks' traditional provision of credit to the private sector via bill discounts and advances, and an expansion of their holdings of government securities. The result was a major shift in the composition of bank assets.

Between the wars Britain suffered greatly from a long-term decline of export sales compared to the pre-1914 years and from the impact of severe world recession in the early 1930s. As the main export industries of coal, iron, textiles and shipbuilding were amongst the banks' largest customers, their persistent problems created difficulties for the banks. On the other hand, once the immediate adjustments to the end of the war had been made, in aggregate the economy experienced a reasonable rate of growth (at 2.2 per cent per annum for real GDP) over the period as a whole from 1924 to 1937. The expansion enjoyed by customers supplying goods and services to the more buoyant home market must have increased their financial requirements and could have provided reasonable compensation for some of the losses of export-customers. If so, this was not reflected in the demand for bank credit from the private sector as a whole, for this underwent a secular decline. In particular, the severe depression of the early 1930s and the uncompetitive rates charged on bank advances during the era of 'cheap money' (after 1931) caused a contraction in the banks' traditional function as suppliers of short- and medium-term loans to firms. For the banks, the vacuum was filled by an increase in their holdings of public debt, the supply of which had expanded dramatically during the Great War of 1914–18. This was the second fundamental change in banking business. During the war there had been a sharp increase in the importance of government as provider of money market securities and this continued to sway the composition of bank assets long after the conflict ceased. Finally, the difficulties facing the international economy during the 1920s and 1930s compounded the long-term decline in the use of sterling bills of exchange for the financing of world trade and, thus, restricted the supply of what had become one of the money market's more popular (and non-government) forms of investment.

In aggregate, the consequence was to skew the composition of bank assets markedly towards public sector securities. The clearing banks became less dependent on intermediation within the private sector and more dependent on intermediation between private sector savers and public sector borrowers.

## CLEARING BANKS' BALANCE SHEETS

In this chapter the main balance sheet items of the banks are examined in turn and, as they dominated the domestic banking sector, most attention is drawn to changes affecting the London clearing banks (LCBs).

## CLEARING BANK LIABILITIES

### *Notes*

By the early twentieth century note-issuing was a non-existent item in the balance sheets of almost all English banks, the last private issue being relinquished in 1921 when the West Country Bank of Fox, Fowler & Co. joined Lloyds Bank.[1] The abolition of country bank notes sought by the 1844 Bank Charter Act had, at long last, been achieved. In England and Wales, coin and Bank of England notes were used for everyday currency purposes, although in Scotland and Ireland local bank notes continued to make important contributions. The First World War and its impact on government finance and on international monetary arrangements, significantly altered existing domestic arrangements. In the war the government sought to pool available specie and yet avoid the dangers of a currency shortage. Thus, the 1914 Currency and Bank Notes Act permitted the issue by the Treasury of legal-tender Currency Notes of £1 and 10/- denominations which were to circulate side-by-side with Bank of England notes whose lowest denomination remained at £5.[2] Also some expansion was allowed in the Bank's circulation and in that of the Irish and Scottish banks whose notes were granted legal-tender status in their respective parts of the kingdom. In consequence there was a sharp increase in currency in the hands of the public, with Treasury and Currency Notes accounting for the bulk of the wartime increase. For instance, at their peak in 1920 these notes stood at £346 million (annual average) compared to £135 million for Bank of England notes, £108 million for coin and £29 million for Scottish bank notes – in total some £618 million, compared to £210 million in 1913.[3] After the war, in 1920, the special status for Scottish and Irish notes was rescinded but Treasury notes were retained, ultimately becoming part of the Bank of England's responsibility, as they were incorporated into its own issues from 1928. Thus, from 1914 the English and Welsh had access to notes of a value low enough to be of use in everyday transactions such as retailing and the payment of wages, a 'privilege' long enjoyed by the rest of the UK.

One permanent effect was the sharp fall in the share of coin in the currency held by the public – low-value, legal tender notes were more convenient to hold and the authorities, with the co-operation of the commercial banks, continued to encourage their use.[4]

The adoption of the new gold standard in 1925 reinforced this, for under its provisions the Bank of England no longer needed to redeem its notes in gold coin. Thus, while the public had held coins to twice the value of notes in 1913, by 1920 coins were less than one-fifth of notes. For the inter-war period as a whole the value of coins languished in absolute terms and continued to decline relatively, so that by 1937 the value of the coin circulation was less than 14 per cent of notes. Finally, in 1928 Bank of England notes were declared legal tender in Scotland and Northern Ireland, as well as in England and Wales, broadening still further their acceptability as cash. The Scottish and Northern Irish banks remained keen to retain their own note issues, though. Patriotism played a part but so, too, did profit. For these banks some economies could be gained in minimising their holdings of Bank of England notes within till money because if customer demand for cash should prove unexpectedly high they could always pay out their own notes.[5] Be that as it may, Table 8.1 shows that compared to the total note circulation in the country Scottish and Irish notes were relatively unimportant, at 5–7 per cent of the total.

From the point of view of the English clearing banks' liabilities, therefore, notes did not figure at all, although they remained of some, if declining, importance to the Scottish and Northern Irish banks. As a result, commercial bank liabilities to the public consisted almost entirely of deposits.

*Deposits*

The figures in Table 8.2 on the LCBs' deposits confirm the overall picture discussed in Chapter 7 of a steady expansion on trend. In detail LCB deposits rose from almost £1.7 billion to £2.2 billion from 1923/5 to 1936/8.[6] As Chapter 2 established, bank deposits already comprised the greatest share of the money supply by World War I. The rise in the public's holding of currency relative to bank deposits during the war soon fell away and net bank deposits (excluding interbank balances) remained at about seven

Table 8.1 UK Bank Note Circulation in the Inter-war Period, £ million (percentage share in total is given in parentheses)

| Date | Monetary Authorities (Bank of England and Treasury Notes) | Scottish Bank Notes | Irish Bank Notes | Total UK Note Circulation |
|---|---|---|---|---|
| 1923/25 | 439.3 (93.5) | 22.3 (4.7) | 8.5 (1.8) | 470.1 |
| 1928/30 | 430.0 (93.7) | 21.2 (4.6) | 7.2 (1.6) | 458.7 |
| 1936/38 | 513.5 (94.8) | 23.0 (4.2) | 5.2 (1.0) | 541.7 |

*Notes:*

All figures are three-year averages (of annual average data) centred on business cycle peaks.

*Source:*

Forrest Capie and Alan Webber, *A Monetary History of the United Kingdom, 1870–1982* (George Allen & Unwin, London, 1985), vol. 1.

times the value of currency until the end of the 1930s.[7]

The main division drawn between different types of deposits is that distinguishing current accounts and deposit accounts; in other words, between deposits subject to withdrawal without notice and those that, formally at least, required the customer to inform the bank of the intention of running down the account sometime before actually doing so. Though not an exact match, this distinction corresponds fairly closely to the theoretical divide between those deposits accumulated, on the one hand, for transaction and precautionary purposes and, on the other, those viewed as highly liquid investments. As the clearing banks paid no interest on most current accounts it is often assumed that people accumulated such balances largely in order to have a pool of available money on which to draw in order to make everyday payments and conduct routine cash transactions. This is known as the 'transactions motive' for holding money and it was

Table 8.2 : London Clearing Banks' Balance Sheets, 1924-1937 (£ millions)

| DATE (end of year) | TOTAL DEPOSITS | ASSETS (ratio to total deposits given in parentheses) | | | | | |
|---|---|---|---|---|---|---|---|
| | | Cash | Money at call and short notice | Bills Discounted | Investments | Advances | Total |
| 1923/25 | 1698 | 208 (12.2%) | 118 (6.9%) | 256 (15.0%) | 318 (18.7%) | 822 (48.4%) | 1722 |
| 1928/30 | 1843 | 207 (11.2%) | 151 (8.2%) | 271 (14.7%) | 265 (14.4%) | 959 (52.0%) | 1852 |
| 1936/38 | 2220 | 236 (10.6%) | 164 (7.4%) | 287 (12.9%) | 614 (27.7%) | 914 (41.2%) | 2215 |

*Source:* London clearing bank monthly returns, available in Forrest Capie and Michael Collins, *The Inter-War British Economy: A Statistical Abstract* (Manchester University Press, Manchester, 1983), pp. 92-9.
All figures are three-year averages centred on business cycle peaks. For the sake of consistency the District Bank has been excluded throughout.

Table 8.3 : Composition of London Clearing Banks' Deposits, 1924-1937 (£ millions)

| DATE (end of year) | CURRENT ACCOUNTS | DEPOSIT ACCOUNTS | RATIO OF DEPOSIT ACCOUNTS TO CURRENT ACCOUNTS |
|---|---|---|---|
| 1923/25 | 980 | 672 | 0.69 |
| 1928/30 | 992 | 817 | 0.83 |
| 1936/38 | 1262 | 1001 | 0.79 |

*Source:* *Bank of England Statistical Summary.* Figures are three-year averages centred on business cycle peaks. There is a break in the series in 1936 but the overall proportions are not seriously affected. These deposit series have a different coverage from that in Table 8.2 - see Forrest Capie and Michael Collins, *The Inter-War British Economy: A Statistical Abstract* (Manchester University Press, Manchester, 1983), pp. 90, 96-8.

the frequent transactions use of cheques, bankers' drafts and bankers' orders that ensured the greater turnover of funds on current account than on deposit account.

It is assumed that another element in the demand for current account balances was the need to set aside some cash (no matter how unconsciously) in order to meet occasional exigencies, for such unpredictable expenses as, say, repairs to the car. This is the 'precautionary motive' for holding money. In this manner current account deposits performed the same functions as currency in a person's pocket, with the added security and convenience of knowing that the funds were held safely in a bank. It is assumed, therefore, that a major determinant of the size of current accounts would be the level of business activity in the economy as a whole. If the economy were in the upswing of a business cycle, then the value of transactions being conducted would be increasing and this, in turn, would increase the demand for money on current accounts. Similarly, a fall in the general level of prices – of the kind that occurred from 1924/5 to 1932/3 – would, *ceteris paribus*, reduce the value of transactions and lower the demand for current accounts.

Formally deposit accounts were subject to notice of withdrawal (of seven days in London) and, therefore, were less suitable for transaction purposes. Also interest was paid to customers on these deposits. At this time, of course, the LCBs and Scottish banks operated price–fixing cartels, with the rate being set in relation to Bank rate (from 1920 onwards the LCBs normally paid 2 per cent below Bank rate, with a minimum of 0.5 per cent). Thus, a major determinant of the level of commercial bank deposit accounts would usually be the level of interest paid by the banks or, more specifically, the differential between that rate and the rate paid on alternative means of holding very liquid funds such as building society shares.

On a strict interpretation of the differences between deposits on current account and those on deposit account, therefore, the level of each would have been determined by different economic variables. However, in practice the distinctions were blurred. In the case of current accounts, while no formal interest was paid, customers with a reasonable credit balance did not have to pay charges to the bank for operating the account. This can be viewed as a hidden or implicit interest payment. Moreover, between the wars some English provincial bank offices, as well as banks in Scotland and Ireland, did make an explicit payment of interest on some types of current accounts while covering their administrative costs by charging a commission. Even in London interest was paid on 'foreign deposits' held on current account.[8] For deposit accounts, too, their distinguishing feature is less obvious when it is recalled that in practice customers could withdraw funds without notice (with, perhaps, just the loss of a few days' interest) and that the bankers themselves claimed that they organised their asset portfolios on the assumption that both current accounts and deposit accounts were subject to immediate withdrawal.[9]

Thus, practice seriously sullied the theoretical divide between current accounts and deposit accounts and it has been partly for this reason that economists and historians have often lumped both together in their discussion of the money supply.[10] Even so, the division was considered important enough for the banks to provide separate figures for both types of deposits, and Figure 8.1 plots annual movements in the series from 1921 to 1936. Both rose across the period as a whole, the most notable features being the stagnation of current accounts in the 1920s and their sharp expansion in the 1930s, and the knockbacks to both series in the 'crisis' year of 1931 and in 1934. Table 8.3 (above) shows how their relative importance changed as a whole between the wars, although the dates shown here have been chosen purposely to highlight trend movements and minimise the impact of business cycle fluctuations.[11] It can be seen that on trend LCB deposit accounts became much more important relative to current accounts during the 1920s,

Figure 8.1: London Clearing Bank Liabilities, 1921-39
(£ millions)

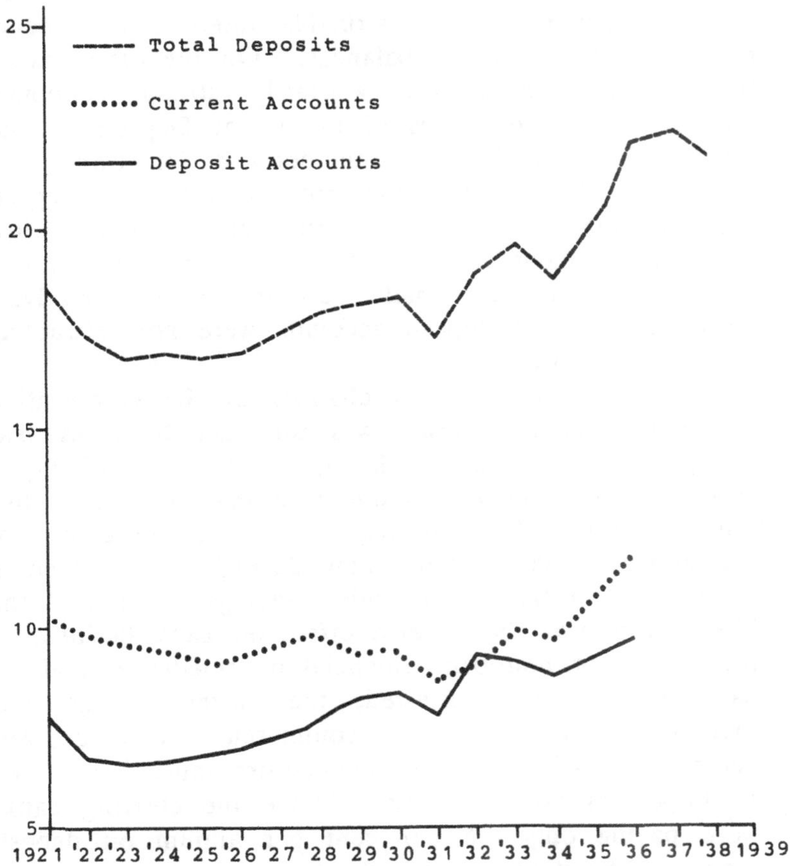


October figures for each year have been used.

Source: Forrest Capie and Michael Collins, *The Inter-War British Economy: a Statistical Abstract* (Manchester University Press, Manchester, 1983), pp.96-8.

then the position was reversed somewhat with a relative rise in current accounts, a rise which continued until the mid–1940s.

The change in the 1920s may be explained in terms of the generally depressed state of the economy which would have limited the demand for current accounts, coupled with reasonable interest rates being paid on deposit account balances. On the other hand, from 1932/3 there was a fairly strong economic recovery from the depths of the Great Depression and this would have boosted the demand for transaction balances. Significantly, too, interest rates on deposit accounts during the 1930s were at historically low levels, being fixed at only 0.5 per cent per annum and this, too, could have made current accounts relatively more attractive as deposit accounts were now attracting such little reward.

More significant than changes in the composition of clearing bank deposits was the fact that, whereas the public overall did build up its holdings of liquid assets (money and near–money) during the 1930s, this was achieved less through the accumulation of commercial bank deposits than through the acquisition of deposits in building societies, savings banks and the like. Here was the adverse effect on bank business of the growth of non–bank financial intermediaries and, as has already been suggested, the cartel arrangements that kept rates paid on commercial bank deposits below those of non–bank competitors must have been an important factor in this. While the clearing banks were paying only 0.5 per cent per annum on deposit accounts, building society shares were attracting over 3.5 per cent and savings bank ordinary depositors were receiving 2.5 per cent.[12]

*Proprietors' Capital*

At the end of 1938 shareholders' capital in the seven largest English banks stood at £236 million.[13] Of this, £72.7 million was paid–up, with another £134 million of reserved capital which shareholders could be called upon to pay only in the event of liquidation. In addition these banks had available some £57 million of published capital reserve funds, plus an unknown amount of 'hidden' reserves.[14] Hidden reserves had been accumulated largely out of undeclared gains on the appreciating market values of such assets as government securities and property holdings which were generally 'marked down' in the banks' balance sheets. While an estimate of their value is largely guesswork, they were none the less substantial – at the time an informed comtemporary, R.J. Truptil accepted suggestions that by 1929 these hidden reserves were equal to the total of paid-up capital and declared reserves.[15]

The size of the ratio of bank capital to liabilities was the subject of some discussion in the period, more especially as commercial banks in other developed countries seemed to maintain higher ratios and because ratios in Britain fell to a new low after the First World War.[16] On the basis of revealed capital resources (i.e. published paid-up capital and acknowledged reserve funds) the ratio maintained by the large London banks fell gradually from about 12–14 per cent of public liabilities in the 1890s, to 10 per cent just before the First World War. There was, then, a significant fall during the war, to some 6–7 per cent, where the ratio remained for most of the inter-war years.[17] Scottish banks' capital ratios were somewhat higher (averaging about 9 per cent in the 1920s and 1930s) but they underwent a similar decline to that of the English banks.[18] Part of the fall can be explained by the failure of capital resources to keep pace with the underlying, real growth of deposits but more significant was the impact of wartime inflation. The money value of deposits grew rapidly between 1913 and 1920 and this inevitably depressed the ratio. The bank amalgamation movement in England also had some impact because merged banks tended to write-down their combined capital value compared to the sum of the previously separate capital stocks of constituent banks.

Although of some concern to contemporaries this falling capital ratio carried no great risks for the banks. For a start, they had their hidden reserves which, like the value of deposits, would have appreciated greatly during the inflationary period. Moreover, the banks were operating on such a large scale that, on the one hand, public confidence was such that a heavy drain on their deposits was extremely unlikely and, on the other, they could more easily accommodate any losses when they did occur. In fact, by drawing on their hidden reserves the banks were able to keep secret the true extent and timing of losses, providing them with the opportunity to make good, or reduce, any published losses and to spread the accounting impact over a longer period. Anyway, as will be shown shortly, the composition of bank assets was such that a high proportion could be quickly liquidated in case of an emergency, and at little cost. Thus, while the banks were to suffer losses during the Great Depression of 1929–32 they were able to maintain public confidence throughout – there was no internal banking crisis of the sort that occurred in other developed economies. In the event, the drop in the capital ratio was not significant to stability.

## CLEARING BANK ASSETS

### *Cash*

In England, banks' cash holdings consisted of 'till money' – namely, coin and Bank of England notes – and balances at the Bank of England. Between the wars there was almost a 50:50 split in the composition with the balance marginally favouring Bank of England balances. Scottish and Irish banks treated holdings of their own notes as part of their till money, although for any notes issued in excess of the quite small authorised limit an equivalent value of legal tender had to be held in reserve. For the UK as a whole there were no legislative regulations governing the ratio of cash to liabilities, yet in practice it was 'remarkably stable'.[19] The ratio of cash to deposits (the cash ratio) for the LCBs as a group was at about 12 per cent during the 1920s and at some 11 per cent for the 1930s (see Table 8.2 and Figure 8.2) and, after allowance is made for changes in definition, this was

Figure 8.2: London Clearing Bank Assets, 1921-39 (£ millions)

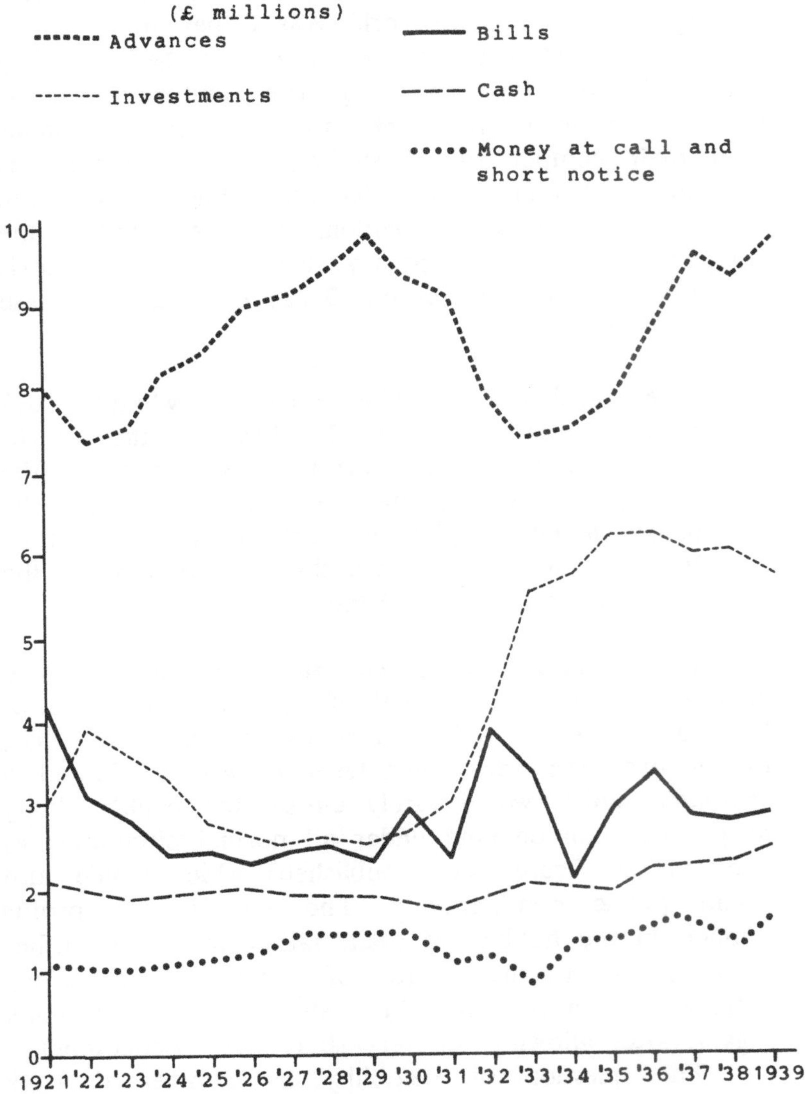


October figures for each year have been used.

Source: Forrest Capie and Michael Collins, *The Inter-war British Economy: a Statistical Abstract* (Manchester University Press, Manchester, 1983), pp.92-6

not much different from that of the early twentieth century nor of the post–World War II period.[20]

The LCBs' cash ratios were published monthly from 1921 but there was no strict uniformity across banks as some operated at ratios greater or smaller than their competitors, depending on such factors as the nature of their deposit liabilities, their overall size and the accounting conventions practised within the company. A contemporary banker, Walter Leaf, Chairman of the Westminster Bank, claimed that these published ratios were:

> purely arbitrary .... The percentage whether 10% or 15%, was fixed upon, I believe, as the sort of thing that the public might fairly expect of the banks; it was a matter of self–respect that the banks should sacrifice so much of their profits ... It is, in fact, much more than is required for the ordinary working of a bank...[21]

But the important thing was that for an individual bank there was a great deal of rigidity in the size of the cash ratio.[22] The assumption must be that, except over the very short–term it was considered a *minimum* which would safely ensure the bank's ability to pay cash on demand under all normal circumstances and (as the figures were published) which would also retain public confidence. The sacrifice of profits implicit in the holding of cash, rather than some other asset giving a direct rate of return, is a strong argument for also seeing the cash ratio as a *maximum* (again, after allowing for very short–term oscillations).

The question of flexibility in commercial bank cash ratios was given much prominence by contemporaries. In particular, the most important enquiry into the monetary system, that conducted by the Macmillan Committee, 1929–31, emphasised the need for banks to maintain fixed cash ratios in order to strengthen the Bank of England's control over money markets.[23] It was argued that if they kept to a rigid ratio, then any alteration by the authorities in the supply of cash to the money markets would show itself fairly quickly in a change in the level of commercial bank cash reserves and the banks would be obliged to alter their loans and investments in order to re-establish the desired ratio. In other words, rigid cash ratios would ensure that the monetary authorities could operate on commercial bank lending quickly and effectively.

It would be mistaken, however, to view inter-war bankers as slaves to their cash ratios, altering advances and investment decisions with every fluctuation. In practice there were elements of flexibility, especially on a day-to-day basis. In any one day the great bulk of a bank's assets were 'tied up' in bills, loans and securities and, at the margin, the demands on the bank for cash and the flow of cash into the bank were bound to vary. These oscillations revealed themselves in the bank's residual asset item, cash. It would have been little short of a miracle, therefore, if the level of cash holdings (and the ratio to deposits) had not fluctuated daily; and it would have been imprudent of any banker to respond too readily by changing other parts of the assets portfolio.[24] Only if the daily changes persisted, adding up to a longer-term tendency for the cash ratio to alter, could the bank justify taking remedial action to re-establish the desired ratio. The lending and investment policies of the commercial banks were not altered at every whim of the cash ratio.

The clearing banks also gained some flexibility in the manner in which they drew up and presented published balance sheets. The LCBs' monthly returns incorporated the practice of 'window-dressing' whereby most of the large banks compiled their balances on different days of the week and ensured that on that day they borrowed cash from a bank that was not striking a balance at the same time. Once the balance had been struck the extra cash would be returned and short loans offered in order for the other bank to go through a similar exercise. As a result, published accounts showed false and inflated cash positions, presumably in the belief that the public preferred to see the banks flush with cash. 'Window dressing' also meant that changes in real cash ratios could be kept from public view, accounting manipulations enabling the banks to merely keep up the appearance of rigid cash ratios.[25] If the banks had all struck their balances on the same day then the cash 'merry-go-round' could not have operated, of course, and it was just such a reform that the Macmillan Report decided to include amongst its recommendations.[26] However, the clearers resisted public pressure and 'window-dressing' was not effectively eliminated until after the close of World War II.[27] Incidentally, when this change was agreed in 1946 the clearing banks also agreed to operate with a cash ratio of 8 per cent to deposits, and as 'window-dressing' was no longer allowed this ratio was probably little different than what the 'true' ratio had been in the 1930s.

When the clearing banks drew up their half-yearly and end-of-year statements the same accounting day was used and, therefore, the 'merry-go-round' was not available and they had to resort to other means of dressing the window. They augmented their cash holdings for that day by borrowing elsewhere in the money market and their 'true' cash position was again obscured in the published data. Although preparation for these annual and half-yearly returns was a special case, the ability of the commercial banks to borrow from the money market was obviously another important, general element of flexibility in their reserve manipulations. For instance, if an individual bank was experiencing pressure on its cash reserve it could ease the situation by liquidating some 'near-cash' or other liquid assets, say by calling in loans to discount houses or by not renewing discounts as bills fell due. Moreover, the commercial banking sector as a whole could take such action although, if the collective demand for new loans was high, the discount houses may have been obliged to borrow from the Bank of England in order to replenish their cash holdings.

In fact, it was the Bank's position as a lender of last resort who was always prepared to accommodate the discount houses which, in turn, guaranteed that the clearing banks could make good any deficiency in their cash reserves.[28] This was even more the case once the closest ties between the Bank of England's liabilities, its reserves and the foreign exchange rate had been severed with the suspension of the gold standard in 1931. Questions of policy will be dealt with in the next chapter but it should be noted here that after the suspension of the gold standard, the Bank no longer operated an active interest rate policy. Instead during the 1930s policy was geared to keeping interest rates low. This meant, in effect, that the commercial banks could always replenish their cash reserves (via the discount houses) without incurring penal rises in Bank rate. Bank rate was fixed at 2 per cent and the Bank of England's willingness always to supply the money market with adequate cash meant that the Macmillan Committee's supposition that banks' cash ratios could be an important instrument of monetary control did not hold.

*Liquid Assets*

The distribution of commercial bank assets is often portrayed as being determined by two forces pulling in opposite directions: liquidity and profitability.[29] Generally, the greater the liquidity of an asset, the lower its yield – thus, the most liquid of assets, cash, earns no interest, whereas a long-term illiquid loan such as a mortgage will carry a relatively high interest rate. Obviously as a profit-making enterprise a bank is keen to hold assets that earn as high a return as possible, subject to maintaining the capacity of meeting all demands on it for cash. It is the immediacy of deposit liabilities, of course, which makes the question of liquidity of such importance to financial institutions. Banks not only have to meet all depositors' demands for legal tender but they must also maintain public confidence (thus retaining deposits) by publicising the fact that they hold an adequately liquid asset portfolio. As a textbook of the 1930s explained:

> To earn profits at all the banker must maintain confidence, [and] to satisfy depositors' claims a

> bank must be able to convert its assets into cash *quickly*. But that is not all. If the depositors' claims are to be fully satisfied the bankers' assets must be convertible into cash *without loss*. When bankers have said that they aim at liquidity they have generally included *both* these attributes...[30]

The eligibility of particular assets to qualify as 'liquid' has varied over time – according to market conditions and conventions – but the definition always encompassed a spectrum of assets which together constituted a 'secondary reserve' standing behind the 'primary reserve' of cash. Between the wars these items included money at call and short notice, and bills (see Figure 8.2 for annual movements). Money at call and short notice was one of the first sets of assets that bankers could turn to if they needed to supplement cash reserves. These were loans of 1 – 14 days' duration to the discount and stock markets, equivalent in all to about 7–8 per cent of the LCBs' deposits (Table 8.2).[31] They constituted a very flexible item in the banks' portfolios and enabled them to offset fluctuations in cash reserves with minimum effort merely by altering the rate of loan renewal. For the LCBs they were also the channel through which they sought extra legal tender from the Bank of England. As was shown earlier in the book, through the nineteenth century the convention had become firmly established that these banks did not rediscount their bill holdings; this potential means of raising money from the central bank was not available in England. Instead the commercial banks' demands on the Bank were felt only indirectly as they altered the volume of money lent to the discount market.[32]

The main class of liquid assets was 'bills', including commercial bills and Treasury bills. Since the First World War the latter had been the more important. They were 91-day promissory notes issued by H.M. Treasury, and the credit-standing of the British government ensured that they were 'a perfectly liquid form of investment which [was] instantly realizable when needed.'[33] Their issue had first been authorised in 1877 but they were not used on a large scale until the financing of the 1914–18 War necessitated the rapid expansion of all forms of government debt. So many were then issued that at their peak, of £1.2 billion in 1921, they totally dominated the London bill market and, thus, the bill holdings of all the major financial institutions. Even though the amount outstanding was reduced during the 1920s – and again in the funding operations of the 1930s – the dominance of Treasury bills remained, and over the years from 1927 to 1934 they were worth from two to four times that of the next largest group of money market bills, bank acceptances.[34]

Bank acceptances were the commonest form of commercial bill held by the clearing banks. These were normally bills of fairly short duration (three to six months) which arose out of international transactions and which had been accepted by a reputable British merchant bank or commercial bank. Such an acceptance raised the bill's status in money markets and lowered the discount rate charged. To be recognised as 'fine' bills by the Bank of England they needed to have been accepted by banks whose assets were held in the UK, as well as bearing the signature of a British bank other than the acceptor. The commercial banks also held bills of varying quality that did not quite meet the 'first-class' criteria of Treasury bills and bank acceptances, but they were only a small proportion of their total holdings. It is clear, therefore, that the great bulk of bank bill holdings comprised highly liquid assets that could find a ready market in the City. Even so, the LCBs did not re-sell any of their bills, including Treasury bills. Rather, their bill portfolios were so large and consisted of bills at all stages of maturity, that a certain proportion would be falling due (i.e. the debt being repaid in cash) on any one day. Therefore, if the banks should find that they needed to adjust their cash reserves they could do this very easily by altering the extent to which they replaced bills falling due. Indeed, the degree of flexibility afforded by this 'rolling-over' of their huge bill portfolios minimised the extent to which the banks had to call in loans made to the discount houses.[35]

There was a growing bill shortage between the wars and this enforced some alterations in bank liquidity. Long-term changes in the methods of financing international transactions and the general uncertainties in the international economy during these years prescribed the supply of commercial bills, with the collapse of world trade in the early 1930s creating an acute shortage in London. In such circumstances the commercial banking sector became increasingly dependent on the Treasury for its supply of liquid assets. Even so, the commercial bill shortfall was not fully met by a significant rise in Treasury bills. Indeed, successive peacetime governments were keen to reduce the size of the National Debt and, in the first half of the 1930s in particular, the Treasury took advantage of prevailing low interest rates to fund the Debt, shifting the balance away from short-term paper like Treasury bills to longer-term bonds. As a result the commercial banks found themselves actively competing with other financial intermediaries, including overseas banks and the discount houses, for the limited supply of Treasury bills that was available. The ease with which the government could raise money is shown by the fact that the interest paid on Treasury bills fell to historically low levels, in fact to below 0.25 per cent per annum in 1933 and 1934.[36]

One result of the dearth of bills was a fall in bank liquidity in the 1930s. It can be seen from Table 8.2 that the proportion of bills to deposits fell from around 15 per cent in the 1920s to just under 13 per cent by the late 1930s. In fact, this modest fall in liquidity remains evident even when the secondary reserve assets (money at call and short notice *and* bills) are added to cash – in aggregate these three items fell from about 34 per cent to 31 per cent of deposits until the trend was abruptly reversed by the sharp expansion of liquid assets during World War II.[37] It should be emphasised, though, that the lumping together of these three balance sheet items into a 'liquidity reserve' (or 'liquidity ratio' if they are expressed as a percentage of deposit liabilities) was not officially instigated until 1951 when the Bank of England laid down guidelines that the LCBs' ratio of liquid assets to deposits should be 28–32 per cent, with an absolute minimum of 25 per cent.[38]

There was no great oscillation in the aggregated liquidity ratio for the LCBs as a group during the inter-war period, but there were important differences across banks (as was the case with the cash ratio). Practice among the non-clearing banks varied even more. In fact, it was not until 1960 that the Scottish banks agreed on a common definition of 'liquid assets'. Nevertheless, although convention did not stipulate the maintenance of rigid liquidity ratios, bankers probably operated within a desired ratio band[39] and they would have been influenced in their lending and deposit-creating decisions by the overall liquidity of their assets. The bill shortage of the 1930s served to heighten their awareness of this constraint.[40] Thus, between the wars the size of, and changes in, the liquidity ratio could have been significant in influencing bank lending but in no precise, automatic manner, and certainly before the 1930s, many commercial bankers would not have held the 'sum of cash, money at call and short notice, and bills' to have been of unique significance.[41]

*Investments*

Between the wars investments showed the greatest change of all items in bankers' asset holdings, with movements responding largely to alterations in government debt policy (Figure 8.2). During World War I government borrowing requirements increased out of all proportion to peacetime needs, with the nominal value of the National Debt rising ten-fold. The banks partly financed this during the war and in the immediate post-war years by increasing their holdings of cash and Treasury bills, but they also met the state's needs by buying longer-term securities. Traditionally the banks held such government securities because they were readily-marketable and carried a higher interest rate than bills (although somewhat lower than loans and overdrafts). Before the war, assets equal (on average) to about 15 per cent of bank deposits were held as 'investments' by the large London clearers and most were held in the form of British government stock.[42] During the 1920s and 1930s, over 90 per cent of the LCB investments were in British government securities with the residual held in Colonial and Dominion government securities, public corporation and local authority paper and, perhaps, a very small holding of public company securities.[43] Given this traditional position it is not surprising that 'the war saw a rapid expansion of the investments of the banks both absolutely and relatively, as the banks were called upon to ensure the success of the war loans both by their direct purchases and by their lending to clients for the purpose.'[44] Government funding operations in the early twenties increased bank investments still further, until they peaked in the autumn of 1922, at some 23 per cent of deposits. Figure 8.2 and Table 8.2 show that the aggregate ratio of LCB investments to deposits contracted through the rest of the 1920s, falling to about 14 per cent by the end of the decade, as government needs became less pressing and as the demand for loans from the private sector increased.

As with other asset ratios there was much variation between clearing banks, and practice in Scotland and Ireland also varied. For instance, while Barclays' ratio stood at 16–18 per cent in 1929, the Midland's was as low as 8–9 per cent. Nevertheless the trend in the LCBs' aggregate ratio of investments to deposits gives a fair indication of the general picture. This shows that the long-term decline in the ratio from 1922 was rudely reversed in the 1930s. In Table 8.2 the nominal value of investments is seen to rise almost two-and-one-half times from 1929 to 1937, with the ratio to deposits increasing from 14.4 per cent to almost 28 per cent. Again the main reasons were a change in government debt policy and in private sector demand for bank credit.

Britain's suspension of the gold standard in 1931

removed a major constraint on the operation of domestic monetary policy. By 1932 official policy was to encourage low interest rates both as an aid to economic recovery and as a means of reducing expenditure on National Debt charges.[45] In that year the government successfully carried out the biggest conversion operation in the history of the National Debt by converting the 5 per cent War Loan, which at the time represented over one-quarter of total government debt, to a new 3.5 per cent loan. Although this was a substantial reduction in the nominal interest rate, the emerging low market rates meant that the rate of return on the new loan was still attractive to investors, including banks. Indeed, policy and market conditions combined to pressurise the banks to take up an increasing proportion of gilt-edged securities from the government. The Bank of England sharply increased the cash reserves of the banking system in 1932, at a time when means of employing the new resources were limited: the supply of Treasury bills was not greatly increased and the economic depression meant that both commercial bills were in short supply and the demand for advances was languishing. Expansion of investments seemed the only traditional area open to the banks.

The general pressure to hold this higher ratio of gilts persisted throughout the decade as governments took advantage of prevailing conditions to reduce the proportion of Debt covered by short-term borrowing and to shift its composition towards longer-term loans.[46] Thus, while 32 per cent of the National Debt had been in the form of securities of over 25 years' maturity in 1930/1, this ratio had risen to 40 per cent by 1938/9.[47] In turn, such changes affected the average life of securities held by the banks, their gilts became longer and their portfolios less liquid. Towards the end of the nineteenth century British government Consols had been viewed by many commercial bankers as extremely liquid assets, but the long-term price decline (rise in interest rates) that began at the end of the 1890s started to tarnish this impeccable reputation, for it raised the possibility of capital loss on any sale. These risks increased between the wars, especially in the 1930s when gilt-edged security prices fluctuated a great deal. For instance, the price of 2.5 per cent Consols had risen by over 70 per cent between 1928 and 1935, yet had then fallen by some 17 per cent by 1937. Clearly, while government securities retained one essential element of liquidity, namely marketability (for they could still be readily sold in the City) the other facet of liquidity, the absence of any loss on resale, was no longer there. 'Investments' now had to be placed somewhere between 'bills' and 'advances' in the liquidity spectrum. In fact, the sharp expansion of the banks' holdings of government securities had in itself reduced the liquidity of these assets. By the mid-1930s the banks held such a large proportion of total National Debt that it would have proved impossible to 'off-load' any substantial part of it without adversely affecting the price.[48] In effect, these large security holdings became 'frozen' or 'locked-in' assets.

Another important consequence of the increase in government security holdings was a proportionate decline in the volume of commercial bank accommodation given to the private sector. Commercial bill discounts were already down, and loans and overdrafts also began to suffer. Compared to pre-World War I years the business of domestic banks had become increasingly concerned with diverting deposits raised from the private sector, into buying public sector debt. The Second World War sharply reinforced this trend and, in fact, it was not until the late 1950s and early 1960s that private sector loans were to regain their former importance among bank assets. The growing dependence of the commercial banks on the government sector becomes fully apparent when the banks' holdings of investments (essentially government securities) are added to their Treasury bills, to their cash reserves (in effect loans to the authorities) and to that proportion of their loans to the money market which was indirectly invested in government securities. It has been estimated that in this way, by 1950 the banks' holdings of government debt totalled some two-thirds of their deposits.[49] Private sector lending had become a minority activity.

*Advances*

Between the wars English bank advances were essentially of the two types common today: loans and overdrafts. Writing of the period, T. Balogh explained:

> Loans are credited on the current account of the borrower and he is debited with the total amount of the loan immediately, even if he only utilizes part of the credit. Overdrafts are permissions to draw on the bank within certain limits over and above the credit balance of the client. The borrower is only debited when he actually uses the credit.[50]

Usually the former were granted for fixed periods against collateral, while the latter were frequently covered by no specific security but depended upon the bank manager's assessment of the customer's honesty and ability to pay. In the mid-nineteenth century loans had been usual in London and overdrafts in the English provinces and Scotland, but by the end of World War I overdrafts had become the most usual form of bank advance throughout the country.

The great majority of advances were granted for short periods, of a few months with the possibility of renewal often available. Most advances were also for relatively modest amounts, with the average being somewhat under £1,000, although much larger advances were granted to industrial and commercial borrowers and much smaller to private and professional clients. If the public utterances of the banks' own supporters are to be believed the giant commercial banks had learnt the lessons of history. They could now avoid the worst dangers of the nineteenth century when it had been possible for locally-based banks to tie up their resources for years at a time and become over-dependent on the fortunes of one or two dominant firms in the locality. The national banks of the twentieth century had been able to establish clear guidelines for their 10,000 or so branch managers:

> Modern bankers have learnt their lessons from the past, and have formulated certain principles: flexibility, liquidity, adequate distribution of risks, inadvisability of lending long while deposits are repayable on demand or at short notice, and the maintenance of adequate reserves for bad debts directly they appear to be doubtful.[51]

Advances were 'illiquid' because the debts could not be resold readily. Therefore, a banker had to be especially cautious to ensure safe repayment within a short period. According to the propagators of sound banking practice, advances...

> ...should be running only for a limited time, with provision for reduction at least, if not full repayment, in periods to be measured in months rather than years. It is a cardinal point of sound English banking that there must be no 'lock-up' of capital ... It is not the business of the banks to supply fixed capital to their customers...[52]

As the least liquid of a bank's assets, apart from its holding of physical property, advances also carried the highest rate of return. For this reason, provided adequate cash and near-cash reserves were held the large joint-stock banks aimed to lend 50–60 per cent of their deposits in the form of advances.[53] During World War I this ratio had been drastically reduced (standing at just 32 per cent in 1919) as the banks faced both increased demands from government and a reduction in the private market for their loans. However as Table 8.2 shows, by the second half of the 1920s the LCBs had been able to recover quite quickly and to establish a ratio of advances to deposits of about 50 per cent.

This had partly been an automatic consequence of the return to peace, with a diminution in the financial needs of the state and an expansion of the private sector within the economy. Before the war it had been the private sector that had demanded most of the banks' financial accommodation and its post-war expansion seems to have been a return to a more normal position. Indeed it was in the provision of short-term credits to the private business sector – in the form of discounted bills of exchange, loans and overdrafts, in the nineteenth century, and predominantly as overdrafts by the 1920s – that British commercial bankers saw their traditional role in the financing of industry and commerce. However, during the 1920s part of this accommodation undoubtedly represented 'frozen' loans made during the boom of 1920–21 when the economic outlook had been good, loans which many firms found difficult to repay in the economic troubles of the next few years.[54] Firms heavily dependent on export sales – firms in the coal, textiles, iron and shipbuilding industries – were particularly badly hit in this period and it seems that the banks may have 'carried' a number of them, with what had started out as temporary advances being regularly renewed for fear that recall would enforce closure of the client's business.[55]

During the Great Depression of 1929 to 1932 the demand for advances fell away again and, though there was to be some recovery, the depression marked the beginning of a prolonged period of decline. This was reinforced by the expansion of state borrowing in the Second World War and, in fact, a determined rehabilitation of advances amongst bank assets was not achieved until the relaxing of government controls in 1958. Table 8.2 shows that LCB advances were down to just 41 per cent of deposits in 1937, compared to 52 per cent in 1929, and this despite a sharp recovery in the domestic economy from 1932 and despite the declared 50–60 per cent objective (see Figure 8.2 for annual changes).

Why did the decline in advances occur? On the demand side, economic conditions in the 1930s were obviously not favourable. But supply factors were also critical. In particular, the competitiveness of the clearers was important. It has already been stressed that the business of non-bank financial intermediaries was expanding in this period and some, such as building societies and insurance companies, made significant progress in attracting funds which may otherwise have gone to the commercial banks. But for advances the price-fixing arrangements of the clearing banks were critical: bank advances, with a minimum charge of 5 per cent per annum for 'prime' customers, were expensive compared to other forms of raising money. Naturally the banks lost business. Low interest rates elsewhere encouraged large numbers of bondholders, including firms, to sell off securities whose value had risen. This, too, reduced the need for bank finance. Indeed, the irony is that the willingness of the commercial banks to buy securities as they added to their own investments, in effect meant that they were supplying cash to the public in this manner rather than through a rise in more expensive – and from the bank's point of view, more lucrative – advances.[56] For some industrial and commercial companies the cheapness of raising capital through the issue of such long-term securities as debentures also reduced their demand on the banks. At the time the number of amalgamations amongst industrial firms was thought to be important in decreasing the demand for loans by allowing economies in the use of financial resources[57] but, if true, the continued movement towards industrial concentration since the 1950s does not appear to have had a similar overriding effect.

In a mechanistic manner, of course, the fall in the relative importance of advances in the LCBs' balance sheets was a result of the rise in the share of investments. Though not rigid, the combined ratio of investments and advances to deposits tended to stay around 66–69 per cent (Table 8.2). From the point of view of profits the banker would have seen the two sets of assets as close substitutes – if advances could not be increased, and liquid reserves were adequate, then more securities would be bought. However, the general consensus is not that expansion of the banks' holdings of government funded debt 'crowded out' advances to the private sector but that, at prevailing interest rates, the demand for advances evaporated and the banks fell back on investments to make good the shortfall. If it had been possible the banks would have lent more at their cartelised rate of interest but, despite some relaxation of traditional vetting criteria, enough customers were not forthcoming at the going price.

## INDUSTRIAL AND COMMERCIAL FINANCE

The question of whether or not the banks were willing to lend – whether they were merely responding to demand or actively restricting loans – had become a political issue during the 1920s. The economy was performing badly. Large-scale unemployment had emerged in 1921 and persisted at about 10 per cent of the insured labour force; British export sales never recovered their pre-1914 level; and the pound sterling came under frequent pressure on foreign exchange markets. As the decade wore on, more commentators, including Treasury and Bank of England officials, became convinced of the need to 'rationalise' British industry, to invest in new productive techniques, reduce costs and become more efficient. A number of people believed the commercial banks had been deleterious in this respect, for they had failed to employ their vast financial resources to the best effect in aiding industry. Some critics thought that in the special circumstances in which the economy found itself the banks should alter their traditional lending stance in order to encourage the 'rationalisation' of industry.[58] The climate of high interest rates until 1932 and the 'City *versus* Industry' conflict that many saw in the government's decision to re-establish the gold standard in 1925 added a whiff of vitriol to the debate. It was in this context that in 1932 the Labour Party conference at Leicester adopted a resolution calling for the nationalisation of the banks.

However, economists were generally supportive of the commercial banks, if somewhat less enthusiastic about the Bank of England and the merchant banks.[59]

Representative of these views was the Report of the Macmillan Committee whose members included two leading economists on monetary affairs, J.M. Keynes and T.E. Gregory. The appointment of this Committee in 1929 was in itself a reflection of the mounting concern for the parlous state of Britain's economy. It was empowered to investigate the organisation and operation of the full range of the country's financial institutions and to consider means to 'enable these agencies to promote the development of trade and commerce and the employment of labour.'[60]

In general, the Committee's conclusions (published in 1931) were that most financial needs of the economy were being met satisfactorily. Specialisation of function meant that different types of financial institutions had evolved to meet different financial needs – the discount houses to service a highly-specialised short money market in the City; the clearing banks to provide conveniently-sited retail banking services and to supply short-term credits to trade and industry; merchant banks to aid the issue of securities and the finance of international trade; stock exchanges to provide formal markets for new and existing securities when firms wished to raise long-term capital; building societies to finance the purchase of properties through mortgages; and so on. Implicit was the view that critics of the commercial banks, who called upon them to make long-term capital available for industry, overlooked the facilities available from other institutions.[61]

The Report did point to a number of deficiencies – especially in money market provision of capital for medium-sized firms wishing to raise funds of up to, say, £200,000, and in providing finance for exporters – but it contained no major criticisms of existing financial institutions. It did seek to encourage the development of consumer credit and hire-purchase but no specific role for the clearing banks was mentioned. In general, the Report supported the view of the bankers themselves, that they were largely passive in the process of granting advances. Banks were dependent, on the one side, on the supply of cash from the Bank of England and, on the other, on the demand for overdrafts from the public.

Thus what criticisms there were, were muted and directed towards financial agencies other than the clearing banks. On the central question of the provision of long-term industrial capital, the Committee concluded:

> that there is substance in the view that British financial organisation concentrated in the City of London, might with advantage be more closely co-ordinated with British industry, particularly large-scale industry, than is now the case; and in some respects the City is more highly organised to provide capital to foreign countries than to British industry.[62]

However, the Macmillan Committee did not see any important, direct role for the clearing banks in the provision of industrial capital. Rather they suggested only a limited involvement, seeking instead the establishment of new institutions which could provide the necessary finance and advice to industry with the 'big banks' involved only indirectly through the purchase of shares in the new institutions and through supplying them with short-term credit facilities.

In fact, for the clearing banks the traditional provision of short-term advances remained dominant. However, trying economic circumstances and the need for the banks to maintain profits did result in a number of innovations and variations in lending policy which proved important in individual cases. It is known that, on occasions, the difficulties facing particular industrial sectors, especially in the export industries, involved the banks in the provision of credit beyond their traditional limits – in economic depression the bankers' dilemma has always been whether to call in doubtful debts and risk precipitating the client's bankruptcy and possible loss of the loan, or to continue the accommodation in the hope of eventual commercial viability. In the circumstances of the inter-war period the consequences for unemployment could have been another significant consideration. Undoubtedly such decisions would have entailed acquiring a more detailed knowledge of their client's businesses than was normal for English banks.

There is information on a number of specific, well-publicised instances of more-than-usual provision of industrial capital. For instance, the Bankers' Industrial Development Company was established in 1930 on the initiative of the Bank of England with finance being supplied through a consortium consisting of the Bank itself, London and Scottish clearing banks and other financial institutions. It was a temporary expedient to help in the reorganisation of the depressed export industries and operated in a similar manner to an issuing house by helping to raise capital for such firms as the National Shipbuilders' Security Corporation, the Lancashire Cotton Corporation and the Lancashire Steel Company.[63] Lloyds Bank and the Midland, in conjunction with the Prudential Assurance Company, also participated in the financing and ownership of a similar firm, the Charterhouse Industrial Development Company, which was established in 1934.

The clearers were directly involved also in a number of large-scale 'rescue operations'. For instance, between 1931 and 1936 the banks had to act together to prevent the liquidation of the Royal Mail group of shipping companies and associated shipbuilding interests (including Harland and Wolff of Belfast).[64] The scale of the difficulties is apparent from the Midland Bank's commitment which, together with those of the affiliated Belfast Bank, amounted to £3.4 million in loans and overdrafts.[65] Similarly, under the leadership of the Bank of England three banks – Lloyds Bank, the National Bank of Scotland and the Royal Bank of Scotland – became entangled in the reorganisation of the Scottish engineering giant, Beardmore.[66] Amongst other commitments this involved the three banks holding £1,386,000 of perference shares in the company, far from the normal form of bank security. Another example of large-scale industrial involvement by the clearers occurred in the depths of the slump in 1932, when Lloyds Bank provided the steel firm of Stewarts and Lloyds with whom the bank had a very long business and family connection, with a £3 million advance to develop the Corby Scheme. The loan was not repaid until 1935 when a debenture issue could be successfully completed. In fact, Truptil described this as 'the first occasion on which an English deposit bank has undertaken an industrial participation, thus following the methods of the continental banks.'[67] This comment is revealing. The historical accuracy of his claim of uniqueness for the loan is less important than the assumption that such action by a British commercial bank was very much out of the ordinary. The fact that such loans did occur provides a fair measure of the dire straits in which parts of British industry and their bankers found themselves during these years.

Such dealings remained the exception, however. British banks did not undertake a wholesale reform of their lending and investment practices. Even so *ad hoc* changes were introduced in response to problems on particular accounts and in deference to the often critical posture of public opinion. But the clearers did not meet the demands of their most ardent critics and mobilise their massive resources in active development of an industrial finance programme. Instead they continued to emphasise liquidity, remained at the short end of the money market and, given the maintenance of high prices for their loans in a difficult market, they suffered a protracted contraction in their advances.[68]

## CUSTOMER SERVICES

Before summarising the major changes in bank liabilities and assets attention should be drawn, albeit briefly, to those parts of the banks' business not captured in balance sheet figures – to the provision of ancillary banking services.

The deposit banks had always offered customers a range of safe deposit services, remittance facilities and advice on financial matters. Some of these were offered gratis, others for a commission. The emergence of the giant clearing banks of the twentieth century meant that their operations were on such a scale as to make feasible the consolidation and formalisation of traditional services. Moreover, the suppression of price competition for deposits and advances meant that the range and quality of these services was one means by which the banks could compete for deposits. The inter–war years witnessed an expansion of these facilities and in the larger cities specialised departments were formed to provide a more professional service. The large banks were willing to act as trustees, executors and administrators of family trusts and, in some cases, they acted as intermediaries between customer and broker, or unit trust. Their foreign exchange dealings were expanded rapidly, especially after the abandonment of sterling's fixed exchange rate in 1931 and their subsequent nurturing of both a forward and spot exchange market. They similarly expanded their foreign bill acceptance business to such an extent as to dominate the market in London. All in all, therefore, although the commercial banks lost ground to other financial intermediaries and did not participate in such growth areas as consumer credit, insurance and house mortgages, they nevertheless continued to develop and extend many of their traditional areas of business. Their decline was relative, not absolute.

## SUMMARY

The general economic environment in which the banks operated from 1914 to 1939 was a difficult one. There was growth in the economy and some sectors were expanding rapidly, but the UK faced major long–term problems associated with the contraction in export sales. Mass unemployment persisted – indeed tended to get worse – and some regions of the country suffered from deep economic depression. The amplitude of business cycle fluctuations, especially downturns, was also worse than before 1914. In common with many other sectors, the banks were faced with major problems. Data deficiencies make an assessment of the impact on bank profits unclear but it should be emphasised that in sharp contrast to many other countries, no British commercial bank of any substance failed in this period. Within the more immediate business environment of the money markets, the banks found themselves operating in – indeed, helped bring about – a less competitive, more regulated system. This was especially true in the bill market and in the deposit–taking and advance–making parts of their business. The greater concern of government and the Bank of England to control money markets, was a critical factor here. Nevertheless, at times non–price competition among the banks could be keen. More significant, though, was the expansion elsewhere, with the clearing banks losing ground to non–bank financial intermediaries within the overall provision of encashable assets. By the end of the period the public had increased its holdings of money and near–money, but relatively less was in the form of domestic bank deposits. On the asset side, the main change was the relative decline of the private sector as takers of bank loans and the corresponding rise of public sector securities. There was a marked decline in the banks' traditional function as suppliers of short–term credit to the private sector and a corresponding rise in the importance of loans to the state, a trend sharply reinforced by the effects of the Second World War.

## FURTHER READING

Edward Nevin and E.W. Davis, *The London Clearing Banks* (Elek Books, London, 1970), chs. 6–9.

T. Balogh, *Studies in Financial Organisation* (Cambridge University Press, Cambridge, 1947).

A.R. Holmes and Edwin Green, *Midland. 150 Years of Banking Business* (Batsford, London, 1986), chs. 5–8.

NOTES

1. R.S. Sayers, *Lloyds Bank in the History of English Banking* (Oxford University Press, Oxford, 1957), pp. 267–8.

2. 4 & 5 Geo. V, c. 14.

3. Figures on currency are from Forrest Capie and Alan Webber, *A Monetary History of the United Kingdom, 1870–1982* (Allen & Unwin, London, 1985), vol. 1, pp. 326–8.

4. *Report of the Committee on the Currency and Bank of England Note Issues* (1925), Cmd. 2393, paras. 42–6, reproduced in T.E. Gregory, *Selected Statutes, Documents and Reports Relating to British Banking, 1832–1928* (2 vols., Cass & Co., London, reprint 1964), vol. 2, pp. 381–2.

5. This argument was to be made much later by the Scottish banks to the *Committee to Review the Functioning of Financial Institutions* [Wilson Committee] – see *Appendices*, Cmnd. 7937 (HMSO, London, 1980), 3, pp. 410–11.

6. Figures exclude the District Bank.

7. Capie and Webber, *Monetary History*, pp. 76–7.

8. Walter Leaf, *Banking* (Williams & Norgate, London, 1926), pp. 107–8.

9. *Report of the Committee on Finance and Industry*, [Macmillan Committee], Cmd. 3897, PP 1931, *Minutes of Evidence*, vol. 1, Evidence of F. Hyde of the Midland Bank, para. 866, p. 56.

10. Milton Friedman and Anna J. Schwartz, *Monetary Trends in the United States and the United Kingdom* (University of Chicago Press, Chicago and London, 1982) – see their chapter 4 for a discussion of data.

11. The figures shown are aggregates and they hide the fact that there was much variation in the ratio of deposit accounts to current accounts across different banks and in different parts of the country.

12. E.J. Cleary, *The Building Society Movement* (Elek Books, London, 1965), p. 190; and H. Oliver Horne, *A History of Savings Banks* (Oxford

University Press, London, 1947), pp. 328, 330.

13. Barclays, the District, Lloyds, Martins, the Midland, the National Provincial and the Westminster.

14. Figures are from T. Balogh, *Studies in Financial Organization* (Cambridge University Press, Cambridge, 1947), pp. 100–5.

15. R.J. Truptil, *British Banks and the London Money Market* (Jonathan Cape, London, 1936), p. 86.

16. *Report of the Treasury Committee on Bank Amalgamations*, Cd. 9052, PP 1918, vol. VI, pp. 337–8.

17. Michael Collins, 'The Business of Banking: English Bank Balance Sheets, 1840–80', *Business History*, vol. 26, March 1984, pp. 43–58.

18. S.G. Checkland, *Scottish Banking. A History, 1695–1973* (Collins, Glasgow and London, 1975), pp. 747–9.

19. Balogh, *Financial Organization*, p. 37, speaking of England and Wales.

20. Edward Nevin and E.W. Davis, *The London Clearing Banks* (Elek Books, London, 1970), p. 141; Balogh, *Financial Organization*, pp. 43–5.

21. Leaf, *Banking*, p. 130.

22. Balogh, *Financial Organization*, p. 38 – the Midland Bank did make a stepwise change, downwards, in the late 1920s.

23. *Report of the Committee on Finance and Industry*, pp. 155–8. Also see the implications for policy in R.S. Sayers, *The Bank of England, 1891–1944* (3 vols., Cambridge University Press, Cambridge, 1976), vol. 1, pp. 310–11.

24. Although changes in the scale of overnight loans to money markets did offer one low-cost means of accommodating such fluctuations.

25. R.M. Goodwin, 'The Supply of Bank Money in England and Wales, 1920–1938', *Oxford Economic Papers*, no. 5, June 1941, pp. 8–11.

26. *Committee on Finance and Industry*, pp. 156–7.

27. Sayers, *Bank of England*, vol. 2, pp. 556–7; and 'Bank Liquidity in the United Kingdom', *Bank of England Quarterly Bulletin*, vol. 2, 1962, p.

251.

28. *Report of the Committee on the Working of the Monetary System* [Radcliffe Committee], Cmnd. 827 (HMSO, London, 1960), p. 128.

29. *Committee on Finance and Industry, Report*, pp. 36–7; J.F. Ashby, *The Story of the Banks* (Hutchinson & Co., London, 1934), pp. 252–3; and A.J. Brown, 'The Liquidity Preference Schedules of the London Clearing Banks', *Oxford Economic Papers*, no. 1, Oct. 1938, pp. 69–71.

30. R.S Sayers, *Modern Banking* (Oxford University Press, Milford, 1938), p. 213.

31. For further details see Balogh, *Financial Organization*, pp. 60–63; Barnard Ellinger, *The City. The London Financial Markets* (King & Son, London, 1940), pp. 137–40; and D. Spring-Rice, 'London Money Markets since the War', *Bankers' Magazine*, March 1923, pp. 417–31.

32. Truptil, *British Banks*, pp. 99–100.

33. Ibid., p. 238.

34. Ibid., p. 262. See Spring-Rice, 'Money Markets', pp. 428–31, for details of the emerging dominance of Treasury bills during the First World War.

35. Ellinger, *The City*, pp. 139–40.

36. Balogh, *Financial Organization*, p.65.

37. H.G. Johnson, 'Some Implications of Secular Changes in Bank Assets and Liabilities in Great Britain', *Economic Journal*, vol. 61, 1951, p. 546.

38. 'Bank Liquidity', *Bank of England Quarterly Bulletin*, p.252.

39. *Committee on Finance and Industry, Minutes*, vol. 1, Evidence of F. Hyde of the Midland Bank, paras. 869–70, 872–5, pp. 56–7; paras.974–5, p. 63; W.H.N. Goschen of the National Provincial, para. 1905, p. 116; and J. Rae of the Westminster Bank, paras. 2415–7, p. 141.

40. Nevin and Davis, *Clearing Banks*, pp. 148–50.

41. Ibid., pp. 141f. For evidence on the 1930s see Edward Nevin, *The Mechanism of Cheap Money* (University of Wales Press, Cardiff, 1955), pp. 126–42.

42. C.A.E. Goodhart, *The Business of Banking, 1891–1914* (Weidenfeld and Nicolson, London, 1972), p. 140. In practice there was much variation from bank to bank.

43. Balogh, *Financial Organization*, p. 70; Truptil, *British Banks*, p. 100; Nevin and Davis, *Clearing Banks*, p. 159.

44. Balogh, *Financial Organization*, p. 71. Generally see F.W. Paish, 'The Floating Debt, 1914–39, and its effects on the British Banking System', Appendix to Part II of Balogh, ibid, pp. 191–212.

45. Susan Howson, *Domestic Monetary Management in Britain, 1919–1938* (Cambridge University Press, Cambridge, 1975), pp. 86–91. Also see Forrest Capie, Terence C. Mills, Michael J. Thomas and Geoffrey E. Wood, 'Was the War Loan Conversion a Success?' City University Discussion Paper on Monetary History of the UK, no. 5, Feb. 1983 (to be printed in *Applied Economics*, forthcoming).

46. H.G. Johnson, 'Clearing Bank Holdings of Public Debt, 1930–1950', *London and Cambridge Economic Service Bulletin*, vol. 29, 1951, pp. 105–7.

47. Nevin and Davis, *Clearing Banks*, p. 167.

48. Nevin, *Cheap Money*, pp. 134–5. As a large proportion of the National Debt was held by government departments and the Bank of England, the commercial banks held about 45 per cent of the 'marketable portion' (i.e. more easily traded in).

49. Johnson, 'Assets and Liabilities', pp. 547–8.

50. Balogh, *Financial Organization*, p. 74. See also H.C.F. Holgate, 'Loans, Overdrafts and Deposits', *Bankers' Magazine*, Nov. 1938, pp. 739–40.

51. Ellinger, *The City*, pp. 143–4.

52. Leaf, *Banking*, p. 157.

53. *Committee on Finance and Industry, Minutes*, vol. 1, Evidence of F.Hyde of the Midland Bank, para. 877, p. 57; F.C. Goodenough of Barclays, paras. 610–5, p. 40; J.W. Beaumont-Pease of Barclays, paras. 2089–2105, pp. 126–6; J. Rae of the Westminster, paras. 2411–4, 2419–25, pp. 111–2; and the Scottish bankers, G.J. Scott and A.K. Wright,

para. 2763, p. 161.

54. Balogh, *Financial Organization*, p.78.

55. *Committee on Finance and Industry, Minutes*, vol. 1, evidence of London Clearing Banks' and Scottish Banks' representatives, *passim*.

56. Nevin, *Cheap Money*, pp. 250–1.

57. Sayers, *Modern Banking*, pp. 238–45; Ellinger, *The City*, p. 158.

58. H.S. Foxwell, 'The Financing of Industry and Trade', *Economic Journal*, vol. 27, 1917, pp. 502–22; Sir Arthur Clay, *Recovery. The Second Effort* (Bell & Sons, London, 1932), pp. 288–9; and Henry Clay, *The Post-War Unemployment Problem* (Macmillan, London, 1929), pp. 186–9.

59. *Committee on Finance and Industry, Report*, pp. 169, 172–3; Balogh, *Financial Organization*, pp. 74–85, 105; and S. Evelyn Thomas, *British Banks and the Finance of Industry* (King & Son, London, 1931).

60. *Committee on Finance and Industry, Report*, p. vi.

61.. Ibid., pp. 161–74.

62. Ibid., p. 171.

63. Balogh, *Financial Organization*, pp. 300–2. On the Bank of England's approach to industry's problems see Sayers, *Bank of England*, vol. 1, ch. 14.

64. Edwin Green and Michael Moss, *A Business of National Importance. The Royal Mail Shipping Group, 1902–1937* (Methuen, London, 1982), especially ch. 8.

65. A.R. Holmes and Edwin Green, *Midland. 150 Years of Banking Business* (Batsford, London, 1986), p. 185.

66. John R. Hume and Michael S. Moss, *Beardmore: The History of a Scottish Industrial Giant* (Heinemann, London, 1979), ch. 7. Also see J. Foreman-Peck, 'Exit, Voice and Loyalty as Responses to Decline: The Rover Company in the Inter-War Years', *Business History*, vol. 23, 1981, pp. 190–207, for another example of (reluctant) financing by Lloyds Bank.

67. Truptil, *British Banks*, p. 105.

68. The effect on profits is not known with certainty, however, for the banks did not divulge their true profits position. See Balogh, *Financial Organization*, pp. 105–8; and Ellinger, *The City*, pp. 182–90. For a more general consideration see Forrest Capie and Alan Webber, 'Profits and Profitability in British Banking, 1870–1939', City University Discussion Paper on Monetary History of the UK, no. 18, May 1985.

Chapter Nine

# MONETARY POLICY, 1914–1939

At the outbreak of World War I the pound sterling was the dominant international currency and the Bank of England, although still a privately-owned institution, operated what monetary policy there was. At that time the chief aims of the Bank were to preserve the gold convertibility of the pound, promote the international standing of the City of London and protect the soundness of the domestic monetary system. World war, the economic disruption that followed in its wake, the economy's continuing weaknesses throughout the inter-war period and the Great Depression of 1929–32 were to test traditional monetary arrangements and enforce change. In the case of policy, most changes affected the determination and defence of the international exchange value of sterling which was in the process of losing its former pre-eminence as a reserve currency. More generally, the economic pressures of the period called for greater discretion in the use of monetary policy and in the choice of instruments for implementing it. Inevitably the exercise of such discretion on matters of high policy became a political issue. Consequently, the inter-war years witnessed a shift of responsibility away from the Bank towards government. The Bank lost much of its nineteenth-century independence but, of course, the Bank governor continued as the government's main adviser on monetary affairs and the Bank retained its central position in the application of policy.

## THE 1914 BANKING CRISIS

The developing European crisis that immediately preceded Britain's declaration of war (on 4 August 1914) seriously disrupted normal international financial arrangements. Growing anxiety and uncertainty led to a sharp increase in the demand for currency, inducing something akin to a banking crisis in Britain, although there was no run on the banks from the general public. Nor was there a serious drain of gold out of the country. Indeed, the crisis proper was largely confined to the country's financial institutions and lasted for just a week or so in late July and early August. In these critical days, the Bank of England was able to provide effective assistance as lender of last resort, and the government introduced a number of special arrangements which restored confidence and enabled the City to resume at least the semblance of normal business for the duration of the war.

The problems were largely focused on London's international financier role. As a growing number of legal, economic and physical impediments were placed on international remittances the Stock Market found itself unable to liquidate claims on foreigners. Of even wider concern was the position of Britain's acceptance business. By the early twentieth century bills drawn on London's acceptance houses and commercial banks were a common means of financing international transactions, and they were a popular investment for many of the country's financial institutions. Under this system of credits British institutions incurred a contingent liability on bills as the acceptors, but in peacetime these liabilities were never called upon to any great extent because the acceptors' clients would ensure that sufficient funds were available in London before payment was due. Thus, the acceptance houses themselves never needed anything like sufficient resources to meet all contingent liabilities. With war in Europe, however, the acceptors found their international clients unwilling, or unable, to remit funds. The acceptors faced bankruptcy. Moreover, their acceptances were extensively held by British banks, other firms and individuals, and they were now in danger of becoming worthless pieces of paper. The failure of the international remittance system struck at the very heart of British financial liquidity.

The role of the commercial banks in the developing crisis has been widely criticised.[1] As individual businesses they acted rationally to build up their own cash reserves and to deflect demands on them for currency. Collectively, however, this added to the pressure for cash and contributed to a growing feeling of crisis. They did this in the first instance by drawing on their accounts at the Bank of England in order to add to their existing holdings of gold. Their motives are not completely clear. It is assumed that, in essence, they were trying to safeguard themselves against a possible surge in demand for currency from their customers, but it has been suggested also that once they had the extra gold they decided to hold on to it for the few critical days of the crisis in the (forlorn) hope that the Treasury and Bank of England would adopt their proposals for the pooling of all bank reserves. According to R.S. Sayers, if this had happened, kudos would have accrued to those banks able to contribute the most gold to the 'national' pool.[2] If this is a true reflection of motives, it was perversity *par excellence* – witholding gold from the Bank of England one day in order to pay it back the next, albeit ostentatiously with due credit and publicity. In the event the authorities rejected the 'pooling' system, and the banks' action served only to weaken the system's central reserve.

The commercial banks also had a hand in increasing the general pressure for liquidity, for as bills became illiquid and bad debts and bankruptcies threatened, the banks called in loans made to the discount houses and Stock Market. This action precipitated further loss of confidence and, again, heightened the demands on the Bank of England for cash. Finally, the commercial banks contributed to public uncertainty in a more direct manner by restricting their normal practice of paying out gold coins to customers. Instead, they offered Bank of England notes. As the smallest English note had a face value of £5 and was, therefore, inappropriate for many everyday retail purposes, queues for coin began to form at the Bank of England on Saturday 31 July. Press comment was adverse, doing little to ease the mounting anxiety. Again the banks' motives are not clear – their refusal to pay gold may have been a clumsy attempt to discourage hoarding by the public – but the impact of their actions attracted much criticism.

Certainly, the authorities were far from pleased with the response of the banks, although this may have been partly the consequence of personal rivalry between the governor of the Bank of England, Lord Cunliffe, and some of the more successful London clearing bank (LCB) chairmen.[3] The banks' plan for pooling reserves was rejected, with the authorities eventually choosing a course of action which mixed the traditional with the novel. Immediate relief was gained by extending the traditional one-day August Bank Holiday by another three days, during which time urgent consultations were held and decisions taken. The aim was to allay anxieties about the central bank's ability to meet the demand for cash at the same time as providing a means by which bill-holders could cope with the sudden threat to their assets. Bank rate had already been raised in three steps, in all from 3 per cent to 10 per cent, but rate changes were unable to fulfil their peacetime function of pulling in overseas funds. Nevertheless, the new Bank rate did increase the penalty on those borrowing from the Bank. The historically high rate also signalled the severity of the problem. This may have been important to the government which sought to follow precedent closely before taking the next step – namely, the granting of legal indemnity to the Bank if it should need to increase its note issue beyond the constraints of the 1844 Bank Charter Act. As in the crises of the mid-nineteenth century this move did not suspend the gold standard – indeed, restricted gold convertibility was maintained throughout the war – but it did increase the pool of reserves available by allowing the Bank to run down the gold held against its note issue. Direct relief to bill-holders came from a general moratorium on payments, with the Bank 'buying in' the affected bills for the duration of the war. Finally, in order to meet public demand for currency and yet, at the same time, centralise specie for national purposes, the issue of 10s. and £1 Treasury notes was authorised by the Currency and Bank Notes Act. This legislation was passed by Parliament in the one day (6 August) and gave England and Wales low note denominations for the first time in almost a century.

These measures were effective in checking the immediate crisis. Bill holdings were rendered liquid, bankruptcies avoided and confidence restored. As pressure eased, Bank rate was reduced (within a week) to 5 per cent. However, while the immediate liquidity problem was resolved the international acceptance business remained devastated by the effects of war. The bill on London was never to regain its former pre-eminence as a means of international payment.[4]

## IMPACT OF WORLD WAR I

The financial crisis of 1914 was but a short-lived episode of the First World War. Never before had Britain been involved in a conflict of such magnitude and it was to have fundamental consequences for the future course of economic affairs.[5] The conduct of monetary policy was no exception. By the close of the war in 1918 the government controlled or regulated the capital markets, the purchase of foreign imports, the supply of materials and foodstuffs, many retail prices, retained profits and the conscription of labour into the armed forces. It also directly 'managed' the coal mines, the railways and sections of the engineering/armaments industry. Such state activity had been unheard of in peacetime and, inevitably, the scale of resources involved had important financial consequences. Taxes had to be raised and money borrowed, both on an unprecedented scale. As the government's banker, the Bank of England had the responsibility of organising and securing the successful issue of long- and medium-term war bonds, as well as the sale of shorter-term securities such as Treasury bills, which were rapidly established as a 'popular' asset within the portfolios of City institutions. The Bank also made direct loans to the government on its own account and it dealt with the paying out and redemption of the new 10s and £1 Treasury notes.

The impact remained long after the war had finished. For instance, the increase in government borrowing was so great that as late as 1925 the value of government securities still outstanding was equal to one-quarter of total private property, whereas at the start of the war in 1914 it had been merely one-fortieth.[6] This much enlarged National Debt had to be serviced: interest payments made, redemptions arranged and new securities issued when the need arose to replace loans falling due or when government sought to alter the composition of the total. Through these transactions the Bank remained an important influence in capital and money markets during peacetime. Government wartime needs had also nurtured closer ties between the Treasury, as the organ of government economic and financial policy, and the Bank, and at another level, between the authorities and money market institutions.[7] Collaboration in the money markets became a central element in government debt management and was extended into the broad arena of monetary policy. For the Bank of England, the greater association with the state and with the conduct of monetary policy increased its influence within the domestic economy. At the same time greater responsibilities for the National Debt could well constrain its powers of independent action as there was no certainty that Treasury aims would coincide with those of the Bank.

The war also had much wider economic consequences which were to have an important bearing on monetary policy. The conflict had disrupted developments within the international economy and the following decades were to experience a period of instability in international financial arrangements and a general slowdown in the growth of world trade. After the signing of the Armistice in 1918 the immediate need was for demobilisation and economic reconstruction in Europe. The form this took was undoubtedly influenced by the nature of the Peace Settlement itself.[8] The old empires of the defeated nations were broken up, Germany was partitioned and partially occupied and a number of new nation–states were created. Disruption to the pre–war pattern of trade was inevitable.

Financial arrangements were also distorted. Two particular war–related problems were war debts and reparations.[9] By the end of the war the allies were enmeshed in a network of debt, with the USA, Britain and France as the main creditors, and France (in net terms, a debtor), Italy and Belgium as important debtors.[10] In all, inter–allied debt amounted to some $26.5 billion. Britain had sold off overseas assets during the war and had run up debts to the USA, although much larger credits had been extended to other allies. Largely on American insistence, these debts were not written off as part of the war effort but treated essentially as commercial debt. They, therefore, incurred interest charges and needed repaying when due, although some concessions were to be negotiated during the 1920s. Reparations were economic penalties imposed on the defeated nations, especially Germany which in 1921 was deemed to owe $33 billion to the allies, a sum far in excess of the amount she could reasonably be expected to pay. Not surprisingly, the issue of reparations (and war debts to a lesser extent) continued to fester during the 1920s, giving rise to a series of tortuous, and sometimes acrimonious, international attempts to reconcile rival objectives.

Both war debts and reparations created major transfer problems for the countries involved, for they had to find a means of paying in a form (gold, foreign currency, or goods?) acceptable to creditors on top of their 'normal' trading and capital requirements. International capital flows and foreign exchange transactions were directly implicated but so, too, was trade in commodities. In other words, the war had created a major international debt problem which continued to have serious repercussions for the world's financial system up until the Great Depression of 1929–32/3 when the recession obliged most debtor countries to suspend or renege on debt payments.

As the main trading nation, Britain was seriously affected by the changed circumstances caused by war. In particular, the balance of payments and the level of unemployment in the export sectors suffered greatly. During the 1920s British exporters met stiff resistance as income growth in their traditional markets slowed down; as the world generally moved towards greater restrictions on foreign competition through the imposition of tariffs and other controls; as changing technology and tastes shifted demand away from Britain's staple export goods, and as the continuing effects of wartime inflation and an over-valued exchange rate reduced price competitiveness. In real terms the export of goods and services from Britain never exceeded the peak of 1913 – in the twenties as a whole the annual average reached only four-fifths of the immediate pre-war figure, and the world depression of the thirties pushed this down further, to just two-thirds.[11] As a proportion of Gross Domestic Product exports fell from 24 per cent in 1913 to 21 per cent in 1929, down even further to just 15 per cent by 1937.[12] The external account was becoming much less important to the economy, but the expanding sectors providing houses and new consumer goods and services to the domestic market were unable to absorb the unemployed from the depressed export trades. Consequently, throughout the inter-war period unemployment rates remained extremely high in a number of major industries with, for example, unemployment amongst insured workers in coalmining and cotton textiles averaging around 21 per cent between 1924 and 1938, with some 37 per cent unemployed in shipbuilding.[13]

The direct consequences of these external weaknesses on the conduct of Bank of England policy were two-fold: unemployment heightened political sensitivity to the use of high interest rates; and the altered international relations necessitated major readjustment in the operation of the gold standard.

## RETURN TO GOLD, 1925

The partial suspension of the gold standard during the First World War meant that as victory approached, some thought had to be given to the timing and form of a return to full exchange convertibility for the pound.[14] A committee under the chairmanship of the recent Bank of England Governor, Lord Cunliffe, was set up in 1918. Its Reports of 1918 and 1919 were unambiguous in their recommendations: they sought a speedy return to gold convertibility at pre-war parity.[15] However, the successful maintenance of exchange convertibility required not only that the authorities should have a gold reserve adequate to meet the likely demands on it, but also an effective means of replenishing that reserve should it come under pressure. In pre-war years the Bank of England had relied heavily on Bank rate changes to influence short-term demands on the reserve, but in 1918 Bank rate would have been ineffective because of the great wartime expansion in money balances. At the close of the war both the banks and public were holding cash and near-cash assets in excess of normal peacetime requirements. Thus, financial institutions were keen to lend and the rate charged by the Bank on its loans would have had only minimal impact on market rates; Bank rate would be effective only if the money market had to go to the Bank to replenish its own reserves but, with such high cash holdings at the close of the war, this was unnecessary.

In these circumstances the immediate re-establishment of pre-war conditions of control was probably impossible. At the very least, it would have required a severe monetary deflation. This, Lloyd George's government was not prepared to contemplate.[16] Instead, it opted for the greater flexibility of a 'floating' exchange rate, a flexibility considered essential to easing the mammoth task of demobilising the armed forces and restructuring industrial production away from war to peacetime uses. Hence, in March 1919 gold standard convertibility was suspended and the international value of sterling was left largely to the foreign exchange markets.

It was to be another six years (in the budget speech of April 1925) before the then Chancellor of the Exchequer, Winston Churchill, announced the return to an international gold standard at the pre-war parity of £1:$4.86.[17] This decision proved highly controversial, with controversy revolving around two main issues: over whether or not the decision was correct at the time; and over the subsequent economic impact of that decision.

The Bank of England had direct responsibility for operating the gold standard and it was also the government's chief source of advice on monetary affairs. The Bank's position therefore has been central to the whole debate on the gold standard. Not unreasonably the Bank has been portrayed as the bastion of orthodox views on exchange rate matters. Its governors and ex-governors – notably Cunliffe, Cockayne and Norman – argued consistently that the country's best hope of recovering pre-war prosperity lay in a return to the pre-war gold standard. According to the Bank's most recent historian, R.S. Sayers, this policy:

> was inspired throughout by the desire to establish and maintain an international monetary system that would facilitate the revival of international trade and international investment. It was through these that the Bank saw its major chance of promoting economic health and prosperity at home: sceptical of its powers to make much impact directly on internal economic conditions, the Bank shared in the general view that the roots of trouble were in the great export trades, and held that it could and should help these by

> promoting world conditions propitious for their revival... the men of 1919 believed that the best monetary system was that of 1913: a world gold standard centred on London, with the Bank of England controlling the system by manipulation of Bank rate and acting as the watchdog of financial practice.[18]

This opinion was shared by the Treasury and it is not surprising, therefore, that policy was 'almost continuously deflationary from 1920 onwards'[19] as anxieties over demobilisation disappeared and the authorities began to prepare for the eventual return to gold.

The general aim in returning to gold, then, was a positive one: the re–establishment of a once–stable system of international finance in which British exports had prospered, in which sterling had operated as the world's major reserve currency and the City of London had acted as entrepôt for a worldwide system of payments. It was felt that the restoration of gold convertibility for such an important currency as sterling would in itself contribute to general stability, boost confidence and encourage commerce. In such circumstances a trading nation like the UK could not fail to benefit and move some way towards obtaining the overall objectives implicit in gold standard policy – namely, full employment, a surplus on the current account of the balance of payments and the maintenance of free trade. From a national standpoint, the return of the pre–war system of exchange was seen as a means of restoring the prestige of the City as a leading financial centre. Another important motive stemmed from the fear of inflation. Policy–makers generally welcomed the degree of domestic monetary discipline associated with the operation of a convertible currency and fixed exchange rate. They saw it as a means of preventing a return of the rapid price rises of the war and immediate post–war years (not only in the UK but throughout Europe) because under the rigours of convertibility the monetary authorities' freedom of action (in particular, their ability to maintain an expansionary monetary policy) would be closely prescribed. In fact, the re-establishment of an exchange rate such as the gold standard regime, which relied heavily on legislation and implicit 'rules' rather than discretionary action by the authorities, conformed to the prevailing orthodoxy of liberalism and *laissez-faire* in economic affairs.

In the event, inflation was avoided, but not one of the authorities' other main objectives was achieved: unemployment remained at historically high rates; exports continued their long-term decline; on trend, Britain's current account was weaker; in 1931 free trade was jettisoned and import tariffs adopted; and the severity of the Great Depression was eventually to force most nations, including the UK, to alter their exchange rates and abandon the gold standard itself.

Not surprisingly the 1925 decision has drawn flak from a wide range of critics. At the time the most influential opposition came from the leading economist, J.M. Keynes, but his was very much a minority view amongst contemporaries.[20] On the basis of a comparison of price changes in the UK and the USA since before the war, Keynes argued that the pre-war parity of £1:$4.86 over-valued sterling by about 10 per cent and this at a time when export sales were already suffering.[21] Thus, British competitiveness would be damaged and as domestic wage costs were unlikely to fall to any great extent, the balance of payments would be weakened and the unemployment problem aggravated.

At the time the authorities accepted that £1:$4.86 might overvalue the currency but they believed any necessary adjustment to British prices and costs would be slight and may well be rendered unnecessary by inflation overseas, especially in America. To the Bank and Treasury, the gains far outweighed any possible costs. Indeed, as sterling had been on the same exchange rate with gold since 1821 (and with the gold dollar since 1834) the authorities gave no serious consideration to changing the parity – it was the war and the immediate post-war years which were seen as wholly exceptional. The decision to return to gold was to be a return to normalcy; the actual rate chosen was not an important policy issue.

Critics argue that this was short-sightedness verging on irresponsibility, for sterling should have been devalued in recognition of the country's weaker trading position. The suspension of the gold standard had given the authorities an opportunity to consider the most appropriate exchange rate for the country's needs but they failed to rise to the occasion and the opportunity was lost. Instead, emotional and jingoistic feelings (for keeping the pound as a leading international currency) seriously clouded judgement on what should have been a largely technical issue. Some commentators believe the authorities' myopia was understandable given the extremely long period since the last change in the exchange rate, but even these accept that overvaluation subsequently damaged the economy. In other words, while the motives of the Bank and Treasury may have been sound, in the event the economic outcome of the 1925 decision was adverse.[22]

The decision to return to gold has faced a much broader onslaught, however. Developing a theme propagated by Keynes at the time, Sidney Pollard presents the issue as a conflict between the financial interests of the City of London and the needs of industry and commerce.[23] He sees the 1925 decision as a victory for the City. This argument stresses the fact that on exchange rate matters the government relied heavily on Bank of England advice and that the Bank, in turn, reflected City prejudices. The businesses of most London financial institutions, and most directors of the Bank of England, were closely tied to the international economy and, not unnaturally, these institutions gave priority to re-establishing world prosperity. A stable and 'fully-valued' pound would not only help generally, but was an essential step in the rehabilitation of London as an international financial centre. The City's profits were closely dependent on sterling's international role and devaluation could undermine confidence and threaten this role. It is not surprising, therefore, that the City sought a return to pre-war conditions at the old exchange rate.

Pollard accepts that in advising government the directors of the Bank 'would not consciously favour their own pockets at the expense of the nation, but [that] it was only human to assume that they would tend to believe that those policies were in the national interest which also happened to be in their own.'[24] For him, the political effectiveness of such a narrow interest group was to be disastrous for the rest of the economy. At the time Keynes, too, emphasised the broad consequences of the decision – it placed the burden of adjustment to loss of international competitiveness upon the domestic economy and necessitated a general fall in money wages and other costs. Thus, just a few months after the return, the question of wage cuts was to be the central issue in a protracted and bitter coal dispute which produced the only General Strike in British history. The over-valuation of sterling and the government's general calls for wage cuts as part of the necessary adjustment to the world situation were integral elements in the conflict. Even if devaluation could not have solved the coal industry's problem of a permanently contracted export market, it may have prolonged the adjustment period available to the industry and, thus, eased the social and political consequences. It was this failure of policy makers to take into account such broader consequences (particularly the impact on existing high rates of unemployment) that has drawn the strongest venom from critics.

The question of the impact on the economy has in itself been a bone of contention. An important general criticism is that the 1925 decision restricted policy options. The re-establishment of a fixed exchange rate with gold convertibility meant that other policies had to be subordinated to the needs of sterling. Critically, once the decision had been taken, an expansion within the domestic economy to reduce unemployment rates could not be countenanced if there was any danger that this might weaken the balance of payments and endanger the reserves. In particular, the overvalued exchange rate and weakened external account meant that the Bank had to maintain relatively high interest rates in order to attract inflows of overseas capital and prevent reserve losses. At this time interest rate policy still performed a largely external role, despite evidence of a growing political sensitivity to the implications for domestic investment and unemployment. In consequence, domestic investors faced 'dear money', with short-term bill rates generally above 4 per cent per annum despite a general fall in the price level (see Figure 9.2 below). Domestic monetary growth also slowed down in the late twenties and this may have depressed growth in home demand. It is for these reasons that such economists as H.G. Johnson, M. Friedman and A.J. Schwartz have emphasised the damaging effects of the monetary deflation associated with the return to gold.[25]

Similar constraints existed for *any* possible reflationary budgetary policy. Contemporary fiscal orthodoxy was to maintain tight control over government expenditure, but the need to defend the exchange rate also imposed a general constraint on government budgets. The Great Depression of 1929–32 highlighted the nature of the problem. As severe recession cut tax revenues and increased state expenditure on unemployment pay, the government's growing budget deficit quickly brought into focus the conflicts inherent in policies aimed at maintaining the fixed exchange rate and any policies that may have sought to increase (or just maintain) current levels of government expenditure. In the event, external stability was once again given preference and government expenditure suffered a sharp cut-back in 1931 (see below).

In general, therefore, between 1925 and 1931 – and, indeed, in the years before 1925 when preparations were being made for the return to gold – the country's exchange rate policy operated as a major brake on other policy options available to government. More directly, the overvalued currency adversely affected the level of exports and imports, with subsequent deflationary effects on income growth and employment opportunities. D.E. Moggridge has estimated that a ten per cent devaluation in 1925 could have improved the current account by some £70 million within three years; and that if the authorities had chosen to use this to reduce unemployment the rate could have fallen from 8.2 per cent to 4.7 per cent.[26] On less generous assumptions, N.H. Dimsdale has suggested that a ten per cent devaluation may have reduced unemployment from 8.2 per cent to 5.8 per cent after four to five years.[27] In other words, he suggests a more modest improvement than Moggridge but one still in a favourable direction. In fact, the thrust of Dimsdale's calculations represents what has come to be a fair degree of common ground in the debate over the return to gold. It is now generally accepted that while over-valuation worsened the plight of the export sectors and of the unemployed, devaluation in itself would not have eradicated the more fundamental problems facing the economy.[28] Moreover, any favourable effects of devaluation would have been offset to the extent that overseas nations retaliated (a reasonable expectation in the 1920s) through devaluations of their own currencies or through greater trade restrictions.

In summary, a more realistic valuation of sterling would have had favourable effects on income and employment, but the long-term changes that were taking place in world markets would still have necessitated painful readjustment within the British economy.

## THE 1931 CRISIS AND DEVALUATION

On 19 September 1931, Britain suspended the gold standard. In other words, the authorities were no longer prepared to guarantee convertibility of paper pounds to gold, nor guarantee that the pound's value remained fixed in terms of other major currencies. So the position remained until after the Second World War. This action was a crisis measure, taken after four months of mounting pressure for international liquidity and of deteriorating confidence in the ability of the Bank of England to maintain the official exchange rate. In the later stages of the crisis, as fears of British devaluation became widespread, those with the ability to do so sold their sterling assets in exchange for 'safe' currencies such as dollars and francs, or for gold itself. The pressure on the Bank's reserves became intense and withdrawals of cash further fuelled anxieties. This speculative run on sterling, thus, became a self-fulfilling prophesy: the more widespread the fear of devaluation, the greater the Bank's reserve losses and this, in turn, increased the likelihood of devaluation. The proximate cause of Britain's abandonment of gold was, therefore, the shortage of liquid reserves available to the Bank relative to the extraordinary demands placed on it in the summer and early autumn of 1931.[29]

Suspension of gold payments, then, was not a planned policy but quite the reverse, with the Bank and Treasury being forced to take the ultimate step only after strenuous efforts to avoid it. An important part of the defence of sterling had been the raising of international loans. The first of these loans (raised at the end of July 1931) was a product of the co-operation between central bankers which had been developing in the 1920s.[30] The Federal Reserve Bank of New York and the Bank of France agreed to provide some £100 millions of short-term credits to the Bank of England for the defence of sterling, a fair indication of the extent of the Bank's demise as the world's lender of last resort. A second loan (of £80 millions) was negotiated when the pound had fallen into much deeper crisis, at the end of August, and, again, it was in the form of credits on New York and Paris. This time, however, the Labour administration's financial advisers and creditors insisted on controversial cuts in government expenditure as a precondition to the successful floating of the loan. The proposed cuts provoked a political crisis for the government. Parliament, nevertheless, agreed to them. The commitment to gold ran very deep indeed – given their loyalty to the exchange rate, the authorities left themselves with little option than to deflate (tariffs were also rejected) and this at a time when unemployment was soaring.

However, defence of the pound had not involved the most obvious of the Bank's traditional responses. There was no determined effort to raise Bank rate in an attempt to avert the drain on the reserves. Why was this? Before the onset of the crisis proper the Bank had been acutely aware of the implications for the domestic economy of any Bank rate change.[31] Official unemployment rates were already high, at about ten per cent throughout most of the 1920s, but as the world plunged into the Great Depression in 1929 unemployment rose sharply to even more depressing levels – peaking at 23 per cent in August 1932. There was an urgent need to encourage enterprise and investment at home. In such circumstances a policy aimed at maintaining or increasing interest rates could be portrayed as insensitive in the extreme. Moreover, Treasury pressure was for keeping market rates down in order to ease the burden of interest payments on the National Debt.

The Bank, therefore, sought to encourage a reduction in rates, and as late as 14 May 1931 Bank rate was cut, from 3 per cent to 2.5 per cent. During the currency crisis itself, however, there was a modest response in the opposite direction with Bank rate being raised on two occasions, to 3.5 per cent on 23 July and to 4.5 per cent one week later. Given the severity of the crisis these moves cannot be portrayed as an active Bank rate policy and it has been suggested that domestic considerations continued to inhibit Bank action, thus weakening its defence of the pound.[32] However, in the circumstances of 1931 it seems most unlikely that a higher rate of interest in London would have made any significant difference. When financiers are fearing a capital loss on their assets through currency devaluation, the rate of return they can earn on those assets becomes largely irrelevant. Confidence is much more important and if there had been a sharp rise in Bank rate this may well have added to anxieties by signalling the desperate plight of the pound. In fact, this seems to have been the view of the French and Americans who forwarded the short-term credits to London.[33] These overseas financial interests also wanted to avoid further instability being caused by 'foot-loose' capital flowing from one financial centre to another in response to competitive changes in interest rates. In the trying circumstances of the crisis the Bank of England itself was more inclined to rely on higher rates but, in the event, the Bank bowed to overseas opinion.

In all other respects the authorities were determined to defend the exchange rate for as long as possible. Why, then, did their policy fail, especially as Britain had successfully maintained the gold standard for almost a century up until 1914? Why were the demands on London in 1931 so great as to deplete the reserves to this unprecedented extent? The answer lies both in the changed nature of Britain's international position and in the character of the demands for international liquidity.

C.P. Kindleberger has claimed that a major weakness was the absence of one predominant country to provide economic leadership, of one dominant financial centre to offer direction to the course of events.[34] The international monetary system of the 1920s was served by multiple financial centres, no single one of which prevailed. In the pre-1914 world, the London money and capital markets had dominated international transactions but during the war the USA emerged as a major creditor nation and New York began to play an increasing role in financing world trade and investment. Also, by the late 1920s French currency stabilisation and strong surpluses on the current account of the balance of payments had enhanced the status of Parisian financial institutions and the franc. An important consequence for the general stability of the international financial system was that the distribution of the world's gold reserves was skewed towards the USA and France. One estimate suggests that between 1925 and 1929 the US imported some $306 million of gold and – of even more significance for the Bank's ability to accumulate gold – that the Bank of France's gold holdings soared by almost $1 billion in the two and a half years to December 1930.[35] London's hegemony had been lost as changes in the means of financing trade led to a decline in the use of bills on London and as weaknesses in the balance of payments reduced the amount available for overseas investment. The fact of London's relative decline is beyond doubt. On the other hand, it is far from obvious why the existence of more than one international financial centre would in itself be destabilising, the more so as co-operation among monetary authorities seems to have been much greater in the 1920s than before the First World War. The existence of a multi-centre system was a weakness only in the sense that it provided speculators with alternative locations for their investments should confidence be lost in one of those centres. But the main issue must be concerned with why there was a loss of confidence in the first place.

Another suggested reason for the pound's greater vulnerability to speculative runs in the 1920s compared with the pre-1914 era, is the claim that in the later period the economy had developed a net debtor position on its short-term capital account with the rest of the world. The Macmillan Report drew attention to the fact that foreigners had lent more in the form of deposits and short-term loans to banks, discount houses, the Stock Market and other financial institutions and to local and central government than British residents' short term credits to the rest of the world.[36] The scale of Britain's accumulated overseas investments meant that, overall, the country was still a net creditor, but most of these British investments were long-term and could not be quickly encashed. For instance, the Macmillan Committee estimated that in 1931 there were at least £407 million of sterling bills and deposits in the hands of foreigners, whereas the UK's short-term assets amounted to just some £153 million plus a similar sum held in the Bank's gold reserve. The country's vulnerability seemed to lie in the fact that if there were a general loss of confidence – with increased demand for gold and overseas currencies – the claims on Britain could be liquidated more quickly than British claims on foreigners. In such circumstances the reserves – and, thus, the ability of the Bank of England to maintain convertibility – could disappear despite the overall surplus on capital account.

However, estimates by A.I. Bloomfield and P.H. Lindert suggest that a debtor position on short-term capital account was no new experience for the UK, nor was the ratio of reserves to liabilities unusually low in the early 1930s. The position had not been very different before 1914, yet then there had been no threat to sterling.[37] Neither the vulnerability of the short-term capital account nor the size of the Bank's reserves was a fundamental cause of the 1931 crisis. Nevertheless, in the changed circumstances of the early 1930s both became important. Once confidence began to crumble, the knowledge of Britain's short-term liabilities added to anxieties over the exchange rate. Indeed, publication of the Macmillan Report in July 1931, in itself, increased awareness of the precarious reserve-to-liabilities ratio.

Once again, the critical element was the loss of confidence and the deeper cause of the 1931 sterling crisis revolves around the reasons for this. It was the loss of confidence which created conditions in which the existence of rival financial centres and awareness of London's short-term debts became important.

The basic cause was the continuing Great Depression, an economic recession which had embraced the world's industrial nations since 1929 and which amounted to one of the worst slumps ever suffered by the international economy. The cumulative collapse and stagnation of the world's leading economies led to a universal contraction of income, severe price deflation, a fall in profits, a rise in bankruptcies and a sharp jump in unemployment. In international payments, the recession impacted unevenly and increased disparities between deficit and surplus countries. Deficit countries borrowed more, while debtor and creditor nations alike resorted increasingly to trade restrictions, currency depreciation and/or devaluation. It was against this backcloth of recession and instability that sterling's position came under close scrutiny in the summer of 1931, a backcloth against which a breakdown in confidence was a real possibility.

Britain's already depressed export and international service sectors felt the full impact of the world recession. In real terms, exports fell by one-third between 1929 and 1932. The volume of imports fell by less than one-tenth, however, and despite a sharp fall in the price of imported foodstuffs and raw materials, the current account of the balance of payments showed a deficit of £103 million for 1931.[38] This deterioration in Britain's international trading position in itself increased pressure on the exchange rate and rekindled fears that the pound was overvalued at $4.86. London's financier status was closely tied to the country's overall economic performance; it was not merely a narrow question of financial technicalities.[39]

Britain was not the only one to suffer a current account deficit. Countries such as Argentina, Malaya and Australia, whose export earnings and/or national incomes depended heavily on primary produce, were also experiencing severe difficulties.[40] Prices of foodstuffs and raw materials had begun a long decline from as early as the mid-1920s. The 1929 recession in manufacturing countries greatly worsened the plight of primary producers, blighting prospects for domestic growth and threatening exchange rates and debt repayments. Many of these countries were to seek protection in import restrictions, currency devaluations and, ultimately, in moratoria on payments of international debts. More conventional methods were also used as they depleted their international currency reserves and sought fresh loans from overseas. It was here that the problems of the agricultural producers added directly to the drain on London, for many of them were Empire countries holding their reserves in London and enjoying access to British capital markets.[41] Yet of still more importance to the sterling crisis proper was the general impact on international confidence. The Great Depression was fertile ground for sowing doubts and raising anxieties.

It was in such circumstances that there were serious failures amongst European banks in the summer (May–July) of 1931: first in Austria and, then, in Germany. In both cases loss of overseas confidence was critical and, as Kindleberger and others emphasise, the absence of an effective international lender of last resort to supply these banking systems with reserves, was a major deficiency in existing financial arrangements. The two major surplus countries, France and the USA, failed to recycle international reserve assets to an adequate extent. The continental bank failures in themselves reduced British reserves by locking up financial claims on Vienna and Berlin. In particular, continental bills drawn on London acceptors, and held extensively by British financial institutions, became illiquid. It was in such an atmosphere of international crisis that devaluation of sterling could be seriously contemplated.

The economic recession was responsible for one other major element in the loss of confidence in London: the government's growing budget deficit. Recession reduced government tax revenues and sharply increased the cost of unemployment benefits as the numbers out of work rose to over 20 per cent of insured workers (or about 16 per cent of the labour force) in 1931. A minority Labour government had been in power since 1929 and the government's left-wing political complexion in itself was unlikely to have inspired confidence amongst international financiers and speculators. More specifically, these financiers doubted that a socialist government would impose the stringent cuts in state expenditure demanded by orthodox opinion in order to balance the budget. The issue was brought starkly before the public in the midst of the run on the pound in the first week of August, when the Report of the May Committee was published. This Treasury Committee had been set up by the Chancellor of the Exchequer to find means of cutting government spending. In the event the Report represented the most orthodox of views on fiscal policy by portraying the government's deficit in the worst possible light and by calling for severe cuts.[42] American and French creditors were also pressing for government economies before providing further credits for the defence of the pound.

The Prime Minister, Ramsay Macdonald, was unable to carry his party with him in implementing the cuts, for the bulk of the Labour Party refused to back the proposed reduction in unemployment pay. Political crisis was added to economic crisis. However, the political situation seemed resolved when Macdonald and a few other Labour leaders joined with the Conservatives and some Liberals to have the retrenchment measures approved by Parliament. Swingeing cuts were implemented, including a 10 per cent reduction in unemployment benefit and state employees' salaries.

However, despite this display of political commitment to financial orthodoxy, and the speedy election of a national government which avowed traditional budgetary measures, sterling's basic problems remained. Table 9.1 reproduces some estimates made by R.S. Sayers and A.K. Cairncross and B. Eichengreen for the reserve position during the last few weeks of the crisis. Withdrawals continued throughout September, with constant pressure on the pound. On reports of naval ratings protesting about their proposed pay cut, the run on the Bank's reserves became intense, with almost £18 million withdrawn during the one day, 18 September. No more options were left, the struggle for the pound was over and the gold standard was suspended on 19 September 1931.

## MONETARY POLICY IN THE 1930s

### *Cheap Money and Managed Exchange Rates*

The 1931 sterling crisis proved to be a 'blessing in disguise'. There was no internal collapse of the banking system and confidence at home was not as badly shaken as in many other countries. Moreover, the abandonment of the gold standard removed an important element of rigidity in the conduct of monetary policy and it increased the options available to the authorities. By imposing a fixed exchange rate

Table 9.1 : The Reserves during the Crisis of 1931

a) The Bank of England's Gold and Foreign Exchange in August and September 1931

| Reserves | £ millions |
|---|---|
| 26 August 1931 | 150 (+ £80 m. of agreed credits) |
| 2 September | 219 |
| 9 September | 204 |
| 16 September | 148 |

*Source:*

R.S. Sayers, *The Bank of England, 1891-1944* (3 vols., Cambridge University Press, 1976), vol. 2, p. 401.

b) Withdrawals from the Reserve during September 1931

| Date | £ millions | Date | £ millions |
|---|---|---|---|
| 1 Sept. | -0.8 | 10 Sept. | -3.4 |
| 2 Sept. | -2.0 | 11 Sept. | -3.3 |
| 3 Sept. | -2.0 | 12 Sept. | -1.8 |
| 4 Sept. | -3.7 | 14 Sept. | -3.3 |
| 5 Sept. | -1.9 | 15 Sept. | -2.8 |
| 7 Sept. | -3.1 | 16 Sept. | -3.9 |
| 8 Sept. | -1.5 | 17 Sept. | -6.2 |
| 9 Sept. | -1.8 | 18 Sept. | -17.8 |
| | | 19 Sept. | -10.5 |

*Source:*

Alec Cairncross and Barry Eichengreen, *Sterling in Decline. The Devaluations of 1931, 1949 and 1967* (Basil Blackwell, Oxford, 1983), p. 68.

in 1925 the actions of the central bank within the domestic economy had been seriously constrained by external conditions. Under the gold standard, movements on the foreign exchanges or in the gold reserve necessitated preventive action which may or may not have been compatible with domestic policy objectives. In theory, the gold standard was a non–discretionary system of monetary management, the central bank's role being to maintain currency convertibility in as technically efficient a manner as possible by applying clearly recognised rules (e.g. by raising interest rates when gold was lost). In practice, the Bank of England had been no automaton and the degree of discretion required – the number of policy decisions called for – had irrevocably increased under the pressures of the Great War and of the heavy unemployment of the 1920s. However, it was not until 1931 that the options were dramatically increased.

The suspension of the gold standard shifted the Bank's basic terms of reference. Decisions were now needed on a whole array of monetary matters. Should an early return to the gold standard be sought or should some other exchange rate regime be adopted? In future should the exchange rate be fixed or variable? Now that interest rates were no longer as dependent on external conditions, should the Bank leave market forces to determine rates in Britain, or should it seek to influence them? If so, in what direction and to what end? Similarly, now that the direct bond between the money supply and foreign exchange markets had been broken, should the authorities try to control monetary growth and, if so, to what purpose? Inevitably, the exercise of greater discretion on such matters of policy led to the greater involvement of government in monetary affairs and a corresponding decline in the Bank's independence. Through the 1930s the Treasury and Bank co–operated more closely than before. In 1934, for instance, the Chancellor of the Exchequer, Neville Chamberlain, emphasised that, 'now we are not on the Gold Standard, of course, the relationship between the Treasury and the Bank of England has to be necessarily closer than ever.'[43] Similarly, in 1936, the Bank's Governor, Montagu Norman, recognised the need for an effective partnership with government, but one in which the Bank was very much the junior:

> I assure the Ministers that if they will make known through the appropriate channels what they wish to do in the furtherance of their policies they will at all times find us willing with good will and loyalty to do what they direct, as though we were under legal compulsion.[44]

While still nominally independent, the Bank was becoming an organ of state machinery. The Second World War was to demand even greater co-operation and the Bank's position as the nation's central bank was to be formalised in 1946 when it was taken into public ownership under the Bank of England Act.

Thus, policy in the 1930s was more complex. A series of monetary measures was implemented at the outset.[45] Not only was gold convertibility suspended but it was decided to allow the value of the pound to depreciate on foreign exchange markets in an attempt to promote export sales and stimulate the economy. The relative rise in the sterling price of imports would also have encouraged a switch by consumers towards domestically-produced goods. Many other nations devalued or depreciated their currencies at the same time but others, including the USA and France, did not do so until some years later (in 1933 and 1936 respectively). Figure 9.1 plots John Redmond's trade-weighted indices of the value of the pound against the dollar, franc and a 'basket' of world currencies.[46] For the composite index the initial depreciation was in the region of some 15 per cent but from 1933 there was a steady erosion of this competitive advantage as the value of sterling rose and/or as other currencies were devalued. Other measures of British international competitiveness differ as regards timing but generally indicate early gains being gradually whittled away.[47] In the 1930s as a whole the rate of decline in Britain's share of world

Figure 9.1: Indices of Sterling Rates of Exchange, 1931-8 (1929/30 = 100)

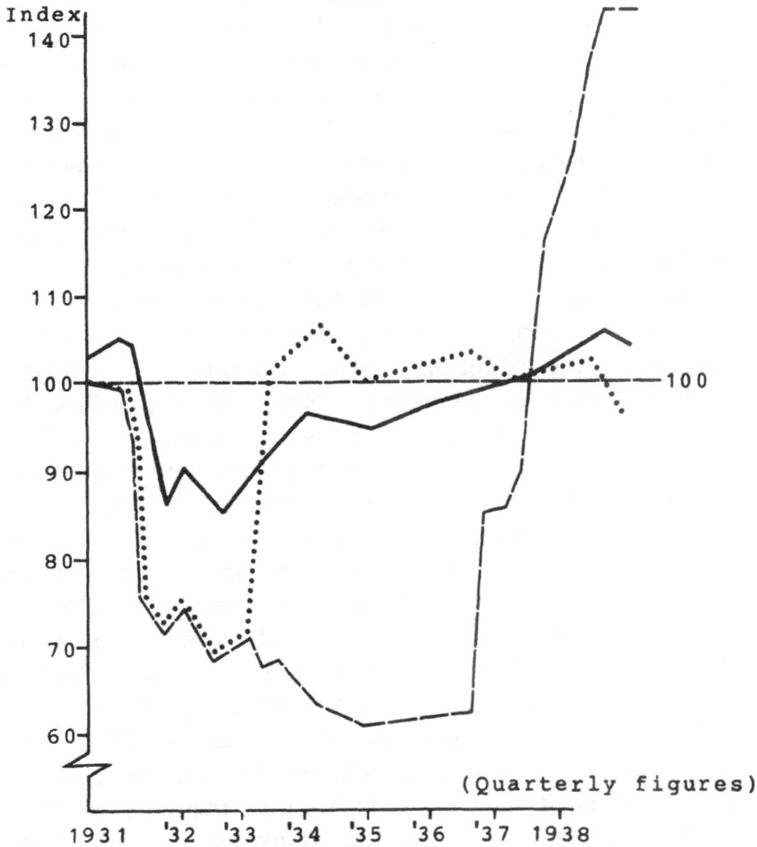


——— Composite index of the effective exchange rate of the £ against 'basket' of world currencies.

........ Pound: US dollar index.

——— Pound: Franc index.

Note: When index falls it represents a depreciation of the pound.

Source: John Redmond, 'An Indicator of the Effective Exchange Rate of the Pound in the Nineteen-Thirties', *Economic History Review*, 2nd. ser., vol. 33, 1980, pp. 83-91

trade slowed down, but it still fell; and whereas the volume of exports recovered from the abysmal levels of 1932, in 1937 it was still one-fifth lower than in 1929. Thus, while depreciation may have prevented the export problem from becoming even worse, it did not lead to an export-led recovery. Balance of payments pressures were eased by a fall in imports but it is difficult to disentangle the effects of currency depreciation from the impact of the imposition of tariffs from 1931 or from the consequences of the general world recession and subsequent recovery.

Apart from the early decision to depreciate the currency, the Treasury also instigated a period of exchange rate management. Some of the inflexibilities of a fixed exchange rate were avoided, with the exchange market value of the pound being determined by what has come to be known as a 'dirty float'. That is, demand and supply in foreign exchange markets were allowed to determine the pound's exchange value subject to various degrees of direct and indirect intervention by the authorities. The most direct intervention was exercised by the Exchange Equalisation Account (E.E.A.) which was set up in 1932 with initial resources of just under £170 million with which to buy and sell on foreign exchange and gold markets.[48] The E.E.A. was formally under the control of the Treasury, but Bank of England officials were in charge of day-to-day operations and ministers relied heavily on Bank advice. The initial objective of the Account's intervention was to keep down the exchange rate, but later, when this proved impossible, the aim was to reduce the amplitude of fluctuations without seriously influencing long-term trends in sterling's value – a policy of 'leaning into the wind'. The hope was that in this way uncertainty would be reduced, exports would be encouraged and the domestic economy would be given some protection from the destabilising effects of short-term capital flows. After 1931 the Treasury also tightened controls on the export of investment capital, whereby the Stock Market was effectively prevented from issuing foreign securities and the supply of funds to Empire countries was subject to official approval. Within the context of these fairly narrow official aims, both exchange rate policy and capital export controls seem to have been effective during the 1930s. After the dollar devaluation, sterling's international value remained relatively stable. However, muted export sales and recurrent deficits on the balance of payments meant that serious problems remained on Britain's external account.

Domestically, the main plank of government policy was that of 'cheap money' – a policy which was to be followed for some two decades after the 1931 crisis. It was explicitly an interest rate policy whereby the authorities tried to keep rates at historically low levels mainly in order to stimulate general economic recovery by cheapening borrowing and encouraging investment.[49] However, more than one motive was involved and a number of ancilliary objectives were present at different times. Thus, Edward Nevin suggests that in 1931/2 the authorities were keen that British rates should fall in order to prevent an inflow of overseas capital which might have increased the value of the pound (and, thus, counteracted exchange rate policy) and, perhaps, have added to London's vulnerability to future speculative outflows.[50] It was critical that a recurrence of the capital flight of 1931 be avoided, and a low rate of return in London seemed a sure way to discourage the accumulation of 'hot money' balances.

A relatively minor, though politically popular, argument in favour of lower interest rates was that they would redistribute income from money lenders to borrowers. Of course, the government itself was a major borrower and lower interest rates would also reduce the amount taxpayers would have to pay. In fact, given contemporary concern for keeping government expenditure within strict bounds, a reduction in interest payments on the National Debt offered a relatively painless means of achieving budget economies. By 1932 such motives were to the fore and the government took full advantage of the dip in market interest rates early in that year by successfully carrying through the biggest conversion exercise in the history of the National Debt. The 5% War Loan, 1929–47, which constituted about 40 per cent of British government securities quoted on the London Stock Exchange, was repaid within six months, with over 92 per cent of debt holders taking 3.5 per cent War Loans in exchange.[51] The new loan was repayable at the government's option some time after 1951. In other words, the government had both reduced the interest rate payable on a large part of its debt – from 5 per cent to 3.5 per cent – and had postponed the repayment date.

Until this conversion had been effected, the sheer size of the 5 per cent loan had made a general reduction in long-term rates less likely, but from 1932 the way was open for a general fall in rates. At the short end of the market Bank rate was reduced in several steps from 6 per cent to 2 per cent, by June 1932, and it remained at this level for almost all the time until 1951. As Figure 9.2 shows, these moves by the authorities were wholly consistent with the experience of market rates which also fell to historically low levels. Long-term interest rates, as represented by the yield on Consols, fell from 4 per cent at the end of 1931 to under 3 per cent by the close of 1934; and the short, three-months' bill rate was down from 5.7 per cent (November 1931) to 0.6 per cent (August 1932). The 1930s became the decade of 'cheap money'. This is even true when account is taken of the fact that general prices were falling until 1934/5. As Table 9.2 shows the fall was not so great as to prevent real interest rates (adjusted for prices) also falling a long way from the rates that had prevailed in the 1920s. Compared to recent experience, money and credit were indeed 'cheap' from 1932 and interest rates remained low even after the revival in prices in the second half of the decade.

### *The Effects of Cheap Money*

Coincidental with the inauguration of cheap money, Britain's depression stopped getting worse and from 1932/3 there began a fairly strong economic recovery which lasted until 1937. Serious problems remained,

Figure 9.2: Rates of Interest, 1920-39 (annual average)

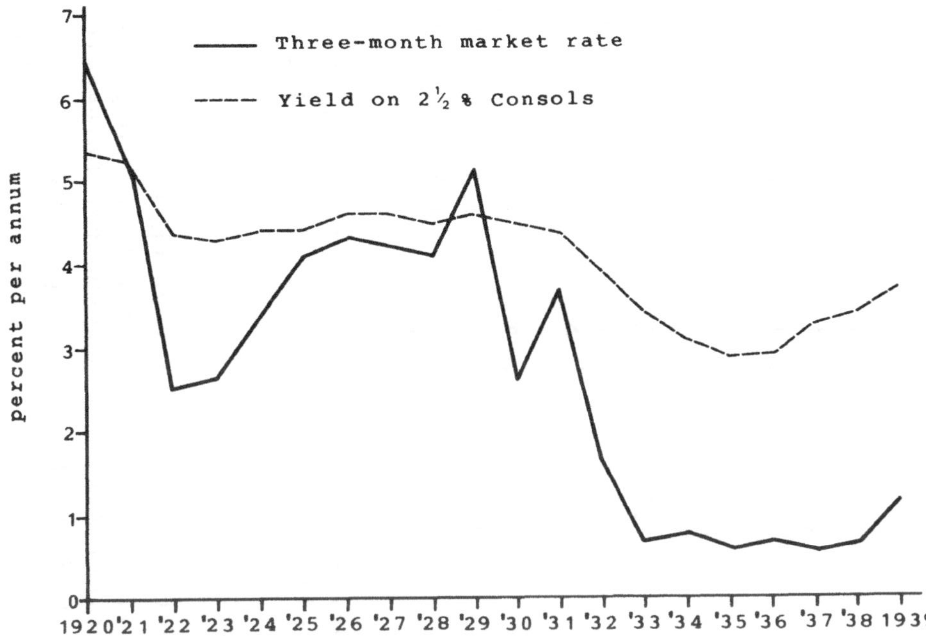


Source: Forrest Capie and Michael Collins, *The Inter-war British Economy: a Statistical Abstract* (Manchester University Press, Manchester, 1983), pp.104, 106.

Table 9.2 : Nominal and Real Interest Rates, annual averages, 1920-39 (per cent per annum)

| | Three Month Market Rate | | Yield on 2.5% Consols | |
|---|---|---|---|---|
| | Nominal Rate | Real Rate | Nominal Rate | Real Rate |
| 1920 | 6.4 | 4.1 | 5.3 | 3.5 |
| 1 | 5.1 | 3.7 | 5.2 | 3.8 |
| 2 | 2.6 | 2.3 | 4.4 | 3.8 |
| 3 | 2.7 | 2.5 | 4.3 | 4.1 |
| 4 | 3.4 | 3.3 | 4.4 | 4.2 |
| 5 | 3.9 | 4.1 | 4.4 | 4.2 |
| 6 | 4.4 | 4.3 | 4.6 | 4.4 |
| 7 | 4.2 | 4.1 | 4.6 | 4.5 |
| 8 | 4.1 | 4.1 | 4.5 | 4.5 |
| 9 | 5.1 | 5.1 | 4.6 | 4.6 |
| 1930 | 2.6 | 2.6 | 4.5 | 4.5 |
| 1 | 3.7 | 3.8 | 4.4 | 4.5 |
| 2 | 1.7 | 1.8 | 3.8 | 4.1 |
| 3 | 0.7 | 0.7 | 3.4 | 3.7 |
| 4 | 0.9 | 0.8 | 3.1 | 3.4 |
| 5 | 0.6 | 0.6 | 2.9 | 3.1 |
| 6 | 0.7 | 0.7 | 2.9 | 3.1 |
| 7 | 0.6 | 0.6 | 3.3 | 3.4 |
| 8 | 0.6 | 0.6 | 3.4 | 3.4 |
| 9 | 1.2 | 1.1 | 3.7 | 3.6 |

The real rate is the nominal rate deflated by the implicit GDP price index (1929 = 100).

*Sources*:

Interest rates from Forrest Capie and Michael Collins, *The Inter-war British Economy: A Statistical Abstract* (Manchester University Press, Manchester, 1983), pp. 104, 106 -

(continued)

figures are annual averages of monthly data. GDP price index from C.H. Feinstein, *National Income, Expenditure and Output of the United Kingdom, 1855-1965* (Cambridge University Press, Cambridge, 1972), pp. T132-3. The series has been converted to a 1929 base.

-------------------

especially in the form of low export sales and high unemployment rates, but sectors producing for the home market experienced strong growth. In all, Gross Domestic Product (constant factor costs) grew at an annual rate of 4.7 per cent between the beginning of the recovery in 1932 and its peak in 1937; industrial production grew at a rate of 7.8 per cent.[52]

All commentators agree that the general thrust of monetary policy was favourable but there is no consensus as to its importance as a causal factor. Positive effects could have been transmitted through both an expansion of the money supply and through low interest rates. Figure 9.3 plots annual movements in one measure of the money stock (M2), high–powered money (currency plus bank reserves) and two measures of economic activity (real Net National Product and numbers in employment). The general timing relationship is consistent with a hypothesis that expansion of the money stock boosted recovery. The nominal money stock rose 5.2 per cent between June 1932 and June 1933, largely as a result of the 6.3 per cent rise in high–powered money which, in turn, was a consequence of the authorities increasing bank reserves in order to facilitate the Debt conversion exercise – the rise in reserves making it easier for the banks to buy the new bonds and helping to push down interest rates.[53] As prices in general were falling at this time, government action to reduce the Debt burden resulted in a sharp rise in real money balances. Some economists, such a Milton Friedman and Anna J.Schwartz, would argue that if, in consequence, real money balances exceeded desired balances, then the public would 'seek to dispose of what they regard as

Figure 9.3: Monetary Variables and Economic Activity, 1920-39

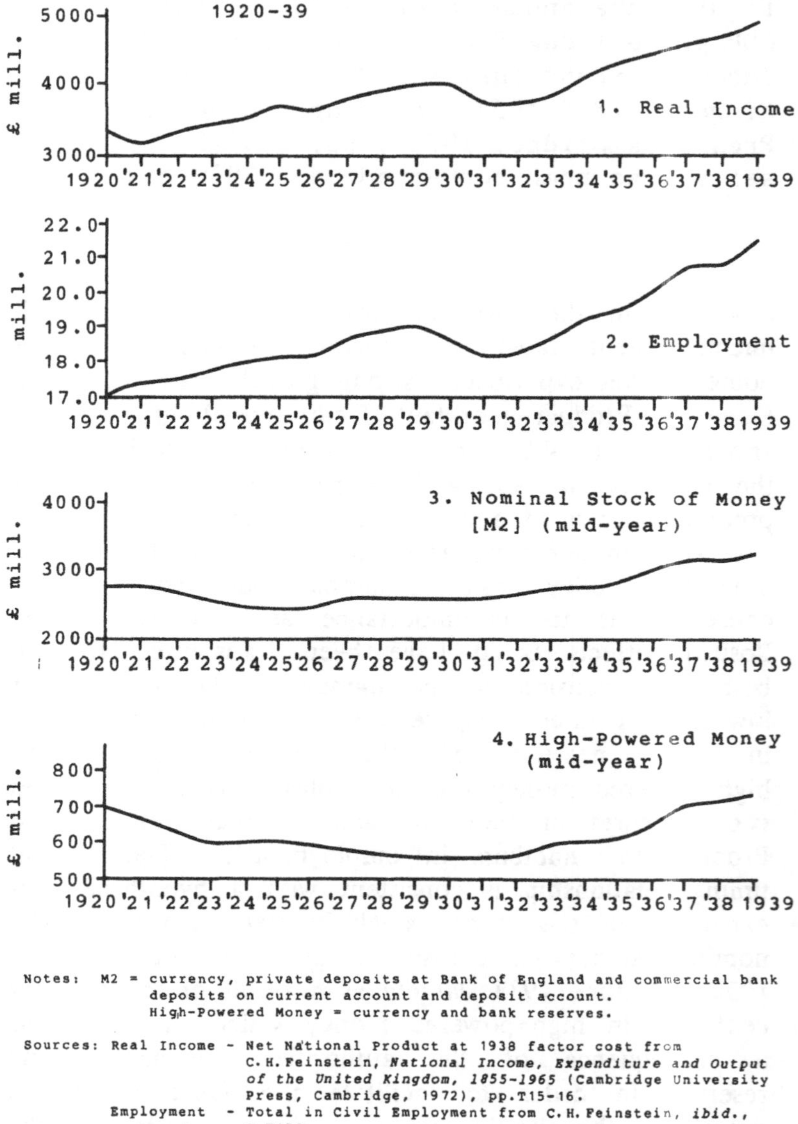


Notes: M2 = currency, private deposits at Bank of England and commercial bank deposits on current account and deposit account.
High-Powered Money = currency and bank reserves.

Sources:

| | | |
|---|---|---|
| Real Income | - | Net National Product at 1938 factor cost from C.H. Feinstein, *National Income, Expenditure and Output of the United Kingdom, 1855-1965* (Cambridge University Press, Cambridge, 1972), pp.T15-16. |
| Employment | - | Total in Civil Employment from C.H. Feinstein, *ibid.*, p.T126. |
| Nominal Stock of Money and High-Powered Money | - | Milton Friedman and Anna Schwartz, *Monetary Trends in the United States and the United Kingdom* (University of Chicago Press, Chicago and London, 1982), Table 4.9. |

their excess money balances; they [would] try to pay out a larger sum for the purchase of securities, goods and services, for the repayment of debts, and as gifts...'[54] The result could be a rise in aggregate demand of the kind that occurred in the 1930s, a rise which would help explain both the increase in output and the slow-down, and subsequent reversal, of the general price fall. In other words, according to such a monetarist interpretation the expansion of the nominal stock of money in the 1930s could have been a major factor in the economic recovery.

However, even if the theoretical underpinnings of such arguments are accepted, important questions over the timing and magnitude of monetary change in the early 1930s remain unanswered. More thorough research is required. Indeed, few commentators have explicitly emphasised the role of changes in the money stock during Britain's recovery from the Great Depression. Instead most assessments of monetary policy have been concerned with the effects of the fall in interest rates but, again, no consensus has emerged.

In general terms the fall in the cost of borrowing removed a potential constraint on growth and, all things being equal, should have encouraged investment and consumption. Firms with investment plans and individuals planning to buy houses or consumer goods could now borrow more easily and more cheaply. In the case of the housing market, mortgage rates on new loans fell from around 6 per cent to 4.5 per cent per annum, between 1932 and 1935.[55] For industry, Nevin has estimated that between 1932 and 1936 the cost of borrowing on long-term debentures and preference shares fell substantially, by one-quarter.[56]

It seems a matter of common sense, therefore, that these favourable monetary conditions would have stimulated the housebuilding boom of the 1930s and the general recovery in capital investment. But, of course, no matter the rate of interest, producers would borrow only if they expected to make a profit on their investment. Anyway, it is often said that the cost of funds for many firms was not great when compared to other costs. Some economists, of course, have emphasised that it would have been the factors affecting entrepreneurs' profit expectations that were the most decisive in determining the demand for funds. Similarly for housebuilding, the demand for mortgages would have depended not only upon the cost and availability of funds but also on such factors as the growth of real incomes, the fall in building costs and the relative attractiveness of property as a form of investment (important in this period when 40 per cent of houses were built for rented accommodation).[57] In this view the cost of borrowing would obviously have been one element in the calculation but it may not have been decisive – cheap money was but one of a number of factors favourable to economic growth in the 1930s.

A major complication in calculating the impact of cheap money arises from the fact that the 1931 crisis ushered in a number of important changes in other spheres of government activity. The depreciation of the exchange rate has already been mentioned. In addition, a General Tariff was imposed on foreign imports and the budget deficit was eliminated after the election of a conservative national government committed to orthodoxy in fiscal matters. It is very difficult to disentangle the impact of cheap money from that of other changes. The thrust of cheap money was favourable to recovery but its relative importance remains an open question.

Some commentators stress the role of non–monetary factors, pointing to favourable conditions on both the supply and demand side of the economy, conditions which interacted in such a way as to produce a cumulative process propitious to a higher rate of output growth and to rising living standards for the employed. For instance, H.W. Richardson has singled out the buoyancy of domestic consumption as providing an important springboard for retailing and other service industries, and for those manufacturing sectors which were exploiting 'new' technologies to mass–produce such consumer durables as motor vehicles, radios and other household gadgets.[58] Larger production brought important economies of scale, reducing costs and improving productivity. Such savings raised real incomes which, in turn, increased consumer demand and enabled the 'virtuous circle' of falling costs and an expanding home market to continue. Living standards were also boosted by falling prices – especially those of foodstuffs and raw materials. Within Richardson's schema, monetary impulses played a subsidiary role and, then, largely through the impact of falling interest rates which encouraged general investment to some extent, particularly in the construction industry. Within such an analysis the rise in the nominal stock of money shown in Figure 9.3 would have been either a *response* to rising incomes – as people required larger money balances to finance the higher level of economic activity – or, if initiated by the authorities, would have had little impact on demand as the 'extra' money would have been added to cash balances rather than used to finance more transactions. The economic impact of policy is seen as marginal.

A more recent attack upon the importance of cheap money has been made by Michael Beenstock, Forrest Capie and Brian Griffiths.[59] These authors accept that monetary experience was favourable to recovery but deny that monetary expansion resulted from the adoption by the authorities of a conscious and active policy. Instead they see it as having arisen out of general market conditions. More radically, they argue that an approach based on New Classical economic theory, which stresses changes on the supply side, offers the best explanation for both the recession of 1929 to 1932 and the subsequent recovery. In particular, they claim that for the manufacturing sector own-product real wage costs rose sharply after 1929, essentially because prices of internationally-traded manufactured goods fell faster than nominal wages. As a consequence, manufacturing profits were squeezed and there was large-scale job shedding in that sector. From 1932, however, real wages in manufacturing stabilised and this 'played a major role in the economic recovery from the supply side '[60] ... 'the recovery of the nineteen-thirties was not prompted by an increase in exogenous demand.'[61]

This controversial account of the recovery has, in turn, been severely criticised by G.D.N. Worswick and N.H. Dimsdale who cast doubt on the statistics used by Beenstock *et al* and, in general, give much greater weight to demand factors.[62] Worswick follows former writers in stressing the importance of the construction industry as a 'leading sector' in the recovery:

> If allowance is made for employment in producing building materials, the direct and indirect employment given by building amounted to as much as 30 per cent of the total rise [in employment] between 1932 and 1935.[63]

Moreover, housebuilding accounted for 17 per cent of the increase in Gross Domestic Product in the first two years of the recovery. According to Worswick it was through the stimulus given to housebuilding (with lower mortgage rates, etc.) that cheap money had its most obvious impact on investment and employment, but he also accepts that the effects could have been more pervasive, for example in stimulating other forms of investment and personal consumption. More generally, Worswick argues that government policy was much more important in the recovery than Beenstock, *et al* admit. Tariffs, exchange rate depreciation and especially cheap money were important.

In summary, it can be said that the differences of historical and economic interpretation remain more obvious than any agreement. The extent to which monetary policy aided the economic recovery of the 1930s remains unresolved. Nevertheless, there is almost complete unanimity in accepting that the shift in the *direction* of monetary policy from 1931 was favourable to growth.

## CONCLUSION

Because of the nature of the controversy over the impact of changes in monetary policy, judgement must necessarily be circumspect. There is general agreement that the commitment to the gold standard in the 1920s had a detrimental impact on the country's economic growth, whereas monetary expansion in the 1930s was favourable. There is less agreement over the relative importance of monetary change, or over what was the most effective transmission mechanism through which monetary impulses affected the economy. The main change in policy stance came in 1931 with the suspension of gold convertibility, but it was a crisis decision forced on the authorities by the pressure of circumstances. It was not planned. Nevertheless, abandonment of the fixed exchange rate did permit greater discretion in the use of monetary policy and during the following decade it led to government taking more responsibility for the conduct of that policy. The First World War had already sharply increased the general influence of the state in economic affairs and World War II was to confirm the permanent nature of this change.

## FURTHER READING

N.H. Dimsdale, 'British Monetary Policy and the Exchange Rate, 1920-1938' in W.A. Eltis and P.J.N. Sinclair (eds.), 'The Money Supply and the Exchange Rate', Supplement to *Oxford Economic Papers*, new ser., vol. 33, July 1981, pp. 306-49.

Sidney Pollard (ed.), *The Gold Standard and Employment Policies between the Wars* (Methuen & Co., London, 1970).

Susan Howson, *Domestic Monetary Management in Britain, 1919-38* (Cambridge University Press, Cambridge, 1975).

Edward Nevin, *The Mechanism of Cheap Money* (University of Wales Press, Cardiff, 1955).

## NOTES

1. J.M. Keynes, 'War and the Financial System, August, 1914', *Economic Journal*, vol. 24, Sept. 1914, pp. 460-86; J.M. Keynes, 'The Prospects of Money, November, 1914', *Economic Journal*, vol.

24, Dec. 1914, pp. 633–4; Marcello De Cecco, *Money and Empire* (Basil Blackwell, Oxford, 1974), pp. 128–32; E. Victor Morgan, *Studies in British Financial Policy, 1914–25* (Macmillan, London, 1952), p. 9; and R.S. Sayers, *The Bank of England 1891–1944* (3 vols., Cambridge University Press, Cambridge, 1976), vol. 1, pp. 69–74. For a recent assessment of many aspects of the crisis see Teresa Seabourne, 'The Summer of 1914' in Forrest Capie and Geoffrey E. Wood (eds.), *Financial Crises and the World Banking System* (Macmillan, London, 1986), pp. 77–119 [with 'Comment' by Charles Goodhart].

2. Sayers, *Bank of England*, vol. 1, pp. 72–3.

3. Ibid., p. 69.

4. Morgan, *Financial Policy*, p.32.

5. For a broad assessment see Arthur Marwick, *Britain in the Century of Total War* (The Bodley Head, London, 1968), chs. 3–5; and Alan S. Milward, *The Economic Effects of the Two World Wars on Britain*, 2nd edn (Macmillan, London, 1984).

6. Morgan, *Financial Policy*, pp. 122, 155–6.

7. Ibid., ch. 6,; Sayers, *Bank of England*, vol. 1, ch. 5.

8. One of the best accounts of the economic implications of the Treaty of Versailles remains J.M. Keynes, *The Economic Consequences of the Peace* (Macmillan & Co., London, 1919), especially chs. 6 and 7. For a view that is highly critical of Keynes see Etienne Mantoux, *The Carthaginian Peace or the Economic Consequences of Mr. Keynes* (Oxford University Press, London, 1946).

9. For a general discussion see Derek H. Aldcroft, *From Versailles to Wall Street, 1919–1929* (Allen Lane, London, 1977), ch. 4.

10. The new Soviet government of the USSR renounced all debts incurred by the Czarist regime.

11. C.H. Feinstein, *National Income, Expenditure and Output of the United Kingdom, 1855–1965* (Cambridge University Press, Cambridge, 1972), p. T.22.

12. Ibid., pp. T15–16.

13. Brian R. Mitchell and Phyllis Deane,

*Abstract of British Historical Statistics* (Cambridge University Press, Cambridge, 1962), p. 67.

14. For details on wartime exchange rate policy see Sayers, *Bank of England*, vol. 1, pp. 83–94; and Morgan, *Financial Policy*, ch. 9.

15. *Committee on Currency and Foreign Exchanges* [Cunliffe Committee], *First Interim Report*, Cd. 9182 (HMSO, London, 1918); and *Final Report*, Cmd. 464 (HMSO, London, 1919).

16. Susan Howson, *Domestic Monetary Management in Britain, 1919–38* (Cambridge University Press, Cambridge, 1975), p. 11.

17. Under the Gold Standard Act, 1925 (15 & 16 Geo. V, c. 29) Bank of England notes were convertible only to gold bullion in the form of bars, and not to coin as under the pre-1914 standard. In effect, under the new gold standard convertibility was largely confined to international transactions.

18. Sayers, *Bank of England*, vol. 1, pp. 110–11.

19. Howson, *Monetary Management*, p. 33. Also see D.E. Moggridge, *British Monetary Policy, 1924–1931* (Cambridge University Press, Cambridge, 1972), pp. 23–8.

20. J.M. Keynes, 'The Economic Consequences of Mr. Churchill' in Sidney Pollard (ed.), *The Gold Standard and Employment Policies between the Wars* (Methuen & Co., London, 1970), pp. 27–43. For a survey of the views of other contemporary critics see L.J. Hume, 'The Gold Standard and Deflation: Issues and Attitudes in the Nineteen-Twenties', *Economica*, new ser., vol. 30, 1963, pp. 225–42.

21. See Dimsdale, 'British Monetary Policy and the Exchange Rate, 1920–1938' in W.A. Eltis and P.J.N. Sinclair (eds.), 'The Money Supply and the Exchange Rate', Supplement to *Oxford Economic Papers*, new ser., vol. 33, July 1981, pp. 314–17, for a general survey of the evidence on overvaluation.

22. R.S. Sayers, who has been one of the stauncher supporters of the Bank's decision argues that while the adverse effects were probably not great, they were nevertheless present – see his 'The Return to

Gold, 1925' in Pollard, *Gold Standard*, pp. 92, 95; and his *Bank of England*, vol. 1, pp. 218–19.

23. Pollard, *Gold Standard*, pp. 1–26. This book contains a very useful collection of essays dealing with the 1925 decision.

24. Ibid., p. 25.

25. Dimsdale, 'Policy and Exchange Rate', pp. 320–1.

26. Moggridge, *Monetary Policy*, pp. 249–50.

27. Dimsdale, 'Policy and Exchange Rate', p. 322.

28. For a recent assessment see J.F. Wright, 'Britain's Interwar Experience' in Eltis and Sinclair, 'Money Supply', pp. 282–305.

29. For a recent re-assessment of the evidence see Alec Cairncross and Barry Eichengreen, *Sterling in Decline. The Devaluation of 1931, 1949 and 1967* (Basil Blackwell, Oxford, 1983), pp. 72–83.

30. Charles P. Kindleberger, *The World in Depression, 1929–1939* (Allen Lane, London, 1973), ch. 7 provides a very useful summary of the various attempts at international cooperation during 1931 and, indeed, of the developing international crisis generally. For a less sanguine view of international co-operation on financial matters see Stephen V.O. Clarke, *Central Bank Cooperation, 1924–31* (Federal Reserve Bank of New York, New York, 1967).

31. Sayers, *Bank of England*, vol. 2, pp. 389–91.

32. On the inadequacies of interest rate policy see David Williams, 'London and the 1931 Financial Crisis', *Economic History Review*, 2nd. ser., vol. 15, 1963, pp. 522–7.

33. Sayers, *Bank of England*, vol. 2, pp. 405–6.

34. Kindleberger, *World in Depression*, ch. 14.

35. Tim Congdon, 'Comment on "What Happened in 1931?"', in Capie and Wood (eds.), *Financial Crises*, p. 150.

36. *Committee on Finance and Industry* [Macmillan Committee], *Report*, Cmd. 3897 (HMSO, London, 1931), pp. 147–51. A point that has often

been repeated – see Williams, '1931 Crisis', pp. 519–20.

37. Arthur I. Bloomfield, *Short-term Capital Movements Under the Pre-1914 Gold Standard*, Princeton Studies in International Finance, no. 11 (Princeton University Press, Princeton, 1963), pp. 71–7 and Peter H. Lindert, *Key Currencies and Gold 1900–1913*, Princeton Studies in International Finance, no. 24 (Princeton University Press, Princeton, 1969), pp. 37, 40–1.

38. Feinstein, *National Income*, pp. T16, T22, T82 for balance of payments figures.

39. For a contrasting emphasis see Forrest Capie, Terence C. Mills and Geoffrey E. Wood, 'What Happened in 1931?' in Capie and Wood (eds.), *Financial Crises*, pp. 120–59 [including 'Comments' by Tim Congdon and Michael Wagner].

40. C.H. Lee, 'The Effects of the Depression on Primary Producing Countries', *Journal of Contemporary History*, vol. 4, 1969, pp. 139–55.

41. Williams, '1931 Crisis', pp. 518–22. On the operation of the sterling area in this period see L.S. Pressnell, '1925: The Burden of Sterling', *Economic History Review*, 2nd ser., vol. 31, 1978, pp. 67–87; and Ian M. Drummond, *The Floating Pound and the Sterling Area, 1931–1939* (Cambridge University Press, Cambridge, 1981).

42. Donald Winch, *Economics and Policy. A Historical Study* (Fontana, London, 1972), pp. 135–42.

43. Quoted in Edward Nevin, *The Mechanism of Cheap Money* (University of Wales Press, Cardiff, 1955), p. 111.

44. Ibid., pp. 111–12.

45. Sayers, *Bank of England*, vol. 2, pp. 416–30; Howson, *Monetary Management*, pp. 79–89.

46. John Redmond, 'An Indicator of the Effective Exchange Rate of the Pound in the Nineteen-Thirties', *Economic History Review*, 2nd. ser., vol. 33, 1980, pp. 83–91.

47. Dimsdale, 'Policy and the Exchange Rate', pp. 332–6; and Cairncross and Eichengreen, *Sterling in Decline*, pp. 90–8.

48. Susan Howson, 'The Management of Sterling, 1932–1939', *Journal of Economic History*, vol. 40, 1980, pp. 53–60; and Susan Howson, *Sterling's Managed Float: The Operations of the Exchange Equalisation Account, 1932–39*, Princeton Studies in International Finance, no. 46 (Princeton University Press, Princeton, 1980). For a critical assessment of some aspects of exchange rate manipulation in the 1930s see D.S. Lees, 'The Technique of Monetary Insulation, December 1932 to December 1937', *Economica*, new ser., vol. 20, 1953, pp. 341–55.

49. Howson, *Monetary Management*, pp. 86–9; 118–19.

50. Nevin, *Cheap Money*, p. 217

51. Ibid., p. 92.

52. Feinstein, *National Income*, p. T.25.

53. Howson, *Monetary Management*, pp. 99–101. For a sceptical interpretation of the impact of the conversion exercise on interest rates see Forrest Capie, Terence C. Mills, Michael J.Thomas and Geoffrey E. Wood, 'Was the War Loan Conversion a Success?' City University Discussion Paper on Monetary History of the UK, no. 5, Feb. 1983 (to be printed in *Applied Economics*, forthcoming).

54. Milton Friedman and Anna J. Schwartz, *Monetary Trends in the United States and the United Kingdom* (University of Chicago Press, Chicago and London, 1982), p. 18.

55. R.M. Macintosh, 'A Note on Cheap Money and the British Housing Boom, 1932–37', *Economic Journal*, vol. 61, 1951, p. 169.

56. Nevin, *Cheap Money*, p. 217.

57. See Howson, *Monetary Management*, pp. 111–17, for a survey of the evidence on the impact of cheap money on the construction boom.

58. H.W. Richardson, *Economic Recovery in Britain, 1932–9* (Weidenfeld and Nicolson, London, 1967).

59. Michael Beenstock, Forrest Capie and Brian Griffiths, 'Economic Recovery in the United Kingdom in the 1930s', Bank of England Panel of Academic

Consultants, Panel Paper No. 23, pp. 57–85.

60. Ibid., p. 65.

61. Ibid., p. 69.

62. G.D.N. Worswick, 'The Sources of Recovery in the 1930s', *National Institute Economic Review*, vol. 110, November 1984, pp. 85–93; and N.H. Dimsdale, 'Employment and Real Wages in the Inter-War Period', *National Institute Economic Review*, vol. 110, November 1984, pp. 94–103.

63. Worswick, 'Sources of Recovery', p. 86.

# PART III: 1939–1986

Chapter Ten

# WAR AND POST-WAR ADJUSTMENTS, 1939-51

It is important to begin the study of money and banking in the modern period with a review of the Second World War. Changes carried through during the conflict had significant post-war consequences for the conduct of policy and for the business of money markets. In addition, wartime financial transactions on the country's external account were to have important long-term effects.

## TOTAL WAR, 1939-45

### *Wartime Fiscal and Monetary Policy*

In September 1939 the UK declared war on Germany and in December 1941 on Japan. It was not until May 1945 that Germany capitulated, and August for Japan. During these six years of conflict the economic means of the nation were geared to total war, in the sense that the allocation of resources and the pursuit of higher economic growth and rising living standards were subordinated to the greater need of defeating the enemy. The Second World War, much more than the First, saw the state take over the management and planning of the economy. This was achieved through the extension of direct controls in the form of rationing, licensing, requisitions, prohibitions, the conscription of labour (although not used extensively for civilians), price and rent controls, subsidies and the physical management of such productive sectors as the steel and coal industries. Effective central planning necessitated an array of powerful state controls. Within this, the role of monetary policy was secondary but not unimportant.

In very general terms monetary policy was harnessed towards ensuring that financial factors did not impede the physical utilisation of resources needed for the war effort, and in this it was largely successful. Its main functions were to facilitate government fiscal and borrowing requirements and to expedite capital and exchange transactions on the external account.

Experience during World War I had made policy-makers keenly sensitive to the risk of inflation.[1] Basically, the risk arose from the potential excess of aggregate demand over supply. Normal supply conditions were badly disrupted through enemy action and the transfer of resources from non-essential (e.g. consumer goods) to war-related production; whereas the arming and maintenance of the armed forces necessitated a sharp increase in the demands made by the state for goods and services. Here were the roots of a potentially sharp inflation and, in the absence of other action, permissive monetary policy would allow the money supply to rise and, so, accommodate the price rises. Inflation could act as the channel through which resources were redistributed from the private to the public sector (as higher taxes were paid on inflated incomes and as consumers and producers alike faced increased costs) and to some extent this did happen during the war. The official cost of living index rose by some 31 per cent, from the end of 1938 to the end of 1945 (the broader GDP price deflator rose by 45 per cent).[2] Yet given the scale of disruption – with the share of the public authorities' current expenditure in Gross National Product rising from 14.5 per cent in 1938 to a peak of 54 per cent in 1943 (it was still at 46.5 per cent in 1945), and consumers' expenditure falling from almost 85 per cent in 1938 to 56.3 per cent in 1943 (69.8 per cent in 1945)[3] – the inflation incurred was relatively modest when compared to the doubling of prices during World War I.

Success over inflation was attributable, partly, to price controls, to the subsidisation of items included in the cost of living index and to the use of direct rationing and licensing as means to restrict private sector demand for scarce commodities. But the government also developed a new strategy for fiscal policy which aimed at constraining the overall level of demand. This was first done in Sir Kingsley Wood's 1941 budget and it was to form the basis of all subsequent war budgets.[4] By 1941 the Treasury had accepted the fiscal concepts advocated by J.M. Keynes (who, in fact, had moved to the Treasury in 1940), permitting the budget to be organised in such a way as to mitigate the inflationary threat.[5] In essence this involved the estimation of total resources available in the coming year (national output or supply) and the estimation of demand for that output from the main economic sectors – namely, from private consumption, investment, exports and government expenditure.[6] The difference between the estimates for aggregate supply and aggregate demand could then be used to calculate the likely 'imbalance' in the economy.

In principle, such an approach could be used to calculate likely deficiencies in demand associated with unemployment, but during the war the problem was one of excess demand. An 'inflationary gap' between total demand and total supply was the main concern of fiscal policy-makers at that time. So, although the collection and organisation of national output and income data in this form – and the underlying concepts – can be viewed as a radical change in government procedures[7], in effect they were consistent with the Treasury's own view of the need to contain inflation and were, therefore, more readily accepted.[8] With the calculation of the size of the inflationary gap, the Treasury was then in a position to know by how much *private* demand had to be reduced (public sector demand could not be suppressed during the war). From 1941 fiscal policy was fixed accordingly.

Fiscal policy employed two main methods to curtail private consumption: increased taxes and increased government borrowing. The lower thresholds and higher rates for income tax, increased purchase tax and an excess profits tax made the main contributions to current revenue. In all, about half of the government's wartime expenditure was met out of current revenue (compared to less than one-third in World War I).

The other half of expenditure was met by increased borrowing, and here monetary policy had a direct role to play. At an early stage of the conflict, the authorities decided not to depend upon the price mechanism for diverting private sector savings into their own coffers. On the outbreak of war Bank rate had been raised from 2 to 4 per cent, but this was no more than an immediate reaction to the uncertainty then existing. Within a few weeks a decided preference for low rates emerged and this remained the view of the authorities through to the post-war years.[9] Bank rate was cut back to 2 per cent and as early as October 1939 the government determined upon a 'Three Per Cent War', with 3 per cent becoming the basic long-term rate for all major capital projects. The main motivation was to minimise the cost of government borrowing. Inevitably, during the conflict the National Debt would grow and a clear lesson of World War I had been that high interest rates would make sharp and continuing inroads into tax revenues. Moreover, the cheap money period of the 1930s had not only accustomed public opinion to low rates but had also persuaded the authorities that they now had the necessary technical skills to ensure the continuation of 'cheap money'. Finally, neglect of the price mechanism in allocating scarce financial resources during the war was fully consistent with government action in the goods market: there, rationing and direct regulation were the preferred instruments of policy.

Such abrogation of an active interest rate policy spawned a series of direct controls. Regulations introduced in 1939 and 1940 imposed effective control over the export of gold, foreign currencies and securities denominated in certain currencies. The

Treasury was to become the sole trader in gold and foreign currency (with specified banks permitted to act as agents) and private hoardings of gold and foreign currency were compulsorily purchased. Unlike the First World War there was to be no attempt to retain Britain's position as an open economy at the centre of a multilateral system of international trade and finance. Instead, in 1939 there was clear recognition of the precariousness of the position in which capital flight had to be prevented and the reserves had to be carefully marshalled in order to optimise the purchase of supplies from overseas. Multilateralism was overthrown for a series of tightly-controlled bilateral arrangements for financing trade with other countries. In essence these foreign exchange controls sought to conserve scarce gold and foreign currency resources, ensuring that they were at the disposal of the authorities for the conduct of the war.

On the domestic front, the authorities conducted a propaganda campaign in which patriotic appeals were made to the public to lend as much as possible to the state. One general principle accepted by the authorities was 'that the Treasury would get the best terms if it split its security offerings to suit the peculiarities of the various broad sectors of the capital market.'[10] They sought maximisation through differentiation and some finesse was acquired in mobilising funds from the various sections of the saving public. Small savings were channelled through the National Savings Movement which raised money through the sale of Savings Certificates and Defence Bonds; and savers were exhorted to accumulate balances at the Post Office and Trustee Savings Banks. Larger individual sums were the target of War Loans, Savings Bonds, Exchequer Bonds and War Bonds; with each issue attempting to attract funds from new sources through some innovation (real or contrived) in the terms governing the loan. Another innovation was the issue of Tax Reserve Certificates, first made in 1941, as a means of tapping idle funds held by firms in anticipation of tax payments.

At the short end of the market, the government

continued to issue Treasury bills. Since 1934 these had no longer been sold direct to the clearing banks; rather, it was the discount houses that took them from the Bank, with the banks then buying their requirements from the discount houses.[11] Through late 1939 and early 1940 the authorities expanded the supply of Treasury bills but it was fast becoming clear that if expansion was to go much further, major changes would be required. The established arrangements between the Bank of England, the discount houses and the clearing banks could not bear the increase in scale. It was partly for this reason that Treasury Deposit Receipts (TDRs) were first issued in July 1940.[12] These were to become an important new source of short-term funds used to meet the 'residual' cash needs of the Treasury (i.e. the fluctuating balance between outgoings on the one hand and tax revenues and loan receipts on the other). In fact, by the end of the war slightly more (net) had been raised on TDRs than on Treasury bills. TDRs were of six months' duration (Treasury bills were three months') and they were non-negotiable except to the government in specified circumstances (Treasury bills were of higher liquidity, being readily resaleable) although there was a tacit agreement that the banks' liquidity would be assured by the willingness of the Bank of England to encash their holdings of Treasury bills without recourse to the sort of 'penalty' rates that might be applicable in peace time. TDRs earned interest at 1.125 per cent per annum, and they were sold directly to the banks, with the scheme covering the London and Scottish clearers and those central banks operating in London (namely, the Commonwealth Bank of Australia and the National Bank of Egypt).

Apart from tailoring state securities to the particular needs of different sections of the capital market, government intervention also took the form of direct rationing of funds. The Capital Issues Committee was empowered to vet applications for new issues (and renewals) of capital securities to the public. The Committee's brief was to ensure that the capital market provided new funds only to essential sectors like the armaments industry, and that its operations did not conflict with the overall needs of state finance. For similar reasons the government operated controls over bank lending. This took the form of 'guidance' from the Treasury and, after consultation with the Bank of England, the banks agreed to limit their advances to applications that could be justified in terms of 'national interest' (in effect, loans which would aid the essential sectors of defence, coal-mining, agriculture, and exports). Obviously, such controls further distorted the banks' normal, peacetime asset and liability ratios. However, the importance of controls over the banks within overall government economic policy was greatly tempered by the heavy reliance on direct, physical controls in the goods and labour markets. In fact, this was true of wartime monetary control in general; in a planned economy monetary policy was of secondary importance.

*The External Account in Wartime*

Another major economic concern which had direct monetary implications was the impact of the war on the UK's trading and capital accounts with the rest of the world. Enemy action and occupation of other countries obviously created major disruption but, more generally, there was the constant need to secure overseas supplies which could help the war effort. At the same time, of course, resources were sorely depleted. One aspect of the authorities' response was the imposition of exchange controls which helped retain foreign reserves but (especially until American aid began flowing on a large-scale in 1942) other methods were needed to acquire the means of paying for imports. For this reason exports continued to be given priority in the allocation of resources. The dire need to get hold of foreign currency was also an influence behind the decision to stop the depreciation of the pound and peg its value at $4.03 in September 1939. Its value had fallen earlier from $4.80 to about $4.00, during the few weeks of August and September, in response to large-scale sales of sterling on foreign exchange markets.[13] Physical constraints such as the availability of shipping space severely limited the potential volume of exports, so the authorities could see little wisdom in allowing their value to fall too rapidly - a relatively high sterling value in terms of other currencies would help sustain export earnings on a much reduced volume of trade. Inevitably, though, exports were lower than pre-war, while there remained the urgent need for imported foodstuffs, raw materials and munitions. In fact, maximisation of import levels could only be achieved through changes on Britain's capital account. Sales of British-held overseas securities and increased borrowing from foreigners were, thus, inevitable.

Imports from the USA were particularly important and, initially, American neutrality meant that Britain had to liquidate her dollar securities. Indeed, in the early years the Americans were to insist upon the British using their gold and dollar resources before any special aid could be provided, and even later the size of Britain's reserves remained a sensitive political issue. In 1939 marketable American securities were valued at some £500 million, the overwhelming bulk of which were privately-owned.[14] The authorities, thus, took powers to ensure the dollar proceeds of any private sales were deposited with the Treasury, or conducted 'vested' sales whereby the authorities sold the securities directly and provided compensation to the owners. In this way Britain managed to pay for limited essential supplies from the USA during the early days of the conflict. With the American entry into the war, though, direct aid began to flow on a large scale. In 1941 President Roosevelt inaugurated the 'Lend-Lease' programme. Under this scheme the UK received a massive $27 billion of aid (almost $6 billion went from the UK to the USA under reciprocal arrangements), enabling the importation of a much greater volume of American war-related goods and even permitting a small build-up of the country's currency reserves in preparation for the end of the war.[15]

While generally recognised as extremely generous, the operation of 'Lend-Lease' did entail a number of difficulties for Britain, difficulties which contributed to a degree of inter-ally tension. These arose mainly from conditions attached to the aid. In general, the Americans continued to press for the liquidation of as much as possible of Britain's own gold and dollar securities. From the point of view of the US administration there was great reluctance to be seen as providing aid which was then used to augment Britain's international reserves; whereas the British were anxious to maintain a minimum of reserves not only during the conflict but as a contingency against the needs of the immediate post-war years. Restrictions were also imposed by the USA on the use of aid materials for the manufacture of British goods which were to be exported, for they might compete with American suppliers. The Americans also won a British commitment to the establishment of a non-discriminatory trade system after the war. This was generally interpreted as an attack not only upon the Nazi trading arrangements of the 1930s but also upon Britain's system of Imperial Preference. From a British perspective, of course, while American aid was extremely welcome, there was some disappointment, if not irritation, at American conditions at a time when major sacrifices were being made. Undoubtedly, too, there was some irksomeness in having to recognise that Britain was very much the junior - and dependent - partner in the financial relationship.

The USA, of course, was not Britain's only overseas supplier and throughout the war the UK continued to trade with non-Axis countries. The desperate need for essential imports - and the inadequacy of exports - applied here, too; so heavy debts were incurred. Of particular importance were the so-called Sterling Balances which were accumulated British debts to those countries that were prepared to allow their holdings of sterling to build up. Most of these countries were from the 'Sterling Area', they had long-standing political or commercial ties with Britain and they commonly used sterling to settle international debts. Included among them were the British colonies, Australia, New Zealand, South Africa, Eire, India, Burma and a number of Middle Eastern countries.

Table 10.1: UK Cumulative Balance of Payments during World War II (£ billions)

| | |
|---|---|
| CURRENT ACCOUNT DEFICIT: | -10.0 |
| FINANCED BY FOLLOWING CAPITAL TRANSACTIONS: | |
| Net grants from USA | 5.4 |
| Net grants, other | 0.0 |
| Sales of overseas investments | 1.1 |
| Accumulation of liabilities (sterling & dollar) | 3.5 |
| Other (requisition of gold & dollar balances) | 0.1 |
| | 10.1 |
| Balance added to reserves | 0.1 |

*Source*: R.S. Sayers, *Financial Policy, 1939–45* (London: HMSO & Longman, Green & Co., 1956), p. 499

During the war these countries accepted sterling credits in exchange for goods and services, or transferred their gold and dollar reserves to London for conversion to sterling. 'While [the sterling balances] accumulated, they allowed Britain to fight the war with resources greater than her own, without bankruptcy and without damage to the international value of the pound sterling.'[16] But they also represented future claims on the British economy and should be seen in the broad context of the weakening of the UK's external capital account.

Table 10.1 provides a summary of Professor R.S. Sayer's estimates of overall UK balance of payments changes during the war. The urgent need to import and the constraints on exports combined to create a massive cumulative current account deficit of £10 billion. The table makes clear how important

American aid and rising overseas debts were in financing this deficit. US grants financed just over half, with another third covered by extra borrowing. Sales of British-owned overseas securities - which reduced pre-war holdings, by almost one-half - also made a significant, though relatively small, contribution, at £1.1 billion. On the cessation of hostilities it became clear that the overall effect of the war had been to reverse the UK's traditional status as a net international creditor. It has been estimated that by mid-1945 the Sterling Area balances stood at £2.7 billion and that, in total, British indebtedness had risen from £0.6 billion in 1939 to £3.4 billion. Post-war reconstruction meant, of course, that the need to import from abroad remained pressing, yet with the export position apparently weak and with heavy indebtedness on capital account, it was inevitable that Britain's balance of payments should dominate the country's monetary policy in the immediate post-war years.

## THE YEARS OF RECOVERY, 1945-51

### *Domestic Monetary Policy in the Immediate Post-War Years*

The Labour government elected in 1945 initially chose to retain the bulk of direct wartime economic controls and, indeed, the implementation of its socialist programme extended the area of state activities, especially through nationalisation. The 1944 White Paper on Employment explicitly rejected a return to mass unemployment and committed the authorities to much greater intervention in economic affairs:

> The Government accept as one of their primary aims and responsibilities the maintenance of a high and stable level of employment ... [and submit] proposals for an extension of State control over the volume of employment ... [17]

Retention of controls would enable the government to

influence aggregate demand so as to attain this end. There was an acceptance by both leading political parties that war had created major imbalances and distortions, with a general restriction of peacetime supplies and a frustration of peacetime demands. Return to a free market would most likely lead to a sharp inflationary boom, followed by a deep recession – a repeat of post-World War I experience. In the event, full employment was readily achieved and the problem for policy-makers became one of restricting domestic demand rather than having to boost it to create jobs. But, of course, realisation of the true nature of this position was to take some time.

In the monetary sphere, retention of direct controls included the continuation of foreign exchange regulations (incorporated into the 1947 Exchange Control Act[18]) and of controls over capital issues and borrowing via a new Issues Committee and through directives regulating bank advances (the 1946 Borrowing Act[19]). The Bank of England was also nationalised under the Bank of England Act, 1946, and its powers over the commercial banks were given legal status.[20] Since its creation in 1694, throughout its nineteenth-century evolution as a central bank and even during the twentieth-century periods of close co-operation with the government (especially close in wartime), the Bank had remained a private institution. The 1946 Act brought this to an end. It formally recognised that the conduct of monetary policy was the proper province of a modern state and ended the anachronistic legal position.

Although it was accepted that monetary policy was the responsibility of government, the authorities' decision to retain direct controls over the economy severely downgraded its importance. During this government's life, from 1945 to 1951, neither changes in interest rates nor in the money supply were explicitly considered to be of much significance in determining aggregate demand which, under the influence of 'Keynesianism', was to become increasingly the authorities' ultimate target. In the early years the government relied most heavily on direct controls (rationing, licensing, import restrictions and the like) and even when these began to be gradually relinquished (from about 1947) fiscal policy was adopted as the main policy instrument. As during the war, monetary policy remained something of a Cinderella.

In the first two years of the Labour administration, Dr Hugh Dalton was Chancellor of the Exchequer, responsible for the overall conduct of monetary policy. Under him the main monetary aim was to push interest rates even lower than they had been during the war – he hoped to convert cheap money into ultra-cheap money.[21] Wartime experience had shown that if the state retained direct controls over the economy then it could adopt an expansionary monetary policy to keep interest rates down, yet avoid most of the inflationary consequences. And all things being equal, low interest rates were to be preferred. One consideration was the fear of post-war depression of the type that had occurred in the 1920s. Economists were arguing at the time that interest rate movements were not important determinants of the rate of investment, but it was still generally agreed that if unemployment should threaten, then cheap money would be more beneficial than dear money. Fiscal motives were also to the fore in the mind of the authorities. The National Debt had trebled during the war and it was in the government's – and taxpayers' – interest to keep charges to a minimum. As the state's additional borrowing requirements were likely to be less once the war had finished, it was thought that a fall in interest rates might, indeed, be possible. Also, as some of the debt was held by non-residents, lower interest payments would help the balance of payments. The Chancellor himself stressed the beneficial redistributional effects of lower rates, favouring the borrower over lender, 'the active producer as against the passive *rentier*.'[22]

The first attack was aimed at short rates, with immediate success as rates on Treasury Deposit Receipts and Treasury bills fell by about 0.5 per cent, to 0.625 and 0.5 per cent respectively. Success here was always likely because of the government's great influence over the bill market. This influence was exercised through the Bank of England's standing arrangement to discount Treasury bills for the commercial banks and discount houses at close to market rate, rather than at a penal Bank rate. The arrangement had originated in the war but had been carried through into peacetime. In consequence:

> the authorities had virtually complete control over the rate of interest on Treasury bills. The rate in the market was unlikely to depart significantly from the rate at which the Bank was prepared to operate, and the market was always able to obtain sufficient funds to take up whatever amounts of the new bills the Treasury decided to issue.[23]

Such techniques had, by the end of 1945, enabled the government to halve interest payments on the floating (short-term) debt which comprised some 30 per cent of the total.

The authorities then turned to longer-term securities where the aim was to get the rate down from 3 to 2 per cent. In effect, they had to persuade the investing public that low rates would continue into the foreseeable future and may yet fall further (causing security prices to rise) and, that it would, therefore, be worth lending to the government on the new terms. Operations in the short-term market had been part of this public persuasion campaign, and they were reinforced by small-scale conversion operations and open-market operations in medium- and long-term securities. Thus, supplies of 2.5 per cent National War Bonds (1954–6) and 3 per cent Savings Bonds (1965–75) were stopped; and in 1946, 1.75 per cent Exchequer Bonds (1950) were offered in exchange for two types of 2.5 per cent bonds. Rates of interest on small savings in the form of Savings Certificates and Defence Bonds were also reduced. However, the government met strong resistance in the market in October 1946 when the Chancellor announced the issue of 2.5 per cent

Treasury Stock (1975) – known as 'Daltons' – and as security prices rose, the new issue proved a failure. In fact, it is assumed that it was purchases by various government 'departments' (e.g. the National Debt Commissioners) which had been successful in easing the absorption of the new low rate up until then[24], but the real cost had been in the rise in bank reserves with the subsequent sharp rise in deposits. In order to support the gilts market, the authorities had been buying bonds and financing these purchases (and any shortfalls from the lack of bond sales) through loans from the banks in the form of Treasury bills and Treasury Deposit Receipts.[25] In fact, deposits of the London clearing banks rose sharply through 1946 and into 1947. As Figure 10.1 indicates, the rate of monetary expansion was similar to that of wartime, but it was rapid compared to the relative contraction after 1947.

In essence government policy foundered on an immutable truth of monetary control: that the authorities can choose *either* to set rates of interest, with the supply of money being determined by the public's demand for money at those rates; *or* they can determine the supply of money, with rates altering in response to demand – they cannot do both. In 1946 and 1947 growing scepticism over the authorities' ability to maintain very low rates was persuading a growing number of holders of gilt-edged securities to sell them and build up cash balances in anticipation of price falls. Such falls could only be avoided if the authorities offered general support to the market, buying gilts themselves and, in the process, creating money.

> The theory is that if, at the chosen level of interest rates, the public's appetite for securities flags and it seeks cash instead, the threat to the interest structure can be countered by giving it what it wants – by starving it of new securities and glutting it with new money until it turns back with relief to securities on the Government's terms.[26]

Figure 10.1: London Clearing Banks' Total Deposits, 1943-51 (Annual, £ billion)

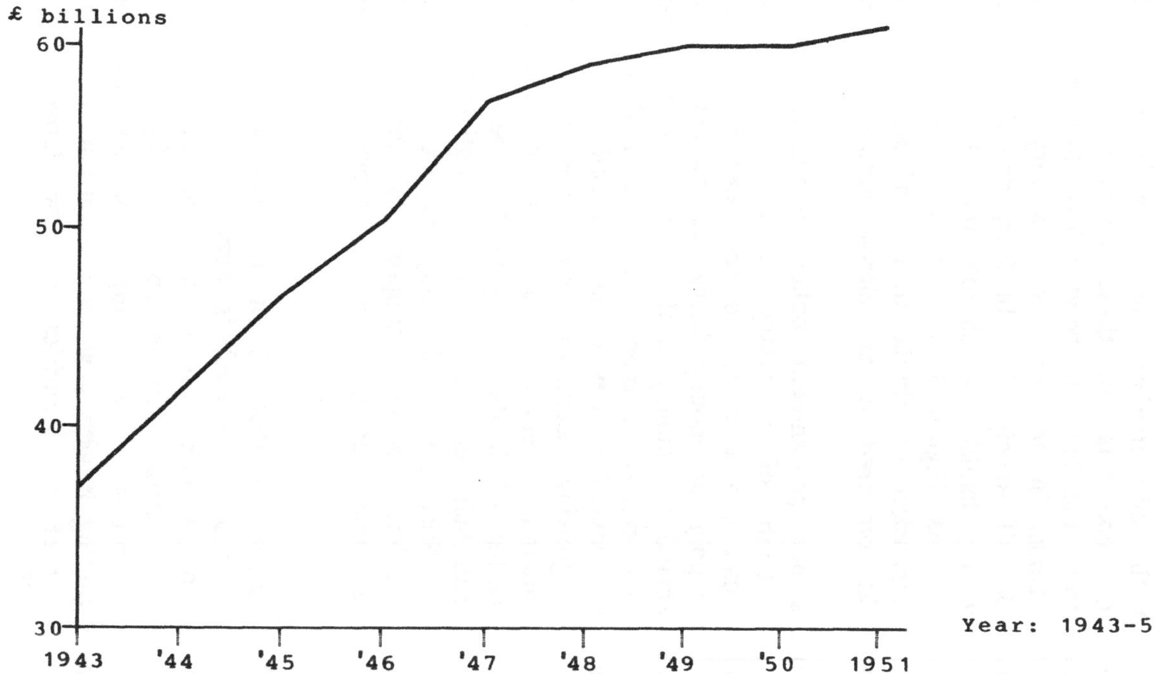


Source: Forrest Capie and Alan Webber, *A Monetary History of the UK, 1870-1982* (Allen & Unwin, London, 1985), vol. 1, p.436.

But the government was not prepared to follow the logic through to the extreme. They were not willing to create money *ad infinitum*. Thus, during the disruption caused by fuel shortages at the beginning of 1947 and, again, during the exchange crisis of the summer, government market support was lacking and gilt prices fell - marking the end of the ultra-cheap money policy.

The policy can be criticised for being inflationary through its money supply effects. However, pursuit of that policy is readily understandable in the context of government motives. Official thinking was shaped by the need to avoid the likely post-war depression. Avoidance of inflation was not a major concern and, besides, the retention of direct controls necessarily dampened down the inflationary price effects of monetary expansion (as it had during the war).

Dalton was replaced as Chancellor by Sir Stafford Cripps in 1947 and this marked a general change in the direction of policy. The authorities continued to influence short-term markets in order to keep rates low but more freedom was permitted the gilts market and here rates rose from under 3 per cent in late 1947 to almost 4 per cent by late 1951. The rate of increase in the money supply also fell away quite markedly in these years, but this was not the conscious outcome of policy. Rather, it was a consequence of the tight budgetary policy adopted. Indeed, monetary policy in this period from 1947 to 1951 is generally portrayed as one of 'neutral money'. As wartime controls were gradually dismantled, the government relied increasingly on fiscal policy to achieve its economic objectives and monetary policy slipped further into the background. In fact, at this time there were barely any government pronouncements even mentioning credit or interest rates.[27] The authorities did on occasions call for restrictions on bank advances and capital issues, but always as supplementary measures to general fiscal squeezes (as in the exchange crisis of 1947 and devaluation crisis of 1949). Monetary policy lay largely in abeyance and interest in monetary techniques of control were not to be revived until the Conservative election victory of 1951.

*External Difficulties, 1945-51*

Post-war conditions necessitated major adjustments in Britain's external relations. In order to pay for the imports needed for reconstruction and for the hoped-for increase in living standards, a steep rise in exports was required. In the short-run this demanded a sharp increase in the proportion of resources employed in the export sector, but in the longer-term it called for a rise in productivity in order to regain and improve upon the country's competitiveness. In retrospect, it is obvious also that a general realignment in currency values was necessary. The most striking change was the new economic hegemony of the USA, and for Britain this was to mean a devaluation of sterling relative to the dollar. Satisfactory British recovery was also dependent upon general expansion in the international economy, and much economic diplomacy in the immediate post-war years was directed towards devising means of strengthening the world economy. Britain's role here, however, was clearly subordinate to that of the USA.

Such an overview of Britain's economic position in the world undoubtedly exercised the minds of policy-makers, but in the course of everyday decision-making it was often the immediate, pressing problems that absorbed their energies. On the ending of the war the balance of payments presented such a problem. Britain already had a weak balance of payments in the 1930s; indeed, her share of world trade had been declining on trend since the late nineteenth century, and the world contraction of the 1930s had severely aggravated the rate of unemployment in the UK. It was true that in that decade the current account had usually been close to balance - if with an increasing tendency to deficit - but this was achieved only with the imposition of tariffs on imports and with informal restrictions on capital exports (formal exchange regulation had lasted for only five months following the 1931 currency crisis).[28] Moreover, the trade balance had benefited greatly from a sharp fall in agricultural prices which had lowered the cost of imports. Above all, there had been mass unemployment in the 1930s. If the one million or so unemployed had been working, then they would have consumed many more imports and Britain could have faced massive balance of payments deficits. Hence, even in the absence of war, drastic action on the external account would have been needed in the 1940s.

The war, though, added dramatically to the UK's external weakness.[29] Resources had been diverted from the export sector, resulting in a 45 per cent fall in exports, between 1938 and 1945, after allowance is made for price changes.[30] British withdrawal from overseas markets had encouraged expansion by both home producers and third-party suppliers. Much of the important Latin American market, for instance, had been lost to US exporters. It would necessarily take time for the UK to redirect resources to export-production and for exporters to win back custom.

The capital account had also been weakened. At least, £1.1 billion of UK-owned overseas investments had been sold and a staggering £3 billion or so of external liabilities incurred. At the time the Treasury argued:

> It is estimated that the net income from overseas investments in 1945 will be less than half that received in 1938. This reflects the extensive liquidation of foreign securities, the repatriation of loans by overseas debtors, and the increased interest payments to holders of sterling debts caused by the heavy war expenditure which the UK has had to incur overseas.[31]

Loss of revenue on overseas securities reduced service income on the current account, but the weakening of the capital account also carried implications for the international role of the pound. In particular there was the sharp increase in the Sterling Balances that has already been noted.

Since 1933 there had existed a bloc of countries which maintained fixed exchange rates between their national currencies and sterling (which, since 1931, had no longer been freely convertible to gold). However, it was the imposition of formal exchange controls by the British at the outbreak of the war in 1939 that had truly created a 'Sterling Area', for bloc members were granted privileged exemptions from the controls.[32] After the war, exchange controls were retained and the exemptions continued, extending to the British colonies, Australia, New Zealand, India, Pakistan, Ceylon and a number of non-Commonwealth states such as Eire, Burma and Iceland.[33] All these countries continued to maintain stable exchange rates amongst themselves – with the value of national currencies tied to the 'key' currency, sterling – and to permit currency convertibility within the area.

Membership thus bestowed the advantages of belonging to a large trading bloc at a time when attempts to establish a truly multilateral system of international finance and currency convertibility came to nought. Members also gained from the arrangements to pool their gold and 'hard' currency (essentially US dollar) reserves in London. Within limits these reserves could be drawn upon by individual members (though not by all members at the same time) to an extent greater than their own contribution and, therefore, their trade with the non-sterling world was not strictly limited by their own ability to earn hard currencies. Another advantage to members was that they were exempted from British exchange controls on capital exports, so that they could raise loans in the London capital market. The UK benefited, too – from the reserve pooling arrangements and from being able to trade and invest within a large, fixed exchange rate area. The political prestige which derived from being 'leader' of an important trading bloc was also important to the UK. The UK also benefited in an even more fundamental sense. The Sterling Balances were international debts which, it was generally recognised, the country was unable to repay in the circumstances of the immediate post-war years. The Sterling Area could, thus, be represented as a mutually-beneficial arrangement between debtor and creditors. It enabled the UK to delay repayment (interest was still paid, of course) and, at the same time, it offered the UK's creditors some recompense through the advantages accruing from being a member of a large trading bloc.

However, leadership of the growing Sterling Area also carried some important disadvantages for the UK. Prior to World War II, the UK had effectively settled her deficits with dollar countries through the overall surplus enjoyed with sterling-using countries which, in turn, had a collective surplus with North America. After 1945 the Sterling Area countries also had a keen appetite for American goods and, so, incurred dollar deficits. This added to the strain on Britain's reserves and contributed to the exchange crises of 1947 and 1949. In fact, it was not until after 1949 - when sterling was devalued, tighter controls were imposed on dollar imports and export sales increased - that the Sterling Area began to acquire a surplus with the dollar states. Yet, even though the pooled dollar reserve began to grow after 1949, so too did Britain's short-term capital liabilities to the rest of the Sterling Area (the Sterling Balances). In other words, unlike the previous position the surplus earned by the Sterling Area was no longer used to buy British goods but to accumulate claims on Britain's reserves. Here, potentially, was a serious threat to the stability of the value of sterling, although it was not to become a real problem until the close of the immediate post-war period.

The government's commitment to full employment was another consequence of war that held major implications for the balance of payments. Compared to the thirties, it implied a higher demand for imports and, therefore, a weaker current account. It meant also that, in future, if current account deficits arose then there would be strict limits to the extent to which a correction could be sought through deflating the domestic economy: the commitment to full employment imposed a major constraint on policy options.

The fact that there had just been six years of austerity and that full trade restrictions were in operation already, also meant there was little room for further cut-backs on imports. The problem was perceived, then, as the need to increase exports. In 1945 exports paid for just 30 per cent of imports and official estimates assumed that a very sharp rise, of 75 per cent over the pre-war volume, would be required if aspirations of a current account surplus were to be achieved. Even then, a straightforward drive for exports would not be enough because there was a serious mismatch in the direction of trade - between the countries from where Britain imported and the markets to which she exported.[34] This mismatch manifested itself in a dollar shortage. The UK needed to buy dollar goods (especially agricultural produce but also capital goods) yet given the low level of reserves she needed to finance those imports by sales of British goods to dollar countries. However, there was inadequate demand for British produce from this quarter.

Nor was this just a British problem. American producers had been able to build up such a commanding lead over the debilitated European and Far Eastern combatants, that peacetime trading patterns had been altered in such a way that it would take some years before America's share of world trade fell back to a 'normal' level. The immediate need in Europe and Japan was for reconstruction and this heightened the demand for American goods. In a nutshell, the problem was that demand for American goods was high but reserves of dollars were low and the ability to sell in America had been reduced. This was the nature of the post-war dollar problem. Globally, the dollar shortage undermined attempts to establish a genuine multilateral payments system; for Britain, it seriously threatened the national recovery programme.

In the event, the UK was successful in raising exports - in constant price terms they rose by 53 per cent between 1946 and 1951 (imports rose by 14 per cent).[35] Government policy played a part - with propaganda encouraging exporters, the discriminatory use of licensing in favour of exporters, the extension of import controls and the use of rationing to restrict other claims on the national output. But export success was partly fortuitous in that military defeat meant neither Germany nor Japan (who together had accounted for 15 per cent of world trade in 1938) were in a position to re-establish their own exports immediately. Thus, Britain's achievement was perhaps less firmly-based than it first appeared.

In the immediate post-war years, though, it was the dollar shortage which proved more intractable and which, on occasions, seemed dramatically to threaten the government's reconstruction programme.

The use of atomic weapons against Japan brought a sudden end to the war in August 1945, immediately bringing Britain's dollar shortage into sharp focus. The 'Lend-Lease' programme ceased with hostilities, stemming the flow of American aid to the UK. It was imperative that the British authorities should seek alternative forms of relief. Theoretically, the government could have devalued sterling immediately but, in practice, devaluation would have been inappropriate in 1945. Price competitiveness was not seen as a major constraint on export sales and the authorities already possessed the necessary controls to restrict imports of a non-urgent kind.[36] For the same reasons still greater contraction of domestic consumption offered a limited solution, in addition to being politically unpopular after the austerity and hardships of the war years. Negotiations for more financial aid from the USA seemed much more acceptable, securing the precious dollars necessary to provide a breathing-space in which economic recovery could commence. 'After six years of war the impulse to accept almost any terms was all but overwhelming.'[37]

In the event, Lord Keynes headed a delegation to Washington in 1945 to negotiate a loan which he portrayed as 'though it is imperfectly satisfactory to us, does represent a compromise and is very considerably removed from what the Americans began by thinking reasonable...'[38] He was not happy with the sum negotiated, because it 'did not allow a margin for unforeseen contingencies' and he deplored the American insistence on a loan rather than a grant. Nevertheless, he pointed out that this sum of dollars could be critical in the years of reconstruction and he emphasised that the US credit was the best available in the circumstances. The commercial terms of the loan were relatively generous - Lend-Lease debts were written-off, a new loan of $3.75 billion was granted at 2 per cent per annum, repayments were not to begin until 1951 and were to be spread over fifty years.[39] General British appraisal, however, was (and continues to be) critical. *The Economist* accepted that there was:

> no real option... There is, however, one compulsion to which we are not subject. We are not compelled to say we like it. And we do not... Our present needs are the direct consequences of the fact that we fought earliest, that we fought longest, and that we fought hardest. In moral terms we are creditors; and for that we shall pay $140m. a year for the rest of the twentieth century. It may be unavoidable; but it is not right.[40]

At the time the loan was seen as 'dollars with strings', the 'strings' being the non-financial conditions the Americans attached to the loan. The most important were that Britain had to accept a policy of 'non-discrimination' in international trade and to restore full convertibility of the pound. These were two of the tenets of the agreement struck with the USA at Bretton Woods in 1944, but the British had perceived them as long-term aims in the post-war world. Now they were to be implemented within the year.

Given the parlous state of the UK economy *vis à vis* the USA, 'non-discrimination' seemed a charter for American exporters to take over, world-wide, and the state of Britain's balance of payments cast serious doubts on her ability to maintain convertibility. From the American point of view, of course, the loan could be portrayed as not ungenerous - after all Britain was a potential trade rival and she was but one (and amongst the best-equipped) of many nations seeking US aid.[41] Moreover, the American administration had to be wary of Congressional opinion, and the furthering of American aims to remove trade discrimination was an important means of carrying public support.

For Britain the commitment to early convertibility seemed a gamble at the time and, in the event, it was a complete failure.[42] In general, the world faced a dollar shortage (relative to the demand for American goods) and a sterling surfeit. Thus once convertibility became possible, a large-scale attempt to switch from the latter to the former was almost certain. In addition, during 1947 Britain's trade balance with the dollar countries deteriorated sharply, and a fuel crisis in the spring restricted productive capacity. Thus, when on 15 July (one year after the granting of the American loan) sterling convertibility was re-established, the situation was already precarious. Armed with the ability to acquire dollars, domestic and overseas sterling-holders sold pounds. By the end of the month the movement out of sterling became a flood, and on 20 August convertibility had to be abandoned. It had lasted just five weeks and had seriously added to the drain on the UK's reserves which the trading account had already depleted. The abandonment of sterling convertibility also ended American hopes for the early establishment of a liberalised, international monetary and commercial system.

On the government's part it could be said that there had been little choice in the matter. An American loan was essential and the economic reality of Anglo-American relationships was that the USA was dominant. Critics of the American authorities declared the terms too onerous. British ministers, in fact, had been hopeful of getting a grant - not a loan - and a much larger amount.[43] Morally, America owed it to her allies to help with reconstruction for they had suffered more physical destruction and disruption, whereas the US economy had grown strongly during the war. Economically, too, it was in America's own interest to foster the recovery of Europe (and the Far East) in order to establish a thriving international economy.

Indeed, the American authorities fairly quickly came to a position close to this, and they altered their attitude towards overseas aid. The failure of sterling convertibility was an obvious factor in this change of policy. Another was the deepening ideological conflict with the USSR whose troops occupied much of Eastern Europe at the end of the war.[44] American politicians accepted that rapid recovery in Western Europe was an important defence against the spread of communism and that large-scale government aid could contribute to the recovery. The Marshall Plan (named after the American Secretary of State) was the most important of the USA's aid programmes and through it almost $10 billion was distributed throughout Europe in the years, 1948 to 1950. Under the scheme not only did Europe receive capital imports but the US also encouraged greater European co-operation and accepted the need for war-torn countries to discriminate against US goods. The UK received over one-fifth of the total American payments made in the European Recovery Programme. As was the case for the rest of Europe, the scale of American aid meant that it was not of overwhelming importance to British recovery but it did make a significant contribution in the early years after the war.[45]

Despite American aid the dollar shortage remained. Even with general discrimination against American imports, the US amassed a cumulative current account surplus of $30 billion between 1946 and 1949.[46] Countries like Britain remained vulnerable and when the USA went into recession (reducing the importation of overseas goods) in 1949 the British balance of payments ran into deficit, especially on the dollar account. As the reserves reached a low point a speculative run against the pound developed, finally forcing a devaluation in September.[47] The dollar parity was changed from $4.03 to $2.80 - a devaluation of some 30 per cent, and one which has generally been considered unnecessarily large. Even so, the fact of a chronic dollar shortage pointed to the need for some realignment between the dollar and the pound after the war. The authorities were already employing restrictions on imports and using exchange controls, and they were in receipt of American aid. By a process of elimination, devaluation was one of the few options available to a government committed to maintaining full employment. With hindsight, the regret must be that it was not a planned, calculated decision but was an involuntary reaction to a run on the reserves: 'to that extent devaluation was a capitulation to market opinion and another of many demonstrations of the weakness of government in the face of an exchange crisis.'[48]

In essence, of course, sterling devaluation was more a reflection of the new strength of the USA within the international economy than of an overall weakness in Britain's external account. Indeed, sterling devaluation was accompanied, or followed, by general devaluation against the dollar in both Europe and the Sterling Area.

*International Monetary Arrangements, 1945-51*

The war had heightened the need to reform international monetary arrangements, but it had also provided the opportunity for the victorious nations to consider how best to implement change. The fall of France in 1940 left the UK and the USA in a unique position to plan for the future, to devise institutional reforms for the world economy that might avoid the pitfalls of the 1920s and 1930s. The inter-war years had seen the failure to re-establish a multilateral system of payments of the sort that had existed under the pre-World War I gold standard. In the 1930s in particular, international economic relations were characterised by nationalistic 'beggar-thy-neighbour' policies whereby nations indulged in competitive devaluations, the abandonment of convertibility and practised discriminatory trade (e.g. tariffs) and financial arrangements (e.g. exchange control). On both sides of the Atlantic such policies were seen as major contributors to the depressed state of trade, to the high rate of unemployment and even to the political tensions of the decade. Planning for something better was to become an essential part of the war effort.

The two allies began exchanging ideas on possible post-war financial arrangements as early as 1941. These negotiations culminated in 1944 with a conference at Bretton Woods, New Hampshire, which was attended by representatives from forty-four nations.[49] The British negotiators, under the leadership of J.M. Keynes, had sought a more radical reform than that which was eventually ratified. However, the reality of international economic relations was that the USA was in a dominant position, and the fundamentals of the Bretton Woods Agreement were to resemble closely the designs of the chief American negotiator and Treasury official, H.D. White. In essence, the Bretton Woods Agreement sought to establish a multilateral payments system with stable exchange rates, but a system which allowed for greater flexibility than the gold standard. A permanent institution, the International Monetary Fund, was set up to oversee the new regime and to encourage international co-operation and collaboration. Member-states were to maintain their own currencies at fixed rates, or 'par-values', in terms of each other's currencies (with the US dollar emerging as the common unit of account). This was to be achieved by active intervention in exchange markets to prevent market values deviating beyond a narrow 1 per cent margin either side of par-value. More broadly, signatories sought to reverse the slide to bilateralism and protectionism by condemning discriminatory currency and trading practices, by encouraging the progressive liberalisation of trade. Currency convertibility - essential to the creation of a truly multilateral system of payments - was also an eventual aim, although restrictions on convertibility were to be permitted during a transitional phase immediately following the war. Convertibility was to be maintained in terms of each other's currency, although as for all practical purposes the acceptable reserve (or 'key') currency became the US dollar, this meant that the link with gold was retained because the dollar itself remained convertible to gold.

It was by these means that the members of the IMF hoped to gain the perceived advantages of a regime of stable exchange rates. Critically, though, provisions were written into the agreement which allowed for greater flexibility than under the gold standard. The transitional phase before the adoption of convertibility has already been noted. Another important interim provision was that which allowed for an alteration of up to 10 per cent in initial par values if these should prove inappropriate. Beyond this, currency realignments (devaluations or revaluations) were to be permitted if a country's balance of payments fell into 'fundamental disequilibrium', but only with the formal agreement of the IMF. In other words, though provided for under the rules, alterations to exchange rates were to be unusual. Potentially, therefore, member-states with balance of payments' deficits could well encounter problems similar to those under the gold standard - if their reserves were inadequate they would be obliged to deflate the domestic economy in order to maintain exchange rate parity. Here, though, the Bretton Woods Agreement offered some improvement on previous systems, by permitting the IMF to lend to (supplement the international reserves of) member-nations which developed temporary deficits, thus obviating the need - at least in the short-run - for deflation and, or, devaluation.

On 27 December 1945 thirty countries met in Washington DC and formally signed the Agreement. In the event, though, war disruption and the dollar shortage meant IMF provisions were not generally applied until much later. Indeed, Britain's aborted attempt to re-establish convertibility in 1947 illustrated the inappropriateness of adopting the rigours of the new system in the difficult circumstances of the immediate post-war world. In fact the most important West European countries, including the UK, were not to adopt general convertibility into dollars until the end of 1958.

Members of the IMF also had to join the International Bank for Reconstruction and Development, making a proportionate contribution to its reserves. The main concern of this, the second of the Bretton Woods institutions, was to be with the provision of long-term development capital. In the immediate post-war years it did, in fact, provide some reconstruction capital for a number of war-torn countries but its efforts in this respect were overwhelmed by direct US government aid of the sort already discussed. In later years the IBRD's main involvement was to be with developing nations.

Both Bretton Woods institutions were to have substantial international roles in the future - especially the IMF - but they were of little significance until the mid-1950s. The reason was their inappropriateness to the needs of post-war reconstruction. In the case of the IMF, its provisions for marginal adjustments to payments' disequilibria stood much greater chance of success in an expanding world economy with no fundamental imbalance. In the 1940s, though, universal currency convertibility and stable exchange rates were not feasible. They were to become attainable only after recovery in the non-dollar world. In the meantime, international payments were arranged under the auspices of other organisations. It has already been shown, for instance, that for Britain the Sterling Area remained important. Also, under the Marshall Plan Europeans were encouraged to plan their own recoveries and advise on the allotment of US aid. By the time of the UK's precipitous attempt at convertibility, the Americans were prepared to countenance the development of regional groupings and accepted that even with financial aid these regional groups would have to discriminate against American produce in order to cope with the dollar shortage. It was for the purpose of responding to the offer of Marshall Aid that the Organisation for European Economic Co-operation was created with seventeen members in 1948 (it had first met in 1947 as a largely Anglo-French initiative under the title, the Committee of European Co-operation). Within this geographical framework, the European states were able to move gradually from inconvertibility and bilateralism towards a freer system which led ultimately to general convertibility for OEEC countries at the end of 1958. An important development had been the creation of the European Payments Union in 1950 (preceded by less formal arrangements) which increased the supply of liquid assets and mutual credit so as to widen and strengthen the multilateral payments mechanism maintained by member-states. This reform of the intra-European payments system turned out to be an important step towards the attainment of the full Bretton Woods multilateral system, but progress was slow.

Thus, the outcome of wartime plans was markedly different than envisaged:

> The American scenario for the post-war period had been one in which after a brief transition period, possibly smoothed by *ad hoc* financial assistance, the IMF would play a central role in establishing full convertibility of currencies, a multilateral system of payments free from discriminatory controls and would, when necessary, provide temporary assistance to member countries in balance of payments difficulties. At or near the centre of these affairs, the United States...would exercise a beneficent but stern influence... All this had been too optimistic. The scale of postwar payments disequilibrium had been much greater than expected.[50]

It should nevertheless be emphasised that under the alternative arrangements European recovery was successful. Britain's record, too, was commendable: GDP (constant factor costs) grew at an average of 3 per cent per annum between 1946 and 1951, with industrial production and exports (constant market prices) recovering sharply, at 5.7 per cent and almost 9 per cent per annum respectively.[51] Full employment was maintained and the average rise in retail prices was held down to 4.6 per cent per annum until the inflationary surge associated with the Korean War in 1951. Such achievements surpassed what many had hoped for in the closing stages of the war. However, with hindsight it is necessary to point to the absence of German and Japanese competition at this time. Once recovery was achieved in those economies even more disrupted by the war than the UK, international comparisons revealed the relative weakness of Britain's growth, a weakness which was to underlie many of the country's post-war economic problems.

## FURTHER READING

R.S. Sayers, *Financial Policy, 1939-45* (HMSO and Longmans, Green & Co., London, 1956)

Alec Cairncross, *Years of Recovery. British Economic Policy, 1945-51* (Methuen, London, 1985)

Robert Triffin, *Europe and the Money Muddle. From Bilateralism to Near Convertibility, 1947-1956* (Yale University Press, New Haven, 1977)

## NOTES

1. R.S. Sayers, *Financial Policy, 1939-45* (HMSO and Longmans, Green & Co., London, 1956), pp. 3-5; and W.K. Hancock and M.M. Gowing, *British War Economy* (HMSO and Longmans, Green & Co., London, 1949, 2nd impression, 1953), pp. 325-43, 501-11.

2. Department of Employment and Productivity, *British Labour Statistics. Historical Abstract, 1886-1968* (HMSO, London, 1971), p. 170. See C.H. Feinstein, *National Income, Expenditure and Output of the United Kingdom, 1855-1965* (Cambridge University Press, Cambridge, 1972), p. T133 for GDP prices.

3. Feinstein, ibid., Table 19, p. T49.

4. R.S. Sayers, '1941 - The First Keynesian Budget', in Charles Feinstein (ed.), *The Managed Economy* (Oxford University Press, Oxford, 1983), pp. 107-17.

5. J.M. Keynes, 'How to Pay for the War' [1939-40], in *The Collected Writings of John Maynard Keynes* (Macmillan for the Royal Economic Society, London, 1972), vol. 22, pp. 40-155.

6. Sayers, *Financial Policy*, pp. 58-98; Hancock and Gowing, *War Economy*, pp. 501-11.

7. Richard Stone, 'The Use and Development of National Income and Expenditure Estimates' in D.N. Chester (ed.), *Lessons of the British War Economy* (Cambridge University Press, Cambridge, 1951), pp. 83-101.

8. For a general assessment see Michael Collins, 'Did Keynes Have the Answer to Unemployment in the 1930s?', in John Hillard (ed.), *J.M. Keynes in Retrospect* (Edward Elgar, London, 1988).

9. Sayers, *Financial Policy*, ch. 5.

10. Ibid., p. 197.

11. See pages 219-20.

12. Sayers, *Financial Policy*, pp. 219-25.

13. Ibid., pp. 460-4.

14. Ibid., p. 363. For more details on Anglo-American relations see Hugh Weeks, 'Anglo-American Supply Relationships' in Chester (ed.), *Lessons*, pp. 69-82; and D.F. McCurrach, 'Britain's US Dollar Problems, 1939-45', *Economic Journal*, vol. 58, 1948, pp. 356-68.

15. Figures from R.G.D. Allen, 'Mutual Aid between the US and the British Empire', *Journal of the Royal Statistical Society*, vol. 109, 1946, pp. 252, 257.

16. Sidney Pollard, *The Development of the British Economy, 1914-1980*, 3rd edn (Edward Arnold, London, 1983), p. 219.

17. *White Paper on Employment Policy*, Cmd. 6527 (HMSO, London, 1944), p.3.

18. 10 & 11 Geo. 6, c. 14.

19. 9 & 10 Geo. 6, c. 58.

20. *Committee on the Working of the Monetary System* [Radcliffe]. *Principal Memoranda of Evidence*, (3 vols., HMSO, London, 1960), vol. 1, pp. 4-5 on the Bank of England's constitution.

21. For an account of policy in this period see J.C.R. Dow, 'The Economic Effects of Monetary Policy, 1945-57', which was submitted to the Radcliffe Committee, *Memoranda*, vol. 3, pp. 76-105; J.C.R. Dow, *The Management of the British Economy, 1945-60* (Cambridge University Press, Cambridge, 1964), especially chs. 2 and 9; and Alec Cairncross, *Years of Recovery. British Economic Policy, 1945-51*, (Methuen, London, 1985), especially ch. 16.

22. Hugh Dalton's budget speech, 15 April 1947, *Parliamentary Debates. Commons*, vol. 436, p. 64.

23. C.M. Kennedy, 'Monetary Policy' in G.D.N. Worswick and P.H. Ady (eds.), *The British Economy, 1945-1950*, (Oxford University Press, Oxford, 1952), pp. 195-6.

24. Some figures are given in 'Exchequer Financing and the National Debt, 1945-51', *Economic Trends*, no. 98, Dec. 1961, pp. vii-xvii.

25. Cairncross, *Years of Recovery*, pp. 433-8.

26. W.T.C. King, 'Gilt-edged and the Volume of Money', *Banker*, vol. 80, 249, Oct. 1946, p. 16.

27. Dow, 'Monetary Policy', p. 78.

28. Sayers, *Financial Policy*, p. 227.

29. White Paper (prepared by the Treasury) on *Statistical Material Presented during Washington Negotiations*, Cmd. 6707, Dec. 1945.

30. Feinstein, *National Income*, p. T16.

31. *Statistical Material*, p. 4.

32. J.R. Sargent, 'Britain and the Sterling Area' in Worswick and Ady (eds.), *British Economy*, pp. 531-49; and A.R. Conan, *The Problem of Sterling* (Macmillan, London, 1966), especially chs. 2 and 3.

33. Detailed membership varied - for example, South Africa and Egypt withdrew in 1947, and in 1950 South Africa negotiated 'special status'.

34. P.D. Henderson, 'Britain's International

Position' in Worswick and Ady (eds.), *British Economy*, pp. 62-71.

35. Feinstein, *National Income*, p. T16. See T. Balogh, 'The International Aspect' in Worswick and Ady (eds.), *British Economy*, pp. 491f. (Here different figures are used).

36. Sir Richard Clarke (edited by Sir Alec Cairncross), *Anglo-American Economic Collaboration in War and Peace, 1942-1949*, (Oxford University Press, Oxford, 1982), pp. 172-5 for the flavour of internal discussions on the exchange rate.

37. Balogh, 'International Aspect', p. 489.

38. From Keynes' House of Lords speech, 18 Dec. 1945, in *Collected Works*, vol. 24, p. 612.

39. In addition there was a Canadian loan of $1.25 billion.

40. *The Economist*, vol. 149, 8 Dec. 1945, p. 821.

41. Details of Anglo-American attitudes and negotiations are in Richard Gardner, *Sterling-Dollar Diplomacy*, 2nd edn (McGraw-Hill, New York, 1969), especially, pp. 192-9. Also see Robert Triffin, *Europe and the Money Muddle. From Bilateralism to Near-Convertibility, 1947-1956* (Yale University Press, New Haven, 1957), pp. 138-47.

42. For an account of the crisis see Dow, *Management of the British Economy*, pp. 22-8.

43. Cairncross, *Years of Recovery*, ch. 5.

44. Edward Meade Earle, 'The American Stake in Europe. Retrospect and Prospect', *International Affairs*, vol. 27, 1951, pp. 423-33.

45. Alan S. Milward, *The Reconstruction of Western Europe, 1945-51* (Methuen & Co., London, 1984) provides a general assessment within a European context.

46. Triffin, *Money Muddle*, p. 1.

47. Alec Cairncross and Barry Eichengreen, *Sterling in Decline* (Basil Blackwell, Oxford, 1983), ch. 4; and Dow, *Management of the British Economy*, pp. 40-5.

48. Cairncross and Eichengreen, *Sterling in Decline*, p. 151.

49. Overviews appear in Victor Argy, *The Postwar International Money Crisis: An Analysis* (Allen & Unwin, London, 1981), chs. 2 and 3; Brian Tew, *The Evolution of the International Monetary System, 1945-81*, 2nd end, (Hutchinson, London, 1982), ch. 1; W.M. Scammell, *The International Economy since 1945* (Macmillan, London, 1980, reprinted 1982), chs. 2 and 3. More details are given in W.M. Scammell, *International Monetary Policy*, 2nd edn (Macmillan, London, 1961), chs. 5-8; and J.K. Horsefield (ed.), *The International Monetary Fund, 1945-1965: 20 Years of International Monetary Co-operation* (3 vols., IMF, Washington DC, 1969), vol. 1; and Armand Van Dormael, *Bretton Woods. Birth of a Monetary System* (Macmillan, London, 1978).

50. Scammell, *International Economy*, p. 37.

51. Calculated from Feinstein, *National Income*, pp. T25 and T16.

Chapter Eleven

# NON-CLEARING BANKS AND OTHER FINANCIAL INTERMEDIARIES SINCE WORLD WAR II

## BANKS AND OTHER FINANCIAL INTERMEDIARIES

The classification and definition of banks and other financial institutions has changed over time in response to changing functions and to the altered needs of official policy. Under the 1979 Banking Act[1] the Bank of England is required to issue formal lists of 'recognised banks' and licensed deposit-takers (LDTs). By November 1981 the list covered some 578 institutions varying from giant American banks such as Citibank which conducts business in the UK, from the familiar names of the high street clearing banks such as Lloyds and the Midland Bank, to more modest concerns like the Cooperative Bank and Moneycare Ltd. It is this mixed group which constitutes the largest section of the officially-recognised 'monetary sector'.[2] Other institutions officially considered by the mid-1980s to have been part of the monetary sector were the National Girobank, certain institutions in the Channel Islands and the Isle of Man, the Trustee Savings Banks, and the Banking Department of the Bank of England.

In practice the chief distinction between these monetary sector institutions and other financial intermediaries was the authorities' judgement that their deposit liabilities formed part of the money supply and, in fact, data for their deposits were used to calculate the then-preferred official measure of 'broad money', sterling M3 (£M3). The identity of deposits with money is easiest to appreciate in the case of the main clearing banks such as Barclays or the National Westminster, for their deposits are freely transferable (by cheque, credit card, etc.) and generally acceptable in payment. However, in the early eighties building societies were not included in the official classification of 'banks' although they were obviously deposit-gathering institutions and their deposits (most of which are called 'shares') were highly liquid. The Trustee Savings Banks were similarly excluded from the official money supply figures until 1981. In other words, while the nature of liabilities may have generally provided a means of determining if an intermediary should be a 'bank' within official classifications, there has (inevitably) been a certain degree of arbitrariness in drawing the distinction.

Table 11.1 lists the main categories of financial intermediaries frequently distinguished in the early 1980s, separating the official monetary sector institutions from other intermediaries known as 'non-bank financial intermediaries' (NBFIs). Further sub-division in Table 11.2 identifies the more important groups within the list of recognised banks and deposit-takers. The prominent position attained by such groups as the overseas banks and other British banks emphasises the importance of distinguishing among different types of banks in the post-World War II period. The varied growth experienced by both bank and non-bank intermediaries during these years reveals significant changes in the business of banking in the UK; and this and the following chapter consider the nature of those changes, the reasons behind them and their consequences. Detailed consideration of the clearing banks (groups 1, 2 and 3 in Table 11.2) is delayed until Chapter 12. This chapter's main concern is with the other banks and financial institutions. Most attention is directed to the development of the so-called parallel or wholesale money markets and to the consequences for the stability of the banking system and the authorities' regulatory role. There

Table 11.1: Categories of Financial Intermediaries

| I. <u>The Monetary Sector</u> | II. <u>Non-bank Financial Intermediaries</u>* (selected categories only) |
|---|---|
| 1. Recognised Banks | 1. Building Societies |
| 2. Deposit-Takers | 2. Finance Houses |
| 3. National Girobank | 3. Insurance Companies and Pensions Funds |
| 4. Trustee Savings Banks | 4. Unit Trusts and Investment Trusts |
| 5. Certain Institutions in the Channel Isles and Isle of Man | |
| 6. Banking Department of the Bank of England | |

* The official classification of such institutions is now, 'Other Financial Institutions' (See *Financial Statistics. Explanatory Handbook*, 1985 edition (HMSO, London, 1985)), pp. 59-77.

---

then follows brief comment on the main NBFIs and on recent institutional change in the retail banking sector.

## RELATIVE GROWTH OF FINANCIAL INSTITUTIONS

Table 11.3 enables a rough comparison to be made of the scale of growth across different groupings of financial institutions.[3] Unfortunately, the data for these different institutions are not always directly comparable, breaks in coverage and definition do occur over time and, of course, the rapid inflation of the 1970s seriously swelled the nominal figures for that decade. Nevertheless, the data do provide a general

Table 11.2 : Main Groups of Institutions Among Recognised Banks and Deposit-Takers, as Dec. 1978

| | Number of Instit-utions | Total Assets/ Liabili-ties (£ bill.) | Share of Total (%) |
|---|---|---|---|
| 1. London Clear-ing Banks | 6 | 44.4 | 20.0% |
| 2. Scottish Clearing Banks | 3 | 5.3 | 2.4% |
| 3. Northern Ireland Banks | 4 | 1.3 | 0.5% |
| 4. Accepting Houses | 35 | 9.1 | 4.1% |
| 5. Other British Banks | 70 | 30.2 | 13.6% |
| 6. Overseas Banks | 201 | 118.1 | 53.3% |
| 7. Consortium Banks | 29 | 9.6 | 4.3% |
| 8. Discount Market Institutions | 18 | 4.2 | 1.9% |
| | Total | 222.2 | |

*Source*: *Committee to Review the Functioning of Financial Institutions. Report*. Cmnd. 7937 (London, HMSO, 1980), Appendix 3, p. 394.

---

impression of relative scale (the size of savings banks' deposits compared to building societies', etc.). They also highlight the sharp growth experienced by the

Table 11.3 : Selected Financial Institutions' Liabilities/Assets, 1957-1978
(£ billions)

| end of:- | 1957 | 1967 | 1978 |
|---|---|---|---|
| Deposit liabilities of 'All Banks' in the U.K.+ | 8.7 | 21.2 | 203.9 |
| Discount houses ('borrowed funds') | 0.9 | 1.7 | 4.1 |
| Trustee savings banks ('total deposits') | 1.1 | 2.3 | 5.0 |
| National savings banks ('total deposits') | 1.7 | 1.8 | 3.0 |
| Finance houses: | | | |
| a) Deposits | 0.1 | 0.6 | 0.4* |
| b) Total selected liabilities | 0.3 | 1.1 | 1.1* |
| Building societies (shares & deposits) | 2.2 | 7.0 | 37.5 |
| Unit trusts (total assets) | 0.06 | 0.8 | 3.9 |
| Insurance companies (total funds/assets) | 4.9 | 12.9 | 46.8 |
| Pension funds (total funds/assets) | 2.1 | 6.4 | 31.1 |

*Notes*

\+ 'All Banks' = London clearing banks, Scottish clearing banks, Northern Ireland banks, accepting houses, overseas banks and other British banks.

* end, March 1976 - excludes finance houses listed as banks.

*Source:*

*Committee to Review the Functioning of Financial Institutions. Report*, Cmnd. 7937 (HMSO, London, 1980), Appendix 3, pp. 393-485.

building societies, insurance companies and pension funds and, from a much smaller base, by the unit trusts. The remaining institutions underwent more modest expansion, except for the 'All Banks' group, where deposits grew most rapidly of all.

Table 11.4 provides a breakdown of changes in the liabilities of these banks and of the discount houses. Again, there are many pitfalls in using data for the non-clearing banks (through changes in coverage, through difficulties of 'double-counting' for institutions active in wholesale money markets where the practice of 'on-lending' to other banks is central to their business, through the effects of inflation, etc.). But no amount of modification of the data would alter the main message of the table. It shows starkly the phenomenal post-war growth of banks other than the traditional money market institutions. The London and Scottish clearing banks, the Northern Ireland banks and the discount houses all grew in the period, but the most dramatic expansion was elsewhere. In particular, overseas banks based in London developed from being relatively unimportant (at 8 per cent of the banking liabilities shown) within the total banking sector of the 1940s and early 1950s, to being the dominant component (at 65 per cent) by the close of the 1970s when their total liabilities were some two-and-a-half times those of the London clearing banks. The table also shows that the accepting houses were another group of banking institutions to enjoy relatively high growth. Other British banks and Consortium banks have only recently been separately identified but these diverse groupings were also important sections of the total banking sector by the 1970s.

## THE LONDON MONEY MARKET

> The money markets are the mechanisms through which wholesale funds are channelled from lenders to borrowers. The London money markets are made up of a series of highly integrated groups of financial institutions which facilitate the borrowing and lending of these funds, which are

Table 11.4 : Deposit Liabilities of Selected Monetary Sector Institutions, 1951-1979
(£ billions)
[percentage share of sub-total in brackets][1]

| | 1951 | 1965 | 1979 (*total* liabilities) |
|---|---|---|---|
| London clearing banks | 6.3[2] (70%) | 9.5 (54%) | 54.3 (25%) |
| Scottish clearing banks | 0.8 (8%) | 1.0 (5%) | 5.9 (3%) |
| Northern Ireland banks | 0.1 (1%) | 0.2 (1%) | 1.4 (1%) |
| Discount market | 1.0⁺ (11%) | 1.4⁺ (8%) | 4.7 (2%) |
| Overseas banks | 0.7* (8%) | 4.6 (26%) | 141.7 (65%) |
| *of which* American | 0.1* (1%) | 1.4 (8%) | 59.2 (27%) |
| Accepting houses | 0.1* (1%) | 1.0 (6%) | 10.3 (5%) |
| Sub-total | 9.1 | 17.6 | 218.4 |
| Consortium banks | - | - | 10.6 |
| Other British banks | - | - | 39.00 |

*Notes:*

1. Rounding-up is responsible for the apparent discrepancies with the 'small' figures.
2. Gross deposits (i.e. including 'items in transit', etc.).

* Total deposits and current accounts.

\+ 'Borrowed funds', excluding capital and reserves.

*Source: Bank of England Quarterly Bulletin*

> mainly short-term money. There is no physical market-place, transactions being primarily conducted by telephone and telex.
>
> (Wilson Committee[4], 1980, Appendix 3, p. 504)

In practice there is a fair degree of integration across the various money markets, often with some of the same institutions active in more than one market, but it is convenient to distinguish, in the first instance, between the traditional money market (or discount market) and the newer, parallel money markets. The parallel markets can be further sub-divided so as to highlight the different functions performed.[5] All these markets deal in 'wholesale' money in the sense that transactions involve large sums and are mainly conducted between financial institutions and/or corporations. While there is some blurring of distinction on the margin, activity in these markets is generally distinguishable from retail banking transactions where funds are raised, and loans made, at a much lower average value and with many more customers (many of whom are individuals) from the personal sector.

## THE DISCOUNT MARKET

The traditional short-term money market was the one created by the London discount houses.[6] This has continued to operate throughout the post-war period - but starting as *the* money market, it has become just one among a number of wholesale markets. Earlier chapters showed that during the nineteenth century, the discount houses emerged as an important bridge between the Bank of England and the clearing banks. Their principal activity was the provision of a market for short-term bills of exchange. In the nineteenth century commercial bills - originating in the domestic and overseas private sectors - had been the mainstay, but twentieth-century wars increased the government's short-term debt so sharply that by the beginning of the post-war period (and earlier in the inter-war years) Treasury bills predominated (see Table 11.5). Agreements which had been in operation since the 1930s between the Bank of England and market institutions had created a situation whereby the discount houses' weekly tender guaranteed to make good any shortfall in the demand for Treasury bills. A crucial feature was the authorities' preparedness to ensure that the discount houses could always meet this undertaking – in effect, through its commitment as lender of last resort the Bank of England was always ready to advance cash to them when they needed it.

Thus, the discount houses first function has been to provide a market for bills originating in both the private and public sectors. Another traditionally important function has been the provision of very short-term assets for domestic and overseas banks. The discount houses' main liabilities were funds borrowed from banks 'at call and short notice' (usually overnight or of a few days' duration). As the banks did not borrow directly from the Bank of England, the discount houses formed an important link between the banking sector and the central bank. Thus, if the banks found themselves in need of cash they could call in their loans to the discount houses who (if short of cash themselves) could, in turn, borrow from the Bank of England. Throughout the period the authorities laid great store by the Bank's ability to influence short-term money markets in this way, by altering the supply of cash through open market operations and by varying the terms on which the Bank would lend (the rate charged was known as Bank rate or, since 1972, as Minimum Lending Rate).[7]

The main change in the discount market since World War II has been the decline of Treasury bills. Table 11.5 shows that in 1957 these constituted some 67 per cent of the total amount of indentified short-term sterling instruments, but by 1979 this had shrunk to just 6 per cent. During the late 1950s and 1960s the decline reflected the waning influence of war-time finance as the money markets turned from public sector debt to private sector securities. Government funding policy (switching from short- to

Table 11.5 : The London Sterling Money Markets, 1957-79. Amounts outstanding, £ billions (percentage share of total in brackets)

| | 1957 | 1967 | 1979 |
|---|---|---|---|
| Money at call with discount market | 0.9 (18%) | 1.7 (18%) | 4.4 (11%) |
| Treasury bills | 3.4 (67%) | 3.2 (34%) | 2.5 (6%) |
| Commercial bills | 0.3 (5%) | 0.7 (8%) | 5.6 (14%) |
| Local authority temporary debt | 0.5 (9%) | 1.8 (19%) | 5.7 (15%) |
| Deposits with finance houses | 0.1 (2%) | 0.6 (6%) | 1.1 (3%) |
| Interbank deposits | n.a. [1962: 0.6 (8%)] | 1.3 (14%) | 16.4 (42%) |
| Sterling certificates of deposit | - | - | 3.7 (9%) |
| Total of those identified above | 5.1 | 9.2 | 39.5 |
| Other market loans by the banking sector | n.a. | n.a. | 5.3 |

*Notes:* There are discontinuities in some of the original data series - see source for details.

*Source: Committee to Review the Functioning of Financial Institutions, Report,* Cmnd. 7937 (HMSO, London, 1980), Appendix 3, p. 510.

long-term debt) reinforced the process. More recently, in the late 1970s and early 1980s the authorities' anti-inflationary efforts reduced the supply of Treasury bills still further. The discount houses compensated for this contraction in government bills partly by expanding their holdings of short-term government bonds (which have up to five years to maturity) though they have rarely held a significant amount of longer-dated bonds. Within the market itself, though, the strong revival of commercial bills was a more obvious counter to the demise of Treasury bills. This is clearly shown in Table 11.6, with Treasury bills falling from 61 to 14 per cent of the discount houses' main assets between 1951 and 1979, whereas 'other bills' rose from just 6 per cent to 51 per cent during the same period. The discount market institutions have also expanded their sphere of business into the newer money markets, holding bankers' certificates of deposits (CDs) and local authority short-term debt in their portfolios. However, into the 1980s they have remained mainly holders of bills.

One consequence of the development of other short-term money markets was that the traditional suppliers of funds to the discount market (the banks) had a broader choice of very liquid assets available. Interbank loans and CDs generally paid high rates and, in part, they became very attractive alternatives to the discount houses' 'call money' which was, subsequently, kept to a minimum.[8] Nevertheless, the intervention of the monetary authorities has ensured that this process has been constrained. The authorities endowed reserve status on call money held with the discount markets and, thus, ensured a minimum demand for it (this special status was also largely responsible for the lower interest rate paid). First, the clearing banks and, then after the introduction of 'Competition and Credit Control' in 1971, all banks, were obliged to hold call money as part of their reserve assets.[9] Even when the reserve asset requirement was abolished in 1981, the authorities insisted on safeguarding the discount houses' position by obliging all listed banks to place funds with them (and/or money brokers and gilt-edged

Table 11.6: The Discount Market: Holdings of Selected Assets, 1951-79 £ billion (percentage share in brackets)

| End of | Government Stocks | Treasury Bills | Other Bills |
|---|---|---|---|
| 1951 | 0.3 (30%) | 0.6 (61%) | 0.06 (6%) |
| 1965 | 0.5 (34%) | 0.5 (34%) | 0.3 (23%) |
| 1979 | 0.8 (15%) | 0.7*(14%) | 2.5+(51%) |

*Notes:*

* For 1979 British and Northern Ireland Treasury bills; for other dates Northern Ireland Treasury bills are classed with 'other bills'.

\+ Excluding local authority and other public sector bills.

*Source: Bank of England Quarterly Bulletin*

---

jobbers) as secured 'call money' to an average value of 6 per cent (with a minimum of 4 per cent) of a bank's eligible liabilities (mainly sterling liabilities plus net non-sterling liabilities).[10] Thus, the liabilities of the discount market institutions have retained their special official status, just as the institutions have retained the privilege of direct access to the Bank of England.

The Green Paper on *Monetary Policy* initiated a major change in 1980. The authorities abolished the practice (first established in 1935) whereby the discount houses were allowed to collude on the price they tendered for Treasury bills. Even so, discount market institutions continued to attract official 'favours'. The reasons given by the authorities for this supportive stance were not too dissimilar to those operative since the 1940s (if not since the 1930s): the authorities wished to maintain an active market for bills and they wanted to continue influencing conditions in that market so as to be able to affect short-term market rates as part of monetary control policy.[11]

## PARALLEL MONEY MARKETS AND INSTITUTIONS

Since the late 1950s a second money market - or group of parallel markets - has developed. The result has been a tremendous expansion in the total and type of short-term market instruments available to banks and others. These instruments are traded in ostensibly discrete markets - in both sterling and non-sterling currencies - but, in practice, there is much inter-connection amongst them. The new markets were initially developed by existing specialist institutions which took on extra business as opportunities were created by changes in official policy and regulations. From the early 1950s, 'the prime mover in the new markets [was] competition in rates of interest, and the springboard for later developments was the change in monetary policy from cheap money to the use of interest rates towards the close of 1951.'[12] Higher and more variable rates increased the margin for potential profit for financial intermediaries prepared to compete for funds which did not originate in domestic retail banking. There emerged new highly-competitive markets, free from the restrictive practices that continued to govern the clearing banks and discount houses until 1971. Further boosts came from the intermittent application of 'monetary squeezes' which concentrated upon restricting clearing bank advances. The resultant rationing of conventionally-supplied bank funds, and the retention of cartelised prices by the clearers, both encouraged dissatisfied customers to seek alternative supplies and enabled interest rates to rise high enough to attract other supplies of money into the new markets. Once established, the new services and new monetary instruments offered by the parallel markets helped ensure their continuation, even when the early favourable conditions receded.

Initially the main participants in the new markets were merchant banks, such as the accepting houses, and overseas banks with offices in London. Indeed, much of the subsequent growth of these institutions was to become closely intertwined with the continued development of the parallel money markets.

When the Radcliffe Committee reported in 1959 there were eighteen members of the Accepting House Committee; by the time of the Wilson Committee Report in 1980 this was down one, to seventeen.[13] In the late fifties their traditional business of 'accepting' bills of exchange for commission was predominant but they were already engaged in a variety of financial activities such as the advisory and issuing services they offered to the long-term capital market. Because their acceptances were eligible for discount (or as security for loans) at the Bank of England and, therefore, were potentially a part of the clearing banks' official reserve assets, the Bank had oversight of the accepting houses' asset structure. There was a keen emphasis on liquidity, with short-term loans to the discount market and local authorities, and holdings of short-term government debt figuring large in their balance sheets.

Since then they have continued their specialised accepting business but, in addition, they have become extensively engaged in wholesale banking. They compete actively for wholesale funds, offering interest on almost all their deposits which are predominantly in the form of time deposits and certificates of deposit (CDs). Of their assets, market loans (CDs, local authority loans and interbank loans) are the most important, at some 53 per cent of total assets by the end of 1981; whereas advances at that time were mainly in non-sterling currencies and almost always in the form of term loans, not overdrafts.[14] The scale of expansion over the three decades since 1951 is apparent from Table 11.4. Their liabilities rose some 75-fold [15] over the period and in 1979 they accounted for 5 per cent of the total banking liabilities identified (a sum equivalent to those of the Scottish banks and discount houses combined).

The overseas banks have been another major group of principals in the parallel markets. They have always been a diverse group of institutions.[16] The

Radcliffe Committee identified seventy-five such banks in London in the late fifties. These were 'the London offices of British [banking] companies whose other offices are in other countries...' and '...branches of banks whose head offices are in other countries.'[17] At that time their main business arose directly out of international trade (e.g. foreign exchange dealing and the provision of international credit facilities) although some American banks had developed UK domestic banking services to a small degree. The next two decades saw a tremendous expansion of these banks.[18] By the beginning of 1985 there were 346 overseas banks and subsidiaries in London, with firms from the USA (64 in number) and Japan (25) providing the biggest national contingents.

The expansion of their liabilities was little short of miraculous, making the accepting houses' boom seem very modest in comparison. Table 11.4 shows that total liabilities stood at £142 billion at the close of 1979. This was equivalent to 65 per cent of the total identified liabilities (consortium and other British banks excluded), or some two-and-one-half times the liabilities of the London clearing banks (LCBs); and representing close to a 200-fold increase over the deposits of 1951. The figures also make clear the importance and relatively faster growth of the American banks (accounting for 13 per cent of overseas banks' deposits in 1951, and 42 per cent in 1979). By the late 1970s some of these banks were still active within the traditional area of financing international trade, and as a group they were important in the international acceptance business, but many of these banks had also been attracted to London by the strength of the euro-currency and euro-bond markets. The overwhelming proportion of their business (in fact, some 90 per cent of both liabilities and assets by the early 1980s) has been in non-sterling currencies and almost all their business has been conducted in wholesale money markets. The scale of their activities is so great, however, that they have inevitably impinged on business that may otherwise have gone to the domestic banks. For instance, in 1978 overseas banks were responsible for 15 per cent of total sterling advances and some 60 per cent of foreign currency advances to UK residents.

The discount houses and clearing banks, too, have participated in the business of the new money markets. The former did so from an early stage through the purchase of short-period local authority bills, and as deposit-takers and lenders in the inter-bank (and, later, the CD) markets. At first the participation of the clearers was somewhat tardy and indirect. Through the sixties the clearers found themselves largely under-lent, not least because of government restrictions on their advances and their asset structures. Thus, there was little need to seek actively fresh sources of funds from the wholesale markets. Adherence to their cartelised price agreements and traditional lines of business also played a part in determining entry into the new, more competitive, markets.[19] However, the clearers were to stake a share in the new business through the creation of merchant bank subsidiaries and affiliates - such as Lloyds Associated Banking Company - which eventually developed a full range of merchant bank services, including investment advice and acceptance facilities. Later, after 1971, when government constraints were removed, the LCBs' parent banks began to participate actively in the markets as principals, although some also retained their more specialist subsidiaries. As a consequence, by the mid-seventies wholesale deposits were of great importance to the clearers as a source of funds, representing over 40 per cent of the LCB groups' total deposits.

The other two groups of banks included in Table 11.4 for 1979 are 'consortium banks' and 'other British banks', both of which include banks heavily committed to the wholesale money markets. By the end of 1978 there were 29 consortium banks (23 in early 1985), created by international consortia of various banks including UK clearing banks and accepting houses. The first of this type of consortium had been formed in the mid-1960s but their numbers were not to expand significantly until the end of the decade.[20]

They were formed to provide specialist international facilities, servicing multinational corporations, often on a large-scale and perhaps with a geographical specialism. Ninety per cent of their deposits have been denominated in non-sterling currencies, the great bulk being raised in the wholesale euro-currency markets for interbank funds and CDs. Similarly 90 per cent of their assets have been held in non-sterling currencies, one-half of which in the late 1970s were in the form of money market loans.

'Other British banks' is a mixed group which at the time of the Wilson Committee enquiry included domestic retail banks such as the Cooperative Bank, the Yorkshire Bank and the National Girobank.[21] But it also included the merchant bank subsidiaries of the clearing banks, and some international banks, such as Standard Charter and Grindlays, which were important participants in the wholesale money markets.

*Secondary Banks*

The various institutions involved in the parallel money markets have been grouped together as 'secondary banks'.[22] From the 1960s they differed from the retail deposit banks (such as the London and Scottish clearers) by raising the bulk of their deposits wholesale, involving a relatively small number of large accounts and almost all their advances were for fixed periods. Their most liquid assets (excluding cash) were held in the form of loans to the parallel money markets, not as bills or loans to the discount market. In contrast, the clearers did not attain a similar liquid asset structure until the late seventies. Another difference from the deposit banks used to be that both the assets and liabilities of the secondary banks were denominated in sterling and non-sterling.

The fact that terms for both loans and deposits were fixed meant that there was a greater 'matching' of one with the other by the secondary banks, matching for both time of maturity and type of currency. Fixed time periods themselves reduced uncertainty and in the seventies this became an increasingly important attribute. Rapid inflation, high and variable nominal interest rates and fluctuating exchange rates all added to the volatility of the banking environment. Thus, methods of reducing uncertainty, such as the greater matching of liabilities with assets, became more valuable. Moreover, the ability to draw on the wholesale markets for fresh deposits – of a specified amount, of a specified currency and, perhaps, for a specified time period – greatly increased the flexibility of a bank's response to an increased demand for loans. The existence of parallel money markets meant, perhaps, that the secondary banks were not as closely circumscribed as the clearers who (until their own excursions into the wholesale markets) were more dependent on a relatively stable supply of retail deposits:

> In this type of business the banks have considerable freedom to vary the volume of lending they carry on their books, since they are usually able to increase the funds at their disposal when necessary by bidding for deposits at the going rate or by issuing negotiable time certificates of deposits.[23]

This flexibility, of course, was one of the main attractions to the clearing banks when the removal of government constraints enabled them to use the facilities developed in the parallel markets. As they did so during the 1970s, some of the distinctions between them and the secondary banks became somewhat blurred, though their much heavier dependence on retail deposits has remained.

## STERLING MONEY MARKETS

It is common to divide the parallel markets between sterling and non-sterling markets. Of the sterling markets four are frequently distinguished: the local authority market; the finance house market; the inter-bank market; and the certificate of deposit market.[24] Before describing developments in each of these, it is worth examining the figures in Table 11.5.

These reveal the size and relative importance of the short-term sterling assets/liabilities created in the various markets. The long-term decline of Treasury bills and revival of commercial bills has already been discussed, but the other principal change was the sharp rise of inter-bank deposits – from 8 per cent of the total identified in the early 1960s to 42 per cent at the end of 1979. By this latter date sterling CDs were also of considerable significance (valued at one-and-a-half times Treasury bills) and the importance of the local authority short-term market, which had been established in the 1960s, was still apparent. Deposits with finance houses had also expanded in the 1960s but, overall, they remained a relatively modest part of the total stock of wholesale money.

*Local Authority Market*

From 1955 a change in government policy obliged local authorities to diminish their previous dependence on the Public Works Loan Board from which they could borrow at favourable rates. Instead they were to seek loans from the market at current rates. With the issue of long-term stock also regulated, local authorities began to devise various means of raising short-term loans – mainly in the form of deposits, at first. Thus emerged the local authority money market. Only large (or wholesale) deposits were acceptable to the local authorities, generally in sterling, often overnight or for two or seven days, although some loans were fixed for up to 364 days. The authorities also began to issue large denomination bills, money market instruments that were usually rediscountable at the Bank of England and eligible as bankers' reserve assets. The main holders of the local authorities' short-term debt (deposits and bills) have been banks and other financial intermediaries although, on occasions, industrial and commercial companies and even other local authorities have also been holders. Table 11.5 gives some impression of the amount involved, with local authority temporary debt rising from £0.5 billion in 1957 to £5.7 billion in 1979, and with its relative importance peaking in the mid–1960s at just under one–fifth of short–term sterling instruments.

As with the other new markets, brokers were active in placing funds with the authorities and specialist firms emerged which handled all forms of local authority debt. In addition to their very short–term debt, in the past local authorities have also borrowed for one or two years on mortgage and, since statutory authorisation in 1963, they have issued a variety of bonds – of one to five years' maturity. These bonds have not been 'eligible' securities at the Bank of England but they are, nevertheless, highly marketable securities.

*Finance House Market*

The finance houses have always raised a significant proportion of their resources in the form of deposits (about 46 per cent liabilities in 1958 and 60 per cent in 1966, but down to 28 per cent by 1976).[25] These have been mainly wholesale deposits raised from industrial and commercial companies, from banks, accepting houses and other financial institutions, as well as from overseas residents. In addition, the finance companies have borrowed directly from the banking sector and from the other short–term money and bill markets.

*Inter–Bank Market*

As Table 11.5 shows, during the seventies the inter–bank market became by far the largest of the sterling parallel markets. By 1979 inter–bank deposits accounted for 42 per cent of total indentified sterling short–term instruments, dwarfing all other components by comparison. The Wilson Committee summarised the main features as they existed in the late 1970s:

> Dealings on this market between banks are on an unsecured basis and are ordinarily in amounts of £0.5 million and £1 million or more. Deposits are not negotiable or transferable. Money may be lent on an overnight basis, at call, or for a fixed term, [and] the bulk of transactions are for

periods of under 3 months.[26]

A major consequence of the development of inter–bank loans on such a scale was that it allowed participating banks to adjust liquidity positions very easily and very quickly through borrowing or lending amongst themselves, usually with a broker as a go–between. Before the 1960s financial institutions had had to rely upon changes in their call money with the discount market or bill discounts in order to adjust their cash and liquidity positions. The extremely flexible inter–bank loan facility provided an effective (and often more profitable) alternative. Only on those occasions when the banking sector as a whole required liquidity, was there recourse to discount market call money or sales of Treasury and other eligible bills. Until 1971 the main principals in the market were merchant banks (including the accepting houses), overseas banks, and clearing bank subsidiaries and affiliates. Since then, the removal by the authorities of discriminatory liquidity constraints, and the abolition of the interest rate cartels, has led to a much greater involvement in inter–bank loans from the clearing banks and discount houses. Transactions are in large, round amounts, both deposits and advances are generally for short, fixed periods, and loans are unsecured, depending on the creditworthiness of the institutions involved.

*Certificates of Deposit*

Certificates of deposit are negotiable (i.e. saleable) instruments which testify that a certain sum has been deposited with the issuing bank under specified terms regarding interest rates and maturity date. Interest is paid on maturity to the holder (not necessarily the depositor). The minimum amount has been £50,000, though up to £500,000 or more is common. USA dollar certificates of deposit were first issued in London in 1966 but it was not until 1968 that the authorities permitted the issue of sterling CDs. Initially it was the secondary banks that used the facility to any degree, but from 1971 the clearing banks also participated.[27]

From the borrower's point of view there is little difference in the cost of CDs and fixed-term deposits, but CDs do provide the depositor with a highly marketable instrument. CDs can be readily resold - the discount houses having developed a secondary market in their dealing - and, thus, they enable depositors to encash the funds if the need arises. The new owner can then reclaim the deposit plus interest at the maturity date, or a CD may be re-sold a number of times before it matures. In turn, this resale ability has perhaps induced depositors to take up CDs for longer periods than would have been the case for non-negotiable deposits, thus providing the banks with some extra security and enabling a better 'match' of resources with their medium-term loans.[28] CDs are not rediscountable at the Bank of England but they are, nevertheless, highly liquid assets and, as with short-term inter-bank loans, they have helped facilitate day-to-day adjustment to liquidity positions. In fact, the Wilson Committee found that most holders of sterling CDs were other banks and discount houses although building societies and other financial institutions, as well as some commercial and industrial firms, were all holders to a lesser extent.[29]

## EUROCURRENCY MARKETS

> The term 'eurocurrency transaction' applies to any transaction in a currency undertaken by the parent company, subsidiary or branch of a commercial bank operating outside the country of origin of that particular currency.[30]

London became the main financial centre for such transactions and, while other currencies have been of significance, US dollars have been the main currency involved.[31] Some British banks accepted foreign currency deposits on a small scale before World War II but it was not until after the 1950s that transactions became large-scale. This was made possible by the re-establishment of exchange convertibility for a number of major currencies (including sterling) in 1958 and the associated revival of foreign exchange markets. The accumulation of dollars in financial centres like London signalled the end of the world-wide dollar shortage that had characterised the immediate post-war period, as capital movements and US government overseas expenditure during the sixties ensured a mounting outflow of dollars from America. Moreover, official monetary constraints (such as 'Regulation Q' which had first imposed ceilings on the rates payable on US time deposits in the 1930s) kept down interest rates in the USA compared to those prevailing in Europe.[32] As a result large-scale holders of dollars could find more profitable employment for them outside the USA. Meanwhile repeated bouts of monetary constraint in America left an unsatisfied demand for bank accommodation – for some corporations, borrowing dollars overseas became an attractive proposition.

The City of London's existing financial experience and extensive international banking links helped attract the new business to the UK. Opportunities for remunerative and secure investment were either available or were developing rapidly (e.g. in the inter-bank and local authority markets) and an active foreign exchange market already existed. Inter-bank transactions quickly established a secondary market in eurocurrencies where funds could be readily lent and re-lent. These funds were generally foreign currency deposits at offices of financial institutions operating outside the currency's country of origin. Most were sited in Europe (hence the term 'eurocurrency') but they could be European banks or other financial institutions, or European offices of institutions from non-European countries such as the USA. It was through these institutions that eurocurrency transactions were conducted. As is often the case with markets, once the specialist facilities were established in London the process developed its own momentum: existing facilities attracted an influx of overseas banks and, as the market grew, facilities improved.

The benign attitude of the British monetary

authorities was also of significance. The Bank of England welcomed the expansion of the City's international business. Of practical importance was the exempting of foreign currency deposits (or advances) from the various constraints applied by the authorities to sterling deposits (or advances) in the pursuit of credit and monetary policy. Eurocurrency deposits were free to grow unrestrained by official directives. The effect of the oil crises of the 1970s has been another important element in the expansion of international banking. The sharp increases in oil prices and the severe recessions endured by the non-oil producing world greatly increased the scale of financial imbalance within the international economy. A major re-cycling problem emerged, creating important opportunities for financial intermediaries able to attract funds from the surplus countries and redirect them to deficit areas. The eurocurrency markets played a critical role here, with the new business underpinning the sharp expansion experienced in the seventies.

From the early days of the developing market there was participation from a wide range of banks, including the clearers through their merchant bank subsidiaries, but overseas banks in London were the main dealers. As in the sterling inter-bank market, transactions were in large round amounts (usually, by the late 1970s, in excess of £1 million) and purchases and sales of currency were arranged through brokers (generally foreign exchange brokers). This remained the case into the 1980s. Deposits are generally 'at call' or for short periods up to six months, though some have been for as long as five years.

Although breaks in the data series again make difficult any accurate measurement of growth over the period as a whole, the phenomenal expansion of the eurocurrency market is marked in Table 11.4 by the rise of the 'overseas banks' to such a prominent position within the monetary sector. Table 11.7, which is based on data presented by the Wilson Committee, provides more detail on the scale of international banking activities. The aggregate figures

Table 11.7: UK Institutions' International Banking Activity, 1962-1969. Amounts outstanding (£ billions)

| end of: | 1962 | 1967 | 1979 |
|---|---|---|---|
| Liabilities | | | |
| Foreign currency deposits and advances from: | | | |
| Other UK banks | 0.3 | 1.6 | 36.6 |
| Other UK residents | 0.1 | 0.3 | 4.9 |
| Overseas banks | 1.0 | 4.4 | 91.5 |
| Other non-residents | | | 17.4 |
| Other foreign currency liabilities | n.a. | n.a. | 21.4 |
| Total foreign currency liabilities | n.a. | n.a. | 171.8 |
| External liabilities in sterling | 0.6 | 2.0 | 9.9 |
| Assets | | | |
| Foreign currency deposits, etc., with: | | | |
| Other UK banks | 0.3 | 1.6 | 37.2 |
| Other UK residents | - | 0.3 | 10.6 |
| Overseas banks | 1.0 | 4.4 | 90.9 |
| Other non-residents | | | 29.5 |
| Other foreign currency assets | n.a. | n.a. | 3.9 |
| Total foreign currency assets | n.a. | n.a. | 172.1 |
| External assets in sterling | 1.5 | 1.0 | 6.9 |

*Notes:* Important differences of definition occurred with the introduction of new returns in 1974. The data for foreign currency liabilities to, and claims on, UK banks and other UK residents before 1972 are

(continued)

from the domestic banking returns and only cover institutions in the banking sector. See source for further details.

*Source:* *Committee to Review the Functioning of Financial Institutions. Report*, Cmnd. 7937 (HMSO, London, 1980), Appendix 3, p. 512.

---

reflect the fact that during the 1970s the eurocurrency market became the largest of the money markets based in London. The very rapid expansion of overseas banks is again apparent. The disaggregated figures show that most eurocurrency transactions were of an inter–bank nature, with over 74 per cent of both liabilities and assets owed to, or held with, UK and overseas banks in the late 1970s. Within this it is assumed that in general the larger, better–known banks with large retail networks (such as some of the large US banks) would be net lenders to the market, while smaller banks, or those with restricted access to retail deposits (such as consortium banks), would be net borrowers.[33] The eurocurrency inter–bank market permits the matching of deposit–givers with deposit–takers, rarely directly but eventually through an efficient system of multiple on–lending between banks.

One important development in eurocurrency markets that deserves specific mention was the first issue of dollar certificates of deposit in 1966. These are similar to sterling CDs but obviously denominated in US dollars and they are subject to their own set of Bank of England requirements governing amounts and maturity. After their introduction dollar CDs quickly emerged as the most important of the market instruments used in the eurocurrency market, providing the same advantages of sterling CDs already discussed.

## SUMMARY ON DEVELOPMENTS IN PARALLEL MARKETS

It is clear from the above account that the late 1950s and early 1960s marked the beginning of a period of important structural change and innovation within British banking. The lengthy Bank of England quotation that follows serves to emphasise both the scale of change occurring in the wholesale money markets and the degree of cross-fertilisation and integration between these new markets:

> ... the most remarkable growth among the [secondary] banks has come in the form of foreign currency deposits - mainly euro-dollars and, since 1966, dollar negotiable certificates of deposit - mostly owned by non-residents, so that much of this business represents purely financial intermediation between foreigners ... [with] ... negligible impact on domestic financial conditions ... These [secondary] banks ... have also been able to attract a rapidly increasing total of sterling deposits, and with the addition of such foreign currency funds as they have switched into sterling, have been able to command a growing total of funds for investment in UK assets. These banks have played a major role in the rapid development of the parallel money markets in London, through which they both extend and take short-term liquid finance. Their sterling funds are largely employed in loans to other banks and to local authorities, besides advances to private customers...[34]

## BANK STABILITY AND PRUDENTIAL SUPERVISION

The emergence by the early twentieth century of a small group of dominant clearing banks with massive retail deposit resources, and the mutual understanding they developed with the Bank of England, left few fears for the basic stability of the UK banking system. The banking crises and failures of the nineteenth century had faded far into history by the time of the post–World War II period. Even so, banking has never been a riskless enterprise, even for large banks, and there have always been smaller concerns operating on the fringes of conventional banking activities, concerns whose resources were small enough and business unconventional enough to raise questions of security, even probity. In all forms of business the innovators incur the most risk; some reap the rewards of high profits but others suffer the ultimate corporate penalty of bankruptcy. Any call for special treatment of bank failures – or, more generally, bank stability – must rest either on the fact that a large number of depositors might lose money in the event of liquidation or (and probably of more practical importance) that as ultimately all banking depends on the maintenance of confidence, there is a danger that the collapse of any one bank could undermine faith in other institutions and so pose a wider threat to the credit system. For these reasons most monetary authorities take a keen interest in banking stability. Historically, in the UK this took the form of establishing a general legislative framework thought to be conducive to stability, but with little detailed prudential regulation of a bank's business. However, as earlier sections on the nineteenth century have shown, legislative regulation tended to be manifest reactions to problems, lagging behind changes in business practice. In the post–war period, too, official action has tended to follow events.

In particular, the mushrooming of the secondary bank sector during the 1960s was to highlight serious deficiencies in the regulatory framework operating after the war. As the country's central bank, it was the Bank of England, of course, which carried the ultimate responsibility for the liquidity and stability of banks in the UK. The Bank acted as lender of last resort to the banking system and, in pursuit of wider monetary aims, it imposed certain asset ratio requirements on the clearing banks. But, in fact, it had few formal powers of supervision over financial institutions. Instead it relied upon informal agreements with the most important money market institutions, the clearing banks, the discount houses and the accepting houses. These controls were not intended so much to ensure commercial viability of these institutions – for they were generally of undoubted respectability – but to help promote Bank policy with regard to the market for government securities and/or broader credit policy. With a small number of institutions involved, personal contact and mutual trust among top management ensured that the Bank would receive information and proffer advice on the general nature of business conducted. The Bank claimed that the advantage of such a system, based as it was on convention rather than law, was that it permitted maximum flexibility (allowing for changing circumstances) and yet still secured effective control.[35] However, the proliferation of secondary banks magnified the deficiencies in such a loose means of regulation. The much larger numbers meant personal contact was impracticable. Also the size, nature of business and nationality of these institutions was so diverse as to render inapplicable any set of simple regulations governing liquidity or capital adequacy.

The authorities' decision in 1971 to extend the requirement to maintain specified reserve asset ratios from the clearers alone to *all* banks, concentrated attention on what were the most appropriate definitions of 'liquidity' for the secondary banks, as well as on the more basic question of what institutions should be considered to be 'banks' and, therefore, subject to official control. But it was the secondary bank crisis of 1973–4 that instilled urgency into the search for reform. The crisis was the most serious experienced by the UK banking system since the Great Depression of the 1930s, or even since the Baring Crisis of 1890.[36]

The crisis arose in the secondary bank sector where a number of relatively small banks had been engaged in a speculative spree in the property market. Much of their finance had been raised in the inter–bank market. In particular, it was through the use of inter–bank loans that money raised from a wide range of financial institutions (including the high street banks and insurance funds) had helped fire the speculation. As the general expansionary phase in the economy (which had begun in 1971) started to falter and difficulties began to be experienced in the property market, one particular bank, London and Counties Securities, faced severe liquidity problems. In November 1973 it approached the Bank of England for help. In the circumstances, the well-publicised problems of the London and Counties undermined confidence and deposit withdrawals hit other banks that had come to rely heavily on inter-bank funds. The unfolding international oil crisis and failures among similar banks in other countries were important factors in this respect. Indeed, the Bank of England believed the threat of a broader loss of confidence encompassing some substantial banks was so grave as to call for extraordinary action. 'The problem was to avoid a widening circle of collapse through the contagion of fear.'[37]

In December the Bank established a Control Committee - the so-called 'Lifeboat' - in which the London and Scottish clearers were prominent. Its function was to identify banks in trouble and to provide extra loans from the participating banks most closely associated with troubled institutions. At its peak in late 1974/early 1975 the 'Lifeboat' was advancing over £1.1 billion to help beleaguered secondary banks. In all, eighteen 'fringe' banks received aid. For a time - in late 1974 - conditions were so bad that the clearers felt that questions of their own capital adequacy prevented them offering any more aid, and the Bank of England had to take sole responsibility for additional loans. In fact, so extraordinary was the damage to confidence at this time that, in December 1974, the National Westminster Bank felt it necessary to issue a public denial that it was itself receiving Bank of England aid. Problems continued into 1975, with the two most prominent firms then in liquidity difficulties being Slater Walker and Edmund Bates & Sons. At the end of March 1978 the 'Lifeboat' was still advancing some £656 million to help carry recipient banks. In the event eight secondary (or fringe) banks were liquidated; many more incurred losses. Indeed, the whole system had endured scares not previously experienced by most living bankers.

As a result of the crisis, the Bank of England increased its supervisory staff and strengthened its form of control. The authorities had accepted the need for more effective supervision over a greater number and a broader range of financial institutions. Moreover, legislative action became imperative with the issuing in 1977 of the first European Economic Community 'Directive on Credit Institutions', which obliged member–states to establish a system of official authorisation before institutions were permitted to raise deposits from the public. The 1979 Banking Act was the outcome. For the first time this Act established a general–purpose definition of an institution carrying on the business of banking. Previously–used legal definitions had had specific meanings – 'authorised banks' had been those institutions permitted by the authorities to carry on foreign exchange dealings; 'Schedule 8 banks' had been those banking institutions exempted from full disclosure of their profits under this particular section of the 1948 Companies Act; and 'Section 127 banks' (which had included most of the secondary banks) had been those banks exempted from the provision of the Protection of Depositors Act, 1963, which was largely concerned with advertising for deposits.[38] None of these classifications was intended to bestow a general stamp of official approval of liquidity or capital adequacy, and Section 127 in particular encompassed a wide range of institutions of differing character. Nor was the granting of any of these official forms of 'recognition' subject to stringent tests as to commercial viability, or to continuing reappraisal and subsequent supervision. Yet after the secondary bank crisis it was recognised that such a loose form of classification had been open to abuse and misinterpretation, blurring the great differences in status that existed between different financial institutions.

The 1979 Banking Act formalised both the status

of banks and the supervisory responsibilities of the Bank of England. Under the Act all firms operating deposit–taking business had first to be licensed to do so by the Bank. Thus, for the first time the Bank was able to control entry to the market, withdrawal or refusal of a licence providing the ultimate sanction against imprudent management and unworthy institutions. Two separate classes of licensed institutions were created: 'banks' and 'deposit–takers' (deposit–taking institutions such as building societies were governed by different legislation). Both types had to meet prudential criteria established by the Act, although in practice the rules were more lenient for fully–fledged banks. The status of a full–fledged 'bank' was bestowed only on those institutions which had had a good reputation for some time and which already provided a wide range of banking services in the UK. The last proviso could have meant, of course, that overseas banks of high reputation could be refused this higher–status recognition if they did little domestic business in the UK. Generally, however, the largest and most reputable institutions were found among the fully–fledged banks.

One novelty of the legislation was that it provided for the insurance of retail deposits (of up to 75 per cent of value) in the case of bank failure but this clause has not yet (1985) been activated. The Act's main contribution had been to provide for the application of broad prudential criteria relating to liquidity and capital adequacy, managerial integrity and the judicious conduct of the overall business. The Bank of England was made responsible for applying and interpreting these criteria not only at the time of licence application but subsequently, through regular supervision of licensed institutions. Supervision was to be carried out by gathering regular accounting information from the institutions and through frequent meetings between Bank staff and repesentatives of supervised institutions. The prudential criteria were drawn so as to allow a great deal of flexibility and discretion which the Bank thought essential if satisfactory controls were to be established over the many different types of banking institutions based in the UK and over the very different types of business they conducted.

Subsequent to the passage of the legislation, the Bank had discussions with the different types of institutions in order to find acceptable criteria. In specifying the size of capital base or ratio of liquid assets to other assets the Bank tried to follow general principles. Aggregate ratios - such as the 'capital to public liabilities' or 'liquid assets to deposit' ratios - were rejected as too crude. Instead the Bank has sought to give due weighting to the different types of risks involved in a bank's business (longer-dated securities are of higher risk than short-dated, etc.). The greater detail and complexity involved in the Bank's new approach adopted after the secondary bank crisis is apparent from the following decision in 1975 of a joint working party of the Bank and the London and Scottish clearers:

> It is agreed that ... it would normally be necessary to evaluate a bank's liquidity position in sterling and foreign currencies separately; and in some cases it may be necessary to evaluate the liquidity of a bank's sterling wholesale book separately from its retail book.[39]

After prolonged discussion and revision, the Bank of England issued a paper in July 1982 which set out the basis on which the adequacy of liquidity of all banks was to be judged (there were separate rules for capital adequacy):

> Banks must be capable of meeting their obligations when they fall due. Such obligations mainly comprise deposits at sight and short notice, term deposits and commitments to lend, including un-utilized overdraft facilities. The mix of these obligations and their incidence in any time period will vary between different banks but the maintenance of an assured capacity to meet them is an essential principle of banking which is

common to all. This capacity may be provided in the following ways:

(i) by holding sufficient immediately available cash or liquifiable assets...

(ii) by securing an appropriately matching future profile of cash flows from maturing assets...

(iii) by maintaining an adequately diversified deposit base...[40]

This, then, is a much more sophisticated approach than previously adopted, based as it is on regular contact between supervisors and the supervised. The 1979 Act established the general principles, but detailed application was to be tailored by the Bank of England to the circumstances of individual (or specific groups of) institutions. There was inbuilt flexibility with regular reviews enabling the rules to be altered to changing conditions. The Bank hoped that in this way it could operate an equitable system which, at the same time, was flexible enough not to stifle innovation and, yet, was effective enough to ensure stability.

Problems remain, however. The Bank has continued to grapple with the difficulties of establishing effective supervision of overseas banks engaged in multinational financial business in which the authorities were keen to retain the UK's share.[41] There have also been problems with domestic banks. One particular scandalous case was that of the Johnson Matthey Bank which got into such dire straits in 1984 that it had to be bought out by the Bank of England in order to avoid collapse. Here was a licensed bank under regular supervision of the Bank of England and apparently meeting the necessary prudential criteria, yet by the end of 1983 its exposure on just two accounts amounted to 76 per cent of its capital base. By the end of 1985 bad debts amounted to £254 million and the cost to the Bank of England of the rescue was then put at no less than £39 million.[42] Even the best administered prudential criteria can be confounded by criminal fraud, of course, but the Johnson Matthey Bank affair came at a time of public concern over the wider regulation of City institutions (e.g. the Stock Market and Lloyds insurers) and it brought down a great deal of criticism on the Bank of England. As a consequence, in December 1985 the government announced its intention of modifying the 1979 Act in order to increase the effectiveness of bank supervision.[43] The distinction between 'bank' and 'deposit-takers' is to go, both are to be subject to the same degree of control and all banks are to have a minimum of £5 million paid-up capital. The Bank of England remains the body with principal responsibility for bank supervision but the Governor is to be assisted by a Board of Banking Supervision and the government is to be given more information when difficulties emerge. Misreporting of information to the Bank is to be made a criminal offence.

It has yet to be seen if these proposed reforms will make much impact but they do retain the essentials already established by practice in the seventies and by legislation in 1979. In particular, the Bank of England retains the major responsibility for operating a supervisory system that still incorporates a great deal of flexibility in its detailed application. Critics can still point to the inadequacy of resources devoted to supervision. The system is also much less open than, say, the American system. In the UK secrecy is maintained by the supervisors and even where evidence of imprudence is uncovered, no warning is given to depositors or investors. The success of such a system depends on trust, and the Johnson Matthey affair has raised serious doubts about the effectiveness of the Bank of England, as well as that of the 1979 Act. As a result the Bank's record under the revised regulations will undoubtedly be subjected to very close public scrutiny.

## NON-BANK FINANCIAL INTERMEDIARIES

In this study of banking the development of non-bank financial intermediaries (NBFIs) – the building societies, insurance and pension funds, finance houses and unit and investment trusts – can only be dealt with in the barest manner. Such institutions compete with the banks, whether directly or indirectly, for deposits and borrowers and the pace of their growth in the post-war years provides a yardstick against which to measure growth amongst the banks. As the figures in Table 11.3 have indicated, it was the building societies, insurance and pension funds and unit trusts that grew the fastest, although changes in data coverage make assessment of recent expansion very difficult.

The Wilson Committee stressed the importance to all financial institutions of the sharp increase in personal savings, especially in the 1970s when as a percentage of Gross Domestic Product personal savings more than doubled (to just under 11 per cent in 1979)[44] with falls in corporate and public sector saving. The resultant financial imbalances between sectors created major opportunities for financial intermediaries in general as they transferred funds from surplus units to deficit units within the domestic economy. (The international financial imbalances consequent upon the oil crises of the 1970s had similar effects on international intermediation.) The domestic banks obviously shared in this increased business, but some NBFIs also grew rapidly. Of the deposit-gathering NBFIs, growth was particularly rapid for the building societies. The number of societies fell as a result of mergers, from 480 in 1970 to 270 in 1980 but the number of branches increased from some 1,500 in 1955 to 2,500 in 1970 and reached about half the total of clearing bank offices, at 6,000, in 1980.[45] As Table 11.3 shows, deposits more than trebled between 1957 and 1967, and rose again by over five-fold between 1967 and 1978. The societies' share of domestic sterling deposits increased from 18 per cent in 1964, to 38 per cent in 1978,[46] mainly at the expense of the savings banks and national savings certificates and bonds, but the London clearing banks also suffered a declining share.[47] The Wilson Committee attributed the societies' success to the growing demand for home ownership (for the building societies were the only institutions seriously meeting the demand for home mortgages); to favourable tax concessions which cheapened the cost of borrowing on mortgage and enabled the societies to offer more favourable rates of interest on deposits; and to the ready-encashability of their deposits which made them an attractive means in which the public could hold its increased savings.[48]

## DEVELOPMENTS IN RETAIL BANKING

The building societies' success in attracting deposits has been an important element in the erosion of the once apparently-impregnable position of the London clearing banks in the provision of retail banking services.[49] (In Scotland the building society movement has not been as strong as in England but it has, nevertheless, been a growing sector offering alternative places of deposit to the clearing and savings banks.) The societies '...offer a simple, efficient, easily understood service to depositors for which no explicit charges are levied. They provide a range of deposit facilities to attract investors with different liquidity requirements. [and] Their large and growing branch networks mean that they are easily accessible...'[50]

The degree of competition between the societies and the clearing banks was heightened in the early 1980s. The Conservative government elected in 1979 was committed to promoting 'market forces', and for banking this meant a phase of 'de-regulation' similar to that of 1971. In particular the authorities removed the supplementary special deposits scheme which had held bank lending in check. An early response of the clearing banks was to enter for the first time into home mortgage provision on a large scale. The building societies were also facing stiffer competition from the increase in state borrowing from the personal sector in the form of savings bonds and the like. The societies' response was innovative – the long–standing cartel arrangements over mortgate rates were modified to allow for greater flexibility for individual societies, and societies enhanced their appeal to savers by experimenting with a variety of different share and deposit accounts which offered a range of interest rates and terms governing withdrawal.[51] Customer services were expanded, with some societies introducing chequeing accounts, installing automatic cash dispensers and offering credit card facilities through affiliates. The authorities continued to encourage this more competitive approach: fiscal changes (effective, 1985/6) placed the societies and banks on a more equal footing as regards tax liability; and a Green Paper of 1984 foreshadowed legislation which would give building societies greater balance sheet freedom.[52] Under these new arrangements societies are still obliged to invest the great majority (90 per cent) of their assets in first mortgages; and at least 80 per cent of liabilities have to consist of money placed with them by individuals. However, with the residual 10 per cent of assets societies can undertake lending of a type either completely new to them or rarely provided previously; and the 20 per cent margin on liabilities opens up the possibility of greater flexibility in raising resources – for instance, from the inter–bank market. Government expressly encouraged the societies to offer a new range of financial services:[53]

> These services will include money transmission and foreign exchange, estate agency and management of mortgage investments, and agency services, including the making or receiving of payments and giving access to authorised investment to businesses. They will also include insurance broking for all types of insurance.[54]

Stiffer competition in the provision of retail banking services has also come from the trustee savings banks (TSBs) and the National Girobank. Until 1976 the business of the TSBs was tightly regulated by statute. They provided a restricted range of services for savers, paid uncompetitive interest rates and almost all their funds had to be invested in public sector debt. Along with most forms of national saving, including the Post Office Savings Bank, the TSBs suffered a long-term decline in the share of total sterling deposits - falling from 8 per cent in the mid-1960s to about 5 per cent in 1978. It was within this context that the 1973 Report of the Page Committee on National Savings felt that their future viability called for a broadening of both their deposit and borrowing services.[55] Subsequently the Trustee Savings Bank Act,[56] 1976, relaxed the regulations governing their business. The TSBs responded positively. Mergers produced a small group of regionally-based institutions and they began to provide '... a wide range of personal banking services including chequing accounts, a Visa affiliated credit card, and also an increasing though still limited amount of mortgage and consumer instalment credit.'[57] The long-term decline in their relative share of domestic deposits has been arrested - having recovered to 7.5 per cent by 1983 - and in 1986 the government floated the TSB as a single, privately-owned corporation. Thus, the ground has been prepared for establishing the TSB as an important new force in British retail banking, but from the perspective of the mid-1980s it is impossible to predict how this might develop.

Similarly the National Girobank (established in 1968) which provides '...an inexpensive, convenient and speedy money transmission service'[58] operating through the country's extensive Post Office network, has been officially encouraged to extend its customer services and to compete more effectively.

In sum, like the wholesale markets since the 1960s, the retail banking market has undergone important changes since the early 1970s. Improved technology - electronic clearing and credit transmission, automatic counter-service tills, and the like - have played a part in changing the nature of services as presented to the personal customer; and technical change promises more radical transformation in the near future. However, throughout this chapter a main theme has been the importance of changes in government policy and how they have responded to, and interacted with, market pressures. Since the early 1970s in particular, the authorities have sought to weaken oligopoly arrangements and encourage greater competition, not just between the clearers themselves but also between the clearers and other banks. The impact on the clearers and their response is considered in the next chapter.

## FURTHER READING

J.E. Wadsworth (ed.), *The Banks and the Monetary System in the UK, 1959–1971* (Methuen & Co, London, 1973).

J.S. Fforde, 'Competition, Innovation and Regulation in British Banking', *Bank of England Quarterly Bulletin*, vol. 23, Sept. 1983, pp. 363–76.

Paolo Savona and George Sutija (eds.), *Eurodollars and International Banking* (Macmillan, London, 1985).

Margaret Isabel Reid, *The Secondary Banking Crisis, 1973–75* (Macmillan, London, 1982).

## NOTES

1. Banking Act, 1979, Eliz. II, c. 37.

2. 'Money and Banking Figures: Forthcoming Changes', *Bank of England Quarterly Bulletin (BEQB)*, vol. 21, Dec. 1981, pp. 531–8. Updated lists and amendments appear frequently in the *BEQB* – eg. see *BEQB*, vol. 25, March 1985, 'Statistical Annex'.

3. A useful survey of postwar growth until the late 1960s appears in 'The UK Banking Sector, 1952–67', *BEQB*, vol. 9, June 1969, pp. 176–200.

4. *Committee to Review the Functioning of Financial Institutions* [Wilson Committee] *Report*. Cmnd. 7937 (HMSO, London, 1980).

5. Through the 1960s a number of useful articles appeared in the *Midland Bank Review*

describing many of the changes taking place in the London money markets. These articles have been conveniently reproduced in J.E. Wadsworth (ed.), *The Banks and the Monetary System in the UK, 1959–1971* (Methuen & Co., London, 1973), pp. 141–200. The present section draws heavily on these articles and on Wilson, *Report, Appendices*, 3, XV.

6. For a concise summary of the historical development see 'The London Discount Market: Some Historical Notes', *BEQB*, vol. 7, June 1967, pp. 144–56. For a much fuller account see G.A. Fletcher, *The Discount Houses in London* (Macmillan, London, 1976).

7. Changes in policy techniques are dealt with in Chapters 13 and 14.

8. *The London Clearing Banks. Evidence by the Committee of London Clearing Bankers to the Committee to Review the Functioning of Financial Institutions* (Committee of London Clearing Bankers, London, 1978), pp. 192–3.

9. 'Competition and Credit Control' *BEQB*, vol. 11, June 1971, pp. 189–93.

10. 'Monetary Control – Provisions', *BEQB*, vol. 21, Sept. 1981, p. 348. In 1983 the average value of 'call money' was reduced to 5 per cent of eligible liabilities and the minimum to 2.5 per cent – 'Operation of Monetary Policy: Monetary Control Arrangements', *BEQB*, vol. 23, Sept. 1983, p. 346.

11. 'Monetary Control: Next Steps', *BEQB*, vol. 21, March 1981, pp. 38–9; and 'The Role of the Bank of England in the Money Market', *BEQB*, vol. 22, March 1982, pp. 86–94.

12. Wadsworth, *Banks and the Monetary System*, p. 160.

13. *Committee on the Working of the Monetary System* [Radcliffe Committee], Cmnd. 827, *Principal Memoranda*, (3 vols., HMSO, London, 1960), vol. 2, pp. 3–12; Wilson, *Appendices*, 3, pp. 412–4. In 1978 the six largest were Kleinwort Benson, Schroder Wagg, Hambros, Hill Samuel, Samuel, Samuel Montagu and Morgan Grenfell.

14. Aggregated accounts are published regularly

in the *BEQB* – see the March 1981 issue (vol.21), Table 3.5.

15. Though changes in the series mean that too much weight cannot be given to precise figures, the overall magnitude is unlikely to change markedly, no matter the statistical adjustment.

16. Radcliffe, *Report*, pp. 70–2; Wilson, *Appendices*, 3, pp. 416–7.

17. Radcliffe, *Report*, p. 70.

18. For instance, see 'Overseas and Foreign Banks in London, 1962–68', *BEQB*, vol. 8, June 1968, pp. 156–65; and 'The Euro-Currency Business of Banks in London', *BEQB* , vol. 10, March 1970, pp. 31–49.

19. *London Clearing Banks*, p. 48–9.

20. Michael von Clemm, 'The Rise of Consortium Banking', *Harvard Business Review*, vol. 49, May–June 1971, pp. 125–36.

21. Wilson, *Appendices, 3,* pp. 414–6. In 1983 there was a major reclassification and these banks were transferred to the new 'retail banks' class – see 'Revised Presentation of Banking Statistics', *BEQB*, vol. 23, Dec. 1983, pp. 562–3.

22. Jack Revell, 'A Secondary Banking System', *Banker*, vol. 118, no. 511, 1968, pp. 798–812; and *Changes in British Banking. The Growth of a Secondary Banking System*, Hill, Samuel & Co., Occasional Paper, no. 3 (Hill, Samuel & Co., London, 1968).

23. Wilson, *Report,* p. 41.

24. In the late 1960s there emerged a fifth, the inter-company market, where firms lent directly to other firms. However, as with trade credit generally, the scale of such transactions is unknown.

25. Radcliffe, *Report*, p. 74; Wilson, *Appendices,* 3, pp. 433; and Wadsworth, *Banks and the Monetary System*, pp. 163–5.

26. Wilson, *Appendices,* 3, p. 507.

27. 'Sterling Certificates of Deposit and the Inter-Bank Market', *BEQB*, vol. 13, Sept. 1973, pp. 308–14.

28. Jack Revell, *The British Financial System*

(Macmillan, London, 1973), p. 248.

29. Wilson, *Appendices*, 3, p. 507.

30. Ibid.

31. Wadsworth, *Banks and the Monetary System*, pp. 164–8, 191–6.

32. 'UK Banks' External Liabilities and Claims in Foreign Currencies', *BEQB*, vol. 4, June 1964, pp. 102–4; and Brian Scott Quinn, *The New Euromarkets* (Macmillan, London, 1975), pp. 35–6.

33. 'Eurobanks and the Inter-bank Market', *BEBQ*, vol. 21, Sept. 1981, pp. 351–64. Also see Richard J. Herring, 'The Interbank Market' in Paolo Savona and George Sutija (eds.), *Eurodollars and International Banking* (Macmillan, London, 1985), pp. 111–21.

34. 'The UK Banking Sector', *BEQB*, 1969, p. 181.

35. For the Bank's views see 'The Supervision of the UK Banking System', *BEQB*, vol. 15, June 1975, pp. 188–94; and 'Banking Supervision and the Banking Act', *BEQB*, vol. 20, June 1980, pp. 205–8.

36. 'The Secondary Banking Crisis and the Bank of England Support Operation', *BEQB*, vol. 18, June 1978, pp. 230–9; and Margaret Isabel Reid, *The Secondary Banking Crisis, 1973–75* (Macmillan, London, 1982).

37. 'Secondary Banking Crisis', *BEQB*, 1978, p. 233.

38. For other definitions and classifications see 'Supervision of UK Banking', *BEQB*, 1975, pp. 185–9.

39. 'The Capital and Liquidity Adequacy of Banks', *BEQB*, vol. 15, Sept. 1975, p. 242.

40. 'The Measurement of Liquidity', *BEQB*, vol. 22, Sept. 1982, p. 399.

41. For example, see 'Some Current Concerns of a Banking Supervisor', speech by W.P. Cooke, Associate Director, *BEQB*, vol. 25, June 1985, pp. 219–23; and Richard S. Dale, 'Prudential Regulation of Multinational Banking. The Problem Outlined', *National Westminster Bank Quarterly Review*, Feb. 1981, pp. 14–24.

42. *The Times*, 29 Nov. 1985,; and *Guardian*,

12 Dec. 1985.

43. See reports in *Financial Times*, 18 Dec. 1985.

44. Wilson, *Report*, pp. 57–8.

45. 'Competition, Innovation and Regulation in British Banking' – paper by J.S. Fforde, *BEQB*, vol. 23, Sept. 1983, pp. 369.

46. Wilson, *Appendices*, 3, Table 10.7, p. 595.

47. For a consideration of some broader issues see David T. Llewellyn, 'Do Building Societies Take Deposits Away from the Banks?', *Lloyds Bank Review*, no. 131, Jan. 1979, pp. 21–34.

48. Wilson, *Report*, pp. 71–2.

49. E.J. Cleary, *The Building Society Movement* (Elek Books, London, 1965), pp. 244 ff. and Mark Boléat, *The Building Society Industry* (Allen & Unwin, London, 1982), especially pp. 118–46.

50. Wilson, *Report*, pp. 71–2.

51. 'Competition, Innovation and Regulation', *BEQB*, 1983, pp. 370–1.

52. *Building Societies. A New Framework*, Cmnd. 9316 (HMSO, London, 1984).

53. Although the proposals did not meet all the expectations of the societies – see *The Future Constitution and Powers of Building Societies* (Building Societies Association, London, 1983).

54. H.M. Treasury, *Economic Progress Report*, no. 181, Nov. – Dec. 1985, p. 8.

55. *Committee to Review National Savings. Report*, Cmnd. 5273 (HMSO, London, 1973), PP. 34–99.

56. Trustee Savings Bank Act, 1976, Eliz. II, c. 4.

57. 'Competition, Innovation and Regulation', *BEQB*, 1983, p. 370.

58. Wilson, *Appendices*, 3, p. 416.

Chapter Twelve

# THE CLEARING BANKS, 1939-1986

This chapter surveys the main changes affecting the clearing banks since the 1930s. Three groups are taken to comprise the 'clearers': London clearing banks (LCBs), Scottish clearing banks (SCBs) and Northern Ireland banks (NIBs). The LCBs have been by far the largest of the three and, in fact, they have major shareholdings in both the NIBs and SCBs. Throughout the years since the thirties, it has been these three groups of clearing banks which have dominated retail banking in the various parts of the UK. Together with the building societies and savings banks, they are responsible for the bulk of deposit-gathering from the general public and through their chequeing, giro and other transfer facilities, they are the main providers of the country's money transmission mechanism. But the business of the clearers is not confined to retail banking, of course. They have either retained or actively developed an important presence in other areas of financial activity, too. It is for these reasons that, as for earlier periods, more attention is given here to studying the clearing banks than to any other particular type of financial institution. Moreover, for most of the post-war period, it was the clearing banks that bore the brunt of official attempts to regulate monetary and credit conditions, another reason to pay them particular attention.

## AMALGAMATIONS AND INSTITUTIONAL CHANGE

By the time of the Radcliffe Committee in 1957 there were eleven members of the Committee of London Clearing Bankers. Of these, the 'Big Five' of Barclays, Lloyds, the Midland, the National Provincial and the Westminster all operated national branch networks throughout England and Wales and they accounted for some six-sevenths of total LCB assets.[1] The District and Martins were much smaller concerns, together being responsible for some 8 per cent of assets, with their outlets heavily concentrated in the North of England. Two others, Williams Deacon's (based mainly in Lancashire) and Glyn, Mills (in London) were owned by the Royal Bank of Scotland; while Coutts (also located in London) was owned by the National Provincial. The last of the London clearers, the National Bank, was predominantly an Irish bank with a small group of offices in London and the other conurbations of England. Thus, the general structure was of a highly concentrated retail deposit market dominated by a small number of national institutions (the 'Big Five') plus a few lesser banks – in effect, there had been little change since the immediate post-World War I years.

By 1977, when the Wilson Committee was appointed to investigate the operation of financial intermediaries, there had been significant institutional changes, mainly as a result of mergers which (as Figure 12.1 shows) occurred in the 1960s.[2] Since as far back as 1918, when a Treasury Committee had publicly expressed apprehension over the possibility of creating a 'bankers' trust', the large clearing banks had assumed that the authorities would contemplate mergers only between banks with complementary rather than competing interests. This was thought to have been the case, for instance, when the National Provincial Bank took over the District Bank in 1962, for the District's branch network was concentrated in the north-west where the National Provincial's representation was relatively light. However, in 1966 the government referred the question of bank charges

Figure 12.1: London Clearing Bank Amalgamations, 1957-1986

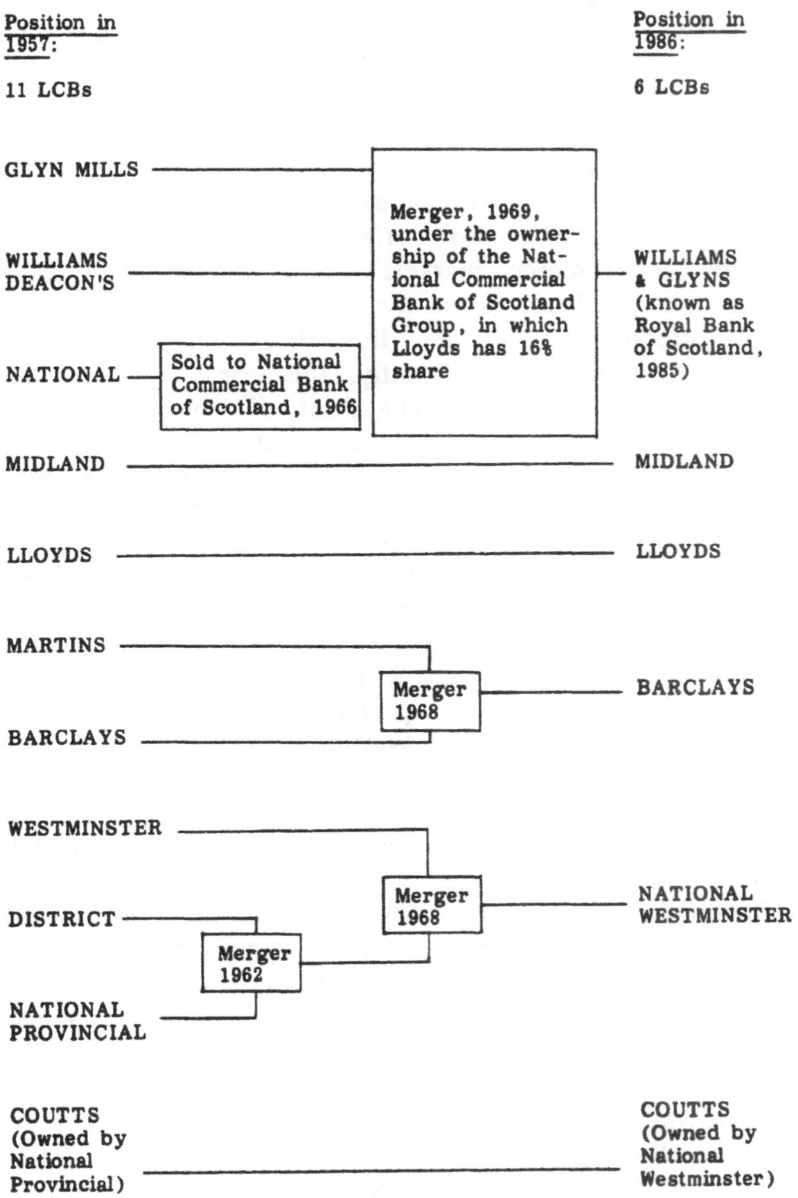

to the Prices and Incomes Board and, in the subsequent report, the Board expressed the view that further amalgamations could reduce costs through the closing down of 'surplus' offices and the rationalisation of branch networks.[3] There was also some awareness that a bank's size affected its ability to provide effective lending facilities on the very large scale required by large national and multinational companies and that size also affected competitiveness in international money markets. Small banks, too, could be at a disadvantage in the provision of such services as credit cards or in the introduction of computerisation. Significantly, the Prices and Incomes Board announced that: 'The Bank of England and the Treasury have made it plain to us that they would not obstruct some further amalgamation if the banks were willing to contemplate such a development.'[4]

The banks were not slow to react. In 1968 it was proposed to merge the Westminster and National Provincial, the new combined business being transferred to the National Westminster Bank in January 1970.[5] Coutts, which had been a subsidiary of the National Provincial retained its separate identity but was now owned by the National Westminster. Other changes came about as a result of Scottish developments. In 1966 the National Bank, which had previously relinquished its Irish business to the Bank of Ireland, was taken over by the National Commercial Bank of Scotland. Thus, when the National Commercial and the Royal Bank of Scotland merged to form the National Commercial Banking Group in 1968, it meant that the three LCBs, the National, Williams Deacon's and Glyn, Mills, came under common ownership. These three were combined to form the new Williams & Glyns in 1969 and this bank has been operating under the name of the parent company, the Royal Bank of Scotland, since 1985.

This, the most recent of the clearing bank merger movements, suddenly lost its impetus however with the other proposal of 1968, the planned merger between Barclays, Lloyds and Martins. If it had been successful, the new group would have controlled about one–half of clearing bank business. The authorities baulked at such a concentration of market power and referred the proposal to the Monopolies Commission. After all, while the Prices and Incomes Board had sought greater cost efficiency through branch rationalisation, it had also strongly supported the introduction of more price competition. Some questioned whether there was much scope for cost savings and the suggested Barclays–Lloyds–Martins merger seemed to threaten the degree of competition already existing. By a majority vote, the Monopolies Commission decided against the merger.[6] Instead, Barclays and Martins alone merged. Lloyds Bank remained independent. For the time being, anyway, it was assumed that the authorities would not support further market concentration, and so the position has remained through to the 1980s.

As a result of the merger, by the time of the Wilson Committee there were just six LCBs: Barclays, Coutts, Lloyds, the Midland, National Westminster and Williams & Glyns (see Figure 12.1). Coutts was owned by the National Westminster and Williams & Glyns by the National and Commercial Banking Group, within which Lloyds had a 16 per cent stake. In 1978 Barclays and the National Westminster were of a similar size and between them they were responsible for almost 60 per cent of total liabilities; Lloyds and the Midland together accounted for just less than 40 per cent; and Williams and Glyns for under 3 per cent.

The Scottish banks had not participated in the early twentieth–century amalgamation wave that had culminated in 1918 for their English counterparts. From 1907 to 1950 the number of Scottish banks had remained at eight (see Figure 12.2). In 1950, though, the Midland Bank merged its affiliates, the Clydesdale Bank and the North of Scotland Bank (the new bank reverting to the title of the Clydesdale in 1963).[7] Other Scottish banks sought economies of scale and in 1952 an agreement was reached whereby the Union Bank was absorbed by the Bank of Scotland and, in 1958, the National Commercial Bank was formed from

**Figure 12.2 : Scottish Clearing Bank Amalgamations, 1949-1986**

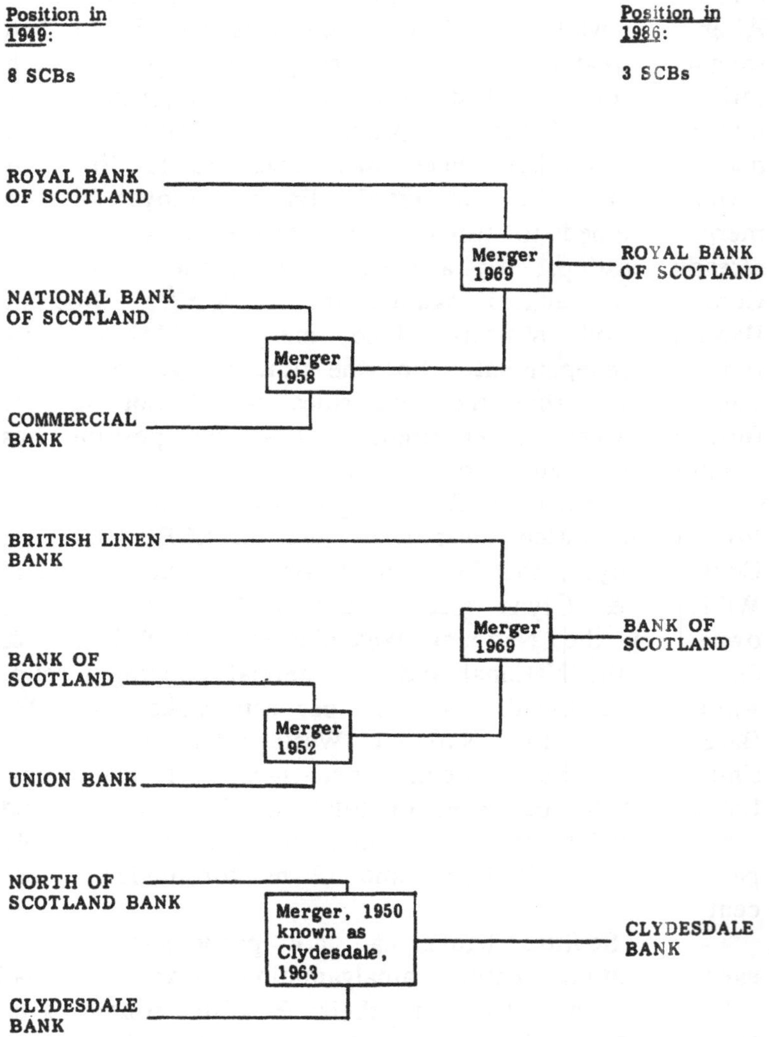

an amalgam of the Commercial Bank and the National Bank of Scotland. As Figure 12.2 shows, two more mergers occurred in the late 1960s. In 1969 agreement was reached on the fusion of the Royal Bank of Scotland and the National Commercial Bank, the new bank bearing the former's name. At that time the Royal accounted for 40 per cent of Scotland's banking business. The other amalgamation was the incorporation of the British Linen Bank into the Bank of Scotland. Thus by the time of the Wilson Committee, the Scottish system was down to three banks: the Royal Bank, the Bank of Scotland and the Clydesdale. All had links with English clearing banks – the Clydesdale was fully owned by the Midland; the Bank of Scotland, 35 per cent owned by Barclays; and the Royal Bank of Scotland, 16 per cent owned by Lloyds through the Royal Bank of Scotland Group which also owned Williams & Glyns.[8] As throughout the history of these Anglo-Scottish affiliations, though, the Scottish banks have retained much of their independence.

To complete the picture of clearing banks in the UK, Northern Ireland must be mentioned. In 1980 the Wilson Committee described the banking system there in the following manner:

> It is dominated by the Northern Ireland branches of the Northern Bank and Ulster Bank, both subsidiaries of London clearing banks [the Midland and National Westminster respectively], which engage in banking throughout Ireland. It also includes branches of two banks registered in the Republic of Ireland.[9]

All four banks operate branches on both sides of the Irish border.

Table 12.1: Deposit Liabilities of the London Clearing Banks, the Scottish Clearing Banks and the Northern Ireland banks, £ billions

| DATE | LCBs | SCBs | NIBs |
|---|---|---|---|
| 1951 | 6.3 | 0.8 | 0.1 |
| 1965 | 9.5 | 1.0 | 0.2 |
| 1979 | 45.8 | 5.0 | 1.3 |

*Source: Bank of England Quarterly Bulletin*

Table 12.1 gives some indication of the relative size of the clearing banks from the three parts of the UK. The London clearing banks have been by far the largest throughout the post–1945 period. This fact, coupled with their ownership links with the Scottish and Irish banks justifies concentrating on the English clearers for the rest of this chapter, although specific reference will be made to Scotland and Northern Ireland on occasions.

## GROWTH OF THE CLEARING BANKS SINCE THE SECOND WORLD WAR

The period since World War II has seen a continuation of some of the more important trends in growth which were apparent by the turn of the century and which had been strengthened between the wars. Commercial bank business, including that of the clearers, has continued to grow but has suffered a relative decline as the range of financial institutions and the services they offer has been broadened.

Tables 12.2 and 12.3 provide some deposit figures as a measure of the long–term growth of the LCBs. In nominal values deposits rose from £6.4 billion in the early 1950s (they had averaged only about one–half of this, at £3.5 billion, 1936/38) to £9.4 billion by the mid–1960s; with a tremendous surge to £45.5 billion by the close of the 1970s. Table 12.3 shows that overall they grew at an annual rate of 7.3 per cent

Table 12.2 : London Clearing Banks' Deposits, 1951-1979

| Date | LCBs' Deposits current values (£ bill) | LCBs' Deposits per head of population (£) | Ratio of LCBs' Deposits to Net National Product (%) | 'Real' LCBs' Deposits, values adjusted for price changes (£ bill) | 'Real' LCBs' Deposits per head of population (£) | Total Bank Deposits in U.K. (£ bill) | Ratio of LCBs' Deposits to Total Bank Deposits (%) |
|---|---|---|---|---|---|---|---|
| | 1 | 2 | 3 | 4 | 5 | 6 | 7 |
| 1951 | 6.4 | 127.3 | 52.0 | 47.0 | 934.4 | 9.2 | 69.6 |
| 1965 | 9.4 | 172.4 | 32.5 | 43.6 | 800.0 | 17.3 | 54.3 |
| *1973* | *21.1* | | | | | *92.8* | *22.7* |
| *1976* | *29.6* | | | | | *159.9* | *18.5* |
| 1979 | 45.5 | 814.0 | 30.3 | 52.8 | 944.5 | 249.0 | 18.2 |

Notes:

1. Figures are three-year averages centred on the dates shown except for 1951, when the two-year average for 1951/2 is used.
2. Data are for December of each year.
3. A major break occurred in the coverage of the series for total bank deposits in 1974/5, seriously affecting the data in columns 6 and 7 (see text).
4. All deposit figures are for sterling and non-sterling balances.
5. Total bank deposits (gross) in the UK = the sum of deposits held by the London clearing banks, Scottish clearing banks, Northern Ireland banks, other UK banks, overseas banks, consortium banks (since 1975), the accepting houses and the 'borrowed funds' of the discount houses.

(continued)

Table 12.2: London Clearing Banks' Deposits, 1951-1979 (Cont.)

*Sources:*

1. London clearing banks' deposits (gross) - *Bank of England Quarterly Bulletin.*
2. Total bank deposits (gross) - *Bank of England Quarterly Bulletin.*
3. UK population - *Social Trends* (HMSO, London, 1979 and 1984).
4. Net National Product - 1978/80 and 1964/6 from *United Kingdom National [Blue Book]*, 1985 edition (CSO, London, 1985), Table 1.2; 1951/52 from C.H. Feinstein, *National Income, Expenditure and Output of the United Kingdom* (Cambridge University Press, Cambridge, 1972), pp. T4-T7.
5. Implicit price deflator (1980=100), used in columns 4 and 5 - derived from *Blue Book, op. cit.*, Table 1.5 and Feinstein, *op. cit.*, pp. T14-17.

NB For columns 4 and 5, Feinstein's series was 'converted' to the *Blue Book* series thus:

Adjusted Feinstein series =

Blue Book Series, where coefficient = coefficient

$$\frac{\text{Blue Book Series, 1963/65}}{\text{Feinstein Series, 1963/65}}$$

---

Table 12.3: Annual Rates of Growth of London Clearing Banks' Deposits, 1951-1980 (per cent per annum)

| Period | LCBs' Deposits, current values | 'Real' LCBs' Deposits | 'Real' LCBs' Deposits per head of population | Total Bank Deposits in UK |
|---|---|---|---|---|
| | 1 | 2 | 3 | 4 |
| 1951/52 - 1964/66 | 2.8 | -0.5 | 4.6 | -1.1 |
| 1964/66 - 1978/80 | 11.9 | 1.4 | 21.0 | 1.2 |
| 1951/52 - 1978/80 | 7.3 | 0.4 | 12.5 | 0.03 |

*Source:* Table 12.2

Table 12.4: Domestic Intermediation by Financial Institutions (additions to liabilities to domestic non-financial sector*), 1958-1979

| | Per cent of GDP at market prices: | | | | |
|---|---|---|---|---|---|
| | 1958/62 | 1963/67 | 1968/72 | 1973/77 | 1978/79 |
| Banking sector | 1.1 | 1.8 | 3.0 | 3.1 | 3.3 |
| Savings banks (investment a/cs) | 0.2 | 0.4 | 0.4 | 0.2 | 0.5 |
| Building societies | 1.0 | 2.0 | 2.8 | 3.4 | 3.1 |
| Finance houses | - | 0.1 | 0.1 | - | 0.1 |
| Life assurance and pension funds | 3.1 | 3.3 | 3.6 | 4.3 | 4.7 |
| Unit trusts | 0.1 | 0.2 | 0.3 | 0.1 | - |
| Total | 5.5 | 7.7 | 10.2 | 11.2 | 11.7 |

* excluding issues of share and loan capital

*Source:* *Committee to Review the Functioning of Financial Institutions.* [Wilson Committee]. *Report*, Cmnd. 7937 (HMSO, London, 1980), p. 65.

(compound), with growth (at 11.9 per cent per annum) much higher in the second half of the period. However, a more realistic assessment of growth rates needs to take account of changes in national income, population and the value of money. This is done in a general manner in columns 3–5 of Table 12.2 and columns 2–3 of Table 12.3. If the clearers had been merely 'holding their own', then over the long term they should have experienced deposit growth which kept apace of these three factors. In fact experience was mixed. As a ratio to Net National Product, the clearers' deposits contracted sharply in the 1951/52 to 1964/66 period; although they then performed much better through to the late 1970s when the rate of decline flattened out. Similarly, if LCB deposits are adjusted to take account of both price and population (column 5 in Table 12.2 and columns 2 and 3 in Table 12.3) there was contraction during the fifties and early sixties but some expansion in the seventies. The result across the three decades as a whole was virtually zero growth in real, per capita terms.

The impact of price inflation was particularly important. The whole of the post-war period has been subjected to continuing price rises and this was especially true of the 1970s when deposits grew most rapidly. With inflation it is reasonable to expect that the demand for money balances (including bank deposits) rises, if only because as prices, salaries, etc, rise, then more money is needed to finance the same volume of transactions. The use of money might be economised if other forms of liquidity are held instead (in effect, an increase in the velocity of circulation of money could occur) but given the high rates of inflation during the 1970s, a sharp rise in money balances would still be a reasonable expectation.[10] Thus, all things being equal, if the LCBs were merely maintaining their relative position as suppliers of liquid assets, their deposit growth should have equalled the rate of inflation. In fact, if the deposit figures are adjusted to take account of price changes alone, it can be seen from Table 12.2 (column 4) and Table 12.3 (column 2) that for the period as a whole deposits did, indeed, just keep ahead of inflation. But experience in the two sub-periods was mixed, with a decline in real terms from 1951/52 to 1964/66 and a rise from 1964/66 to 1978/80.

By far the highest rates of inflation were experienced in the later period and it has been suggested that at such high rates bank deposits were boosted not only by the fall in the value of money, but also by a proportional rise in the volume of bank business.[11] First, in the uncertainty created by the high and variable rates of inflation of the 1970s there was an increase in the public's preference for liquid assets (including bank deposits) and, secondly, low business profitability and the poor showing for equities at that time, encouraged firms to rely less on long-term external financing and more on short-term funds such as bank loans. The argument is that, at the time firms were much less willing to commit themselves to long-term finance because of the uncertain course of future prices. If they had done so and the pace of inflation had then unexpectedly eased they would have been burdened with high 'real' interest rates. In the circumstances, they turned to their bankers.

Another factor accounting for LCB growth in the 1970s was the introduction in 1971 of 'Competition and Credit Control'.[12] This removed the authorities' quantitative constraints on bank lending and the clearers' greater competitiveness and price-oriented approach arising from this change in policy probably helped increase the rate of real deposit growth.

The clearers thus attracted new business and slowed down the rate of decline in their market share. However, it is important to view the clearing banks' achievements in the context of the strong upsurge in total financial assets that was occurring during the 1970s.[13] To a significant degree this reflected the sharp increase in the personal sector's financial surplus, which rose from some 2 per cent of GDP during the 1960s and early 1970s to over 5 per cent from 1973.[14] The personal sector showed a strong preference to hold its invested earnings in the form of liquid assets, and as the personal sector's financial surplus was responsible for over 40 per cent of total savings over the period from 1976 to 1984, a high proportion of total earnings was thus directed into such financial assets.[15] Here was a major source of growth not only for banks but for financial institutions in general. In fact, the influence of the personal sector was even greater than the financial surplus figures alone suggest, for as the Wilson Committee noted:

> ...since part of consumption (particularly the purchase of consumer durables) and a large proportion of capital spending on house purchase is financed by borrowing, and since individuals have for many years been realising some of their financial assets, the gross flow into the financial institutions and certain categories of government debt has substantially exceeded the personal sector's net financial surplus.[16]

The provision of financial assets for the personal sector has, of course, been one of the traditionally strong areas for the clearing banks and they did benefit from the expansion. However, most of the growth in personal sector financial assets since the 1960s has been in the form of building society deposits, life assurance and pension funds, and national savings. Personal sector bank deposits have grown, but less so. In consequence, the banks have suffered a relative decline. Table 12.4 reproduces some relevant figures from the Wilson Committee's *Report*. The overall growth of domestic financial intermediation is apparent – its value rising from 5.5 per cent of GDP in the late 1950s/early 1960s to 11.7 per cent by the late 1970s. The figures for individual sectors suggest that after increases in the proportionate share of the banking sector in the 1960s there was stagnation during the 1970s. Building societies increased their share overall, although there were signs of a slow-down at the end of the 1970s.

Moreover, within the banking sector the LCBs have undergone a long-term comparative decline.

Column 7 in Table 12.2 shows that their share of total bank deposits fell from just under 70 per cent in the early 1950s, to somewhat over 54 per cent by the mid-1960s. There was then a dramatic fall, with the LCBs down to just under 23 per cent in 1972/4 (Table 12.3 gives the contrasting growth rates for LCB and 'total' deposits).[17] However, a serious complication in showing the extent of the LCBs' relative decline in market share is the major break that appears in the statistics compiled by the Bank of England. In 1975 new definitions and a wider coverage greatly increased the number of institutions included in the 'banking sector', so that comparison of the LCBs' relative position before and after 1975 overstates the extent of their decline. Even so, a real decline there has been.

To accommodate the discontinuity in the statistics additional base periods are used on the right hand side of Table 12.2 for the total UK bank deposit series. The figures for the latter half of the 1970s are not directly comparable to the earlier ones, but they nevertheless suggest that the meteoric decline in the LCBs' share of deposits had been arrested during those years. Even so, any review of the post-war period as a whole must stress the LCBs' relative contraction.

One area of particularly high growth has been in the business of overseas banks operating in the UK. Much of their business has been conducted with overseas firms and in overseas currencies but they have also made inroads into UK domestic banking and, on trend, the extent to which they compete with the clearing banks has increased. By 1980, for instance, overseas banks were providing almost one-third of all bank loans to British manufacturing industry.[18] Moreover, the total deposit figure in Table 12.2 does not include the shares of building societies - for they are not classed as 'banks' - which have also been increasing rapidly. In fact, by the mid-1980s they accounted for about 44 per cent of resident sterling deposits compared with the LCBs' share of (just) 33 per cent. According to Sir Timothy Bevan, Chairman of Barclays Bank: 'It is now the Building Societies, not the Clearers, which dominate the retail deposits markets.'[19] The extent of the LCBs' relative decline is fully apparent.

In sum, while banks in general, including LCBs, have participated in the growth of financial assets and intermediation associated with the inflationary period – and, indeed, the clearers' deposits have grown faster than the rate of inflation – since the 1960s, the LCBs have none the less been experiencing a declining market share.

## REASONS FOR CLEARERS' RELATIVE DECLINE

Much of the relative decline was a consequence of the greater expansion experienced by overseas banks operating in the UK, by the merchant bank sector and by non–bank financial intermediaries (NBFIs) such as building societies and insurance companies. Developments concerning these institutions have already been dealt with in the previous chapter but, generally, it seems that the LCBs' shrinking market share reflected the continuing process of 'financial sophistication'. In a developed economy like the UK rising real incomes are associated with a broadening of asset portfolios, with a relatively higher growth of non–money financial assets. Surveying the whole period from 1880 to the early 1960s, D.K. Sheppard has stressed the long–term changes that were occurring in the distribution of the community's financial assets:

> Total financial savings grew considerably faster than national income; an increasing proportion of these savings tended to be placed with the non–banking institutions; concurrently, relative to the banks, these other institutions became increasingly important both as sources of credit and as providers of relatively liquid savings instruments.[20]

Within these general trends some specific factors (most of which were also emphasised for the inter–war period) have been singled out as having inhibited the clearers' relative performance. Tax policy played a part in favouring the accumulation of some financial assets over others. Thus, successive governments have maintained fiscal incentives which reduce the real cost of payments on life assurance, pension schemes and national savings. The same has been true of mortgage loans for home purchase, yet the tax exemptions on interest payments on bank loans were severely restricted in 1969 and abolished in 1974. The banks have also claimed that the building societies gained an advantage from their privilege of being able to 'compound' tax on the interest paid on their shares (thus, paying the tax 'on behalf' of customers) and from favourable rates of corporation tax.[21]

Another feature has been the traditional demarcation of function within British financial markets. In the years following the Second World War the LCBs largely subscribed to this notion of specialisation and it was not until the late 1960s or early 1970s that established demarcation lines were seriously breached. Such compartmentalisation of markets favoured those institutions concentrating on the higher growth sectors, to the detriment of the clearers. This was the case, for instance, in home mortgage financing. Here the terms of the (often) 20–25 year loans granted for home purchase were considered to be outside the clearers' traditionally short-term credit provision for the non-corporate sector. In the event, it was not until 1980 that the two largest clearers, Barclays and the National Westminster, decided to commit significant resources to this type of business – by the mid-1980s the banks had captured about 16 per cent of the mortgage market, with the building societies responsible for 76 per cent. Similarly, it was not until the 1970s that the clearers themselves participated more actively in the provision of consumer credit, or competed fully for deposits in the wholesale money markets, although there was earlier participation through subsidiary companies and affiliates. Specialisation, then, while never sacrosanct, worked against the LCBs for much of the post-war period, although it must be readily acknowledged that the last decade and a half has seen a determined effort to break down many of the traditional barriers.

Consideration of demarcation lines in the provision of financial services raises the more general issue of LCB competitiveness, an additional factor in their relative decline. There has always been keen competition for the business of large customers (industrial concerns and the like) for these have greater choice over which institution to borrow from, or lend to. The clearers' participation in the wholesale money markets – both international and domestic – which emerged during the 1960s has also necessarily been on a competitive basis. However, as was shown in earlier chapters, by the 1920s retail banking business had become highly concentrated into the hands of a small number of clearers who suppressed competition through the operation of effective price cartels. The economic uncertainties of the 1930s and the impact of World War II reinforced these oligopolistic elements.

As in the inter-war years, the attitude of the monetary authorities was crucial to the stifling of price competition. The sharp rise in National Debt during the war increased the government's dependence on the banks for the maintenance of a market in such debt. State securities such as Treasury bills, Treasury Deposit Receipts and Consols figured greatly in the clearers' portfolios. The authorities also benefited in the conduct of their interest rate and credit, or money, control policies by being able to channel policy changes through a small number of large clearers who acted in concert. For instance, the fact that the LCBs always altered their interest rates in line with official rates simplified the authorities' control over short-term market rates. More generally, through to the 1970s an increasing range of controls over bank lending, interest rates and asset ratios was applied to the clearing banks. From the point of view of control there was much to recommend these arrangements, because the LCBs accounted for the bulk of bank deposits – and, thus, of the money supply – and their bill discounts and loans formed a large proportion of the total credit provision from financial institutions. In return the clearers were able to suppress price competition, and they were exempted from Schedule 8 of the 1948 Companies Act which meant that they did not have to disclose their true profit position to the public.

Over time, the burden of war finance lessened and through the 1960s there was increasing criticism of these arrangements.[22] Disquiet arose, first, over inefficiencies resulting from the stifling of price competition because this forced banks to compete in the provision of services (in itself, not unwelcome) and raised suspicions that the clearers were wastefully 'duplicating' branch offices that remained underused. In 1968, the Monopolies Commission which was investigating the proposed merger between Barclays, Lloyds and Martins, severely criticised the price-fixing arrangements, believing them to 'have such a soporific effect on the banks that, so long as they exist, no foreseeable change in the structure of the clearing bank system could greatly increase the degree of competition in it.'[23] Already, in the previous year, the Report on Bank Charges by the National Board for Prices and Incomes had explicitly called for the abolition of collective agreements on deposit and lending rates.[24] There was also recognition of the rapid growth of NBFIs and other banks which were providing services in markets where the clearers did not actively compete.[25] This fact helped gain support for change from the clearers themselves – a more adventurous entrepreneurial spirit could, perhaps, win them a larger share in these alternative markets. The Prices and Incomes Board Report had urged British banks to follow the example of their American counterparts:

> Historically, the British banks have stood aside from the main development of mortgage loans and instalment credit. These fields have been taken over by building societies and finance houses. Nor have the British banks diversified their liabilities. In other countries it has not been so. There is nothing in the nature of banking as such

> which prevents the British banks from following the example of, say, the American banks in these respects. Banks in the United States issue a wide variety of time deposits, including negotiable certificates of deposit which may be traded in the money market. And they are prominent in the field of instalment credit and in making mortgage loans.[26]

Official action came in 1971 when Edward Heath's Conservative government adopted a new approach in its 'Competition and Credit Control' policy.[27] The London and Scottish clearers lost the right to collude on interest rates, use of the price mechanism was lauded and the clearers were urged to compete more vigorously with each other and with rival institutions. Thus ended the price-fixing cartels which had originated in the nineteenth century and which had been formalised, with official blessings, before World War II. Subsequently, rates have not varied much between the banks but the rates have more closely followed changes in market rates and, of course, identity of rates could be as much a sign of keen competition as of (implicit) collusion. By the end of the 1970s, the LCBs themselves were publicly applauding 'the increased competition in financial markets because it fosters efficiency and benefits customers.'[28] The figures in Table 12.2 have already shown that one result of this more adventurous approach may have been to arrest the long-term decline in market share.

The clearers were also able to point out that they had responded positively to the 1971 changes by extending their areas of activity and by giving more weight to price competition. Some of these extra activities had previously been almost exclusively conducted through the medium of affiliates and subsidiary companies but, since the 1970s, in-house development by the clearers has given rise to something akin to 'universal' banks, whereby the LCBs provide a very broad range of services. In this way the two decades following the mid-1960s witnessed a severe weakening of the institutional specialisation that had so characterised British money markets in the first half of the century.

As early as the 1950s (beginning with the Commercial Bank of Scotland's acquisition of the Scottish Midland Guarantee Trust) the clearers had taken shareholdings in finance companies and this interest in hire-purchase provision has continued, so that a great part of this sector is now owned by one or other of the banks.[29] In addition, from the late 1960s and the early 1970s, the clearing banks became more active in competing for the deposits of large customers in the wholesale money markets; they began to increase sharply their medium-term borrowing (i.e. borrowing with an initial term of one to two years); and they developed a range of services formerly associated with the merchant banks. These services have included, 'corporate financial advice, capital issue facilities, investment management, loan syndication and acceptance credits...'[30] Again the clearers operated partly through subsidiaries although there was continued diversification in the services offered by parent banks. There has been great development of international banking business, too. At home the clearers have been keener to compete for and develop services such as credit cards, consumer credit, mortgage financing, insurance services and financial advisory facilities. A number of the clearers were also prepared to take advantage of the relaxation of the rules on participation in stock market activities which was introduced in 1986 (the year of the so-called 'Big Bang') through the infusion of fresh capital into existing firms of stockbrokers and other dealers in securities. As an illustration of the extensive range of services offered by the major clearing banks, Table 12.5 lists the main divisions within Barclays Bank group as of November 1985. From this it is possible to give meaning to the label 'universal banking'.

The 1971 reforms seem, therefore, to have been effective in removing one likely cause of the clearers' relative decline: the official feather-bedding of the 'soporific' clearers has now gone and its removal

**Table 12.5 : The Activities of the Barclays Bank Group of Companies, November 1985**

**BARCLAYS PLC**
**Group Holding Company**

**BARCLAYS BANK PLC**
**Principal Operating Company**

| UNITED KINGDOM OPERATIONS | | OVERSEAS OPERATIONS |
|---|---|---|
| Domestic Banking<br>Almost 2,900 Barclays Bank branches in England, Scotland, Wales, Channel Isles and Isle of Man<br>31 Local Head Offices | Barclays Investment Management Ltd<br>Corporate investment management | With subsidiary and associated companies almost 2,400 branches in some 80 countries |
| Barclaycard | Barclays Property Investment Management Ltd<br>Property investment and management | A wide range of banking and related services is offered throughout the world |
| Barclays Merchant Bank Ltd<br>Corporate advice<br>Company flotations<br>Capital issues<br>International securities<br>Acceptance credits<br>Medium term loans, etc. | Barclays Unit Trusts and Insurance Ltd<br>Management company for all unit trust and insurance operations<br>- Barclays Unicorn Ltd<br>Unit trust management in the UK and overseas<br>- Barclays Life Assurance Co Ltd<br>Unit-linked life assurance and pension policies<br>- Barclays Insurance Services Co Ltd<br>Insurance and broking and advice<br>- Barclays Insurance Brokers International Ltd<br>World-wide insurance broking and advice | |
| Barclays Development Capital Ltd<br>Development and replacement capital<br>Management and employee buy-outs | Barclays Bank Finance Company (Jersey) Ltd<br>Barclays Finance Company (Guernsey) Ltd<br>Barclays Finance Company (Isle of Man) Ltd<br>Acceptance of sterling and foreign currency deposits | |
| Mercantile Credit Co Ltd<br>Over 100 branches | Share Registration and New Issues<br>For companies and local authorities | |
| Highland Leasing Ltd<br>Leasing<br>Hire purchase<br>Instalment finance | Barclays Futures Ltd<br>Financial futures - broking and research | |
| Barclays Bank Trust Co Ltd<br>39 offices in the UK and offices in the Channel Islands and Isle of Man<br>Trust administration<br>Personal investment management<br>Personal taxation and financial planning<br>Self-administered pension | | |

seems to have contributed to an awakening of a more enterprising spirit. The clearers have become more competitive and their business more diversified. As the data presented earlier suggested, one consequence may have been to check the sharp fall in their share of total deposits. However, the nature of the data makes it difficult to draw firm conclusions. The significance of the break in the statistical series in 1975 has already been commented upon. Another influence has been the changing relative importance of the clearers' subsidiary and in-house business. Many of the clearers' subsidiary companies and affiliates are not grouped with the parent company, or even within the 'banking sector' (because they are not banks), but more strictly belong to other sectors (e.g. insurance companies). Thus, the failure of the data to capture their growth understates the extent to which the LCBs innovated in the period as a whole, whereas the degree to which the clearers shifted business from subsidiaries to in-house departments during the late 1970s might over-state their success in defending market share. Even so, the main conclusion from the data still holds: during the post-war period banks other than the clearers grew much more rapidly than the clearers themselves. The clearers may have become more price-competitive and innovative than during the rest of the twentieth century, but 'outsiders' proved even more effective.

Another factor offered in explanation of the clearers' partial eclipse has been the discriminating impact of government credit and monetary control – an explanation favoured by the clearers themselves. Until the reorientation of policy in 1971 the clearing banks bore the brunt of official controls. In particular, during the fifties and sixties there were frequent phases when the authorities sought to constrain domestic demand by restricting the creation of credit. The clearers and the finance companies were singled out for special control. Thus, the clearing banks received frequent 'requests' to restrain growth of their advances, they were required to maintain specific asset ratios and, on occasions, they were subjected to more direct controls in the form of 'special deposits' (whereby part of their cash holdings were requisitioned by the Bank of England in order to stem the growth of bank lending). In this, the controls were very effective and 'their prolonged use resulted in a substantial frustration of the demand for bank credit.'[31]

As other banks and NBFIs (except the finance houses which were partially-owned by the clearers) were not subjected to these controls, it is not surprising that the clearing banks raised objections on the grounds of discrimination. A general condemnation was expressed by the Wilson Committee: 'The system inhibited competition among banks and between them and other financial institutions, thus protecting market shares and discouraging innovations.'[32] The authorities' justification was pragmatic. By controlling clearing bank (and finance house) advances they were able to control the bulk of financial credit, especially consumer credit, and the effective link between Bank rate and the clearers' interest rates meant that they could directly influence short-term market rates.

It was generally recognised, though, that a long-term consequence had been to give the clearers' competitors an unfair advantage. It was for this reason that the reforms of 1971 sought not only to encourage price competition but also to remove the main discriminatory effects of credit policy. Accordingly, most official controls over assets and liabilities were extended beyond the clearers, to *all* banks. An exception was made in the case of the cash ratio, however, and until 1981 the clearers alone were obliged to maintain balances at the Bank of England, to the extent of 1.5 per cent of their eligible liabilities. Also NBFIs such as building societies have remained largely outside the direct application of monetary controls. The changes introduced in 1971 thus helped the clearers to an important extent but did not remove all discriminatory effects. Moreover, in practice, controls over banking were retained. For example, on a number of occasions during the 1970s, the supplementary deposit scheme (known as the 'corset') was applied so as to inhibit directly the growth of bank liabilities. Compared to the NBFIs, therefore, the banks (though not just the clearers now) continued to feel official constraints most strongly.

With the election of a new Conservative government under Margaret Thatcher in 1979 there were renewed attempts to place financial institutions on a more equal footing under the operation of monetary policy. Even here, though, as the government's central aim was to reduce inflation by restricting the growth of the money supply and as the banks' sterling deposits – but not NBFIs' deposits – were the main component of the authorities' chosen target variable (sterling M3), restriction of the growth of the banks' business remained an important feature of government policy.

## THE CLEARING BANKS' BALANCE SHEETS

Figures 12.3 and 12.4 graph changes in the distribution of the LCBs' liabilities and assets over the period from 1938 to 1982. Despite some detailed problems in using such data, they nevertheless provide a summary picture of major trends in the clearers' business over time. It is important to bear in mind, though, that they refer to the clearers' parent companies (Midland Bank, Lloyds Bank, etc) and not to the clearers' groups of companies (i.e. parent and subsidiary companies).

The rest of this chapter highlights the more important changes affecting specific groups of liabilities and assets, but before doing so it is appropriate to draw attention to some significant general features. A critical factor influencing the composition of bank assets has been government policy. Throughout, there were periods of official constraint on bank advances and for most of the post-war years there were stipulations regarding reserve ratios. During the 1940s and 1950s, however, the influence of government was most obvious in the predominance of public sector liabilities in the LCBs' portfolios. These state liabilities took the form of cash, Treasury bills (which

Figure 12.3: Distribution of London Clearing Banks' Liabilities, 1938-82
(Liabilities as a Percentage of Total Liabilities)

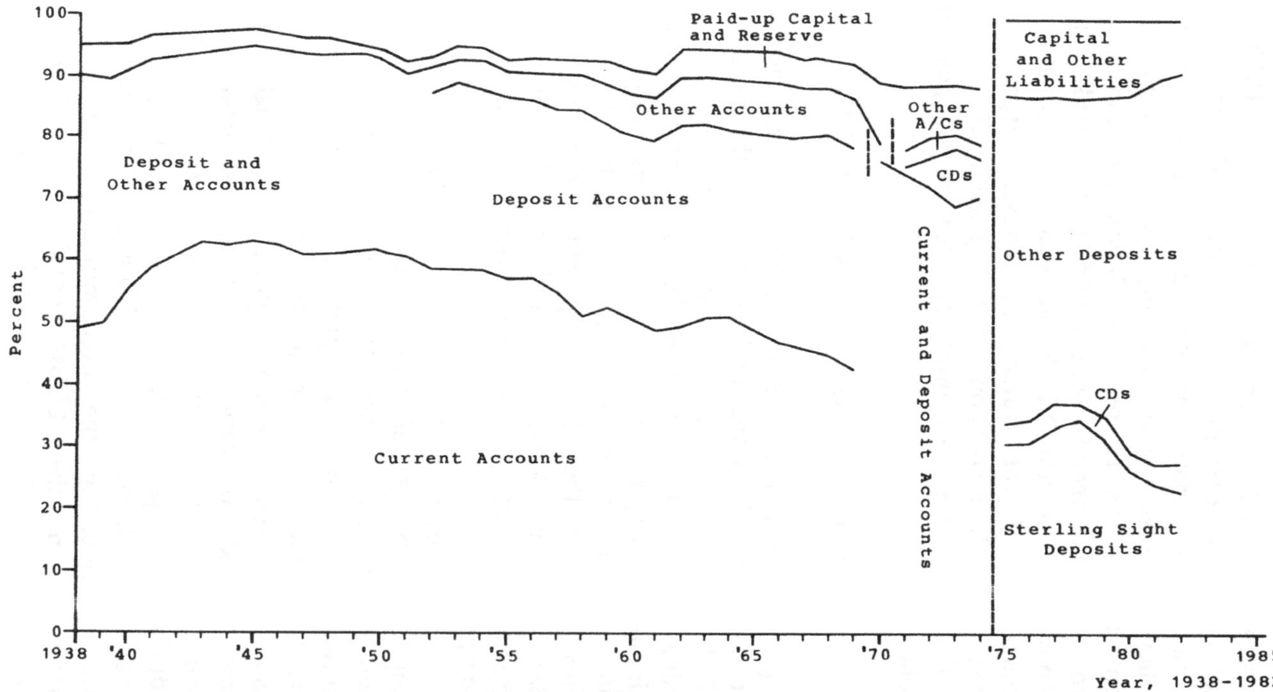


Sources: *Annual Abstract of Statistics* and *Bank of England Quarterly Bulletin*

Figure 12.4: Distribution of London Clearing Banks' assets, 1938-82
(Assets as a percentage of total deposit [gross])

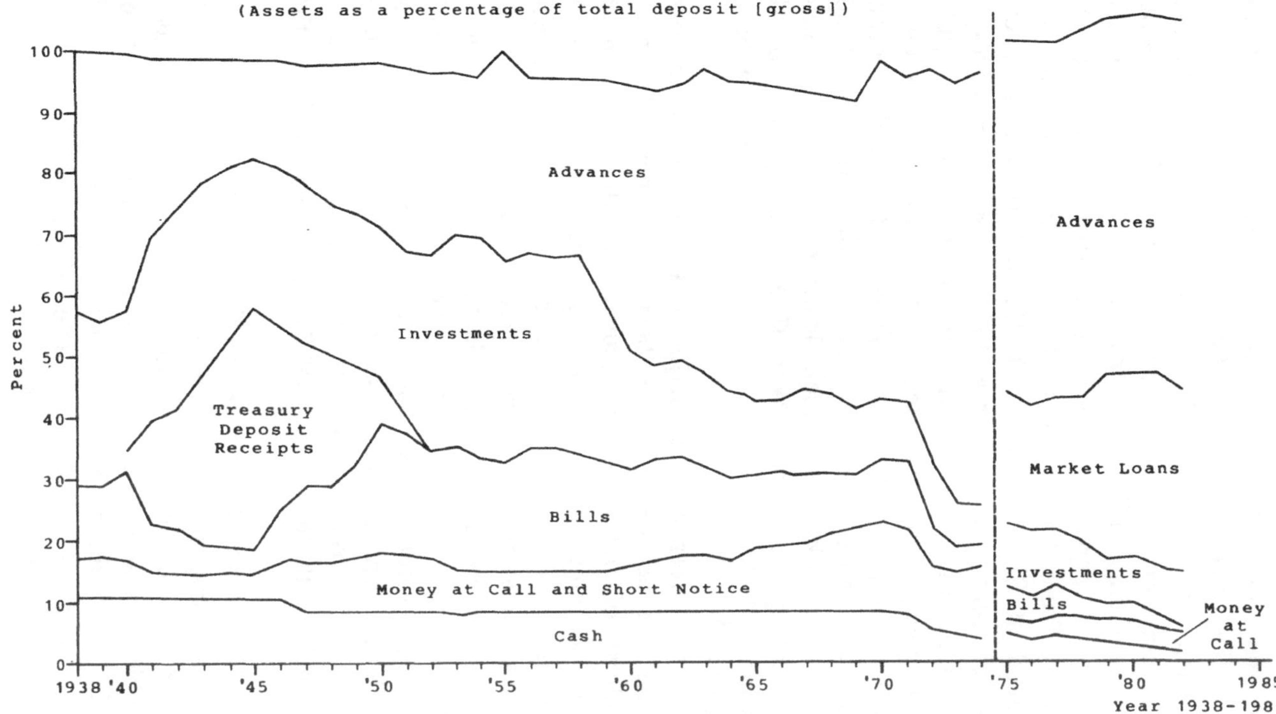


Sources: *Annual Abstract of Statistics* and *Bank of England Quarterly Bulletin*

accounted for the bulk of the 'bills' category in Figure 12.3), Treasury Deposit Receipts (TDRs) and longer-term government securities (accounting for the bulk of the banks' 'investments'). Even the item, 'money at call and short notice', was indirectly lent to the state in that most of the balances were deposited with the discount houses which, in turn, invested most of them in Treasury bills. Thus, if we lump together all these assets - cash, money at call and short notice, Treasury bills, TDRs and investments - it can be seen that as a percentage of total deposits they rose very sharply from 56 per cent at the outbreak of the war, peaked at 82 per cent in 1945, and remained at over 65 per cent until the late 1950s. In other words, at this time the government's financial needs and public debt policy dominated the clearers' asset portfolios to an extraordinary degree. They had already become relatively more important during the troubled 1930s, when the banks found their loans to the private sector contracting, but World War II and the growth of the National Debt were undoubtedly the most important factors.[33]

In retrospect the major post-war trend in bank assets can be seen to have been the general decline in holdings of public sector securities as the needs of the state became less demanding and as the LCBs diversified and contributed increasingly to the financial requirements of the private sector. In the 1950s and 1960s this switch occurred largely in the form of an increase in advances and decline in investments, although within bills, too, there was a move from public to private sector assets. The surprise, perhaps, is that the return towards asset ratios more closely resembling those of the 1920s took such a long time to achieve.

Developments in the 1970s confirmed this switch in the composition of the clearers' assets, from the public to the private sector. The seventies was a troubled decade with serious national and international problems, culminating in lower economic growth and high rates of inflation. The rising personal sector financial surplus that has already been discussed was concomitant with rising deficits in the corporate, public and overseas sectors. Because of inflation, the government sought to slow down the growth in the money supply (including bank liabilities) and, therefore, sought to finance more of its own debt through sales of securities to the personal sector, rather than to the banks. Simultaneously, the effects of inflation made bank loans more attractive to business firms. The net effect was to increase the banks' intermediation between the (surplus) personal sector and the (deficit) corporate sector, at the same time as the authorities were reducing the banks' financing of public sector debt – within bank balance sheets the share of advances rose and that of public sector liabilities fell. The outcome was that advances came to dominate the clearers' assets. Thus, in 1973/74 they stood at some 70 per cent of deposits, with the grouping of government–dominated assets down to under 30 per cent (even if no account is taken of the smaller share of Treasury bills within total bill holdings). In effect, then, the history of the post–war period has been one of the banks gradually breaking from the extraordinary constraints created by war and establishing a more normal position, where their resources became largely committed to the private sector.

Of liabilities, the main changes in deposits have been the declining share of current accounts, or sight deposits, from the high levels created during World War II and, since the 1960s, the greater dependence of the clearers on wholesale deposits and non–sterling deposits (not apparent from the graphs).

Finally in emphasising general trends, attention should be focused on three particular time periods in which significant changes occurred: the war and immediate post–war decade in which government securities dominated the banks' assets; from 1958 to 1960, when there was an upsurge in advances and concomitant decline in investments which proved permanent; and from 1971 to 1973, when there was another stepwise expansion in advances which establised a new long–term pattern in the composition of bank assets. Further details are given below.

## LIABILITIES

### *Scottish and Northern Ireland Bank Notes*

The Scottish clearing banks and Northern Ireland banks continue to circulate their own notes, although for every pound issued above a small authorised amount (of under £3 million for Scotland, and some £2 million for Northern Ireland) they have to hold an equivalent value of Bank of England notes (held mainly at the Bank of England). At the end of the 1950s, notes represented some 12 per cent (or £127 million) of the combined public liabilities of the Scottish and Northern Ireland Banks, although by the early 1980s this was down to about 6.5 per cent (some £624 million).[34] The retention of note-issuing powers is to an extent a reflection of patriotism, of the long tradition of maintaining separate identities for their systems of banking, and it is partly due to the absence of any convincing arguments in favour of abolition. Before the Wilson Committee, the Scottish clearers also argued an economic case. They claimed that it was 'worthwhile to issue their own notes because it enables them to avoid holding Bank of England notes [effectively non-interest-bearing government debt] in their tills. Instead they hold their own notes which can be provided at much lower cost.'[35]

### *Deposits*

The clearing banks have remained the dominant force in retail deposit banking throughout the period, although most recently they have faced stiffer competition from the National Girobank, the Trustee Savings Banks and, most effectively, from the building societies. Their dominance rests on the great convenience that extensive branch networks provide customers and the fact that they 'carry out the bulk of the nation's cash distribution and money transmission activities.'[36] It has been the attraction to customers of these services (chequeing, cash tills, standing orders, etc.) that enabled the clearing banks to secure such a large proportion of their deposits in the form of current accounts, on which no interest was paid.

Surveying the period as a whole, the overwhelming proportion of deposits has been repayable on demand, held either as current accounts or deposit accounts (which, despite a formal seven-day notice before withdrawal, have been immediately encashable). Other forms of deposit where withdrawal has not been so immediate, as in the case of savings accounts, have remained comparatively insignificant.

From Figure 12.3 it can be seen that the relative importance of current accounts rose strongly during wartime from 50 per cent to over 60 per cent of total liabilities. Just before the war, balances on deposit account had been some four-fifths of current accounts but by the early fifties the impact of wartime changes was still apparent, with the ratio still below one-half. Indeed, there was no significant change in the relative shares until 1956/7, with current accounts then beginning a gradual decline. By the early 1970s the relative importance of deposit accounts had so increased that they were equal to 86 per cent of current accounts.

In general terms, the overall growth of bank deposits – and even the distribution between types of deposits – was greatly dependent upon the conduct of monetary policy. During the war and immediate post-war years, the rise in the money supply and the general increase in liquidity throughout the economy undoubtedly added to the growth of current accounts, the most liquid of deposits. Prevailing interest rate conditions contributed to the mix between current accounts and interest-bearing deposits. Balances on current account are an extremely convenient means in which to hold money and, all things being equal, an inducement (in the form of interest payments) would have to be paid in order to persuade the public to hold more of its liquid assets in another form such as deposit accounts. Thus, the lower the rate of interest being paid on deposit accounts, the greater the amount that is likely to be held on current account. The official policy of cheap money, which was first introduced in the thirties and maintained throughout the 1940s, may have been important here. During this time – until November 1951, in fact – a rate of only 0.5 per cent per annum was paid on deposit accounts and this probably buoyed-up balances held on current account. Conversely, when interest rates began to rise during the 1950s, 1960s and (even more so) during the 1970s, this heightened awareness of the cost of holding bank balances on current account. Interest-bearing accounts became more attractive. The years between 1971 and 1976 provide a good example. These were years of sharply rising inflation and high nominal interest rates, and they were also years when the number of deposit and savings accounts (on which interest was paid) rose by almost one-quarter, to 11.4 million.[37] In the early 1980s, too, there was a period of historically high 'real' interest rates (adjusted for inflation) and this must have been a factor in the continuing decline in the share of sterling sight deposits (Figure 12.3), so much so that by 1981/2 they represented less than one-quarter of the total of LCB liabilities.

From the banks' point of view, a significant consequence of this relative decline in the importance of sight deposits was that an increasing proportion of their resources became more 'market-oriented' or 'price-conscious'. The banks had to pay more attention to their own competitiveness if they were to slow-down the loss of retail deposits to institutions such as the building societies. It has already been noted that official pressure forced the abandonment of the interest-rate-fixing cartels. Under these agreements all the LCBs had paid a common rate on seven-day deposit accounts, set at 2 per cent below Bank rate.[38] In Scotland interest was paid on deposits which were encashable on demand provided that they had been 'inactive' for at least a month. Here, too, a price-fixing cartel ensured a uniform rate (of 2.5 per cent below Bank rate by the 1960s).[39] The Northern Ireland banks also operated a cartel – on seven-day deposits, 2 to 3 per cent below Bank rate was payable, depending on the size of the total balance. Similar agreements covered interest and commission charges. In 1971 'Competition and Credit

Control' abolished these agreements in England and Scotland, thus opening the way for a greater competitive response from the clearers in their search for deposits.[40]

One effect of the changing distibution of deposits was that the clearers no longer got the majority of their balances interest-free. Yet, as deposit accounts were effectively withdrawable on demand, the short-term nature of their liabilities remained. Similarly, the relative decline of sight deposits has not greatly reduced the retail nature of most of the clearers' accounts, a big attraction of having a bank account remains the access that this gives to the banks' money transmission services. Thus for the banks, the reduction in interest-free deposits has reduced this form of financial contribution towards retail banking costs but it has not reduced the costs themselves. At first, the banks sought to recoup these costs by charging more commission for the use of cheques, bankers' orders, and the like, unless a minimum current account balance was maintained (details differed from bank to bank, but in mid-1985 the National Westminster, for instance, insisted on a minimum credit balance of £100). However, competitive pressures forced changes here, too. Other institutions such as the building societies and savings banks made no charges for the maintenance of their retail accounts and when, in 1985, the Midland Bank decided to abolish charges for all accounts staying in credit – and in so doing successfully increased its market share – the other clearers quickly followed suit by offering 'free' current accounts.

The greater influence of competitive forces was even more apparent in the clearers' attempts to obtain deposits other than their traditional sterling retail balances. Until the 1960s almost all the clearers' deposits came from either current accounts or deposit accounts and mainly from the personal sector. However, as was discussed in the previous chapter, during the 1960s a market developed for deposits of larger sums lodged mainly by financial institutions and large corporations for varying periods and receiving higher rates of interest than the clearing banks' 7-day deposit rate. These larger balances became known as wholesale deposits. At first the clearing banks competed for such deposits through specially-created subsidiary companies, but since gaining greater freedom from official controls with the introduction of 'Competition and Credit Control' in 1971, the parent banks have also operated in the wholesale money markets.

Three main channels to wholesale markets were open to the LCBs: large deposits (of over £10,000) were raised through the branches; inter-bank and other large deposits (e.g. local authority funds) were raised directly or through money brokers; and certificates of deposit (CDs) were issued for balances usually in excess of £50,000. In all cases the interest that was paid reflected prevailing, competitive market rates. In Figure 12.3 the only one of these three forms of deposit that is shown separately is CDs. These are issued by banks to certify that a fixed-term deposit has been made and they carry an undertaking by the bank to pay the bearer on maturity. In the UK they were first issued in dollars in 1966 and in sterling in 1968, with the Bank of England regulating the number of issues. CDs proved advantageous to both banks and depositors. For the banks they provide a means of raising large amounts for a fixed period on terms which can be individually negotiated. Depositors are paid a rate which is competitive with those payable on other forms of large deposits. In addition, CDs have the advantage of being negotiable, they can be sold to a third party if cash is required immediately. Indeed, after their introduction CDs quickly became readily saleable in a market organised mainly by the discount houses. However, while CDs were an interesting innovation and, at times, a useful and flexible supplement to normal deposit sources, it can be seen from Figure 12.3 that they have remained a small part of the LCBs' total liabilities – peaking in 1973 at 8 per cent, but falling to around 3.4 per cent in the late seventies and early eighties.

Nevertheless, wholesale deposits generally have had

great significance on the nature of banking in the UK. With traditional retail banking, with the great proportion of resources coming from the personal sector's balances held in relatively small amounts throughout thousands of branches, it could be argued that the clearers were 'deposit–driven' – their ability to lend was directly governed by the growth of deposits. This has been less true since the development of wholesale deposits. Personal sector deposits remain the main source of the clearers' resources but much less so than in earlier periods. As early as 1971, in fact, wholesale deposits accounted for some 45 per cent of the LCB group's total deposits. This enabled them to 'modify the traditional approach, since they can now enter into lending commitments in the knowledge that any shortfall in branch deposits can be made good in the [wholesale money] markets.'[41] This extra flexibility means the clearers are able to match more readily the size and maturity of commitments to resources.

While the clearers' involvement in wholesale money markets has been conducted partially in sterling, another important dimension has been the growth of non–sterling business. This arose out of the development from the early 1960s of the euro–currency markets, wherein banks have bought and sold deposits denominated in currencies of countries other than those in which the banks were located. Before 1971, official liquidity reserve requirements prevented the clearers' parent banks from participating directly, but they were able to set up subsidiaries to acquire non–sterling deposits. After the 1971 reforms, the clearers themselves became very active in the market for funds, with non–sterling balances accounting for some 15 per cent of total LCB deposits by the mid–1970s. Also after the abandonment of exchange controls in 1979, and the boost this gave to foreign currency trading, there was a period of rapid expansion in non–sterling (mainly US dollar) deposits, so much so that they accounted for some 27 per cent of the clearers' deposits by the early 1980s.

In sum, while the clearing banks have remained

the main institutions in the provision of retail deposit services and other banking facilities, their importance here has declined on trend and they have lost much of their overwhelming predominance. For the banks, an increasing proportion of their deposit resources has been raised in the more competitive environment of the wholesale and (increasingly) non-sterling money markets.

## ASSETS

### *Cash*

As shown in Figure 12.4 – and as defined for official control purposes for most of the period – the most liquid of the clearers' assets, cash, consisted of coin and notes in their tills, plus ordinary balances at the Bank of England. In pursuit of credit or monetary policy, on occasions the authorities have required the clearers to place with the Bank of England 'special deposits', or 'supplementary special deposits', but as the banks did not have free access to these funds they have not been included among their cash assets. The ratio of cash to total deposits – the 'cash ratio' – was more-or-less fixed for most of the period. It can be seen from Figure 12.4 that it stood a fraction above 10 per cent between 1938 and 1946. It then fell to 8 per cent, where it remained from 1947 to 1971 and even this fall was more apparent than real in that it reflected an alteration in reporting conventions. It arose from an agreement of 1946 between the London clearers and the Bank of England to cease the practice of 'window-dressing' which had falsely inflated the published figures for cash, and the LCBs subsequently agreed to abide by an 8 per cent 'true' ratio.[42] Bank of England controls seem to have turned this conventional ratio into a binding regulation, hence the stability in the graph.[43] (The Scottish and Northern Ireland banks, however, were exempted from these controls.[44])

For the LCBs there proved to be little difficulty in maintaining the ratio, for if they found their cash holdings falling below requirements, they could always readily sell their holdings of Treasury bills for cash. In effect it was the Bank of England's management of the public debt that ensured the saleability of Treasury bills because during the 1940s, 1950s and 1960s the authorities were always keen to support the market in bills – they would always supply cash for bills.[45] One important consequence, however, was to reduce whatever importance the cash ratio may have had as a fulcrum for monetary control. So, in spite of the Bank of England's insistence on a fixed cash ratio, in practice the authorities' support for short-term public debt meant that they relinquished control over the supply of cash to the banks.

In 1971, the 'Competition and Credit Control' reforms abolished this system. The requirement on the LCBs to maintain an 8 per cent cash ratio (and 28 per cent liquidity ratio) was removed and replaced by new liquidity regulations covering *all* banks. The overall effect was to reduce immediately the clearers' holdings of traditionally-defined 'cash' – the ratio was halved, down to 4 per cent between 1971 and 1974, and there it remained until 1978. Most of this was held in the form of 'till money', cash ready to pay out to customers. However, at the insistence of the authorities a sum equivalent to 1.5 per cent of 'eligible liabilities' (representing some £300 million in the mid-1970s) had to be held as non-interest bearing balances at the Bank of England. This latter requirement was the only one of a discriminatory nature that had been retained after 1971, for it applied only to the LCBs. The Bank of England argued that these balances were important in providing it with a fulcrum for its everyday management of the short-term money market, but the Bank also acknowledged that these 'free' funds came to form 'a substantial part of the Bank's resources and income'.[46]

Not surprisingly the LCBs were dissatisfied, for they believed that the amount involved was considerably in excess of the amount necessary to meet their clearing settlements with other banks.[47] It was not until 1981, however, that the authorities responded to the clearers' pressure for change. The clearers' exclusive 1.5 per cent requirement was abolished and replaced by a new obligation on *all* banks to hold balances at the Bank of England equivalent to 0.5 per cent of eligible liabilities (0.25 per cent for Northern Ireland banks). At the same time, it was agreed that the LCBs would, in addition, retain operational balances at the Bank for clearing purposes. As Figure 12.4 shows, the cash ratio (calculated on the old basis) fell further after these changes and it was down to under 2 per cent of total deposits by 1982. The clearers seem to have cut their cash holdings down to what must be an operational minimum.

The story of the cash ratio since 1945, then, is one of substantial shrinkage. Initially, the authorities had sought to use it as a (not too effective) control instrument over the LCBs. However, as soon as official regulations were relaxed in 1971 it became apparent that the amount of cash conventionally held was far in excess of what the banks themselves thought necessary in the interest of prudence. They were then free to hold a higher proportion of interest–bearing assets, causing a rundown of cash balances to levels never previously experienced in the UK. One consequence has been to raise the potential effectiveness of official action on cash balances – the banks have little choice but to respond to pressure on their minimal cash holdings – and, indeed, the 1980 Green Paper on 'Monetary Policy' emphasised the central role that the cash ratio requirement could play in the authorities' attempts to influence short–term interest rates.[48]

*Liquidity*

The minimisation of cash balances does not mean that questions of liquidity are no longer important to the clearing banks. Ultimately, concern for liquidity arises from the need to meet depositors' (and to a lesser extent, borrowers') demands for cash. Because the clearers are so large and because so many firms and households have bank accounts, in aggregate retail deposits are fairly stable. An individual might run down deposit balances for payment purposes, say, but the chances are that the person or firm receiving payment will add the sum to their bank account, leaving the aggregate of bank balances unchanged. Undeniably, this, and the general level of confidence in the clearers, was a factor in permitting the reduction of the cash ratio once official constraints were relaxed. However, most retail deposits are subject to immediate withdrawal and wholesale deposits (which, as has been shown, have grown in importance) tend to be of a fairly short-term nature and are generally more volatile than retail deposits. Thus, both during and since the years of large cash ratios the clearers have had to maintain a high degree of liquidity amongst their assets. In particular, they have sought to hold an adequate proportion of assets in forms that can be quickly encashed at little risk of capital loss. The nature of their liabilities ensures that this has remained generally true even in the absence of official stipulations.

For the period up to 1971 the LCBs were obliged by the monetary authorities to maintain a minimum 'liquidity ratio'. Such a ratio had arisen out of the banks' own practice before World War II, but in 1951 they agreed with the Bank of England to keep it within the range of 28 to 30 per cent of total deposits. In practice this settled at 30 per cent, until it was officially reduced to 28 per cent in 1963. The ratio expressed the value of a batch of officially-recognised liquid assets as a proportion of the banks' total deposits. The permitted liquid assets were essentially cash, money at call and short notice, and bills.[49] Cash has already been dealt with. Money at call and short notice were overnight and very short loans made mainly to the London discount market, although some very short loans to the Stock Exchange, bullion brokers and others were included. Bills were mainly Treasury bills (negotiable government paper of, usually, 91 days' maturity) although some private sector commercial bills of exchange were also permitted. After the war, in fact, Treasury bills dominated this category of liquid assets, but as the authorities sought to fund the nation's debt (substituting long-term for short-term debt) the banks' holdings of Treasury bills declined, so that by the mid-1960s commercial bills comprised about one-half of the total of bill holdings.[50]

Figure 12.4 shows how the share of liquid assets in the LCBs' balance sheets changed over time. During World War II the formal liquidity ratio fell, but at this time an additional, highly liquid asset, the Treasury Deposit Receipt (TDR), was created. TDRs, which first appeared in 1940, were very similar to Treasury bills but of six months' duration and, unlike bills, they were non-negotiable. As was shown in Chapter 10 they were intended to divert yet more funds into the government's coffers in order to help the war effort. In effect, the banks had little choice but to buy them. If the TDRs are added to the conventional liquidity ratio, the impact of the government's extension of its short-term debt during the war becomes apparent. The combined group of liquid assets rose very sharply, reaching 57 per cent of total deposits. This represented a tremendous distortion of the banks' peacetime asset structure and it was to take some years after the war for a more normal pattern to re-emerge. Through the second half of the 1940s the authorities reduced the liquidity of the banking system and by 1953 TDRs had been withdrawn completely, being partially replaced by the issue of more Treasury bills. In 1951 the authorities also reduced the supply of Treasury bills. This measure pushed the liquidity ratio down to 32 per cent and it remained at 32–35 per cent until 1963 when (after the introduction of the new 28 per cent minimum) it fell closer to 30 per cent.

While relatively stable over time, the liquidity ratio always proved a rather imprecise means of controlling the scale of bank advances (the main policy target during the 1950s and 1960s) because it was not a fixed rate, but a minimum, and as the banks always kept somewhat above it they were in a position to absorb Bank of England attempts to reduce their liquidity, at least in the first instance. Perhaps more important in frustrating the authorities' policy was the fact that the banks found that they could counter any contraction in their liquid assets by selling off public securities from their 'investments', leaving advances untouched. However, government restrictions did have important long-term effects, for these liquidity ratios – in excess of 30 per cent – were far above the level necessitated by normal prudential requirements. As early as the 1950s, the Radcliffe Committee had expressed the view that:

> The convention that the ratio of 'liquid assets'...to total deposits should normally be not less than 30 per cent has been inherited from the period when the banks...were many more in number and much smaller in size than they are now...it is difficult to believe that ordinary banking prudence would, left to itself, require the maintenance of so high a ratio...for the very large banks of today.[51]

In 1971, 'Competition and Credit Control' abolished the clearers' existing liquidity ratio requirement and replaced it with a less onerous reserve ratio which was to be applicable to all banks. As with the relaxation of the cash ratio regulations, one important result was to free bank resources for use in less liquid, but more profitable, assets such as advances. Figure 12.4 shows how great an impact the change had, with the liquidity ratio (defined as formerly) falling sharply from 32 per cent in 1971 to under 19 per cent by the close of 1973. Under the new regulations, reserve assets were deemed to include:[52]

> Balances at the Bank of England (coin and notes held as 'till money' and 'special deposits' were excluded);
>
> Treasury bills;
>
> Tax reserve certificates;
>
> Money at call with the London money market;
>
> Local authority and British commercial bills

eligible for rediscount at the Bank of England (a ceiling of 2 per cent of eligible liabilities was imposed on commercial bills);

British government securities with one year or less to maturity.

As a group these reserve assets were not permitted to fall in value below 12.5 per cent of a bank's 'eligible liabilities' which, in turn, were essentially a bank's liabilities denominated in sterling plus its net liabilities in non–sterling currencies.[53]

This new reserve ratio proved much less burdensome for the LCBs and when inaugurated in October 1971 the reclassification of assets gave them a collective reserve ratio of 16.5 per cent, well in excess of official requirements. There was, thus, a switch to less liquid assets, although the LCBs continued to hold their reserves somewhat above the minimum so as to allow for short–term fluctuations in deposit withdrawals.[54] Further policy changes came in 1981 when the official reserve ratio requirements were abolished altogether, although less precise liquidity requirements were retained for prudential purposes (as opposed to 'monetary control' purposes) and the discount market's position was bolstered by official insistence that each bank place funds with the market to an average value of no less than 6 per cent (with a minimum of 4 per cent) of the bank's eligible liabilities. Subsequently, in 1983, these ratios were reduced to 5 per cent for the average, and to 2.5 per cent for the minimum, but the obligation to retain call money has remained.[55]

The impact on the LCBs' asset structure is somewhat obscured by the break in the data series between 1974 and 1975, but, even with this, the movements in Figure 12.4 point to a further dwindling of bills, to just 1 per cent of total deposits in 1982. Taking a long–term perspective, the recent low level of bills among the banks' liquid assets provides a major contrast to the position during the earlier decades of the 1940s, 1950s and 1960s. Also the item specified as 'money at call' seems much smaller since the statistical change in 1974/5 but this is probably offset by the appearance of the new and large category, 'market loans', which subsumes some of the items defined earlier as 'money at call and short notice' and as 'advances'. The growth of market loans reflects the clearers' greater involvement in inter-bank, local authority, CD and eurocurrency markets. By the early 1980s their combined value was equivalent to 30 per cent of total deposits. It is important to realise that 'market loans' are made for short periods and are of a highly liquid nature. In consequence, even before the 1981 change, 'the liquidity buffer function that call money [lent to the discount market] used to fulfil [had] been taken over by the "parallel markets", especially the inter-bank and certificate of deposit markets.'[56]

Overall, then, there have been fundamental changes in those assets at the liquid end of the clearers' balance sheets. The importance of cash and bills fell sharply from the early 1970s. So, too, did loans to the discount market. However, other 'market loans' greatly expanded. The general effect, though, was to reduce the liquidity of the clearers' assets. In particular, government debt became less pervasive, and as the authorities relaxed their reserve requirements, the clearers were able to respond to the growing demand for bank credit. They reduced their holdings of liquid assets and extended their advances.

*Advances and Investments*

The long-term expansion of advances since the war, with the accompanying decline in holdings of state liabilities of all kinds, has been the dominant and most persistent feature of the clearers' changing asset distribution.

During the economic troubles of the 1930s, advances had already lost some of their former importance but the war was to cause much greater contraction. As the clearers took on large amounts of government securities (especially TDRs) and general war controls constrained the private sector's ability to borrow, the share of advances fell sharply, reaching a record low of some 16 per cent of total deposits at the end of 1945. During the late 1920s this share had been up to over 50 per cent, and evidence to the Macmillan Committee in 1929–31 suggested that bankers thought a peacetime ratio of 60 per cent was desirable.[57] There was, thus, much room for expansion when the war ended and, in absolute terms, bankers' advances more than doubled between 1946 and 1952. But the continuing importance of public sector securities and the retention of wartime controls over the private sector, and over the banks themselves, meant that in relative terms only a modest recovery had occurred by 1951. By that time the share of investments was some 26 per cent, and advances stood at about 30 per cent, still well below expected peacetime levels. It is clear from Figure 12.4 that what had happened within the LCBs' portfolios had been the nigh–elimination of TDRs which had allowed for expansion of advances, but that this had been moderated by the growth of bills (mainly Treasury bills) and investments (mainly longer–term government securities). Overall, the government was funding the National Debt and this is reflected in the clearers' balance sheets, as the very high level of wartime liquidity was run off and investments expanded.

There then followed a period of stability with no sharp changes in the asset structure between 1951/2 and 1958. This was a decade of overall economic expansion but one in which problems on the country's external account induced the authorities to seek ways of constraining domestic demand. Controls over bank lending became an integral part of this policy and the impact on the share of advances is clear. However, the bankers themselves were keen to extend their loans to the private sector[58] because advances generally carried a higher return than government securities. In fact, all the signs are that the banks were grossly underlent and in 1958, when there was a (temporary) removal of government restrictions and the economy began to experience a phase of economic growth, there took place a dramatic expansion of bank advances.

This lasted for two years. In absolute terms, the value of advances rose very sharply, by 64 per cent, between 1958 and 1960. The share of advances in total bank assets increased from 29 per cent to 43 per cent. The surge in advances was accommodated mainly by a fall in the share of investments, from 32 per cent to 20 per cent, as the banks off-loaded government securities on a massive scale.[59] The return of economic troubles and the reimposition of government controls, checked the rapidity of expansion in advances but throughout the 1960s their relative growth continued, if at a more modest pace, and investments declined. In fact, during this decade the share of advances managed to rise to the 50 per cent mark, a proportion which had not been achieved since the 1920s. The banks' asset structure was at long last recovering from the distortions of wartime finance.

The importance of government restraints was again revealed by the tremendous expansion of advances from £5.9 billion to £13.4 billion in 1971 to 1973. This resulted in the share of advances among LCB assets rising from 53 per cent to 69 per cent. As has already been stressed, the inauguration of 'Competition and Credit Control' in 1971 removed the official quantitative ceilings that had been imposed on bank lending and relaxed the LCBs' liquidity requirements. This relaxation of controls also coincided with a decidedly expansionary budgetary policy from the government. The banks responded strongly. They sharply increased loans to the private sector and ran down (in relative terms) all other assets.

Both demand and supply factors were influential. The removal of liquidity constraints encouraged the banks to seek more profitable employment of resources, but rapid rates of inflation had seriously increased the danger of capital losses on investments and had shrunk the real value of interest receipts on fixed-term securities. Thus, advances became relatively more attractive. Government policy had a particular influence here, too, for the authorities formally abandoned their active support of government security prices in the market and the new liberal regime on bank loans pointed to an expansion of advances as the best means of improving bank profitability. From the point of view of bank customers, it seems likely that quantitative constraints on bank advances had led to unsatisfied demand and, once the constraints were removed, customers could seek loans afresh or transfer from the other forms of (non–clearing bank) credit that they had been obliged to use during the restriction period. Also firms were finding bank loans an attractive alternative to debenture and equity finance at a time when high and variable inflation rates were both undermining stock market rates and discouraging firms from borrowing at fixed rates over a long period. Simultaneously, inflation was reducing the real cost of bank loans and declining company profits were reducing the supply of companies' internal funds.

One particular feature was the emergence of a money 'merry–go–round', whereby money was shuffled between financial institutions. This served to inflate the advances figures, perhaps to a significant degree. This 'merry–go–round' owed its existence to the peculiar circumstances of the early 1970s: to the rapid inflation; to the oil crisis; and to the collapse of sterling in 1973. Money market rates rose so sharply in response that they left the clearers' rates on advances so far behind as to make it worthwhile for corporate customers to draw on their bank credits and relend in the money markets.[60] The overall result, then, was to generate another tremendous burst in bank lending on a scale similar to that of 1958–60. The banks greatly expanded their lending facilities and their customers sharply increased their take–up rate of these loans. In fact, the upsurge was so dramatic as to force government action against the resultant inflationary pressures. The expansion was brought to an abrupt halt in 1973, with the re–imposition of official controls in the form of 'supplementary special deposits' (the 'corset'). For the rest of the decade the authorities retained a watching brief over bank advances, with the 'corset' being applied on three different occasions before its eventual abolition in June 1980.

Even though the rehabilitation of advances in the LCBs' balance sheets was marked by two dramatic bursts of expansion these should not obscure the fact that the long-term trend was maintained. After each burst there was no contraction in the share of advances. Within the general expansion, too, there have been important changes in the nature and type of advances made by the LCBs. The most significant change was the declining use of traditional overdrafts, whereby customers paid interest only on the amount outstanding up to an agreed level. Typically these accounts were subject to annual review. However, the 1970s witnessed major innovations in the manner in which the clearers provided loans. In particular, the provision of term loans, rather than overdrafts, came to play a significant part in the extension of credit, especially to business firms.[61]

By the late 1970s the clearers' medium-term loans were typically granted for fixed periods of over two years' duration, and commonly for between five and seven years. Illustrative of changing practice was the publicity (in 1981) given to the Midland Bank's willingness to lend up to £500,000 with repayment over as long a period as twenty years, although the average maturity of all its term loans at this time was about seven years. The interest charged on these loans has usually been variable, bearing a close relation to market rates, although fixed rates are sometimes agreed.

In the late 1950s the overdraft had still been the typical form of granting a bank advance in England for both the personal and the corporate sectors. By the late 1970s, however, contractual term loans accounted for as much as 40 per cent of the LCB groups' total advances to UK residents other than those to the personal sector.[62] By the early eighties, for instance, the Midland Bank seems to have been fairly representative, with 40 per cent of the Midland Bank Group's lending to industry in the form of such term loans, the overwhelming bulk of which were being provided for small businesses.[63] However, it is assumed that the general short-term nature of the parent banks' liabilities will continue to impose a limit on the extent to which their resources can be committed to fixed period loans (overdrafts are, at least nominally, repayable on demand), although such considerations are offset to the degree that the clearers can rely upon the overall stability of their retail deposits, and upon the greater flexibility gained from being able to raise deposits in wholesale money markets.

In the past there had always been a core of customers' overdrafts that were regularly renewed – which were, in effect, medium-term loans – although the annual review had been retained. It is possible that the trend towards term loans may have been an attempt to place this type of medium-term credit on a more formal basis. From the banks' point of view, fixed period loans mean more certainty, because with overdrafts there was always an element of customer autonomy in determining how much of the agreed limit to overdraw. Fixed period loans also offer greater certainty to customers in that overdrafts are formally recallable on demand and the terms governing them can be varied.

Apart from the development of medium-term loans for the corporate sector, during the 1970s the clearing banks (along with other banks, finance houses and specialist institutions) also committed more resources to instalment credit and leasing facilities for firms. With leasing, the banks took ownership of equipment (with most in the range of £5,000 to £100,000 by the late 1970s) and leased it to firms, making a profit on the charges levied.[64] Tax laws were particularly instrumental in making this form of credit attractive to business firms and banks alike.[65] Innovations have also occurred in the area of personal credit. In addition to overdrafts, the clearers offer more consumer credit on fixed terms, credit cards (most notably Access and Barclaycard), home improvement loans and – on a large scale since mid-1980 – mortgages for home purchase.[66] Moreover, the clearers have retained their substantial interest in consumer credit through their shareholdings in the finance houses.

The break in the statistical time series in 1974/5 masks some of the important changes that were taking place in the 1970s but it can be seen from Figure 12.4 that 'advances' retained a large share in the clearers' assets – close to the 60 per cent that bankers historically have sought – although this was somewhat less than in the early seventies. However, it is assumed that part of the new category of those assets labelled 'market loans' had previously been grouped with 'advances'. As already noted, these market loans represent the banks' credit facilities offered in parallel money markets, mainly in the inter–bank market, in both sterling and non–sterling currencies. As was the case for the liabilities side of the balance sheets, it is the development of wholesale money markets, including eurocurrency markets, that explains why 'market loans' were such an important asset item by the 1970s.

Even allowing for the break in the time series, the main post–war trends are still apparent: loans and advances to the private sector have expanded greatly and holdings of government liabilities have dwindled. In particular, investments have come down to an 'irreducible minimum' and are 'held primarily for liquidity purposes...'[67], a dramatic change from the position of thirty years earlier. By the 1970s advances and market loans had become the main sources of revenue for the banks, with investments being bought only in periods of deposit growth unaccompanied by an increased demand for loans.

## BANKS AND INDUSTRY

As discussed in earlier parts of the book, a recurring theme on the role of banks in the UK economy has been the expression of doubts over the banks' willingness and ability to meet the needs of industry for outside finance. Such alleged deficiencies figured in the debate on the slowdown in British growth rates from the late nineteenth century, and they were raised again between the wars and considered by the Macmillan Committee. In the post–war period the banks continue to have their critics and the possibility of nationalisation by a future Labour government remains a possibility. However, both the Radcliffe and Wilson Committees formally considered the relative merits of the banks in providing industrial finance and both were generally sympathetic to the clearing banks.[68] Radcliffe noted the importance of short-term bank loans to firms and also spoke favourably of the Industrial and Commercial Finance Corporation. This Corporation had been established in 1946 by the Bank of England and the London and Scottish clearing banks to provide credit for small- to medium-sized industrial and commercial concerns where capital requirements were not large enough to justify raising funds on the stock market but where needs exceeded normal bank credit facilities. The banks' involvement won some praise. However, Radcliffe did point to a gap in provision, between the seven-year or so time limit imposed on loans by the clearers and the minimum fifteen-year or so limit of the finance houses.[69] The Radcliffe Committee also urged the banks to replace their renewable overdrafts to small businesses and farmers with a system of fixed-period loans, so as to instil greater certainty into the repayment period.[70] However, there was no serious criticism of the clearers.

In 1971 the Bolton Committee reported on its enquiry into the financial problems facing small firms. Again, the clearing banks emerged largely unscathed. What criticism there was, was indirect, for they pointed out that (for a variety of reasons) the imposition by the authorities of quantitative controls on bank advances tended to operate disproportionately against small firms.[71] In 1980, the Wilson Committee considered many of the same issues as Radcliffe, although by then it was possible to point out that the clearing banks had met part of Radcliffe's recommendations by having reduced the importance of overdrafts and expanded the use of fixed period loans.[72] They also noted that during the rapid inflation of the 1970s firms had turned increasingly to bank credit, including leasing.[73] Indeed, during the decade 'the main new domestic source of medium-term finance had been the banking system itself', reaching such a point that by the end of the decade 'companies [came] to rely almost entirely on the banks to meet their needs for outside finance'.[74]

The Wilson Committee's anxiety was not over the banks' provision, then, but over the decline in long-term industrial securities, a decline which arose out of the uncertainty created by high rates of inflation.[75] In fact, subsequent upon the return of lower inflation rates in the first half of the 1980s, the equity market did recover but (of significance here) bank lending continued to be the main source (about 80 per cent) of external financing for industrial and commercial companies.[76] As had been the case for Radcliffe, the Wilson Committee was quite satisfied with the role of the banks.[77] The Committee accepted the basic proposition that the nature of bank liabilities was such that long-term loans (of twenty years or more), or equity shares in business firms, could form but a very small portion of a bank's lending. Even the minority dissenting note called not upon the banks, but upon long-term investing institutions such as the insurance companies and pension funds, to provide capital for a joint private and public sector national investment bank which could help rejuvenate British industrial investment.[78] The clearing banks' short-term liabilities apparently excluded them from such a commitment (or threat). On the specific issue of the clearing banks' facilities for business firms, and on the more general question of a possible link between deficiencies in these facilities and Britain's poor investment record, all three major official enquiries of the twentieth century – under Macmillan, Radcliffe and Wilson – have been generally satisfied with the banks' record.

## SUMMARY

Although a spate of mergers in the 1960s concentrated still further the corporate ownership of the clearing banks in the UK, this and the previous chapter have shown that the pressures for increased competition were much more significant for the post-war period as a whole. Part of the greater market-orientation has come from the clearers themselves, as they developed important innovations in the provision of financial services and as they extended their businesses into new areas at home and abroad. They did this through the creation of specialist subsidiary companies and through 'in-house' developments. More significant for UK financial provision in general, though, was the growth of strong and effective rivals in the shape of other banks and NBFIs. The clearers remained dominant in money transmission and retail banking provision but, even here, there was greater competition from institutions such as the building societies, the Trustee Savings Banks and the National Girobank. Commercial pressure was much greater in the wholesale money markets where a myriad of financial institutions and overseas banks competed on more-or-less equal terms with the clearers, as both lenders and borrowers. More generally, the post-war rise of the insurance and pension funds has meant that the pre-war decline in the banks' share of aggregate financial assets has quickened.

The clearers were always inclined to engage in effective price competition for the deposits of large customers, but it was the development of the wholesale money markets from the early 1960s that noticeably increased the clearers' ability to raise funds from other than current accounts and deposit accounts. In the wholesale markets the banks had to compete on market terms, there existed no strong oligopoly power of the sort in retail money markets. In retail banking it was government action that eventually attacked this oligopoly and instilled a greater degree of competition, especially in 1971 when the 'soporific' clearing banks were obliged to abandon their price-fixing cartels.

Government influence has been pervasive: official blessing was bestowed on the clearers' restrictive agreements throughout the period until 1971; in pursuit of the wider aims of credit control, the authorities insisted that the clearers alone abide by rigid reserve requirements; and, periodically, they imposed quantitative ceilings on advances, only reducing the 'discriminatory' nature of the controls in the 1970s. In the decades following the war, the authorities placed heavy reliance on the clearing banks' willingness to buy and hold government securities and tax policy, too, had an influence by favouring some institutions over the clearing banks. From the early 1970s, changes in policy and control techniques continued to have important consequences but the trend in monetary policy was towards general and more price-oriented controls. These allowed greater room for the clearers to compete both with each other and with other institutions. Finally on the influence of government, this chapter has shown the protracted nature of the recovery from the impact of the expansion of the National Debt during World War II and the subsequent distortions this caused to the clearing banks' asset structure. A major theme has been the contrast between the composition of assets in the 1940s and that of the 1970s and early 1980s. In particular, the data highlight the declining importance of government securities and the greater involvement by the clearers in the provision of credit to the private - and more market-oriented - sector.

## FURTHER READING

*The London Clearing Banks* (Committee of London Clearing Bankers, London, 1977).

*Committee to Review the Functioning of Financial Institutions* [Wilson Committee], *Report*, Cmnd. 7937 (HMSO, London, 1980), especially ch.4 ; and *Appendices*, 3, pp. 393–421.

Jack Revell, *The British Financial System* (Macmillan, London, 1973), ch. 6.

## NOTES

1. *Committee on the Working of the Monetary System*, [Radcliffe Committee], *Report*, Cmnd. 827, (HMSO, London, 1960), p. 42, *Principal Memoranda*,

vol. 2, pp. 49–61 for further details on the structure and function of the London clearing banks.

2. *Committee to Review the Functioning of Financial Institutions* [Wilson Committee] *Appendices*, Cmnd. 7937, (HMSO, London, 1980), 3, pp. 407–9.

3. For a consideration of the arguments see Harry Johnson, 'Observations on the Bank Merger Proposals', *Bankers' Magazine*, 206, July/Dec. 1968, pp. 135–7; and J.R. Harrod, 'Why Not Two Clearers?', *ibid*, pp. 139–43.

4. National Board for Prices and Incomes, *Report No. 34, Bank Charges*, Cmnd 3292 (HMSO, London, 1967), p. 53.

5. Details from *The London Clearing Banks. Evidence by the Committee of London Clearing Bankers to the Committee to Review the Functioning of Financial Institutions* (Committee of London Clearing Bankers, London, 1978), pp. 20–2.

6. Monopolies Commission, *Barclays Bank Ltd, Lloyds Bank Ltd and Martins Bank Ltd: A Report on the Proposed Merger*, (HMSO, London, 1968), pp. 44–63. The story from the viewpoint of one of the parties to the proposed merger is told in J.R.Winton, *Lloyds Bank, 1918–1969* (Oxford University Press, Oxford, 1982), pp. 194–200.

7. On Scottish mergers see S.G. Checkland, *Scottish Banking. A History, 1695–1973* (Collins, Glasgow & London, 1975), pp 639–44, 675–8.

8. Wilson, *Appendices*, 3, pp. 409–11.

9. Ibid., p. 411. See Norman J. Gibson, *The Financial System in Northern Ireland* (Northern Ireland Economic Council, Belfast, 1982), especially pp. 4–31.

10. For a detailed treatment of the long-term velocity of circulation see Milton Friedman and Anna J. Schwartz, *Monetary Trends in the United States and the United Kingdom* (University of Chicago Press, Chicago & London, 1982), ch. 6, especially relevant are pp. 253–9.

11. M.G. Wilcox, 'Inflation and its Effects on Banks and Finance Houses', *Midland Bank Review*, Aug. 1975, pp. 10–16; and 'Bank Lending in a

Changing Environment – A Response to Recent Criticisms', *Midland Bank Review*, Autumn/Winter 1981, p. 17.

12. See 'Banking Regulations and Competition', *Midland Bank Review*, Nov. 1971, pp. 3–11, for a considered discussion of the changes.

13. Wilson, *Report*, pp. 27–34.

14. 'The Financial Scene in the 1970s', lecture by the Deputy Governor, *Bank of England Quarterly Bulletin* [*BEQB*], vol. 21, March 1981, p. 71.

15. *United Kingdom National Accounts* [*The CSO Blue Book*], 1985 edn (HMSO, London, 1985), Table 13.1. For a broad perspective see Richard T. Coghlan and Peter M. Jackson, 'The UK Personal Savings Ratio; Past, Present and Future', *Scottish Journal of Political Economy*, vol. 26, 1979, pp. 307–24; and Graeme Dorrance, 'Savings in the 1970s', *Lloyds Bank Review*, 138, Oct. 1980, pp. 12–26.

16. Wilson, *Report*, p. 32.

17. Non-Bank Financial Intermediaries are not included in the figures. As early as the late 1950s the Radcliffe Committee had been aware of the relative expansion of other institutions (banks and non-banks) *vis á vis* the clearers. See G. Clayton, 'British Financial Intermediaries in Theory and Practice', *Economic Journal*, vol. 72, 1962, pp. 869–86; and W.T.C. King, 'Should Banks Bid for Deposits?', *Banker*, vol. 112, 1962, pp. 761–72.

18. Kevin W. Wilson, *British Financial Institutions: Savings and Monetary Policy* (Pitman Books, London, 1983), p. 85.

19. Sir Timothy Bevan, 'The Banking Environment', *Barclays Review*, vol. 60, Feb. 1985, p. 2.

20. David K. Sheppard, *The Growth and Role of UK Financial Institutions, 1880–1962* (Methuen & Co., London, 1971), p. 103.

21. For the clearers' general viewpoint see *London Clearing Banks*, pp. 189f. For the building societies' case see Leonard Williams, 'A Competitor's View' in Institute of Bankers, *The Banks and Their Competitors* (Institute of Bankers, London, 1980), pp.

43–55.

22. Brian Griffiths, *Competition in Banking* (Institute of Economic Affairs, London, 1970); and N.J. Gibson, *Financial Intermediaries and Monetary Policy* (Institute of Economic Affairs, London, 1967).

23. *Report on Proposed Merger*, p. 46.

24. *Report*, Cmnd. 3292, pp. 60–1.

25. Ibid, pp. 28, 35. See F.W. Paish, 'Deposit Rates after Mr. Jones', *Banker*, vol. 117.2, 1967, pp. 845–9.

26. *Report*, Cmnd. 3292, p. 30.

27. The authorities' new approach was formally presented in 'Competition and Credit Control', *BEQB*, vol. 11, June 1971, pp. 189–93. See Chapter 14 for more details on policy matters.

28. *London Clearing Banks*, p. 189.

29. Radcliffe, *Report*, p. 74; Wilson, *Appendices*, 4, p. 430.

30. *London Clearing Banks*, p. 27.

31. M.J. Artis, 'Monetary Policy' in F.T. Blackaby (ed.), *British Economic Policy 1960–74: Demand Management* (Cambridge University Press, Cambridge, 1979), p. 264.

32. Wilson, *Report*, p. 178.

33. H.G. Johnson, 'Clearing Bank Holdings of Public Debt, 1930–1950', *London and Cambridge Economic Service Bulletin*, vol. 29, 1951, pp. 105–7.

34. *The Annual Abstract of Statistics* and the *Bank of England Quarterly Bulletin* provide regular series of data. 'Public Liabilities' are defined as total deposits plus notes.

35. Wilson, *Appendices*, 3, pp. 410–11. Also see Maxwell Gaskin, *The Scottish Banks. A Modern Survey* (Allen & Unwin, London, 1965), pp. 99–103.

36. Wilson, *Appendices*, 3, p. 408.

37. *London Clearing Banks*, p. 48.

38. Prices and Incomes Board. *Report*, Cmnd. 3292, p. 28.

39. Gaskin, *Scottish Banks*, pp. 167–9.

40. 'Competition and Credit Control', p. 189. Northern Ireland Banks continued to charge rates recommended by the Northern Ireland Bankers'

Association. (Gibson, *Financial System in Northern Ireland*, p. 10).

41. *London Clearing Banks*, p. 46. See H. Carter and I. Partington, *Applied Economics in Banking and Finance*, 2nd edn (Oxford University Press, Oxford, 1981), pp. 110–1, 119–20, on the importance of wholesale deposits to the clearers.

42. Pages 241–2.

43. Radcliffe, *Report*, p. 119.

44. The Radcliffe Committee suggested that the note issues complicated the question of establishing ratios that would be directly comparable with those of the LCBs and that the relative smallness of these other banks meant that the establishment of controls was not crucial (*Report*, p.54).

45. Ibid., p. 128.

46. 'Monetary Control – Provisions', *BEQB*, vol. 21, Sept. 1981, p. 347. Also see 'The Role of the Bank of England in the Money Market', *BEQB*, vol. 22, Mar. 1982, pp. 86–94.

47. *London Clearing Banks*, pp. 61, 183–4.

48. 'Monetary Control', Cmnd. 7858 (HMSO, London, 1980), p. 7.

49. Radcliffe, *Report*, pp. 52, 119. Before 1971 the Bank of England occasionally varied the detailed list of assets considered eligible for the liquidity reserve.

50. J.E. Wadsworth (ed.), *The Banks and the Monetary System in the UK, 1959–1971* (Methuen & Co, London, 1973), pp. 152–9.

51. Radcliffe, *Report*, p. 119.

52. See Jack Revell, *The British Financial System*, (Macmillan, London, 1973), pp. 151–6.

53. 'Competition and Credit Control', pp. 190–1.

54. *London Clearing Banks*, p. 62.

55. 'Operation of Monetary Policy: Monetary Control Arrangements', *BEQB*, vol. 23, Sept. 1983, p. 346.

56. *London Clearing Banks*, p. 192–3.

57. Pages 252–3 for interwar figures.

58. Radcliffe, *Report*, pp. 47, 55.

59. King, 'Should the Banks Bid?', pp. 762–3.

60. 'Analysis of Financial Statistics', *BEQB*, vol. 13, Sept. 1973, p. 298.

61. Wilson, *Report*, pp. 222–4.

62. For an industrial analysis of advances see W.A. Thomas, *The Finance of British Industry, 1918–1976* (Methuen & Co, London, 1978), pp. 198–209; and *London Clearing Banks*, ch. 9 for more details.

63. 'Bank Lending in a Changing Environment', p. 18.

64. *London Clearing Banks*, pp. 102–3.

65. In a period when industrial profits were low and banking profits high, tax legislation enabled the banks, as lessors, to reduce their corporation tax liability at a time when low rates of profit prevented many industrial customers from directly doing so.

66. For a general picture see Edward Nevin and E.W. Davis, *The London Clearing Banks* (Elek Books, London, 1970), ch. 12.

67. *London Clearing Banks*, p. 61.

68. For a defence of the banks' role see 'Bank Lending in a Changing Environment', pp. 17–22. Also see Ben Fine and Laurence Harris (eds.), *The Peculiarities of the British Economy* (Lawrence and Wishart, London, 1985), chapter 4, where these critics of the City argue that there is no evidence that the banks 'starved' industry of funds.

69. Radcliffe, *Report*, p. 312; and Oliver Francks, 'The United Kingdom Deposit or Clearing Banks' in Institute of Bankers, *The City of London as a Centre of International Trade and Finance* (Institute of Bankers, London, 1961), pp. 76–8.

70. Radcliffe, *Report*, pp. 322, 325–6.

71. *Committee of Inquiry on Small Firms* [Bolton Committee], *Report*, Cmnd. 4811 (HMSO, London, 1971), especially pp. 158–66, 192.

72. Wilson, *Report*, pp. 222–3.

73. 'Financial Scene in the 1970s', p. 73.

74. 'The Banks' Role in Financing Industry'. Speech by the Governor, *BEQB*, vol. 21, Mar. 1981, p. 77.

75. Wilson, *Report*, pp. 32–3, 225, 263–8.

76. 'Company Profitability and Finance'. *BEQB*, vol. 25, June 1985, pp. 224–32.

77. For a review favourable to the banks see 'Reflections on the Role of the Institutions in Financing Industry'. Lecture by the Governor, *BEQB*, vol. 21, Mar. 1981, pp. 79–85.

78. Wilson, *Report*, pp. 274–87.

Chapter Thirteen

# MONETARY POLICY IN THE 1950s AND 1960s

The Bank of England's formal independence ended with the passing of the 1946 Bank of England Act which legally acknowledged the importance of monetary affairs to government by taking the Bank into public ownership.[1] Since then, the Bank has been an integral part of the machinery of state and its policies have been those of 'the authorities'. This is not to claim that the Bank no longer retains some independence as a source of advice to government, nor to deny that Bank governors and government ministers have not always seen eye-to-eye, even on major policy issues[2], but in most respects Bank officials now have the same status and role in policy-making as public servants in such departments of state as the Treasury. In the last resort, it is government that is responsible for monetary policy.

The aims of policy and the instruments employed to achieve those aims have varied over time and it is important to survey the main chronological developments since the last war. However, before doing so, some consideration should be given to the more apparent constraints within which the authorities (the Bank and Treasury) have had to operate – a keen awareness of the nature of such constraints is essential to any judgement on the authorities' choice of objectives and instruments, to an assessment of the effectiveness of monetary policy since the 1940s.

The first section of this chapter examines these

constraints and, then, a history of policy during the 1950s and 1960s is presented. Policy in the 1970s and 1980s is dealt with separately in Chapter 14.

## CONSTRAINTS ON THE OPERATION OF MONETARY POLICY

### *The External Account*

For most of the post-1945 period the UK has exported over one-fifth of the Gross National Product, and imported goods and services to a similar value – between 1979 and 1984 the average proportions were about 25 per cent.[3] It is obvious that variations in trade of this magnitude have important direct effects on the volume of payments into, and out of, banks based in Britain. More generally, the fact that British producers have had to compete in international markets has also imposed an overall constraint on the conduct of macroeconomic policy. In addition to the impact of changes on the trading account, the UK's position as 'a relatively small country with a relatively very large financial centre exposed to international monetary forces acting in a turbulent world'[4] has meant that, at times, capital movements into, and out of, the country have been important determinants of domestic monetary conditions. Long-term capital transfers – such as the investment overseas of over £89 billion of capital (gross) from 1979 to 1985 – have been a factor; but, historically, short-term capital flows have had a more immediate impact on monetary and exchange rate policy.

Because of London's position as a major international financial centre, at any one time non-residents hold large amounts of short-term claims on British financial institutions in the form of currency, bank balances and short-maturity securities. Historically, these claims have been large relative to the size of the official foreign currency reserves which are available to meet demands to convert sterling assets into other currencies. The ease with which sterling claims can be liquidated, and the volatility of short-term capital flows, has rendered them an important element in Britain's external account. Indeed, on many occasions in the post-war period the rapid withdrawal of such funds put pressure on the country's foreign currency reserves and on the international value of the pound, precipitating a 'sterling crisis' and often provoking major changes in overall government economic policy. How such pressure manifested itself depended upon the exchange rate regime then in operation. With a convertible pound and fixed exchange rate (as existed from 1958 to 1972) the degree of pressure could be gauged by the extent to which the authorities needed to use the official reserves (or borrow from abroad) in order to maintain the par value of the currency. Since June 1972 when the fixed exchange rate was abandoned, pressure has led more directly to a fall in the international value of sterling.

Irrespective of the exchange rate regime, large withdrawals of short-term capital from London necessarily impinge upon government monetary policy and, of course, such external pressures may – and often have – run counter to the objectives of that policy. For instance, the Labour government of the mid-1960s was initially committed to achieving a high rate of economic growth, which implied an expansionary monetary policy. However, recurrent balance of payments difficulties and accompanying periods of large international capital withdrawals, forced the government to impose and retain tight monetary controls alongside deflationary fiscal policy and more direct constraints on incomes and imports, in a vain attempt to defend the par value of sterling[5] (see Chapter 15 for more details). Indeed, the second half of the 1960s provides a striking illustration of how government policy can be severely hamshackled by changes in the balance of payments.

Even with the apparently greater flexibility permitted since 1972 by a floating exchange rate, governments have still found themselves 'blown off course' by a flight of capital and precipitous fall in the value of the pound. A recent example occurred in 1984. By then the current Conservative government had long been proclaiming the need for lower interest rates. This would aid economic recovery by cheapening costs to industry and, in fact, at the end of June, wide publicity was given to the Bank of England's view that there was no need for UK interest rates to rise. Within a week, the large-scale withdrawal of capital from London had produced a 'sterling crisis' with the value of the pound reaching a new low (of less than $1.30), resulting in a general rise in British interest rates.[6] Undoubtedly external factors continue to be of the utmost importance to the conduct of monetary policy.

### *The Bank of England's Relationship with the Money Market*

As a modern central bank, the Bank of England accepts responsibility for the regulation and support of commercial money markets. This involves both a general oversight of mandatory and prudential regulations governing the banking sector, and the more traditional role of lender of last resort. The large-scale money market operations that derive from the Bank's management of government accounts have meant also that the Bank has maintained close daily contact with other financial institutions throughout the post-war period. While such contact has undoubtedly facilitated the detailed implementation of policy, it has also restricted the channels through which monetary impulses have operated, limiting the Bank's freedom of action. Policy cannot be pursued irrespective of the impact on the money market institutions with which the Bank is in daily contact and to which it has long-established responsibilities for supplying cash in an emergency and for ensuring orderly market conditions.

As has been shown in earlier chapters, the two types of institutions that have traditionally been the most important vehicles to bear policy changes are the commercial banks (especially the London and Scottish clearing banks) and the London discount houses. The discount houses in particular have retained a special relationship with the Bank, a relationship that dates back to the last century and one which illustrates well how the Bank's traditional links with money markets aid the implementation of policy yet, at the same time, impose their own constraints. It has been the discount houses alone that have had direct access to loans from the Bank, with the commercial banks relying on calling up (or not renewing) their loans to the discount houses in times of cash shortages. In return for this privilege, since 1940 the members of the London Discount Market Association (LDMA) have undertaken to ensure that the Bank succeeded in selling all the Treasury bills offered weekly for sale as part of its National Debt transactions. The LDMA did this by purchasing any remaining bills not bought by other bidders. Until 1971 the discount houses – with the permission of the authorities – tendered a syndicated (or cartelised) price for their Treasury bills; and although since that year there has been more competition over the rate offered to the Bank, the commitment to take up any residual bills has remained.[7] The advantage to the Bank and Treasury has been the certain knowledge that the full amount of funds sought would be obtained, i.e. that all Treasury bills would be sold. The impact on the discount houses has been to confirm their institutional importance to the operation of policy in the short-term money market.

For much of the period since World War II an important feature of policy was the Bank's attempts to control short-term interest rates, including the rate on Treasury bills, and obviously the arrangements with the LDMA were central to the transmission mechanisms used. The Bank was able to manipulate the supply of Treasury bills (and, with their growing importance in the 1970s and 1980s, of commercial and other bills, too) in such a way as to help determine short-term interest rates. For instance, at least until 1980, it often sought to induce cash shortages amongst monetary institutions in order to make sure that the market was to some extent dependent on Bank loans and would, therefore, be influenced by the rate charged by the Bank on such loans.[8] Over the post-1950 period a favourite means of inducing a cash shortage was to sell more Treasury bills which, according to the terms of the tender agreement, the discount houses were obliged to buy. Thus, it was often through the medium of the discount houses that the cash shortage was first felt. However, the Bank has had to develop a finely-tuned 'feel' for the market. It is a question of judgement. In such operations the Bank has had no wish to provoke a severe cash shortage which might embarrass the discount houses' liquidity positions, but it has had to create enough pressure to oblige the discount houses to resort to loans from the Bank in order to replenish their holdings of cash. By so ensuring that it became the ultimate supplier of cash to the money market, the Bank was then in a position to influence the rate paid on bills and, thus, was able to signal to the market what it considered an appropriate level, or direction, for short-term interest rates.

However, the cost to monetary policy of such transactions was that the Bank's general willingness to supply funds to the discount houses meant that the authorities lost control over the supply of cash. The Bank could fix the price (i.e. short-term interest rates) but the supply was determined by the market's demand for loans at that price. Thus, by operating through the discount market the authorities precluded an important means of implementing monetary policy, i.e. through the use of cash supply controls. Moreover, seen from another aspect, the authorities' arrangements for the bill tender contained an element of financial masquerade. Under the system the discount houses guaranteed to buy Treasury bills, but if they had inadequate funds to do so, the Bank guaranteed to supply the necessary cash. In such a case as this, the Treasury would, in effect, not be borrowing from the money market but indirectly from the Bank of England. The outcome could well be a situation where the authorities were financing the sale of Treasury bills by increasing the liabilities of the central bank and, so, increasing the supply of reserves to the banking system - a procedure akin to 'printing money'.

It was partly in recognition of such constraints that since 1971 the Bank has attempted to distance itself somewhat from the LDMA. Under arrangements introduced since then, continuous borrowing facilities are no longer available to the discount houses – loans are now offered 'exceptionally', as a last resort facility, and at such a rate of interest as to deter borrowers. In general terms, the Bank has aimed to give much greater scope to the market in determining short-term rates. (These changes will be dealt with more fully in Chapter 14.)

*Management of the National Debt*

The Bank of England acts as the government's bank. Apart from responsibilities for the official currency reserves, this involves the Bank in the organisation of current government finances (receiving tax revenues, arranging disbursement, smoothing financial transfers between the public and private sectors, and so on) as well as in managing central government debt. The Bank 'services' the National Debt by paying dividends to bondholders and arranging for repayment when Debt matures. Through the agency of the Government Broker, it is also active in the purchase and sale of new and existing government securities. Such transactions can be on a very large scale.

> The gilt-edged market dominates the UK capital market. Net new issues of gilt-edged over the years 1977–81 inclusive amounted to nine times all new private sector issues of equity and debt combined, and turnover in gilts accounted for 75 per cent by value of the total on the UK stock exchanges.[9]

Obviously National Debt transactions on this scale have important implications for money and capital markets. They not only impinge on the operation of monetary policy but may well constitute an important technique of control.

It has been emphasised that in short-term money markets the need for the Bank of England to support sales of Treasury bills played a significant role, but the long-term capital needs of the state have been important, too. During the post-war period a large amount of Debt has been maturing regularly and, therefore, has necessitated frequent renewals. For this reason, until the late sixties an overriding aim of the Bank was to support the market in long-term government securities (so-called 'gilts', which are mainly government and nationalised industry bonds). Indeed, the Bank was - and still is - the dominant buyer and seller of gilt-edged stock. For most of the post-war period the authorities believed that the market for gilts (and, therefore, the prospects for refinancing the National Debt cheaply) could be seriously damaged if prices were unstable and, more especially, if there was a significant fall in the price. They, therefore, decided to intervene actively in the market in order to moderate price falls.[10]

The effects of such intervention on monetary policy could be perverse, however. For example, in 1960 government policy aimed to tighten monetary conditions by, among other measures, calling for 'special deposits' from the clearing banks in order to reduce bank reserves which, in turn, should have led to a cut-back in bank loans. However, at the same time the Bank continued to pursue its longer-term policy on the National Debt, by maintaining its general support for the market in gilts. According to this approach, when demand for gilts was rising the Government Broker sold, and bought when the market was weak - a policy of 'leaning against the wind'. However, one effect of the government's call for special deposits in 1960 was to force the clearing banks to sell some of their gilt holdings in order to make good the deficiency in reserves. But because the Government Broker was willing to buy these securities from the banks, the impact of the call for special deposits was seriously weakened.[11] On the one hand, government policy was reducing clearing bank reserves by draining them off as special deposits yet, on the other, the Government Broker was supplying the banks with alternative reserve assets at very little cost (for the fall in gilt prices had been mitigated by the Broker's purchases). This episode illustrates clearly the type of inconsistency that could arise in the post-war years between the Bank's long-term strategy for government securities and the short-term objectives of monetary policy. It also highlights the importance of Debt management as a constraint on policy.

This particular example in which National Debt management rendered monetary controls ineffective was, in fact, but one instance of the general conflict inherent in a policy aimed at resisting sharp, especially upward, movements in interest rates. An important implication of the use of quantitative controls (such as the special deposit scheme) to bring about a contraction in bank deposits and loans was that interest rates had to rise. But, up until the late 1960s and early 1970s, traditional National Debt management aimed at keeping government interest payments down. The philosophy behind Debt management was firmly against interest rate flexibility, hence the conflict. This conflict the authorities increasingly recognised. Consequently, as monetary policy came to play a more active role in government economic management, the authorities moderated their attitude towards interest rates and accepted the need for greater variability. In particular, the adoption from the mid-1970s of targets for the rate of growth in monetary aggregates forced a considerable change in the Bank's objectives regarding gilt-edged operations. The authorities came to accept that the sale of gilts to the non-bank private sector was one important means of reducing the money supply. Consequently, attempts through the 1970s and early 1980s to slow-down monetary expansion sharply increased the sale of securities to the public, even if this raised interest rates. Indeed, by the end of the seventies gilts management was seen as an integral part of monetary policy techniques; important in its own right, if subordinate to monetary aggregate objectives.[12]

This shift in emphasis was quite gradual but, in total, the thrust of gilt-edged management had altered markedly by the late 1970s. The long-term aim remained the support of the market in government securities so as to ensure that the state could acquire adequate finance, but there was less active intervention by the authorities to influence interest rates. In recent years, therefore, at times of market weakness the Bank has been less concerned than in the past to uphold prices. In addition to this, increased sales of government debt to the non-bank private sector have been viewed by the authorities as a major means of reducing bank liabilities (as the public ran down its bank deposits to purchase gilts). Sales of gilts have, thus, been seen as one important means of reducing the expansion of the money supply and as this became a central feature of monetary policy from the mid-1970s so, too, did the need to sell gilts. An important corollary, though, is that the authorities have had to permit greater variability of gilt prices and, thus, more freedom to long-term interest rates.

*General Policy Environment*

The programme of an elected government covers broad areas of social, political and economic policy and there is no certainty that inconsistencies and conflicts will not arise as government pursues a diversity of objectives. Even within economic policy there has often been friction between the stated aims of different components of that policy. For post-war governments important economic goals have been the pursuit of full employment, wage and price stability, higher growth, improved balance of payments, exchange rate stability (until 1972, a fixed exchange rate) and effective regional development programmes. In broad terms, the main instruments employed to achieve these goals have been fiscal policy, direct controls such as restrictions on capital exports or various prices and incomes constraints, and monetary policy. However, the mutual use of these different techniques of economic management has not always been internally consistent and achievements in one area have been necessarily affected by action elsewhere. In particular, a retrospective view of the period needs to take account of the changing role and status of monetary policy within the battery of policy instruments available to the authorities.

In the early decades after the war all major political parties espoused 'Keynesian economics' in the sense that they believed that, left to its own devices, the market economy was most unlikely to produce full employment; that the attainment of full employment should be a top priority; and that government had the power to manipulate the level of aggregate demand in the economy in such a way as to achieve full employment. Thus, if unemployment did exist this was interpreted as resulting from a deficiency in aggregate demand, a deficiency which could be made good by the government either raising its own demand for goods and services through increased government expenditure, or by offering inducements such as reduced taxes and higher welfare benefits to the private sector to raise its demand. In other words, fiscal measures occupied the central position within policy instruments considered by the state, and belief in their efficacy justified their use.

In the event, the goal of full employment was readily attained through the 1940s, 1950s and 1960s. Indeed, the authorities found that in general 'economic management' measures were required to dampen down demand rather than stimulate it. As earlier anxieties about the possible return of mass unemployment on the scale of the 1930s faded, the emphasis of policy shifted towards the attainment of higher growth rates and improved balance of payments. Lack of success in these areas through the 1950s and 1960s encouraged a broadening of the use of policy instruments, especially credit controls and monetary measures, as well as prices and incomes policies. Meanwhile, greater use of monetary instruments was gaining more support in academic circles. In particular, a number of studies publicising the theoretical reasoning and empirical findings of a group of economists under the leadership of Professor Milton Friedman of the University of Chicago – a group collectively known as 'monetarists' – offered intellectual underpinning for a greater reliance on monetary policy. Even so, until the 1970s this academic influence had no great impact on the British authorities who continued to use changes in monetary policy in a pragmatic manner, usually as part of a 'package' of measures, including fiscal and other changes. Monetary policy was just one of the policy instruments used by government, and it was often a subordinate one.

When mass unemployment re–emerged in the late 1970s and 1980s the authorities no longer believed that expansionary fiscal measures could provide a remedy and, anyway, economic priorities had changed. The preoccupation of the 1970s was with the rate of inflation – a rate which peaked in 1974 when the annual rate of price increases was running at over 24 per cent per annum – and the traditional Keynesian prescription for unemployment of an expansionary budget was seen as a threat to price stability. A much–quoted passage from a speech made by the then Prime Minister, James Callaghan, in 1976 to the Labour Party Conference illustrates how far official thinking had changed from the immediate post–war decade:

> It used to be thought that a nation could just spend its way out of recession and increase employment by cutting taxes and boosting government spending. I tell you in all candour that that option no longer exists.[13]

The election of a Conservative government in 1979 reinforced these trends in official thinking, for the new administration under Margaret Thatcher overtly embraced the monetarist views of Professor Friedman and raised monetary policy to a new status, with a corresponding decline in the use of fiscal and direct means of influencing economic activity.

It is apparent even from this very curt survey that the weight given to monetary policy by different governments since World War II has varied greatly. For the bulk of the period monetary policy performed a subsidiary role and was greatly constrained by other aspects of policy. In the late 1950s and early 1960s, for instance, balance of payments difficulties had led

Conservative administrations to impose a series of deflationary monetary controls – with higher interest rates and restrictions on bank lending – yet budgetary policy (e.g. in 1955, 1957, 1960 and 1964 [Spring]) was often expansionary.[14] In the early 1970s, too, the Bank of England was publicly critical of the government's expansionary fiscal policy at a time when, in the Bank's view, the poor condition of the external account and the high rate of monetary growth called for retrenchment.[15] A deflationary policy was subsequently imposed. Even in the 1980s, of course, the new primacy given to monetary instruments of control is still subject to many constraints and, in the real world, other government preoccupations continue to compromise the pursuit of monetary policy objectives.

## THE 1950s – REVIVAL OF MONETARY POLICY

In the years immediately following the war, the Labour government's reliance on, first, direct controls and, then, on fiscal policy meant that monetary policy was largely in abeyance. However, as the remainder of wartime controls were being relaxed or abolished by the close of the 1940s, and as market forces were given more leeway, expediency dictated that governments which now accepted a general responsibility for managing the economy, should be prepared to develop new instruments of control. It was in this context that the 1950s saw a revival in the use of monetary policy, if still largely as an adjunct to Keynesian-type demand management policies which retained their heavy reliance on budgetary measures.

The revival of official interest in monetary policy was associated with the election of a Conservative government in 1951 and, in particular, with the predilections of the Chancellor of the Exchequer, R.A. Butler.[16] Since the early 1930s, the authorities' attitude towards interest rates had remained fairly rigid: rates were to be kept as low as possible. The sharp rise in the size of the National Debt during the Second World War had reinforced the desire to minimise government interest payments – a main factor in the cheap money policy – and, as part of their overall strategy, the authorities had continued to hold Bank rate at 2 per cent. However, the willingness of the new Conservative administration to use a more active monetary policy inevitably entailed a break with the policy of the previous two decades, for it implied a preparedness to accept a greater degree of interest rate flexibility. Thus, in the early fifties there was the beginning of a revival in Bank rate policy and even some willingness to permit a fall in the price of government securities (a rise in long-term interest rates) when this was considered to be of general benefit to overall monetary objectives.[17] Interest rate changes were made 'effective' – i.e. market rates were brought into line with them – partly through the conventional setting of some market rates with reference to Bank rate (as in the case of rates on the clearing banks' deposit accounts and advances). But it was the authorities' dealings in short-term markets that underlay their influence over interest rates because, as already noted, they were able and willing to induce cash shortages through the manipulation of the supply of Treasury bills.

Even so, this shift in policy in 1951 must be seen in relative terms only. It was true that the extreme rigidity of the immediate post-war years had gone, but the demands of state finance continued to bear heavily on monetary policy and the authorities would still not countenance too sharp a drop in government security prices.[18] Similarly, while the Bank of England did use Bank rate on occasions to effect changes in short-term market rates, the initial alterations in the official rate were made somewhat tentatively and infrequently. As Table 14.1 shows, Bank rate was first raised by 0.5 per cent, to 2.5 per cent, in November 1951 and then increased to 4 per cent in March 1952; but no further change was made for another 18 months. In all, by the middle of the decade, Bank rate had been altered four times only. In fact, it was not until the late 1950s that Bank rate policy could be described as 'active' to any degree. Officially-induced rises were invariably defensive in their nature and usually accompanied by a series of measures intended to oblige market rates to follow suit.[19] In general, therefore, the new policy aimed to keep interest rate oscillations within narrow limits and it was not designed to give free play to money market forces. Instead, monetary policy was seen as a useful addition to the instruments available to government for managing the economy.

Table 13.1: Bank Rate Changes during the 1950s

| Bank Rate (% per annum) | Date of Change (month/ year) | Bank Rate (% per annum) | Date of Change (month/ year) |
|---|---|---|---|
| 2.5 | 11/51 | 7 | 9/57 |
| 4 | 3/52 | 6 | 3/58 |
| 3.5 | 9/53 | 5.5 | 5/58 |
| 3 | 5/54 | 5 | 6/58 |
| 3.5 | 1/55 | 4.5 | 8/58 |
| 4.5 | 2/55 | 4 | 11/58 |
| 5.5 | 2/56 | 5 | 1/60 |
| 5 | 2/57 | | |

In a period of full employment the main pressure for government intervention came from difficulties on Britain's balance of payments, although the persistence of price inflation was also a factor.[20] The low level of foreign currency reserves, relative to the potential claims on them, meant that the authorities were acutely sensitive to movements on the external account. In fact, recurrent deficits on the current account of the balance of payments (in 1951, 1955 and 1960) and/or the threat of significant withdrawals of capital funds (with sterling crises in 1955, 1957 and 1961) provoked a series of economic policy 'packages' during the first decade of post-war Conservative rule. Invariably, such packages involved the greater use of monetary and credit controls other than Bank rate. The circumstances of their introduction meant that these controls, too, were restrictive in nature, aimed largely at curtailing consumer demand as a means of improving the balance of payments. In the process, the authorities broadened the scope of peacetime monetary instruments beyond Bank rate and began to evolve a range of monetary and credit controls, which were to form the basis of implementing policy into the 1970s.

## POLICY IN THE 1950s and 1960s

### *The Radcliffe Committee*

In 1957 the Treasury appointed a committee with a broad brief to 'inquire into the working of the monetary and credit system, and to make recommendations.'[21] Apart from the secretary and the chairman, Lord Radcliffe, there were eight committee members, including two economists, A.K. Cairncross and R.S. Sayers. It was these two who were to have a marked influence on the theoretical tenor of the investigation. The Radcliffe Committee held wide-ranging interviews with representatives from the Bank of England, the Treasury, other government departments, the main financial institutions and with economists and other interested parties. The Committee's unanimous Report was published in 1959 and, together with the Minutes of Evidence and three volumes of Memoranda, it still provides the most comprehensive description of the main money market institutions of the day and of government monetary and debt policy as then practised. The theoretical emphases made within the Report and its recommendations on policy matters were not uncontroversial even at the time[22], but the Radcliffe Committee's interpretation of how monetary impulses affected the economy were doubtlessly influential, especially with policy-makers. Thus, a Bank of England paper printed in 1969 claimed that over the previous decade:

> Broadly...the approach to policy has been similar to that of the Radcliffe Committee in that the authorities have consistently believed that it was right to pay attention to and try to understand the general financial position of all sectors of the economy and insufficient to concentrate exclusively on a single variable such as the quantity of money...[23]

This quotation from the Bank of England refers to one of the central findings of the Radcliffe Committee, namely that what determined the level of expenditure by firms and individuals was not the quantity of money held, but the ability of the private sector to borrow and raise credit. In a mature economy such as the UK, a sophisticated financial sector had been developed, with a broad range of borrowing facilities available (e.g. bill discounting, bank loans, or hire-purchase arrangements) and, to the Committee, it was the availability and cost of this credit which directly affected the public's willingness to spend. In supplying this credit the country's financial institutions created a continuum of assets of varying liquidity, ranging from cash, through bank deposits, to a host of financial securities as diverse as bank acceptances and insurance policies. To Radcliffe it was this liquidity spectrum which constituted a major determinant of aggregate demand within the economy. Moreover, the supply of liquid assets was remarkably flexible because financial institutions, in particular, were forever finding new means of providing credit – restrict one sort and it could be replaced quickly by a close substitute.

The Radcliffe Report recognised that those assets generally conceived of as money (i.e. Bank of England notes and bank deposits) did have special attributes but their uniqueness was played down, because other assets, too, could be used to make purchases. Goods and services could also be bought on credit. Thus, any attempt by the authorities to restrict demand in the economy, by restricting the quantity of money, could be nullified as economic agents maintained their purchases through the greater use of credit, permitting the same level of expenditure on a smaller money base.

> We have argued...that our financial institutions are so highly developed and so prone to further development that control of 'the supply of money' – whatever that may be made to mean – is not by itself a reliable policy measure, and that the authorities must seek rather to influence the general liquidity situation by operating on rates of interest.[24]

Such views were accepted by the monetary authorities to a lesser or greater extent throughout the 1950s and 1960s. Even so, there is a danger of exaggerating the influence of Radcliffe. The Report was in many respects a creature of its own time. In particular, its views on government responsibilities towards the economy soundly reflected prevailing Keynesian orthodoxy. Thus, monetary and credit policy was examined within the context of it being but one instrument for managing aggregate demand, and a subordinate one at that. Even within the narrower inquiry of how best to implement monetary policy itself, in many respects the Report largely reflected practice as it was already developing in the 1950s. This was true of the Bank of England's greater reliance on direct controls in addition to Bank rate policy, of the Bank's opposition to a strict money supply policy and of the authorities' recognition of the need to extend controls beyond the clearing banks. The tenor of the Report was to extol the virtues of existing financial institutions and condone the authorities' willingness to permit the established price cartels and other non–competitive practices in the money markets. The Bank of England's approach remained pragmatic – doing what seemed both necessary and practicable to effect changes – rather than following a clear theoretical line. As a result, controls were often developed piecemeal, with more types of institutions (e.g. finance companies) and credit instruments (e.g. hire–purchase) being covered as required.

The Radcliffe Report reflected this non–dogmatic, practical approach both in its analysis of the effects of monetary policy and in its recommendations for policy changes. Indeed, the absence of a clear theoretical framework attracted a series of criticisms. As one critic put it: 'The most common complaint has related to the ambivalence, ambiguity, and indeterminateness of the report...the Committee produced a document that appeared to be all things to all men...the Committee has confused counsel rather than clarified it.'[25]

It would be mistaken, therefore, to portray these years as the 'Radcliffe Era' if the implication is that monetary policy took a radical turn as a result of the Committee's report. Nevertheless, in the main, the Committee's views reasonably represent the thrust of official thinking in the 1950s and 1960s.[26]

*Economic Problems and Policy Response*

The national economic backcloth against which monetary policy was unfolding was one in which an unprecedented rate of growth in output and real income was achieved and full employment maintained. Thus, Gross Domestic Product grew at an annual rate of 2.8 per cent between 1951 and 1973, with GDP per man–year growing at 2.4 per cent per annum.[27] However, these achievements are less impressive in the light of international comparison. British growth rates were not as good as those achieved by many other industrial nations and domestic prices continued to rise, and at a rate somewhat in advance of the country's main competitors. Also, once Western Europe and Japan had recovered from the war, Britain's share of world exports suffered a secular decline. Nevertheless, British export growth in itself was quite respectable and, over the long term, the balance of payments current account tended to a slight surplus. Critically, though, short–term oscillations led to intermittent deficits which had a disproportionate impact on policy because of sterling's legacy as a former international reserve currency.[28] The same was true of fluctuations in international capital flows. Sterling's international role meant that the authorities were often struggling to maintain fixed exchange rates with gold and foreign currency reserves which, at times, looked woefully inadequate in comparison to the scale of capital and trade flows on the external account.

In dealing with these difficulties, successive governments continued to be influenced greatly by Keynesian economic theory with its commitment to demand management. Short-term disequilibrium provoked official reaction: both balance of payments deficits and rising prices were seen as symptoms of excessive demand, the remedy lying in the government dampening down that demand. Conversely, rising unemployment and improved balance of payments were evidence of underutilised capacity (deficient demand) which called for reflationary measures. Budgetary changes (e.g. in tax rates and tax thresholds, or in the investment plans of nationalised industries) and – increasingly through the 1960s – direct controls on wages and prices, played the central role in governmental response but monetary measures, too, were given a greater role.

*Techniques of Monetary Control*

The greater willingness of the authorities to follow a more active Bank rate policy as part of the broadening of the techniques of post-war monetary management has already been noted. Another aspect of policy in the 1950s and 1960s was a preparedness to adopt more direct regulations over the country's main financial institutions. In particular, the imposition of controls on the London and Scottish clearing banks became a central feature. The controls took a number of forms but an important element was the authorities' attempt to regulate bank liquidity. It was assumed that control over commercial banks' reserves of liquid assets would provide control, in turn, over the general level of their loans and liabilities. Thus, in an extreme case where commercial banks operated on a fixed ratio of reserves to liabilities, and where the authorities could control the supply of reserve assets, then the government would have a powerful weapon by which to determine the size of bank liabilities – a reduction in the supply of reserves to the banks would cause a fall in their reserve ratio, obliging them to reduce liabilities in order to restore that ratio.

By the 1950s the emphasis that the Macmillan Committee had placed on the cash ratio as a potential control instrument had all but evaporated, because (as noted earlier) the Bank of England's willingness always to supply cash to the market in exchange for government securities (both as lender of last resort and as support to the market in government paper) rendered ineffective any attempt to control this ratio.[29] In practice, the commercial banks could always replenish their cash holdings. Attention, thus, turned to the broader range of 'liquid' assets held by the banks – assets which could be quickly converted to cash at little cost. In effect, these assets were cash itself, money lent at call and short notice to the London discount market and Stock Exchange, Treasury bills and commercial bills of exchange.[30] Together they constituted a sort of 'liquidity reserve', a reserve whose traditional importance was well-established in British banking because of the short-term nature of deposit liabilities.

It seemed to the authorities that the clearing banks would be more responsive to any move to tighten monetary conditions (i.e. to push up interest rates and, or, restrict the supply of credit) if the banks normally worked close to the minimum of some agreed or customary 'liquidity ratio' of reserves to liabilities. Difficulties could arise if the clearing banks held liquid reserves in excess of minimum requirements for it would afford them some immunity from Bank of England attempts to reduce their liabilities (or loans) by restricting the supply of such assets to the market. Provided the banks remained above the minimum in the face of such action by the authorities, they could merely allow their holdings of liquid assets to decline without reducing liabilities or loans. No legal reserve requirements existed in Britain – nor did the new monetary policy introduce any – but, in general terms, the authorities sought a greater degree of discipline. In 1951 the Governor of the Bank suggested that the London clearing banks (LCBs) should hold liquid assets to the value of some 28–32 per cent of their deposits, with a minimum of 25 per cent. By 1957 a firm 30 per cent minimum had been established and this was reduced to 28 per cent in 1963.[31] Also in 1951, a Treasury funding operation reduced the supply of Treasury bills by about £1 billion and, as these securities were the main item in the banks' liquid assets, this action largely explains the very sharp drop in bank liquidity from October to November 1951, when the average liquidity ratio for the LCBs fell from 39 per cent to 32 per cent.[32] (see Figure 12.2 for more details). In other words, the authorities' action reduced the liquidity of the banking system and made commercial banks more sensitive to any further falls, thus increasing the power of the Bank to effect its policies.

As operated in the UK, however, the use of liquidity ratio controls was but an imprecise instrument of policy. As the clearing banks did not have to operate at a *fixed*, minimum ratio, but continued to hold liquid reserves somewhat in excess of the recommended target, the impact of any official action could be cushioned. More importantly, the authorities did not strictly control the supply of liquid assets to the banks. First, some of the assets that clearing banks were permitted to count as part of their liquid reserves (e.g. commercial bills of exchange) were not state liabilities, and, secondly, a large proportion of the state's existing short-term liabilities (such as Treasury bills) were held by the non-bank, private sector. In other words, tight quantitative control of the supply of liquid assets by the Bank of England was impossible because if it bought Treasury bills in an attempt to reduce bank liquidity, the commercial banks were still able to replenish their reserves by buying some of the existing stock of Treasury bills from the non-bank sector, or by buying more commercial bills. The imposition in 1961 and 1965 of limits on the proportion of commercial bills permitted in the reserve was only a partial solution to this problem.[33] In addition, as has been shown, the authorities' general support for the market in government bonds weakened the effects of liquidity controls, for the banks could respond to falling liquidity reserves by selling off some of their holdings of gilts and, as the Government Broker was generally willing to buy, the cost of doing so was nominal. The authorities' attempts to prevent too sharp a fall in the price of government stocks weakened their ability to restrict the supply of liquid assets.[34]

In fact, in these decades the authorities did not operate on the basis of any coherent theoretical model of monetary impulses within the economy. Their approach was pragmatic and their means of control largely *ad hoc*. Policy on liquidity reserves should be seen in this light, too – it was felt in a general sense that greater influence over banks' liquidity reserves would bolster attempts at monetary restriction, but stringent control from this single policy instrument was not expected. The Bank of England was not operating a reserve base system of control during these years; rather, it was using its ability to affect clearing bank liquidity reserves as a practical means of bolstering interest rate policy.

Pragmatism was evident also in the increasing reliance on more direct measures of credit control. Thus, 1960 saw the Bank employing special deposits for the first time.[35] By this technique the authorities were able to reduce commercial bank liquidity at a stroke by enforcing the London and Scottish clearing banks to deposit a set proportion (0.5 – 1 per cent) of their own (gross) deposit liabilities with the Bank. Once designated, 'special deposits', these funds could no longer be classed amongst the clearers' cash or liquidity reserves, although some pecuniary compensation was provided through the Bank making interest payments on the balances. Potentially this technique provided the authorities with a very flexible instrument for controlling bank liquidity – the banks' access to cash could be altered merely by government dictate. However, the authorities were to call for clearing bank special deposits on only five occasions – in 1960 (twice), 1964, 1966 and 1970 – before this particular scheme was abandoned in September 1971. In practice, during the 1960s special deposits were not used flexibly to effect detailed regulation but were essentially supplementary to other, even more direct, controls over the banks.

In particular, the authorities resorted to constraints on bank advances. The common response to pressure on the country's external account was to restrain domestic demand and, as an important part of that demand was financed through bank credit, bank advances became prime targets for regulation. For the authorities, the clearing banks presented a convenient and politically-acceptable channel through which to implement policy: only a small group of very large banks was involved, banks with a tradition of acting in unison and of co-operating closely with the central bank. The means of control took the form of simple 'requests' from the Chancellor of the Exchequer, or the Bank of England, to the banks to reduce their advances. Legislation proved unnecessary, with the authorities appealing to the bankers' sense of public responsibility – sometimes referred to as 'moral suasion' – and relying upon the glare of publicity to ensure that the banks' response was monitored widely.

Initially the requests were couched in general terms. In July 1955, the Chancellor had called for 'a positive and significant reduction'[36] in bank advances, and in the following year his successor reminded bankers that 'the contraction of credit should be resolutely pursued and that there should be no relaxation in the present critical attitude towards applications for bank finance.'[37] In one guise or another, these requests maintained controls over bank lending until 1958 when fear of a recession persuaded the authorities to remove restrictions in order to expand the economy. The outcome was the very sharp increase in bank advances discussed in Chapter 12.

When a worsening external account led to the reimposition of constraints in 1964, the authorities' requests became more directive as to the priorities to be followed (e.g. with preference to be given to exporters). The constraints also became more specific in the sense of setting detailed targets for total advances or by specifying a percentage growth rate for the coming year. Controls were also extended to cover UK banks other than the clearers. In general, controls over bank loans were tightened when the authorities sought to contract domestic demand and relaxed when expansion was desired – they were part and parcel of the so-called 'stop-go' policies of that period. As such, the authorities' approach was similar to their position over liquidity controls – no watertight regulation was sought, the aim being to establish a general ability to influence overall monetary and credit conditions. In this context, the government was fully aware that widely-publicised policy changes could have significant short-term effects on money and foreign exchange markets, and as short-term considerations played such an important role in determining the timing and nature of the policy measures adopted, the theoretical nicety of any particular measure was of secondary importance.

The logic that justified controls over bank advances led to another policy innovation in the 1950s, the use of hire-purchase regulations. Finance companies began to expand during this decade, with a growing volume of a limited range of consumer durable goods such as motor vehicles and furniture commonly paid for by instalments. Hire-purchase controls provided an opportunity to extend government influence over domestic demand beyond the clearing banks. These controls took the form of the authorities specifying the minimum deposit and maximum repayment period required for specified goods bought on this type of credit. Action was first taken in February 1952, and again in February 1955, when hire-purchase terms were tightened in order to dampen aggregate demand.[38] By the 1960s such constraints had become a recurring feature of government economic 'packages' designed to counter rising prices and balance of payments difficulties.

## POLICY APPRAISAL

By the late 1960s, the general tenor of British monetary policy was coming under increasingly critical scrutiny from both outside the government machine and from within (from those responsible for implementing policy). The influence of the close government direction of the economy during the war and the immediate post-war years had all but evaporated and the use of selective controls over private institutions was becoming less acceptable. The discriminatory impact of policy was one source of criticism. As the previous chapter stressed, the business of the clearing banks had borne the brunt of government constraints (witness the sharp surges in bank advances when constraints were removed temporarily in 1958 and, again, in 1971[39]) and this at a time when other foreign and domestic institutions were taking an increasing share of Britain's financial business. In fact, the imposition of constraints on the clearers may well have encouraged the growth of their competitors. The finance companies probably suffered in a similar manner and although hire-purchase controls affected directly only a small proportion of aggregate sales, changes in government regulations could have a significant impact on the demand for such products as motor vehicles.[40]

The problem of lack of ubiquity in monetary controls was inherent in the Radcliffe-type approach to manipulating credit creation within the economy. If it is accepted that a continuum of money and quasi-money substitutes exists, then there can be no theoretical justification for confining controls to a limited number of credit institutions and instruments. As we have seen, the Bank of England's response was a practical one - clearing banks and finance company controls captured the bulk of domestic institutional credit-creation. This approach still left the Bank open to charges of inequity if it allowed competitors to expand. Anyway, could such controls be effective in determining aggregate demand (the ultimate objective) if other institutions were free to provide alternative sources of credit?

Expression of more fundamental dissatisfaction with the approach of policy in these decades stemmed from the authorities' strong predilections to play down the economic importance of changes in the money stock, and to treat monetary policy as subservient to fiscal policy within the overall strategy adopted to manage short-term economic fluctuations. The short-term nature of many government objectives leaves an impression of the authorities experimenting – sometimes with a touch of desperation – with new methods of plugging leaks as fresh cracks appeared in the dyke, with a series of economic packages hastily devised to meet immediate difficulties. Disillusionment with post-war attempts to 'manage' the economy grew as Britain's economic problems persisted, more especially with the emergence in the 1970s of 'stagflation' (the simultaneous existence of high rates of price inflation and high rates of unemployment). Earlier optimism about the effectiveness of short-term government economic intervention had largely dissipated and an increasing number of commentators called for greater emphasis on longer-term goals and on the use of monetary policy to combat inflation.[41] Thus, by the beginning of the 1970s, changes were in the offing, changes which would enhance the role of monetary policy within the authorities' overall economic strategy.

## FURTHER READING

Bank of England, *The Development and Operation of Monetary Policy, 1960–1983* (Oxford University Press, Oxford, 1984).

A.R. Nobay, 'The Bank of England, Monetary Policy and Monetary Theory in the United Kingdom, 1951–1971', *Manchester School*, vol. 41, 1973, pp. 43–58.

David R. Croome and Harry G. Johnson (eds.), *Money in Britain, 1959–1969* (Oxford University Press, London, 1970).

NOTES

1. The Bank of England Act, 9 & 10 Geo. VI, c. 27.

2. For example, see Harold Wilson, *The Labour Government, 1964–1970. A Personal Record* (Weidenfeld & Nicolson and Michael Joseph, London, 1971), pp. 34–8, 128–9, 251, 452–5.

3. Data are from C.H. Feinstein, *National Income, Expenditure and Output of the United Kingdom, 1855–1965* (Cambridge University Press, Cambridge, 1972), pp. T16–7; and *Economic Trends* (HMSO, London), 379, May 1985, pp. 8, 14.

4. 'Recent Changes in the Monetary and Regulatory Framework' (Bank Governor's speech, 28 Jan. 1982) *Bank of England Quarterly Bulletin.* [BEQB], vol. 22, March 1982, p. 102.

5. C.D. Cohen, *British Economic Policy, 1960–1969* (Butterworths, London, 1971); and F.T. Blackaby (ed.), *British Economic Policy, 1960–74: Demand Management*, students' edn (Cambridge University Press, Cambridge, 1979), pp. 28–52.

6. Sterling was to fall lower still in the autumn, and a surge in the value of the US dollar in 1985 provoked talk of a £1:$1 parity. Throughout, the external pressure helped keep UK real interest rates at unprecedented heights.

7. G.A. Fletcher, *The Discount Houses in London* (Macmillan, London, 1976), pp. 49–51, 183–94, 202–3.

8. 'The Management of Money Day-by-Day', *BEQB*, vol. 3, March 1963, pp. 15–17; and 'The Bank of England in the Money Market', *BEQB*, vol. 22, March 1982, pp. 87–9.

9. 'The Bank's Operational Procedures for Meeting Monetary Objectives', *BEQB*, vol. 23, June 1983, p. 210.

10. *Committee on the Working of the Monetary System.* [Radcliffe Committee] *Minutes of Evidence* (HMSO, London, 1960), Evidence of the Bank's Cashier and the Government Broker, Qs. 11967, 12009; 'The Operation of Monetary Policy since

Radcliffe' (a paper prepared by the Bank of England in consultation with the Treasury), *BEQB*, vol. 9, Dec. 1969, pp. 455–6. The article is reprinted in David R. Croome and Harry G. Johnson (eds.), *Money in Britain, 1959–1969* (Oxford University Press, London, 1970), pp. 211–30; and 'Official Transactions in the Gilt-Edged Market, *BEQB*, vol. 6, June 1966, pp. 141–8 reprinted in Bank of England, *The Development and Operation of Monetary Policy, 1960–1983* (Oxford University Press, Oxford, 1984), pp. 75–82.

11. J.H.B Tew, 'Monetary Policy – Part I' in Blackaby, *Economic Policy*, pp. 230–3. For a discussion of the general implications for the control of bank credit and deposits see W. Manning Dacey, 'The Floating Debt Problem', *Lloyds Bank Review*, April 1956, pp. 24–38.

12. 'The Gilt-Edged Market', *BEQB*, June 1979 reprinted in Bank of England, *Monetary Policy*, pp. 86–97; and 'The Bank's Operational Procedures for Meeting Monetary Objectives', ibid, pp. 98–104. Chapter 5 in *Monetary Policy* provides an overview of the main changes in the Bank's policy on government securites.

13. Quoted in Charles Feinstein (ed.), *The Managed Economy* (Oxford University Press, Oxford, 1983), p. 25.

14. Blackaby, *Economic Policy*, pp. 12–76; Sidney Pollard, *The Development of the British Economy, 1914–1980*, 3rd. edn (Edward Arnold, London, 1983), pp. 410–6.

15. 'Speech by the Governor of the Bank of England' [19 Oct. 1972], *BEQB*, vol. 12, Dec. 1972, especially pp. 516–7.

16. J.C.R. Dow, *The Management of the British Economy, 1945–60* (Cambridge University Press, Cambridge, 1964), pp. 66–70; and Charles Kennedy, 'Monetary Policy' in G.D.N. Worswick and P.H. Ady (eds.), *The British Economy in the Nineteen-Fifties* (Oxford University Press, London, 1962), pp. 301–25.

17. *The Economist* was a leading advocate of the 'new' approach – see comments in 'Tory Touchstone', vol. 165, 11 Oct. 1952, pp. 69–70;

'Towards Flexible Money', vol. 174, 8 Jan. 1955, pp. 125–7; and 'Flexible Money in Action', vol. 175, 7 May 1955, pp. 489–91.

18. For an example of where support of the market in securities ran counter to the aims of monetary policy see 'Flexible Money in Action', ibid, p. 490.

19. Radcliffe, *Report*, Cmnd. 827, (HMSO, London, 1960, reprint), pp. 138–42.

20. For a discussion of the objectives and effectiveness of policy see David Williams, 'Some Aspects of Monetary Policy in England, 1952–8', *Yorkshire Bulletin of Economic and Social Research*, vol. 12, 1960, pp. 96–110.

21. Radcliffe, *Report*, p. 1.

22. Arthur Seldon (ed.), *Not Unanimous. A Rival Verdict to Radcliffe's on Money* (Institute of Economic Affairs, London, 1960); W.T. Newlyn, 'The Radcliffe Report: A Socratic Scrutiny', *Bankers' Magazine*, 189, Jan. 1960, pp. 21–6. R.S. Sayers, 'Monetary Thought and Monetary Policy in England', *Economic Journal*, vol. 70, 1960, pp. 710–24, discusses the 'Radcliffe View' in the context of nineteenth and twentieth-century theory. The last two papers are reprinted in H.G. Johnson (ed.), *Readings in British Monetary Economics* (Oxford University Press, London, 1972), pp. 507–33.

23. 'The Operation of Monetary Policy, *BEQB*, 1969, p. 448. This important paper has been reprinted in Croome and Johnson (eds.), *Money in Britain*, pp. 211–30, where it is accompanied by 'Discussion Papers' by R.F.G. Alford (pp. 231–4) and J.R. Winton (p. 235). The original paper also appears in Bank of England, *Monetary Policy*, pp. 7–13.

24. Radcliffe, *Report*, p. 179.

25. Seldon (ed.), *Not Unanimous*, p. 102. Seldon suggests that the Committee's lack of precision may have resulted from the desire to produce a unanimous report: 'Agreement between a lawyer, two business men, two bankers, two trade unionists, and two economists was conceivable on the technical

aspects, but it was too much to expect agreement on the broad issues of policy that necessarily rest on political assumptions and value judgements.' (pp. 102–3). For a more sympathetic review of some of the ambiguities see R.F.G. Alford and H.B. Rose, 'The Radcliffe Report and Domestic Monetary Policy', *London and Cambridge Bulletin*, no. 32, printed in *The Times Review of Industry*, Dec. 1959, pp. ii–vi.

26. For an appraisal of the Radcliffe Report's place in the history of monetary policy see A.R. Nobay, 'The Bank of England, Monetary Policy and Monetary Theory in the United Kingdom, 1951–1971', *Manchester School*, vol. 41, 1973, pp. 43–58.

27. R.C.O. Matthews, C.H. Feinstein and J.C. Odling-Smee, *British Economic Growth, 1856–1973* (Oxford University Press, Oxford, 1982), p. 22.

28. See Chapter 15.

29. Radcliffe, *Report*, p. 128.

30. In practice there was some variation in the permitted assets.

31. 'Bank Liquidity in the United Kingdom', *BEQB*, vol. 2, Dec. 1962, p. 252; Radcliffe, *Minutes*, evidence of the Bank Governor, C.F. Cobbald, Q. 1754, p. 130; and 'The UK Banking Sector, 1952–67', *BEQB*, vol. 9, June 1969, p. 177.

32. Bank of England, 'Principal Changes in the British Monetary System since 1931', Radcliffe, *Principal Memoranda of Evidence* (3 vols., HMSO, London, 1960) vol. 1, p. 22.

33. Ibid, p. 30. Also see 'UK Banking Sector', *BEQB*, 1969, pp. 190–1.

34. On the Bank's support for gilt prices see 'Official Transactions in the Gilt-Edged Market', in Bank of England, *Monetary Policy*, pp. 75–82.

35. 'The Procedure of Special Deposits, *BEQB*, vol. 1, Dec. 1960, p. 18.

36. Bank of England, 'Principal Changes', p. 29.

37. Ibid., p. 31.

38. 'Memorandum of Evidence Submitted by the Board of Trade', Radcliffe, *Memoranda*, vol. 1, pp. 234–5.

39. Radcliffe, *Report*, p. 148; and 'The Travails of Competition and Credit Control' and 'What Went Wrong?', in Bank of England, *Monetary Policy*, pp. 42–4.

40. *Committee [on] Consumer Credit. Report*, Cmnd. 4596, (2 vols, HMSO, London, 1971), vol. 1, pp. 354–7.

41. The collection of essays contained in Johnson (ed.), *British Monetary Economics*, provides a convenient source for the currents of British thought in the late sixties. Also see Harry G. Johnson, 'Recent Developments in Monetary Theory – A Commentary' and 'Discussion Papers' by David Laidler and R.T. Armstrong in Croome and Johnson (eds.), *Money in Britain*, pp. 83–128.

Chapter Fourteen

# MONETARY POLICY IN THE 1970s AND 1980s

Changed economic circumstances and changed economic and political philosophies have been responsible for a pronounced shift in British monetary policy in recent years. The publication in 1971 of the Bank of England's consultative document, 'Competition and Credit Control', can conveniently be seen as the inauguration of this shift in policy stance, and the 1979 Banking Act and 1980 Green Paper on *Monetary Control* provided formal confirmation of the change in official sentiment. Three main aspects have been involved: prudential control; greater market freedom; and new techniques of monetary control.

## PRUDENTIAL CONTROLS

These controls are concerned with the Bank of England's responsibilities for oversight of the propriety and financial soundness of market institutions. The 1979 Banking Act[1] and subsequent discussions between the Bank and other financial institutions have led to a formal broadening and deepening of the authorities' supervisory role over markets. Even so, criticisms persist and the reader is referred to Chapter 11 for more details.[2] For present purposes it is sufficient to note that these prudential controls have been carried out in conjunction with, and as part-response to, changes in the methods of monetary control. In particular, one aspect of the reforms has been to extend their applicability beyond a select group of institutions (based on the clearing banks) to a much wider range of deposit-taking businesses. Equity has been an important goal here; so, too, has been the pursuit of greater efficiency through increased competition.

## GREATER MARKET FREEDOM

The previous chapter stressed that by the late 1960s there was growing disillusionment with the techniques used to implement credit control. In particular, the heavy reliance on controls over bank liquidity and on quantity restrictions on bank lending and borrowing by instalments was distorting competition and innovation in money markets.[3] For one thing, the burden fell unduly on the clearing banks and finance houses (and, indirectly, on the building societies through the effects of interest rate changes on house-buying) while other types of financial institutions remained largely outside the Bank of England's jurisdiction. During the sixties acceptance houses, foreign banks in London and other deposit-taking institutions had expanded rapidly, and the authorities' concentration on the clearing banks was seen as both discriminatory and inadequate. Attempts to check the expansion of the clearing banks and finance houses had probably contributed to the growth of these competing institutions; but also the growing importance of the non-clearers in the supply of credit highlighted the need to extend the range of the chosen methods of control. In addition, the heavy reliance on direct and usually quantitative constraints was seen to have frustrated the operation of the competitive price mechanism.

Thus, in its 1971 paper on 'Competition and Credit Control'[4] the Bank of England proposed a shift from discriminatory, quantitative techniques to more generally applicable controls relying heavily on changes in the price of credit, in the rate of interest. As in 1951, it was a philosophy which amply suited the political predilection of the newly-elected Conservative government. The Governor of the Bank described it as 'a new approach to credit control designed to permit the price mechanism to function efficiently in the allocation of credit, and to free the banks from rigidities and restraints which have for far too long inhibited them from efficiently fulfilling their intermediary role in the financial system.'[5]

Thus, the existing cash and liquidity ratios imposed on clearing banks were abolished and replaced by a 12.5 per cent reserve asset ratio for *all* banks. Similarly, the Special Deposit Scheme which had hitherto applied only to the clearing banks was also extended to include other banks. In addition, the document proposed that the Bank should no longer impose ceilings on bank advances, and so removed the chief quantitative constraint currently operating. The authorities felt that greater reliance on interest rate changes would be more pervasive in effect – affecting credit conditions for many institutions beyond the clearing banks – and would also be more compatible with the efficient operation of the market mechanism within money markets. In other words, the 1971 document was an attempt to rekindle the flame of an active interest rate policy which had but flickered briefly in 1951. The implementation of this more variable interest rate regime also necessitated some important changes in existing Bank operations. In particular, the Bank proposed reducing its involvement in – and general support for – the market in government securities. This would entail a readjustment to the policy that the Government Broker had been pursuing actively since at least 1958. Henceforth prices could move more freely, removing an important constraint on long-term market rates. Another important measure outlined in 'Competition and Credit Control' was the abolition of the long-standing rate-fixing cartel among the London and Scottish clearers. In future, the banks were encouraged to compete more actively among themselves and with other institutions.

The 1971 paper did inaugurate some important changes, therefore. But despite its declared intentions, the central decision to rely more heavily on interest rate changes and less on direct controls turned out to be far from sacrosanct - principle proved expendible in the face of economic pressure. In practice, there was no inflexible adherence to the reforms of 1971 but, as in the 1950s and 1960s, so in the 1970s, there was a preparedness to use *ad hoc* controls if these were considered useful. Thus in the face of inflationary pressure from August 1972 all banks were subject to official guidance on lending priorities; from December 1973 the terms of instalment credit were once again controlled; a ceiling was imposed on rates paid on bank deposits of up to £10,000, 1973–75; for a time after 1978 the authorities sought to influence building society interest rates; and from December 1973 the Supplementary Credit Control Scheme - the 'corset' - was used to restrict the growth of bank liabilities on a number of occasions. Thus, while it is possible to discern some important moves towards greater 'market freedom' during the seventies, any general tendency was severely modified by the continuing use of direct, quantitative controls.[6]

Even so, the emphasis on the market and the price mechanism was to be strongly revived in the Government's 1980 Green Paper on *Monetary Control*.[7] Artis and Lewis see this document 'as a reaffirmation of the original aims of Competition and Credit Control that, as far as possible, the special controls upon banks should be removed, not imposed on other institutions, and the "market instrument of interest rates" should regulate credit creation.'[8] The Green Paper saw fiscal policy and interest rate policy as the two main means of controlling the growth of the money supply.

> Direct quantitative controls are not an alternative, since to the extent that they do not change interest rates, they tend, over time, to divert and change the forms of liquidity and credit without affecting underlying monetary conditions.[9]

The distorting impact of direct controls was emphasised

and the salutary effects of the pricing system extolled. Thus, the phasing out of the 'corset' was proposed (it ceased in June 1980); the reserve asset ratio was abolished; and the requirement to hold cash balances with the Bank of England was to be generalised beyond the London clearing banks to all banks. The document also questioned whether market rates should be automatically tied to Minimum Lending Rate (the name given to Bank Rate since 1972), and subsequently the Bank stopped publishing MLR in August 1982 in order to allow greater play to market forces in determining short-term interest rates. Henceforth, the discount houses could no longer buy and sell bills, or borrow, at the Bank of England at a well-publicised, pre-determined rate, but had to compete among themselves. Another important break with tradition was the Bank's withdrawal of its undertaking to lend to the discount houses at all times. Strictly such loans were the channel through which the Bank in its capacity as lender of last resort ensured that the banking system had adequate cash, but in practice loans had been made frequently as a means of influencing short-term interest rates. In future, these loans were to be exceptional, used only when there was a technical shortage of cash in the bill market (due, for example, to an oversubscription to an issue of government stock) or when the Bank especially wished to influence market rates.[10] In normal circumstances, the Bank was no longer seeking to maintain a specific rate but was adopting an approach similar to that used by the authorities in the USA since 1979, and aiming to keep short-term rates within an undisclosed band in order to allow competitive forces greater latitude.[11]

More detailed consideration of the changing methods of control will be taken up shortly, but it is already clear from what has been said that while the stress on the market mechanism and competitiveness has been closely related to alterations in the government's overall monetary strategy, the greater encouragement of 'market forces' has also been an important trend in its own right. The 1970s and early

1980s thus witnessed some effort to recognise the discriminatory and distorting effects of the credit controls practised since the Second World War and determination to take action was greatly stiffened by the election of a right-wing Conservative government in 1979. The government was intent on placing financial institutions on a more equal footing and on establishing greater competition in the provision of financial services. The clearing banks, building societies and the Trustee Savings Banks were all urged to extend the range of their businesses and to compete more actively. In general, the new government sought to relax regulations in both money and capital markets and to encourage more open competition.

The Bank Governor's speech to the Finance Houses Association in January 1982 sums up how the new attitude was to affect monetary policy:

> Recent experience serves...to confirm the judgement that arrangements that allow maximum flexibility of response, that leave as much room as possible to the free play of market forces, and that enable us to operate with a somewhat lower profile than before, are best suited to our times...[12]

Nevertheless, official action inevitably involves non-market 'distortions' - by definition, a 'free market' is only possible in the absence of monetary policy and it is inconceivable that any British government would abandon this tool of economic management. Even if greater reliance on interest rate policy imposes less obvious restrictions on competitive forces than direct controls, the commitment to use rate changes in itself highlights the authorities' willingness to 'distort' the price mechanism in pursuit of the public interest. Anyway, while it is not yet possible to assess properly the changes implemented in the early eighties, it is clear from post-war history that the Bank of England, at least, has always favoured a somewhat pragmatic approach which has meant the use of *ad hoc* constraints if the need should arise.

## TECHNIQUES OF MONETARY CONTROL

### *Competition and Credit Control*

The 1971 document on 'Competition and Credit Control' and the 1980 Green Paper on *Monetary Control* can again be used as convenient signposts of changing policy techniques and objectives.

The main aim in 1971 was to combine 'an effective measure of control over credit conditions with greater scope for competition and innovation.'[13] The Bank of England's pronouncements did speak of 'monetary policy' but the use throughout of the term, 'credit control', indicates the transitional nature of the changes launched in 1971 – standing somewhere between the Radcliffe Committee's emphasis on a wide range of liquidity and credit, and the much stronger concern in the 1970s with monetary aggregates. The Chancellor, Anthony Barber, made it clear that the ultimate objective was still to influence aggregate demand and that monetary policy was to be used as a flexible policy instrument:

> And so monetary policy will be used in future...as an integral part of the general management of demand. Because one of the main qualities of monetary policy is flexibility I do not propose to lay down numerical targets. The policy will be geared to the needs of the situation, and will change as those needs change.[14]

As has been noted, there was a new awareness that the prior concentration on restricting bank advances had been too narrowly-based; it had failed to encompass non-bank credit and, indeed, had contributed to the growth of this unregulated sector. This was part of the reason why the authorities increasingly favoured the use of broader monetary aggregates as the target variables to control, and the 1971 reforms were largely concerned with the means by which these broader monetary variables were to be regulated.

Two main (if related) influences were present: the

eschewment of specific controls in favour of more general ones, and the downgrading of quantitative controls in favour of the price mechanism. The use of a more active interest rate policy was to the fore of official thinking. Faith in the efficacy of such a policy was based on a belief that the demand for credit was price-elastic and, thus, if the authorities could affect changes in market interest rates they could affect the general demand for credit and, in turn, the growth of monetary aggregates.[15] Crudely, if the authorities could make loans dearer, this would discourage borrowing and depress general demand. However, this new interest rate policy was not to be channelled through the long-standing price fixing arrangements that the Bank, discount houses and clearing banks had been formally operating. Bank rate changes would still signal the authorities' views on short-term rates but, as already shown, the price fixing cartels were to be abolished. In future, competition was to be more evident, and interest rates were to be more variable and to reflect market conditions more accurately.

In this spirit it was proposed to abolish direct ceilings on bank lending, although qualitative guidance ('priority should be given to exporters', 'borrowing for the purchase of consumer durables should be discouraged', etc) was to remain. The specific reserve ratio requirements imposed on London clearing banks - with minimum cash holdings equal to 8 per cent of liabilities and liquid assets to 28 per cent - were also to go, but control over the liquidity of the banking system was still considered essential to monetary policy and a new reserve asset ratio of 12.5 per cent of eligible sterling liabilities was introduced for the *whole* banking system (with a ratio of 10 per cent being agreed for the 'non-bank' finance houses).[16] For the same reason the authorities extended the special deposit scheme beyond the clearers to all banks (except those in Northern Ireland). Under this scheme, the banks could be called upon to place extra deposits with the Bank of England and such deposits could not be counted as part of reserve assets. So, if they wished, the authorities could reduce the banks' cash holdings at a stroke and reduce the liquidity of the whole banking system. The authorities would continue to use open-market operations to influence the supply of reserve assets available to the banks, but they intended to increase the penalties on those banks seeking liquid assets through sales of government securities. In future, they proposed to reduce their own support to the gilts market, so restricting the ease with which banks could redistribute their asset holdings in order to accommodate official pressure on liquidity. Henceforth, if banks in general sought to sell off holdings of gilts in return for bills or cash, they would find the market weaker, with a greater risk of capital losses as gilt prices fell.

'Competition and Credit Control' stressed that control over bank liquidity was not considered a main method of monetary regulation in its own right; rather it was intended as a supplement and support to interest rate policy:

> It is not expected that the mechanism of the minimum asset ratio and Special Deposits can be used to achieve some precise multiple contraction or expansion of bank assets. Rather the intention is to use our control over liquidity...to influence the structure of interest rates. The resulting changes in relative rates of return will then induce shifts in the asset portfolios of both the public and the banks...We expect rather to achieve our objectives through market mechanisms. Special Deposits can be used not only to mop up any abnormal excess liquidity, but also to oblige the banking system to seek to dispose of assets not eligible for the liquidity ratio...[17]

At the time the Governor was surprisingly assured of the efficacy of the new controls: 'no limitation is envisaged on the authorities' ability to neutralise excess liquidity or to bring about sufficiently strong upward pressure on bank lending rates.' At least publicly, the authorities heralded in the new flexible interest rate policy with some confidence.

*Experience of the 1970s and Monetary Targets*

In the event, monetary policy during the 1970s was to rely as heavily on direct intervention as in the 1960s. Inflation was to become the most pressing concern of economic policy-makers during the decade. On trend the annual rate of increase in retail prices rose very sharply, to a peak of 20–23 per cent in 1974/5. Inflation was occurring against a background of decline in the British manufacturing sector and the emergence of large-scale unemployment for the first time since the 1930s. Internationally, there was increased disruption to financial and commercial relations established in previous decades. In particular, the abandonment of fixed exchange rates and the dramatic increases in oil prices engineered by the Organisation of Petroleum Exporting Countries - with the price of crude oil rising fourfold during 1973–4 and more than doubling in 1979–80 - had serious consequences for developed countries such as the UK.

With hindsight it can be argued that these problems were as daunting as any that have ever faced British macroeconomic policy-makers and it is not surprising that a variety of management 'tools' was tried. The use of fiscal policy continued to the fore, yet with waning conviction.[18] Both Labour and Conservative governments turned to incomes policies as a means of reducing wage costs; but there was also an increasing acceptance that monetary policy could have an important part in dampening inflationary pressures. One consequence was that from the mid-seventies more attention was directed towards the monetary consequences of fiscal policy, with the authorities becoming more receptive to arguments that a rising Public Sector Borrowing Requirement (PSBR) could directly inflate the growth of the money supply and, thus, that tighter fiscal control was needed. Also much greater credence was given to the view that changes in the stock of money were important determinants of changes in the general price level. For this reason the emphasis moved much more towards controlling bank liabilities than had been explicit in the 1971 document on 'Competition and Credit Control'. In 1971 many of the techniques to be employed by the Bank were geared to controlling bank reserve assets and it was not clear if the relevant 'monetary aggregates' were to be bank advances (as in the sixties) or bank deposits. In subsequent years, the Bank monitored movements in both bank assets and liabilities but the emphasis switched decidedly towards variables measuring aggregate liabilities.

For a while Domestic Credit Expansion (DCE) attained some prominence as a monetary indicator, although it is difficult to know if this reflected the British authorities' own preference or was largely the result of having to abide by the terms of International Monetary Fund (IMF) loans made in 1967 and 1976 when the balance of payments was weak.[19] The IMF was particularly keen on DCE control and in 1967, for instance, a ceiling was imposed on British DCE as a pre-condition of a loan. The British authorities also set DCE targets for 1977–9. The Bank of England calculated DCE as:

| | |
|---|---|
| | public sector borrowing requirement (PSBR) |
| *minus* | non-bank private sector purchases of public sector debt |
| *plus* | sterling bank lending to the private sector |
| *plus* | sterling bank lending to the overseas sector |

DCE was seen as, '...the total arrived at after adjusting the increase in the money supply to take account of any changes in money balances directly caused by an external surplus or deficit.'[20] Thus, it was an attempt to capture the change in a broad definition of the money stock arising from *domestic* sources. The IMF wanted national authorities to take responsibility for controlling this, for if the increase in DCE rose faster than the total demand for money, the deficiency would show in an adverse balance of payments. It was as an indicator of potential external imbalance that use of DCE as a target variable appealed to the IMF.

The Bank of England continued to calculate and publish figures for DCE amongst its regular money stock data until the end of 1981, but by the late seventies whatever significance it had had as a target variable seems to have already waned.[21] The concept had been criticised on a number of counts[22] but with Britain's abandonment of a fixed exchange rate in 1971, and of exchange controls in 1979, its relevance to monetary policy faded. Under a fixed exchange rate regime the authorities might be able to control domestic credit but not international capital flows. It was this that had previously provided some justification for the use of DCE as a target variable. In theory, with floating exchange rates, external flows should be minimal and, thus, control of the domestic money stock could be within the grasp of the authorities.

Though closely related to monetary variables, DCE was strictly a measurement of assets and its declining fortunes were mirrored by the increasing stress on monetary liabilities. The authorities began to collect and closely monitor data for a variety of measures of the money stock. Precise definitions have varied over time but Table 14.1 shows the measures used as of mid-1980 and lists some of the main components that the authorities have been concerned with.

The narrowest measure shown is M1, which consists of notes and coin plus private sector sterling sight deposits (mainly current accounts). Another measure, M2, is not distinguished in the table but it has been used in a number of important empirical studies. It is a somewhat broader measure of the money supply as it includes M1, plus private sector sterling time deposits within the banking sector. Of the broad money aggregates, sterling M3 (£M3) is equivalent to M1 plus private sector sterling time deposits *and* public sector sterling deposits (definition as of mid-1980); while M3 is the sum of £M3 and UK residents' deposits held in foreign currencies.

In the 1970s M3 (and later, £M3) was to become the preferred target for monetary policy. At first the

Table 14.1: Selected Measures of the Money Stock and their Main Components

1. Notes and coin in circulation with public

   *UK private sector sterling sight deposits*

2. (i) Non-interest bearing
3. (ii) Interest bearing
4. *M1* (=1+2+3)
5. UK private sector sterling time bank deposits, including sterling certificates of deposit
6. UK public sector sterling deposits
7. *Sterling M3* (= M1+5+6)
8. UK residents' deposits in other currencies
9. *M3*(=£M3+8)

*Source:* *Economic Progress Report (H.M. Treasury)*, No. 123, July 1980, p. 3

---

Bank worked towards unpublished targets for growth in monetary aggregates but since 1976 (when DCE accompanied M3) it began to publish these targets in the form of preferred ranges of growth. The initial decision to publish targets was an attempt to influence financial opinion.[23] By the mid-1970s the annual inflation rate was exceeding 20 per cent and there was widespread anxiety about the future value of the pound at home and abroad. The authorities felt that the setting of targets for future money supply growth within reasonable, and diminishing, bounds would help restore confidence by illustrating their determination to control inflation. A public criterion of monetary descipline was also important to the authorities' application for the IMF loan of 1976. At this time the target variable chosen was M3 and its use was as an 'over-riding constraint' on macroeconomic policy.

Under the Labour government of the time, fiscal policy was still conducted on broadly Keynesian lines but the urgent need to check inflation had led to a situation where the authorities were willing to limit monetary growth and conduct other policies within this constraint. In particular, there was a clear recognition that growth of the PSBR affected monetary growth, and the open use of targets for M3 was a public admission that the monetary consequences of policy were to be given a high priority.

The general reasons for this greater concern with money supply aggregates will be considered shortly, for now it is important to emphasise the break with the Radcliffe heritage that it represented. The Radcliffe Committee had denied the significance of changes in the stock of money, seeing its control as 'incidental to interest rate policy.'[24] In contrast, during the 1970s the British authorities were to place its control at the centre of economic policy.

In developing methods of controlling the new monetary aggregates, however, the 1971 techniques based on a flexible interest rate policy proved inadequate to the task. In this highly inflationary period the magnitude of interest rate rises necessary to constrain monetary growth was considered too great, political expediency and economic necessity combined to make acceptable more direct measures for slowing down the growth of the money supply. Thus, there was a return to a position somewhat similar to the 1960s. Quantitative ceilings on bank lending were not reimposed but as the previous section on market freedom showed, whenever inflationary pressures became too great or the exchange rate was threatened, the Bank resorted to a variety of *ad hoc* measures. The Bank portrayed their use as supplementary to interest rate policy but, in effect, they were substitutes.

Problems for the authorities began shortly after the introduction of the new, 'freer' regime. The rate of growth of the money supply rose very sharply, from an annual rate of 13 per cent for M3 in 1970–1, to 20 per cent, 1972–3. It seemed that the banks were keen to adapt to the new system, actively competing for business and increasing their loans. In the early stages the authorities took little action to dampen down this growth. Part of the reason for their passivity was that a large component of the expansion in measured monetary aggregates was seen by them as a statistical quirk arising from the abandonment of ceiling controls on bank advances. The imposition of controls had forced some potential borrowers to go to non-bank financial intermediaries, or to resort to other means of raising credit, and abandonment of such controls inevitably entailed a readjustment as the banks won back customers or met previously unsatisfied demands.

Overall government strategy was an important factor in the authorities' response. This strategy was geared to reducing unemployment through fiscal expansion. Under the Chancellor, Anthony Barber, taxes were cut and a sharp expansion in PSBR was budgeted for. Monetary expansion was seen as the lesser evil when compared to unemployment. Barber's 'dash' for growth caused inevitable pressures on the balance of payments and in June 1972 the government tried to remove a major constraint to its budgetary policy by allowing the external value of sterling to 'float'.[25] By the second half of that year the authorities were decrying 'excessive' monetary growth while still welcoming the economic stimulus arising from continued credit expansion. Tentative measures were taken to moderate the 'excess' – MLR was raised and special deposits called for – but bank lending continued to surge. In fact, it was not until after the sterling crisis of July 1973 (when the pound fell by almost 10 per cent) that the authorities found the strength of their convictions and implemented the new controls. In November 1973 another 2 per cent of special deposits were called for (already 1 per cent had been called in November 1972, and 2 per cent in December 1972), and MLR was raised from 11.5 per cent to 13 per cent (it had been at 7.5 per cent in June).

However, M3 growth continued unabated, so the authorities abandoned their nascent reliance on the price mechanism, sought more immediate response and reimposed direct controls over the money market. Thus, hire-purchase restrictions were reintroduced in December 1973. For the banks, though, the main constraint was in the form of reimposed ceilings, this time on their liabilities rather than on their loans. This last constraint was known as the Supplementary Special Deposits scheme (commonly referred to as the 'corset' because of its restraining effects) and in all it was in operation for three periods[26]: from December 1973 to February 1975, from November 1976 to August 1977, and from June 1978 to June 1980, when it was abolished. Under the scheme the banks and finance houses had to place non-interest earning deposits with the Bank of England if their own individual interest-bearing 'eligible liabilities' (essentially sterling deposits) grew faster than a rate fixed by the authorities. The amount of supplementary deposits required increased progressively with the amount of excessive growth. In this way the Bank was able to impose a financial penalty on any bank exceeding the official target, a constraint which was considered to be more in sympathy with 'Competition and Credit Control' than the reimposition of ceilings on bank lending. Nevertheless the corset directly interfered in the market mechanism which had been so loudly extolled in 1971 and it produced distortions not dissimilar to the direct controls of the 1960s.

In particular, it encouraged 'disintermediation' whereby borrowers and lenders developed alternative forms of credit which were not subject to the same controls as eligible liabilities.[27] For instance, on finding their powers to provide advances constrained, the banks instead expanded the granting of acceptances to customers. These acceptances were almost as saleable as certificates of deposit, so customers could readily obtain cash, but as acceptances were not included among 'eligible liabilities' the banks incurred no official penalty. The problems for monetary control of such developments was essentially that while the 'corset' slowed down the growth in eligible liabilities (and, therefore, in M3) the actual impact on aggregate demand - on inflation - was offset to the extent that alternative sources of money were being supplied. It was in full knowledge of these 'distorting' effects that a new Conservative government was to reaffirm the authorities' previous commitment to 'market controls' in 1980.

*Green Paper on 'Monetary Control', 1980*

The election of Mrs Thatcher's government in 1979 gave greater impetus to the already existing tendency to rely more heavily on monetary policy.[28] The new administration avowed the need to reduce government controls and to encourage 'market forces'. It was claimed that the solution to the UK's long-term problems of low growth and uncompetitiveness lay in 'privatisation' of public sector industries (the sale of publicly-owned assets such as British Telecom and British Petroleum equities), greater tax incentives to wealth accumulation and discouragement of 'irresponsible' trade union power in the labour market. The money markets were affected directly by the decision to abolish exchange rate controls in October 1979, for this increased competition and further integrated British markets into world markets.

Another policy objective was the long-term contraction of the Public Sector Borrowing Requirement (PSBR) which is the amount the government has to borrow to cover the difference between its expenditure and its revenue. This had ideological attractions for a government seeking to minimise state involvement in the operation of the economy, but it also had important implications for the conduct of economic management in the UK. Within the Keynesian orthodoxy which had been established since the 1940s, it had been generally accepted that planned alterations in the government's borrowing requirement were an important policy tool for influencing the level of aggregate demand - the government could budget for a deficit if it wished to boost demand, or a surplus if it wished to deflate. From the mid-1970s, successive governments moved away from this position and, in response to a continuing rise in the PSBR during the inflationary period of the 1970s, they sought greater constraints on government borrowing.[29] Since 1979 in particular, the Conservative government's intention (if not the reality) has been a more rigid adherence to stabilising or reducing the PSBR.[30] If applied strictly, such a policy implies the end of short-term demand management, constituting a major break with post-war practice.[31]

Under this new regime, fiscal policy was to be subservient to monetary policy in the sense that rises in the PSBR were seen as a major contribution to increases in the money supply and, as priority was to be given to monetary control, government had to plan for an overall level of the PSBR that was compatible with its monetary targets. An increase in the PSBR can be financed in four ways: (i) increased sales of public debt to the UK private, non-bank sector; (ii) a rise in external financing of the public sector (e.g. a fall in the official reserves); (iii) increased sterling lending by banks to the public sector; and (iv) a rise in notes and coin held by the public (in effect, a special form of borrowing from the public). To the extent that (i) and (ii) account for an increase in the PSBR there would be no rise in the money supply but rises in bank lending (iii) and in notes and coin (iv) would add directly to the money supply in the UK. The relationship with the official measures of the money supply is set out more formally below:

| | |
|---|---|
| | PSBR |
| *less* | net acquisitions of public sector debt by UK non-bank private sector |
| *plus* | increase in sterling bank lending |
| *equals* | DCE |
| *less* | increase in external and foreign currency finance |
| *less* | increase in banks' net non-deposit liabilities |
| *equals* | increase in sterling M3 |

Because of the 'leakages' (through increases in the sales of government securities to the non-bank private sector or external financing) the statistical relationship between movements in the PSBR and in £M3 has not been very close, in fact, but the Thatcher government continued to lay great stress on the need to contribute towards 'the fight against inflation' by reducing the PSBR. Its contraction was seen as an important prop to monetary policy.[32]

The authorities' views on monetary policy were set out separately in the 1980 Green Paper on *Monetary Control*. This Green Paper placed eradication of inflation to the fore, arguing that 'a progressive reduction in the rate of growth of the money stock is essential to achieving a permanent reduction in inflation.'[33] At a practical level the Green Paper reiterated the importance of using monetary targets:

> The government believes that its monetary policy can best be formulated if it sets targets for the growth of one of the aggregates, against which progress can be assessed. This gives the clearest guidance to those concerned in both financial markets and domestic industry, on which to assess the direction of Government policy and to formulate expectations.[34]

Published targets, then, were seen as establishing the overall parameters within which public sector finance (government borrowing requirements, wages policy, etc) should be formulated. They were also to provide a yardstick against which to measure the effects of policy. Finally, in themselves, they were seen as potentially important determinants of market action through their effects on expectations and attitudes (e.g. in affecting wage negotiators' views on future rises in the cost of living, or lenders' and borrowers' views on the future course of real rates of interest). The Green Paper did reflect current Bank of England practice by acknowledging the need for the authorities to take account of a wide range of monetary aggregates (including broad measures of liquidity as well as money supply figures), but despite the dangers inherent in placing undue weight on a single statistical series, the Green Paper firmly established £M3 as the preferred measure of monetary growth.

In its analysis of monetary policy the Green Paper distinguished between two time-periods: the short- and medium-terms. It expressed a basic belief in the underlying stability of the statistical relationship between the rate of change in prices and the rate of change in the money stock over the medium-term (2-5 years?). Within this time-scale, fiscal policy and interest rate policy were seen as the main means of controlling the growth of the money supply. The government believed a long-term contraction in the size of the PSBR relative to national output was the best contribution fiscal policy could make to slowing monetary growth. In the short-term, however, time lags could cause important distortions in the response of the money supply to changes in policy. For this reason, the authorities needed techniques of short-term monetary control and it was here that the Green Paper introduced reforms.

As already outlined, the Green Paper attacked the distortions caused by direct controls. For this reason it proposed the abolition of the Supplementary Special Deposits scheme. Not only had this device encouraged 'disintermediation' at home but it was recognised that once exchange rate controls had been removed, banks based in Britain could easily avoid the corset by booking 'excess' deposits overseas.[35] The Green Paper also reiterated the authorities' faith in the importance of the Bank of England's influence over interest rates. As a statement from the Bank explained: '...the desire to retain a fairly direct influence over interest rates rests on the view that these may have a significant effect on, for example, the demand for money, the demand for credit and the exchange rate, with consequences for the development of the economy more generally.'[36] This influence over interest rates was to be exercised through the Bank's involvement in the daily operations of the money market, although a change in arrangements was introduced. In particular, the Bank was to rely more on open market operations (buying and selling securities, especially bills), less on direct lending, and it was to aim at maintaining not a specific short rate but to allow fluctuations within an undisclosed band of rates. As a consequence, in August 1981, Minimum Lending Rate was 'suspended'. On the face of it, the passing of a published rate at which the Bank was prepared to lend to the discount houses seems a sharp break with Bank of England history but, in fact, it was largely a technical matter. The important link with tradition was retained in the declared intention of operating an active interest rate policy. Even MLR could be revived if need be (as it was temporarily during the sterling crisis of January 1985). The justification for the change was to allow greater leeway to market forces in determining precise rates, while the authorities 'continue to exercise substantial influence over very short-term rates as a positive element of economic policy.'[37]

As an aid to interest rate policy the Bank retained controls over bank liquidity. The reserve asset requirement established in 1971 was seen by the Green Paper as an unnecessary distortion of the market in short-term public debt and, in practice, of little use in controlling liquidity. It was abolished in 1980. However, the 1.5 per cent cash ratio which since 1971 had applied to the clearing banks only, was extended in August 1981 to all banks so as to provide a 'fulcrum' for Bank policy if need be.[38] Similarly, the special deposit scheme which already covered all banks was retained as a means of preventing the build-up of excess liquidity within the banking sector.

In summary, therefore, the election of a Conservative government in 1979 can be seen to have confirmed the authorities' growing concern with monetary aggregates, with control of the money supply. It also revived the 1971 belief in the efficacy of competitive forces and (within the chosen techniques of monetary control) it led to a greater emphasis on interest rate policy.

## REASONS FOR THE INCREASED IMPORTANCE OF MONETARY POLICY

There is an undeniably sharp difference between the views of the authorities in the 1960s on the importance of the money supply and those of the 1980s. The Radcliffe view was that the objective of monetary policy should be control over interest rates; by the 1980s interest rates were seen essentially as the technique to be used in achieving the new objective, control over the money supply. The process by which the general philosophy underlying policy underwent change is obviously complex, but it is possible to identify a number of important general influences. Undoubtedly the inflation of the 1970s was a critical factor, a factor which affected Chancellors from both major political parties.[39] The persistence of historically high inflation rates over an unprecedentedly long period concentrated the authorities' attention on methods of controlling prices. While theoretically feasible, both incomes policy and fiscal policy were subject to major practical and political limitations; and the emergence in the 1970s of 'stagflation' – the simultaneous presence of high rates of unemployment and high inflation rates – seriously undermined confidence in the efficacy of fiscal controls. Conventional wisdom had assumed a trade-off between unemployment and price stability, with a fiscal boost reducing the former and a fiscal contraction constraining inflation. Stagflation, thus, presented a major policy dilemma, raising serious doubts over Keynesian-type management techniques which had held sway since the late 1940s. The greater reliance on monetary policy was an attempt to fill the vacuum.

Moreover, a growing body of theoretical and empirical work was pointing to the importance of monetary aggregates.[40] These academic developments were especially associated with the work of Professor Milton Friedman and his followers at Chicago University, but by the early seventies Friedman's ideas had permeated into many scholarly studies. The authorities seem to have been particularly influenced by a series of empirical investigations of data for the 1960s which appeared to confirm the Chicago view of a stable relationship between the demand for money in Britain and the level of income and interest rates.[41] The Bank believed the case for monetary policy was established, leaving the practical choice of whether to make interest rates or the money supply the proximate objective of policy. In the event it was the impact of inflation which persuaded the authorities to opt for the latter. According to the Bank Governor:

> With increased inflationary expectations interest rates also have risen greatly. We can...think of the nominal interest rate as having an "expected inflation" component and a "real" interest element. But we can never observe expectations, which are in any case likely both to differ from person to person, and to be volatile. The real rate of interest is an abstract construct. This has made it very difficult to frame the objectives of policy in terms of nominal interest rates.[42]

The authorities, therefore, concentrated on the money supply.

These two trends – the growing importance of monetary policy within overall techniques of economic management and the shift within that policy towards control of monetary aggregates – were international in nature. The IMF's attitude towards DCE (above) was a case in point. Undoubtedly this, too, influenced the British authorities.[43] A specific international influence in the 1970s came from the break-up of the Bretton Woods agreement on fixed exchange rates. The pound was 'floated' in 1972 and this in itself had important consequences for the possibilities of money supply policy. Flexible exchange rates theoretically insulated the UK money supply and made it feasible for the authorities to control it. But abandonment of a stable exchange rate also removed a significant constraint on monetary policy. During the 1960s, inflationary pressures led to frequent exchange rate crises, forcing the authorities to dampen domestic demand in order to fulfil their commitment to the par value of the pound. 'Floating' removed this constraint, encouraging the Bank to seek other means of checking inflation. Control over the money supply came to be seen in this light.[44]

One final point should be made about the contrast in policy aims between the 1960s and 1980s, and that is the need to acknowledge the high level of continuity in the methods used to implement policy. There have been some significant technical changes but the transition in objectives has been eased by these elements of continuity. Throughout, policy changes have been channelled mainly through the banking sector and (at least until the 1980s) the implementation of policy has involved a mix of quantity and price controls. In addition, although the 'targets' of policy have been different it could be argued that even the most recent emphasis on interest rate techniques follows a long tradition established by the Bank of England through the nineteenth and twentieth centuries.

## VALIDITY OF THE 'NEW' MONETARY POLICY

It is possible to see the transmission mechanism underlying recent monetary policy in the following manner:

| *Policy Instruments* | | *Target Variable* | | *Ultimate Objective* |
|---|---|---|---|---|
| Interest rate policy, open market operation, special deposits, reduction of PSBR, base control[?] | → | Rate of change in the money supply | → | Rate of change in general prices |

The main objective of policy since 1979 has been to slow down the rate of price increases and the authorities have seen the main contribution from monetary policy as the reduction of the growth rate of the money supply.[45] As the 1980 Green Paper made clear, fiscal policy's contribution would be to bring about a long-run cut in the relative size of the PSBR. As has already been emphasised, in determining which monetary policy instruments to use the authorities reiterated their dislike of direct quantity controls such as the 'corset' and these were to form no part of the new regime. However, they did give some early consideration to a potentially new control instrument, 'money base control'. Under such a system the authorities would seek to control that group of public sector liabilities commonly regarded as 'cash' (normally, notes and coin held by the public; notes and coin held by the banks; and bankers' balances at the Bank of England).[46] If the authorities chose to act only on cash held by the banks (the last two items), then they could require the banks to hold a fixed ratio of cash reserves to liabilities. Control over the supply of reserve assets should then ensure the authorities' control over bank liabilities. Thus, if the authorities chose to alter the supply of bank cash reserves, this would have a multiply impact on bank liabilities as the banks sought to maintain the required cash ratio. However, the Bank of England envisaged major problems in operating such a money base system – both technical problems and problems affecting the Bank's fundamental relationship with the money markets – and did not introduce it in the early 1980s although there has since been closer official monitoring of movements in the money base and it may yet have a role to play.

By a process of elimination, therefore, under the new regime control of the money supply was to rely heavily upon interest rate policy in the short term and upon the reduction of the PSBR in the medium term (formally, too, special deposits could still be called in order to reduce bank liquidity but they had not been so used by July 1986).

The justification for heavy reliance on monetary policy depends crucially on the robustness of the two main channels of transmission: upon whether there is a predictable relationship between changes in the money stock and changes in the price-level; and upon whether the authorities can control the money stock (in the context of the Green Paper, do interest rate changes bring about money supply changes?). In fact, both issues are hotly debated and the authorities' emphasis on a monetary remedy for inflation remains controversial.

During 1980 a committee of the House of Commons – the Treasury and Civil Service Committee – investigated the theoretical and practical aspects of monetary policy. The Committee took evidence from the Treasury, Bank of England, some overseas central banks and a representative range of (non-Marxist) economists. A report was produced in 1981.[47] The Committee distinguished between four different schools of thought on the effectiveness of monetary policy: the monetarists were divided between the 'New Classical' school and the 'Gradualists', and the non-monetarists were split into 'Pragmatists' and 'Anti-Monetarists'.

Professor A.P.L. Minford[48] was the only witness considered to be of the 'New Classical' school whose ideas are centred on the rational expectations theories developed by Professors Robert Lucas and Thomas Sargent.[49] According to the Committee two assumptions made by the 'New Classical' school are critical to their assessment of the impact of monetary policy: the assumption (in the absence of state intervention, monopolies, etc.) of price flexibility in all markets and the assumption that economic agents of all sorts (financiers, trades union negotiators, etc.) act 'rationally' in forming expectations of the future course of economic affairs. As the Report explained:[50]

> Possessing rational expectations means that one's expectations are formed in a way *consistent* with one's view of reality. If wages, prices and expectations all respond quickly to policy (and they only will if the announcement is credible) there will be no costs involved in combating

> inflation. With flexible prices, rational expectations and credible policy the rate of inflation equals – even in the very short run – the excess of the rate of growth of the money supply over the rate of growth of real output, where the latter is determined by real 'supply side' factors.
>
> The way to change the rate of inflation quickly and without disruption to the real economy, is to reduce the rate of growth of the money supply and to announce firmly that this policy will be adhered to in the future.

In this extreme view, then, changes in the money supply have a rapid and direct impact on prices, and *only* on prices. Minford criticised the procedures adopted by the authorities in Britain, but he was wholly sympathetic to the thinking that underlay the change in policy announced in the 1980 Green Paper. His main criticism was that it would have been better to have introduced an immediate and much sharper cut in the PSBR and in monetary growth.

Professors M. Friedman and D.E.W. Laidler are two well-known monetarists who gave evidence to the Committee.[51] These, too, argued strongly that changes in monetary aggregates determine the rate of price increases but they were 'Gradualists' when it came to policy advice. In contrast to Minford, they recommended a gradual reduction in the rate of increase in the money supply over a period of years. According to Laidler:

> The case for gradualism rests on the proposition that, *ultimately*, the main burden of adjustment will be borne by the price-level. I stress the word, ultimately, because in my view, the brunt of the *impact* of monetary policy falls not upon the price level at all, but rather upon interest rates and real income (and therefore employment). Only later do effects on the price level begin to come through.[52]

> ...the whole case for gradualism in monetary policy rests upon the recognition that tight monetary policy does have adverse effects on unemployment and on the judgement that those effects are highly undesirable.[53]

The shock to unemployment arises because the initial impact of tighter monetary control is a rise in interest rates and a fall in aggregate demand which (because all prices are not flexible and because of lags in reaction) reduces real output. Only after some time (perhaps two years or so) is there a noticeable effect on the price level. Thus, instant, sharp monetary contraction of the sort advocated by Minford was rejected in favour of a more gradual reduction in monetary growth of the sort announced by the government in 1980.

However, while in general terms both Laidler and Friedman supported the new government's declared intention of restraining monetary growth as a cure for inflation, they expressed doubts and serious criticisms over important aspects of that policy. The two economists denied that there was a close link between changes in the PSBR and the money supply, a link which formed a central prop of the authorities' Medium Term Financial Strategy.[54] Professor Friedman also made a special point of dismissing the Green Paper's claim that the money supply could be controlled through interest rate policy. In his view, the correct means of gaining control would be to establish a money base system, with the Bank of England employing open market operations in short-term bonds to control the supply of reserve assets available to the commercial banking sector.[55]

To the Committee, Professor J. Tobin[56] was representative of the 'Pragmatists' who were '...sympathetic to the idea that the money supply should be controlled, but were not inclined to place sole reliance on monetary policy in combating inflation or to pursue money supply targets with single-minded zeal.'[57] The Pragmatists criticised the over-simple view of the economy portrayed by some monetarists and emphasised the complexity of responses (with variations in scale and timing) to policy initiatives. In particular they believed that the unemployment consequences of the authorities' Medium Term Financial Strategy would be much worse than the monetarists acknowledged and they emphasised the importance of the labour market to the inflationary process, stressing the usefulness of incomes policies for reducing inflation.

Finally, of those from whom evidence was taken by the Committee the most outspoken opponent of the authorities' new monetary policy was Lord Kaldor, an 'Anti-Monetarist'.[58] Kaldor dismissed the most fundamental claims of the monetarists. To him, the £M3 measure was not especially meaningful nor susceptible to close control, because in an advanced economy like the UK there are many alternative assets that have (or could have) the same attributes as money – control one such asset and the public will use others. Essentially the demand for money is the critical determinant, not the supply. As the Committee explained:

> Economic policies adopted in the name of money supply control do *not* operate directly on the monetary aggregates, but operate instead on the flow of income, the general price level and the level of interest rates or interest differentials that generate the demand for money. Hence, as Kaldor argues, they will, if successful, achieve control of the money stock by controlling the demand for money.[59]

Thus, as the disinflationary policies adopted by the government impacted on income and output, Kaldor predicted serious unemployment consequences. He called instead for greater priority to be given to maintaining full employment and higher growth through an interventionist approach involving wages and prices controls and import restrictions.[60]

As Kaldor's evidence emphasised, the basic theoretical difference is that monetarists believe that (at least over the long term) changes in the money stock are the main determinant of changes in the general price-level; while non-monetarists argue that the line of causation of any relationship is likely to run more strongly from prices *to* money (e.g. as prices rise and the nominal value of transactions increases, then individuals and firms require larger money balances). At the heart of this debate is a disagreement over the relative stability of the demand for money. Those who believe 'money matters' contend that the demand for real money balances is reasonably stable and predictable, so the velocity of circulation, too, is reasonably stable. Opponents argue otherwise.

The importance of the stability of the demand for money can be briefly illustrated with reference to the familiar quantity equation,

$$MV=PY$$

Where the value of nominal income (PY) generated in any one year is equivalent to the number of times (V) that the money stock is used to purchase that money income, multiplied by the nominal value of the money stock (M). The effect on nominal income (PY) of changes in M depends critically upon the stability of the income velocity of circulation, V. Within the equation, PY can change as a result of either changes in the supply of money available (M) *or* changes in the amount of money people wish to hold (i.e. the demand for money) for this directly affects V. For instance, if the demand for money should double with the supply remaining constant, then the available supply would have to be turned over twice as often, doubling V, if there was to be no change in PY. From the point of view of monetary policy, there would be no merit in trying to influence PY through changes in M if V behaved erratically. For this reason the stability of the demand for money with respect to interest rates and income has been considered critical, and it has formed the focus of most empirical studies.

Evidence of a stable demand for money function

during the 1960s was important in persuading the authorities to opt for controls (through interest rate policy) over the money supply during the early 1970s. However, important differences of interpretation persist. Laidler and Friedman, for instance, continue to emphasise the underlying stability of the demand for money.[61] In contrast, Kaldor points to the variability of the income elasticity of the demand for money[62] and Professor D. Hendry, adviser to the Committee on Monetary Policy, concluded on the basis of Treasury data for the 1960s and 1970s that: 'velocity is rather adaptable and can accommodate big changes in the money supply and/or demand both in the UK and the rest of the world.'[63]

A recent, well-considered survey of the evidence by Artis and Lewis, emphasised that up-to-date studies on 1970s data pointed to a breakdown in the stability of the demand for money function. This was most noticeable for estimates of the short-run demand for money when the authorities' once-preferred measure of the money supply, M3, was used, but recent results also called for caution in interpreting stability over the long term.[64] One possible reason for the breakdown during the 1970s is technological change which has led to major innovations in retail banking, such as the greater use of credit cards and the speedier means of cheque clearing, and has created the reality of rapid worldwide communications in the wholesale money markets. Another reason is the major break in institutional and market practices consequent on the introduction of the 'Competition and Credit Control' reforms. But whatever the reasons, statistical results cast doubt on a fundamental relationship underlying much of the authorities' approach. Writing in 1981, Artis and Lewis stressed:

> Despite this lack of evidence, the authorities have, almost as an act of faith, gone ahead and set money supply targets for M3 (and later £M3), an exercise which seems of doubtful value if the demand function really is inherently unstable or is subject to institutional change, the impact of

which upon demand cannot be predicted in advance.[65]

Artis and Lewis also considered statistical analyses of the relationship between changes in the money supply and price changes in the UK. These suggest a weak relationship for the 1960s, but a much stronger one for the 1970s. However, the timing relationship between changes in the money stock and prices was not uncomplicated. For instance, it appears from Figure 14.1 that for the early and mid–1970s there was a two–year or so time–lag between changes in M3 and in retail prices, but that by the end of the decade and into the 1980s, prices no longer seemed to be lagging. The reasons either for such a long lag as two years or for marked variability in the lag are not self–evident and as Artis and Lewis conclude: 'it is fair to say that the transmission mechanism of monetary policy to ultimate goal variables remains shrouded in mystery.'[66]

A practical issue for those conducting statistical analyses is the choice of variable to represent 'the money supply'. In the past, M1, M2, M3 or £M3, have each been used, but there are other possibilities. In 1984, for instance, the authorities began publishing targets for a 'wide' monetary base series, MO (notes and coin held by banks and the public, plus banks' operational balances at the Bank of England).[67] For investigations of policy under a fixed exchange rate, DCE may be a more appropriate measure of the components the authorities can influence; and Private Sector Liquidity (PSL2) provides a very broad measure, comprising mainly £M3, private sector bills, local authority deposits, tax deposits, and building society deposits. If movements over time in all these series possessed a close statistical correlation, then the actual choice may not be too important but, in fact, their behaviour has been markedly different on occasions. Figure 14.2 shows the annual percentage changes over the period, 1970–1985, in four of these monetary aggregates, M0, M1, £M3 and PSL2. There are both similarities and dis–similarities, but it is instructive to

Figure 14.1: Retail Prices and the Money Stock (M3), 1969-1985 (percentage change over previous twelve months)

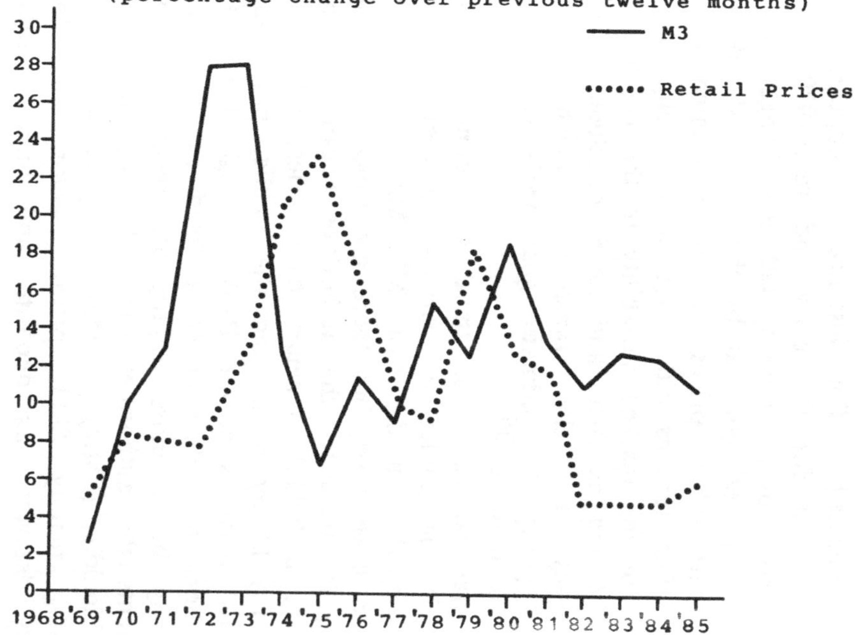


Sources: Retail prices - Department of Employment *Gazette*

M3 - *Bank of England Quarterly Bulletin* and *Annual Abstract of Statistics*

Figure 14.2: Monetary Aggregates, 1970-1985 (percentage change over previous twelve months)

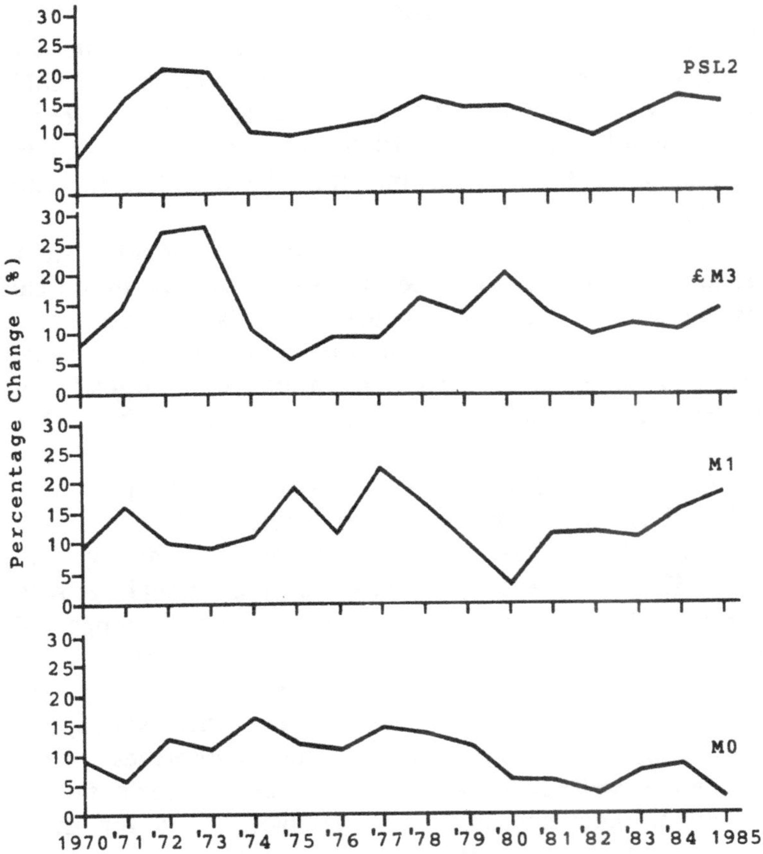


Sources: M0 - *Bank of England Quarterly Bulletin*, vol. 24, Mar. 1984 and CSO, *Economic Trends*, May 1986.

M1 - *Annual Abstract of Statistics*, 1980 and 1985 edns.

£M3 and PSL2 - CSO, *Economic Trends, Annual Supplement*, 1986 and CSO, *Economic Trends*, May 1986.

emphasise the latter. Between 1973 and 1974 the annual rates of change in both M0 and M1 rose, while they fell for £M3 and PSL2. There was another important divergence across the years, 1977 to 1980, with the rate of growth in M1 falling from some 22 per cent per annum to 3.3 per cent; whereas for £M3 there was a rise from 9.4 per cent to 18.7 per cent. More recently, in 1984 to 1985, the rates of change in M1 and £M3 have risen, but they have fallen for M0 and PSL2.

It is obvious that the actual money stock measurement chosen will be important to any empirical investigation. Such a choice has also presented a critical practical problem for the monetary authorities, especially since they began to announce 'targets' for the rate of expansion in monetary variables.[68] One serious problem with announcing targets and emphasising the performance of one or two particular statistical series is apparent from Table 14.2.

Here the Treasury's forecasts of monetary growth for £M3 are presented alongside the actual growth experienced. Even though quite a broad range of figures was used for the forecasts, the actual growth rate was well in excess of the top of this range in three of the six periods shown. In other words, by announcing monetary targets the authorities have provided a well-publicised advertisement of their failure to control their chosen target-variable. It is for these reasons that the authorities have recently begun to play down their earlier enthusiasm for monetary targets, preferring instead to emphasise the importance of evaluating a wide range of monetary measures (including the exchange rate) in order to assess the thrust of policy.[69]

Difficulties in finding a reliable measure of the money stock are important, of course, not only for assessing the relationship between money and prices but also in determining the extent of the authorities' control over their chosen target-variable.[70] As has been emphasised, in the 1980 Green Paper the authorities thought the main contribution of fiscal policy lay in the long-term reduction of the PSBR

Table 14.2: Comparison of Official Forecasts and Actual Growth of the Target Monetary Aggregate, £M3, 1980-86

| Period: 12 months beginning | Growth Forecast at beginning of period (% p.a.) | Actual Growth (% p.a.) | Discrepancy between Actual and Maximum Forecast (% p.a.)* |
|---|---|---|---|
| Feb. 1980 | 7-11 | 17.0 | +6.0 |
| Feb. 1981 | 6-10 | 14.5 | +4.5 |
| Feb. 1982 | 8-12 | 10.0 | -2.0 |
| Feb. 1983 | 7-11 | 9.9 | -1.1 |
| Feb. 1984 | 6-10 | 9.5 | -0.5 |
| Feb. 1985 | 5-9 | 14.75 | +5.75 |

* A minus (-) sign indicates that actual performance fell within the forecasted range; a plus (+) sign means it was outside the range

*Source:* *Financial Statements and Budget Reports*, 1980/81 - 1986/87 (HMSO, London, 1980-86)

---

and they declared their intention of effecting shorter-term changes in the money supply mainly through short-term interest rate policy. Short-term rates were to be controlled through the Bank's open market operations mainly in bill markets and, although there was no longer to be a clear signal of the authorities' desired rate in the form of MLR, the Bank was actively to influence short-term rates to keep them within an undisclosed band. But the authorities have failed to keep £M3 growth within their target range, thus raising the critical question of whether indeed the authorities can adequately control the money supply in the short- and medium-term.[71] Two general features affecting their degree of control are, first, whether the necessary money supply components, such as bank lending, are responsive enough to interest rate changes; and, secondly, whether the authorities are prepared to alter rates frequently enough and by sufficient amounts, if such changes (especially rate rises) are viewed as politically unpopular and potentially damaging to financial and industrial stability (e.g. through their impact on expectations and investment decisions). Serious doubts still surround both these points.

In fact, latterly the Thatcher government has acknowledged these difficulties and has shifted somewhat from the position it took up in 1980. In October 1985 the Chancellor of the Exchequer, Nigel Lawson, announced that targets for £M3 would no longer be central to monetary strategy.[72] Instead the authorities intend to give greater weight to the 'more stable' M0 series, although its movements will also be considered in the light of other measures such as foreign exchange rates and the actual behaviour of £M3 in relation to the authorities' (now downgraded) target for this variable. The Chancellor presented his impotence over £M3 as being the result of institutional change and altered practice in the money markets (continuing innovation and competition) but, more fundamentally, he recognised his inability to identify a statistical series which both measures 'the money supply' and which can be empirically and theoretically linked to changes in the price level. In many respects this admission of failure seriously questioned the whole of the government's monetary strategy launched in the Green Paper of 1980. In practice, the links between policy instruments and target variable, and between target variable and final objectives, have not been as precise as the 'new' monetary policy envisaged.

As is invariably the case in economics, the real world rarely provides an unambiguous example of a particular theory being applied to policy. It is possible for the 'New Classical' economists and other monetarists to claim that there has been no true 'monetarist experiment' in Britain because the government was not prepared to follow the strength of its own stated convictions and to cut the PSBR enough, or to raise interest rates enough - or to adopt money base control - so as to keep £M3 within target, especially in 1979/80,1980/81 and 1984/5. Nor did the government ensure a steady diminution of the rate of monetary growth, year after year. Even so, the rigours of political economy are lax enough to enable supporters of the Conservative government to claim (on the basis of such data as that in Figure 14.1) that monetary policy did eventually have the desired impact on the inflation rate. But even if critics conceded this (and many point to other reasons for the drop in inflation) they would argue that the costs of monetary deflation and tight fiscal policy have been very high, with unemployment rates rising to new peaks and with unprecedented losses in potential output. True, Mrs Thatcher's government believed the control of inflation to be a medium-term strategy and implicitly accepted that bankruptcies and rising unemployment would occur in the short-run, but (by 1986) they were still awaiting the market recovery in the labour market which, they believed, the greater stability of prices would produce. Seven years on from the election of Mrs Thatcher the number unemployed remained at some three million - the long-term reward for the harsh medium-term had not materialised.

## PRACTICAL MONETARISM

Careful reading of Bank of England pronouncements on the objectives and techniques of monetary policy, in fact, reveals few dogmatic statements. Compared to those of government ministers, or even Treasury comment, the Bank's public utterances have tended to be well-guarded, hedged-in with qualifications. Indeed, a study of the Bank's history since nationalisation shows cautious pragmatism to be a traditional element in its policy, an element that has been retained even since 1979. The Bank, of course, does not formulate policy in a vacuum. Its actions come under close scrutiny from academics, professional financiers and politicians. It has to hold a line between those who favour discretionary, interventionist policies and those who extol the virtues of *laissez faire*; between those who believe changes in the money supply are the critical determinant of price changes and those who think that money is largely passive, accommodating forces in the 'real' world; and, of course, it has had to carry through policy under both Labour and Conservative masters. In this context the Bank's lack of dogmatism is hardly surprising.

Even within the recent shifts in monetary policy the Bank has not been wholly committed to one particular interpretation of monetary theory. The Bank's preparedness to use *ad hoc* measures of control (at least, until 1979) has already been commented upon. The Governor, himself, has spoken approvingly of the term, 'practical monetarism', to describe the Bank's recent approach.[73] Although there have been preferred monetary targets, in 1978 the Governor was stressing that the 'main role...for monetary targets is to provide the framework of stability within which other policy objectives can be more easily achieved.'[74] Moreover, while the usefulness of a single target was admitted for the reasons given in the 1980 Green Paper (above), in practice the Bank considers changes in £M3 (and, since 1984, M0) in the context of a range of financial and economic indicators.

The Bank's pragmatism may offer part of the explanation why in the early 1980s the authorities apparently continued to hold beliefs (e.g. on the short- and medium-term stability of the demand for money) which were not supported by the statistical facts. Monetary management is more of an 'art' than the 'scientific' presentation of monetary theory sometimes implies. Even if a target variable can be shown to have lost (or to never have had) important statistical properties it could be that the Bank still needs to acquire a 'feel' for the money markets, and monetary aggregates can be used for this purpose – they may still act as valuable, if imprecise, indicators of the thrust of policy or of market conditions. Moreover, the authorities claim that retention of monetary targets at least provides them with a means of influencing money market expectations - the City has a general belief in these aggregates, which in itself adds to their importance and requires the Bank to take account of them.

Even within the public concern for £M3 , changes in bank lending continue to be carefully monitored. So, as the notation outlined earlier showed, the definition of £M3 subsumes bank lending, enabling the Bank to go some way to placating those who argue that bank credit rather than liabilities is crucial to overall demand. Similarly, the Bank collects and monitors broad measures of liquidity such as PSL2 and recently these have been given greater weight by the authorities. In practice, the Bank has sought to keep its eggs in more than one basket. Of course, such a compromising stance risks drawing fire from all sides, with charges of inadequate conviction or woolly-minded theoretical interpretation. As the history of twentieth-century monetary policy puts beyond doubt, the Bank's actions are so important to economic management that they will continue to attract close scrutiny and criticism of this sort.

## FURTHER READING

Bank of England, *The Development and Operation of Monetary Policy, 1960-1983* (Oxford University Press, Oxford, 1984).

C.A.E. Goodhart, *Monetary Theory and Practice. The UK Experience* (Macmillan, London, 1984).

M.J. Artis and M.K. Lewis, *Monetary Control in the United Kingdom* (Philip Allan, Oxford, 1981).

David Gowland, *Controlling the Money Supply* (Croom Helm, London, 1982).

Treasury and Civil Service Committee, *Memoranda on Monetary Policy*, PP 1979-80, 720, I-II (2 vols., HMSO, London, 1980).

NOTES

1. Banking Act, 1979, Eliz. II, c. 37.

2. Pages 379–87.

3. *Committee on the Working of the Monetary System* [Radcliffe Committee] *Report*, Cmnd 827 (HMSO, London, 1959, reprinted 1969), pp. 179–83. The Committee itself recognised the 'distorting' effects of controls but thought the benefits outweighed the costs.

4. 'Competition and Credit Control', *Bank of England Quarterly Bulletin (BEQB)*, vol. 11, June 1971, pp. 189–93.

5. 'Key Issues in Monetary and Credit Policy', *BEQB*, vol. 11, June 1971, p. 198. This paper, along with other important statements on Bank policy, is reprinted in Bank of England, *The Development and Operation of Monetary Policy, 1960–1983* (Oxford University Press, Oxford, 1984), pp. 39–41.

6. Bank of England, *Monetary Policy*, pp. 42–4; 'Monetary Policy and Regulations Imposed on Listed Banks', *Midland Bank Review*, Summer 1979, pp. 15–9; Brian Griffiths 'The Reform of Monetary Control in the United Kingdom', *Annual Monetary Review*, No. 1, especially pp. 32–5; Richard Coghlan and Carolyn Sykes, 'Managing the Money Supply', *Lloyds Bank Review*, 135, 1980, pp. 1–13; and Charles Goodhart, 'Problems of Monetary Management: The UK Experience' in Anthony S. Courakis (ed.), *Inflation, Depression and Economic Policy in the West* (Mansell and Alexandrine Press, London and Oxford, 1981), pp. 111–43.

7. *Monetary Control*, Cmnd 7858 (HMSO, London, 1980).

8. M.J. Artis and M.K. Lewis, *Monetary Control in the United Kingdom* (Philip Allan, Oxford, 1981), p. 8.

9. *Monetary Control*, p. 15.

10. 'The Role of the Bank of England in the Money Market', *BEQB*, vol. 22, Mar. 1982, p. 90.

11. Ibid., pp. 86–94; and Brian Tew, 'The Implementation of Monetary Policy in Post–War Britain', *Midland Bank Review*, Spring 1981, pp. 13–4.

12. *BEQB*, vol. 22, Mar. 1982, p. 102.

13. 'Competition and Credit Control, p. 189.

14. Budget Speech, 1972, *Parliamentary Debates. Commons*, vol. 833, 1971–72 Session, 21 March 1972, p. 1347.

15. There was a noticeable vagueness in both 'Competition and Credit Control' and the Governor's account in 'Key Issues' regarding the meaning of 'monetary aggregates'. Again, this is suggestive of a transitional phase, between the fifties' and sixties' stress on financial institutions' assets (advances and credit) and the late seventies'/early eighties' emphasis on liabilities (deposits).

16. In addition, the clearing banks alone were to keep an average balance with the Bank of England equivalent to 1.5 per cent of eligible liabilities. Details of the various arrangements concerning the variety of institutions are given in Chapters 11 and 12.

17. 'Key Issues', p. 197.

18. Charles Feinstein (ed.), *The Managed Economy* (Oxford University Press, Oxford, 1982), Introduction, pp. 18–30, for a succinct survey of this process.

19. Tew, 'Implementation of Policy', p. 6.

20. 'Domestic Credit Expansion', *BEQB*, vol. 9, Sept. 1969, p. 363.

21. After 1981 Domestic Credit Expansion was relegated to 'Additional Notes' among the regular statistical tables given in the *Bank of England Quarterly Bulletin*.

22. H. Carter and I. Partington, *Applied Economics in Banking and Finance*, 2nd edn (Oxford University Press, Oxford, 1981), pp. 151–3.

23. 'Setting Monetary Objectives' (paper by Governor's assistant, J.S. Fforde, 1982) in Bank of England, *Monetary Policy*, pp. 65–73.

24. Radcliffe, *Report*, p. 135.

25. See pages 555–8.

26. For official accounts of the scheme see 'Credit Control: A Supplementary Scheme', *BEQB*, vol. 14, Mar. 1974, pp. 37–9; and 'The Supplementary Special Deposits Scheme', *BEQB*, vol. 22, Mar. 1982,

pp. 74–85.

27. Griffiths, 'Reform', pp. 34–6.

28. For the political context of the new economic ideology see William Keegan, *Mrs Thatcher's Economic Experiment* (Allen Lane, London, 1984); and Leo Pliatzky, *Getting and Spending. Public Expenditure, Employment and Inflation* (Basil Blackwell, Oxford, 1982), ch. 6.

29. *Committee to Review the Functioning of Financial Institutions* [Wilson Committee] *Report*, Cmnd 7937 (HMSO, London, 1980), p. 33, 79–81.

30. *The Government's Expenditure Plans, 1980–81*, Cmnd 7746 (HMSO, London, 1979).

31. Tew, 'Implementation of Policy', pp. 8–9.

32. P.M. Jackson, 'The Public Expenditure Cuts: Rationale and Consequences', *Fiscal Studies*, 1, No. 2, Mar. 1980, pp. 66–82.

33. *Monetary Control*, p. iii.

34. Ibid., p. iv.

35. 'Supplementary Special Deposits', p. 82.

36. 'The Role of the Bank of England in the Money Market', *BEQB*, vol. 22, Mar. 1982, p. 94.

37. Ibid., pp. 93–4.

38. This was the view of the Green Paper on *Monetary Control* (p. 15); but the Bank claimed the scheme was more a means of providing resources and income for the Bank ('Role of the Bank in the Money Market', *BEQB*, vol. 22, p. 89).

39. David Gowland, *Controlling the Money Supply* (Croom Helm, London, 1982), especially chs. 9 and 10.

40. Among the pioneering works see Milton Friedman, 'The Quantity Theory of Money: A Restatement', in M. Friedman (ed.), *Studies in the Quantity Theory of Money* (University of Chicago Press, Chicago, 1956), pp. 3–21; Milton Friedman and Anna Jacobson Schwartz, *A Monetary History of the United States, 1867–1960* (Princeton University Press for NBER, Princeton, 1963); Phillip Cagan, *Determinants and Effects of Changes in the Stock of Money, 1875–1960* (Columbia University Press for NBER, New York, 1965); and A.H. Meltzer, 'The

Demand for Money: The Evidence from the Time Series', *Journal of Political Economy*, vol. 71, 1963, pp. 219–46.

41. 'Reflections on the Conduct of Monetary Policy' (Governor's lecture), *BEQB*, vol. 18, Mar. 1978, p. 32; C.A.E. Goodhart, assisted by A.D. Crockett, 'The Importance of Money', *BEQB*, vol. 10, June 1970, pp. 181–97. Among the 'early' empirical work on the UK: Appendix II to 'Importance of Money', ibid; N.J. Kavanagh and A.A. Walters, 'Demand for Money in the UK, 1877–1961: Some Preliminary Findings', *Bulletin of the Oxford University Institute of Economics and Statistics*, vol. 28, May 1966, pp. 93–116; and David Laidler and Michael Parkin, 'The Demand for Money in the United Kingdom, 1955–1967: Preliminary Estimates', *Manchester School*, vol. 38, 1970, pp. 187–208.

42. 'Reflections', p. 32.

43. Wilson, *Report*, pp. 16, 79.

44. 'Setting Monetary Objectives' in Bank of England, *Monetary Policy*, pp. 66–8; and 'British Economic Policy over the Last Decade' (Governor's address to Italian Senate, April 1983), ibid., p. 63.

45. Of course, the government claims that price stability will, in turn, lead to an increase in British competitiveness, a restoration of confidence among investors, more growth and a fall in unemployment.

46. M.D.K.W. Foot, C.A.E. Goodhart and A.C. Hotson, 'Monetary Base Control', *BEQB*, vol. 19, June 1979, reprinted in Bank of England, *Monetary Control*, pp. 129–36; and the Green Paper on *Monetary Control*, pp. 8–11, 21–31.

47. Third Report from the Treasury and Civil Service Committee, *Monetary Policy* [*Report*], vol. 1; *Minutes of Evidence*, vol. 2; *Appendices*, vol. 3, PP 1980–81, 163.I–III (HMSO, London, 1981). Also see *Memoranda on Monetary Policy*, PP 1979–80, 720.I–II (2 vols., HMSO, London, 1980).

48. *Report. Minutes of Evidence*, vol. 2, pp. 8–40; and *Memoranda*, vol. 1, pp. 131–43.

49. Robert E. Lucas and Thomas J. Sargent (eds.), *Rational Expectations and Econometric Practice*

(Allen & Unwin, London, 1981) and R.E. Lucas and T.J. Sargent, 'After Keynesian Macroeconomics', in Federal Reserve Bank of Boston, *After the Phillips Curve: Persistence of High Inflation and High Unemployment*, Conference Series, No. 19 (Federal Reserve Bank of Boston, Boston, 1978), pp. 49–72. For a non-technical presentation of the arguments of the 'rational expectations' school see Arjo Klamer, *The New Classical Macroeconomics* (Wheatsheaf Books, Brighton, 1984).

50. *Report*, vol. 1, pp. xxxiii–iv.

51. For Professor Friedman's evidence see *Memoranda*, vol. 1, pp. 55–61; and for Professor Laidler's see *Report. Minutes of Evidence*, vol. 2, pp. 156–80 and *Memoranda*, vol. 1, pp. 48–54.

52. *Minutes*, vol. 2, p. 158.

53. Ibid., p. 160.

54. A general consideration appears in Maximilian Hall, *Monetary Policy since 1971. Conduct and Performance* (Macmillan, London, 1983), ch. 7. A more considered analysis can be found in P.E. Middleton, C.J. Mowl, J.C. Odling-Smee and C.J. Riley (HM Treasury), 'Monetary Targets and the Public Sector Borrowing Requirement' in Brian Griffiths and Geoffrey E. Wood (eds.), *Monetary Targets* (Macmillan, London, 1981), pp. 135–75, and 'Comments' by David Laidler (pp. 176–9) and James Trevithick (pp. 180–2).

55. *Memoranda*, vol. 1, pp. 57–9.

56. *Minutes*, vol. 2, pp. 208–22. Also memoranda from Professor M. Artis, *Memoranda*, vol. 2, pp. 40–7; and from the National Institute of Economic and Social Research, *Memoranda*, vol. 1, pp. 147–59.

57. *Report*, vol. 1, p. xxxviii.

58. *Memoranda*, vol 1, pp 86–130. Also see Nicholas Kaldor, *The Scourge of Monetarism*, 2nd edn (Oxford University Press, Oxford, 1982).

59. *Report*, vol. 1, p. xli.

60. *Memoranda*, vol. 1, pp. 99–100.

61. D.E.W. Laidler, *The Demand for Money*, 2nd edn (Dun-Donelley, New York, 1977); and Milton

Friedman and Anna J. Schwartz, *Monetary Trends in the United States and the United Kingdom* (University of Chicago Press, New York and London, 1982). Two criticisms of the latter's evidence for the UK are contained in 'Papers Presented to the Panel of Academic Consultants' of the Bank of England, 1983. These are David F. Hendry and Neil R. Ericson, 'Assertion Without Empirical Basis: An Econometric Appraisal of "Monetary Trends..."'; and A.J. Brown, 'Friedman and Schwartz on the United Kingdom'.

62. *Scourge*, pp. 78–83.

63. *Minutes*, vol. 2, Appendix 4, p. 94.

64. Artis and Lewis, *Monetary Control*, ch. 2. Also see C.A.E. Goodhart, *Monetary Theory and Practice. The UK Experience* (Macmillan, London, 1984).

65. Artis and Lewis, *Monetary Control*, p.25.

66. Ibid., p. 51.

67. M0 replaced M1 as the preferred narrow money variable.

68. Griffiths and Wood, *Monetary Targets*, for a collection of studies assessing the problem.

69. HM Treasury, *Economic Progress Report*, No. 166, Mar.–Ap. 1984, p. 2, where the budget strategy was outlined.

70. David Savage, 'Monetary Targets and the Control of the Money Supply', *National Institute Economic Review*, No. 89, Aug. 1979, pp. 44–52; and David Savage, 'Some Issues of Monetary Policy', *NIER*, No. 91, Feb. 1980, pp. 78–85.

71. Griffiths, 'Reform'. Artis and Lewis, *Monetary Control*, ch. 4, consider the major constraints; and 'Setting Monetary Objectives', pp. 65–73, illustrates the shortcomings.

72. For elaboration see 'Assessing Monetary Aggregates', HM Treasury, *Economic Progress Report*, No. 184, May–June 1986.

73. 'Reflections', p. 37. Similarly see 'British Economic Policy over the Last Decade' in Bank of England, *Monetary Policy*, pp. 63–4; and 'Setting Monetary Objectives', ibid., pp. 65–73.

74. 'Reflections', p. 34.

Chapter Fifteen

# THE UNITED KINGDOM AND INTERNATIONAL FINANCIAL ARRANGEMENTS SINCE 1951

## GENERAL BACKGROUND

The modern British economy has always been heavily dependent on trade with the outside world. In the early 1950s the UK was exporting some 20 per cent of Gross National Product and this proportion has increased over time, so that by the early 1980s it was up to 27 per cent.[1] Imports accounted for similar amounts. International capital movements into and out of the country have also been significant. However, while the external account has remained of crucial importance to the UK, on trend the UK's importance in the world has declined sharply. The country's share of world exports of manufactures fell from around 25 per cent in 1950, to 14 per cent in 1964, to under 10 per cent in 1979 and, down again, to below 8 per cent in 1985.[2] Naturally, the UK's diminished economic importance on the global scene was accompanied by a commensurate political demise.

In general, therefore, the UK remained heavily dependent on conditions in the world economy throughout the post-war period but she was no longer a dominant world power, her influence over the external economy became marginal. A relative decline would be expected, of course, as other nations developed, but the particularly worrying aspect of the decline was the extent to which it was derived from Britain's inability to grow at a similar pace to other developed nations.[3] By the 1980s there was widespread concern about the seemingly intractable inability of British suppliers to compete in international markets. By this time the UK economy was becoming increasingly dependent on imports of manufactured goods and in 1983, for the first time since industrialisation, the country incurred a deficit in her international trade in manufactured goods. This, and the contraction of the manufacturing sector, with its concomitant long-term rise in unemployment, has raised widespread fears of British 'deindustrialisation'.[4]

Deindustrialisation and a higher rate of import penetration are just the latest manifestations of a long-term problem of relatively poor output, productivity and real income growth. Britain's poor competitiveness throughout the post-war period meant that successive economic managers had difficulty in maintaining a satisfactory balance of payments at full employment (a major objective for most of those years). It was within the context of these external difficulties that the country's internal monetary and other policy arrangements became directly relevant.

In the face of balance of payments deficits the UK authorities could seek adjustment in a number of directions, most of which have been tried at some time or other since the war. First, they could draw on the foreign currency reserves, but obviously there were definite limits here, limits which were tighter for the UK than most because of the high level of short-term sterling liabilities relative to the size of the reserves. The reserves did provide a marginal buffer but they were rarely sufficient to cover current account deficits of even modest duration. The authorities could augment the reserves, of course, by borrowing from overseas. Loans could be raised in the private financial markets or through official institutions. In the post-war period, it was the latter that were generally most important at times of 'crisis', with the UK authorities arranging credit facilities with the International Monetary Fund (IMF) in 1956, 1964-5, 1967 and 1976-7, and with other monetary authorities in 1964, 1966-7 and 1977. A third form of adjustment could be to restrict imports through tariffs and quotas and/or to subsidise exports. Some trade restrictions have been constantly present in post-war years although the formal objective of the IMF and the General Agreement on Tariffs and Trade (GATT) has been the eradication of import constraints. In the UK an extraordinary 15 per cent surcharge (tariff) was imposed on imported manufactures in order to cope with the record trade deficit of 1964, but this was a temporary measure and the tariff was reduced to 10 per cent in 1965 and abolished in 1966. Nevertheless, the persistence of Britain's poor competitive performance has meant that there continues to be strong advocacy for the imposition of tariffs over the longer term. The Cambridge Economic Policy Group, for instance, argues for the use of a strategic tariff on overseas manufactured goods so as to check the contraction of Britain's manufacturing sector[5]; and the Labour Party, trade unions and some industrialists express sympathy with this view. In contradiction, though, it is often said that international treaty obligations especially within the European Economic Community (EEC) severely constrain the UK's freedom of action and unilateral trade restrictions could provoke damaging retaliatory measures from other nations.

Other adjustments to balance of payments problems have included cutbacks in British government military and other expenditure overseas. On trend this has been curtailed, especially since the 1960s. Outflows of private capital were also subject to official regulation to some degree or other until 1979 when exchange controls were removed. More generally, successive governments have also operated on private capital flows through the international money markets by seeking to raise (lower) interest rates in order to induce (deter) inflows of funds.

A more obvious wholesale adjustment to persistent imbalance would be to devalue sterling relative to other currencies for, all things being equal, this would make it cheaper for foreigners to acquire British goods and services while increasing the sterling price of imports. Moreover, the negotiated realignment of par-values was allowed for under IMF rules. However, the British authorities showed themselves to be reluctant to take such a measure, partly because of sterling's international role and partly because devaluation was perceived as damaging to the country's prestige. Nevertheless, sterling devaluation was forced on a reluctant government in 1967 (the 1949 devaluation is discussed in Chapter 10) and since 1973 the commitment to a fixed exchange rate has been 'suspended'. Even under the floating rate regime of the seventies and eighties, though, the authorities have been keen to avoid too sharp a depreciation of the pound because of the feared inflationary consequences.

Given their reluctance to devalue the currency, successive British governments (with or without overt pressure from international creditors) have sought to turn balance of payment deficits around through domestic deflation. For this, both fiscal and monetary policies were usually employed, plus *ad hoc* measures designed to check the growth of domestic wages. On trend monetary policy has played an increasing role as an instrument of constraint. In general terms, the aim has been two-fold: in the immediate-term a reduction in domestic demand has been sought, for this should curtail demand for imports and encourage export substitution; and for the medium- and long-term, it was hoped that the rate of inflation would slacken and so increase British international competitiveness as to correct the underlying weakness of the balance of payments. It is this long-term aim - the fundamental adjustment designed to make the UK economy more efficient, more competitive in international markets - that has proved so elusive. The methods used by individual governments during the period took a variety of forms, reflecting fashions in economic theory and political persuasion. In general, though, there was little 'directive' intervention by the state at the micro-level, although many relatively minor *ad hoc* exceptions could be cited. Most governments, whether under the influence of orthodox Keynesian economics or not, concentrated on macroeconomic pursuits (often supplemented by exhortations to employers and trade unionists to 'improve efficiency') rather than resort to the use of direct state action. In the 1960s, for instance, the Wilson government sought export-led growth as the ultimate objective.[6] From 1979 the Thatcher government believed the answer lay in greater freedom for competitive forces and looked to a spontaneous market recovery. Assessment is not easy, and it is bound to be subjective, but it can be said that such 'fundamental reforms' were unsuccessful in raising long-term British growth rates to the level achieved by most other developed nations. They also failed to slow down the decline of Britain's share in world manufactured exports. Thus, throughout the post-1951 period Britain's exchange rate and balance of payments policies have had to be conducted from the perspective of a declining industrial power.

With this broad backcloth in mind, the rest of this chapter examines the general chronology of Britain's experience, concentrating on the international role of sterling, the nature of international capital flows and exchange rate policy - factors of direct relevance to domestic monetary conditions.

## THE 1950s: THE STERLING AREA AND STERLING BALANCES

### *The Viability of the Post-war Sterling Area*

Sterling occupied a special position in international finance for much of the post-World War II period. Into the 1960s it was an important 'key' currency, second only to the US dollar as the preferred reserve currency of the world's monetary authorities and as the currency in which companies held their working balances. On trend, though, as Britain's economic and political importance declined, so too did the international role of sterling. It has been suggested, for instance, that in the period of dire dollar shortage immediately after World War II perhaps one-half of world trade was settled in sterling.[7] However, relatively slower growth in the UK and the emergence of chronic payments deficits in the USA (which turned the rest of the world's dollar scarcity to a surfeit) meant a decline in the importance of sterling. By the early 1960s, the proportion of world trade financed with sterling was down to one-third. A series of sterling crises in the sixties and the devaluation of 1967 reduced the pound's popularity still further, and by the time fixed parity was abandoned in 1972, just one-fifth of trade was settled in sterling.

The pound's relative importance as a reserve currency was never as great as its use for trade, but this too declined. Thus, sterling assets accounted for about one-fifth of international reserves held by monetary authorities at the close of World War II, for one-tenth in 1962 and for something like one-twentieth by 1974. On trend the world's monetary authorities found it more suitable to hold an increasing supply of other reserve assets - US dollars, Eurodollars, leading European currencies such as the Deutsche Mark and the Special Drawing Rights (SDRs) of the IMF. In other words, the story of sterling's international role mirrored that of the UK's international economic performance - it was one of decline.

At the beginning of the 1950s, though, the pound and the Sterling Area were important props to existing international currency arrangements. As earlier chapters have shown, Britain's international economic and imperial role had meant that sterling balances were extensively held by non-residents. In particular, the monetary authorities of a number of overseas countries with which the UK had close links - mainly members of the Commonwealth - had found it either convenient or expedient to hold their monetary reserves in the form of sterling assets (largely British government securities).[8] These officially-held balances rose sharply during the war as the UK ran up debts with a number of countries, especially with India, Pakistan and Ceylon.[9] Private sector sterling balances (largely in the form of bank deposits) had also been accumulated by the banks and other institutions of these and other countries. As a result, foreign-owned sterling balances were far in excess of what would have been justified on the basis of the UK's trading position alone. In fact, the Radcliffe Committee estimated that during the war net sterling liabilities to foreigners rose seven-fold from £540 million to £3,700 million[10], around which level they hovered until the mid-1960s. Table 15.1 presents some summary figures of gross sterling liabilities, showing their size relative to the country's official reserves. It is clear that important changes in British indebtedness and in Britain's reserve position could arise not only from changes in the country's own trading position, but also from changes in the external role of the currency.

Table 15.1: Gross Sterling Liabilities and UK Reserves (average of amounts outstanding at the end of year, £ billion)

| Period | Gross Sterling Liabilities* | | Official Gold and Currency Reserves |
|---|---|---|---|
| | Total | Overseas Sterling | |
| 1951/4 | 4.0 | 2.7 | 0.8 |
| 1962/5 | 5.2 | 2.9 | 1.0 |

* reclassification in 1962 reduced the size of liabilities (by some £0.4 billion from the total for that year)

*Source: Bank of England Quarterly Bulletin*

---

Immediate post-war conditions were favourable to the maintenance of a currency bloc based on sterling. The Sterling Area provided a means by which to participate in a multilateral (though not world-wide) system of payments and commerce at a time when the strength of the US economy, and the dollar shortage, ruled out the early realisation of a fully international, liberalised and competitive Bretton Woods system. Here the attitude of the USA was crucial. The realities of the Cold War and of the relative weakness of West European economies meant that the USA accepted that full implementation of the Bretton Woods principles was for the future (especially after the failure to establish the dollar-convertibility of sterling in 1947). From the late forties the USA was prepared, in effect, to provide diplomatic and financial support for discrimination against its own produce and currency, by tolerating the existence of the Sterling Area.

According to Susan Strange the central characteristic of the Sterling Area was that:

> Sterling countries allied themselves in trade and payments policies in a discriminatory club against the dollar. They openly combined to exclude dollar imports by rationing, to restrict capital transfers outside the club, and to foster dollar-saving trade between themselves as much as possible.[11]

Members maintained fixed exchange rates and practised mutual currency convertibility - but restricted convertibility into other currencies, especially into dollars (until 1958). Sterling was held as part of the official reserves of the various members and was used to settle inter-country debt within the Area. At the same time accumulated reserves of gold and dollars were pooled in London, depositing authorities taking sterling in exchange.

The advantages of such a currency and trading bloc to its members were that they could liberalise trade and financial transactions among themselves (by reducing tariffs, permitting international capital flows, etc.) without endangering their limited reserves of scarce currency. Moreover, the pooling of reserves reduced the sum of gold and dollars needed compared to an alternative system of individually-held reserves. 'The possibility for economy arises when the pattern of payments and receipts varies widely among the members of the group, either on a seasonal basis or from year to year.'[12] If this were the case, then as some members incurred net deficits with the dollar–using world others would be accumulating surpluses. Thus, dollar–deficit countries would be able to draw on the pooled reserve, the impact on the aggregate amount being offset by the net surpluses of other members. In a like manner, the group as a whole benefitted from the dollar–earning capacity of some of the least–developed colonies such as the Gold Coast (later, Ghana). Moreover, as the arrangements reduced the danger to Britain's dollar reserves, the UK was in a better position to allow member countries to borrow more freely in London. The British reaped what gains there were from being at the head of a quasi–imperialistic organisation and, of course, avoided having to liquidate the sterling balances *en masse.* In fact, as the fiasco of the 1947 attempt at convertibility had shown, wholesale liquidation was not a realistic option. Rather, official holders of sterling were 'locked into' their sterling reserves – the UK had insufficient gold and dollar reserves to liquidate them and was not in a position to provide goods and services in exchange. Even after the restoration of dollar convertibility in 1958 any attempt by Sterling Area holders to swap sterling *en masse* for 'hard' currencies would have precipitated a reserve crisis for the UK, raising the spectre of sterling devaluation which, of course, would have devalued the reserves of Sterling Area members.

*Decline of the Sterling Area*

The degree of mutual benefit derived from Sterling Area membership declined over time. With the appearance of an American deficit during the 1950s, the need to conserve dollars became less pressing. Politically, the UK's position within the Commonwealth became less important and, economically, trade with the UK became less central to many members' interests. Indeed the general complementarity of trade within the Area seems to have waned.[13] In the 1940s and 1950s the UK tended to have trading surpluses with the world when the rest of the Sterling Area had deficits, and *vice versa.* In such circumstances there was a clear advantage in pooling reserves. However, from the late 1950s the British trade balance more closely paralleled that of the rest of the Sterling Area, reducing the advantages of pooling. In general terms, too, the *raison d'être* of the Sterling Area was being weakened by the worldwide move towards greater freedom of trade and finance. If the advantages of multilateralism were available in the world at large – if the major key currency, the dollar, was now more readily accessible – why continue membership of a bloc tied to a 'second best' currency?

The UK government's own policies, in fact, helped to undermine the economic advantages of Sterling Area membership. From the election of a Conservative administration in 1951 policy was more eagerly geared to international 'liberalisation' and, gradually, steps were taken which led to the eventual convertibility of sterling into dollars from the end of 1958.[14] For the British this seemed the road to rehabilitation of the pound, with the hope of recapturing a greater share of the business of international money markets for City of London institutions. However, the greater success in establishing a more truly international payments system diminished the attraction of exclusive currency blocs such as the Sterling Area; whereas at the same time, the relative decline of Britain's economic importance undercut the attractiveness of sterling as a key currency for Commonwealth and other Sterling Area countries.

As the restrictions between Sterling Area and non-Sterling Area trade and finance were being relaxed, the nature of the UK's sterling liabilities was altering. In all, some 68–75 per cent of sterling liabilities were held within the Sterling Area. In total this component of the aggregate amount remained relatively stable, but on trend the independent Commonwealth countries reduced their balances as the Colonies and Middle East countries built up theirs.[15] In aggregate such Sterling Area balances were not subject to sharp short-term capital flows – in or out of the UK – presumably because, in the main, they comprised either official reserve holdings or privately-owned working balances. Balances held outside the Sterling Area were much less stable. In general this element - one-quarter to one-third of the total - were privately-owned, were much more market-orientated and less politically tied to sterling. Moreover, the relaxing of foreign exchange restrictions and the freer convertibility of currencies introduced in the late 1950s increased the volatility of this form of short-term capital. This part of Britain's short-term debt became more sensitive to changes in interest rate differentials between financial centres such as London and New York, and much more sensitive to any rumours, or actual danger, of capital loss from devaluation.

By the late 1950s and early 1960s, the UK's gold and convertible currency (mainly dollar) reserves hovered around 25-30 per cent of outstanding sterling balances, more or less the same as the total of sterling balances held outside the Sterling Area.[16] Under the Bretton Woods agreement, the UK was committed to maintaining a fixed exchange parity for sterling and with the successful introduction of convertible at the end of 1958, the conduct of domestic economic policy was to become much more sensitive to external factors. Changes on Britain's trading balance continued to be important, but the ability of overseas holders of short-term sterling balances (in the form of bank deposits and the like) to convert them into dollars or gold greatly enhanced the importance of potential capital flows. In future, British governments had to be more careful in avoiding circumstances that might lead to the liquidation of sterling balances, for any sudden conversion of a large proportion could quickly exhaust the international reserves and threaten both convertibility and the par-value of the pound. The presence of the sterling balances undoubtedly increased the UK's vulnerability. Whatever the initiator of such a capital outflow, once a rundown of the sterling balances began this in itself could provoke a 'run' on the pound by highlighting the relative smallness of available reserves. Confidence in the ability of the UK authorities to maintain convertibility and avoid devaluation would be of the utmost importance and even though there was a powerful element of stability governing the bulk of sterling balances under normal circumstances, their potential threat to Britain's reserves could become a factor in the breakdown of confidence. Such considerations were to play an important role during the exchange crises of the 1960s.

## THE 1960s: EXCHANGE INSTABILITY

A retrospective of British economic policy in the 1960s could be readily forgiven for identifying the weakness of the external account as imposing the most serious constraint on the authorities' broad objectives of achieving higher growth rates and preventing any significant increase in unemployment rates.[17] Balance of payments difficulties and the weakness of sterling seemed at times to be the central economic preoccupation, especially under the Labour administrations of 1964–70.

Table 15.2 summarises the main annual changes in balance of payment aggregates over the years, 1961–71. It can be seen that the balance on current account (column 3) while not particularly healthy before the close of the 1960s, was not particularly weak either, except for 1964, 1967 and 1968. However, throughout the sixties there was a net export of capital (column 4) and this was generally larger over the years from 1964 to 1968. In combination, then, the current and capital accounts caused quite substantial currency outflows (column 6) during this period. Bearing in mind that in 1964 the gold and convertible currency reserves available to finance this deficit were just over £800 million, a consequence of these outflows was that the authorities had to resort to large-scale borrowing from overseas (column 7).

### *Labour's Exchange Rate Policy*

When the new Labour government came to power in the autumn of 1964 it was immediately confronted with a currency crisis. The outgoing Conservative administration had boosted domestic demand through

Table 15.2 : UK Balance of Payments Aggregates, 1961-71 (£ millions)

| | Visible Balance | Invisible Balance | Current Account Balance (1 + 2) | Investment and Other Capital Transactions etc.* | Balancing Item | Balance of Capital and Current Accounts (3 + 4 + 5) | Financed by#: Net Transfers with Overseas Monetary Authorities | Financed by#: Official Reserves (drawing on + / additions to -) |
|---|---|---|---|---|---|---|---|---|
| | 1 | 2 | 3 | 4 | 5 | 6 | 7 | 8 |
| 1961 | -140 | 187 | 47 | -316 | -70 | -401 | 370 | -31 |
| 1962 | -100 | 255 | 155 | -3 | 40 | 192 | -375 | 183 |
| 1963 | -119 | 244 | 125 | -99 | -84 | -58 | 5 | 53 |
| 1964 | -543 | 185 | -358 | -311 | -26 | -695 | 573 | 122 |
| 1965 | -260 | 230 | -30 | -316 | -7 | -353 | 599 | -246 |
| 1966 | -108 | 238 | 130 | -632 | -98 | -591 | 625 | -34 |
| 1967 | -599 | 330 | -269 | -609 | 207 | -671 | 556 | 115 |
| 1968 | -712 | 468 | -244 | -1006 | -160 | -1356 | 1296 | 114 |
| 1969 | -209 | 714 | 505 | -169 | 351 | 687 | -643 | -44 |
| 1970 | -34 | 857 | 823 | 682 | -85 | 1420 | -1295 | -125 |
| 1971 | 190 | 934 | 1124 | 1917 | 230 | 3271 | -1735 | -1536 |

* Including: Exchange Equilization Account loss on forward commitment in 1967, -105; and in 1968, -251. Allocation of Special Drawing Rights in 1970, 171; in 1971, 125. Gold subscription to International Monetary Fund in 1966, -44; in 1970, -38.

\# Plus net foreign currency borrowings in 1969, 56; in 1971, 82. Here a negative sign (-) indicates a decrease in liabilities to Overseas Monetary Authorities (e.g. through repayment of debt). So that in 1964 the balance of payments deficit of £695m was financed by drawing £122m from the reserves and by borrowing £573m from OMAs.

*Source:* CSO, *United Kingdom Balance of Payments* (HMSO, London, 1983), p. 7.

expansionary monetary and fiscal policies in the previous two years. With full employment, signs of inflationary pressures had appeared and the balance of payments deteriorated. However, the Conservative government decided not to respond by a sharp cut-back in demand, but hoped instead for moderation in wage claims as continued expansion encouraged investment and the adoption of new working practices and technology, thus raising British productivity and international competitiveness.[18] Before this hope was tested, though, government had changed hands and the country was faced with a large balance of payments deficit in 1964. This quickly spawned a crisis of confidence in the ability of the authorities to maintain the par-value of sterling - a large-scale liquidation of sterling balances threatened.

Shortly after taking office the new Prime Minister, Harold Wilson, decided against devaluation as a solution to the crisis.[19] With hindsight this would have been the most politically astute time to have devalued, for the previous Conservative administration could have been blamed for creating the crisis. In the event, Wilson seems to have been unwilling to have risked Labour being dubbed the 'devaluation party', for Labour leaders had been responsible for earlier devaluations in 1931 (under a Coalition government) and 1949.[20] International opinion was also a factor. Devaluation of sterling would have directly devalued the reserves of Sterling Area monetary authorities, of course, and there was naturally some reluctance to accept this. More generally, devaluation of one of the world's two key currencies - even if only the junior one - could undermine confidence in the world authorities' ability to maintain the Bretton Woods system of stable exchange rates and, more particularly, could call into question the power of the US authorities to defend dollar parity in the face of continuing balance of payments deficits. Finally, one other factor was surely the optimism of a newly-elected government that hoped to 'regenerate' the British economy in such a way as to greatly raise the country's productivity growth rates and its international competitiveness. Success here would render devaluation unnecessary.

Having rejected devaluation, the government had to find means of protecting the reserves in the short-term, while its longer-term policies had time 'to transform' British productive performance. However, available options were somewhat limited. The electoral commitment to higher growth had been accompanied by scathing attacks on previous administrations for their 'stop-go' policies.[21] The new government hoped to avoid the post-war pattern of discontinuous growth: to break the cycle of fiscal and monetary expansion ('go'), quickening economic growth, inflationary pressures and balance of payments difficulties, followed by contractionary fiscal and monetary policy ('stop'). The objective was a smoother growth path, one which would achieve higher growth rates in the long run. Therefore, at the outset, if the new government followed the established reaction to balance of payments deficits and imposed monetary and fiscal contraction, it risked endangering its own preferred strategy.

The new government, thus, rejected two of the methods for dealing with payments deficits: devaluation and domestic deflation. As a result resort was made to *ad hoc* measures. A temporary 15 per cent tariff was immediately imposed on imports of manufactured goods (reduced to 10 per cent in April 1965 and abolished in November 1966) even though this was contrary to the GATT agreements to which the UK was a signatory. Also Bank rate was raised from 5 to 7 per cent in an attempt to attract short-term capital to the UK.

The reaction of the exchange markets was perverse, however.[22] The rise in Bank rate was interpreted as a sign of weakness, with the fact that the government had broken with tradition by announcing the new rate on a Monday, instead of Thursday, serving to highlight the seriousness of the crisis facing the pound. As a result, the government was obliged to augment the reserves by borrowing funds from overseas monetary authorities. The Bank of England arranged for credits of $3 billion with eleven central banks and the Bank for International Settlements. Such a massive addition to Britain's reserves - in effect, more than doubling them - lifted the immediate crisis, for it made plain to holders of sterling balances that the British authorities had the means to meet all likely demands for foreign currency. But raising the loans was not costless. Interest had to be paid and international indebtedness weakened Britain's negotiating position *vis à vis* the rest of the world, giving her creditors some leverage over the determination of domestic policy as it affected the external account. What is more, short-term credits did not solve the underlying problem of British uncompetitiveness. The government had to resort to domestic 'disinflation' (e.g. tighter credit conditions and restrictions on wage increases) but the hoped-for transformation of Britain's productivity record did not emerge. The pressure on sterling was bound to reoccur.

*Sterling Devaluation, 1967*

Serious problems built up again in 1966, culminating in a 14.3 per cent devaluation against the US dollar in November 1967. The persistent weakness of the balance of payments (Table 15.2) was a basic factor but the existence of the sterling balances was an important destabilising element which increased vulnerability to speculative runs on the reserves.[23] The mobility of privately-held balances had been growing since the late fifties, so as pressure on the pound developed - as fears of devaluation spread - it became incumbent upon a large number of holders of sterling to avoid potential capital loss/make capital gains by converting their balances into 'hard' currencies. Through 1967 a number of short-term factors combined to reduce confidence and feed speculation. In May the French President rejected Britain's application to join the EEC, in June the Arab-Israeli conflict closed the Suez canal and in the autumn a British dock strike seriously affected the immediate prospects for exports. Moreover, there was a general conviction in financial markets that the Labour government would not countenance a (further) domestic contraction of sufficient severity to obviate the need to devalue. By the autumn, then, speculators had little to lose by selling sterling for other currencies, because with a fixed parity they could always buy back at the same rate once the crisis had passed; while there was much to be gained if their fears proved justified and sterling was to be devalued. 'Speculative' actions of this sort, in fact, became a decisive factor.[24] Thus in the last few days of the crisis some £200 million seems to have been withdrawn from the reserves in this way – the Bank of England used $1 billion supporting the pound in exchange markets in just one day, 17 November – fatally adding to the drains on the trading and long-term capital accounts.

Two other aspects of the 1967 devaluation are important for what they reveal of Britain's position within the world monetary system. The first concerns the ability of the international community to co-operate and agree on an orderly realignment of the sterling parity. The second highlights the degree of friction between international and national economic objectives.

There has been general criticism of the British government for, first, deciding to defend the par-value of the pound with the consequential large international indebtedness and domestic constraint; for failing to take the eventual decision earlier in the autumn of 1967 when the likelihood of devaluation was widely accepted; and for then succumbing to market pressure, devaluing and presenting speculators with a handsome profit.[25] However, criticism does not usually extend to the international arrangements for devaluation itself. In contrast to earlier currency realignments the 1967 devaluation of sterling was orderly. The British consulted with the central banks of other leading industrial nations and with the IMF.[26] Agreement was reached with the IMF about the extent of the devaluation and about the provision of $1.4 billion of IMF credit to augment the UK's reserves. Another

$1.5 billion credit was arranged directly with other central banks. IMF officials also won the agreement of other countries to accept British devaluation without retaliation in the form of competitive devaluations of the type that had occurred in 1949. In 1949 a host of non-dollar nations had followed Britain in devaluing, but in 1967 only fourteen countries - ten, including Denmark, New Zealand and Eire, closely linked to the UK - devalued in the wake of the British move. In this sense the 1967 devaluation was much more effective for the UK than that of 1949.[27] Of course, the muted retaliatory response of the 1960s was a clear reflection of the UK's declining importance since the 1940s, but it also marked a success for IMF policy in supervising an orderly realignment of what after all was still a key currency.[28]

In this light, then, the 1967 devaluation could be viewed as a technical success for the 'managed' international monetary system which had evolved out of the Bretton Woods agreements. On the other hand, prior to the crisis the IMF and that institution's main paymaster, the USA, had been keen to avoid sterling devaluation altogether. In part, this reflected the commitment to a system of stable exchange rates (although IMF rules formally allowed negotiated realignments); in part, too, there was a reluctance to reward speculators. But a critical element was the anxiety felt over how sterling devaluation might affect the standing of the system's principal currency, the dollar.[29] Although on a different scale, the USA was experiencing balance of payments problems similar to the UK's and sterling devaluation exposed the weakness of the dollar still further, encouraging speculation about the ability of the US authorities to maintain parity. The mechanics of sterling devaluation may have been a technical success but for the IMF and its 'managed' system of stable exchange rates it was to be a Pyrrhic victory. Balance of payments disequilibria, especially the American deficit, continued to threaten chosen par-values, forcing a series of *ad hoc* adjustments before the American break with gold and dollar devaluation in 1971.[30] In the event sterling devaluation was a significant step in the general break-up of the Bretton Woods arrangements.

The other general issue raised by devaluation concerns the degree to which a sovereign state relinquishes control over economic policy once it incurs large-scale international debts. In any financial arrangement of this type, the expectation would be that the debtor would be under some obligation to meet minimum requirements set by creditors. Within the IMF framework it has been legitimate for officials to enquire of debtors as to how they intended to correct the payments deficits which underlay the need to borrow; and the IMF has attached conditions to loans which it felt would aid correction of the imbalance within IMF rules. Such restrictions as import tariffs have not normally been countenanced. Rather, the IMF has favoured the debtor nation imposing disinflationary domestic policies through tighter monetary controls, cuts in government expenditure, increased taxes, wage controls and the like. Such strictures have drawn serious criticism from debtor nations, especially from underdeveloped countries where incomes are already low by Western standards, with allegations of the "rich men's" club of the IMF constraining development in poorer nations.[31] In fact, such restrictions were also attached to the loans made to the UK and these, too, had political consequences.

The Labour government had been elected in 1964 on a manifesto which promised to break the mould of the previous thirteen years of Conservative economic policy. More egalitarianism was promised, but within the context of a better growth performance. Thus, the need to constrain domestic demand - first, to defend the chosen exchange rate and, then, under the strictures of the IMF - created political friction. Yet on taking office it had been the Cabinet's, and especially the Prime Minister's, choice to retain a fixed exchange rate and defend existing sterling parity. The decision obviously ruled out adjustment through currency devaluation or depreciation, leaving the government to face the remaining options of restrictions on imports and capital outflows, domestic deflation and/or increased competitiveness through productivity gains significantly ahead of other trading nations. The last was not achieved and within IMF rules trade restrictions were limited (the 'illicit' import surcharge of 1964 had been a temporary measure only). The government had little choice, therefore, but to incur debts and to deflate the economy. In fact, deflation would have been needed with or without IMF strictures, but the international body did provide a convenient target for critics from within the governing political party. Of course, the government itself drew fire from other political parties.

As has already been noted, the government may have won itself a greater degree of freedom of action if it had devalued immediately on taking office, but even then a careful exercise in demand management would have been necessary. In the mid-sixties the unemployment rate was at historically low levels, at 1.5–2.5 per cent of the labour force, so if devaluation were to succeed in boosting export-demand for British goods, higher rates of inflation would have resulted unless constraints were imposed on domestic demand in order to 'release' resources into the export sector.[32]

It was believed by such government advisers as Nicholas Kaldor that, if successful, export-led growth would ensure the maintenance of full employment at the same time as keeping the balance of payments in surplus and protecting the reserves.[33] And when devaluation was eventually forced on the government it was this type of argument that was used to present the decision in a positive light – devaluation would cheapen British goods overseas, boost export sales and, so, meet the twin objectives of a higher rate of growth and a current account surplus.

How effective was the devaluation of 1967? In the short-term, pressure on sterling remained – with periods of intense selling reoccurring over the following eighteen months or so. This activity in exchange markets was part reflection of a broader international uncertainty, which included speculative waves against other currencies, but for sterling it was the failure of the balance of payments to improve quickly that continued to feed the doubts. In the short-run devaluation had a perverse effect, with the balance of payments deficit worsening in 1968 and there was no noticeable turnround until into 1969.[34] It seems that while devaluation had an immediate impact on trade values - raising the cost of imports in sterling and reducing the non-sterling price of exports - there was a time lag before volumes adjusted. In the short-term, then, more was paid for imports and less earned on exports, so the deficit deteriorated. Eventually though, volumes adjusted to the new prices and the balance of payments improved. This has become known as the 'J-curve' effect, with the external balance worsening before it improved. Domestically this meant that the government had to continue for some years with a policy of fiscal, monetary and income constraint, measures which attracted considerable criticism. Nevertheless, in strictly economic terms, most commentators agree that devaluation was having a significant, favourable impact on the balance of payments by the close of the 1960s, especially through the beneficial effects on export sales.[35]

Finally on the sterling devaluation of 1967, attention should be drawn to the effect it had on the pound's international role. Devaluation further diminished sterling's popularity as a reserve currency. Devaluation, of course, reduced the international value of the reserves of those monetary authorities holding sterling and encouraged them to reduce their vulnerability to future devaluations by diversifying their reserve holdings away from sterling. Even before devaluation there had been increasing pressure to convert sterling balances (although at this stage there was no significant rundown of Sterling Area reserves) and in 1966 at Basle the Bank of England had had to negotiate an agreement with a number of other leading central banks for the provision of credits to offset the conversion of sterling balances.[36] Soon after devaluation, these central bank credits were enlarged to $2 billion, in September 1968. On the basis of these extra 'reserves' the Bank of England was able to offer official holders of sterling, such as Australia, a guarantee of the US dollar value of some 90 per cent of their sterling reserves in exchange for an agreement that the monetary authorities concerned would hold an agreed minimum of their reserves in the form of sterling. The aim was to improve mutual security and, in all, guarantee agreements were drawn up with 64 countries for an initial period of from three to five years (generally extended until the end of 1974). Such agreements may well have been a factor in encouraging a small group of overseas monetary authorities (Australia, New Zealand, Hong Kong and Eire) to hold more sterling but, as stressed earlier, other components of the world's monetary reserve grew even faster. The long-term decline of sterling's reserve currency role continued unabated.

## 1970s AND 1980s: FLOATING EXCHANGE RATES

### *The Floating of the Pound, 1972*

Despite the severe adjustment problems that confronted the UK during the 1960s, governments had remained committed to the par-value exchange rate regime. Yet in June 1972 the decision was taken to 'suspend' this 28-year-old commitment and to float the pound. Since then, whether under Labour or Conservative governments, the authorities have not been prepared to defend a publicly-declared exchange rate through the use of currency reserves in the foreign exchange markets. Instead the international value of the pound has been allowed greater freedom to change in line with market conditions, although it has been a managed or 'dirty' float, with the authorities maintaining an interventionist posture in exchange markets.

The immediate prelude to the June 1972 decision was another speculative run on sterling. This time, though, the authorities were not willing to repeat the politically and economically damaging currency-defence policies of the 1960s. Abandonment of the fixed exchange rate was to increase the government's options: domestic deflation and international indebtedness were apparently no longer the only responses available.[37]

A new Conservative government under Edward Heath had come to power in late 1970, and faced with rising unemployment in 1971 the Chancellor of the Exchequer, Anthony Barber, decided on the introduction of reflationary fiscal and monetary measures. The aim was to boost economic growth to the historically high rate of 5 per cent per annum. Hire purchase controls were abolished, quantitative restrictions on bank lending were removed, Bank rate was reduced, taxes were cut and government subsidies increased. Although high inflation rates were being experienced, further tax cuts and public spending increases in 1972 confirmed this strategy of a 'dash for growth'. Significantly, in his budget speech the Chancellor made clear his attitude to the exchange rate. If need be, he was prepared to remove the constraint imposed on domestic policy by the exchange rate:

> ... I am sure that all honourable members in this House agree that the lesson of the international balance of payments upsets of the last few years is that it is neither necessary nor desirable to distort domestic economies to an unacceptable extent in order to maintain unrealistic exchange rates, whether they are too high or too low.[38]

Some professional economists had already established a theoretical case for greater exchange rate flexibility[39] and in the real world practical pressures were pushing in the same direction, away from rigid exchange rates. Through the sixties, underlying balance of payments disequilibria had increasingly weakened the ability of the Western powers to maintain their chosen exchange rate parities. Sterling devaluation has already been catalogued, but the problem was more widespread than this. In particular, the US payments deficits associated with large outflows of capital and military expenditure and the higher growth rates of countries such as Germany and Japan, created a fertile seedbed for volatile capital movements, out of weak currencies into strong.[40] It was within this unstable context for the West's international monetary arrangements that the group of ten leading industrial nations agreed to a package of reforms at a meeting in December 1971 at the Smithsonian Institute, Washington.[41] One of their main decisions was to relax the fixed parity rule. In future the extent of exchange rate fluctuations permitted under IMF rules was raised from 1 to 2.25 per cent either side of par-values. The international background to Britain's decision to float was, thus, one of increasing derangement to the established par-value regime of Bretton Woods, and also one in which less rigid adherence to fixed parities was being implemented.

Yet, shortly after Anthony Barber's budget speech, the UK authorities took steps in the opposite direction, to commit themselves to a greater fixity in the exchange rate. The EEC nations sought more stability than allowed for under the Smithsonian Agreement and they arranged to restrict fluctuations among their own currencies to half the agreed Smithsonian margin, thus creating the so-called 'snake in the tunnel'.[42] In anticipation of gaining full EEC membership the UK joined the 'snake' on 1 May 1972. It now seems hardly surprising that there should have been a speculative run against sterling as soon as doubts arose over the strength of Britain's balance of payments: the government was committed to an expansionary programme, inflation was worsening and the Chancellor had publicly cast doubts on his willingness to support sterling parity. So, when in April and May 1972 the reported balance of payments figures showed some deterioration, many sterling holders decided the wise course of action was to swap their pounds for one of the strong currencies. At its height, the run on the pound depleted the reserves by some $2.5 billion in just six days. The UK was forced to leave the European snake and the pound was floated. In fact, within the following eighteen months many other nations followed the British example, gave up the struggle to maintain stable rates and introduced various forms of floating exchange rate regimes. The Bretton Woods system of stable par-value exchange rates had ended; Britain's decision of June 1972 had ushered in an new era in international monetary arrangements.

In Britain the initial intention had been to suspend the fixed parity commitment temporarily but economic circumstances quickly deteriorated, making continuance of the float imperative. Fundamentally, sterling's problems were a consequence of inflation and the subsequent derangement this caused to existing currency alignments. For the UK the steep rise in the international price of primary products in the early seventies sharply raised the import bill and weakened the current account. Non-oil commodity prices more than doubled, 1971-4, while the Organisation of Petroleum Exporting Countries (OPEC) was able to take advantage of increased demand (as the industrial world, in particular, was nearing the end of an expansionary phase) and restricted supply (the Arab-Israeli conflict and an effective cartel arrangement) to quadruple 'official' oil prices between the end of 1972 and the beginning of 1974.[43] The individual decisions of most other industrial nations to follow the UK's lead, and float, also diminished the prospects of an early return to a stable rate for sterling. By raising costs the commodity price rises of the 1970s added to Britain's already high inflation rate. As Table 15.3 shows, British consumer prices were rising at an annual rate of about 7-9 per cent during 1972 and 1973, but this rose sharply to 16 per cent in 1974, peaked at 24.3 per cent in 1975 and remained at historically high levels (with a dip in 1978) into the next decade. Even in the early seventies, Britain's inflation rate was out of line with that of other industrial nations but the discrepancy widened sharply during the rest of the decade.

There is much debate as to the relative contribution of the main 'causes' of Britain's inflation in this period and, in particular, a divide exists between those who emphasise rising costs through increased import prices and/or greater wage-push, and

Table 15.3: Inflation in the Industrial World, 1970-84. Consumer prices, percentage change over previous year.

| Year, 1970-84 | UK | USA | Japan | France | Germany | Italy | Industrial Countries |
|---|---|---|---|---|---|---|---|
| '70 | 6.4 | 5.9 | 7.6 | 5.9 | 3.4 | 4.9 | 5.6 |
| '71 | 9.5 | 4.3 | 6.1 | 5.5 | 5.2 | 5.7 | 4.6 |
| '72 | 7.1 | 3.3 | 4.5 | 6.2 | 5.5 | 5.7 | 4.6 |
| '73 | 9.2 | 6.2 | 11.7 | 7.3 | 7.0 | 10.8 | 7.6 |
| '74 | 15.9 | 11.0 | 24.4 | 13.7 | 7.0 | 19.1 | 13.3 |
| '75 | 24.3 | 9.1 | 11.8 | 11.8 | 5.9 | 17.0 | 11.1 |
| '76 | 16.6 | 5.8 | 9.3 | 9.6 | 4.3 | 16.8 | 8.3 |
| '77 | 15.8 | 6.5 | 8.0 | 9.4 | 3.7 | 17.0 | 8.4 |
| '78 | 8.3 | 7.6 | 3.8 | 9.1 | 2.7 | 12.1 | 7.2 |
| '79 | 13.4 | 11.3 | 3.6 | 10.7 | 4.1 | 14.8 | 9.1 |
| '80 | 18.0 | 13.5 | 8.0 | 13.8 | 5.4 | 21.2 | 11.9 |
| '81 | 11.9 | 10.4 | 4.9 | 13.4 | 6.3 | 17.8 | 9.9 |
| '82 | 8.6 | 6.2 | 2.6 | 11.8 | 5.3 | 16.5 | 7.5 |
| '83 | 4.6 | 3.2 | 1.8 | 9.6 | 3.3 | 14.7 | 5.0 |
| '84 | 5.0 | 4.3 | 2.3 | 7.4 | 2.4 | 10.8 | 4.8 |

*Source:* International Monetary Fund, *International Financial Statistics Yearbook*, vol. 38 (IMF, Washington DC, 1983), p. 105.

---

those who stress monetary growth.[44] Undoubtedly, if the commodity price boom was one major factor, so, too, was monetary expansion. There was rapid monetary growth in the UK after the government's decision to 'dash for growth' through fiscal and monetary expansion. The removal of restrictions on bank lending with the introduction of 'Competition and Credit Control' in 1971 was significant in sharply accelerating measured monetary growth. The budget concession of March 1972 which made most interest payments tax deductable, made borrowing yet more attractive. In all, between October 1971 and December 1973 bank loans to UK residents rose some two–and–one–half times. Although there is some uncertainty as to the extent that this measured 'actual' expansion as opposed to re–intermediation, monetary growth on such a scale offers an important explanation of the ensuing inflation.[45]

*Exchange Rate Volatility*
Supporters of floating rates suggested that such a regime would be more stable than the par–value system in the sense that there would be no sharp discontinuities of the sort caused when major balance of payments disparities arose for countries wedded to fixed exchange rates.[46] Here, government–inspired deflations/inflations, or devaluations/revaluations, had proven to be disruptive, more so than the continuous adjustment of a floating rate. Theoretically, if the currency were allowed to float freely (without government intervention) changes in the currency's value would be continuous, with instant response to changing demand and supply conditions in the foreign exchange markets. Each change would, thus, be relatively small and over the long–term adjustments would be gradual as they reflected changes in, say, relative inflation rates in different countries. If higher inflation in the UK, for example, threatened to make British goods less competitive, the effect on the pound would be a continuous depreciation (theoretically at the same pace as the change in the ratio of British to world prices), obviating the impact on the balance of payments. A floating exchange rate, it was argued, provided an efficient and effective means of exchange adjustment to a country's underlying trading position.

Moreover, supporters of floating exchange rates claimed that the overall effect of free market speculation would be to increase the degree of currency stability. The argument was that profit–maximising action by speculators would tend to smooth out random price deviations around the 'normal' exchange rate which reflected underlying economic conditions. For instance, if the market price rose above the 'normal' level, speculators as a group would anticipate a fall in the near-future and sell the currency, thus checking the price rise. The reverse would happen with a rate depreciation. Any change in the underlying conditions (e.g. disparities in national inflation rates) would still cause exchange rate movements, but speculation would reduce the degree of oscillation around these normal, or 'trend' movements.

In the late 1960s and early 1970s, such attributes seemed very attractive when compared to the Bretton Woods par-value system, within which changes in sterling (especially the 1967 devaluation) had been the cumulation of tortuous political decisions and had been accompanied by – indeed provoked by – large-scale speculative movements. In a freely floating regime, it was argued, the opportunities for speculative gains would be severely circumscribed as rate changes would be the outcome of thousands of individual market decisions, rather than the result of governmental judgement.

Figure 15.1 shows quarterly movements in the dollar-sterling exchange rate, 1972–85, and in the more broadly-based index of sterling's value against a weighted average of overseas currencies, 1975–85. Over the period as a whole the pound depreciated considerably – from $2.6 in early 1972 to around $1.2–1.4 in 1985, a decline of around 50 per cent; and for the index, from a peak value of 105 in the spring of 1975 to about 80 by 1985, a fall of some 24 per cent. In general terms, this depreciation reflected the fact that the UK experienced higher inflation rates than most other developed nations. However, the correlation between currency depreciation and inflation rates was far from precise; other factors had important effects, too. Of particular interest here was the sharp reversal of trend registered in the sterling index between 1978 and 1980 when there was a rise of 25 per cent before a further long-term decline set in.

Part of the explanation for the buoyancy of sterling during 1979 and 1980 lay in the strength of Britain's current account as the economy went into

Figure 15.1: Sterling Exchange Rates, quarterly, 1972-1985.

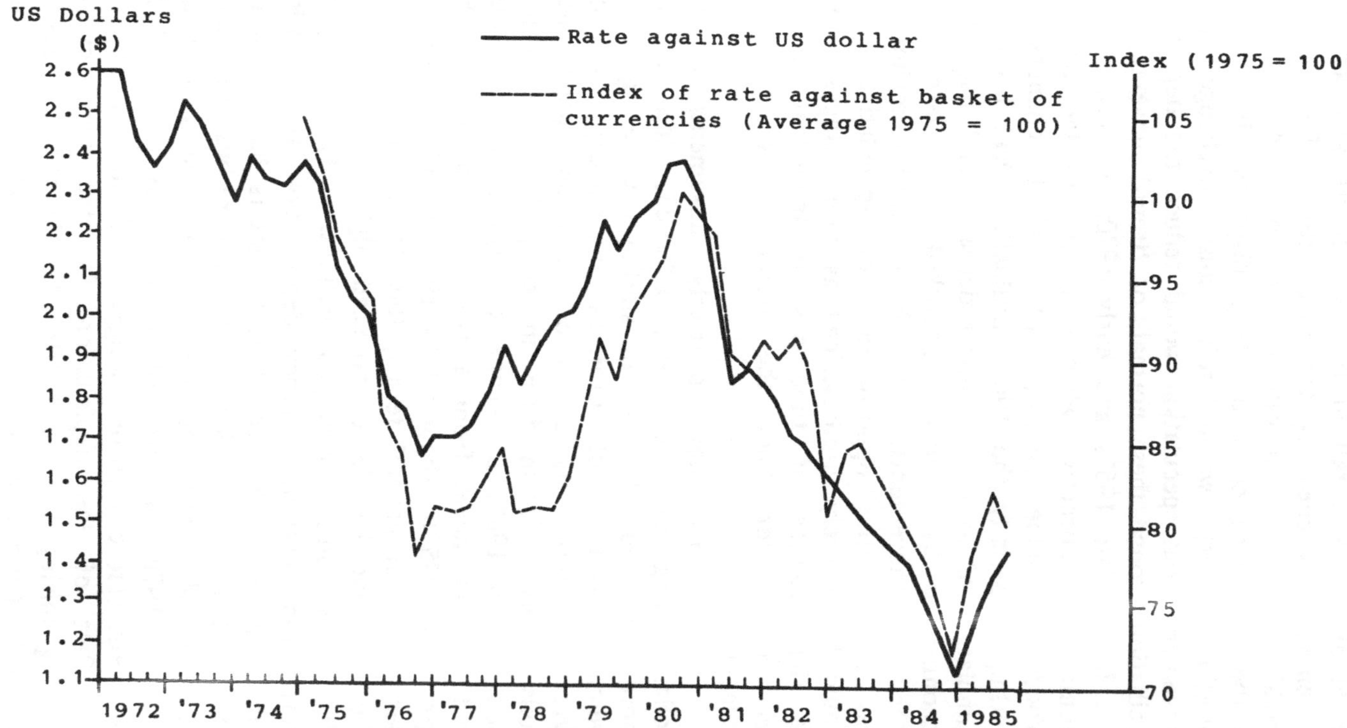


Source: Central Statistical Office, *Economic Trends*

deep recession. Recession eased the demand for imports of raw materials and other goods. Of significance, too, was the growing oil output from the North Sea. The commodity and oil price rises of the early 1970s obviously damaged the trading account of large commodity-importing nations like the UK. However, by the time of the second set of oil price hikes in 1978-9 the UK had become an important producer of oil in her own right. As a result Britain's current account balance was much stronger. This in itself increased demand for sterling and greater confidence encouraged an inflow of capital funds - sterling seemed to offer a haven for capital funds seeking protection from the potential depreciation of the currencies of oil-importing nations such as Japan and Germany. It seems that there was also a speculative element as demand for sterling was boosted by a growing belief that the rate would continue to rise. At this time the appreciation of the pound went so far, in fact, as to attract major criticism, particularly from the Cambridge Economic Policy Group (CEPG) which bemoaned the adverse effects on the competitiveness of British manufacturing.[47] The CEPG argued that British manufacturers were not only having to cope with a world-wide recession but were also suffering from a rising exchange rate which sharply reduced exporters' revenue per unit of sales. In 1979 unemployment already stood at historically high rates when the UK entered its most severe recession since 1929-32 and the 'uncompetitive' pound severely handicapped exporters and added to unemployment. Manufacturers found it more difficult to compete, export markets were lost, importers won a larger share of the domestic markets and the decline in manufacturing employment quickened. The CEPG acknowledged that the lack of manufacturing competitiveness - indeed, the whole 'de-industrialising' process - was a long-term phenomenon the origins of which went back much further than the 1970s, but they were highly critical of government for 'allowing' an appreciation of sterling at this critical time. For them, the rising pound greatly exacerbated the manufacturing sector's underlying problems, forcing severe contraction in the midst of an international recession.

In other respects, too, government monetary policy was a factor in keeping the exchange rate higher than critics such as the CEPG considered appropriate. In response to the problems caused by inflation, the Labour government of the late 1970s and, more ostentatiously, the Conservative government elected in 1979, avowed tight monetary policies. The associated high[48] interest rates further encouraged capital flows into the UK, adding to the buoyant demand for sterling. More recently (1984–6) the authorities have been concerned to 'lean into the wind' in foreign exchange markets, particularly to discourage too rapid a fall in the exchange rate because of the inflationary impact it could have in pushing up import prices.[49] In other words, the authorities have been prepared to use the reserves to buy sterling when demand has fallen too sharply and to discourage so rapid a fall in short-term interest rates that demand for the currency could be badly affected.[50] The float has not been 'free' or 'clean', either in the UK or elsewhere.

Apart from significant changes on trend since the float, on occasions the exchange rate has been volatile over the very short-term (daily or weekly) and, as Figure 15.1 shows, there has also been a significant degree of oscillation over somewhat longer periods (quarterly averages are plotted). Indeed, in terms of exchange rate instability the period since 1971 has been unique in modern British history. Previous sections of the book have emphasised the contrasting stability of earlier periods: the narrowness of fluctuations after the establishment of gold convertibility in 1821; the relative rigidity of the classical gold standard after the 1870s; the return to fixed rates in the 1920s; the managed stability of the pound after devaluation in 1931; and the establishment of official par-values under the IMF. Since 1972, though, the certainty inherent in a successful par-value regime has been lost. On a day-to-day basis, private traders and financiers have been able - at a cost - to militate against the uncertainty for individual transactions (e.g. whether or not the price agreed would be worth the same in sterling when the balance was paid in the future) through dealings in the forward exchange markets. In general, though, importers and exporters have had to operate in a much less certain environment - for the short, medium and long-terms the values of the currencies in which traders conduct their business have been less predictable. Figure 15.1 illustrates the extent of oscillation. In the headlong tumble of the pound during 1975-76, the broadly-based based index of sterling fell by about 20 per cent in all (2nd quarter, 1975 to 1st quarter, 1977), a greater amount than the devaluation of 1967. Between the first and second quarters of 1976 alone, the pound's international value dropped by 8 per cent. There were also sharp movements in the opposite direction. For instance, between the third quarter of 1977 and the first quarter of 1978 the pound appreciated by about 5 per cent, although it fell back again, by almost 6 per cent over the next quarter. Another sharp about-turn occurred at the beginning of 1985; and there have been many examples of shorter-term oscillations.

*The Importance of Capital Flows*

Short-term capital flows have continued to be important under the new system and these have been significant transmitters of instability.[51] For instance, not long into the float the pound came under heavy pressure in the summer and autumn of 1973 with the current account in a weak position, and with general uncertainty over the government's ability to contain domestic inflation. At one point in September, sterling temporarily fell by about 7 per cent in just one day, in response to a sharp withdrawal of short-term balances.[52] Here sterling assets were being offloaded by 'speculators' in exchange for strong currencies such as the mark. The German authorities sought to hold the value of the mark relative to sterling (and dollars) by direct intervention in exchange markets but, if anything, this further encouraged expectations of a realignment (sterling depreciation/mark appreciation). Indeed, generally, speculative movements of this sort have continued to be generated by official interventions. There have also been episodes of speculative buying of sterling, as in 1977 after the UK authorities had concluded an agreement for IMF credits which the foreign exchange markets viewed favourably because of its stipulations about the control of domestic inflation. Also as Britain's North Sea oil became of greater importance to the balance of payments from the late 1970s, fluctuations in world oil prices have been the source of speculation about the future course of exchange rates and have affected sterling accordingly. Finally, very recently, in the mid-1980s, there have been sharp speculative movements in and out of dollars which on occasions seriously altered the international value of sterling.

It is obvious that the influence of capital account movements did not diminish after the abandonment of the fixed exchange parity and, as the above illustrations show, they continued to have significant effects on the exchange rate irrespective of underlying trading positions. In other words, speculative activity has not always been benign in smoothing out fluctuations in exchange rates along the lines suggested by some supporters of floating rates. Instead it is commonly accepted that speculative capital movements have just as readily reinforced deviations in rates. As sterling's experience shows, when market price has fallen, a common response has been for market agents to sell, strengthening the price fall. The reverse has happened when the rate has appreciated, with a 'halo effect' attracting speculative purchases and further price rises.

In this period, in fact, UK money and capital markets have become more closely integrated into world markets and this has enhanced the potential role of international capital flows. One particular step towards greater integration was taken in October 1979 when the British government removed all restrictions on the freedom of UK residents to buy foreign currencies.[53] Tight controls over foreign exchange transactions had been imposed during World War II and although they were relaxed after the war, they were never abolished. Indeed the balance of payments weakness of the 1960s reversed the process of relaxation. Even after the pound was floated, difficulties on the balance of payments continued to offer justification for the retention of controls, although membership of the EEC since 1973 established a formal commitment to their abolition for inter–Community transactions. By the late seventies, however, Britain's healthier balance of payments weakened the arguments for retaining controls. Not only did the stronger pound mean that it was difficult to argue for the need to protect the reserves, but also a case could be made for encouraging the purchase of overseas assets so as to prevent the exchange rate rising too high in the wake of North Sea oil euphoria. At the end of 1977 constraints on direct investment in other EEC countries were relaxed and after the election of a government with a general commitment to encouraging greater market freedom, restrictions on capital flows to other parts of the world were removed in October 1979.

A more pervasive influence on the greater integration of world financial markets was the development and operation of off–shore financial institutions, particularly in the eurocurrency markets which have already been discussed in Chapter 11.[54] The British offices of many foreign banks and the overseas departments and subsidiaries of British banks have been very active in developing a market for *ex patria* liquid balances, particularly dollar balances in Europe. Competition for both borrowing and lending has been keen, in all creating an integrated international money market with a common interest rate structure. Continuing technical improvements in communication methods used by financiers have facilitated this move to a unified market. In effect it has become even easier to transfer funds internationally. A main advantage has been increased allocative efficiency within international money markets.

The creation of eurodollars has also added - some say significantly - to the world's supply of liquid balances and to the world's supply of monetary reserves, as monetary authorities have added dollar claims on eurobanks to their foreign currency holdings.[55] But there have also been disadvantages associated with the increased international mobility of short-term capital funds, for it has meant that 'destabilising' flows can occur more readily in response, say, to interest rate differentials between one financial centre and another, or in response to speculation about the future course for exchange rate movements. According to Robert Roosa, for instance:

> ... earlier this century, the preponderance of international capital flows ... reflected business decisions to finance trade or to establish producing facilities in foreign countries. Now ... it seems apparent that the dominant proportions of the investment funds actually in movement internationally today reflects instead decisions concerning portfolio holdings (both short term and long term), as financial or business concerns attempt to diversify their risks and improve their financial returns.[56]

According to this view, then, the emergence of large-scale off-shore money and capital markets has meant that international investment flows have occurred less in response to decisions about the purchase of physical capital assets than to more strictly financial considerations. These movements can be destabilising in the sense that the currency flows may be inconsistent with national objectives regarding, say, the appropriate exchange rate, the size of the reserves or the level of domestic interest rates. From an international perspective, if monetary authorities collectively seek to moderate the extent of exchange rate fluctuations, the greater ease with which speculative funds can be transferred may well run counter to official policy.

The existence of 'footloose' international liquid

assets was not a new phenomenon of the seventies and eighties, however. None the less, the scale of expansion has been impressive. Worldwide, the foreign liabilities of deposit banks rose more than eleven-fold, to $2,505 billion between 1970 and 1984, with the UK's bank liabilities to foreigners going up fifteen-fold (to $531 billion) in the same period.[57] The expansion was partly a result of greater intermediation and partly a result of the sharp increase in the supply of reserve assets, especially US dollars. One important source of funds for eurocurrency institutions was the re-investment of the large oil revenues from the OPEC countries consequent upon the price hikes of 1973 and 1979-80.[58] These price rises forced major balance of payments readjustments. The oil exporters initially accumulated massive surpluses, a significant part (some 40 per cent) of which they re-invested with the eurocurrency banks where they could earn a competitive interest rate on quite liquid balances. The oil importers, especially developing nations like Brazil and Mexico which could not readily boost exports to OPEC members, sought to finance their balance of payments deficits through borrowing in commercial financial markets, including from eurodollar banks. Thus, the monetary institutions of the West were able to exploit the intermediation potential inherent in this massive recycling problem, although subsequently some of the debtor-nations found great difficutly in meeting repayment schedules (or even interest rate commitments) and a significant number of banks have had to 'roll-over' or even 'write-off' the debts.

It was this participation in the international intermediation boom that helped retain the importance of City of London institutions within world money markets; they are no longer dependent upon the international role of sterling. Indeed, the floating of the pound reduced further that currency's already diminished reserve function because its value was no longer guaranteed to those monetary authorities holding sterling. The decline of the pound during 1975 and 1976 (Figure 15.1) was so steep, in fact, that remaining official holders of sterling were obliged to consider diversifying into other currencies on a significant scale. The British authorities responded by contracting a new Basle agreement in 1976, winning central bank credits of $3 billion to offset such official withdrawals. In the event the turnround in sterling's fortunes in the late seventies meant that there was no need to draw on this facility. Such manoeuvrings were but the vestiges of the once extensive international reserve function; in effect the floating of the pound marked the end of the Sterling Area. Even so, privately-held balances of sterling have remained important, and the rapid expansion of Euro-currency markets has helped retain and strengthen the international business of London-based banks.

*Overview*

In conclusion it is worth emphasising the obvious, lest it be overlooked. Since 1972 not just the value of the pound but the conduct of monetary and other economic policy - indeed, the course of British economic fortunes - have continued to be heavily influenced by external factors. A floating exchange rate has been no panacea for the country's main economic problems of high inflation rates, low productivity growth and mass unemployment. On the other hand, given the shocks administered to Britain's economy by sharp changes in the terms of trade, world recession and the historically high and variable inflation rates at home and abroad, it is inconceivable that a fixed exchange rate could have been maintained. The economic and political strains would have been too great. In this sense floating the pound was acknowledging the inevitable. It undoubtedly eased some of the constraints on domestic policy, allowing a greater degree of discretion to the authorities in their response to changes on the external account. Real constraints have remained, however - the greater amount of discretion gained is only a question of degree. In practice, the authorities could not act irrespective of the exchange rate; they could not permit inflation to go on unabated without incurring a sharp depreciation of the exchange rate which involved 'real' costs in the form of dearer imports of raw materials and commodities.

The experience of the floating pound has also highlighted the broader question raised throughout history whenever flexible exchange rates have been allowed: what determines the rate of monetary expansion? With an international system of stable exchange rates, monetary growth and the rate of price changes in any one country cannot get much out of line with that of competitors without affecting the reserves. Floating exchange rates relax that check and permit divergent monetary growth and inflation rates. Indeed, removal of the constraint was the major motive for Britain's float in the first place, but its continuation enabled British monetary and price experience to diverge from that of other manufacturing nations. Hence the policy dilemma - floating eased the adjustment to the oil price shocks and international trade fluctuations of the seventies, but it also removed an important constraint on the inflationary process. In turn, it was the high rates of inflation experienced in the period that provoked repeated government attempts to impose tight monetary and fiscal constraints and to use incomes policies. The abandonment of a fixed exchange rate may have increased policy options but the paramount importance of the external account to domestic policy has remained.

## FURTHER READING

Alec Cairncross and Barry Eichengreen, *Sterling in Decline. The Devaluations of 1931, 1949 and 1967* (Basil Blackwell, Oxford, 1983).

Susan Strange, *Sterling and British Policy* (Oxford University Press for the Royal Institute of International Affairs, London, 1971).

Robert Solomon, *The International Monetary System, 1945–1981* (Harper & Row, New York, 1982).

Victor Argy, *The Postwar International Money Crisis: An Analysis* (Allen & Unwin, London, 1981).

W.M. Scammell, *The International Economy since 1945* (Macmillan, London, 1980, reprinted 1982).

NOTES

1. Details in C.H. Feinstein, *National Income, Expenditure and Output of the United Kingdom, 1855–1965* (Cambridge University Press, Cambridge, 1972), Table 5, p. T17; and CSO, *United Kingdom National Accounts* [Blue Book], (HMSO, London, 1985), Table 1.2, pp. 2–3.

2. London and Cambridge Economic Service, *The British Economy. Key Statistics, 1900–1970* (Times Newspapers Ltd, London, 1971), Table N; and *National Institute Economic Review*, 116, May 1980, Table 22.

3. For a lively polemical view see Sidney Pollard, *The Wasting of the British Economy* (Croom Helm, London, 1982). Also see John Eatwell, *Whatever Happened to Britain? The Economics of Decline* (Duckworth for the BBC, London, 1982).

4. Frank Thomas Blackaby, (ed.), *De-Industrialisation* (Heinemann, London, 1979); and David Coates and John Hillard (eds.), *The Economic Decline of Modern Britain* (Wheatsheaf Books, Brighton, 1986).

5. *Economic Policy Review* (later *Cambridge Economic Policy Review*), *passim*; Francis Cripps and Wynne Godley, 'Control of Imports as a Means to Full Employment and the Expansion of World Trade: The UK's Case', *Cambridge Journal of Economics*, vol. 2, 1978, pp. 327–34. For a similar view see Douglas Jay, *Sterling. Its Use and Misuse: A Plea for Moderation* (Sidgwick & Jackson, London, 1985), pp. 107, 130, 240–1.

6. N. Kaldor, 'Conflicts in National Economic Objectives' in Charles Feinstein (ed.), *The Managed Economy* (Oxford University Press, Oxford, 1983), pp. 169–84.

7. 'Overseas Sterling Balances, 1963–1973' *Bank of England Quarterly Bulletin (BEQB)*, vol. 14, June 1974, p. 162, for estimates. Also see 'Sterling in the World Today', *Midland Bank Review*, Feb. 1956, pp. 1–7.

8. 'New Series of External Liabilities and

Claims in Sterling', *BEQB*, vol. 3, June 1963, pp. 103–5.

9. A.R. Conan, *The Problem of Sterling* (Macmillan, London, 1966), p. 83.

10. *Committee on the Working of the Monetary System*, [Radcliffe]. *Principal Memoranda* (HMSO, London, 1960), vol. 1, p. 16.

11. Susan Strange, *Sterling and British Policy* (Oxford University Press for the Royal Institute of International Affairs, London, 1971), p. 62. More generally see Phillip W. Bell, *The Sterling Area in the Postwar World* (Oxford University Press, Oxford, 1956); A.R. Conan, *The Sterling Area* (Macmillan, London, 1952); Benjamin J. Cohen, *The Future of Sterling as an International Currency* (Macmillan, London, 1971).

12. Richard N. Cooper, 'The Balance of Payments' in Richard E. Caves *et al*, *Britain's Economic Prospects* (Allen & Unwin, London, 1968), p. 181.

13. Ibid., p. 182.

14. On the internal debates over how quickly to re-establish convertibility – and even over the desirability of a floating exchange rate – see J.C.R. Dow, *The Management of the British Economy, 1945–60* (Cambridge University Press, Cambridge, 1964), pp. 80–90.

15. Conan, *Problem of Sterling*, p. 80.

16. 'The Position of Sterling: Background Material', *Midland Bank Review*, Aug. 1960, pp. 8–16; and 'Sterling as a "Key" Currency', *Midland Bank Review*, Aug. 1963, pp. 3–12.

17. Strange, *Sterling*, for instance, argues that the *main* cause of poor British economic performance 'has not been the British economy but rather the decline of sterling and the failure of British policy to adapt to that decline.' (p. 300). On the consequences for domestic policy of the political commitment to a fixed exchange rate in the 1960s see Roger Opie, 'Economic Planning and Growth' in Feinstein (ed.), *Managed Economy*, pp. 147–68.

18. For a narrative of these years see F.T.

Blackaby (ed.), *British Economic Policy, 1960–74: Demand Management*, students' edn (Cambridge University Press, Cambridge, 1979), pp. 23–8.

19. Harold Wilson, *The Labour Government, 1964–1970: A Personal Record* (Weidenfeld & Nicolson and Michael Joseph, London, 1971), p. 6.

20. J.H.B. Tew, 'Policies Aimed at Improving the Balance of Payments' in Blackaby, *British Economic Policy*, pp. 312–4; Also see Samuel Brittan, *Steering the Economy. The Role of the Treasury* (Secker & Warburg, London, 1969), especially pp. 178–180.

21. Harold Wilson, *The New Britain: Labour's Plan* (Penguin, Harmondsworth, 1964), especially chs. 2 and 3.

22. *Financial Times*, 23–28 Nov. 1964.

23. Brinley Davies, *The United Kingdom and the World Monetary System*, 3rd edn (Heinemann, London, 1979), p. 118.

24. Alec Cairncross and Barry Eichengreen, *Sterling in Decline. The Devaluations of 1931, 1949 and 1967* (Basil Blackwell, Oxford, 1983), pp. 215–6. For a brief, 'factual' account of devaluation see 'Devaluation – For the Record', *Midland Bank Review*, Feb. 1968, pp. 15–18; and the *Financial Times* in the weeks before and after 17 November for the atmosphere of 'crisis'.

25. See, for instance, *The Economist*, vol. 225, 25 Nov. 1967, pp. 868–73. The profit for speculators was gained by selling high priced sterling for 'hard' currencies and, then (after devaluation), buying it back at the new, lower price.

26. Gerald Meier, *Problems of a World Monetary Order*, 2nd edn (Oxford University Press, Oxford, 1982), pp. 65–8.

27. Although the main problem in 1949 had been the rate with the 'scarce' dollar.

28. Brinley Davies, *The United Kingdom*, pp. 118–20.

29. 'Strains' that the Dollar will have to Bear', *Financial Times*, 22 Nov. 1967, p. 16, for an illustration of how contemporaries viewed the link

between sterling and the dollar.

30. Among the best general surveys see Robert Solomon, *The International Monetary System, 1945–1981*, (Harper and Row, New York, 1982), especially pp. 96–113; Meier, *World Monetary Order*, chs. 3–5; W.M. Scammell, *The International Economy since 1945* (Macmillan, London, 1980, reprinted 1982), Part Three; and Brian Tew, *The Evolution of the International Monetary System, 1945–81* 2nd edn (Hutchinson, London, 1982), ch. 14.

31. Cheryl Payer, *The Debt Trap. The IMF and the Third World* (Monthly Review Press, New York and London, 1974).

32. Cairncross and Eichengreen, *Sterling in Decline*, chs. 5 and 6. The more general case for easing the balance of payments and inflationary difficulties through depressing aggregate demand relative to capacity is made in F.W. Paish, 'Inflation and the Balance of Payments in the United Kingdom, 1952–67', in Feinstein (ed.), *Managed Economy*, pp. 133–46. For an insight into the advice being given by the Bank of England at the time see *Bank of England Quarterly Bulletin*, vol. 8, June 1968, pp. 171–4.

33. Kaldor, 'National Economic Objectives', for instance. See W. Beckerman and Associates, *The British Economy in 1975* (Cambridge University Press, Cambridge, 1965).

34. In fact, contemporary estimates showed the position to be worse than we now know it to have been.

35. An excellent summary of some of the more important assessments appears in Cairncross and Eichengreen, *Sterling in Decline*, pp. 197–213. On the theoretical arguments over whether or not the effect of devaluation on the balance of payments is permanent see R.J. Ball, T. Burns and J.S.E. Laury, 'The Role of Exchange Rate Changes in Balance of Payments Adjustment – the United Kingdom Case', *Economic Journal*, vol. 87, 1977, pp. 1–29.

36. 'Overseas Sterling Balances', *BEQB*, June 1974, especially pp. 164–71.

37. For a succinct discussion of the general

policy implications of a floating exchange rate see J.S. Metcalfe, 'Foreign Trade and Balance of Payments' in A.R. Prest and D.J. Coppock (eds.), *The UK Economy. A Manual of Applied Economics*, 9th edn (Weidenfeld & Nicolson, London, 1982), pp. 151–4.

38. *Parliamentary Debates. Commons*, vol. 833, 1971–72 Session, 21 March 1972, p. 1354.

39. For instance, M. Friedman, 'The Case for Flexible Exchange Rates', in *Essays in Positive Economics* (University of Chicago Press, Chicago, 1953), pp. 157–203; J.E. Meade, 'The Case for Variable Exchange Rates', *Three Banks' Review*, No. 27, Sept. 1955, pp. 3–27; and Harry G. Johnson and John E. Nash, *UK and Floating Exchanges*, Hobart Paper No. 46 (Institute of Economic Affairs, London, 1969).

40. Victor Argy, *The Postwar International Money Crisis. An Analysis* (Allen & Unwin, London, 1981), pp. 36–43, and 'A Return to Bretton Woods?', *Midland Bank Review*, Autumn/Winter 1981, pp. 30–1 for a brief assessment; also see references in Note 30.

41. *World Economic Survey, 1971: Current Economic Developments* (United Nations, New York, 1972), pp. 3–8; John Williamson, *The Failure of World Monetary Reform, 1971–74* (Nelson, Sunbury-on-Thames, 1977), especially pp. 53–60.

42. On the Eurosnake see Rainer Hellmann, *Gold, the Dollar and the European Currency System* (Praeger, London, 1979), especially ch. 3.

43. Angus Maddison, *Phases of Capitalist Development* (Oxford University Press, Oxford, 1982), pp. 139–44.

44. Two representative views of different theoretical approaches are D. Laidler, 'Inflation in Britain: A Monetarist Perspective', *American Economic Review*, vol. 66, 1976, pp. 485–500; and John Hicks, 'What is Wrong with Monetarism?', *Lloyds Bank Review*, Oct. 1975, pp. 1–13.

45. J. Ball and T. Burns, 'The Inflationary Mechanisms in the UK Economy', *American Economic Review*, vol. 66, 1976, pp. 479–82; and John Williamson and Geoffrey E. Wood, 'The British

Inflation: Indigenous or Imported?', ibid., pp. 520–31.

46. Two recent, succinct summaries of the case for and against floating exchange rates can be found in Bo Södersten, *International Economics*, 2nd edn (Macmillan, London, reprint 1981), ch. 27; and in Peter H. Lindert and Charles P. Kindleberger, *International Economics*, 7th edn (Richard D. Irwin, Homewood, Illinois, 1982), ch. 21. An early case for floating rates was made in M. Friedman, 'The Case for Flexible Exchange Rates'. Also see A. Lanyi, *The Case for Floating Exchange Rates Reconsidered*, Essays in International Finance, No. 72 (Princeton University, Princeton, New Jersey, 1969); and Johnson and Nash, *UK and Floating Exchanges*.

47. 'Will British Industry Recover?', *Cambridge Economic Policy Review*, vol. 8, April 1982, p. 25; and 'Britain's Economic Crisis and Possible Remedies', *CEPR*, vol. 6, April 1980, pp. 7, 11, 15–16. For a more general assessment of the impact of North Sea oil see P.J. Forsyth and J.A. Kay, 'The Economic Implications of North Sea Oil Revenues', *Fiscal Studies*, vol. 1, July 1980, pp. 1–28; and Marian E. Bond and Adalbert Knobl, 'Some Implications of North Sea Oil for the UK Economy', *International Monetary Fund Staff Papers*, vol. 29, Sept. 1982, pp. 363–97.

48. That is, higher than in the absence of a tight monetary stance.

49. Such action is wholly consistent with the advice from the International Monetary Fund. See 'Guidelines for Management of Floating', *IMF Survey*, 17 June 1974, pp. 181–3.

50. *Financial Times*, 7 June 1986.

51. Robert V. Roosa, *Economic Instability and Flexible Exchange Rates* (Institute of Southeast Asian Studies, Singapore, 1983).

52. *Financial Times*, 7 Sept. 1973.

53. *Bank of England Quarterly Bulletin*, vol. 19, Sept. 1979, pp. 260, 274; and Dec. 1979, pp. 370–1. For an historical background to Britain's use of exchange controls and the argument for their abolition see Robert Miller and John B. Wood, *Exchange Control for Ever?* (Institute of Economic

Affairs, London, 1979).

54. Pages 374–8.

55. For an assessment see Argy, *Postwar International Money Crisis*, ch. 7; and C. Freedman, 'The Euro-Dollar Market: Five Recent Studies', *Journal of Monetary Economics*, vol. 3, 1977, pp. 467–78.

56. Roosa, *Economic Instability*, p. 4.

57. International Monetary Fund, *International Financial Statistics. Yearbook*, (IMF, Washington DC, 1985), vol. 38, p. 63.

58. On the general re-intermediation and transfer problems created by the oil price rises see P.M. Oppenheimer and W.B. Reddaway, 'World Recession and World Debts', *Midland Bank Review*, Spring 1983, pp. 7–15.

Chapter Sixteen

# RETROSPECTIVE

It is opportune in this final section to provide an overview of the whole 160–year period by reiterating the more important, broad historical developments highlighted by the study. Once again it seems sensible to look, in turn, at each of the three functional divisions used throughout: at the commercial banking sector; at monetary policy; and at the UK's international financial position.

## COMMERCIAL BANKING SECTOR

It has been a main contention of this book that after a period of rapid expansion in the early and middle nineteenth century, the commercial banks suffered a long–term relative decline (in the rate of growth of bank liabilities, in the ratio of bank liabilities to total encashable assets and in the ratio of money balances to National Product). It was a decline which was discernible by the turn of the century, but one which has continued into recent times. This developmental profile, in itself, is not particularly controversial, although the early dating of the beginning of the decline – and its persistent nature – may be more of a surprise.

During the nineteenth century (as during the eighteenth), the developing British economy underwent a period of rapid monetisation. Earlier times had witnessed a decline in the use of barter and of payments in kind, with a corresponding rise in the use of money. But for the nineteenth century the most obvious process by which the public added to its money balances was through the expansion of commercial banking. More people opened bank accounts, bank liabilities (notes and deposits) formed a growing proportion of total money balances and these were increasingly used to effect payments. However, legal restrictions on the minimum face value of bank notes limited their use for retail and other small value transactions, especially in England and Wales where the lowest note denomination was £5. Legislation in the 1840s had imposed restrictions, too, on the total size of bank note circulations and such constraints helped ensure the continuing importance of coin right through until the First World War. But over the long term notes were not that important for bank growth – it was bank deposits that comprised by far the fastest growing component of the money stock. In effect, monetisation in the nineteenth century was almost synonymous with the expansion of bank deposits and the greater use of bankers' drafts and cheques.

It was within this context that there was a mushrooming in the number of banking offices. It was to be the joint-stock banks (permitted in England and Wales for the first time in 1826 and in Ireland in 1825, but with a much longer lineage in Scotland) that were to the fore in this pioneering phase, as their new branch networks stretched out to most parts of the country and encouraged more of the high and middle income groups to acquire the 'banking habit'.

Until the last quarter of the nineteenth century, the structure of the English banking system was characterised by a large number of relatively small banks. Indeed, for much of the century, there was a large body of private banking partnerships although, in aggregate, these were responsible for a dwindling proportion of total bank liabilities. Even the typical joint-stock bank in England was operating on a relatively small scale and confined its retail outlets to a particular town or district. For instance, in the mid-1870s there were 122 joint-stock banks in England

and Wales, on average operating ten branches in addition to their head offices and with each bank holding about £2 million of deposits. Up until this time retail banking was operating in a competititive market with a large number of suppliers of bank services. This was not true of Scotland, though. In Scotland a small number of 'national' banks had dominated the market from an early stage and restricted competition. This was to be the pattern of developments in England, too.

In the five decades before World War I there was a dramatic increase in the degree of market concentration within retail banking. It arose partly from the continued expansion of the larger joint-stock banks, as they built up branch systems into national networks, but, above all, it was the result of numerous mergers which sharply reduced the number of companies. By 1918 the 'Big Five' of Barclays, Lloyds, the Midland, the National Provincial and the Westminster controlled between them some 80 per cent of English and Welsh bank liabilities. This process of increasing concentration of market power only came to an end in 1918. In that year the Treasury Committee on Bank Amalgamations made clear the authorities' opposition to further mergers amongst the 'Big Five'. But, by then, oligopoly power was already firmly entrenched.

In the pre-1914 period the greater concentration of market power was accompanied by an increasing tendency to suppress price competition, a tendency which had hardened into overt practice by the 1920s. The impact of two world wars and the economic uncertainties of the inter-war years were instrumental in this process of consolidation. Here, the attitude of the authorities was critical. Both wars sharply increased public sector borrowing and the banks were obliged to alter radically the composition of their assets, by contracting loans to the private sector and sharply increasing their holdings of public sector liabilities. From the government's point of view, the rise in the National Debt increased the authorities' dependence on the banking sector and greatly enhanced the significance of stabilising the market for public sector debt and of being able to influence interest rates. Control of interest rates also assumed greater importance in the pursuit of broader economic goals (e.g. the maintenance of cheap money during the 1930s and 1940s). It was within this context that the authorities condoned existing restrictive practices and encouraged the further suppression of price competition in the discount market and amongst the clearing banks. This remained official policy after World War II. In fact, as the major political parties had now accepted a general responsibility for managing the economy, control over the clearing banks was elevated to a new status within the ambit of economic policy instruments. As a consequence, it was to be many years before the composition of the clearers' balance sheets began to resemble (what had been) a 'normal' peacetime structure.

The period of enhanced oligopoly power coincided with a slow-down in the growth of commercial bank liabilities – the end of the phase of rapid monetisation – and a loss of 'market share' for the banks as other financial institutions grew more quickly. The growth of non-bank financial intermediaries and their expanding provision of near-money assets other than bank deposits, has been a common feature of the process of economic maturity within industrial nations – a development commonly labelled, 'financial sophistication':

> By financial sophistication is meant both the emergence of a large number of close substitutes for money [e.g. building society shares] which reduce the demand for money as an asset; as well as the development of various methods of economizing on money balances, such as...the transfer of funds by telegraph, telephone or electronically...which reduce the transactions demand for money.[1]

It is the former process – the growth of financial intermediaries other than banks and the development of liquid assets other than bank notes and deposits - which has been stressed in this study.

The broadly coincidental emergence, on the one side, of a slow-down in the long-term expansion of bank deposits and the decline in the banks' relative position as suppliers of total encashable assets, and, on the other, of greater oligopoly power, begs the question of a causal relationship. Did one tendency reinforce the other? One view is that the relative decline of deposit banking within the total provision of financial services is a 'normal' development in capitalist economies. Taking this viewpoint, there was nothing unusual, in principle, about the course of British banking history. The contention in this study, though, is that, in practice, the creation of strong oligopolies in deposit banking and their propensity to suppress price competition, added to the relative retardation of clearing bank expansion. The merger booms of the late nineteenth and early twentieth centuries were a critical element in the process but, as has been argued, war and the attitude of the authorities helped 'institutionalise' the non-competitive attitude of the clearers.

There were some innovations and there was non-price competition amongst the banks themselves, but for a very long time the clearers remained wedded to a concept of compartmentalisation in the provision of financial services, a concept of specialisation. They concentrated on raising retail deposits from 'respectable' account holders, on maintaining a highly liquid asset structure and on providing credit at the short end of the market. They were slow to diversify and, as a result, it was left to other institutions to exploit the faster growing markets. It is true that after World War II, in particular, the clearers did take a stake in some of the new growth sectors through the creation of subsidiary companies, but it was not really until the 1970s - by which time the burden of war finance had been lifted and the strictures of government controls over lending, liquidity and interest rates had been relaxed - that the clearers displayed any noticeable orientation towards the market. Since then, of course, there has been much greater willingness to diversify and to compete actively on price. The importance of the historical perspective is that it shows how unusual this attitude and experience has been over the past one hundred years.

## MONETARY POLICY

Long-term changes in the nature and aims of monetary policy have been closely bound up with the changing role of the state in economic affairs. The beginning of the nineteenth century was characterised by a phase of liberalisation – with attacks on the Bank of England's monopoly of joint-stock banking in England and Wales (and similar curtailment of Bank of Ireland privileges), with legislative provision for greater freedom of entry of new firms into the banking business and with the repeal of the Usury Laws which had imposed a ceiling on interest rate charges. These measures heralded a long period of *laissez-faire* in monetary matters which, in essence, lasted until the First World War. State intervention was minimal, concerned largely with establishing an appropriate legislative framework (e.g. through changes in company law and controls over the note circulation). Within the classical orthodoxy of the pre-1914 world, in fact, an ultimate objective was to obviate the need for policy, to minimise state interference with the market mechanism.

In the sphere of monetary 'management' this was to be achieved through establishing a more or less automatic system which called for largely non-discretionary action by the authorities. Indeed, in this context, 'the authorities' were not the state, but the privately-owned Bank of England. It was the Bank which conducted the day-to-day operation of the system and it was the Bank which evolved any long-term strategies – ministers were involved only on those relatively rare occasions (such as banking crises) when monetary matters were thrust into the political arena.

The two main pillars of the legislative framework

were, first, the 1819 and 1821 Acts which established sterling as a fully-convertible gold currency on a fixed exchange rate and, secondly, the 1844 Bank Charter Act which sought to ensure that the size of the Bank's note liabilities was closely governed by movements in the level of the gold reserves. Within these constraints the Bank's objectives were closely circumscribed: to abide by its legal obligations, to avoid political controversy and to make a profit for shareholders. In practice, the Bank also accepted 'lender of last resort' responsibility for the City's money market. But it was particularly the obligation to maintain gold convertibility of its notes at par value that gave rise to whatever 'policy' there was. The Bank was obliged to maintain a reasonable level of gold reserves. In consequence, the Bank's management both reacted to threats to those reserves and began to seek ways of anticipating such threats. The Bank had to monitor potential sources of pressure for cash in the London money markets and (through its provincial offices, local banking connections and the like) to garner information on conditions throughout the country.

Over time methods improved. The main long-term development was the growing reliance on Bank rate. The Bank made no overt attempt to regulate the money supply, the focus of control being the 'price of credit', the rate of interest. In essence, Bank rate technique was relatively simple to operate: the rate would be raised when the reserves were falling (or were expected to) and lowered when the reserves were rising. Market rates were brought into line through the Bank's willingness to buy and sell in the money markets, through 'open market operations'. The so-called 'gold devices' were also used on occasions to influence the foreign exchanges but, according to R.S. Sayers, they were very much ancillary techniques of control.[2] In fact, generally in the period the Bank's exercise of discretion was marginal. For the most part it was a willing captive of the gold standard 'rules'.

The First World War brought a sharp break to

these arrangements, marking a watershed in the history of British monetary history. Three main consequences derived from the war. First, the conflict seriously undermined the long-term viability of the international gold standard. Not only was the 'free' operation of the system severely curtailed for the duration of hostilities, but for a number of years afterwards many countries (including the UK) found it impossible either to re-establish convertibility or to stabilise exchange rates. More significantly, though, the war both quickened the pace of Britain's international decline and seriously altered existing financial arrangements (war debts, reparations, etc.). In effect, the buoyancy and stability of the pre-1914 gold standard had been lost. The second major financial impact of the war was the creation of a massive upsurge in the size of the National Debt. Of necessity, this increased the authorities' involvement in money and capital markets. It also added an important, new dimension to the objectives of interest rate policy - all things being equal, the authorities wished to minimise the amount of interest paid on the National Debt. Finally, the war was also associated with an awakening of a greater concern by the state for the direction of economic affairs, a concern reinforced by the chronic nature of the unemployment and export problems which emerged in the 1920s.

Even so, the attempt to re-establish a new version of the gold standard during the 1920s bears witness to the strength of contemporary desires for external stability, even if this should seriously circumscribe domestic monetary autonomy. In the event, a return to the non-discretionary system of the pre-1914 world proved impossible and when the break with gold was forced on the authorities in 1931, it served to strengthen the broader trend towards more political involvement in economic matters. The battery of measures that followed inevitably involved the exercise of greater discretion, of more policy. The exchange rate regime decided upon was that of a 'managed float' and, domestically, the authorities opted for a low interest rate policy which they felt would aid recovery.

The general acceptance of a state responsibility for the conduct of monetary policy was reinforced by World War II and by the growing ascendancy of Keynesian economics which provided a theoretical *raison d'être* for greater political involvement in the management of the economy.

The Bank of England was taken into state ownership in 1946 but, rather ironically, monetary policy was largely neglected as a tool of economic management by the Labour government in the years immediately following the war. More reliance was placed on either direct controls (e.g. rationing) or, later in the life of the administration, on fiscal policy. It was not until 1951 that there was something of a revival in monetary policy, with some tentative moves to initiate a more active interest rate policy. For most of the period since then, monetary measures were commonly used as a supplement to (and support for) the main tool of post-war economic management, i.e. fiscal policy. However, on trend there has been a decline in the prominence of fiscal policy, as doubts have arisen over both the theoretical underpinnings of demand management and the effectiveness of Keynesian techniques in tackling the UK's economic problems in practice. This decline in the fortunes of Keynesian economics has been mirrored by the rise of 'monetarism'. This process culminated in 1979 with the election of a Conservative government which chose monetary policy as the principal weapon in its 'fight against inflation'. Fiscal policy was now playing the supporting role.

Within this general shift in the relative fortunes of macroeconomic policy, there have also been significant changes in both the meaning of 'monetary policy' and the techniques used to implement it. Initially the authorities modified traditional techniques to support the objectives of demand management – for example, by increasing interest rates to restrict domestic demand and/or to attract short-term capital to London. However, the operation of monetary policy within the broad Keynesian umbrella of the

1950s and 1960s was marked by a high degree of pragmatism. This was noticeable, for instance, in the authorities' approach to the imposition of quantitative ceilings on bank lending, in their use of controls over bank reserve ratios and in their *ad hoc* extension of constraints to financial institutions such as the finance houses.

For the 1970s and 1980s, the two main features have been the official sanctioning of a greater freedom for market institutions and agents, and the greater emphasis placed on control of the money supply. The former was partly ideological (especially with the election of Conservative governments in 1970 and 1979) but it also reflected the authorities' realistic acceptance that the use of selective controls of the type used in the 1960s, created serious market distortions and raised criticisms of partiality in the application of policy. A 'freer' market subjected to more general control offered an attractive pathway for future development. By the end of the seventies 'general control', of course, had come to be perceived as the setting of targets for monetary growth, with their attainment being secured through the Medium-Term Financial Strategy and, in the short run, through the use of an active interest rate policy. Despite the apparent political triumph of 'monetarism' in determining the objectives and main instruments of control, it has been suggested, in fact, that the Bank of England continued to uphold its tradition of pragmatism in matters of policy. There has been a greater commitment to economic dogma than in previous decades but the Bank – if not the Treasury – has left room for the return to *ad hoc* controls if the need should arise.

## THE UNITED KINGDOM AND THE INTERNATIONAL FINANCIAL SYSTEM

A major division of opinion exists between those who see the maintenance of stable exchange rates as a means of imposing an important discipline on domestic monetary authorities, and those who see it as an excessive constraint on national economic autonomy.

Such a divide was present in one form or other whenever questions of the exchange rate regime and balance of payments adjustment entered the arena of political debate. This was true of the Bullionist debates of the Napoleonic Wars (prior to the period covered by this book), of the controversy surrounding the passing of the 1844 Bank Charter Act, of the decision to return to the gold standard in 1925, of the determination on a 'managed float' in the 1930s, of the Bretton Woods' negotiations and of the exchange rate difficulties of the 1960s, 1970s and 1980s. The fact is, though, that for almost the whole 160 years covered by this study, the UK conducted its monetary policy within the rigours of a stable exchange rate. Excluding wartime, the only periods when this did not apply were the years from 1918 to 1925, from 1931 to 1939 and from 1972 to the present–day (1986). For the rest of the time British monetary policy was formally tethered to the vicissitudes of international money.

Of course, there were significant differences of detail in the various arrangements adopted over time. Up until the First World War the pound was locked firmly into the international gold standard, with the Bank of England only able to operate discretionary policy at the margin. The Bank may have been able to ride out a temporary disequilibrium - fall in sterling exchange rates and loss of reserves - but if the pressure were sustained, legal obligations left little option. Acceptance of such constraints was firmly entrenched in British political attitudes and it was only the Great War which disrupted these arrangements and raised the question of exchange rate policy. In the event, inflation (especially hyperinflation on the Continent) reinforced official fears of inconvertibility and confirmed the general commitment to a stable exchange rate. In fact, the new gold standard regime of 1925 to 1931 did not allow much more freedom than the 'classical' standard. But the country's economic problems were sorely to test this official faith in the gold standard, as the friction between international and national policy became blatant with the emergence of chronic unemployment. In some respects, then, the suspension of gold convertibility in 1931 (although not planned for) was welcomed as an opportunity to use greater discretion in domestic monetary matters. The fear of inflation did not disappear altogether, but it was less prominent in a period when prices were falling and unemployment rates were unprecedentedly high. Even so, while the creation of a 'floating pound' permitted more national autonomy during the 1930s, for most of the time the authorities, in fact, chose to intervene in such a way as to maintain a high degree of exchange rate stability.

The Bretton Woods' arrangements re-established the formal commitment to external stability, setting up a multilateral system of currency convertibility and fixed exchange rates. The need for some flexibility was now officially recognised, however, with the arrangements allowing national authorities to restrict international capital flows and to make formal adjustments to exchange rates. Nevertheless, in the aftermath of war most countries were unable, or unwilling, to accept the rigours of the new regime immediately and it was not until 1958 that many European states adopted full convertibility. In practice, too, the inbuilt flexibilities proved difficult to operate. The UK, for instance, found it hard to activate the devaluation option. More widely, arrangements were threatened by chronic balance of payments misalignments, especially USA deficits, and the system came to an end in the early 1970s under the strain of a very sharp rise in world commodity prices.

Since then attempts to rehabilitate a system of stable exchange rates have continued (so far, unsuccessfully). One concern has been over the effects of the instability generated by the sharp exchange rate fluctuations experienced during the 1970s and 1980s - for the UK (and many other countries) these have been on an unprecedented scale. There are anxieties, too, that floating exchange rates have greatly added to inflationary pressures by permitting the tremendous expansions that have occurred in domestic money supplies. As the pace of inflation in the UK has slowed down the prospects for the adoption of a greater degree of exchange rate stability have improved. At present (1986) this is acknowledged by the authorities' intervention in exchange markets to stabilise the value of sterling within an unpublished (and movable?) band. It may also be marked in the near future by a decision to join the European Monetary System. Again the critical choice is between, on the one hand, external stability and loss of national autonomy and, on the other, greater external instability wedded to more domestic discretion (or for those who fear inflation, more domestic 'irresponsibility').

Lest concern with the details of exchange rate regimes distract from the obvious, it must be stressed in any survey of international monetary arrangements that the main historical feature has been the UK's long-term economic decline. In the pre-1914 world Britain was the leading commercial and financial nation and, indeed, the gold standard is often portrayed as a British-centred system. Serious competitive weakness became obvious by the 1920s and this has proved to be the long-term pattern. After the Second World War the USA and the dollar dominated, the UK and sterling playing a supporting role. Even the imperial links that had been formalised through the creation of the Sterling Area generated their own strains on an economy which was undergoing a trend decline relative to other developed nations. From the 1960s, this retardation process seems to have accelerated and the UK is now a small economy in global terms. But it is still an economy which is heavily dependent on the external account. It is obvious, too, that the pace and direction of the economy's long-term performance, and its changing world status, were critical in determining the broad parameters in which both monetary policy and commercial money markets had to operate.

NOTES

1. Michael David Bordo and Lars Jonung, 'The Long-Run Behavior of the Income Velocity of

Circulation of Money in Five Advanced Countries, 1870–1975: An Institutional Approach', *Economic Enquiry*, vol. 19, no. 1, 1981, p. 98.

2. R.S. Sayers, *Central Banking after Bagehot* (Oxford Universtiy Press, Oxford, 1957), pp. 17–18.

# BIBLIOGRAPHY

## Official Publications and Reports


Central Statistical Office, *Annual Abstract of Statistics*.

Central Statistical Office, *Economic Trends*.

Department of Employment, *Gazette*.

H.M. Treasury, *Economic Progress Report*.

*Parliamentary Debates. Commons*.

*Select Committee on the Bank Acts*, Parl. Papers 1857 (Sess. 2), vol. 10.

*Report of the Royal Commission...[on] Recent Changes in the Relative Values of the Precious Metals...*, Parl. Papers, 1887, XXII.

*Report of the Royal Commission...[on] Recent Changes in the Relative Values of the Precious Metals...*, Parl. Papers, 1888, XLV.

*Interviews on the Banking and Currency Systems of England, Scotland, France, Germany, Switzerland and Italy*, National Monetary Commission, US Senate, 61st. Congress, 2nd. Session, Document no. 405 (Government Printing Office, Washington, 1910).

*Report of the Treasury Committee on Bank Amalgamations*, Cd. 9052, Parl. Papers 1918, VI, pp. 333–39.

*Committee on Currency and Foreign Exchanges. First Interim Report*, Cd. 9182 (HMSO, London, 1918) and *Final Report*, Cmd. 464 (HMSO, London, 1919).

*Report of the Committee on the Currency and Bank of England Note Issues*, Cmd. 2393, Parl. Papers 1924–5, IX.

*Committee on Finance and Industry. Report.* Cmd. 3897 (HMSO, London, 1931).

*White Paper on Employment Policy*, Cmd. 6527 (HMSO, London, 1944).

White Paper (prepared by the Treasury) on *Statistical Material Presented during Washing Negotiations*, Cmd. 6707, Dec. 1945.

*Committee on the Working of the Monetary System. Principal Memoranda of Evidence*, 3 vols. (HMSO, London, 1960) and *Report*, Cmnd. 827 (HMSO, London, 1960) and *Minutes of Evidence* (HMSO, London, 1960).

National Board for Prices and Incomes, *Report No. 34, Bank Charges*, Cmnd 3292 (HMSO, London, 1967).

Monopolies Commission, *Barclays Bank Ltd, Lloyds Bank Ltd and Martins Bank Ltd: A Report on the Proposed Merger* (HMSO, London, 1968)

*Committee* [on] *Consumer Credit. Report*, Cmnd. 4596 (2 vols., HMSO, London, 1971).

*Committee of Inquiry on Small Firms. Report*, Cmnd. 4811 (HMSO, London, 1971).

*Committee to Review National Savings. Report*, Cmnd. 5273 (HMSO, London, 1973).

*The Government's Expenditure Plans, 1980–81*, Cmnd. 7746 (HMSO, London, 1979).

*Committee to Review the Functioning of Financial Institutions. Report and Appendices*, Cmnd. 7937 (HMSO, London, 1980).

Green Paper on *Monetary Control*, Cmnd. 7858 (HMSO, London, 1980).

Treasury and Civil Service Committee, *Memoranda on Monetary Policy*, Parl. Papers 1979–80, 720. I–II (2 vols., HMSO, London, 1980).

Financial Statements and Budget Reports, 1980/81–1986/87 (HMSO, London, 1980–86).

Treasury and Civil Service Committee *Third Report on*

*Monetary Policy*, vol. 1; *Minutes of Evidence*, vol. 2; *Appendices*, vol. 3, Parl. Papers 1980–81, 163. I–III (HMSO, London, 1981).
*Building Societies. A New Framework*, Cmnd. 9316 (HMSO, London, 1984).
*Financial Statistics. Explanatory Handbook*, 1985 edition (HMSO, London, 1985).
Central Statistical Office, *United Kingdom National Accounts* [Blue Book] (HMSO, London, 1985).
United Nations, *World Economic Survey, 1971, Current Economic Developments* (United Nations, New York, 1972).

Books

Aldcroft, Derek H. *From Versailles to Wall Street, 1919–1929* (Allen Lane, London, 1977)
Argy, Victor *The Postwar International Money Crisis: An Analysis* (Allen & Unwin, London, 1981)
Artis, M.J. and M.K. Lewis *Monetary Control in the United Kingdom* (Philip Allan, Oxford, 1981)
Ashby, J.F. *The Story of the Banks* (Hutchinson & Co., London, 1934)
Bagehot, Walter *Lombard Street* (King, London, 1873)
Balogh, T. *Studies in Financial Organization* (Cambridge University Press, Cambridge, 1947)
Bank of England *The Development and Operation of Monetary Policy, 1960–1983* (Oxford University Press, Oxford, 1984)
Barker, T.C. and C.I. Savage *An Economic History of Transport in Britain*, 3rd edn (Hutchinson & Co., London, 1974)
Barrow, G.L. *The Emergence of the Irish Banking System, 1820–1845* (Gill & Macmillan, Dublin, 1975)
Beckerman, W. and Associates *The British Economy in 1975* (Cambridge University Press, Cambridge, 1965)
Bell, Philip W. *The Sterling Area in the Postwar World* (Oxford University Press, Oxford, 1956)
Bellman, Harold *Bricks and Mortals* (Hutchinson & Co, London, 1950)

Bisschop, W.R. *The Rise of the London Money Market, 1640–1826* (King & Son, London, 1910)
Blackaby, Frank Thomas (ed.) *De-industrialisation*, (Heinemann London, 1979)
Blackaby, F.T. (ed.) *British Economic Policy, 1960–74: Demand Management*, students' edn (Cambridge University Press, Cambridge, 1979)
Bloomfield, Arthur I. *Monetary Policy under the International Gold Standard, 1880–1914* (Federal Reserve Bank of New York, New York, 1959)
Bloomfield, Arthur I. *Short-Term Capital Movements Under the Pre-1914 Gold Standard*, Princeton Studies in International Finance, no. 11 (Princeton University Press, Princeton, 1963)
Bloomfield, Arthur I. *Patterns of Fluctuation in International Investment before 1914*, Princeton Studies in International Finance, no. 21 (Princeton University Press, Princeton, 1968)
Boleat, Mark *The Building Society Industry* (Allen & Unwin, London, 1982)
Bordo, Michael D. and Anna J. Schwartz (eds.) *A Retrospective on the Classical Gold Standard, 1821–1931* (University of Chicago Press, Chicago and London, 1984)
Brittan, Samuel *Steering the Economy. The Role of the Treasury* (Secker & Warburg, London, 1969)
Building Societies Association *The Future Constitution and Powers of Building Societies* (Building Societies Association, London, 1983)
Cagan, Phillip *Determinants and Effects of Changes in the Stock of Money, 1875–1960* (Columbia University Press for NBER, New York, 1965)
Cairncross, A.K. *Home and Foreign Investment, 1870–1913* (Cambridge University Press, Cambridge, 1953)
Cairncross, Alec and Barry Eichengreen *Sterling in Decline. The Devaluations of 1931, 1949 and 1967* (Basil Blackwell, Oxford, 1983)
Cairncross, Alec *Years of Recovery. British Economic Policy, 1945–51* (Methuen, London, 1985)
Cameron, Rondo E. (ed.) *Banking and Economic Development. Some Lessons of History* (Oxford

University Press, London, 1972)
Cameron, Rondo E. (ed.) *Banking in the Early Stages of Industrialisation* (Oxford University Press, London, 1967)
Cannan, Edwin (ed.) *The Paper Pound of 1797–1821. The Bullion Report* (King & Son, London, 1919; reprint Cass & Co, London, 1969)
Capie, Forrest and Michael Collins *The Inter-War British Economy: A Statistical Abstract* (Manchester University Press, Manchester, 1983)
Capie, Forrest and Alan Webber *A Monetary History of the United Kingdom, 1870–1982* (Allen & Unwin, London, 1985), vol. 1
Capie, Forrest and Geoffrey E. Wood (eds.) *Financial Crises and the World Banking System* (Macmillan, Basingstoke, 1986)
Carter H. and I. Partington *Applied Economics in Banking and Finance*, 2nd edn (Oxford University Press, Oxford, 1981)
Chapman, Stanley *The Rise of Merchant Banking* (Allen & Unwin, London, 1984)
Checkland, S.G. *Scottish Banking. A History, 1695–1973* (Collins, Glasgow & London, 1975)
Clapham, Sir John *The Bank of England: A History* (2 vols., Cambridge University Press, Cambridge, 1945)
Clarke, Sir Richard (ed. by Sir Alec Cairncross) *Anglo-American Collaboration in War and Peace, 1942–1949* (Oxford University Press, Oxford, 1982)
Clarke, Stephen V.O. *Central Bank Cooperation, 1924–31* (Federal Reserve Bank of New York, New York, 1967)
Clay, Sir Arthur *Recovery. The Second Effort* (Bell & Sons, London, 1932)
Clay, Henry *The Post-War Unemployment Problem* (Macmillan, London, 1929)
Clay, Sir Henry *Lord Norman* (Macmillan, London, 1957)
Clayton, G *British Insurance* (Elek Books, London, 1971)
Cleary, E.J. *The Building Society Movement* (Elek Books, London, 1965)

Coates, David and John Hillard (eds.) *The Economic Decline of Modern Britain* (Wheatsheaf Books, Brighton, 1986)

Cohen, Benjamin J. *The Future of Sterling as an International Currency* (Macmillan, London, 1971)

Cohen, C.D. *British Economic Policy, 1960–1969* (Butterworths, London, 1971)

Cokerell, H.A.L. and Edwin Green *The British Insurance Business, 1547–1970* (Heinemann, London, 1976)

Collins, Michael 'The Bank of England and the Liverpool Money Market, 1825–50', unpublished Ph.D., University of London, 1972

Committee of London Clearing Bankers *The London Clearing Banks. Evidence by the Committee of London Clearing Bankers to the Committee to Review the Functioning of Financial Institutions* (Committee of London Clearing Bankers, London, 1978)

Conan, A.R. *The Sterling Area* (Macmillan, London, 1952)

Conan, A.R. *The Problem of Sterling* (Macmillan, London, 1966)

Cottrell, P.L. *British Overseas Investment in the Nineteenth Century* (Macmillan, London, 1975)

Cottrell, P.L. *Industrial Finance, 1830–1914* (Methuen, London, 1980)

Crick, W.F. and J.E. Wadsworth *A Hundred Years of Joint-Stock Banking* (Hodder & Stoughton, London, 1936)

Croome, David R. and Harry G. Johnson (eds.) *Money in Britain, 1959–1969* (Oxford University Press, London, 1970)

Crouzet, Francois (ed.) *Capital Formation in the Industrial Revolution* (Methuen & Co., London, 1972)

Dam, Kenneth *The Rules of the Game* (University of Chicago Press, Chicago and London, 1982)

Davies, Brinley *The United Kingdom and the World Monetary System*, 3rd edn (Heinemann, London, 1979)

De Cecco, Marcello *Money and Empire: The*

*International Gold Standard, 1890–1914* (Blackwell, Oxford, 1974)

Department of Employment and Productivity *British Labour Statistics. Historical Abstract, 1886–1968* (HMSO, London, 1971)

Dormael, Armand Van *Bretton Woods. Birth of a Monetary System* (Macmillan, London, 1978)

Dow, J.C.R. *The Management of the British Economy, 1945–60* (Cambridge University Press, Cambridge, 1964)

Drummond, Ian *The Floating Pound and the Sterling Area, 1931–1939* (Cambridge University Press, Cambridge, 1981)

Eatwell, John *Whatever Happened to Britain? The Economics of Decline* (Duckworth for the BBC, London, 1982)

Eichengreen, Barry (ed.) *The Gold Standard in Theory and History* (Methuen, New York and London, 1985)

Ellinger, Barnard *The City. The London Financial Markets* (King & Son, London, 1940)

Feinstein, C.H. *National Income, Expenditure and Output of the United Kingdom, 1855–1965* (Cambridge University Press, Cambridge, 1972)

Feinstein, Charles (ed.) *The Managed Economy* (Oxford University Press, Oxford, 1983)

Fetter, Frank Whitson *Development of British Monetary Orthodoxy, 1797–1875* (Harvard University Press, Cambridge, Mass., 1965)

Fine, Ben and Laurence Harris (eds.) *The Peculiarities of the British Economy* (Laurence and Wishart, London, 1985)

Fletcher, G.A. *The Discount Houses in London* (Macmillan, London, 1976)

Forbes, R.N. *The History of the Institute of Bankers in Scotland, 1875–1975* (Institute of Bankers in Scotland, Edinburgh, 1975)

Ford, A.G. *The Gold Standard, 1880–1914: Britain and Argentina* (Oxford University Press, Oxford, 1962)

Friedman, Milton and Anna Jacobson Schwartz *A Monetary History of the United States, 1867–1960* (Princeton University Press for NBER, Princeton,

1963)

Friedman, Milton and Anna Jacobson Schwartz *Monetary Trends in the United States and the United Kingdom* (University of Chicago Press, Chicago and London, 1982)

Gardner, Richard *Sterling–Dollar Diplomacy*, 2nd. edn (McGraw–Hill, New York, 1969)

Gaskin, Maxwell *The Scottish Banks. A Modern Survey* (Allen & Unwin, London, 1965)

Gayer, Arthur D., W.W. Rostow and Anna Jacobson Schwartz (assisted by Isaiah Frank) *The Growth and Fluctuation of the British Economy, 1790–1850* (2 vols., Oxford University Press, Oxford, 1953)

Gerschenkron, Alexander *Economic Backwardness in Historical Perspective. A Book of Essays*, 2nd impression (Harvard University Press, Cambridge, Mass., 1966)

Gibson, N.J. *Financial Intermediaries and Monetary Policy* (Institute of Economic Affairs, 1967)

Gibson, Norman J. *The Financial System in Northern Ireland* (Northern Ireland Economic Council, Belfast, 1982)

Gilbart, J.W. (ed. Ernest Sykes) *The History, Principles and Practice of Banking* (2 vols., new edition, G. Bell & Sons, London, 1911)

Gillett Brothers Discount Co. Ltd. *The Bill on London* (Chapman & Hall, London, 1952)

Goodhart, C.A.E. *The Business of Banking, 1891–1914* (Weidenfeld and Nicolson, London, 1972)

Goodhart, C.A.E. *Monetary Theory and Practice. The UK Experience* (Macmillan, London, 1984)

Gowland, David *Controlling the Money Supply* (Croom Helm, London, 1982)

Green, Edwin *Debtors to Their Profession: A History of the Institute of Bankers, 1879–1979* (Methuen & Co., London, 1979)

Green, Edwin *The Making of a Modern Banking Group* (private circulation, London, 1979)

Green, Edwin and Michael Moss *A Business of National Importance. The Royal Mail Shipping Group, 1902–1937* (Methuen, London, 1982)

Gregory, T.E., assisted by Annette Henderson *The Westminster Bank through a Century* (2 vols., Oxford University Press, London, 1936)

Griffiths, Brian *Competition in Banking* (Institute of Economic Affairs, London, 1970)

Griffiths, Brian and Geoffrey E. Wood (eds.) *Monetary Targets* (Macmillan, London, 1981)

Hall, Maximilian *Monetary Policy since 1971. Conduct and Performance* (Macmillan, London, 1983)

Hancock W.K. and M.M. Gowing *British War Economy* (HMSO and Longmans, Green & Co., London, 1949, 2nd impression, 1953)

Harris, C.S.R. *Germany's Foreign Indebtedness* (Oxford University Press, London, 1935)

Hawtrey, R.G. *A Century of Bank Rate*, 2nd edn. (Cass & Co., London, 1962)

Hellman, Rainer *Gold, the Dollar and the European Currency System* (Praeger, London, 1979)

Holmes, A.R. and Edwin Green *Midland. 150 Years of Banking Business* (Batsford, London, 1986)

Horne, H. Oliver *A History of Savings Banks* (Oxford University Press, London, 1947)

Horsefield, J.K. (ed.) *The International Monetary Fund, 1945–1965: 20 Years of International Monetary Cooperation* (3 vols., IMF, Washington DC, 1969)

Howson, Susan *Domestic Monetary Management in Britain, 1919–38* (Cambridge University Press, Cambridge, 1975)

Howson, Susan *Sterling's Managed Float: The Operation of the Exchange Equalisation Account, 1932–39*, Princeton Studies in International Finance, no. 46 (Princeton University Press, Princeton, 1980)

Hume, John R. and Michael S. Moss *Beardmore: The History of a Scottish Industrial Giant* (Heinemann, London, 1979)

International Monetary Fund *International Financial Statistics. Yearbook* (IMF, Washington DC, 1985)

Imlah, James Albert H. *Economic Elements in the Pax Britannica* (Cambridge University Press,

Cambridge, Mass., 1958)

Jackman, W.T. *The Development of Transportation in Modern England* (Cambridge University Press, Cambridge, 1916; reprinted by Cass & Co., London, 1962)

Jay, Douglas *Sterling. Its Use and Misuse: A Plea for Moderation* (Sidgwick & Jackson, London, 1985)

Johnson, Harry G. and John E. Nash *UK and Floating Exchange Rates*, Hobart Paper no. 46 (Institute of Economic Affairs, London, 1969)

Johnson, H.G. (ed.) *Readings in British Monetary Economics* (Oxford University Press, London, 1972)

Kaldor, Nicholas *The Scourge of Monetarism*, 2nd edn (Oxford University Press, Oxford, 1982)

Keegan, William *Mrs Thatcher's Economic Experiment* (Allen Lane, London, 1984)

Keynes, J.M. *The Economic Consequences of the Peace* (Macmillan & Co., London, 1919)

Keynes, John Maynard *A Treatise on Money* (2 vols., Macmillan & Co., London, 1930)

Kindleberger, Charles P. *The World in Depression, 1929–1939* (Allen Lane, London, 1973)

Kindleberger, Charles P. and Jean-Pierre Laffargue (eds.) *Financial Crises. Theory, History and Policy* (Cambridge University Press, Cambridge, 1982)

King, W.T.C. *History of the London Discount Market* (Routledge & Sons, London, 1936)

Klamer, Arjo *The New Classical Macroeconomics* (Wheatsheaf Books, Brighton, 1984)

Laidler, D.E.W. *The Demand for Money*, 2nd edn (Dun-Donelly, New York, 1977)

Lanyi, A. *The Case for Floating Exchange Rates Reconsidered*, Essays in International Finance, no. 72 (Princeton University, Princeton, New Jersey, 1969)

Leaf, Walter *Banking* (Williams & Norgate, London, 1926)

Lindert, Peter H *Key Currencies and Gold, 1900–1913*, Princeton Studies in International Finance, no. 24

(Princeton University Press, Princeton, 1969)
Lindert, Peter H. and Charles P. Kindleberger *International Economics*, 7th edn (Richard D. Irwin, Homewood, Illinois, 1982)
London and Cambridge Economic Service *The British Economy. Key Statistics, 1900–1970* (Times Newspapers Ltd., London, 1971)
Lucas, Robert E. and Thomas J. Sargent (eds.) *Rational Expectations and Econometric Practice* (Allen & Unwin, London, 1981)
Maddison, Angus *Phases of Capitalist Development* (Oxford University Press, Oxford, 1982)
Mantoux, Etienne *The Carthaginian Peace or the Economic Consequences of Mr. Keynes* (Oxford University Press, London, 1946)
Marwick, Arthur *Britain in the Century of Total War* (The Bodley Head, London, 1968)
Matthews, Philip W. *The Bankers' Clearing House* (Pitman & Sons, London, 1921)
Matthews, R.C.O. *A Study in Trade-Cycle History. Economic Fluctuations in Great Britain, 1833–1842* (Cambridge University Press, Cambridge, 1954)
Matthews, R.C.O., C.H. Feinstein and J.C. Odling-Smee *British Economic Growth, 1856–1973* (Oxford University Press, Oxford, 1982)
Meier, Gerald *Problems of a World Monetary Order*, 2nd edn (Oxford University Press, Oxford, 1982)
Michaely, Michael *The Responsiveness of Demand Policies to Balance of Payments: Postwar Patterns*, Studies in International Relations, no. 5 (National Bureau of Economic Research, New York, 1971)
Miller, Robert and John B. Wood, *Exchange Control for Ever?* (Institute of Economic Affairs, London, 1979)
Milward, Alan S. *The Economic Effects of the Two World Wars on Britain* 2nd edn (Macmillan, London, 1984)
Milward, Alan S. *The Reconstruction of Western Europe, 1945–51* (Methuen & Co., London, 1984)
Minsky, Hyman P. *Can 'It' Happen Again? Essays*

*on Instability and Finance* (M.E. Sharpe Inc., New York, 1982)

Mitchell, B.R. and P. Deane *Abstract of British Historical Statistics* (Cambridge University Press, Cambridge, 1962)

Moggridge, D.E. *British Monetary Policy, 1924–1931* (Cambridge University Press, Cambridge, 1972)

Morgan, E. Victor *The Theory and Practice of Central Banking, 1797–1913* (Cambridge University Press, Cambridge, 1943)

Morgan, E. Victor *Studies in British Financial Policy, 1914–25* (Macmillan, London, 1952)

Morgenstern, Oskar *International Financial Transactions and Business Cycles* (Princeton University Press, Princeton, 1959)

Munn, Charles W. *The Scottish Provincial Banking Companies, 1747–1864* (John Donald, Edinburgh, 1981)

Nevin, Edward *The Mechanism of Cheap Money* (University of Wales Press, Cardiff, 1955)

Nevin, Edward and E.W. Davis *The London Clearing Banks* (Elek Books, London, 1970)

Nishimura, Shizuya *The Decline of Inland Bills of Exchange in the London Money Market, 1855–1913* (Cambridge University Press, Cambridge, 1971)

Palgrave, R.H. Inglis *Bank Rate and the Money Market* (John Murray, London, 1903)

Payer, Cheryl *The Debt Trap. The IMF and the Third World* (Monthly Review Press, New York and London, 1974)

Pliatzky, Leo *Getting and Spending. Public Expenditure, Employment and Inflation* (Basil Blackwell, Oxford, 1982)

Pollard, Sidney (ed.) *The Gold Standard and Employment Policies between the Wars* (Methuen & Co., London, 1970)

Pollard, Sidney *The Wasting of the British Economy* (Croom Helm, London, 1982)

Pollard, Sidney *The Development of the British Economy, 1914–1980*, 3rd edn (Edward Arnold, London, 1983)

Powell, Ellis T. *The Evolution of the Money Market, 1385–1915* (Financial News, London, 1915)

Pressnell, L.S. *Country Banking in the Industrial Revolution* (Oxford University Press, Oxford, 1956)

Quinn, Brian Scott *The New Euromarkets* (Macmillan, London, 1975)

Rae, George *The Country Banker*, 7th edn (John Murray, London, 1888)

Reid, Margaret Isabel *The Secondary Banking Crisis, 1973–75* (Macmillan, London, 1982)

Revell, Jack *Changes in British Banking. The Growth of a Secondary Banking System* Hill, Samuel & Co., Occasional Papers, no. 3 (Hill, Samuel & Co., London, 1968)

Revell, Jack *The British Financial System* (Macmillan, London, 1973)

Richards R.D. *The Early History of Banking in England* (King & Son, London, 1929)

Richardson, H.W. *Economic Recovery in Britain, 1932–9* (Weidenfeld and Nicolson, London, 1967)

Richardson, Harry W. and Derek H. Aldcroft *Building in the British Economy between the Wars* (Allen & Unwin, London, 1968)

Roosa, Robert V. *Economic Instability and Flexible Exchange Rates* (Institute of Southeast Asian Studies, Singapore, 1983)

Saul, S.B. *Studies in British Overseas Trade, 1870–1914* (Liverpool University Press, Liverpool, 1960)

Savona, Paolo and George Sutija (eds.), *Eurodollars and International Banking* (Macmillan, London, 1985)

Sayers, R.S. *Modern Banking* (Oxford University Press, Milford, 1938)

Sayers, R.S. *Financial Policy, 1939–45* (HMSO and Longmans, Green & Co., London, 1956)

Sayers, R.S. *Central Banking after Bagehot* (Oxford University Press, Oxford, 1957)

Sayers, R.S. *Lloyds Bank in the History of English Banking* (Oxford University Press, Oxford, 1957)

Sayers, R.S. *The Bank of England, 1891–1944*, (3 vols., Cambridge University Press, Cambridge,

1976)
Scammell, W.M. *International Monetary Policy*, 2nd edn (Macmillan, London, 1961)
Scammell, W.M. *The London Discount Market* (St. Martin's Press, New York, 1968)
Scammell, W.M. *The International Economy since 1945* (Macmillan, London, 1980, reprinted 1982)
Seldon, Arthur (ed.) *Not Unanimous. A Rival Verdict to Radcliffe's on Money* (Institute of Economic Affairs, London, 1960)
Sheppard, David K. *The Growth and Role of UK Financial Institutions, 1880–1962* (Methuen & Co., London, 1971)
Simpson, Noel *The Belfast Bank, 1827–1970* (Blackstaff Press, Belfast, 1975)
Soderstern, Bo *International Economics*, 2nd edn (Macmillan, London, reprint 1981)
Solomon, Robert *The International Monetary System, 1945–1981* (Harper & Row, New York, 1982)
Strange, Susan *Sterling and British Policy* (Oxford University Press for the Royal Institute of International Affairs, London, 1971)
Supple, Barry *The Royal Exchange Assurance* (Cambridge University Press, Cambridge, 1970)
Sykes, Joseph *The Amalgamation Movement in English Banking, 1825–1924* (King & Son, London, 1926)
Temin, Peter *The Jacksonian Economy* (W.W. Norton & Co., New York, 1969)
Tew, Brian *The Evolution of the International Monetary System, 1945–81*, 2nd edn (Hutchinson, London, 1982)
Thomas, S. Evelyn *British Banks and the Finance of Industry* (King & Son, London, 1931)
Thomas, S.E. *The Rise and Growth of Joint-Stock Banking* (Pitman, London, 1934)
Thomas, W.A. *The Finance of British Industry, 1918–1976* (Methuen & Co., London, 1978)
Triffin, Robert *Europe and the Money Muddle. From Bilateralism to Near-Convertibility, 1947–1956* (Yale University Press, New Haven, 1957)
Triffen, Robert Adolphe *The Evolution of the International Monetary System: Historical*

*Reappraisal and Future Perspectives*, Princeton Studies in International Finance, no. 12 (Princeton University Press, Princeton, 1964)

Truptil, R.J. *British Banks and the London Money Market* (Jonathan Cape, London, 1936)

Vane, Howard R. and John L. Thompson *Monetarism: Theory, Evidence and Policy* (Martin Robertson, Oxford, 1979)

Wadsworth, J.E. (ed.) *The Banks and the Monetary System in the UK, 1959–1971* (Methuen & Co., London, 1973)

White, Lawrence H. *Free Banking in Britain. Theory, Experience and Debate, 1800–1845* (Cambridge University Press, Cambridge, 1984)

Williamson, John *The Failure of World Monetary Reform, 1971–74* (Nelson, Sunbury-on-Thames, 1977)

Wilson, Harold *The New Britain: Labour's Plan* (Penguin, Harmondsworth, 1964)

Wilson, Harold *The Labour Government, 1964–1970. A Personal Record* (Weidenfeld & Nicolson and Michael Joseph, London, 1971)

Wilson, Kevin W. *British Financial Institutions: Savings and Monetary Policy* (Pitman, London, 1983)

Winch, Donald *Economics and Policy. A Historical Study* (Fontana, London, 1972)

Winton, J.R. *Lloyds Bank, 1918–1969* (Oxford University Press, Oxford, 1982)

**Articles, Essays and Papers**

Anon., 'Tory Touchstone', *The Economist*, vol. 165, 11 Oct. 1952, pp. 69–70

Anon., 'Towards Flexible Money', *The Economist*, vol. 174, 8 Jan. 1955, pp. 125–7

Anon., 'Flexible Money in Action', *The Economist*, vol. 175, 7 May 1955, pp. 489–91

Anon., 'Sterling in the World Today', *Midland Bank Review*, Feb. 1956, pp.1–7

Anon., 'The Position of Sterling: Background Material', *Midland Bank Review*, Aug. 1960, pp. 8–16

Anon., 'Exchequer Financing and the National Debt, 1945–51', *Economic Trends*, no. 98, Dec. 1961, pp. vii–xvii

Anon., 'Sterling as a Key Currency', *Midland Bank Review*, Aug. 1963, pp. 3–12

Anon., 'Devaluation – For the Record', *Midland Bank Review*, Feb. 1968, pp. 15–18

Anon., 'Banking Regulations and Competition', *Midland Bank Review*, Nov. 1971, pp. 3–11

Anon., 'Guidelines for Management of Floating', *International Monetary Fund Survey*, 17 June 1974, pp. 181–3

Anon., 'Monetary Policy and Regulations Imposed on Listed Banks', *Midland Bank Review*, Summer 1979, pp. 15–9

Anon., 'Britain's Economic Crisis and Possible Remedies', *Cambridge Economic Policy Review*, vol. 6, April 1980, pp. 5–18

Anon., 'Bank Lending in a Changing Environment – A Response to Recent Criticisms', *Midland Bank Review*, Autumn/Winter 1981, pp. 17–22

Anon., 'A Return to Bretton Woods?' *Midland Bank Review*, Autumn/Winter 1981, pp. 30–4

Anon., 'Will British Industry Recover?', *Cambridge Economic Policy Review*, vol. 8, April 1982, pp. 18–26

Alford, R.F.G. and H.B. Rose 'The Radcliffe Report and Domestic Monetary Policy', *London and Cambridge Bulletin*, no. 32, printed in *The Times Review of Industry*, Dec. 1959, pp. ii–vi

Allen, R.G.D. 'Mutual Aid between the US and the British Empire, 1941–45', *Journal of the Royal Statistical Society*, vol. 109, 1946, pp. 243–71

Anderson, B.L. 'The Attorney and the Early Capital Market in Lancashire' in Francois Crouzet (ed.), *Capital Formation in the Industrial Revolution* (Methuen & Co., London, 1972), pp. 223–55

Anderson B.L. and P.L. Cottrell 'Another Victorian Capital Market: A Study of Banking and Bank Investors on Merseyside', *Economic History Review*, 2nd. ser., vol. 28, 1975, pp. 598–615

Artis, M.J. 'Monetary Policy – Part II' in F.T.

Blackaby (ed.), *British Economic Policy 1960–74: Demand Management* student's edn (Cambridge University Press, Cambridge, 1979), pp. 258–303

Ashton, T.S. 'The Bill of Exchange and Private Banks in Lancashire, 1790–1830' in T.S. Ashton and R.S. Sayers (eds.), *Papers in English Monetary History* (Oxford University Press, Oxford, 1953), pp. 37–49

Ball, R.J., T. Burns and J.S.E Laury 'The Role of Exchange Rate Changes in Balance of Payments Adjustment – the United Kingdom Case', *Economic Journal*, vol. 87, 1977, pp. 1–29

Ball, R.J. and T. Burns 'The Inflationary Mechanisms in the UK Economy', *American Economic Review*, vol. 66, 1976, pp. 467–84

Balogh, T. 'The International Aspect' in G.D.N. Worswick and P.H. Ady (eds.), *The British Economy, 1945–1950* (Oxford University Press, Oxford, 1952), pp. 476–510

Bank of England 'Principal Changes in the British Monetary System since 1931' in *Committee on the Working of the Monetary System. Principal Memoranda of Evidence*, (3 vols., HMSO, London, 1960), vol. 1, pp. 17–22

Batchelor, Roy A. 'The Avoidance of Catastrophe: Two Nineteenth Century Banking Crises' in Forrest Capie and Geoffrey E. Wood (eds.), *Financial Crises and the World Banking System* (Macmillan, London, 1986), pp. 41–76 [including Comment by L.S. Pressnell].

Beenstock, Michael, Forrest Capie and Brian Griffiths 'Economic Recovery in the United Kingdom in the 1930s' in 'The UK Economic Recovery in the 1930s', Bank of England Panel of Academic Consultants, Panel Paper no. 23, pp. 57–85

Bevan, Sir Timothy 'The Banking Environment', *Barclays Review*, vol. 60, Feb. 1985, pp. 1–4

Bloomfield, Arthur I. 'Rules of the Game of International Adjustment?' in C.R. Whittlesey and J.S.G. Wilson (eds.), *Essays in Money and Banking* (Oxford University Press, Oxford, 1968), pp. 26–46

Bond, Marian E. and Adalbert Knobl, 'Some Implications of North Sea Oil for the UK Economy', *International Monetary Fund Staff Papers*, vol. 29, Sept. 1982, pp. 363–97

Bordo, Michael David and Lars Jonung 'The Long-Run Behavior of the Income Velocity of Circulation of Money in Five Advanced Countries, 1870–1975: An Institutional Approach', *Economic Enquiry*, vol. 19, no. 1, 1981, pp. 96–116

Bordo, Michael D. 'The Gold Standard: The Traditional Approach' (and subsequent discussion) in Michael D. Bordo and Anna J. Schwartz (eds.), *A Retrospective on the Classical Gold Standard, 1821–1931* (University of Chicago Press, Chicago and London, 1984), pp. 23–119 [including Comment by C. Knick Harley]

Brown, A.J. 'The Liquidity Preference Schedules of the London Clearing Banks', *Oxford Economic Papers*, no. 1, Oct. 1938, pp. 49–82

Brown, A.J. 'Friedman and Schwartz on the United Kingdom' in 'Papers Presented to the Panel of Academic Consultants' (Bank of England, 1983)

Capie, Forrest and Ghila Rodrik-Bali 'Concentration in British Banking, 1870–1920' *Business History*, vol. 24, 1982, pp. 280–92

Capie, Forrest, Terence C. Mills, Michael J. Thomas and Geoffrey E. Wood 'Was the War Loan Conversion a Success?' City University Discussion Paper on Monetary History of the UK, no. 5, Feb. 1983 (to be reprinted in *Applied Economics*, forthcoming)

Capie, Forrest and Alan Webber 'Total Coin and Coin in Circulation in the United Kingdom, 1868–1914', *Journal of Money, Credit and Banking*, vol. 15, 1983, pp. 24–39

Capie, Forrest and Alan Webber 'Profits and Profitability in British Banking, 1870–1939', City University Discussion Paper on Monetary History of the UK, no. 18, May 1985

Capie, Forrest, Terence C. Mills and Geoffrey E. Wood 'What Happened in 1931?' in Forrest Capie and Geoffrey E. Wood (eds.), *Financial Crises and the World Banking System* (Macmillan, London, 1986), pp. 120–59 [including 'Comments' by Tim Congdon and Michael Wagner]

Capie, Forrest H. and Geoffrey E. Wood 'The Long Run Behaviour of Velocity in the UK', City University Discussion Paper on Monetary History, no. 23, 1986.

Chapman, S.D. 'Financial Restraints on the Growth of Firms in the Cotton Industry, 1790–1850', *Economic History Review*, 2nd. ser., vol. 32, 1979, pp. 50–69

Clayton, G. 'British Financial Intermediaries in Theory and Practice', *Economic Journal*, vol. 72, 1962, pp. 869–86

Clemm, Michael Von, 'The Rise of Consortium Banking', *Harvard Business Review*, vol., 49, May–June 1971, pp. 125–36

Coghlan, Richard T. and Peter M. Jackson 'The UK Personal Savings Ratio: Past, Present and Future', *Scottish Journal of Political Economy*, vol. 26, 1979, pp. 307–24

Coghlan, Richard and Carolyn Sykes 'Managing the Money Supply', *Lloyds Bank Review*, no. 135, 1980, pp. 1–13

Collins, Michael 'The Langton Papers: Banking and Bank of England Policy in the 1830s', *Economica*, vol. 39, 1972, pp. 47–59

Collins, M. and P. Hudson 'Provincial Bank Lending: Yorkshire and Merseyside, 1826–60', *Bulletin of Economic Research*, vol. 31, 1979, pp. 69–79

Collins, Michael 'The English Banking Sector and Monetary Growth, 1844–80', University of Leeds Economics Discussion Paper, no. 102, 1981

Collins, Michael 'Long-Term Growth of the English Banking Sector and Money Stock, 1844–80', *Economic History Review*, 2nd ser., vol. 36, 1983, pp. 374–94

Collins, Michael 'The Business of Banking: English Bank Balance Sheets, 1840–80', *Business History*, vol. 26, 1984, pp. 43–58

Collins, Michael 'Sterling Exchange Rates, 1847–80', *Journal of European Economic History*, vol. 15,

1986, pp. 511–33.

Collins, Michael 'English Banks and the Mid–Nineteenth Century Business Cycle', in P.L. Cottrell and D.E. Moggridge (eds.), *Money and Power* (Macmillan, London, 1987, forthcoming)

Collins, Michael 'Did Keynes Have the Answer to Unemployment in the 1930s?' in John Hillard (ed.), *J.M. Keynes: A Retrospective* (Edward Elgar, London, 1988, forthcoming)

Cooper, Richard N. 'The Balance of Payments' in Richard E. Caves *et al*, *Britain's Economic Prospects* (Allen & Unwin, London, 1968), pp. 147–97

Cripps, Francis and Wynne Godley, 'Controls of Imports as a Means to Full Employment and the Expansion of World Trade: The UK's Case', *Cambridge Journal of Economics*, vol. 2, 1978, pp. 327–34

Dacey, W. Manning 'The Floating Debt Problem' *Lloyds Bank Review*, April 1956, pp. 24–38

Dale, Richard S. 'Prudential Regulation of Multinational Banking. The Problem Outlined', *National Westminster Bank Quarterly Review*, Feb. 1981, pp. 14–24

Deane, Phyllis 'New Estimates of Gross National Product for the United Kingdom, 1830–1914', *Review of Income and Wealth*, ser.14, 2, June 1968, pp. 95–112

Dimsdale, D.H. 'British Monetary Policy and the Exchange Rate, 1920–1938' in W.A. Eltis and P.J.N. Sinclair (eds.), 'The Money Supply and the Exchange Rate', Supplement to *Oxford Economic Papers*, new ser., vol. 33, July 1981, pp. 306–49

Dimsdale, D.H. 'Employment and Real Wages in the Inter–War Period', *National Institute Economic Review*, vol. 110, November 1984, pp. 94–103

Dornbusch, Rudiger and Jacob A. Frenkel 'The Gold Standard and the Bank of England in the Crisis of 1847' in Michael D. Bordo and Anna J. Schwartz (eds.), *A Retrospective on the Classical Gold Standard, 1821–1931* (University of Chicago Press, Chicago and London, 1984), pp. 233–73

[including 'Comment' by J.R.T. Hughes]
Dorrance, Graeme 'Savings in the 1970s' *Lloyds Bank Review*, 138, Oct. 1980, pp. 12–26
Dutton, John 'The Bank of England and the Rules of the Game under the International Gold Standard: New Evidence' in Michael D. Bordo and Anna J. Schwartz (eds.), *A Retrospective on the Classical Gold Standard, 1821–1931* (University of Chicago Press, Chicago and London, 1984), pp. 173–99 [including 'Comment' by Donald E. Moggridge]
Earle, Edward Meade 'The American Stake in Europe. Retrospect and Prospect', *International Affairs*, vol. 27, 1951, pp. 423–33
Ford, A.G. 'The Transfer of British Foreign Lending, 1870–1913', *Economic History Review*, 2nd. ser., vol. 11, 1958, pp. 302–8.
Ford, A.G. 'International Financial Policy and the Gold Standard, 1870–1914', University of Warwick Discussion Paper in Economics, no. 104, Jan. 1977
Foreman-Peck, J. 'Exit, Voice and Loyalty as Responses to Decline: The Rover Company in the Inter-War Years', *Business History*, vol. 23, 1981, pp. 191–207
Forsyth, P.J. and J.A Kay, 'The Economic Implications of North Sea Oil Revenues', *Fiscal Studies*, vol. 1, July 1980, pp. 1–28
Foxwell, H.S. 'The Financing of Industry and Trade', *Economic Journal*, vol. 27, 1917, pp. 502–22
Francks, Oliver 'The United Kingdom Deposit or Clearing Banks' in Institute of Bankers, *The City of London as a Centre of International Trade and Finance* (Institute of Bankers, London, 1961), pp. 72–84
Fratianni, Michele and Franco Spinelli 'Italy in the Gold Standard Period, 1861–1914' in Michael D. Bordo and Anna Jacobson Schwartz (eds.), *A Retrospective on the Classical Gold Standard* (University of Chicago Press, Chicago and London, 1984), pp. 405–51 [including 'Comment' by Richard E. Sylla]
Freedman, Charles 'The Euro-Dollar Market: Five

Recent Studies', *Journal of Monetary Economics*, vol. 3, 1977, pp. 467–78

Friedman, M. 'The Case for Flexible Exchange Rates' in his *Essays in Positive Economics* (University of Chicago Press, Chicago, 1953), pp. 157–203

Friedman, Milton 'The Quality of Money: A Restatement' in M. Friedman (ed.), *Studies in the Quantity Theory of Money* (University of Chicago Press, Chicago, 1956) pp. 3–21

Good, David F. 'Backwardness and the Role of Banking in Nineteenth Century European Industrialization', *Journal of Economic History*, vol. 33, 1973, pp. 845–50

Goodhart, Charles 'Problems of Monetary Management: The UK Experience' in Anthony S. Courakis (ed.), *Inflation, Depression and Economic Policy in the West* (Mansell and Alexandrine Press, London and Oxford, 1981), pp. 111–43

Goodwin, R.M. 'The Supply of Bank Money in England and Wales, 1920–1938', *Oxford Economic Papers*, no. 5, June 1941, pp. 1–32

[Gregory, T.E.] 'The Treasury Bill: The Story of an Economist's Invention', *Midland Bank Review*, February 1961, pp. 3–9

Griffiths, Brian 'The Determination of the Treasury Bill Tender Rate', *Economica*, n.s., vol. 38, 1971, pp. 180–91

Griffiths, Brian 'The Development of Restrictive Practices in the UK Monetary System', *Manchester School*, vol. 41, 1973, pp. 3–18

Griffiths, Brian 'The Reform of Monetary Control in the United Kingdom', *Annual Monetary Review*, no. 1, Oct. 1979, pp. 29–42

Hall, A.R. 'A Note on the English Capital Market as a Source of Funds for Home Investment before 1914', *Economica*, new ser., vol. 24, 1957, pp. 59–66

Harley, C.K. and D.N. McCloskey 'Foreign Trade: Competition and the Expanding International Economy' in Roderick Floud and Donald McCloskey (eds.), *The Economic History of Britain since 1700* (2 vols., Cambridge University

Press, Cambridge, 1981), vol. 2, pp. 70–98

Harrod, J.R. 'Why Not Two Clearers?', *Bankers' Magazine*, 206, July/Dec. 1968, pp. 139–43.

Henderson, P.D. 'Britain's International Position' in G.D.N. Worswick and P.H. Ady (eds.), *The British Economy, 1945–1950* (Oxford University Press, Oxford, 1952), pp. 62–71

Hendry, David F. and Neil R. Ericson 'Assertion Without Empirical Basis: An Econometric Appraisal of "Monetary Trends..."' in 'Papers Presented to the Panel of Academic Consultants' (Bank of England, 1983)

Herring, Richard J. 'The Interbank Market' in Paolo Savona and George Sutija (eds.), *Eurodollars and International Banking* (Macmillan, London, 1985), pp. 111–21

Hicks, John 'What is Wrong with Monetarism?', *Lloyds Bank Review*, no. 118, Oct. 1975, pp. 1–13

Holgate, H.C.K. 'Loans, Overdrafts and Deposits', *Bankers' Magazine*, Nov. 1938, pp. 739–43

Horsefield, J.K. 'The Bankers and the Bullionists in 1819', *Journal of Political Economy*, vol. 57, 1949, pp. 442–8

Horsefield, J.K. 'The Origins of the Bank Charter Act, 1844', in T.S. Ashton and R.S. Sayers (eds.), *Papers in English Monetary History* (Oxford University Press, Oxford, 1953), pp. 109–25

Howson, Susan 'The Management of Sterling, 1932–1939', *Journal of Economic History*, vol. 40, 1980, pp. 53–60

Hume, David 'On the Balance of Trade' (1752), reprinted in Barry Eichengreen (ed.), *The Gold Standard in Theory and History* (Methuen, New York and London, 1985), pp. 39–48

Hume, L.J. 'The Gold Standard and Deflation: Issues and Attitudes in the Nineteen-Twenties', *Economica*, new ser., vol. 30, 1963, pp. 225–42

Jackson, P.M. 'The Public Expenditure Cuts: Rationale and Consequences', *Fiscal Studies*, 1, no. 2, Mar. 1980, pp. 66–82

Johnson, H.G. 'Some Implications of Secular Changes in Bank Assets and Liabilities in Great Britain', *Economic Journal*, vol. 61, 1951, pp. 544–61

Johnson, H.G. 'Clearing Bank Holdings of Public Debt, 1930–1950', *London and Cambridge Economic Service Bulletin*, vol. 29, 1951, pp. 102–9

Johnson, Harry 'Observations on the Bank Merger Proposals', *Bankers' Magazine*, 206, July/Dec. 1968, pp. 135–7

Johnson, Harry G. 'Recent Developments in Monetary Theory – A Commentary', in David R. Croome and Harry G. Johnson (eds.), *Money in Britain, 1959–1969* (Oxford University Press, London, 1970), pp. 83–128 (including 'Discussion Papers' by David Laidler and R.T. Armstrong)

Johnson, Harry G. 'The Monetary Approach to Balance-of-Payments Theory' in Harry G. Johnson, *Further Essays in Monetary Economics* (Allen & Unwin, London, 1972), pp. 229–49

Jones, Geoffrey 'Lombard Street on the Riviera: The British Clearing Banks and Europe, 1900–1960', *Business History*, vol. 24, 1982, pp. 186–210

Jonung, Lars 'Swedish Experience under the Classical Gold Standard, 1873–1914' in Michael D. Bordo and Anna J. Schwartz (eds.), *A Retrospective on the Classical Gold Standard, 1821–1931* (University of Chicago Press, Chicago and London, 1984), pp. 361–404 [including 'Comment' by Peter H. Lindert]

Kaldor, N. 'Conflicts in National Economic Objectives' in Charles Feinstein (ed.), *The Managed Economy* (Oxford University Press, Oxford, 1983), pp. 169–84

Kavanagh, N.J. and A.A. Walters 'Demand for Money in the UK, 1877–1961: Some Preliminary Findings', *Bulletin of the Oxford University Institute of Economics and Statistics*, vol. 28, May 1966, pp. 93–113

Kennedy, C.M. 'Monetary Policy' in G.D.N. Worswick and P.H. Ady (eds.), *The British Economy, 1945–1950* (Oxford University Press, Oxford,

1952), pp. 188–207

Kennedy, Charles 'Monetary Policy' in G.D.N. Worswick and P.H. Ady (eds.), *The British Economy in the Nineteen-Fifties* (Oxford University Press, London, 1962), pp. 301–25

Kennedy, William P. 'Institutional Response to Economic Growth: Capital Markets in Britain to 1914' in Leslie Hannah (ed.), *Management Strategy and Business Development. An Historical and Comparative Study* (Macmillan, London, 1976), pp. 151–83

Keynes, J.M. 'War and the Financial System, August 1914', *Economic Journal*, vol. 24, Sept. 1914, pp. 460–86

Keynes, J.M. 'The Prospects of Money, November, 1914', *Economic Journal*, vol. 24, Dec. 1914, pp. 610–34

Keynes, J.M. 'The Economic Consequences of Mr. Churchill' reproduced in Sidney Pollard (ed.), *The Gold Standard and Employment Policies between the Wars* (Methuen & Co., London, 1970), pp. 27–43

Keynes, J.M. 'How to Pay for the War' [1939–40], in *The Collected Writings of John Maynard Keynes* (Macmillan for the Royal Economic Society, London, 1972), vol. 22, pp. 40–155

King, W.T.C. 'Gilt-edged and the Volume of Money', *Banker*, vol. 80, 249, Oct. 1946, pp. 7–16

King, W.T.C. 'Should the Banks Bid for Deposits?', *Banker*, vol. 112, 1962, pp. 761–72

Laidler, David and Michael Parkin 'The Demand for Money in the United Kingdom, 1955–1967: Preliminary Estimates', *Manchester School*, vol. 38, 1970, pp. 187–208

Laidler, D. 'Inflation in Britain: A Monetarist Perspective', *American Economic Review*, vol. 66, 1976, pp. 485–500

Lee, C.H. 'The Effects of Depression on Primary Producing Countries', *Journal of Contemporary History*, vol. 4, 1969, pp. 139–55

Lees, D.S. 'The Technique of Monetary Insulation, December 1932 to December 1937', *Economica*, new ser., vol. 20, 1953, pp. 341–55

Llewellyn, David T. 'Do Building Societies Take Deposits Away from the Banks?' *Lloyds Bank Review*, no. 131, Jan. 1979, pp. 21–34

Lucas, R.E. and T.J. Sargent 'After Keynesian Macroeconomics', in Federal Reserve Bank of Boston, *After the Phillips Curve: Persistence of High Inflation and High Unemployment*, Conference Series no. 19 (Federal Reserve Bank of Boston, Boston, 1978), pp. 49–72

McCloskey, Donald N. and J. Richard Zecher 'How the Gold Standard Worked, 1880–1913' in Donald N. McCloskey, *Enterprise and Trade in Victorian Britain* (Allen & Unwin, London, 1981), pp. 184–208

McCloskey, Donald N. and J. Richard Zecher 'The Success of Purchasing-Power Parity: Historical Evidence and Its Implications for Macroeconomics' in Michael D. Bordo and Anna J. Schwartz (eds.), *A Retrospective on the Classical Gold Standard, 1821–1931* (University of Chicago Press, Chicago and London, 1984), pp. 121–70 [including 'Comment' by Robert E. Lipsey and Milton Friedman]

McCurrach, D.F. 'Britain's US Dollar Problems, 1939–45', *Economic Journal*, vol. 58, 1948, pp. 356–68

McGouldrick, Paul 'Operations of the German Central Bank and the Rules of the Game, 1879–1913' in Michael D. Bordo and Anna J. Schwartz (eds.), *A Retrospective on the Classical Gold Standard, 1821–1931* (University of Chicago Press, Chicago and London, 1984), pp. 311–59 [including 'Comment' by Heywood Fleisig]

Macintosh, R.M. 'A Note on Cheap Money and the British Housing Boom, 1932–37', *Economic Journal*, vol. 61, 1951, pp. 167–73

Meade, J.E. 'The Case for Variable Exchange Rates', *Three Banks' Review*, no. 27, Sept. 1955, pp. 3–27

Meltzer, Allan H. 'The Demand for Money: The Evidence from the Time Series', *Journal of*

*Political Economy*, vol. 71, 1963, pp. 219–46

Metcalfe, J.S. 'Foreign Trade and Balance of Payments' in A.R. Prest and D.J. Coppock (eds.), *The UK Economy. A Manual of Applied Economics*, 9th edn (Weidenfeld & Nicolson, London, 1982), pp. 125–192

Middleton, P.E., C.J. Mowl, J.C. Odling-Smee and C.J. Riley (H.M. Treasury) 'Monetary Targets and the Public Sector Borrowing Requirement' in Brian Griffiths and Geoffrey E. Wood (eds.), *Monetary Targets* (Macmillan, London, 1981), pp. 135–75

Minsky, Hyman P. 'The Financial Instability Hypothesis: Capitalist Processes and the Behaviour of the Economy' in Charles P. Kindleberger and Jean-Pierre Laffargue (eds.), *Financial Crises. Theory, History and Policy* (Cambridge University Press, Cambridge, 1982), pp. 13–39

Morgan, E. Victor 'The National Debt and Monetary Policy', *Lloyds Bank Review*, vol. 37, 1955, pp. 18–33

Neuburger, Hugh M. and Houston H. Stokes 'The Relationship between Interest Rates and Gold Flows under the Gold Standard: A New Empirical Approach', *Economica*, vol. 46, 1979, pp. 261–79

Newlyn, W.T. 'The Radcliffe Report: A Socratic Scrutiny', *Bankers' Magazine*, no. 189, Jan. 1960, pp. 21–6

Newmarch, William 'An Attempt to Ascertain the Magnitude and Fluctuations of the Amount of Bills of Exchange... 1828–1847', *Journal of the Statistical Society*, vol. 14, 1851, pp. 143–83

Nishimura, S. 'The Estimates of Bank Deposits in the UK, 1870–1913', unpublished typescript, University of Hosei, 1976

Nobay, A.R. 'The Bank of England, Monetary Policy and Monetary Theory in the United Kingdom, 1951–1971', *Manchester School*, vol. 41, 1973, pp. 43–58

Opie, Roger 'Economic Planning and Growth' in Charles Feinstein (ed.), *The Managed Economy* (Oxford University Press, Oxford, 1983), pp. 147–68

Oppenheimer, P.M. and W.B. Reddaway, 'World Recession and World Debts', *Midland Bank Review*, Spring 1983, pp. 7–15

Paish, F.W. 'The Floating Debt, 1914–39, and its Effects on the British Banking System', Appendix to Part II of T. Balogh, *Studies in Financial Organization* (Cambridge University Press, Cambridge, 1947), pp. 191–212

Paish, F.W. 'Deposit Rates after Mr. Jones', *Banker*, vol. 117.2, 1967, pp. 845–9

Paish, F.W. 'Inflation and the Balance of Payments in the United Kingdom, 1952–67' in Charles Feinstein (ed.), *The Managed Economy* (Oxford University Press, Oxford, 1983), pp. 133–46

Pippenger, John 'Bank of England Operations, 1893–1913' in Michael D. Bordo and Anna J. Schwartz (eds.), *A Retrospective on the Classical Gold Standard, 1821–1931* (University of Chicago Press, Chicago and London, 1984), pp. 203–32 [including 'Comment' by Charles E.A. Goodhart]

Platt, D.C.M. 'British Portfolio Investment Overseas before 1870: Some Doubts', *Economic History Review*, vol. 33, 1980, pp. 1–16

Pollard, Sidney 'Fixed Capital in the Industrial Revolution in Britain', *Journal of Economic History*, vol. 24, 1964, pp. 299–314

Pressnell, L.S. 'Gold Reserves, Banking Reserves, and the Baring Crisis of 1890' in C.R. Whittlesey and J.S.G. Wilson (eds.), *Essays in Money and Banking* (Oxford University Press, Oxford, 1968), pp. 167–228

Pressnell, L.S. '1925: The Burden of Sterling', *Economic History Review*, 2nd. ser., vol. 31, 1978, pp. 67–87

Redmond, John 'An Indicator of the Effective Exchange Rate of the Pound in the Nineteen–Thirties', *Economic History Review*, 2nd. ser., vol. 33, 1980, pp. 83–91

Revell, Jack 'A Secondary Banking System', *Banker*, vol. 118, no. 511, 1968, pp. 798–812

Rich, Georg 'Canada without a Central Bank: Operation of the Price–Specie–Flow Mechanism,

1872–1913' in Michael D. Bordo and Anna J. Schwartz (eds.), *A Retrospective on the Classical Gold Standard, 1821–1931* (University of Chicago Press, Chicago and London, 1984), pp. 277–309 [including 'Comment' by Ronald A. Shearer and Carolyn Clark]

Sargent, J.R. 'Britain and the Sterling Area' in G.D.N. Worswick and P.H. Ady (eds.), *The British Economy, 1945–1950* (Oxford University Press, Oxford, 1952), pp. 531–49

Saul, S.B. 'The Export Economy, 1870–1914', *Yorkshire Bulletin of Economic and Social Research*, vol. 17, 1965, no. 1, pp. 5–18

Savage, David 'Monetary Targets and Control of the Money Supply', *National Institute Economic Review*, no. 89, Aug. 1979, pp. 44–52

Savage, David 'Some Issues of Monetary Policy', *National Institute Economic Review*, no. 91, Feb. 1980, pp. 78–85

Sayers, R.S. 'The Question of the Standard, 1815–44', *Economic History*, vol. 3, Feb. 1935, pp. 79–102

Sayers, R.S. 'Monetary Thought and Monetary Policy in England', *Economic Journal*, vol. 70, 1960, pp. 710–24

Sayers, R.S. 'The Return to Gold, 1925' in Sidney Pollard (ed.), *The Gold Standard and Employment Policies between the Wars* (Methuen & Co., London, 1970), pp. 85–98

Sayers, R.S. '1941 – The First Keynesian Budget' in Charles Feinstein (ed.), *The Managed Economy* (Oxford University Press, Oxford, 1983), pp. 107–17

Scammell, W.M. 'The Working of the Gold Standard', *Yorkshire Bulletin of Economic and Social Research*, vol. 17, no. 1, 1965, pp. 32–45

Schwartz, Anna Jacobson 'Monetary Trends in the United States and the United Kingdom, 1873–1970: Selected Findings', *Journal of Economic History*, vol. 35, 1975, pp. 138–59

Seabourne, Teresa 'The Summer of 1914' in Forrest Capie and Geoffrey E. Wood (eds.), *Financial Crises and the World Banking System* (Macmillan,

London, 1986), pp. 77–119 [including 'Comments' by Charles Goodhart]

Simon, Matthew 'The Pattern of New British Portfolio Foreign Investment, 1865–1914' in A.R. Hall (ed.), *The Export of Capital from Britain, 1870–1914* (Methuen, London, 1968), pp. 15–44

Spalding, W.F. 'The Establishment and Growth of Foreign British Banks in London...', *Journal of the Institute of Bankers*, Nov. 1911, pp. 433–61

Spring-Rice, D. 'London Money Markets since the War', *Bankers' Magazine*, March 1923, pp. 417–31

Stone, Richard 'The Use and Development of National Income and Expenditure Estimates' in D.N. Chester (ed.), *Lessons of the British War Economy* (Cambridge University Press, Cambridge, 1951) pp. 83–101

Tew, Brian 'The Implementation of Monetary Policy in Post-War Britain', *Midland Bank Review*, Spring 1981, pp. 5–14

Tew, J.H.B. 'Monetary Policy – Part I' in F.T. Blackaby (ed.), *British Economic Policy, 1960–74: Demand Management*, students' edn (Cambridge University Press, Cambridge, 1979), pp. 218–57

Tew, J.H.B. 'Policies Aimed at Improving the Balance of Payments' in F.T. Blackaby (ed.), *British Economic Policy, 1960–74: Demand Management*, students' edn (Cambridge University Press, Cambridge, 1979), pp. 304–59

Weeks, Hugh 'Anglo-American Supply Relationships' in D.N. Chester (ed.), *Lessons of the British War Economy* (Cambridge University Press, Cambridge, 1951), pp. 69–82

Whale, P. Barrett 'A Retrospective View of the Bank Charter Act, 1844', in T.S. Ashton and R.S. Sayers (eds.), *Papers in English Monetary History* (Oxford University Press, Oxford, 1953), pp. 126–31

Wilcox, M.G. 'Inflation and its Effects on Banks and Finance Houses', *Midland Bank Review*, Aug. 1975, pp. 10–16

Williams, David 'Some Aspects of Monetary Policy in

England, 1952–8', *Yorkshire Bulletin of Economic and Social Research*, vol. 12, 1960, pp. 96–110

Williams, David 'London and the 1931 Financial Crisis', *Economic History Review*, 2nd. ser., vol. 15, 1963, pp. 513–28

Williams, Leonard 'A Competitor's View' in Institute of Bankers, *The Banks and Their Competitors* (Institute of Bankers, London, 1980) pp. 43–55

Williamson, John and Geoffrey E. Wood, 'The British Inflation: Indigenous or Imported?', *American Economic Review*, vol. 66, 1976, pp. 520–31

Worswick, G.D.N. 'The Sources of Recovery in the UK in the 1930s', *National Institute Economic Review*, vol. 110, November 1984, pp. 85–93

Wright, J.F. 'Britain's Interwar Experience' in W.A. Eltis and P.J.N. Sinclair (eds.), 'The Money Supply and the Exchange Rate', Supplement to *Oxford Economic Papers*, new ser., vol. 33, July 1981, pp. 282–305

**Articles in the Bank of England Quarterly Bulletin**

'The Procedure of Special Deposits', vol. 1, Dec. 1960, p.18

'Bank Liquidity in the United Kingdom', vol. 2, Dec. 1962, pp. 248–55

'The Management of Money Day-to-Day', vol. 3, March 1963, pp. 15–21

'New Series of External Liabilities and Claims in Sterling', vol. 3, June 1963, pp. 98–105

'UK Banks' External Liabilities and Claims in Foreign Currencies', vol. 4., June 1964, pp. 100–8

'Official Transaction in the Gilt-Edged Market', vol. 6, June 1966, pp. 141–8

'The London Discount Market: Some Historical Notes', vol. 7, June 1967, pp. 144–56

'Bank of England Liabilities and Assets: 1669 to 1966', appendix to vol. 7, June 1967

'Overseas and Foreign Banks in London, 1962–68', vol. 8, June 1968, pp. 156–65

'The UK Banking Sector, 1952–67', vol. 9, June 1969, pp. 176–200

'Domestic Credit Expansion', vol. 9, Sept. 1969, bound separately

'The Operation of Monetary Policy since the Radcliffe Report' (prepared by the Bank of England in consultation with the Treasury), vol. 9, Dec. 1969, pp. 448–60

'The Euro-Currency Business of Banks in London', vol. 10, March 1970, pp. 31–49

Goodhart, C.A.E. and A.D. Crockett, 'The Importance of Money', vol. 10, June 1970, pp. 181–98

'Competition and Credit Control', vol. 11, June 1971, pp. 189–93

'Key Issues in Monetary and Credit Policy', vol. 11, June 1971, pp. 195–8

'Speech by the Governor of the Bank of England' (19 Oct. 1972), vol. 12, Dec. 1972, pp. 514–8

'Analysis of Financial Statistics', vol. 13, Sept. 1973, p. 295–305

'Sterling Certificates of Deposit and the Inter-Bank Market', vol. 13, Sept. 1973, pp. 308–14

'Credit Control: A Supplementary Scheme', vol. 14, Mar. 1974, pp. 37–9

'Overseas Sterling Balances, 1963–1973', vol. 14, June 1974, p. 162–75

'The Supervision of the UK Banking System', vol. 15, June 1975, pp. 188–94

'The Capital and Liquidity Adequacy of Banks', vol. 15, Sept. 1975, pp. 240–3

'Reflections on the Conduct of Monetary Policy' (Governor's lecture), vol. 18, Mar. 1978, pp. 31–7

'The Secondary Banking Crisis and the Bank of England Support Operation', vol. 18, June 1978, pp. 230–9

Foot, M.D.K.W., C.A.E. Goodhart and A.C. Hotson, 'Monetary Base Control', vol.19, June 1979, pp. 149–59

'Banking Supervision and the Banking Act', vol. 20, June 1980, pp. 205–8

'Monetary Control: Next Steps', vol. 21, March 1981, pp. 38–9

'The Financial Scene in the 1970s', lecture by the

Deputy-Governor, vol. 21, March 1981, pp. 71-6
'The Banks' Role in Financing Industry'. A speech by the Governor, vol. 21, Mar. 1981, pp. 77-8
'Reflections on the Role of the Institutions in Financing Industry', lecture by the Governor, vol. 21, Mar. 1981, pp. 79-85
'Monetary Control - Provisions', vol. 21, Sept. 1981, pp. 347-50
'Eurobanks and the Inter-bank Market', vol. 21, Sept. 1981, pp. 351-64
'Money and Banking Figures: Forthcoming Changes', vol. 21, Dec. 1981, pp. 531-8
'The Role of the Bank of England in the Money Market', vol. 22, Mar. 1982, pp. 86-94
'The Supplementary Special Deposits Scheme', vol. 22, Mar. 1982, pp. 74-85
'Recent Changes in the Monetary and Regulatory Framework' [Bank Governor's speech, 28 Jan. 1982], vol. 22, Mar. 1982, pp. 101-3
'The Measurement of Liquidity', vol. 22, Sept. 1982, pp. 399-402
'British Economic Policy over the Last Decade [Governor's address to Italian Senate, April 1983], vol. 23, June 1983, pp. 194-9
'Setting Monetary Objectives' [paper by Governor's assistant, J.S. Fforde], vol. 23, June 1983, pp. 200-8
'The Bank's Operational Procedures for Meeting Monetary Objectives', vol. 23, June 1983, pp. 209-15
'Operation of Monetary Policy: Monetary Control Arrangements', vol. 23, Sept. 1983, p. 346
'Competition, Innovation and Regulation in British Banking', paper by J.S. Fforde, vol. 23, Sept. 1983, pp. 363-76
'Revised Presentation of Banking Statistics', vol. 23, Dec. 1983, pp. 562-3
'The Travails of Competition and Credit Control' and 'What Went Wrong?', in Bank of England, *The Development and Operation of Monetary Policy, 1960-1983* (Oxford University Press, Oxford, 1984), pp.42-44

'Some Current Concerns of a Banking Supervisor', speech by W.P. Cooke, Associate Director, vol. 25, June 1985, pp. 219–23
'Company Profitability and Finance', vol. 25, June 1985, pp. 224–32

# GENERAL INDEX

# INDEX OF NAMES